1855 SESQUIC
ST. CLAIR

NTENNIAL 2005
MINNESOTA

Years of Memories

The History and Memories of McPherson Township & St. Clair, Minnesota

1855-2005

Myrtle Westphal
Project Coordinator

For more information, write to:
Minnesota Heritage Publishing
205 Ledlie Lane, Suite 125
Mankato, MN 56001
www.mnheritage.com

ISBN: 0-9713168-8-0

Library of Congress Catalog Number: 2005922869

Published by Minnesota Heritage Publishing

Printed in the United States of America
By Corporate Graphics, North Mankato, MN

First Edition

Cover Photograph: Submitted by Shirley Fitzloff, Scott and Sandy Schaible.
The children on the Hilton Bridge (located just north of St. Clair) are
thought to be the children of Herman and Ottelia Fitzloff.

Cover Design by Sara Boettcher

Dedication

As the history of the McPherson Township-St. Clair area is compiled, special thanks are in order. First of all to our forefathers who left foreign countries, for various reasons, to journey into an unknown territory in order to provide a better living for their families. Although the journey was by no means easy, their determination prevailed.

A mention must also be made of our armed forces that sacrificed dearly over the years to provide the freedoms we are enjoying today. Although things may not be what we always think they should be, we are truly blessed to be able to live in the United States of America. We must give special consideration to our government officials and pray for their guidance so they lead and make wise decisions to protect all of us.

Gratitude is also due to our churches that over the years have always provided the opportunity to care for our spiritual needs. Although they have and still do provide the opportunity to worship, attendance and participation sometimes is a struggle. This is a freedom that our forefathers felt was one of the most important factors in their journey to a better world.

Education in this community has always been important. Special recognition needs to be given to the people who have provided this opportunity: school boards, faculty, support staff, community and parents. Thanks also must be given to the students, who have taken advantage of the opportunities which were provided for them and in return have given back to society the best of themselves.

Lastly, mention must be made of the community—a community that over the years has progressed with pride and sacrifice, which continues to provide the best opportunities, possible to everyone in the surrounding areas. The cooperation which is needed to continue to make us a better place in which to live is not always easy. Many businesses have come and gone. The McPherson Farmers Mutual Fire Insurance Company incorporated on June 6, 1881, and the St. Clair State Bank in July of 1906 have served the community with dedication and dignity throughout the years.

As we look back and see what has been, let us also look ahead and see what our part may be to make the future even better.

Ladies from St. Clair posing in front of the new bank building.

Introduction

This project started as a dream, hoping to put into words and pictures the memories of this little community that once was the home of the Winnebago Indians. It was the site of future dreams of our forefathers who came from different foreign countries looking for a better and more prosperous life for their families. My intent was to encourage people to reminisce about the past in order to preserve for the future. As the sesquicentennial is celebrated in 2005, I feel it is an opportune time to collect and organize this project.

Unwilling to attempt to do a project of this magnitude alone, I solicited the help of several St. Clair area natives. A special thanks to Shirley (DeMars) Fitzloff-Halberg, Norla Hesse and Mary McComb for their help in research, interviewing and in every other way of assisting in this project.

A "special thanks" for the financial assistance from Dale Stolt at the St. Clair State Bank, which was needed to complete this book and for everyone who in any way assisted by contributing stories, pictures and information. Without all of you this would have stayed as a "dream."

It is my intent to make the reading of this book an enjoyable as well as an informative experience. Although I am not a professional author, I have attempted to be as accurate as time allowed. Many people have contributed even though they felt they were not able to submit an appropriate article. It is the desire of the entire committee that you find the contents as exciting as we did while doing the project.

The discrepancies that may be found are inevitable as every one may remember different events in different ways. Exclusion of any family or other portion of life in this production may be due in some part to lack of sufficient time, failure of people to submit information and misinterpretation. Although this book of memories is not a complete history of the area, please be assured that every event that has taken place over the years has played an important role in who and what we are today.

Thank you to the many, many individuals whose contributions are found throughout this publication.

I trust all who read this book will over look any errors with tolerance and in proper perspective.

"God Bless America" and bless everyone who takes the opportunity to read *Years of Memories*.

Myrtle Westphal, Project Coordinator

Behold the Work of the Old...
Let your Heritage not be Lost,
But bequeath it as a Memory,
Treasure and Blessing...
Gather the lost and the hidden
And preserve it for thy Children
Christian Metz, 1846

(Submitted by Nick Cords)

Seated, L to R: Brian Lynch, Mayor; Kathy Seys, City Clerk;
Julie Spear, council member
Standing: council members Collin Scott, Micheal Wheaton and Doug Westphal

St. Clair City Hall and Fire Department

Message from St. Clair Mayor

GREETINGS:

As one of many people who will be celebrating the 150th anniversary of St. Clair, I extend my congratulations. I feel humbled to be your mayor during this great milestone in history. I claim St. Clair as my hometown as I was born in the farming community and became a city resident in 1993. Over the years there have been changes and hopefully, more changes are in the future.

St. Clair has changed considerably over the past forty years for me. I remember in the early 1970's a railroad dividing our school and football field, serving the grain elevator at that time. However, it was the end of the line and soon became the end of the railroad history. Also at that time St. Clair boosted having a hardware store, two grocery stores, a full service gas station, TV repair shop, barber shop, restaurant, a couple of bars, insurance business, bank, school, and district owned school buses as well as the post office. We carried a lot of pride in keeping these businesses but as our needs changed, so did our Main Street. The grocery stores closed, along with the hardware store. Now we have two auto repair shops, car wash, two beauty shops, wholesale pet supply, and the bar. Our grocery line decreased to the convenience store, along with the gasoline need. The post office, bank, insurance company and school have remained: and of these the school is our means of stability.

We do have an excellent school system supported by a strong and proud community. We have been able to meet the needs of our children with a new facility as well as maintaining if not increasing enrollments of children from preschool through grade 12. Our school bus system is now privately owned and operated.

We are a very strong farming community but we have also transitioned into a bedroom community of Mankato. The city itself relies on city jobs rather than the income from grain and livestock as our mainstay. With an annual budget of $400,000 and one full-time city clerk and two full-time maintenance people, the city is doing well.

As I start my second term in office, we are in the early stages of making necessary changes such as replacing the water tower system, as well as the water treatment system. As we grow and the equipment ages, changes are necessary but in order to grow we will have to encourage people to come. At the present, we need land to offer for building houses but we are very much in need of supplying housing for our senior citizens, which is also in the early stage of development. In 15 years we have increased our population by approximately 200 people – proof of steady growth. I hope during my tenure of being in this office, we will complete great accomplishments as listed above and include any others as the need arises. We have been open and will continue to be open to the needs of our residents and those who enjoy what St. Clair has to offer.

City of St. Clair Mayor, Brian Lynch

St. Clair 2004

Table of Contents

DEDICATION i

INTRODUCTION ii

GREETINGS FROM MAYOR v

OUR NATIVE AMERICAN PAST 1

MCPHERSON TOWNSHIP 17

ST. CLAIR 31

OUR CHURCHES AND CEMETERIES 45

OUR SCHOOLS 57

CENTENNIAL CELEBRATION – SEPTEMBER 1955 65

EVENTS OVER THE YEARS 73

OUR FAMILIES – BIOGRAPHIES 161

MEMOIRS 293

PAST BUSINESSES AND ORGANIZATIONS 329

ST. CLAIR IN 2005 335

CLOSING THOUGHTS 357

BIBLIOGRAPHY 359

INDEX 361

Winnebago Agency House from an original oil painting by artist Emm Miller

CHAPTER ONE

Our Native American Past

HOW THE WINNEBAGO SETTLED IN MANKATO

It has not been possible to obtain satisfactory evidence as to the true origin of the Winnebago Indians. (Webster's Dictionary - "muddy water people")

Several hundred years ago the Winnebago had their home on the Turkey River, in Eastern Iowa, near Dubuque. They were removed from there to Long Prairie, Minnesota.

Then they came to Blue Earth County. The government had established a reservation for them here but many refused to come, preferring to stay at Long Prairie. History has some interesting versions of their origin.

(Additional Notation: The reservation that was provided here for this tribe by a treaty made at Washington, on February 27, 1855, included in Blue Earth County the townships of Rapidan, Decoria, McPherson, Lyra, Beauford and Medo. It continued six miles east in Waseca County, there including Alton and Freedom townships. By a later treaty at Washington, April 15, 1859, the Winnebago relinquished the west half of this Reservation, "to be sold by the United States in trust for their benefit." By an act of Congress, February 21, 1863, the east half, comprising McPherson, Medo, Alton and Freedom, was directed to be similarly sold, another reservation having been provided in Dakota. From Warren Upham: *Minnesota Geographic Names*)

One source states they were driven from Mexico by the companions of Cortez or their successors, that they resisted all attempts to drive them from their native lands until the white traders hunted them with dogs of uncommon size and ferocity.

The Winnebago never lost their hatred of the Mexican Spaniards.

Some authors believe they are descendants from the same stock as the Sioux and that their language is proof of this. Other sources reveal that this great nation originally resided somewhere to the north of the Great Lakes, and emigrated south. After a long and tiring journey, a large band of them, calling themselves Ho-ho-ga or "Fish Eaters," separated from the main group, and established other residence on the margin of the lake. This band was supposedly known by the name of Winnebago. During the journey other bands separated from them on the Mississippi and received the name of Conays.

However great and powerful the nation may have been, they were by 1900 fast deteriorating, mentally and morally, on their reservation in Nebraska. They were dying off at the rate of between 50 and 100 per year.

Peaceful Indians

These then, were the Winnebago Indians. Like most Indian tribes they were constantly being driven to different areas. The fact they were predominantly peaceful with whites all during this time distinguished them from other Indian Tribes.

It was in 1848 that the Winnebago, once the proud owners of all southern Wisconsin, were removed from Iowa to Long Prairie, Minnesota. The journey was long and was marked by dissatisfaction and desertion. It was

inspired by parties who were jealous of Hon. H. Rice, (one of the white men leading the tribe northward), by whiskey sellers who hovered about the train and by Wabasha III, who, at Winona, offered the Winnebago a share of his territory in Minnesota.

In fact, it became necessary to invoke the aid of soldiers from Fort Snelling and to arrest Wabasha for inciting sedition among the Winnebago.

Once the reservation at Long Prairie was reached, individual deserters who, in 1848-1850, abandoned it were occasionally apprehended by the soldiers of Fort Snelling and returned.

The Aborigines of Minnesota, published by the Minnesota Historical Society in 1911, says: "This unwillingness to remain at Long Prairie was entirely unjustifiable."

"The country was well adapted to their needs, a United States agent (J. E. Fletcher) was with them, the annuities secured to them by their treaty were dispensed with regularity and they had no trouble with the neighboring tribes. They had as local fur-trader, David Olmsted."

Whiskey Problem

During their stay of seven years (1848-1855) at the Long Prairie Reservation, whiskey seemed to be the big problem, causing discontent and turmoil.

James E. Child's *History of Waseca County* reveals "...there was no danger from the Winnebago; so long as they should remain sober."

After they had outlived their welcome at Long Prairie, the Winnebago were herded further south. This time, their domain was to within three miles of the southern part of Mankato.

The year was 1854; this part of Minnesota was just starting to be settled and some 1,500 "savages" swooping down on Mankato like an avalanche caused widespread protests from the Mankato Populace.

The tribe itself was also very much discontented...upon reaching their new destination, the Winnebago found their new sanctuary located on the Blue Earth River. Arrangements for their settling here had been made in 1855. Their discontent may be found in the fact their tribe had been rather prosperous up until the time they had to pull stakes at Long Prairie.

Plant 700 Acres

In 1852, the Winnebago planted 700 acres: 300 by the Ojibwa and 305 by the Sioux, showing a more prosperous condition among the Winnebago than among either of the other tribes.

Their fears were ill founded, for the time being at least. Their main occupation had been agriculture and the land they were destined to settle on was well adapted for their purpose.

They were pleased with their new location and the energetic guidance of their friend and agent, J. E. Fletcher. The land they were given amounted to 9½ townships according to some sources and to 6½ by others.

It was 30 miles long east and west, by 13 miles wide north and south. Another version has it 25x13 miles wide north and south. Another version has it 25x13 in area.

The reason for the whites in the area complaining lay in the fact that some 12 or 15 had to give up their homesteads.

The government paid them for their loss, of course, but the very real threat of being scalped by these "savages" still remained.

Actually, the Winnebago tribe was a very peace-loving one and was known to side with the white in time of crisis. The Winnebago had a magnificent domain. They were entirely satisfied and they made rapid improvement under the leading of agent Fletcher, but always in the face of neighborhood jealousies, and the evils thrust upon them by the ever-present whiskey-seller.

Hughes' *History of Blue Earth County* says of the situation, "The people raised the most vigorous protest against these confiscations of their territory. They were the main topics of conversation all the time." (1855)

Whites Protest

On the 2nd of June, a mass meeting convened at Mankato to protest against the Indian reservation.

"Resolutions were passed protesting against so many savages menacing the lives and property of the adjacent white settlements, and against taking so much territory from civilization and the County of Blue Earth for the perpetuation of savagery in its midst."

A committee was appointed to present the grievances to Gov. Gorman. But it was to no avail as far as the Indian reservation was concerned, as their cry for redress was too gentle to be heard in Washington.

Arrive at Mankato

About the middle of June the entire Winnebago tribe, over 2,000 strong, arrived at Mankato. Some came up the river in bark canoes; others came upon ponies and dog-carts and still others on foot. General Fletcher decided upon the spot where the village of St. Clair now stands as the headquarters for the tribe. Here he had his own house and the government houses and stores erected and the place was called the "Winnebago Agency."

Agent C. H. Mix in 1858 reported the Winnebago to be an industrious and happy lot, "taking hold in real earnest upon the duties of agricultural life."

Eight hundred acres were under good cultivation, furnishing enough for the Indians and their stock. Carpenters, blacksmiths and other mechanics were occupied.

A brick maker made 200,000 excellent brick and three brick houses were built. One hundred sixty-eight pupils attended the manual labor school.

In 1860 these statistic were reported: total number of red men at agency, 2,100; number of families, 400; females, 706; children, 878; residing off reservation, (Wisconsin especially) 200; acres of land cultivated 1,600; cases of small pox 260 (43 fatal).

The Winnebago tribe included a medicine man by the name of "Baptiste" who used water from the nearby "Morse Mineral Springs" which was located just north of the McPherson Township line, in Section 29 of LeRay Township. The medicinal qualities of the spring were first discovered and utilized by the whites around 1889. Indian folklore praised the water from the springs, claiming it contained health-giving properties and was rich in minerals. In 1889, Daniel Morse, who owned the property on which the springs were formed, had the water from the springs tested and found that the claims were indeed true. A stock company was later formed and the water was bottled.

One School

The agency had one school with two interpreters and 188 pupils enrolled. The branches taught were orthography, reading, writing, arithmetic, geography, grammar, and housework for girls.

Hughes says this glimpse of Indian agency life in Blue Earth County does not incorporate the full report. Left out are: "The number of gallons of whiskey consumed, the quarrels between themselves and between them and the whites, the stealing from the Indians by the whites and from the whites by the Indians, and filth and degradation everywhere."

It might be added that on Saturday, Dec. 20, 1862, the *Mankato Weekly Record* had this to say pertaining to young Indian boys drinking lager beer, "...and the agent, fearing that the morals of his good Indians' might be corrupted, thereby issued an edict prohibiting the beer trafficking." It was in cases like this that bitter quarrels ensued between the agents and government men on one hand and the citizens and soldiers on the other.

Everything up until this time seemed to be progressing reasonably well. The Winnebago were again becoming a self-sufficient, prosperous tribe.

Still, settlers in the area wanted them out of the way. They had in their possession some of the finest cropland in the world and this wasn't doing our ancestors any good.

Sioux Outbreak Contributed to Winnebago Removal

Three events brought a swift and unwarranted removal of the small Winnebago group of Indians settled on a reservation just outside Mankato. The great election of 1860 took place, the Civil War erupted in the south, and the Sioux outbreak began here in Minnesota Aug. 17, 1862.

Winchell, in his book *Aborigines of Minnesota*, had this to say about the unfortunate circumstances about to take place.

"The (promised) allotments were never completed. The Winnebago, curtailed in their annuities, surrounded by hostile, or at least unfriendly white people, unable on account of the unsettling of their land tenure to continue farming operations, finding the reservation destitute of game, and preyed upon by all the wiles of the merciless whiskey-sellers who swarmed about their borders, were reduced to destitution and some of them to the borders of starvation.

Notwithstanding their dire condition in 1867, the Secretary of the Interior stated officially that "no evidence has been discovered calculated to implicate the tribe. Most of them have remained quietly on their reservation during the war (Sioux Outbreak)."

The *Mankato Semi–Weekly Record* during September and October 1862 gave several isolated cases of a Winnebago participating in the outbreak, however.

An October 11, 1862, issue of this paper went on to state, "General Pope, upon his arrival in our state, assured our people that if it could be shown that even one Winnebago had cooperated with the Sioux, he would hold the entire tribe responsible, and deem it sufficient grounds for their removal."

Commissioner Dole had mentioned that the condition of the Winnebago was peculiar. He was satisfied that while it might have been true that a few of them were engaged in the atrocities of the Sioux the tribe as such "is not more justly responsible for their acts than our government would be for those of a pirate who might happen to have been born upon our territory."

But it was true that the people of Minnesota had equally as much hatred toward the Winnebago as against the Sioux, and they demanded that the Winnebago, as well as the Sioux, be removed beyond the limits of the state.

General's Sibley and Pope accused the Winnebago of participating in the outbreak and although several were captured and tried at the military court none were proven guilty.

Daniel Buck, in his book *Indian Outbreaks*, elaborates on this situation. "On the 12th day of October, 1862, Little Priest and eleven Winnebago Indians, who were at the Lower Sioux Agency at the time of the Outbreak, and supposed to have been engaged in the murders there, were arrested by order of General Pope and taken to St. Paul for trial."

No satisfactory reason was given for such discharge, and the people were greatly dissatisfied. They were discharged at night, although the testimony of members of the Indian Counsels showed their complicity with Little Crow.

This release aroused a feeling of alarm and indignation on the part of the people, less the whole of the condemned Sioux should escape.

It was reported that such leaders as Little Priest, Hounka, and Winneshiek gave the whites cause to have some fear of the Winnebago when these few outlaw Indians tried to induce the others to join in the Sioux Uprising. However this was never proven to be fact.

It was such good influence of the older chiefs and headmen, such as Decoria, Good Thunder, La Sallieur, Good Heart, Four Cloud, Yellow Bank and others that kept the Winnebago in favor of the white man.

As a whole the Winnebago were as badly frightened as the whites, and could not have been induced under any circumstances to join the Sioux.

Theodore C. Blegen, in his book, *Minnesota, A History of the State*, says, "Much anxiety in Minnesota centered in the possible participation of the Chippewa and Winnebago in the war, but there is little evidence that these Indians did in fact take part."

The terrible events of 1862 created mass hysteria on the part of the white settlers. So far as they were concerned all Indians were terrible. It had a tragic effect on the Winnebago. Plans for their removal from this area were made by civic minded and well-meaning Mankato citizens.

Hughes remarks, "About January 1, 1862, a secret society called "Knights of the Forest" was organized at a law office in Block 14 of Mankato. Its purpose was to have both the Sioux and the Winnebago Indians removed from Minnesota. Sub-lodges were organized at Garden City and Meridan and perhaps elsewhere."

Through the efforts of this society and of the constant clamor of the people here and elsewhere, Congress was finally induced, during February and March 1863, to pass acts for the removal of both tribes from Minnesota to Nebraska and South Dakota.

It was on April 25, 1863, that the Winnebago were officially notified that a new reservation had been established for them. It was to be located on a barren tract of land on the Missouri in South Dakota.

A council convened for the express purpose of informing them of this action. Batiste LaSallieur, their head chief, told his group that he had seen the country and that it was cold and barren, without timber and not fit for habitation. Councils met to discuss the matter and express their dissatisfaction and dismay, but it was all to no avail.

On May 2, about a fourth of them attended by Marcus Moore went to Wilton, where Judge Donaldson was holding a term of court, and applied for naturalization papers with the intention of filling claims on the land. The judge refused their application and the people had Moore arrested.

Chief Winneshiek with 200 to 300 followers decided to rebel and left for Lake Elysian defying the authorities. This old chief was of strong character and the leader of the conservative party in the tribe, who were bitterly opposed to every mode of civilization life. He thought whiskey was all right, though.

He always went clothed in Indian garb and generally carried an old spear instead of a gun. Because of his opposition to everything pertaining to civilization, he had been dropped from the head chieftainship.

The whites had been dishonest with the Indians, both in the distribution of government annuities and in sale of goods by traders. This, too, caused a great deal of ill feeling among the Indians. In the distribution of the last goods, sent by the government to this county for the Winnebago, 1,420 blankets had been sent, but only 500 were delivered to the Indians; 1,150 yards of blue cloth sent, only 275 yards delivered; 2869.5 yards of other cloth sent, none delivered; four dozen plaid wool shawls sent, none delivered. The goods not delivered were valued at $10,000.

This was bound to create agitation among the Indians toward the whites, for the whites were stealing from them and thought nothing of it.

Winnebago Ouster Resulted in Bloody Savagery

It was the job of Justus C. Ramsey (brother of the governor) to see to the removal of the Winnebago from the Mankato area. They were to be received in a camp located just behind the location of the present Hubbard Mill in Mankato.

This was called "Camp Porter" in honor of John J. Porter, who had been one of the most active participants in the removal of these Indians. The first group arrived on May 5, 1863. There were 100 of them.

Hughes dramatically describes the savagery that followed; "The next day May 6, the Winnebago under Chief Winneshiek, killed two Sioux spies, who had come to visit them at Lake Elysian, and mutilated their bodies in a shocking manner.

"Another Sioux, who had married a Winnebago squaw and had lived with the tribe all winter, left them saying he was going to tell the Sioux.

"They followed him to the Agency and killed him, also, and dismembered his body in a most horrible manner.

"They cut out his tongue and hung it on a pole, because he had said he would tell the Sioux. Another took his scalp and stretched it on a hoop attached to a pole, another took his head, another took his arm, etc.

"The Chief Little Priest cut off his finger nails with strips of skin attached and tied them about his own wrists.

"A party of about twenty young bucks decked in paint and feathers, with wreaths of weeds and grass on their heads, brought the two Sioux scalps and the tongue, adorned with gay ribbons with them and paraded along Main and Front streets yelling and hooting to the accompaniment of half a dozen Indian drums.

"This was done to curry favor with the whites and make them think they were the enemies of the Sioux."

By May 9, Camp Porter was bulging with over 800 Winnebago. Also on this date a group of soldiers were sent to bring in Chief Winneshiek and his party.

The Winnebago began their departure from Mankato; 445 embarked on the steamer Pomeroy and 355 on the Eolian. The war party with the two Sioux scalps was on the first boat and what a sight they must have been.

They sat in a circle on the upper deck with the two scalps hung on poles in the center, pounding wildly on their tom toms and chanting eerie Indian war songs.

Their half-naked bodies were smeared with mud and paint and their long, shaggy hair was full of grease and feathers. This made for a picture of savagery in its ugliest form, and surely made the whites shiver with distaste as the Indians passed down the river.

On May 10, 1863, 338 more Winnebago departed on the Pomeroy, and on the 14th, 300 of Winneshiek's band had been rounded up and left on the same boat.

The rest of the tribe left May 17 for St. Peter by wagon and took the boat from there. The people of Mankato were very happy to see the last of them leave and celebrated by firing cannons and raising flags.

This was the last of the Indians in Blue Earth County and a new era dawned on its history.

The white felt the county's growth had been greatly retarded with the six townships and a half of its very best territory in the hands of the Indians.

Settlers began rushing into this rich vacant land even before the government had time to bring it to market.

Because the Winnebago had not joined in the Outbreak, the Sioux were bitterly disappointed in them.

This and the bitter loss of their Reservation by the Winnebago, which they dearly loved, quickly led to bad blood between the two tribes.

This feeling soon came out as open hostility and by 1864 and 1865, Little Priest and many of his people sided with the whites against the Sioux. They blamed the Sioux completely for their troubles.

Winchell, in his book, tells about the effect the Act of Congress had, from February 21, 1863 onward, on the Winnebago tribe.

"It requires that they be removed peacefully and quietly by the President to a tract of land beyond the limits of any state, equal in extent to their diminished reservation and well adapted for agricultural purposes.

"Their lands were ordered to be appraised and their building and other improvements paid for, the proceeds of such sale to be expanded in necessary improvements on their new reservation.

At the same time a large amount of provisions and agricultural and mechanics tools was purchased by the government for the establishment of the Winnebago on their new reservation.

"The selection of the land was made by Supt. Clark W. Thompson, who also conducted the removal, at the upper side of Sueotka Creek, in South Dakota, about 80 miles above Fort Randall, on the north side of the Missouri. The Sioux were their neighbors immediately toward the east, according to the plan of Supt. Thompson.

"The Winnebago removed were 1,945, of whom 531 were men. The removed Sioux were considerably less in number.

The sterility of this region made the Winnebago dissatisfied and they were permitted, March 6, 1865, to occupy a tract ceded to them by the Omaha in Nebraska.

"In 1890 those on this reservation numbered 1,215, but a considerable number (perhaps an equal number) returned to their old haunts in Wisconsin, Minnesota and Iowa, where they engaged variously in agriculture.

As a tribe the Winnebago have been generally peaceful, at least as far as relates to the whites, tractable and easily inducted to the simpler arts of civilization.

"They have been unfortunate in having been subject to the cupidity of neighboring white settlers, and their lands have been ceded by them no less than seven times in consequence of the encroachments of the whites.

"Though they have been paid liberally for their lands at each change of habitat, they have been retarded greatly in all their efforts at improvements."

After the Indians were removed from the St. Clair area, the lands were sold to the white settlers under sealed bids.

The lowest price paid was $2.50 per acre. The lands were taken with great haste and by 1864 much of it was occupied and improved.

The post office was still called "Winnebago Agency" until 1886, when it was changed to "St. Clair." This name was in honor of General St. Clair.

It should be noted that the view held by Little Decora, a noble Indian, was predominant throughout the small Winnebago nation at the time their agency was located near Mankato.

While watching the lights in the sky from the burning of New Ulm, he said that he had no fear for himself, or for the old men, but that if the Sioux came, he did not know about all the young men. As for himself, he would be found dead at the white man's door, defending it.

His attitude had great influence on his tribe for he was highly respected by them and when some Winnebago wanted to join the Sioux in their uprising, he was one of the very influential chiefs discouraging such action. Always a true friend to the white man, Decoria Township was named after him.

Up until 1927, Rev. Henry Roe Cloud, a Winnebago whose descendents had resided here, was the only Indian to ever graduate from Yale College, and he shared with the son of ex-President Taft the high honors of the class.

It is easily understood, when considering the circumstances of the time, why the Winnebago were evicted from Blue Earth County. We were living in a phase of history when this area was a part of the "Wild West." Men, probably more so than now, were greedy, short tempered and irrational.

Proof of their being short tempered lies in the fact that lynching was a widespread practice; it was not uncommon for a couple of thousand men to be lynched each year in the United States.

Here, in Blue Earth County, our ancestors had suffered severely at the hands of the Sioux. Time was not taken to differentiate between a good and a bad Indian, in this case between a Winnebago and a Sioux.

It was, therefore, felt that the Whites could rid themselves of Indian trouble by sending all Indians in the area as far away from our borders as possible. This was done in 1863, yet Minnesota was to experience more conflict with the Indians.

Blue Earth and other Minnesota counties could expand now, but many people on looking back in our history of expanding at the Indians expense find little comfort in the thought.

By John Haack – *Mankato Free Press* - February 1967

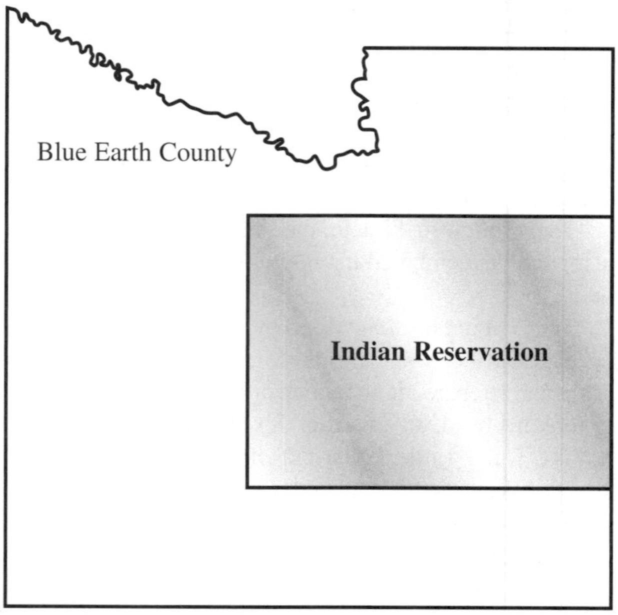

INDIAN CHIEF CHALLENGED COUNTY PIONEER TO DUEL

While visiting the late Captain Keysor some years before his death, he gave the writer an amusing story of his being challenged to fight a duel with one of the Winnebago Indian chiefs, on the Winnebago Indian reservation, which was then located where St. Clair now stands. Captain Keysor was a millwright by trade, and at the time of this incident, in the year 1858, the old pioneer was employed by the government in the erection of a sawmill there. It would appear that Chief Little Priest and Cut Nose, who lived on the reservation during the year 1858 had a great craving for "firewater," and when under the influence of the liquor were always looking for a fight. Captain Keysor was busily chiseling a mortise joint on the end of a log, which was to go into the sawmill, one day, when Little Priest had imbibed too freely. The chief approached him and dared him to fight a duel. The Indian had a murderous looking bow and a number of arrows, which he handled in a way that Keysor did not like.

Captain Keysor refused to accept the challenge, and a little later was laughed at by some of the other white men working there. When the Indian returned and again challenged Captain Keysor, he sent him over to the men who had laughed at him, and told Little Priest that they were just itching for a scrap. "He bluffed the whole lot of them," said Captain Keysor, "and then it was my turn to laugh."

"Had it not been for the level headedness of Chief Winneshiek," said Captain Keysor, "the Winnebago would have joined the Sioux in the outbreak of 1862." This old man had more than ordinary intelligence, and it was his counsel that kept the younger men of the tribe from joining in that massacre. Had they joined the Sioux, Mankato would undoubtedly have shared the fate of New Ulm.

Captain Clark Keysor

"Little Priest, who was the son of Chief Winneshiek, was considered a bad Indian, and was the terror of his entire tribe. He was thought to possess a charmed life. He had killed several of his tribe members in cold blood, so you can easily see that when he came up to me that day armed with a bow and some fierce arrows, I was not very anxious to become engaged in an encounter with him. At the time of the attack by the Sioux on Captain Marsh's command at the Redwood Ferry, it is said that Little Priest, who had gone up there with some of the Winnebago a few days previous, had taken part in the atrocities there and later at New Ulm and Fort Ridgely. He returned to the agency at St. Clair a few days later and described killings, so minutely, that some believed he himself had committed the deeds he attributed to that of the Sioux. This rascal did manage to work up considerable trouble and excitement at the agency. Had it not been for the wisdom of father, Winneshiek, the Winnebago would have attacked Mankato from the south, while the Sioux would have swooped down the Minnesota valley and attacked from that direction.

"Mankato people should hold a warm spot in their hearts for old Chiefs Winneshiek, Good Thunder, Yellow Bank and Four Cloud, for through their wisdom and love for the whites, they dissuaded the Winnebago from joining the Sioux," said the old veteran.

"This ill-natured chief was arrested with some of the others, who had accompanied him to the Redwood Agency, on suspicion of being implicated in the outrages at Redwood and New Ulm. Little Priest and other suspects were taken to Fort Snelling for trial. A short time later they were returned to Mankato to be tried before a court martial before General H. H. Sibley at his camp in what is now Sibley Park. Some very damaging evidence was produced by Indian half-breeds who had been in the fight at New Ulm. One witness stated that after the Sioux had shot a white man and wounded him badly, Little Priest rushed forward and stabbed the victim with a knife several times. Little Priest was cleared of the charge, however.

"The people of this vicinity," said Captain Keysor, "were fed up on Indian atrocities and petitioned Congress to have the Winnebago removed from Minnesota. They were finally bundled on a steamboat at Mankato and started on their journey down the Minnesota and Mississippi and up the Missouri River to their new reservation in Nebraska.

Little Priest, as the boat pulled out into the stream from the levee in Mankato, stood erect and waved adieu to the land where he had reddened his hands in the blood of both his own tribe and that of the white man.

"Later I heard he enlisted in a company of U.S. scouts at Omaha, and distinguished himself in fighting against the Sioux. In an encounter with the Sioux, Little Priest was mortally wounded, but not before he killed three of the party including the chief. Taking the slain Sioux chief's horse he managed to reach the fort, but soon succumbed to his wounds. Thus ended the life of Little Priest, who once dared me to fight a duel with him at Blue Earth County Winnebago Indian agency," said the sturdy old veteran of the Indian and Civil Wars.

In Thomas Hughes "Indian Chiefs of Southern Minnesota (1854-1934)," he vividly describes the events of the 1862 uprising. He talks of Hoonk-Hoo-No-Kaw (Little Chief), commonly called "Little Priest," as being the most active and among the most noted of the Winnebago Chiefs, when that tribe was domiciled in Minnesota. His father, whose Indian name was Mor-ah-tshay-kaw (The Traveler), was also known as "Little Priest." Mr. Hughes also writes of a Dr. M. R. Wickersham, who was the physician at the Agency, and his daughter, who later became Mrs. E. D. B. Porter.

It is noted that Little Priest without doubt was the most courageous, gritty, daring and energetic of all the Winnebago Chiefs, if not also the most able. With all he possessed a very kind and generous spirit. He frequently bought food and clothing and distributed them to those of his band who were in want, because of sickness or old age. The Winnebago included him with Winneshiek, Waukon and Decoria as their three greatest heroes and chieftains.

By Frank Franciscus - *Mankato Free Press* Staff Writer - 1946

Chief Little Priest

WINNEBAGO INDIAN AGENCY

A treaty involving the United States government and the Winnebago Indian chiefs occurred on the 27th of February 1855. It granted the Indians a permanent home: a thirty-mile by thirteen-mile strip of land that encompassed a portion of Waseca and Blue Earth Counties. The reservation extended beyond the junction of the Le Sueur and Blue Earth Rivers.

There were bitter complaints among the settlers against the government's moving the Indians to the Blue Earth County reserve. Twenty-three families had already claimed home sites, had made some improvements, and were forced to relocate.

It was found that the area could not provide adequate food for the two thousand Winnebago. Wild game was not as abundant here as it had been in the forested area of the Long Prairie Reservation farther north and annuities were always delayed. The Indian Agent, Jonathan E. Fletcher, proposed setting up a farm at the Agency where the Indians could learn farming. He thought this would aid them in providing for their needs.

The Winnebago Agency house and farm was located one mile southeast of the village now known as St. Clair, near the Le Sueur River in the township of McPherson. It was twelve miles from Mankato and originally it was on the daily mail route from Winona to Mankato. The village was also known as Winnebago Agency until the year 1886. The Agent's home and farm were located on the prairie south of the Le Sueur River valley and on the southern edge of the "Big Woods." The house was listed on the Minnesota State Register and also on the National Register of Historic Places.

The Agency Complex had a number of buildings: the agent's house, a warehouse, a schoolhouse, a carpenter shop, a physician's office and living quarters, several outhouses, blacksmith shop, a stable and several log houses for the Indian help (such as interpreters). The log school building remained in use as a school and church until 1876.

The Winnebago Agency House was built in 1855 and 1856 and was of Georgian style. It served as the office and dwelling place of the Indian Agent. The building was

A facsimile of the old Agency mission school and Catholic Church. This building was used for services between 1855 and 1874. When the Winnebago Indians were moved from the area in 1863, the first public school was founded.

constructed of salmon colored native brick. A sawmill and a brickyard were constructed by the U.S. government in 1855 to prepare building materials for the Agency complex. Both mill and brickyard were located along the banks of the Le Sueur River at the site now know as the village of St. Clair. It was possible for the sawmill to be converted to shingle making when needed. Native lumber was in abundance in this locale. Black walnut wood was used for the doors and woodwork in the interior. Many Indian were employed in the brick making for the Agency House. Two double paired chimneys were on each side of the structure which had a high pitched roof.

The first agent was General Jonathan E. Fletcher. He served as agent from June 1855 to April 1858. Fletcher taught many of the Indians to plant crops, build houses, and to wear white men's clothes. He persuaded the Indians to send some of their children to school: but he did not succeed in getting many converted to the white man's religion, mainly because of the white man's poor example. Agent Fletcher was succeeded by Charles H. Mix until 1861; and by A. D. Balcombe until 1863.

Soon there was pressure by the white settlers for the reduction of the reservation, and at the end of four years the Indians surrendered the west half for an addition to their annuities. After this there was even better progress among the Indians.

After the Sioux Indian uprising of 1862, public pressure was applied and necessitated the removal of all Indians from this area. The rage among the whites so terrified the Winnebago that they consented with eagerness to a proposal for their removal to a new reservation. The United States Government rescinded all treaties. In the spring of 1862 the Winnebago were loaded on riverboats and were relocated on the Omaha Reservation in eastern Nebraska.

The government announced the sale of the land in newspapers in large cities of the east and Chicago. Land promotions were booming in the middle 1860's and descriptive phrases of Winnebago Lands were often exaggerated. The following paragraph was taken from the *Shoemaker Business Directory of Mankato* (1885-1886) and it presents a more accurate picture.

"The Northwestern part of the county was originally covered with an unbroken forest, the extremity of what is know as the Big Woods. The remainder of the county is interspersed with prairie and timber. The prevailing kinds of wood are oak, maple, elm, ash, basswood, butternut, black walnut, hickory, cottonwood, and hackberry. Wild plums and grapes are found in abundance, as well as strawberries, raspberries, gooseberries, and cranberries. The soil is peculiarly adapted to the raising of grain. All kinds of vegetables grow to great perfection. Apples are cultivated with success and other kinds of fruit are gradually making their way into the country. Wild hay is abundant and very nutritious, and this in connection with the inexhaustible supply of water, makes Blue Earth County a natural stock raising region, and unsurpassed for dairy purposes."

Meanwhile, Henry Truman and his son, Josiah, had purchased the quarter section of the Agency farm, though they were then living in the District of Columbia. In the autumn of 1863, the Trumans and Henry Truman's son-in-law John Boswell, and their families arrived in Blue Earth County to take possession of the property. When the Winnebago were relocated, the Indian Agent had to accompany his assigned people and there were a number of surplus items to sell, such as agricultural items, tools and cattle that were too old to move. Therefore Lucius

Dyer, the former farm manager, was appointed to remain at the Agency House until all was disposed of. Mr. Dyer refused to vacate the premises to the Trumans and Boswells until the following spring. The newcomers sought an abandoned log house for shelter. There were thirteen people in their party, all family members. They remained there over the winter and moved into the Agency House in the spring of 1865.

Josiah Truman had applied for the land patent and chose to operate the Agency House as a hotel. This place was a stage stop on the direct route from Minnesota Lake and an ideal location for a lodging house. The rest of the families also remained here and assisted with the farming and in operating the hotel.

The period between 1867 and 1879 was particularly difficult, for the wives of Henry, Josiah and John died, Josiah Truman returned to the east and Henry Truman and John Boswell families continued the farming operation. Henry Truman died in 1880. John Boswell died in 1893.

In 1880, Duane Rasdall bought the Agency House and acreage. He continued farming and living in the house until his death in 1906. The Agency House was used as a social center with meetings such as ladies aid societies and township board meetings held there.

After Duane Rasdall's death, his wife, Jane, her daughter Grace and her son-in-law, Frank Chase continued residing there. Jane Rasdall died in 1921 and the Chases bought the property from the estate in 1923. They farmed the land and occupied the house until 1941 when they retired.

From 1941 until 1956 the property was owned and operated by Courrier Hubmer. The house stood empty. In 1956 Ralph Preston became the owner and in 1970 his son, Marvin, bought it. However, Marvin Preston and his wife Pat had lived in the house from 1956 until 1983. The brick façade was disintegrating and it was becoming impossible to repair the house. At the Preston's request the Agency House was burned April 15, 1986.

Many attempts were made to save the Winnebago Agency, as it was one of the two remaining Indian Agencies in Minnesota. The other is located at the Lower Sioux Agency in Redwood County.

An interesting notation concerning the Agency Road was that the Mankato's Agency Road was linked to the original Agency Road, which was located on an old Indian trail. Much of this is now Minnesota Highway # 83.

By Marion Boswell Hoffman for
The Heritage of Blue Earth County, MN, 1990

(Additional Notations from Thomas Hughes - *History of Blue Earth County*, 1909)

The delegation of Winnebago, who had accompanied General Fletcher, their agent, to Washington comprised three chiefs namely: Winneschiek or Waunk-annchakugah (the Coming Thunder), Hoonch-ha-haykah (Big Bear), and Hoonkhonokah (Little Priest), and three braves. These returned to St. Paul with General Fletcher by April 20th, 1855, and at once proceeded with him to the Blue Earth County, to inspect their new reservation and to accurately fix its boundaries. These matters had been left somewhat to the agent. On arriving at Mankato about the last of April, General Fletcher employed Evans Goodrich, the County Surveyor, to run the lines of the reservation. In the train of the Winnebago Indians came a few men, who at once took a prominent place in the business affairs of the agency. Among these were Asa White and Henry Foster. At one time this colony contained 2,000 Indians.

About August 1st, the Sioux Indians gave their new neighbors, the Winnebago, a great reception feast at Mankato, which in number of guests and the demonstrations held, far outdid the opening of the white man's wigwam. The streets, the woods, and the river literally swarmed for several days with these dusky denizens of the wilderness. Their costumes, consisting almost wholly of paint and feathers, were gorgeous. Their principle-gathering place was in Warren and Van Brunt's Additions. Four or more of the largest teepees were joined together to form the feast lodges. The sound of the tom toms and dance songs was scarcely hushed day or night.

A military company was organized at the Winnebago Agency on August 2, 1859, with Dr. Coleman as captain and Asa White as first lieutenant. Originally there were thirty members which in a month increased to forty-eight. They were equipped with Minnie rifles and all necessary accoutrements from the state armory. On August 3rd and 4th Major Cullen came to Mankato and paid the volunteers, who had served in the defense of the frontier during the Inkpadutah massacre. Dr. Lewis' company received about $12 to $13 apiece. Congress had appropriated on Jun 14, 1858, $20,000, but $11,163.81 had been used in expenses of investigation of causes of the massacre. The balance was used in paying claims of volunteer expeditions, search for, and ransom of female captives, and loss of property. The aggregate claims reached $446,232.62 and of these $25,114.91 was approved by Major Cullen, and was paid pro rata. The home guard companies did not receive anything for their services.

It is noted that the first 4th of July celebration was held in 1860. In the middle of April 1862 saw in every river a tremendous flood, and the bridge over the Le Sueur on the Agency road, which Mr. McCarty had mostly built at his own expense, was swept away. Also noted that in 1862, during the Sioux uprising, Newell Houghton of the Winnebago Agency was killed.

THE DEATH OF HONK HONKA

Life at an Indian Agency had many a sensation and many a tragedy. In April 1857, when the Inkpadutah trouble was at its height, there lived among the Winnebago, a vicious, drunken Indian named Honk Honka. In one of his wild periodic sprees he assaulted a white man so viciously that the matter could not be overlooked and the sheriff was sent for, who took the culprit to Mankato to lodge in the County Jail. It happened to be the very day that Capt. Lewis' company returned from their skirmish with the Sioux near Madelia, and everybody's attention was taken up with that exciting event. While the deputy sheriff was stopping a minute in the bar room of the Mankato House to discuss the news, he left Honk Honka, handcuffed, sitting on a bench near the door. Suddenly the Indian darted out and disappeared into the neighboring brush, and aided by the gathering darkness escaped. After spending some weeks down in Sibley County where some friends liberated his hands from the irons, he returned unexpectedly one day to the Agency and entered one of the Indian huts. Two papooses were sleeping on a bed in the room and Honk Honka, being drunk as usual, threw himself on the bed crosswise, pinning both children under him. The cries of the youngsters brought the mother at once to their aid, but unable to extricate them, she ran out yelling frantically for help. A white man named John Quinlan, hearing the disturbance, rushed in and jerked the Indian off the bed. Honk Honka drew a long, sharp knife and rushed furiously at Quinlan, who dodged around the stove in the center of the room. For half an hour or more the mad chase was kept up around that stove until Quinlan was nearly exhausted. There was no time to open the door and get out, for the knife in the hand of the whiskey crazed savage was too close to his back. The woman had disappeared and there was no response to his cries for help. At last he spied an axe in a corner of the room, and as he spun around the stove he managed to grab it, and facing suddenly about, he dealt the Indian a blow which severed his head from his shoulder. A number of young bucks soon came and gathered Honk Honka's body up in a blanket and buried it. A brother of the deceased refused to accept Quinlan's plea of self-defense, but threatened to avenge his brother's death. Knowing the man's character, Quinlan concluded the Agency was not the safest place on earth for him, and departed for parts unknown and thus ended the sprees of Honk Honka.

By Thomas Hughes - *History of Blue Earth County* - 1909

OLD WINNEBAGO INDIAN AGENCY IS AT ST. CLAIR

Somebody wrote in, so long ago that I've forgotten who or when, to tell me that there might be something of interest down around the old Winnebago Indian Agency at St. Clair, Minnesota.

I just got around to it and I'm glad I did.

One reason, outside of the pretty drive down Hwy. 169 to Mankato, is that I met Clay Boswell. He is an interesting and engaging source of historical information.

Boswell will be 77 next spring. He's spare and wiry, helps with the farming and climbs telephone poles to wire the barnyard.

"A fellow came in and said, 'You shouldn't be up there. You're too old for that.' I asked him how old he thought I was, and he said, 'Why, you must be nearly 65."

Height never did bother him, Boswell told me. Every year a friend takes him foxhunting in an airplane. He watches the ground as they go skimming along and never gets sick.

Boswell's grandparents on both sides of his family came into the St. Clair area shortly after the Winnebago agency was established in 1855.

I didn't know who or what to look for when I got into St. Clair (12 miles southeast of Mankato on Hwy. 83). But it didn't take me long to find out.

Bill Hager, hardware store proprietor, told me there was nobody who could begin to help me nearly as much as Clay Boswell.

I found him on the farm. He took me to the old agency house, 1.7 miles east of the center of town. He showed me where the timbers were cut and milled from walnut trees by the Le Sueur River and where the bricks were kilned.

Marvin L. Preston and family have lived in the old agency house for the last seven years. He farms the land around it back to the river. Five Preston boys (6 year-old twins, the others 4, 8 and 10) are running around where the Winnebago walked.

After the New Ulm battle with the Sioux (1862), the United States Calvary herded the white settlers around St. Clair into Tivoli, a small settlement three miles to the northwest. Sioux scouts killed one of their cavalry guards. Said Boswell:

"He was watering the horses in the river when he saw the Sioux in the weeds. He might have lived except that he put up a holler. The Sioux shot him. My grandmother saw him die on the doorstep of a little log cabin by the bridge. He is buried in Tivoli Cemetery.

"The Sioux tried to get the Winnebago to join the uprising and help them mop up the whites, but Chief Decora of the Winnebago had too many white friends. He wouldn't help.

"Some of the white settlers saw how good the land was and talked the government higher ups into moving the Winnebago out. This was started before the Sioux uprising. The Winnebago who had a little shack and had settled down weren't bothered. They took title to their land just like anybody else. Some of them made good farmers. They were nice people."

In Boswell's school about a quarter of the children were part or all Winnebago. Eventually, however, all the known Winnebago scattered. He blames the government dole. "They were always looking ahead to the next check."

Summer Tillotson, who built Boswell's grandfather's house (still standing), had a Winnebago wife. They left after selling the house, and Boswell doesn't know what became of them.

Don't imagine from all his interest in the past that Boswell is living in it. Here is a man of 76 who not only works but has a demanding hobby. He keeps flocks of wild geese and wood ducks—feeds them and makes pets of them.

"I suppose you have goose for Christmas," I remarked.

He laughed. "I've never killed a single one."

By Ben Kern - *Minneapolis Tribune* Staff Writer - 1963

INDIAN SKELETONS REVIVE MEMORIES OF THE WINNEBAGO

The excavation and subsequent reburial of six Indian skeletons on the Merlin Goodrich farm three and one-half miles south of St. Clair, brings back some old memories for Merlin's grandmother, a resident of Janesville Nursing Home.

Lottie Goodrich, who will be 87 on October 2, told the Argus that she was born on the farmstead, where the skeletons were unearthed, in 1890.

"I remember my mother telling about them moving the Indians off, she said. "I guess they just herded them up like cattle and took them away."

When Mrs. Goodrich was a little girl, an Indian named Yellow Blanket came to the farm and asked her father if he could camp on Rice Lake, which adjoins the Goodrich farm.

"Dad said he could and they put up a teepee down at the edge of our woods. Back then the lake was full of ducks and mudhens. In the spring you could catch carp and a few bullheads."

The family stayed by the lake for about a month before moving on, Lottie recalls.

During that time she remembers the man coming up to the house for food.

"Mom had just baked some bread so she sat him down and gave him some of it with milk. Then he put the rest of the bread in a leather pouch and poured the milk right in on top of it to take back to his wife."

Lottie recalls another time when an Indian woman named East Lake and her son came to the farm and asked for shelter. The family put them up in the basement.

"She stayed behind when the main group left," Lottie said. "I don't think the Indians were happy about moving."

Mrs. Goodrich also remembers the log pen that lay just to the east of their farmyard.

"It was a square pen lined with logs," she said. The skeleton of an Indian chief was propped up in the corner of the enclosure. It was like he was put there to look after the people buried there."

Lottie said that she and her brothers and sisters were scared to death of Indians, so they never went near the enclosure.

"But someone used to bring the chief food at night and it was always gone in the morning." She recalled. "I guess maybe the neighborhood dogs ate it. We had some dogs around the place too."

The wooden pen came to mind again this summer when Lottie's grandson, Merlin, started excavating for his family's new home. At the north edge of the basement, Merlin discovered the skeletons of six Indians.

All were buried facing west, toward the setting sun, as was the Indian custom. Each had a ring of nails around the skeleton, indicating that they had been buried in some type of coffin.

Among the Indian bones, Merlin found pieces of blankets, beads, brushes and small mirrors. There was also a Pipestone pipe and a French trader's pipe.

At first Merlin wasn't quite sure what to do with the skeletons. That question was settled after he contacted the Bureau of Indian Affairs and some Indians offered to rebury their ancestors.

"My main concern was to find them a proper resting place," he said. "We planned to bury them in the same location where they were originally."

Last Thursday about 30 Indians, some from as far away as Wisconsin, drove to the Goodrich farm and held a burial service. Merlin had collected all the bones and placed them in a sturdy wood coffin.

Following the burial service, which the Indians did alone, everyone was invited to share food and drink. A peace pipe was passed around.

Although the Winnebago Indians have been gone from Minnesota for over 100 years, their memory lives on and was recalled again last week just south of St. Clair.

From the *Janesville Argus* – 1977

HISTORY OF THE WINNEBAGO AGENCY HOUSE

Perched high above the Le Sueur River about one mile south of St. Clair sits a 128-year-old house. Its old walls seem strong, solid, permanent, as if they will shelter many more generations of hard working farm families. The building's major support is three side-by-side layers of soft brick set on a clay base. It is not a wooded frame encased in a veneer of brick. Its walls have therefore been prone to shifting, which might not have been the situation had the building been erected with less haste or put up with the improved engineering that came later in the century.

But looks are deceiving, and the Winnebago Agency House, as it is known to state historians, is deeply wounded from decades of heat and cold, and the shifting earth.

Having been built in 1855, these blows of old age may be fatal.

"The walls are shifting and repair would be extensive and expensive," stated the present owner, Marvin Preston, who with his family, have owned the house, which is on County Road 173, since 1970.

The history of the Agency House is tied to that bitter era in American history when the white man's government took upon itself the relocation and re-education of Native American Indian Tribes. One unfortunate clan was the Winnebago.

In about 1855 the group was moved to a 30 mile-by 13-mile strip of land in Blue Earth County and western Waseca County.

A model farm complex was built for the reservation on the prairie just south of the Le Sueur River valley and on the southern edge of the "Big Woods" of what is now St. Clair. In addition to at least 14 log homes, it included numerous brick buildings; among when a stable, physician's house, warehouse, blacksmith shop, interpreter's cabin, and the building that housed the administration offices and home for Agent Jonathan E. Fletcher. The

Winnebago Agency House after a kitchen and garage were added. ca. 1920

reservation existed for only eight years.

That imposing, Georgian style, two-story, red brick building is all that remains of the self-contained mini-village. Another brick home, just to the north of the present Agency House, was built by a trader who followed the Indians from Wisconsin and used bricks from the same brickyard to fashion his walls. It also remains.

When most of the Winnebago tribe moved to South Dakota, a few Indian families kept their allotted 80 acres, and stayed to farm near the agency until well in to 1900's.

Henry Truman, his son John, and John Boswell, his son-in-law, were adventurous men who perhaps were stifled by the civilization of Baltimore. They bought the Agency House farm in 1863 for $2 an acre and moved there with their families.

The 13-member group lived in a little log cabin for the first year because the reservation farm manager, a Mr. Dyer, was still in residence in the home while he disposed of livestock and cleared the account books.

The Trumans operated the Agency House, which included five huge bedrooms and numerous fireplaces, as a hotel. It also served as a stop on the stagecoach line that ran down to Minnesota Lake. One room, on the bottom story of the building, had a floor four inches higher than any of the other floors.

Legend has it that loggers from the Le Sueur River regularly climbed the banks to drink at the hotel's bar. The heavy traffic wore out the floor, but instead of tearing out the old and putting in the new, different floor was just laid over the top.

That room was known as "The Bar" well into the 1940's.

The period between 1867 and 1870 was particularly difficult, for the wives of Henry, Josiah and John all died. Josiah Truman returned to the east. Henry Truman and John Boswell kept the family together and continued the farming operation. Henry Truman died in 1880. John Boswell died in 1893.

Trumans' wife, who died of old age, was buried in a one-acre cemetery on the farm. When the remains were dug up in 1876 to be moved to another cemetery, the coffin and body weighed more than 400 pounds.

The surprised diggers opened the coffin to investigate and found that her body had petrified and was well preserved even though she had not been embalmed.

In 1882, Duane and Jane Rasdall bought the Agency House and acreage from the Henry Truman estate for $16 an acre. They continued farming and living in the house until his death in 1906. The Agency House was used as a social center with meetings such as ladies aid societies and township board meetings.

In time, the two families would be tied together by the marriage of two descendants. Three great-grandchildren of the Rasdalls and Boswells still live in the Mankato area: Harold Boswell, Marian Boswell Hoffman, and Jane Boswell Kroenke.

After Duane's death, his wife, Jane, her daughter Grace and her son-in-law, Frank Chase continued residing there. Jane died in 1921 and Grace and Frank Chase bought the property from the estate in 1923, for $100 per acre. That same year, the old stables and other outbuildings were demolished. They farmed the land and occupied the house until 1941 when they retired.

The Rasdall family gathered in the parlor at the Winnebago Agency house. ca. 1895

The Rasdall living room at the Winnebago Agency house. ca. 1895

A man named Currier Hubmer bought the place in 1941, but he never lived in the Agency House. (It is noted that Albert and Agatha (Oftedahl) Bollmann and their daughter Carol lived here during this time.)

Mr. Hubmer then sold the property to Ralph and Eleanor Preston in 1956. A son Marvin and his wife Patricia (Rahbeck) and two sons Gary and Joel moved to this site. In 1970 they sold it to their son Marvin and Patricia. They farmed the ground and raised their family here adding three more sons, twins Jim and John, and Peter. He has since painted the old agency's bricks white, done some interior remodeling and removed the south set of double chimneys. Marvin and Pat lived in the house from 1956 until 1983. The brick façade was disintegrating and it was becoming impossible to repair the house. On April 15, 1986, the Preston's requested the Agency House be burned down.

The Preston's youngest son Peter and his wife Jobi (Danberry) built a new home on this building site and continue to live in that home with their three children.

Historically Registered

In April 1973 the Agency House was listed on the Minnesota State Register of Historic Places as well as the National Register of Historic Places. The Application states that Agent Fletcher's house is one of only two agency buildings remaining in Minnesota; the other is located at Upper Sioux Agency in Yellow Medicine County. In addition to the house structure there is a great deal of archaeological potential here, potential, which has been destroyed at Long Prairie where the earlier Winnebago Agency buildings were located.

The simple federal style structure was built between 1855 and 1856 and is a two-story brick structure with a low-pitched gable roof and paired chimneys built into the sidewalls. Exterior decoration is at a minimum; the simple cornice, short eaves and unframed windows give a stark appearance to the structure. The house is rectangular in shape with five openings across each story of the front. The salmon colored brick has been painted white.

Presently the house is in good condition although there has been alteration and remodeling. The original fireplaces have been covered (two on each floor) and the large rooms divided. There is also a stucco addition at the rear.

The grounds of the agency house have been substantially changed since the agency was abandoned, but old foundations of former buildings can still be located.

Winnebago Agency is not salvageable.

(June 11, 1985)

Sometime in the next few weeks, in this the summer of its 130th year, what remains standing of the historic Winnebago Agency near St. Clair will come crashing down in a shower of dust, plaster, mortar, wood and brick.

A bulldozer or other mechanical equipment will finish what 13 decades of weathering had started – a deterioration that was gradual at first, then accelerating to the inexorable and climaxing this spring when the entire southeast corner collapsed under its own weight.

Unless the imposing and unique two level structure in a bucolic rural setting is reconstructed brick-by-brick – not likely – Minnesota will have lost one of two remaining buildings that served the Indian resettlement era of the 1850's-1860's.

The Agency had been converted into a home and modernized over the years – electrical service, plumbing, insulation, and an oil burner and white exterior paint. One of the one-time guestrooms, at the northeast corner, had been fashioned into a kitchen.

"We reared five boys in that house," remarked Mrs. Preston with affection. She and her husband now live in a split-level bungalow at the east limits of St. Clair and adjacent to the cemetery, about a mile from the Agency.

"We gave that house all the tender loving care we could."

The Prestons moved out of the Agency two and one-half years ago, for safety reasons. The brick walls were settling before then, a portion of the east wall having been fortified with concrete tile.

This is the corner-quarter that gave way completely, from eave to foundation, this spring.

What remains is a physical hazard, remarked Mrs. Preston. "We have grandchildren that play out there, so we'll have to tear down what's left."

It had been considered, at one time, to move the structure and restore it at the Farmamerica grounds west of Waseca, Minnesota, but estimated moving and restoration costs were $200,000 to $350,000 – money Farmamerica did not have.

For the Prestons, they will have to be content with having been faithful stewards to the end and consoled by the presence of cabinetry in their new home fashioned from the Agency's butternut fireplace mantles.

Test of stewardship

(April 18, 1986)

Whatever hope Marvin and Pat Preston had for the preservation of the 1860's Winnebago Agency were dashed by the rains of this date a year ago. Overnight, the southeast corner of the imposing structure on an obscure county road east of St. Clair gave way and crashed – from eaves to foundation – as a heap of brick and mortar.

The Prestons appreciated the agency's significance. They gave it all the physical attention they could reasonably afford.

Later, they offered it to any responsible organization, hoping that it could be carefully lifted and moved to a more prominent, public setting—relocated, ironically not unlike the Indians who were once ministered-to from the building.

But last spring's downpours prescribed a different, reluctant, final destiny. Now a hazard, the building's wooden members were purposely burned in a controlled fire this week and the remaining brick surfacing will be pulled down.

The Prestons would like to be regarded as having been good stewards. They certainly were, as somebody with lesser sensitivities would have had it bulldozed long ago.

(Special Notation: The information for the Winnebago Agency house was compiled from information from *The Mankato Free Press* by Ken Berg–1983, Marian Studer-Johnson–1985, Krystal Quinn–1986 and Patricia Preston–Keller.)

The deterioration and demolition of the Winnebago Agency house in 1985.

CHAPTER TWO

McPherson Township

McPherson Township lies to the north of Medo Township in the east tier in Blue Earth County. This township was formerly part of the Winnebago Indian Reservation. The Le Sueur River meanders across the township from southeast to northwest. The portion north of the river was once covered with heavy timber, while to the south of the river was fine prairie land. Rice Lake lay in the southwest corner of the township.

The township was first attached to Mankato for official purposes and was called Rice Lake in August 1855. The name of Rice Lake was chosen after the lake of that name located in the township, which was famous among the Indians for its production of wild rice.

The first settlers were Charles Mansfield and Ansen W. Callen, who settled on the east side of Rice Lake in the fall of 1854. A number of government officials and employees were of the Agency. On August 21, 1855, the town was made an election precinct under the name of Rice Lake.

Charles Mansfield, A. W. Callen and J. L. Alexander were the first election judges and twenty-one votes were cast in the fall of 1855. In 1855 white settlement in the immediate area was suddenly cut off by the National Congress, which had created a new reservation for the Winnebago Indians. Among those connected with the Indian agency, who came here with the Winnebago in June 1855, were: General J. E. Fletcher, Indian agent; Henry Foster, Joshua Ady, A. L. Foyles, W. J. Cullen, Superintendent of Indian School; Charles H. Mix, Asa White, George Culver, Peter Manaige, Newell Houghton and J. L. Alexander. In June 1856, John Johnson, later of Sterling, located at the Agency as blacksmith. In 1861, J. B. Hubbell and Lucius Dyer and other republican officials under Agent Balcome located at the agency. Shortly after Mr. Lincoln became president, Charles Mix superseded Gen. Fletcher as agent and he returned to Boston.

The Winnebago Indians were removed in May 1863, and immediately settlers began pouring into the town. There are many tales connected with the old Winnebago Agency.

By September 2, 1863, sufficient settlers had located in the town to require the County Board to create it into an independent municipality. The name was changed from Rice Lake to McClellan, after the famous Union General. The first town meeting was held at the home of Lucius Dyer on September 19, 1863. The following officers were elected: Supervisors, Asa White; Chairmen, J. Y. Cowell and Lucius Dyer; Clerk, Henry Foster; Treasurer, R.O. Bartlett; Assessor, Charles Manaige; Justices, J. L. Alexander and J. Y. Cowell; constables, Aaron Foyles and Alexander Payer.

Henry Foster was the first postmaster, appointed in 1856. James B. Hubbell succeeded him in 1863, who in turn was succeeded by Lucius Dyer in May 1863. The post office was designated "Winnebago Agency." Dyer had been an Indian farmer under Republican administration, but on the departure of the Winnebagoes, had purchased the land, on which the large brick residence of the Indian agents stood, and occupied it as a hotel.

In March 1865, he sold the place to Josiah C. Truman, who about the same time succeeded him as postmaster.

In February 1865, the name of the town was changed from McClellan to McPherson by act of the Legislature.

The post office of "Belleview" was established in June 1873 and was located in Section 32. James H. Eastman was the first postmaster. He served until January 1876, when Amos H. Eastman was put in charge. A. B. Preston succeeded Eastman in 1879.

The Methodist minister, Rev. B. Y. Coffin, taught the

first school in 1857 for the Indians at the agency. Francis Beveridge taught the first public school in 1863 at the agency. Nine school districts were formed over the years.

In the fall of 1872 schoolteachers in McPherson Township were Morris Wilkins, Frank Wilkins, J. L. Burgees, David Eastman, Eliza Wilson and Julius Dawley.

Taken from *Heritage of Blue Earth County*, by Julie Schrader, 1990

MCPHERSON TOWNSHIP CENTURY FARMS:

1865 Joseph & Catherine May, George & Mary May, Edward & Frances May, Eugene & Patricia May, Jack & Lisa May—1991

1866 Alpheus & Eliza Covel, George & Ella Covel, George & Lottie (Covel) Goodrich, Lyle & Stella Goodrich, Merlin & Elmay Goodrich—2003

1866 Asahel B. Preston, Clark & Lillie Preston, Delmar & Norma Preston—1980

1868 Anton & Anna C. Phillips, Harry & Lucille Phillips, Harold & Vera Phillips—1990

1888 Fred & Mary Thissen, Severin & Katie Thissen, Patrick Thissen & Catherine Thissen—1994

1892 Anton & Mary Lang, Lynden & Mildred Lang, Jerome & Mary Lang, Jerome & Kristine Lang—2003

1901 Paul M. & Anna Westphal, John & Frieda Westphal– Paul & Adeline Westphal, Bernard & Myrtle Westphal – Margie Westphal Fritz—2003

MCPHERSON TOWNSHIP BRIDGES

As mentioned earlier when one looks at a map of McPherson Township one can see the Le Sueur River crossing from the southeast across the entire township to the northwest corner. The Blue Earth County Public Works Department notes having four bridges over the river, three structures over streams and two structures over ditches.

In 2004 McPherson Township was paying an annual "Special Assessment Tax" on 18 county ditch repair assessments for a total of $1,051.90. As one can see the cost and upkeep of our road system has consumed a lot of tax dollars.

Century Farm: Records show this farm was transferred from the United States Government to Martin B. Dungan on August 5, 1869. On September 10, 1901, it was transferred from Thomas H. McGovern and his wife Winford to Paul Westphal, Sr. It was recognized as a "Century Farm" in August 2003.

The Hilton Bridge, which is located over the Le Sueur River on the north edge of St. Clair on Blue Earth County Road #28, was built in 1879 at a cost of $2,918 and was 70' long. It was replaced with Blue Earth County Bridge 07220 in 1958. The new bridge structure length is 135.3 feet and the project cost was $585,000. The children on the bridge are thought to be the children of Herman and Ottelia Fitzloff.

Hilton Bridge

The Hilton Bridge was replaced by a new bridge built in 1958.

The O'Connor Bridge, which was located over the Le Sueur River on McPherson Township Road #326, was built in 1883. It was 146' long and cost $6,345. It was replaced in 1978 with bridge 07541 at a cost of $188,000. It is 170.4' in structure length.

Collapse of the north side of the O'Connor Bridge - ca. 1950

Collapse of the O'Connor Bridge - ca. 1950

The O'Connor Bridge (McPherson Township Road 618th Ave.) as it looked in 1987
before the new bridge was built.

The new Le Sueur River Bridge on McPherson Towhship Road 618th Avenue, built in 1987.
Pictured is Eric Westphal helping his Grandpa Bernie Westphal with the harvest.

The Flitter Bridge, which is located over the Le Sueur River in Section 23 on Blue Earth County Road #172, was built in 1913.

The Flitter Bridge, which was located over the Le Sueur River in Section 23 on Blue Earth County Road #172, was replaced in 1977 with bridge 07540. The structure length is 142.7' and the cost was $132,000.

The Davis Bridge was located over a stream in Section 9 on Township Road #162. The old structure was built in 1910. It was replaced in 1977 with corrugated metal pipe arches and is bridge 05664.

The bridge, on Blue Earth County Highway #15 east of St. Clair
over the Le Sueur River, was built in 1923. The bridge was replaced in 1972
with the structure length of 149.5'. It is bridge 07513.

The Danberry Bridge is located over a stream in Section 13 on McPherson Township Road #111. It was built in 1924. It was replaced in 1973 with bridge L9416 and consists of concrete culverts.

The Freitag Bridge was located over a stream on County Road #172. It was built in 1939. In 1995 it was reinforced with concrete extensions and is bridge 90543.

The Schalow Bridge over a ditch in Section 18 on McPherson Township Road #136 was replaced in 1960 at a cost of $21,000. It consists of steel culverts and is bridge L5662.

The May Bridge over a ditch in Section 19 also on McPherson Township Road #136 was replaced in 1960 at a cost of $19,000. It was replaced with steel culverts and it is known as bridge L6995.

The original bridge on the Waseca County line was constructed in 1908 at a cost of $1,956 and was 60' long. It has now been replaced.

McPHERSON.

Township 107 North. **1895** Range XXV West.

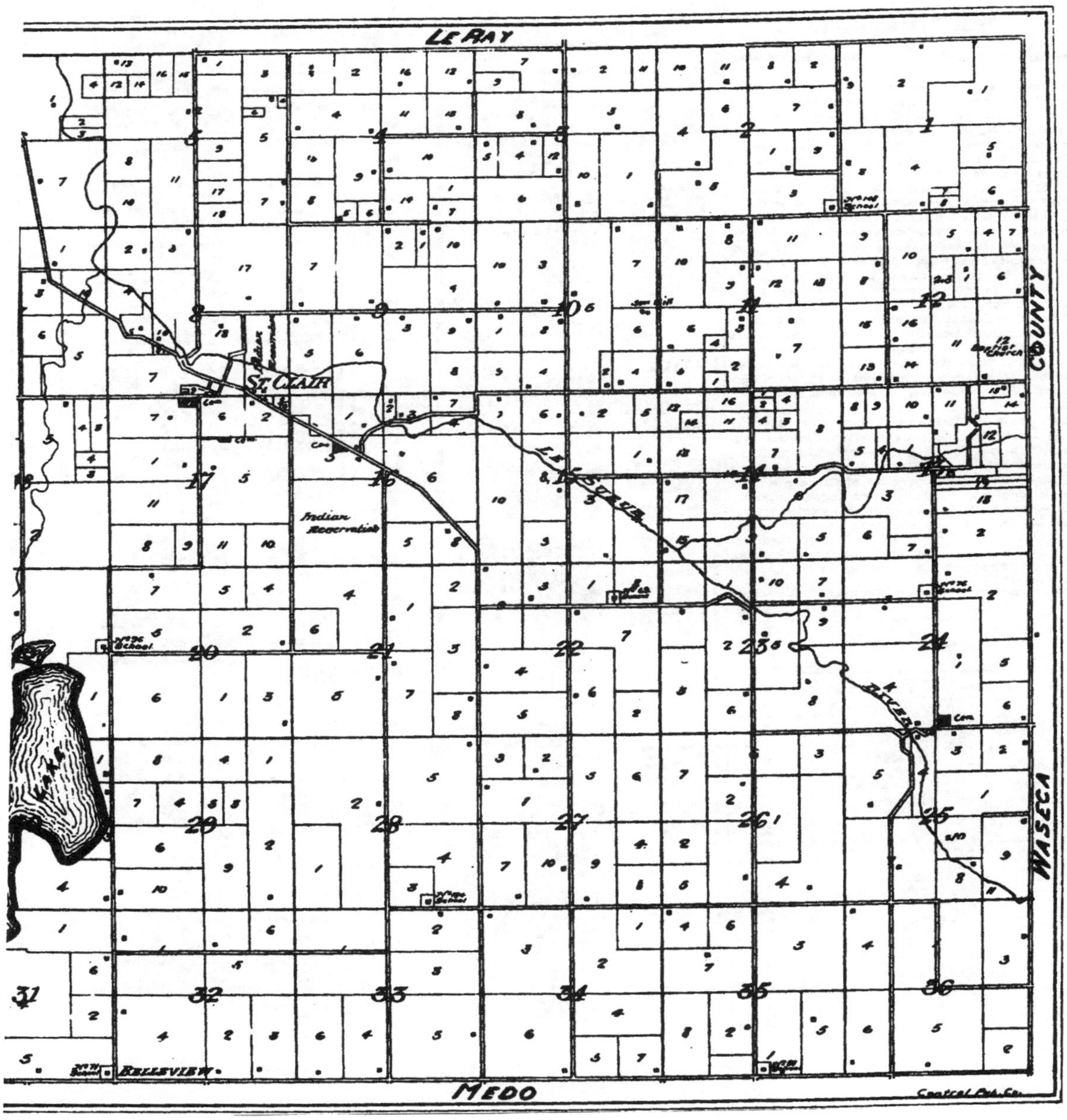

McPHERSON TOWNSHIP.

McPHERSON.

Township 107 North. Range XXV West of 5th Principal Meridian.

McPherson township lies to the north of Medo. This town was formerly a part of the Winnebago Indian reservation; the agency buildings are still standing at the village of Saint Clair, on the LeSueur river, which meanders accross the township from southeast to northwest. That portion north of the river is for the most part covered with heavy timber, while to the south of the river is generally fine prairie land, interspersed with groves and lakes. Smith Mill, on the C. & N. W. Ry., is the nearest railway station.

This town was at first attached to Mankato for official purposes, and was called Rice Lake. The petition for organization was accepted by the county commissioners in September, 1863, and the name changed to McClelland. In 1865 the name of the town was again changed to McPherson.

The name of Lucius Dyer, one of the members of the first town board of Danville township in 1858, appears on the records as moderator of the election for organization of this town, held at his home, September 19th, 1863. John Low was clerk, and the Judges of election were Henry Foster, J. L. Alexander and R. O. Bartlett.

SAINT CLAIR.—In McPherson township, 12 miles from Mankato and 6 from Eagle Lake, on the LeSeuer river is located the old Winnebago Agency, which until late years has been known as Hilton and now as the village of St. Clair. It has a population of 300 people, daily stage to Mankato; 4 churches—Congregational, Lutheran, German Methodist and Catholic; a graded school; 1 boot and shoe store; 2 blacksmith shops; 1 carpet weaver; 1 wagon maker; 1 druggist; 2 mills; 1 furniture store; 2 general stores; 1 hardware store; 1 harness shop; 1 hotel; 1 livery stable; 1 meat market; 1 physician and three saloons.

Sub. Div. No.	NAME	LEGAL SUBDIVISION OR DESCRIPTION	No. of Acres	Land Assessment	Structural Assessment
		Section 1.			
1	Julius Trahms	S½ of NE¼ and NE¼ of NE¼	120	$1,663	
2	Fred Theisen	NW¼ Exc W½ of W½ and NW¼ of NE¼	160.19	1,940	$250
3	Willard & Barney	W½ of SW¼	80	1,109	
4	Nellie L. Nesbitt	E½ of SW¼ and N 112 11-13 R of W 52 R of SE¼	117	1,296	62
5	Catherine Reeder	N½ of E 108 a. of SE¼	54	686	
6	Ellen Coughlin	S½ of E 108 a. of SE¼	54	513	
7	Jas Mahoney	N 15 R 9 5-8 links of N 46 R 3¾ links of W 52 R of SE¼	5	69	
8	Ellen Coghlin	S 30 R 19¾ links of W 52 R of SW¼ of SE¼	10	139	
9	A. Schoen	W½ of W½ of NW¼	40	327	63
		Section 2.			
1	Franz Bruch	NW¼ of SE¼	40	416	
2	A. Schoen	NE¼ of NE¼	40.22	485	
3	L. R. Gilmore	S½ of SE¼ exc½ a. school lot	79.50	1,054	
4	Robt. Brush	W 94 R and 2 ft of N 66 R of SW¼ and SW¼ of NW¼	80	693	62
5	John Roerig	S 92 a. of SW¼ and E 28 a. of N 68 a. of SW¼	120	1,109	125
6	J. A. Willard	SE¼ of NW¼	40	554	
7	R. D. Craig	SW¼ of NE¼ and SE¼ of NE¼	80	693	63
8	Henry Schwarble	NW¼ of NE¼	40	388	63
9	Gottleib Juneyberg	NE¼ of SE¼	40	554	62
10	Wilhelm Kantop	NW¼ of NW¼	40.71	554	
11	E. L. Cook	NE¼ of NW¼	40	443	37
		Section 3.			
1	John Larabee	E½ of SE ¼ and E 20 a. of W½ of SE¼	100	1,386	125
2	Herman Klingbeil	NW¼ of NE¼ and W½ of NE¼ of NE¼	61.36	693	63
3	J. E. Holmquist	S½ of NE¼	80.24	1,080	250
4	M. Wosnock	W½ of NE¼ of SW¼ and E½ of NW¼ of SW¼	40	388	
5	Christian Godman	W½ of NW¼ of SW¼	20	222	
6	Aug. Klingbeil	S½ of SW¼	80	1,035	63
		Section 3.			
7	H. Foster	N 20:91 a. of NW¼ of NW¼ and NE¼ of NW¼	61.79	$591	
8	Chris Brandes	S½ of NW¼	80	970	$125
9	D. F. Rasdell	S 20 a. of NW¼ of NW¼	20	268	
10	Aug. Kupke	W 60 a. of SE¼	60	709	
11	Wilhelm Kostop	E½ of NE¼ of NE¼	20.41	166	
12	W. Klingbeil	E½ of NE¼ of SW¼	20	240	41
		Section 4.			
1	Fred Fischer	N ½ of SE¼ of SE¼	20	222	
2	J. Tolzman	NE¼ of NW¼	40.75	485	
3	Chas Radtke	NW¼ of NW¼	40	347	100
4	J. Kollars	S½ of NW¼	80	1,109	
5	John Gerber	SW¼ of SE¼ of SW¼	10	139	
6	D. Eaton	SE¼ of SE¼ of SW¼	10	139	
7	E. Franska	S½ of SE¼ of SE¼	20	222	
8	Augusta Brandt	SW¼ of SW¼	40	554	
9	T. C. Eaton	N 60 a. of E½ of SW¼	60	762	187
10	Carl Schostag	N½ of SE¼	80	891	156
11	Chas. Schostag	SW¼ of NE¼	40	277	
12	M. S. Kelly	NE¼ of NE¼	40	277	
13	L. Theibault	SE¼ of NE¼	40	485	
14	C. Suderman	SW¼ of SE¼	40	416	62
15	Carl Kruse	NW¼ of SW¼	40	554	
16	Haggard & Humiston	NW¼ of NE¼	40	554	
		Section 5.			
1	Frank A. Stevens	N½ of NW¼ of NE¼	20	208	
2	O. E. Tillotson	SW¼ of NE¼ and S½ of N W½ of NE¼ and S½ of NW¼	140	970	400
3	J. Kollars	NE ¼ of NE¼	40	277	
4	J. Kollars	E 16 r. of N 20 r. of SE¼ of NE¼	2	28	
5	Fred Kruse	W 64 r. of N 20 r. of SE¼ of NE¼ and S½ of NE¼ of SE¼ of NE¼ and S½ of SE ¼ of NE¼ and NE¼ of SE¼	73	832	250
6	Paul Achen	N½ of NW¼ of SE¼ of NE¼	5	56	
7	Augusta Brandt	SE¼ of SE¼	40	416	62
8	A. F. Hilton	NW¼ of SW¼	40	416	
9	Fred Kruse	N½ of NW¼ of SE¼	20	277	
10	Etta Beyersdorf	SW¼ of SW¼	40	451	
11	Chas. Dittman	E½ of SW¼ and S½ of NW¼ of SE¼	100	970	125
12	Wm. Tillotson	SW¼ of NW¼ of NW¼	10	111	
13	Fred Funk	N½ of NW¼ of NW¼	20.20	139	
14	S. Lamm	SE¼ of NW¼ of NW¼	10.80	111	
15	M. Smith	E½ of NE¼ of NW¼	20.44	208	
16	P. Smith	W½ of NE¼ of NW¼	20.46	208	
17	Aug. Krause	N½ of SW¼ of SE¼	20	177	
18	Jos. Jeurisch	S½ of SW¼ of SE¼	20	277	
		Section 6.			
1	E. Schroeder	W½ of NE¼ and W½ of NE¼ of NE¼ and NE¼ of NE¼ of NE¼ and SE¼ of NE¼ exc S 44 R	128.05	901	188
2	J. Hayes	N 30 R of S 44 R of SE¼ of NE¼ and E½ of NW¼	90.37	698	63
3	Wm. Boswell	SE¼ of SW¼ and S 36 R of SE¼ of NE¼	62	305	
4	N. Julliar	SE¼ of N ½ of NE¼	10	111	
5	M. G. Hoagland	SW¼ of NW¼	40	250	
6	Fred Buckholtz	NW¼ of NW¼	38.90	416	38
7	Mary McGovern	SE¼	160	1,313	187
8	Peter McGovern	NE¼ of SW¼	40	308	
9	J. Krause	W½ of SW¼	80	651	
		Section 7.			
1	Wm. Brandt	N½ of NE¼	80	873	125
2	E. B. Weatherbee	SE¼ of NW¼	40	485	31
3	E. J Scott	SW¼ of NE¼	40	471	562
4	Wm Boswell	NE¼ of NW¼	40	437	50
5	Bertha Lassow	E½ of SE¼ and E½ of SW¼ of SE¼	100	1,081	
6	F. W. Lassow	NW¼ of SE¼	40	319	
7	Jas. Fields	SW¼ of SE¼ and E½ of NW¼ exc. E½ of SW¼ of SE¼	100	1,317	613
8	P. McGovern	SW¼ of NW¼	39.23	416	
9	Jos. Krause	NW¼ of NW¼	39.28	451	31
10	Wm. Tillotson	SE¼ of NE¼ exc. ½ a. cemetery	39.50	398	187
11	S. Lamm	W½ of SW¼	81.36	970	
		Section 8.			
1	Aug. Krause	SE¼ of NW¼	40	471	
2	Catherine Gekeler	NW¼ of NW¼	40	451	63
3	Jos. Juriah	NE¼ of NW¼	40	485	250
4	F. S. Wells	SW¼ of NW¼ exc. 3 80-100 a. and 1 42-100 a. in NW corner of NW¼ of SW¼ N of road 23½ r. on ¼ line and 23 r. on road	37.63	340	125
5	Bertha Lassow	E 3 80-100 a. of SE¼ of SW¼ of NW¼ all S of river and NW¼ of SW¼ exc. Wells' 1 42-100 a. and exc. Davis' 1½ a.	43.26	402	212
6	F. J. Shorey	½ a. of NW¼ of SW¼ Rec. Book 28, p. 134 and 1 a. of W½ of NE¼ of SW¼ Rec. Book 28, p. 139	1.13	34	94
7	E. B. Haynes est	S½ of SW¼ exc. 3¼ a. church lot and exc. Deumland's 6-100 a. and exc. Krause's 14-100 and ex. J. Maloney's 3:00 a. in NE¼ of SW¼ and E½ of NE¼ of SW¼ exc. Haynes' add. and exc. Phillips' ¼ a. and exc. Lewis' 50-100 a. and exc. Merchant's 50-100 a	86	901	36
		Section 8.			
8	E. B. Haynes. est.	SW¼ of SW¼ of NE¼ of SW¼	5	$48	
9	Jas. Maloney	E 526½ ft. of SW¼ S of school lot exc. W 214 ft of S 281 ft in SE¼ of SW¼, rec. book 44, p. 178	3.00	69	
10	Frank Airo	NE¼ of SW¼ of NE¼ of SW¼ exc. McGovern's ½ a. and NW¼ of NE¼ of SW¼ exc. Grigons' 30-100 and exc. Davis' 1 a.	13.11	180	$125
11	P. McGovern	50-100 a. in NE¼ of SW¼ of NE¼ of SW¼, rec. book 33, p. 447	.50	55	
12	M. A. St. Cyr	50-100 a. in NE¼ of SW¼, rec. book 30, p. 289	.50	55	94
13	Anna Phillips	25-100 a. in E½ of SW¼ rec. book 46, p. 440	.25	28	12
14	Aug. Krause	14-100 a. in SE¼ of SW¼, rec. book 42, p. 489	.14	3	
15	Grignon & Coughanour	30-100 a. W of lot 13, Haynes' add., rec. book 42, p. 35	.30	42	625
16	Isaac Autrey	All between Hilton townsite and Haynes' Add. N of alley and S of Main-st of SE¼ of SW¼	.15	55	31
17	N. Julliar	NE¼	160	2,010	188
18	Frank Wilkins	NW¼ of SE¼	40	374	13
19	Emily Merchant	½ a. in SW¼ of NE¼ of SW¼ rec. book 32, p. 59	.50	55	156
		Section 9.			
1	E. Franska	E 10 a. of NW¼ of NE¼	10	111	
2	John Lang	W 30 a. of NW¼ of NE¼	30	277	75
3	Aug. Barneska	SW¼ of NE¼ and W½ of SE¼	120	1,109	225
4	Chris. Alpers	SE¼ of NE¼	40	469	
5	Gustaf Schmidt	W 75 a. of SW¼	75	832	162
6	A. D. Axtell	E 85 a. of SW¼	85	538	125
7	W. Frolick	W½ of NW¼	80	693	250
8	D. F. Rasdall	SE¼ of SE¼	40	471	
9	H. G. Getzkow	NE¼ of SE¼	40	478	125
10	Chas. A. Fisher	NE¼ of NE¼	40	473	125
		Section 10.			
1	Fred. Glamm	NW¼ of SW¼	40	554	63
2	John Hintze	E 10 a. of SW¼ of SE¼	10	118	
3	Chris. Alpers	E½ of NW¼	80	1,109	
4	Wm. Miller	SE¼ of SE¼ and SE¼ of SW¼	80	827	125
5	John Hintz	W 30 a. of SW¼ of SE¼ and NW¼ of SE¼ and W½ of NE¼	150	1,871	125
6	F. & H. Gerlick	NE¼ of SE¼	40	464	250
7	A. D. Reid	E½ of NE¼	80	970	125
8	Fred Glamm, Jr	NE¼ of SW¼	40	554	
9	Aug. Fisher	SW¼ of SW¼	40	347	63
10	C. Alpers	W½ of NW¼	80	1,109	125
		Section 11.			
1	F. A. Damelonski	SW¼ of SE¼ of SW¼	10	111	25
2	F. A. Damelonski	S½ of E½ of E½ of SW¼ and NW¼ of SE¼ of SW¼	30	277	
3	Herman Krause	N½ of E½ of E½ of SW¼	20	277	
4	A. B. Preston	S 7½ a. of SW¼ of NE¼ of SW¼	7 50	83	
5	Chas. Wolfet	SW¼ of SW¼	40	664	125
6	Anton Lang	NW¼ of SW¼ and N 13½ a of W½ of E½ of SW¼	53.50	613	125
7	Gerlich Bros	SE¼	160	1,814	63
8	Carl Burch	NE¼ of NW¼	40	446	31
9	Jas. Cross	SE¼ of NW¼	40	564	63
10	Jas. Nesbitt	W½ of NW¼	80	1,064	
11	L. R. Gilmore	N½ of NE¼	80	1,007	
12	U. Maigenski.	SW¼ of NE¼	40	480	31
13	H. H. Gerlich	SE¼ of NE¼	40	330	
		Section 12.			
1	Mary E. Elliott	E½ of SW¼ of NE¼	20	277	
2	Mary E. Elliott, guardian	Und 4-6 of W½ of SW¼ of NE¼	13.34	139	
3	Robt Greiner	Und 2-6 of W½ of SW¼ of NE¼	6.66	56	
4	Oscar Greiner	W½ of NE¼ of NE¼	20	226	
5	Robt Greiner	NW¼ of NE¼	40	485	63
6	Haggard & Merrill	SE¼ of NE¼	40	485	63
7	W. Adkins	E½ of NE¼ of NE¼	20	226	65
8	H. H. Nichols	SW¼ of NW¼	40	499	94
9	L. A. Gilmore	NW¼ of NW¼	40	513	
10	S. F. Barney	E½ of the NW¼	80	1,169	
11	Richard Ash	W½ of SE¼	80	1,081	
12	P. G. Ayars	E½ of SE¼	80	1,109	125
13	Jos. Market	SW¼ of SW¼	40	513	
14	S. S. Larrabee	SE¼ of SW¼	40	485	
15	S. F. Barney	NW¼ of SW¼	40	582	
16	Haggard & Merrill	NE¼ of SW¼	40	540	
		Section 13.			
1	Agnes Simons	SE¼ of NW¼	40	471	
2	Wm. A. Tetzlof	S½ of SE¼	80	741	
3	M. Neary	N½ of SW¼ and N½ of SE¼ of SW¼	100	1,109	125
4	Jos. E. Sonasac	E½ of E½ of SW¼ of NW¼	10	139	
5	Jos. E. Sonasac	W 30 a. of SW¼ of NW¼	30	416	
6	Frank A. Petska	SW¼ of SW¼	40	554	
7	J. H. O'Brien	S½ of SE¼ of SW¼	20	277	63
		Truman's Subdivision of N½ of NW¼ and NE¼ and N½ of SE¼ of Sec. 13, Town 107, Range 25.			
8	Melvina O'Brien	Lots 1 and 2	20	277	
9	Jos. Market	Lots 3 and 4	20	225	

Continued on next page.

1895 McPHERSON TOWNSHIP.—Continued.

Sub. Div. No.	NAME	LEGAL SUBDIVISION OR DESCRIPTION	No. of Acres	Land Assessment	Structural Assessment
		Section 13.			
10	Fred Rix	Lots 5, 6, 7 and 8	40	[illegible]	
11	Chas. R. Larrabee	Lots 9, 10, 11 and 19	38	527	[illegible]
12	Asa Owen	Lots 12, 15, 16, 17, 18, 23 and all E of road of 20	33.25	970	63
13	Emery Cook	W 10 a. of lot 13	10	136	63
14	Jennie Banker	E 28½ E of lot 13 and all of lot 14	20	277	
15	John Cunningham	Lots 21 and 22 and all W of road of lot 20	18.20	277	31
16	Cary H. Barrott	Lot 24	10	124	
17	Gertrude Barrott	Lot 25	10	111	
18	E. A. Peck	Lots 26, 27 and 28	45	546	63
		Section 14.			
1	Herman Krause	N 4 a. of NW¼ of NW¼ of NE¼	4	44	
2	Chas. A. Gekeler	S 6 a. of NW¼ of NW¼ of NE¼	6	85	
3	Albert Fritzloff	SE¼ of NW¼ of NE¼	10	111	
4	Wm. Freitag	NE¼ of NW¼ of NE¼ and SW¼ of NW¼ of NE¼	20	166	
5	Wm. Peek	SE¼ of SE¼	40	554	
6	H. A. Braden	N½ of NE¼	80	985	
7	J. G. Miller	SW¼ of NE¼	40	527	63
8	H. A. Braden	E½ of NE¼	80	[illegible]	63
9	S. Murphy	SW¼ of SE¼ and SE¼ of SW¼	80	1,040	63
10	Wm. Freitag	NE¼ of SW¼ and SE¼ of NW¼	80	1,053	435
11	Anton Wolfel	S½ of NE¼ of NW¼	20	222	
12	Chas. Wolfel	N½ of NW¼ of NW¼ and SW¼ of NW¼ of NW¼	30	392	
13	W. H. Gekeler	SW¼ of NW¼	40	576	
14	S. S. Babcock	SE¼ of NW¼ of NW¼	10	111	
15	W. Seewald	SW¼ of SW¼	40	377	
16	Isaac Autrey	N½ of NE¼ of NW¼	20	208	
17	Joseph Warner	NW¼ of SW¼	40	[illegible]	
		Section 15.			
1	W. H. Gekeler	SE¼ of NE¼	40	361	500
2	Aug. Glamm	W 60 a. of N½ of NE¼ exc. ½ ac. school lot	59.50	609	63
3	John Smith	SW¼ of NE¼ and W½ of SE¼	120	1,046	63
4	Frank Amberg	E½ of SE¼	80	832	250
5	C. Wolfel	E½ of NE¼ of NE¼	20	194	
6	C. A. Gekeler	NE¼ of NW¼	40	554	63
7	Aug. Fisher	NW¼ of NW¼	40	374	
8	P. O'Connor	NE¼ of SW¼ and SE¼ of NW¼	80	832	188
9	Mary O'Connor	SE¼ of SW¼	40	499	
10	Isaac Autrey	W½ of SW¼ and SW¼ of NW¼	120	1,178	
		Section 16.			
1	Archie Gleason	NE¼ of NW¼	40	305	125
2	Henry Mantage	All N of river, of W 21 r. of NW¼ of NE¼	6	69	
3	C. D. Adams	NW¼ of NE¼ exc. N 6 a. of W 10⅔	34	416	
4	C. D. Adams	S½ of NE¼ of NE¼	20	208	
5	Henry Foster	SW¼ of NW¼ of NW¼ and SW¼ of SE¼ and S½ of NW¼	220	2,281	500
6	D. F. Randall	S½ of NE¼ and N½ of SE¼	160	1,868	500
7	D. F. Randall	N½ NE¼ of NE¼	20	208	63
8	Isaac Autrey	SE¼ of SE¼	40	374	125
		Section 17.			
1	L. F. McGovern	S½ of NW¼	80	901	63
2	Fred Schulz	NE¼ of NE¼ all S of road	31.90	332	156
3	Wm. Wagner	All of E 14.36 a. of NE¼ of NE¼ N of road	6.10	84	
4	John Fitzloff	All of W 17.40 a. of E 32 a. of NE¼ of NW¼ N of road	2	42	
5	John Beetman	N½ of SE¼ and S½ of NE¼ exc. 1.22 a. cemetery	158.78	1,782	625
6	L'wr'nce McGovern	NW¼ of NE¼	40	415	
7	F. Reeder	N½ of NW¼ exc. 4 a. ch. lot	76	801	125
8	Nic Phillips	W 60 a. of S½ of SW¼	60	686	
9	Nic Phillips	E½ of SE¼ of SW¼	20	280	
10	S. Lamm	SE¼ of SE¼	40	471	
11	John Beetman	SW¼ of SE¼ & N½ of SW¼	120	1,363	
		Section 18.			
1	A. F. Hilton	N½ of SW¼	80	970	
2	T. Bowe	SE¼ and S½ of SW¼	240	2,495	
3	J. Reeder	E 30 r. of N 106 r. and S 27 r. of E 60 r. of NE¼	20	277	
4	F. Lassow	W 30 r. of E 60 r. of N 106 r. and N 27 r. of S 54 r. of E 60 r. of NE¼	20	319	
5	Chas. Dumbrck	W 100 a. of NE¼	100	1,130	125
6	J. Fields	NE¼ of NW¼	40	540	
7	S. Lamm	NW¼ of NW¼	40	443	125
8	A. F. Hilton	S½ of NW¼	80	1,035	94
		Section 19.			
1	F. W. Wingen	Lots 1 and 2	60.40	617	312
2	T. Bowe	N½ of NW¼ and E½ of SE¼ of NW¼	50.02	970	375
3	Jos. May	Lot 3 and N½ of NE¼ and SE¼ of NE¼ exc. SE ½ a. and W½ of SW¼ and W 60 a. of S½ of NW¼ and lots 4 and 5	379.24	3,336	188
		Section 20.			
1	F. C. Schultz	W½ of SE¼	80	894	94
2	Harriet H. Gilmore	S½ of NE¼	80	985	125
3	Fred Kook	E½ of SE¼	80	860	
4	S. Lamm	NE¼ of NE¼	40	443	
5	F. Beyersdorf	S½ of NW¼ and NW¼ of NE¼	120	1,275	188
6	F. W. Wingen	SW¼	160	1,783	
7	F. L. Beyersdorf	N½ of NW¼	80	887	
		Section 21.			
1	D. F. Randall	W½ of NE¼	80	[illegible]	
2	Isaac Autrey	NE¼ of NE¼	40	499	
3	Ed Lynch	SE¼ of NE¼ and NE¼ of SE¼	80	832	
4	Henry Foster	E½ of NW¼ and NW¼ of NW¼	120	1,381	
5	M. Dooley	SW¼	160	1,668	[illegible]
6	Fred Schultz	SW¼ of NW¼	40	499	
7	Theodore Heinze	W½ of SE¼	80	762	63
8	Albert Fitzloff	SE¼ of SE¼	40	485	31
		Section 22.			
1	M. Smith	NW¼ of NE¼ exc ½ a. school lot	39.75	485	
2	Chas Wolfel	SE¼ of SE¼	40	377	
3	Thos. O'Connor	NE¼ of NW¼	40	461	125
4	Ed Lynch	N½ of SW¼	80	901	188
5	A. Fitzloff	S½ of SW¼	80	908	
6	J. H. Fields	W½ of SE¼	80	970	125
7	John Fields	SE¼ of NW¼ and S½ of NE¼ and NE¼ of SE¼	160	1,940	300
8	Frank Amberg	NE¼ of NE¼, except ½ a school lot	39.75	492	
9	Chas. Smith, Jr	W½ of NW¼	80	775	125
		Section 23.			
1	S. Murphy	NE¼ of NW¼	40	377	
2	Herman Frank	NE¼ of SW¼ and SE¼ of NW¼	80	1,178	63
3	Frank Shandera	W½ of SW¼	80	690	
4	Wm. Seewald	W½ of NW¼	80	1,080	63
5	Aug. Flitter	NW¼ of SE¼ and SW¼ of NE¼	80	868	188
6	T. J. McGovern	SE¼ of SW¼	40	485	
7	Albert Posh	NE¼ of NE¼	40	527	375
8	John Sullivan	E½ of SE¼ and SW¼ of SE¼	120	1,654	125
9	Regina Petska	SE¼ of NE¼	40	416	
10	Mary E. Market	NW¼ of NE¼	40	499	94
		Section 24.			
1	A. Kabuki	SW¼ of NE¼ and W½ of SE¼, except ½ a. cemetery	119.50	1,328	250
2	M. Flemming	N½ of NE¼ and SE¼ of NE¼	120	1,169	
3	Regina Petska	NW¼ exc. ½ a. school lot	159.50	1,995	125
4	Milo Baldwin	SW¼	160	1,595	125
5	C. E. Graham	NE¼ of SE¼	40	495	
6	E. Myeue	SE¼ of SE¼	40	485	
		Section 25.			
1	John Shultz	SE¼ of NE¼ and SW¼ of NE¼	80	832	300
2	David Anthony	NE¼ of NE¼	40	416	
3	Herman Fritz	NW¼ of NE¼	40	513	25
4	Fred Doss	E 40 a. of NW¼ exc. NE 1 a.	39	377	
5	John Doss	W½ of E½ of NW¼ and W½ of NW¼	120	1,237	25
6	Milo Baldwin	NE 1 a. of NW¼	1	9	
7	W. J. Dooley	SW¼ exc. 1¼ a. NE of river	158.75	1,587	
8	Wm Spencer	SW¼ of SE¼	40	388	
9	Julius Stoldt	E½ of SE¼, all N of river	78	585	63
10	Herman Miller	NW¼ of SE¼ and 1¼ a. all NE of river of SW¼	41.75	499	125
11	H. Spencer	All SW of river of E½ of SE¼	4	28	
		Section 26.			
1	H. S. Hilton	NW¼ of SE¼ and SW¼ of NE¼	80	895	
2	Wm. Baumgartner	SE¼ of NW¼ and NW¼ of SW¼	80	868	125
3	Milo Baldwin	NE¼ of NE¼	40	380	
4	P. Lynch	S½ of SE¼ and NE¼ of SE¼ and SE¼ of NE¼ and E½ of SW¼	240	2,680	125
5	W. H Lynch	SW¼ of NW¼	40	530	
6	T. McGovern	NE¼ of NW¼ and NW¼ of NE¼	80	762	125
7	Wm. Baumgartner	W½ of NW¼	80	609	
		Section 27.			
1	Adolph Meyer	S½ of NW¼	80	970	
2	Elizabeth Sherer	NE¼ of NW¼	40	485	63
3	A. Pagenhopf	NW¼ of NW¼	40	388	
4	W. Baumgartner	NE¼ of SE¼	40	499	
5	N. Juliar	W½ of NE¼	80	985	
6	J. A. Willard	E½ of NE¼	80	832	
7	J. F. Lynch	W½ of SW¼	80	832	125
8	N. H. Lynch	SE¼ of SE¼	40	513	125
9	P. Baumgartner	W½ of SE¼	80	787	94
10	John Timmerman	E½ of SW¼	80	868	100
		Section 28.			
1	D. D. Brewer	W½ of SW¼	80	970	
2	C. J. Pagenhopf	NW¼ and E½ of SW¼	240	2,481	250
3	Ed Lynch	SW¼ of SE¼ exc. 1 a. sch. lot	39.50	443	
4	H. Lynch	NW¼ of SE¼ and E½ of SE¼	120	1,333	94
5	A. Pagenhopf	NE¼	160	1,802	375
		Section 29.			
1	S. Lamm	NE¼ of NE¼ exc. NW 1-5 a.	39.80	416	
2	C. R. Brewer	E½ of NE¼ and SE¼ of NE¼	120	1,419	500
3	D. D. Brewer	E½ of SW¼ of NE¼	20	139	
4	Nic. Phillips	SE¼ of NW¼ and NW¼ of NE¼	80	967	
5	Fred W. Wingen	W½ of SW¼ of NE¼	20	139	
6	A. Dittbrenner	N½ of SW¼	80	970	
7	Aug Bierbauer	SW¼ of NW¼	40	495	
8	Mary A. Phillips	N½ of NW¼	80	970	
9	B. Leonard	W½ of SE¼	80	832	
10	Wm. Rage	S½ of SW¼	80	901	
		Section 30.			
1	Nic. Phillips	N 19.67 a. of lot 1	19.67	194	250
2	Joe May	Lots 4, 5 and 6	146.06	1,705	
3	A. Dittbrenner	S 10 a. of lot 1 and N 10 a. of lot 2	20	194	125
4	Geo. C. Covill	Lot 3 and S 40.80 a. of lot 2	119.18	1,317	188
		Section 31.			
1	Geo. C. Covill	N½ of NE¼ and 8½ a. in N part of lot 1	88.50	[illegible]	865
2	J. Mullen	NE¼ of SE¼	40	495	
3	Geo. Albert	Lot 2	40.46	416	
4	Amelia Arnold	N½ of SW¼ and NW¼ of SE¼ and SW¼ of NE¼ and lot 1, exc. Covill's 8½ a.	202.60	2,730	63
5	J. W. Mace	S½ of S½ exc ½ a. school lot	159.50	1,668	63
6	G. B. Preston	SE¼ of NE¼	40	485	114
		Section 32.			
1	Paul Aschen	NW¼	160	1,882	188
2	P. L. Hawkins	W½ of SE¼	80	936	250
3	A. Beyersdorf	E½ of SE¼	80	970	125
4	A. B. Preston	SW¼	160	1,940	250
5	Jos. Wingen	S½ of NE¼ and NW¼ of NE¼	120	1,395	625
6	Chas R. Brewer	NE¼ of NE¼	40	499	
		Section 33.			
1	Jos. Wingen	NW¼	160	1,802	
2	Mat Lynch	N½ of NE¼	80	901	94
3	Fred Koch	S½ of NE¼	80	945	
4	O. E. Hale	E½ of SW¼	80	901	125
5	S. Babcock	SE¼	160	1,830	250
6	H Fitzloff	W½ of SW¼	80	801	94
		Section 34.			
1	W. H Lynch	NE¼ of NE¼	40	416	
2	S. Lamm	S½ of NE¼ and NW¼ of NE¼	120	1,109	
3	Frederick Franz	NW¼	160	1,886	
4	S. Lamm	N½ of SE¼	80	901	
5	A. E. Wilson	SW¼ of SE¼	40	555	
6	John Mahoney	SW¼	160	1,584	63
7	Ann E. Wilson	SE¼ of SE¼	40	530	305
		Section 35.			
1	O. T. Severson	S½ of SE¼ of SW¼ and W½ of SE¼ exc ½ a. school lot	99.75	1,035	125
2	A. Oftedahl	N 60 a. of E½ of SW¼	60	684	63
3	M. Dunsworth	NE¼	160	1,883	63
4	M. H. Lynch	NW¼ of NW¼	40	416	
5	Pat Foley	E½ of SE¼	80	901	125
6	Pat Lynch	NE¼ of NW¼	40	402	
7	Andrew Hanson	S½ of NW¼	80	968	125
8	Ann E. Wilson	W½ of SW¼	80	1,190	
		Section 36.			
1	W. Spencer	E½ of NW¼ and W½ of NE¼	160	1,940	
2	H. S. Taylor	SE¼ of SE¼	40	554	
3	Pat Kelly	E½ of NE¼ and NE¼ of SE¼	120	1,575	
4	Nels Anderson	W½ of NW¼	80	832	63
5	H. G Taylor	W½ of SE¼ and E½ of SW¼	160	2,079	
6	C. F. Timmerman	W½ of SW¼	80	970	125

Main Street looking east, ca. 1901

CHAPTER THREE

St. Clair, Minnesota

On August 11, 1865, Aaron Hilton laid out a townsite in Section 8 of McPherson Township, which is presently St. Clair. He named the townsite Hilton. By 1866 the new village contained about 12 houses, three general stores, two blacksmith shops, three wagon shops, two boot and shoe shops, two saloons, one hotel and a mill. The mill was built by Aaron Hilton in 1864 and had two run of saws with a capacity of 10,000 feet of lumber per day, and attached lath and shingle mill and a capacity of 100 barrels of flour per day.

Aaron Hilton was appointed postmaster and the post office was moved from the agency building to the Brown Brothers General Store (which was opened in 1864 by George and James Brown) in Hilton. A Mr. Koehler had a store there at one time. In January of 1867 J. C. Truman converted the Winnebago Agency House into a hotel. In November of 1869, Hilton sold his mill to Hegle and Reader, and in a year or two, Hegle sold his interests to Peter Pfaff. In 1869 James Brown was appointed postmaster and in 1871 Henry Mohr succeeded him. Brown also had sold his mercantile business to Mr. Mohr in May 1871. Mr. Brown moved to the new townsite of Mapleton and began business there being the first merchant in Mapleton.

Fishing on the Le Sueur River, ca. 1900

Other early businessmen in Hilton included Nick Lang, M. B. Rasdell, who in 1879 became a member of the firm of Brown Bros., J. C. Cook (shoemaker), Charles Young (owned a variety store), Mathias Jost (was in the mercantile business), Fred Gerlich, H. R. King (druggist), and H. Miller (shoemaker). Doctors Eaton and E.B. Haynes were the first physicians and J.C. Nutting, C. Wilbur Ray and W. S. Smith treated the sick in later years. On October 14, 1880, J. H. Barlow started a paper called the *Messenger*, which was only issued a short time.

Up until this time the post office at Hilton had been designated Winnebago Agency. On February 6, 1886 a meeting was held and it was decided that the name would be changed to Hilton. April 1, 1886, it was changed to "St. Clair," a name suggested by Charles O'Connor, after General St. Clair. The village has since gone by the same name. Mr. O'Connor had been a postmaster and later ran a general store in the village. As postmaster he had experienced considerable confusion in the mail between Winnebago Agency and Winnebago, and therefore pressed for a change in the name for the town. It is not clear why the name was changed from Hilton to St. Clair six weeks later.

In February of 1890, Joseph H. Gebbard was appointed postmaster. His successor was Fred Gerlich, who in turn was succeeded in December 1898, by M. G. Rasdall. Until 1887, the village was divided into two school districts, Number 70 and 73, on August 6, of that year, the districts were united, and the fine brick schoolhouse was completed by the fall of 1888 at a cost of $6000. In 1898 the McPherson town hall was erected in St. Clair.

In 1882 William Field and Son built a feed mill. The mill was a 14-inch French burr with a grinding capacity of 300 to 400 bushels per day.

Duemeland's General Store was established December 14, 1882. The store, built by E.A. Duemeland, was operated until 1940 when he sold out and retired. (William Godemann bought it at this time and later sold it to Clair Wolcott and his brother, Harold. They operated the store under the name of Wolcott Brothers. The Wolcott's sold it to Marvin and Lucille Hemshrot.)

Grignon and Coughour started the first creamery in the village in 1891. George B. Caldwell built the hotel in 1895.

By 1895, the village of St. Clair had a population of 300 people. It had a daily stage to Mankato, four churches, a grade school, boot and shoe store, two blacksmith shops, a carpet weaver, a wagon maker, a druggist, two mills, a furniture store, a harness shop, a hotel, a livery stable, a meat market, one physician and three saloons. On March 9, 1897, J. W. Ward started the *St. Clair Star* which survived only a few months.

The party line first came to Decoria and McPherson townships in 1904. In 1904 the St. Clair Bellview Telephone Company was organized, with S.S. Babcock as president and Henry Thielman as manager. The switchboard was in the back of Thielman's store for ten years and then moved above the bank. Andy Quinn was the first lineman and Hulda Fitzloff the telephone opera-

Main Street looking east to west, ca. 1895

Main Street looking west to east, ca. 1895

Main Street looking west. The town hall is pictured at the front left. ca. 1900

tor. A large brick co-op creamery was also built in 1904.

The St. Clair State Bank was organized in 1906 by Henry Thielman, Nicholas Juliar, H. S. Haedt, G. J. Juliar, A. A. Juliar, H. A. Hubmer, Thomas Bowe, F.W. Lassow, F. C. Schultz, S. B. Wilson, George May and John Bestman. The bank building was completed in 1907.

On December 20, 1907, St. Clair was incorporated as a village by a vote of 40 to 9. The first elections were held in 1908. Trustees: Henry Thielman, president, E.F. Duemeland, P. H. Bowe, J. W. Chase; Recorder: Charles O'Connor; Treasurer: M. C. Dalton; Justices: Charles O'Connor, Christ Aplers; Constables: Henry Luedke and A. T. Andrews.

The railroad came to St. Clair in 1908 shortly after the village had incorporated. The route was started by a group of farmers and businessmen and was known officially as the Duluth, St. Cloud, Glencoe and Mankato line. The long list of towns in the title prompted people to label it the alphabet line or the ABC line. St. Clair was to have been on the Mankato to Albert Lea run of the new railroad, but tracks were never laid between the community and Mankato. Among other deterring influences, inter-railroad rivalry entered the picture. The Chicago and Milwaukee were opposed to the idea and began laying a track eastward from Good Thunder. Its plan was to cut across the right-of-way, which the Alphabet would use, between Albert Lea and Mankato. In the face of such a move, the backers of the Alphabet line sold out to the rival railroad and the St. Clair to Albert Lea route became part of the Chicago, Milwaukee, St. Paul and Pacific system. In 1955 two or three trains a week were serving the community.

Huntting Elevator Company built a grain elevator in 1908. The Botsford Lumber Company was also established in St. Clair in 1908.

In 1911 the village built a water tower to hold the community's water supply. The tower made possible the establishment of a volunteer fire department, which could replace the old bucket-brigade method with hoses. Hose carts and other equipment purchased in 1910 have been replaced over the years with the most recent equipment.

The Kuske Harness, Leather and Hardware business was established in 1913 and was located in the west end of town and in 1931 moved downtown. Dr. Richard Juliar established a medical practice in St. Clair in 1913.

Henry Thielman built a new store for his mercantile business in 1915. Later this store was Pagenkopf's Store.

In 1922 a new brick addition was added to the old community school structure, which had been built in 1888. The addition enabled the school to expand to twelve grades. The class of 1923 was the first class to graduate from St. Clair having completed the twelfth grade. Transportation to and from school was provided by four wagons owned by the school district and one wagon and one automobile owned by a driver. Eighteen charcoal foot-warmers and eight blankets provided heating. The horses to draw the wagons were provided by the driver. By 1930 transportation changed rapidly from horse drawn vehicles to motor buses. In 1942 the population of St. Clair was 286.

Over the years changes continued to be made. In 1970 the City Dump was closed and the city contracted for curbside garbage collection. Land was purchased from Carl Rose for a wastewater treatment plant and the Nyquist Addition Plat was approved and construction began. A federal grant was received for the wastewater treatment plant in 1971 and this project was completed in 1972. St. Clair continued to grow and with the Denn and Frank addition plats in 1972 construction of homes also continued. In 1973 the city decided to contract its police protection with the Blue Earth County Sheriff's Department. The new St. Clair City Hall/Fire Department building was constructed on the old Creamery property at 304 West Main Street in 1974. As the city was expanding and lots for building additional homes were no longer available, the Goodrich 1st Addition plat was approved and construction began in 1977. There had been no train service to St. Clair for sometime and in 1977 the railroad tracks were removed and the bed leveled. Street signs were also installed throughout the city. The new well was dug near the water tower in 1978.

In 1983 the cable TV franchise was granted and a City Economic Development Committee was appointed. The water filtration system was replaced and upgraded at the Water System Pump House in 1984 and the Women Jaycees along with the area Actioneers organized the return of a community celebration "St. Clair Days." It was also during this year that the small cities in Blue Earth County (including St. Clair) were awarded a $30,000 Small Cities Economic Development Grant from Blue Earth County. In 1985 the population of the city was 655.

Natural gas lines were installed by NSP in 1992 and the 2nd, 3rd and 4th Goodrich Housing Additions were plat approved. The Memorial Park was developed on 7.8 acres of land and a pavilion, softball field, volleyball court, picnic shelter and playground areas were constructed. It was in this year that the weekly curbside recycling was initiated and the city purchased its first computer system. After some time without hometown news coverage, Jerry and Marie Groebner expanded coverage in the *Lake Region Times* (a weekly newspaper) to include St. Clair. The city of St. Clair then approved the *Lake Region Times* as the official city newspaper. In 1997 the city decided to disband operation of the Municipal Liquor Store and sold it to Troy and Kelly Zabel who currently operate it as the UpTown Tavern. The Goodrich 5th Addition plat was also approved in 1997 and again construction of homes continued.

In 2001 erosion along the south banks of the Le Sueur was in need of attention and the Le Sueur River Streambank Erosion Project was completed along the 200 block of Main Street West. The total cost of this project was $212,000.

St. Clair has grown in population over the years. People like living in smaller towns. Several housing additions, as well as a trailer court and two Schalow Apartment buildings have provided living spaces for continual growth. Population of St. Clair in 2005 is 823.

By Julie Schrader—1990 and
Cathy Seys, St. Clair City Clerk–2005

St. Clair Mayors - 1922-2005

1922	Jacob W. Chase
1924	O. O. Juliar
1925	Rudolph A. Froehlich
1926	Earl W. Pagenkopf
1927	George R. Macomber
1926	O. O. Juliar
1929	Fred Wingen
Jan. 1933 - Dec. 1934	Louis Grams
Jan. 1935 - Dec. 1938	Henry Lubke
Jan. 1939 - Dec. 1945	George H. Hubmer
Jan. 1946 - Dec. 1948	Nicholas Juliar
Jan. 1948 - Dec. 1953	George Hubmer
Jan. 1954 - Dec. 1957	George Miller
Jan. 1958 - Dec. 1963	George Hubmer
Jan. 1964 - Dec. 1965	Ben Winslow
Jan. 1966 - Dec. 1969	Carl Fitzloff
Jan. 1970 - Mar. 1973	Harry L. Miller
Apr. 1973 - Dec. 1976	Lyle Goodrich
Jan. 1977 - Dec. 1982	Ramona Fitzloff
Jan. 1983 - Dec. 1994	Harry L. Miller
Mar. 1995 - Mar. 2003	Dennis Zabel
Mar. 2003 - Present	Brian Lynch

Main Street looking east

Main Street looking west

Main Street looking east. The profile of the wooden Lutheran Church building on Main Street dates this photo as 1926. It is believed the wooden church was moved straight north so that it could be used by the congregation during the construction of the new brick church. Upon completion, the wooden church was dismantled.

North side of Main Street

Railroad Street in St. Clair. These homes were owned by (L to R) Mr. Depuydt, Art Winkelman and Roy Lewis.

Pictured on the left is the hotel and bank on the north side of Main Street.

St. Clair, ca. 1910

St. Clair, ca. 1916

Main Street looking west, ca. 1917

St. Clair in 1920 – looking northwest. The school is pictured on the left, St. John's Lutheran Church is front center and the town hall on the right.

Main Street looking west, ca. 1920

Aerial view of St. Clair in the 1940s.

Aerial view of St. Clair, ca. 1945

Aerial view of St. Clair, ca. 1950

St. Clair in the 1950s. North side of Main Street looking west.

Main Street looking west in 1988

Main Street looking east in 1988

St. John's Lutheran Church (built in 1876) and Parsonage (built in 1905).

CHAPTER FOUR

History of Our Churches

CONGREGATIONAL CHURCH

The Rev. Wallace Bruce organized the Congregational Church in 1874 with less than twelve members. A house of worship was built in 1876. In 1904 the congregation was reorganized and a new church was built. A new parsonage was built in 1908. The church was located in the area where the telephone company's substation is today. The church was disbanded about 1920 and the property was later sold.

The church building was later moved across the street and was remodeled into a house. The Lyle Splinter family lived in it at one time. In 1997 the property was purchase by St. John's Evangelical Lutheran Church, the buildings were removed and the lot is being used as a parking lot.

Congregational Church, ca. 1909

IMMACULATE CONCEPTION CATHOLIC CHURCH

Prior to 1854, there were very few white settlers in the territory. It has been asserted that the Indian missionary Msgr. Augustine Ravoux passed through this area and offered the Holy Sacrifice before 1854, while on a journey to the Indian villages on the Missouri River. The first recorded attempt to establish a more or less permanent settlement was the action taken by the government in 1855 to move the Winnebago Indians from the reservation at Long Prairie, Minnesota, to a new location on the Blue Earth River south of Mankato. Father Francis Vivaldi missionary to this tribe at Long Prairie came with them. He was instructed with the spiritual care of the Winnebagoes and also, with the help of a few Indian women, who he had hoped would form a religious community, conducted the school for Indian children at the Winnebago Agency.

The early history of the Catholic Church of the Winnebago Agency is based largely on the verbal accounts given by a few French and Indian half breeds remaining after the removal of the Winnebago Tribe of Indians in the spring of 1863 to a reservation in Nebraska.

The lands in and adjacent to the present Village of St. Clair to the extent of about four townships was a Winnebago Indian Reservation, occupied by the Tribe from the year 1854 to 1863. During the time the Tribe was here a Catholic Sisterhood maintained an Indian school. Also a chapel was established by Father Ravouz and later attended by a priest named Father Francis Vivaldi.

After the removal of the Indians in 1863, the Mission was organized in 1864, and continued to be known as the Winnebago Agency and was visited two or three times a year by Father Sommereisen of Mankato, saying Mass in private homes at such visits until 1866. There were about thirty families as members. The following formed a parish organization: James Alexander, Mrs. J. Ady, James, John and Patrick O'Connor, Frank Kennedy, Edward Lynch, Peter and Charles Manaige and Michael St. Cyr. A piece of ground of two acres located about one mile southeast of the present village and having on it an old log hotel building was purchased from Henry Foster.

A few of the Catholic men of this new organization set earnestly to work to remodel the old hotel and succeeded by cutting in windows, plastering, building an altar and pews and making it a good frontier church.

The Mission was then placed in charge of Father Bauman, a priest resident at St. Mary's in Waseca County, Minnesota, who visited the Mission once a month until 1874. This was also when a new frame church (30'x50') was built in what is now the present village of St. Clair on the site of the present church. Mrs. James (Mary) Maloney donated the land, which had the rectory, schoolhouse and a barn in which the horses were kept for the school children and parishioners driving in with buggies to the church in memory of her husband, James Maloney, Jr. They were Margaret (Mrs. Walter Grams) grandparents.

During the years 1875-1880, Father Herman Richards, S.J., a Jesuit Father, assistant pastor at St. Peter and Paul's in Mankato, attended the missions from St. Clair to Luverne in southwestern Minnesota. His name was held in benediction by the pioneers. In 1878 it was officially named St. Clair's Catholic Church of St. Clair, MN, and was in charge of the Jesuit Fathers in Mankato, MN, from 1874. The first baptism in the new parish was John Hayes, son of Joseph Hayes and Elizabeth Smith, on December 28, 1874, by Father Schnitzler S.J. The first marriage was of Anthony Callaghan and Helen Shea on November 26, 1876. The first confirmation class was on October 2, 1876, by Bishop Ireland from St. Paul, MN. The first death was that of Patrick Leary who was six years old in 1876. The cemetery records go back to 1876.

From 1874 until 1900 the parish baptized 450, married 68 and buried 73 people. Under Father Kreidler S. J. the church was enlarged in 1892 to 30' x 68' and the name changed to The Church of the Immaculate Conception of St. Clair, MN. During these years Fathers Richard, Aufenkalk, Sigg, Schaaf, Grafweg, and Breymann served at the parish. In 1900 Father Robert Highes and the Fr. Daniel Hughes took care of the parish from St. John's in Mankato, MN. In September 1902 the Mission was made a parish with a resident pastor, a Father E. M. Ryan from New York. That year the rectory was built. Bishop Joseph B. Cotter of Winona, Right Rev. James Coyne, Rev E. M. Ryan, pastor and lay members Herbert Bruels and Martin Bowe, legally incorporated the church in June 1902. Fr. Ryan died in October 1902 and the parish was again under the care of Fr. Hughes from Mankato, MN.

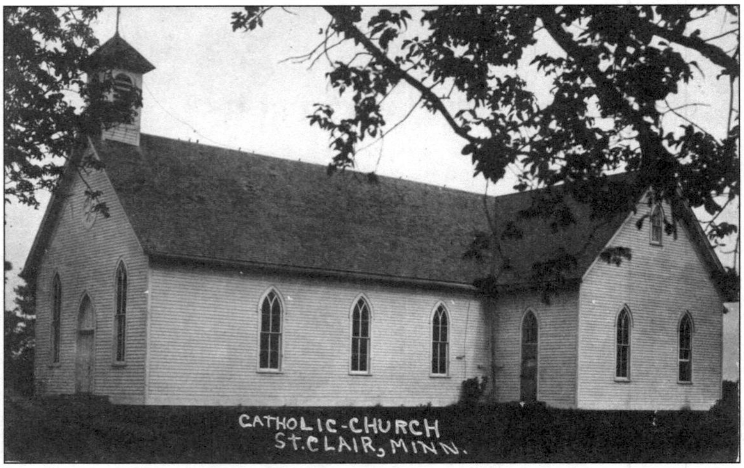

The Catholic Church was built in 1892 and was destroyed by fire in 1914.

The Catholic parsonage was built in 1902.

In 1914 Father James Glendon was pastor somewhat less than a year and it was during this pastorate that the church built by Fr. Schnitzler was completely destroyed by fire. Fr. O'Connor supervised the construction of the present church.

From 1900 until January 15, 1989, there were a total of 1,870 baptisms, 485 marriages and 421 funerals preformed. The resident pastor at this time was Fr. Harold Mountain who came in 1977 and served until 1994. His mother Ada Bowe, was born on July 15, 1894, and was married in 1914. Another son Edward is also a priest in the diocese of Winona.

The priests that have served our parish since Fr. Harold Mountain are Fr. Syl Brown, Fr. James Russell, Fr. Russell Seepaniak and Fr. Kevin Connolly.

An educational building was built in 1963 and a new front with handicap facilities was built onto the church in 2003.

In 2004 Charles Grams and Mark Gens are the trustees. Serving on the cemetery board is Daniel Ireland. The president of the council of Catholic Women is Mrs. Alicia More. Mrs. Kim Bruender is the secretary, Mrs. Kristin Nett the treasurer and vice president is Mrs. Cathy Sargent. The organists are Clifford Schneider, Matt Sieberg, Kathleen Tharp, Abby Ireland and Jamie Chen. The religious education director is Mrs. Loretta Zelasney. The resident Pastor is Fr. Patrick Arens. This is his first assignment as a Pastor.

By Father Syl Brown and Cliff Schneider

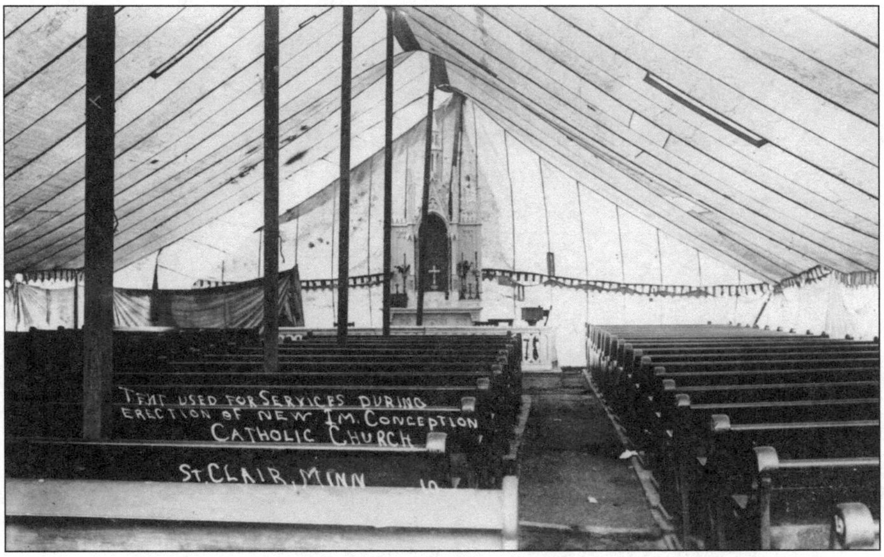

Inside of the tent that was used for services while the new Catholic Church was being built in 1914.

Construction of the Catholic Church in 1914.

Construction of the Catholic Church in 1914

Immaculate Conception Catholic Church

Immaculate Conception Education Building built in 1963

Immaculate Conception Catholic Church

Interior of Immaculate Conception Catholic Church

Interior of Immaculate Conception Catholic Church

ST. JOHN'S EVANGELICAL LUTHERAN CHURCH

The first Lutherans came to this area in 1866. In 1867 church services were held in the District 70 school house which was located one-half mile east of Hilton. On July 31, 1869, the congregation was officially organized with thirteen charter members and was known as St. John's Evangelical Lutheran Church. The Rev. Albert Kuhn served as the pastor. Charter members of this organization were Louis Korth, Carl Pagenkopf, John Flitter, Fred Lassow, August Beerbaum, August Barneske, Fred Cords, Carl Kruse, Fred Luenebury, Fred Koch, Carl Dittman, Henry Mueller and Karl Kurth. Seven years later, in the year 1876, the congregation was incorporated under the name of "St. John's Evangelical Lutheran Church of Winnebago Agency," by the trustees, John Fitzloff, August Barneske, and August Kopke. The minister at this time was Pastor G. E. Ahner formerly of Nicollet, Minnesota, and it was also in this year that the congregation built its first church. In 1880, the congregation numbering only 20 voting members decided to extend a call for a full-time pastor as a self-sustaining congregation. In 1883, the congregation numbering 27 voting members built the first parsonage. By 1892, the congregation numbering 256 souls and 46 voting members, renovated the old church at a cost of $1,200. In 1905 a new parsonage was erected at a cost of $3,000.

It is noted that around the year 1913-1919 several improvements were made on the church property. Cement floors were laid in the basement of the parsonage and barn. A new furnace was installed in the parsonage. Cement sidewalks were laid. Electric lights were installed in the church and parsonage, a new organ was purchased and school desks were installed for instruction classes. A special notation is made that the ladies of the congregation were for the most part, responsible for these necessary improvements. Records show they paid for the entire cost of the installation of electricity and fixtures as

Interior of St. John's Lutheran Church

1918 St. John's Lutheran Church Confirmation Class members, L to R: Alvin Schenk, Fred Kruse and Waldemar Proechel. Pastor Reinhold J. Mueller served the church from 1913-1920.

St. John's Lutheran Church built in 1925-26

St. John's Lutheran Parsonage built in 1995

St. John's Lutheran Educational Unit built in 1965

St. John's Lutheran Church in 2001

St. John's Lutheran Pre-school opened September 8, 2004 with eleven students.

well as half the cost of the new organ.

On September 7, 1920, Pastor G. E. Fritzke was installed as pastor. During his pastorate the water system was installed in the parsonage. It was also during this time because of the extensive repairs needed for the old church building that the decision was made to build a new church. The cornerstone was laid in July 1925. The new facility was dedicated on February 27, 1926. The cost of the entire project was $25,000.

In 1935 Pastor A. H. Mackdanz accepted the call to serve the congregation and a Sunday school program was started. In November 1948 a new Wicks Pipe Organ was dedicated. This organ is still being used at the present time. In April 1949 Pastor Arthur Kell was installed. In 1950 the constitution was reviewed and certain changes were made, the German Services were discontinued, and the independent Lutheran Cemetery Association was dissolved and the cemetery was then absorbed into the congregation. In the spring of 1952, the church was redecorated and new lights were installed in the chancel, and the confirmation class wore gowns for the first time. In 1957 Pastor LeRoy Ristow was installed and in 1958 the choir began to wear gowns. In 1959 Pastor David Kock was installed and a Young Peoples League was organized. In 1962 a set of chimes was added to the organ. On February 6, 1965, the Groundbreaking Ceremony for the new Educational Unit was held. Pastor Donald Lindloff was installed on April 17, 1966 and he served the congregation until 1994. This was also the year the 100th anniversary was celebrated. On August 6, 1968, a severe rain storm caused considerable flooding in St. Clair including the church basement, which was covered with about 2 feet of murky water, however, no major damage was done. Pastor Jeffrey Holtan was ordained and installed on January 8, 1995, and the new parsonage was dedicated on August 27, 1995. In 1997 the Splinter property was purchased and is being used as a parking lot. Pastor Daniel Schmidt was installed on October 22, 2000, and on April 29, 2001, the new entryway was dedicated. The "Follow Me Preschool" program began in the fall of 2004.

Over the years many changes in the physical structure of this congregation have changed as well as the number of members. The original goals of the founders, that being of strictly adhering to the Word of God and the preaching of the Law and Gospel in its truth and purity as well as to the teachings of Doctor Martin Luther, have never changed.

ZION UNITED METHODIST CHURCH

Preaching services and prayer meetings were held in homes and several schoolhouses of the community from 1867 to 1876. On February 24, 1876, a group of people who had been under the ministering influence of pioneer pastors for several years, gathered in School District 70 of the St. Clair community to adopt articles of incorporation and to elect trustees. The trustees that were elected were Frederick Lumberg, president; Otto Schultz, secretary; and John Borchard, treasurer. It was also in 1876 that the first church was built in St. Clair, which was then called the Winnebago Agency. Charter member families were those of the above mentioned trustees and Carl Marzinske, John Buckholtz, H. Miller, C. Dittman, John Gekeler and August Fisher. Several years later came the Nicholas Juliar family and other names were soon added. In 1879 the St. Clair congregation became a part of the Mankato Mission and taken as a regular appointment.

In 1889 the church had a membership of 26 and was part of a "circuit riders charge," which included Willow Creek, Smith's Mill and Amboy. A revival held in 1897 over this circuit resulted in great good. St. Clair experienced a steady growth and membership and Amboy membership reached 80 over a former count of 29.

In 1912 a new church was built at a cost of $6,750 under the direction of Rev. J., D. Moede. Mildred Juliar was the first baptism performed in the new church. A basement the full size of the church was excavated in 1925. In 1947 Mr. and Mrs. George Hubmer presented the congregation with an electric organ and in 1949 an annex was added to the church and presented to the congregation by Currier Hubmer, Frederick Bestmann, Harry Fisher, Robert Zavoral and Elmer Haugen. In 1959-1960 many improvements were made at a cost of $20,000.

Evangelical United Brethren Church (built 1912) and Parsonage (built 1930)

In 1910 a house was purchased in St. Clair for a parsonage and the first pastor to occupy it was Rev. Paul Mueller. In 1930 a new parsonage was built.

In 1924 the church had a membership of 83. From 1924-1929 the church was revived with the help of Evangelist P. A. Lang and O. S. Monson. In 1929 the membership grew to 162 and to 174 in 1930.

Rev. G. H. Knebel organized the first Sunday school. The Sunday school continued to be a strong right arm to the church.

In November 1946 the United Brethren in Christ Church and the Evangelical United Brethren Church united to form the Evangelical United Brethren Church. This step united the Beauford United Brethren in Christ Church and the Zion Evangelical Church in St. Clair into one denomination. Since 1952 these two churches were served together.

In 1966 the General Conference of the Methodist and Evangelical United Brethren Churches started the question of union. In 1969 the Conference met in session in St. Paul to unite the two denomination under the new name of United Methodist.

Zion United Methodist Church celebrated its centennial on September 26, 1976. Over the years the number of families in the congregation had decreased and so the last service for this congregation was held in June 2003.

The church building, as well as the parsonage, was sold to Jonas and Angie Nissen of Mankato, MN. It is now known as "Bell Tower Place" and is a community theatre as well as a cozy, warm and inviting setting for meetings, gatherings, parties and weddings.

CEMETERIES

Bunker Hill Cemetery: This cemetery is located in the SW corner of the SE quarter of Section 24 in McPherson Township. It was owned at one time by the township. It is said to have about fifty people buried here but only fifteen names were found on head stones when the Blue Earth County Historical Society did the transcription of the cemetery. Early burials are C. Wood Ebenezer-1871, Cathrine Cramton-1875 and Marcus More-1882.

Immaculate Conception Catholic Cemetery: This cemetery is located in the N one-half of the NE corner of the NW corner of Section 17 in McPherson Township. The Immaculate Conception Church of St. Clair owns the cemetery. The first burial took place in 1864 and the cemetery was dedicated in 1874.

Immaculate Conception Catholic Cemetery

St. John's Evangelical Lutheran Cemetery: The first burial in this cemetery was in 1902 when the cemetery was established. The cemetery was platted and dedicated in 1905 and is owned by St. John's Evangelical Lutheran Church. It is located in the NE corner of the NE quarter in Section 17 in McPherson Township.

St. John's Evangelical Lutheran Cemetery

What you have inherited
From your fathers, earn
Again for yourselves, or
It will not be yours.
Goethe

(Submitted by Nick Cords)

McPherson/Union Cemetery: This cemetery is located in the SE corner of the NE quarter in Section 7 in McPherson Township and is owned by the McPherson Cemetery Association. The cemetery was established in 1869 when the first burial took place. It was platted and dedicated in 1874. Familiar names include Campbell, Chase, Hilton, Rasdall, Truman, Foster, Reid, Wolcott, Fields, and Manaige.

Union Cemetery

St. Johns (Bestman) Cemetery

St. John (Bestman) Cemetery: This cemetery is located in Section 17 on the south edge of St. Clair. Carl Moede was buried in 1868, Fredrich Schultz in 1872, Wilhelmine Kurth in 1877 and August Bestman in 1876. There is a board of directors that oversees its operation.

Country school in the early 1900s. This school was located northeast of St. Clair in Section 3 about 1¼ miles from the Herman Klingbeil farm.

CHAPTER FIVE

Our Schools

When a settlement first sprang up along the Le Sueur River where St. Clair now stands, a school also was established. The first school in the area was a religious school, which was taught by the pioneer Methodist preacher, Rev. B.Y. Coffin, in 1857 for the Indians. The Jesuit sisters also taught a parochial school during the Indian times. The first public school for the white children was taught in 1863 at the Agency by Francis Beveridge, a noted lawyer from St. Paul, who spent his last years in retirement at this out of the way village. From 1865 to 1887 there were eight schoolhouses in McPherson Township. Later there was a school at each end of the new community. In 1888 these two common school districts were consolidated and the brick building was built. The school built in 1888 after the first consolidation housed ten grades. Over the years, one by one, the country school consolidated with the school located in St. Clair.

In 1922, 34 years later, two more districts were added to the consolidation, and a second brick building, providing facilities for 12 grades, was constructed. In 1923 the first class having completed twelve grades was graduat-

St. Clair School in 1888

St. Clair School house built in 1888

St. Clair High School, ca. 1923

St. Clair's first school bus

ed. The graduates were Mabel Juliar, Nicholas Juliar, Ardela Kruse, Oscar Lubke, Lucile Pagenkopf and Kevin O'Brien. The faculty of four were W.E. Nelson, superintendent, Emma Godeman, W. F. Small, principal, and Isabel McIntosh. The school board members were Henry Lubke, Judge O'Connor, F.E. Juliar, George Hubmer, Walter O'Brien and Grace (Foster) Chase.

In 1942 with the Surplus Marketing Administration (SMA) supplying the food and the Works Progress Administration (WPA) providing labor and supervision, a hot school lunch was made available at the cost of $.03 per day. Meal tickets were sold by the week for $.15. The students lined up in the hall, had their tickets punched, then filed past the Home Economics room door and received a cup filled with hot dish and a spoon. They then filed back to their classrooms and sat at their desks to eat

1941 St. Clair school bus and children
Back row, L to R: Bus driver Andy Riese, Laverna Hemingover, Kate Hemingover, Ellen Schmidt, Lorene Glamm, Doris Freitag, Alvin Fleming, Gene Dumdei, Donald Glamm, Kenneth Freitag, Elmer Danberry.
Middle row: Anita Grams, Donna Pierce, Martha Schmidt, Lyle Fleming, LuJune Pierce.
Front row: unidentified, Karl Grams, Ronnie Heningover, Glenn Pierce, Margie Westphal.

St. Clair School with new addition, 1950

Harold Walton became the St. Clair School Superintendent in 1957.

their lunch. The meals were generally served only during the winter months. Clara Hintze started this service. Another government program at this time was the National Youth Organization (NYO) which was administrated in order to give young people an opportunity to earn money. Robert Fritzke worked under this program and was the only school secretary at this time doing the school paper, memos, mimeographing for school and community. He earned $10 a month for his efforts.

In 1948 the school district again expanded when ten more rural districts joined the consolidation. A third addition to the system, adding eight classrooms and a new auditorium and gymnasium, was added in 1950 to accommodate the constantly swelling needs of the growing district.

Several more rural districts had since joined and now consolidation of 146 districts compose the St. Clair District #75 and the district in 1955 comprised 40,000 acres of land and had an assessed valuation of $1,200,000. Serving on the school board at this time were C. G. Hubmer, chairman, F. J. Bestman, clerk, Walter H. Grams, treasurer, J. C. Wohlrabe, Hugh Russell and Victor Shaver. In 1960 a new elementary wing was added. This addition included twelve elementary rooms,

St. Clair School Mascot

Elementary wing built in 1960

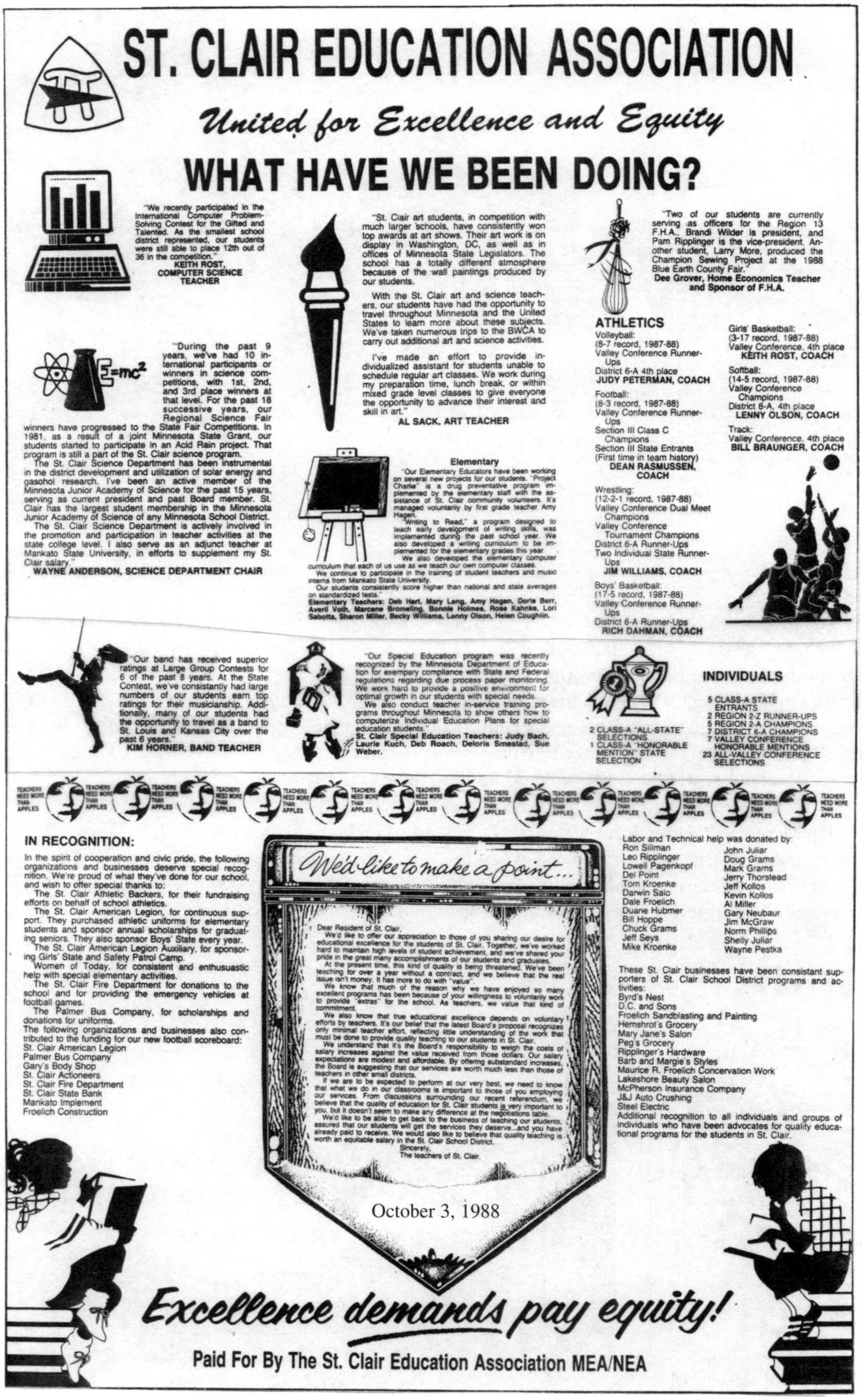

ST. CLAIR EDUCATION ASSOCIATION

United for Excellence and Equity

WHAT HAVE WE BEEN DOING?

"We recently participated in the International Computer Problem-Solving Contest for the Gifted and Talented. As the smallest school district represented, our students were still able to place 12th out of 36 in the competition."
KEITH ROST, COMPUTER SCIENCE TEACHER

"St. Clair art students, in competition with much larger schools, have consistently won top awards at art shows. Their art work is on display in Washington, DC, as well as in offices of Minnesota State Legislators. The school has a totally different atmosphere because of the wall paintings produced by our students.

With the St. Clair art and science teachers, our students have had the opportunity to travel throughout Minnesota and the United States to learn more about these subjects. We've taken numerous trips to the BWCA to carry out additional art and science activities.

I've made an effort to provide individualized assistant for students unable to schedule regular art classes. We work during my preparation time, lunch break, or within mixed grade level classes to give everyone the opportunity to advance their interest and skill in art."
AL SACK, ART TEACHER

"Two of our students are currently serving as officers for the Region 13 F.H.A., Brandi Wilder is president, and Pam Ripplinger is the vice-president. Another student, Larry More, produced the Champion Sewing Project at the 1988 Blue Earth County Fair."
Dee Grover, Home Economics Teacher and Sponsor of F.H.A.

"During the past 9 years, we've had 10 international participants or winners in science competitions, with 1st, 2nd, and 3rd place winners at that level. For the past 18 successive years, our Regional Science Fair winners have progressed to the State Fair Competitions. In 1981, as a result of a joint Minnesota State Grant, our students started to participate in an Acid Rain project. That program is still a part of the St. Clair science program.

The St. Clair Science Department has been instrumental in the district development and utilization of solar energy and gasohol research. I've been an active member of the Minnesota Junior Academy of Science for the past 15 years, serving as current president and past Board member. St. Clair has the largest student membership in the Minnesota Junior Academy of Science of any Minnesota School District.

The St. Clair Science Department is actively involved in the promotion and participation in teacher activities at the state college level. I also serve as an adjunct teacher at Mankato State University, in efforts to supplement my St. Clair salary."
WAYNE ANDERSON, SCIENCE DEPARTMENT CHAIR

Elementary

"Our Elementary Educators have been working on several new projects for our students. "Project Charlie" is a drug preventative program implemented by the elementary staff with the assistance of St. Clair community volunteers. It's managed voluntarily by first grade teacher Amy Hagen.

"Writing to Read," a program designed to teach early development of writing skills, was implemented during the past school year. We also developed a writing curriculum to be implemented for the elementary grades this year.

We also developed the elementary computer curriculum that each of us use as we teach our own computer classes.

We continue to participate in the training of student teachers and music interns from Mankato State University.

Our students consistently score higher than national and state averages on standardized tests."

Elementary Teachers: Deb Hart, Mary Lang, Amy Hagen, Doris Berr, Averil Voth, Marcene Bromeling, Bonnie Holmes, Rose Kahnke, Lori **Sabotta, Sharon Miller, Becky Williams, Lenny Olson, Helen Coughlin.**

ATHLETICS

Volleyball:
(8-7 record, 1987-88)
Valley Conference Runner-Ups
District 6-A 4th place
JUDY PETERMAN, COACH

Football:
(8-3 record, 1987-88)
Valley Conference Runner-Ups
Section III Class C Champions
Section III State Entrants
(First time in team history)
DEAN RASMUSSEN, COACH

Wrestling:
(12-2-1 record, 1987-88)
Valley Conference Dual Meet Champions
Valley Conference Tournament Champions
District 6-A Runner-Ups
Two Individual State Runner-Ups
JIM WILLIAMS, COACH

Boys' Basketball:
(17-5 record, 1987-88)
Valley Conference Runner-Ups
District 6-A Runner-Ups
RICH DAHMAN, COACH

Girls' Basketball:
(3-17 record, 1987-88)
Valley Conference, 4th place
KEITH ROST, COACH

Softball:
(14-5 record, 1987-88)
Valley Conference Champions
District 6-A, 4th place
LENNY OLSON, COACH

Track:
Valley Conference, 4th place
BILL BRAUNGER, COACH

"Our band has received superior ratings at Large Group Contests for 6 of the past 8 years. At the State Contest, we've consistantly had large numbers of our students earn top ratings for their musicianship. Additionally, many of our students had the opportunity to travel as a band to St. Louis and Kansas City over the past 6 years."
KIM HORNER, BAND TEACHER

"Our Special Education program was recently recognized by the Minnesota Department of Education for exempary compliance with State and Federal regulations regarding due process paper monitoring. We work hard to provide a positive environment for optimal growth in our students with special needs.

We also conduct teacher in-service training programs throughout Minnesota to show others how to computerize Individual Education Plans for special education students."
St. Clair Special Education Teachers: Judy Bach, Laurie Kuch, Deb Roach, Deloris Smestad, Sue Weber.

INDIVIDUALS

2 CLASS-A "ALL-STATE" SELECTIONS
1 CLASS-A "HONORABLE MENTION" STATE SELECTION

5 CLASS-A STATE ENTRANTS
2 REGION 2-Z RUNNER-UPS
5 REGION 2-A CHAMPIONS
7 DISTRICT 6-A CHAMPIONS
7 VALLEY CONFERENCE HONORABLE MENTIONS
23 ALL-VALLEY CONFERENCE SELECTIONS

TEACHERS NEED MORE THAN APPLES

IN RECOGNITION:

In the spirit of cooperation and civic pride, the following organizations and businesses deserve special recognition. We're proud of what they've done for our school, and wish to offer special thanks to:

The St. Clair Athletic Backers, for their fundraising efforts on behalf of school athletics.

The St. Clair American Legion, for continuous support. They purchased athletic uniforms for elementary students and sponsor annual scholarships for graduating seniors. They also sponsor Boys' State every year.

The St. Clair American Legion Auxiliary, for sponsoring Girls' State and Safety Patrol Camp.

Women of Today, for consistent and enthusuastic help with special elementary activities.

The St. Clair Fire Department for donations to the school and for providing the emergency vehicles at football games.

The Palmer Bus Company, for scholarships and donations for uniforms.

The following organizations and businesses also contributed to the funding for our new football scoreboard:
St. Clair American Legion
Palmer Bus Company
Gary's Body Shop
St. Clair Actioneers
St. Clair Fire Department
St. Clair State Bank
Mankato Implement
Froelich Construction

We'd like to make a point...

Dear Resident of St. Clair,

We'd like to offer our appreciation to those of you sharing our desire for educational excellence for the students of St. Clair. Together, we've worked hard to maintain high levels of student achievement, and we've shared your pride in the great many accomplishments of our students and graduates.

At the present time, this kind of quality is being threatened. We've been teaching for over a year without a contract, and we believe that the real issue isn't money. It has more to do with "value".

We know that much of the reason why we have enjoyed so many excellent programs has been because of your willingness to voluntarily work to provide "extras" for the school. As teachers, we value that kind of commitment.

We also know that true educational excellence depends on voluntary efforts by teachers. It's our belief that the latest Board's proposal recognizes only minimal teacher effort, reflecting little understanding of the work that must be done to provide quality teaching to our students in St. Clair.

We understand that it's the Board's responsibility to weigh the costs of salary increases against the value received from those dollars. Our salary expectations are modest and affordable. By offering substandard increases, the Board is suggesting that our services are worth much less than those of teachers in other small districts.

If we are to be expected to perform at our very best, we need to know that what we do in our classrooms is important to those of you employing our services. From discussions surrounding our recent referendum, we believe that the quality of education for St. Clair students _is_ very important to you, but it doesn't seem to make any difference at the negotiations table.

We'd like to be able to get back to the business of teaching our students, assured that our students will get the services they deserve...and you have already paid to receive. We would also like to believe that quality teaching is worth an equitable salary in the St. Clair School District.

Sincerely,
The teachers of St. Clair.

Labor and Technical help was donated by:

Ron Sillman	John Juliar
Leo Ripplinger	Doug Grams
Lowell Pagenkopf	Mark Grams
Del Point	Jerry Thorstead
Tom Kroenke	Jeff Kollos
Darwin Salo	Kevin Kollos
Dale Froelich	Al Miller
Duane Hubmer	Gary Neubaur
Bill Hoppe	Jim McGraw
Chuck Grams	Norm Phillips
Jeff Seys	Shelly Juliar
Mike Kroenke	Wayne Pestka

These St. Clair businesses have been consistant supporters of St. Clair School District programs and activities:
Byrd's Nest
D.C. and Sons
Froelich Sandblasting and Painting
Hemshrot's Grocery
Mary Jane's Salon
Peg's Grocery
Ripplinger's Hardware
Barb and Margie's Styles
Maurice R. Froelich Concervation Work
Lakeshore Beauty Salon
McPherson Insurance Company
J&J Auto Crushing
Steel Electric

Additional recognition to all individuals and groups of individuals who have been advocates for quality educational programs for the students in St. Clair.

Excellence demands pay equity!

Paid For By The St. Clair Education Association MEA/NEA

October 3, 1988

cafeteria and industrial arts shop. Remodeling in the high school building doubled the size of the library, science department, home economics department and commercial department. The new music department was relocated in the former lunchroom.

Aerial view of St. Clair School in June 1994

When the Milwaukee Railroad discontinued services to St. Clair ,some land became available and was purchased by the school district. Working with the neighboring church to parcel it out a new athletic complex for the school and a convenient parking lot for the church was developed. The first football game on the new field was played in the fall of 1980, but still was the only school in the Valley Conference forced to host afternoon games, as there were no lights on the field. With cooperation between the school district and the St. Clair Athletic Backers, a group that had been organized in 1972 to help with various athletic related projects, the dream of a lighted athletic complex became reality. Lights from the Mankato State University Lower Campus were purchased and installed and were first used in the summer of 1981 for the community education softball season. The first high school football game played "under the lights" in the history of the St. Clair District took place on September 4, 1981.

In 1988 after many meetings, much discussion and the availability of several options, the school board decided to drop out of negotiations for the development of a pairing program with Janesville and Waldorf-Pemberton School Districts. The possibility of sending secondary students to Mankato East High School was also discussed. The majority of the school board felt that the people of the district should decide the future of the district and presented a referendum on the ballot. This referendum did pass and enabled the present K-12 program to remain at St. Clair. The enrollment at this time was 495 students and there were 57 on the staff. The 1988 assessed valuation of the district was $12 million.

Overcrowding was again becoming a problem and in June 1989 the school board passed a resolution to build a science classroom (2,894 square feet) and to rent the Catholic Church CCD building to address health and safety hazards. The school board members at this time were Thomas Kroenke, chairman, Elaine Marzinske, clerk, Jerry Sader treasurer, Thomas Freitag, Jerry Phillips and Cathy Spear, directors.

St. Clair Media Center built in 1994

In December of 1989 the Hemshrot Grocery property was purchased for $18,366. In January of 1990 an architectural design was approved for the addition of a kindergarten room. In May of 1990 the approval of payment not to exceed $9,900 for the removal of the Hemshrot and Hendricks (old meat market/café) Buildings was passed.

A community-member committee was formed to study facilities and make recommendations to the School Board in January 1991. They presented their recommendations to the board and it was decided to build new elementary classrooms, new shop area and a new media center. The original bids in March 1993 came in too high and had to be re-bid. The final bid was accepted in June 1993, with Met-Con as general contractor. Two portable classrooms had to be moved to the west side of the building. The softball field was also removed. The lights, poles and fencing from the softball field were moved to the St. Clair City Park. The project was completed in 1994 with $1,930,000 in building bonds and $315,000 in capital facilities bonds. The addition added another 21,361 square feet to the existing building. The enrolment was 612. The board members were Thomas Kroenke, chair-

Superintendent Dr. Jerry Olson

man, Cathy Spear, clerk, Jerry Sader, treasurer, Don Larson, vice chairman, Jerry Phillips and Maynard Schwandt. Dr. Jerry Olson was the superintendent.

The new addition did not resolve issues of gym space, locker rooms, band and music storage, office, theater/stage, or weight room needs.

In June of 1995, the school board approval was given to have R.W. Carlstrom making the gymnasium and other class rooms handicap accessible.

The school and community were saddened at the tragic news on October 9, 1996, of the death of Principal James Buysse as a result of injuries sustained in an automobile accident. Mr. Buysse was remembered as an educator with a tireless dedication to students in need. Mr. Buysse came to St. Clair School in 1977 and served as the principal until his death. A Marian Anderson print was dedicated in his honor and is displayed in the school media center.

In November 1996 the school mascot was changed from the "Indians" to the "Cyclones" after many years of pressure from the MCLU and the State Educational Board.

After many years of "temporary use," the two temporary classrooms were removed due to health and safety issues in February 1998. Elementary classrooms were made in the back of the media center to accommodate students.

After a visit by the State Fire Marshal in May 1998 the St. Clair School was cited with several building issues. At that point a "facilities committee" was formed which included community members, staff members, administration and school board members. The committee ultimately formulated a recommendation statement for presentation to the school board, which included a proposed course of action. Staff and community information meetings were held for input and questions.

The all-day, every-day kindergarten was approved by the school board in March 1999. Parents were given the option of half-day dismissal. All-day kindergarten gives the children an advantage of library, music and art, extended interaction with peers, and core subjects of math and reading.

In August 1999 the St. Clair School Board approved

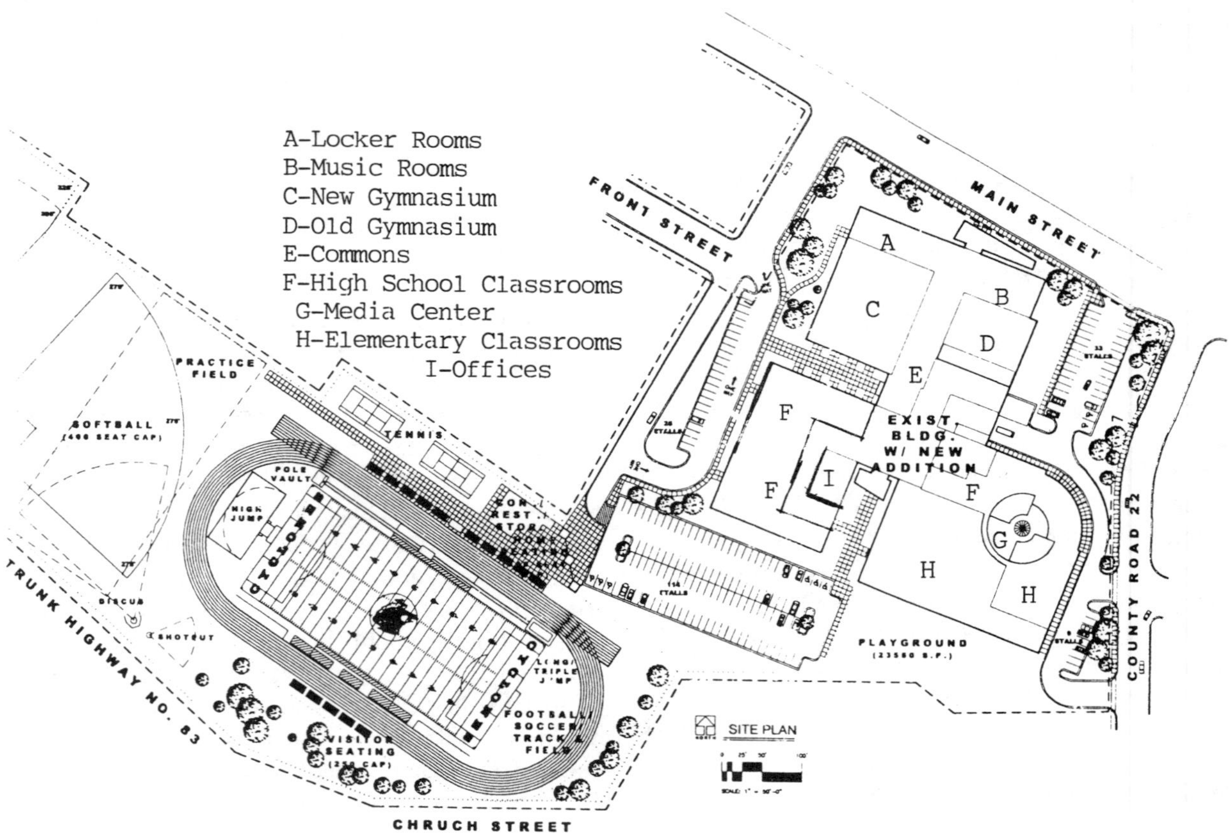

the hiring of the DLR Group to begin a study of options for the school building.

On June 5, 2000, a special election was held in which the voters approved the issuance of general obligation bonds not to exceed 10.5 million dollars for the betterment of the school facilities. The vote passed with 557 "yes" votes and 425 "no" votes. Approximately 44.6% of this was paid by the State through Debt Equalization. The District purchased an additional 10.5 acres of land at a price of approximately $10,000 per acre. A portion of Agency Street was closed to accommodate the athletic complex of the new facility. Enrollment was 670 students and 80 staff members.

A schematic design for the new building was submitted and approved by the school board in October 2000. The members of the school board at this time were Rick Behnke, chairman, Mark Frahm, vice chair, Laura Linde, clerk, Dale Westphal, treasurer, Connie Johns and Len Demert, directors. Mr. Rick Linnell was the superintendent.

The approval by the school board for the building and renovation documents and also the approval for bids to go out to contractors took place in February 2001. Bids were received and awarded on March 8, 2001, with groundbreaking and construction beginning in April and May.

St. Clair Public School in 2004

North entrance of the school

Construction went well and the elementary staff and students were able to move into their new classrooms in December. The old elementary wing was then remodeled and the high school students were able to move into their new areas in April 2002.

After graduation on May 21, 2002, the 1922 three-story section of the school building was demolished. Construction of the new gymnasium in this area as well as the parking lot was begun. The existing playground equipment could no longer be used due to new codes and regulations. The classrooms for a one-level K-12 building were completed. The first basketball game in the new gymnasium was played in February 2003.

On June 20, 2003, the "Dedication Ceremony" was held. Community and staff members, administration, board member, local politicians and local communities were invited for this special event. The school board members at this time were Mark Frahm, chairman, Connie Johns, vice chairman, Laura Linde, clerk, Scott Sonnek, treasurer, Kathy Johnson and Harvey Hesse, directors. Rick Linnell was superintendent, Alan Fitterer was secondary principal and Renee Klinkner was elementary principal. There were 81 staff members and 562 students. The new building boasts the latest in technology with fiber optics, smart boards, new science rooms, music suites, a new gymnasium, a commons area and air conditioning throughout the building. St. Clair is one of few small towns that have survived without becoming a consolidated school district. This community should be very proud of their dedication to the education of their children.

Rick Linnell, current superintendent

As of September 2004, the athletic complex includes a concession/storage building, a new crow's nest and independent well. Work is in progress for a track around the football field and a softball field. This is the first track field for St. Clair School. The new school building and athletic complex cover 136,000 square feet and are worth $22,278,443. Breakfast prices are $.95, elementary lunch $1.65, secondary lunch $1.75. Admission to activities is $5 for adults and $3 for students.

The St. Clair School district consists of 48,352 acres with a total taxable market valuation of $237,767,900.

There are a total number of 19.45 acres in the District #75 School Complex with a valuation of $108,973. The annual budget is $5,035,315. There are 665 students enrolled with a staff of 81.

The shared mission of the St. Clair School District and its community is to foster a student-focused environment that emphasizes critical thinking, educational innovation, and societal contribution for every student attending the school.

South entrance of the school in 2004.

MEMORIES

Memories are heartbeats
Sounding through the years,
Echoes never fading
Of our smiles and tears,
Moments that are captured,
Sometimes unaware,
Pictured in an album,
Or a lock of hair.

Images that linger
Deep within the mind,
Bits of verse we cherished
Once upon a time.
Through the musty hallways
Of the days we knew,
Ever comes the vision
Beautiful and true.

Memories are roses
Blooming evermore,
Full of fragrant sweetness
Never known before.
Life must have a meaning,
Goals for which to strive.
Memories are lights that burn
To keep the heart alive.

by Grace E. Easley

School gymnasium, locker room and commons 2004

St. Clair School Athletic Complex

CHAPTER SIX

St. Clair's Centennial Celebration

SEPTMEBER 1955

OVER 50 IN CAST OF BIG PAGEANT

Dance Climaxes Three-Day Centennial

Mankato Free Press – September 2, 1955

Three days of fun, frolic and festivities will be held in honor of St. Clair's centennial celebration Saturday, Sunday and Monday. The 100th birthday celebration of this village of 250 has been in the planning stage for many months, with all of the village's citizens taking a hand in the work.

St. Clairites trace their history back to 1855 when the Winnebago Agency was first established. The first settlers came to the area some years before that time when the township area was first called Rice Lake.

The St. Clair's annual Labor Day celebration this year has been enlarged to include the centennial celebration. The three-day event will include a giant midway which will be set up on the main street of the village, a horseshoe pitching contest, chaired by Loyal Joos, band concert, two-hour pageant, fireworks display, parade, free acts, drawings for merchandise prizes and a house full of furniture, beard judging contest, kangaroo court, and a centennial dance.

Saturday afternoon, North Star Shows midway attractions will be set up on St. Clair's Main Street for a three-

Driver Roy Lewis, Neil Maloney, Paul Schwwitchenberg, unidentified.
The pink convertible belonged to Gene Baer.

Centennial beard growing final contestants
Back row, L to R: Paul Schwichtenberg, James Winkelman, Roy Lewis and Neil Maloney
Front row: Bernard Hodapp, Bud Mace, Lyle Splinter and Chub Wolcott

day stand. Over 10 truck loads of attractions are being brought into St. Clair for the centennial event. The North Star attractions will include many rides and side shows, and will be running all day Sunday and Monday.

Over 100 entries have been accepted in the beard contest. Almost all of St. Clair's men have gotten into the spirit of the centennial celebration by growing beards.

Prizes in the contest include an electric razor, a fishing pole and reel and many other surprise awards, according to the contest chairman.

The St. Clair high school band will give a concert at 2 p.m. Sunday and the crowning of the centennial queen will also take place in conjunction with the band concert.

There are nine contestants in the queen contest, all living in and around St. Clair. They are Darlene Cords, Barbara Blank, Patty Christnagel, Rosalie Christnagel, Sandra Miller, Carol Phillips, Maxine Witt, Marilyn Fitzloff, and Lois Klingbeil.

The queen will be named immediately following the concert. The panel of judges who were selected to make the queen selection, are Eugene Hunziker of Mankato, Perry Stoffel of Eagle Lake and Lloyd Sandberg of Janesville.

The "Early Days" pageant, will begin at 7:30 p.m. in the high school auditorium on Sunday. The two-hour pageant features over 50 performers made up of St. Clairites and traces the village's history from 1855 to the present.

Following the 23 episodes of the pageant there will be a giant fireworks display. The first of the fireworks are scheduled to be set off at 9:30 p.m., or immediately following the pageant portraying St. Clair's history. They will be shown on the high school grounds. A very crowded schedule has been set up for Labor Day, the last day of the three-day Centennial Celebration.

Events Monday include the centennial parade at 10 a.m., the finals of the horseshoe tourney at 1 p.m., Hal Garven show at 2:30 and 7:30, drawings for merchandise prizes and the house full of furnishing, the beard judging and kangaroo court and the centennial dance.

The one-hour centennial parade will open the festivities on Labor Day at 10 a.m. There will be approximately 30 different units in the parade, which will start from the west end of St. Clair and wind through town.

High school bands from St. Clair, Nicollet, Janesville, Pemberton, Waseca, and Mankato will take part in the parade. All of the floats, sponsored by the St. Clair merchants will have a centennial theme.

Drawing for the house full of furniture will be held at 9 p.m., Monday. There will be three prizes; first prize a complete living room suite, second prize a bedroom suite, and third prize a kitchen suite. In addition there will be a drawing for many small merchandise prizes, all over $5.00, during the afternoon.

PAGEANT IS FEATURE OF CENTENNIAL
Will Be Given Sunday Night in School Building

A two-hour pageant, written by two St. Clair schoolteachers, Marcella Glamm and Sylvia Gunsolus, will be featured at the town's centennial celebration. The pageant will be given Sunday in the St. Clair high school auditorium beginning at 7:30 p.m.

Over 50 St. Clair people will make up the cast. The pageant portrays, through narration and scenes, the history of St. Clair. The scenes begin in 1855 and carry tales and stories about St. Clair, its life and times, through 1955.

Episode one, entitled Early Rice Lake, begins as follows:

"Hello, St. Clair! A century ago you were but a dream, a land of trees, lakes, and rice swamps. An abundance of wild animals, game, birds, but few settlers inhabited the area.

"Imagine an Indian summer day, beautiful in its sunshine and shadows, with its falling leaves, and the languid Le Sueur River winding its way slowly to the closing of another season.

"Beaver, deer, bears, and wolves were using this last reprieve from winter in securing more food and better lodging in preparation of the season to follow. On the east side of Rice Lake, more specifically where the Bowe, Phillips, Hodapp and Goodrich farms are now, the first settlers of this area were also making the same sort of preparations. The adventurous families of Charles Mansfield and A.W. Callen set up a homestead, very crude and humble, but nevertheless it was our beginning."

In the town's early history it shows that in the beginning of St. Clair, it was known as Hilton for a period of time, and also as the Winnebago Agency, after the Indians of the same name.

As the year 1855 opened, the pageant continued, more and more settlers began to build around St. Clair. But then the Territorial Legislature passed a law on February 20, opening up the land to the Winnebago Indians.

The third episode of the pageant depicts the mass movement of the Winnebago Indians to the agency. Those white people who lived on the agency land soon were afraid of the Indians and also distrusted them, the pageant related.

Pests of the time are told about in the fourth episode. Mosquitoes and grasshoppers were the chief offenders.

The downfall of the Indian was described in the fifth episode of the pageant. The Indians downfall was laid to the free use of liquor.

Secret societies of the Indians were described in the sixth episode. This part of the pageant told how the young Winnebago chiefs wanted to join the Sioux against the whites. Through the efforts of the Knights of the Forest and other groups, Congress passed an act in February and March of 1863 for the removal of both

Indian Chief played by Don Lewis. Playing the family is Paul and Ruth Schwichtenberg as the parents and Gayle Hubmer and Leon Schwichtenberg as the children.

tribes from the area.

Some Indians did not want to leave. The seventh section of the pageant tells about the heartbreak that was caused by Congress' order. The heartbreak was due to intermarriages between the whites and the Indians.

When the Indians finally left, there was a great rejoicing and celebration in the St. Clair area. The ending of the Indian era in St. Clair's history is described in the eighth episode.

The 14 final episodes in the St. Clair pageant describe different portions of life at St. Clair.

They are entitled: the first store; the village smithy; communication and transportation; down by the old millstream; cheers for the churn' hardware business; sleep, eat and drink; the shoemaker; for safety's sake; the three R's; remember the Sabbath messengers of mercy; public utilities and fire fighting; fun and frolic; and the wheel of fortune.

The cast of the pageant follows:

Narrators – Curtis Pederson and Courrier Hubmer, General Fletcher – Orville Christnagel, Knights of the Forest – L. A. Froehlich, Henry Lynch, Cornelius Maloney and Hubert Johnson.

Mansfield family – Wanda Froehlich, Loyal Joos and the Joos children, Callen family – Carl and Lillie Fitzloff and the Page boys.

Mr. Guinlan – L. A. Froehlich, Indian chiefs – William Hager, Lyle Nicolai, James Riese and Donald Lewis, Joyce – Donavan Schwichtenberg, Peter Manaige family – Paul and Ruth Schwichtenberg, Gayle Hubmer and Joos children.

Storekeeper – Lowell Pagenkopf, Village blacksmith – Fred Bestmann, Creamery operator – John Fossum, Hardware store – E. F. Hager.

Saloon keeper – Eugene Phillips, Shoemaker – Paul Schwichtenberg, Farmers insurance company – Nick Juliar, Bank – G.H. Hubmer, School master – R. V. Kafka, Fire department – Lyle Splinter.

Fun and frolic – Harold Wolcott, Clay Boswell, Laura Brewer, L. A. Froehlich, Nadine Lewis, James Riese, Ruth Schwichtenberg, Lyle Nicolai, Barber chair – Duane Sanborn, Post office – Robert and Gertrude Fritzke.

ST CLAIR ENTERTAINS CENTENNIAL CROWDS

Mankato Free Press - September 5, 1955

"One with onions coming up" was the comment of Bert Denn and Gene Phillips as they fried their "Commercial Club T-bones" at the St. Clair Centennial. Adding the onions was Mrs. Gerald Mace and Charles Russell was ready to deliver the goods. The Commercial club, which co-sponsored the community centennial observance with the American Legion, did a land office business at their big lunch stand on Sunday. One wondered if the stand might have stood where the land office used to be.

PICK "QUEEN" AT ST. CLAIR

Darlene Cords, 15, daughter of Mr. and Mrs. Eddy Cords of St. Clair, was crowned the monarch of the celebration and St. Clair Centennial Queen.

The St. Clair high school sophomore was chosen Sunday afternoon before the large crowd, which turned out to hear the high school band in concert and see the lucky beauty crowned queen.

Darlene's attendant was Marilyn Fitzloff.

A capacity crowd was also reported at the Centennial pageant, presented Sunday evening in the high school auditorium. The two-hour production brought St. Clair's earlier years back to life for a brief moment on the stage as a running narrative explained the pantomime actions.

St. Clair on Monday morning was again alive with centennial festivity as the observance's parade marched its way up the village's main street.

On Monday afternoon activity included the finals in the horseshoe tournament at 1 p. m., the Hal Garven free acts and drawing for the merchandise prizes at 2:30 p.m. and the beard judging at 3:30 p.m.

Monday also included another presentation of the Hal Garven shows, including The Roy and Helene, a magician, John Shirley as master of ceremonies, Gordon Smith, (a dog act), the Jay sisters, (a tumbling act) accordionist Betty McCall and entertainer King Cole, at 7:30 p.m. The grand drawing was held at 9 p. m. and the centennial dance at 9:30 p.m. in the open-air dance floor, winding up the community's big three-day centennial celebration.

ST. CLAIR FETE CALLED SUCCESS

Mankato Free Press - September 6, 1955

St. Clair's 100th birthday celebration held over the Labor Day weekend, was rated a satisfying success today by George Hubmer, secretary of the Commercial Club, which co-sponsored the three-day observance with the St. Clair American Legion.

About 5,000 people packed into the village Monday, Hubmer said, to make it the centennial celebration's best day, climaxing months of planning and three days of actual activities and programs.

The centennial event included a midway attraction, dances, free acts, a historical pageant, and a horseshoe pitching tournament and a beard-growing contest.

The top doubles team in the horseshoe tourney, according to Loyal Joos, was Harold and Orville Beelow of Janesville. Clarence Tosch and Lincoln Ahlstrom of North Mankato placed second. In singles competition Harold Beelow was top man, and Arnold Erickson of Rapidan was second.

Between 30 and 40 St. Clairites added to the centennial spirit with healthy beards, which John Sanborn, contest chairman, described as ranging from "pretty good looking" to "just hair on the face."

The top eight beards, selected Monday afternoon by Judges Frank Cords, Roy Schulz, George Ward, Clarence Pohl and Leo Nenno were grown by Neil Maloney, Roy Lewis, James Winkelman, Bernard Hodapp, Harold Wolcott, Lyle Splinter, Clement Mace and Paul Schwichtenberg in that order. There were over 100 entrants for this contest.

The St. Clair Centennial Parade Highlights Gala Celebration.

Leading the Centennial Parade at St. Clair Monday was their American Legion color guard and Auxiliary, followed by the St. Clair High School band. A long line of floats, bands, antique autos and commercial units made up a long, colorful parade. Visitors from near and far jammed the streets to witness the spectacle. One of the top floats in the parade was a colorful unit entered by the McPherson Farmer Mutual Insurance Co., one of the oldest organizations in the area. A two-horse family unit complete with top was an apt entry advertising the Morristown Centennial, which was held the week of Sept. 8, 9, and 10.

Janesville was well represented in the St. Clair parade. The Little German Band riding the Chamber of Commerce's Centennial float aroused a very nice reaction from the people along the street. The Jubilee Queen, Anna Marie Pischner, and her two attendants, Shelby Mullerleile and Sharon Beccue, and the high school band, under the direction of Mr. William Sandon, made impressive entries.

St. Clair Centennial Parade in 1955.

Parade float

McPherson Farmers Mutual Fire Insurance Company parade float.

St. Clair State Bank float. L to R: Ruth (Nyquist) Schwichtenberg and Betty Lou (Kruse) Mabee

Miller's Produce float. Back-right: Lois Klingbeil.
Front-left: Marilyn Fitzloff

Fitzloff's Store Float

St. Clair Feed Mill float

Bill Hager (left) and James Riese (right)

Dressed and ready to celebrate

CHAPTER SEVEN

Events Over the Years

-1849-

Through a provision of the Northwest Ordinance the United States Government gave the rights to two sections of land in McPherson Township, sixteen and thirty-six, to be used for school purposes. This did not include the area within the boundaries of the Indian Reservation.

March 3 - The Territory of Minnesota was organized.

-1851-

Treaty of Traverse des Sioux opened the area to settlers.

-1854-

The year settlements began in McPherson Township. In November Charles Mansfield and Ansen W. Callen located upon claims on the east bank of Rice Lake, in McPherson Township on sections nineteen and twenty.

-1855-

February 27 - The United States Government granted a reservation to the Winnebago Indians of about 149,760 acres or about one-third of the land of Blue Earth County. This included McPherson, Medo, Decoria, Beauford, Rapidan and Lyra Townships plus parts of seven more townships. It was thirty miles long east to west and thirteen miles wide.

There was no white population on the reservation, so no school districts were established within its boundaries until later.

The Winnebago Agency House was built in 1855.

-1860-

Winnebago Indian Agency: Major Mix, agent, reported there were about 400 families at the Agency. Of the number 706 were females and 878 children. About 200 resided off the reservation, mostly in Wisconsin. The Indians cultivated 675 acres of land, with fourteen families of them raising enough wheat and oats for their own use. There had been 260 cases of small pox; forty-three of them proved fatal. The school at the agency had been in charge of Supt. W. E. Cullen; two interpreters had been employed; 118 pupils enrolled, 62 males and 58 females, and the average attendance was 71.5. The classes taught were orthography, reading, writing, arithmetic, geography, and grammar. The girls were also taught housework. The number of gallons of whiskey consumed; the quarrels between themselves, and between them and the whites; the stealing from the Indians by the whites, and from the whites, by the Indians; and the filth and degradation everywhere was not included in the report.

Ginseng Roots Source of Money to Pioneers: Women and children earned considerable money in pioneer days, gathering ginseng roots. In one year, 1860, a total of 83,000 pounds of this Chinese drug was marketed in Blue Earth County, and netted the gatherers some $6,640.

-1861-

Winnebago Indian Agency: The number of acres cultivated by the Winnebago Indians was 675: 200 plowed by the department and 475 by the Indians. 112 acres were in wheat, 49 in oats, 440 acres in corn, 22 in potatoes, and

40 acres in beans. There were 129 pupils in the Indian schools.

-1862-

Caldwell family moves to the Winnebago Agency.

Sioux Indian uprising led by Chief Little Crow. On August 19 and 20 the farmers all over the county abandoned their partly harvested fields, their stock and their homes and fled with their families into the villages. The whole country was deserted and the villages were crowded with refugees. During the uprising 360 white died.

December 26 - 38 Sioux Indians were hanged in Mankato.

-1863-

There were a sufficient number of settlers in the community to justify the establishment of a separate township. It was named McClellan after General George B. McClellan, short-time commander of the Union forces during the Civil War.

February 21 - The Congress of the United States made a treaty with the Winnebago Indians that would remove them from Blue Earth County. The Indians left the reservation in May.

May 16 - The United States government started to sell the land that was in the reservation. This amounted to 149,760 acres in Blue Earth County, 234 sections in all. One hundred seventy-nine sections were to be sold to the highest bidder and fifty-five sections for preemption. This opened the way for settlers to move in.

August 8 - After a short debate, the government gave sections sixteen and thirty-six of each township in the reservation to the state school system, or eighteen sections in all.

September 2 - State legislature prevailed to change the name of the township from McClellan to McPherson after General McPherson, who was killed during the siege of Atlanta because McPherson emerged from the war a brighter hero the McClellan.

-1864-

The Catholic Church was organized by Father Sommereisen with about thirty families and purchased a log building about l mile east of the village for a church.

George and James Brown opened a general store known as "Brown Brothers."

A sawmill and gristmill were fitted up and put into operation by Aaron Hilton at the Winnebago Agency.

-1865-

August 11 - Aaron Hilton laid out a town site, which he called "Hilton" (presently St. Clair) in the southeast quarter of section #8 of McPherson Township.

Population of McPherson Township was 596.

-1866-

Immigration into our county was very large. During June and July alone over 6,200 acres of land belonging to the Winnebago Agency in Blue Earth County were sold at the St. Peter Land office.

True Story of Old Mill

The Historic Mill was built by Gotfried Schostag, brother-in-law of Fred Schmidt, who lived with the Schmidt's on their farm on the old Winnebago Agency road a few miles from Mankato. A windmill built on the farm in 1866 for the purpose of operating a sawmill, to cut lumber for building purposes, proved impractical because of insufficient wind. By then the construction bug had already bitten Mr. Schostag. Undaunted by this first failure, he prepared plans for a much larger mill that could grind wheat and grain for flour and feed.

He must have been a public minded citizen, for with evidently but little persuasion, the farmers of the Minnesota Lake vicinity induced him to build his masterpiece there.

The various parts of the mill were hewed on the Schmidt farm, where lumber was plentiful, and then the finished work was hauled to Minnesota Lake. This in itself was a sizeable task, and too much for Mr. Schostag to accomplish single-handed, so the farmers formed a hauling bee, and gayly transported the timbers to the present site of the mill.

Mr. Schostag, presumably assisted by some of the farmers, set to work on the actual construction of the building. Anyone who has ever inspected the edifice will realize the extent of the work involved. Not only was it of astonishing size, but all the gears and working parts are made of wood. Only the grinding equipment is of differ-

Log cabin built in 1866

Windmill built by Gottfried Schostag and later moved to Minnesota Lake.

ent material, and that is of course stone.

For the thirty years following the mill whirled and groaned, and made white and coarser flours and feed. Then in 1906, Gotfried Schostag died from injuries received while repairing his structure. The mill was closed, though whether from respect or disintegration, it is not known.

The roller mill, popularizing itself at about this time, made it impractical for windmills to compete with its alert, economical maneuvers, and cast the Minnesota Lake mill into oblivion and unimportance.

Since that time, Gotfried Schostag's masterpiece has stood silently, scornful of the modern generation of mills, and feeling, no doubt, fearfully neglected.

(This story was told to the newspaper reporter by Mrs. Fred Schmidt (Julia Schostag), the sister of Gotfried Schostag, in 1944. Gotfried was born in 1834.)

-1867-

A group of people met in homes and several schoolhouses for preaching services and prayer meetings. The group later became the Zion United Methodist Church.

July 1 - Rafts of 50,000 feet of saw logs were floated from Lake Elysian through its outlet into the Le Sueur River. At the present village of St. Clair a number of the logs got stuck and were sold to the mills there.

-1869-

St. John's Evangelical Lutheran Church congregation was organized July 31.

-1870-

March 4 - Reported that the mail was routed to the post office semi-weekly from Mankato to Minnesota Lake by way of Tivoli, Winnebago Agency, Medo, and Sherman.

March 16 - A meeting was held at the Belleview School House and the Medo-McPherson Cemetery Association was formed. Charter members were A. J. Eastman, S. Elzea, H. Eastman, F. S. Mace, J. H. Eastman, George Donald, Alfred Eastman, N.S. Hill, J. D. Hawkins, W. H. Norton, A. L. Redner and A. B. Preston. S. Elzea was elected chairman and A.B. Preston secretary.

Population of McPherson Township - 903.

-1873-

In 1873 the matter of building the railroad from Mankato to Wells, was a very live issue. On February 27, 1873, Lyra voted $15,000 bonus to the Wells road by a majority of one in a poll of 107. April 1, Mankato voted $70,000 in bonus to the Wells road. April 3rd, Mapleton voted $12,500 bonus to the Wells Railway. These amounts were in lieu of the former bonuses voted a year or two before, which had in some way fallen through.

June - A new post office was established in McPherson, under the name of "Belleview" with J. D. Hawkins as postmaster.

At this time the salary of the county superintendent of schools was $200 per year. The first teacher in the new Belleview schoolhouse was David Eastman and his wages were forty dollars per month.

Much of the farming done by the pioneers was done by hand, but in 1873 farm machines advanced to seeders for sowing, and harvesters to cut and bind the ripened grain. Two men being carried along with the machine tied up the bundles. These laborsaving contrivances enabled the farmers to greatly enlarge their fields.

-1874-

The Catholic Church of St. Clair of the Winnebago Agency purchased the present site and a frame building was erected.

The Congregational Church organized.

Grasshoppers invaded the area and destroyed entire crops. The county paid ten cents per quart for dead grasshoppers. About 16,000 bushels were collected in ten days. They were buried.

-1875-

Janesville Argus - August 3 - Aaron Hilton, an old resident of the Winnebago Agency is dead.

Population of McPherson Township - 957.

-1876-

February 24 - Zion Church of Evangelical Association adopted Articles of Incorporation.

St. John's Evangelical Lutheran Church was incorporated and a church was built.

Janesville Argus - May 30 - The Old Agency building at Winnebago Agency in McPherson Township with 280 acres of land adjoining was lately sold to J.H. Boswell for $11,000 payable $1,000 yearly.

-1877-

Janesville Argus - February 27 - Parties at Winnebago Agency have perfected a hopper dozer and will send a model to St. Paul. It can be made at a cost of $12 to $15.

Janesville Argus - October 16 - Mel Rasdall of the Agency is off to Iowa picking up cheap horses. When he returns we expect he will give every fellow two or three for a hundred dollars each.

-1878-

Janesville Argus - And now comes an old settler of Indian notoriety and says "Mankato" means in Indian, blue earth, just what it was intended to mean, but Mankah-to as some scientific chaps desire to spell it, means in Indian talk, Blue Skunk. "That's just the plain Indian of it. Now which will the scientific chaps take."

The diphtheria is now affecting the people of Winnebago Agency, several cases occurring we understand.

-1879-

Janesville Argus-

Mel Rasdall was elected Constable of McPherson. The Agency voted license by 120 against 74. That's surprising, as we have heard all the voters of that place were temperance men, except Mel Rasdall, who sanctions whiskey now and then for medical purposes only.

...the greatest excitement at present in this community (McPherson) is the Alma City and Winnebago Agency railroad, which probably will extend as far as Austin or the State line...No doubt it will be put through immediately, as several farmers propose to vote for any required bonus, on condition that the depot be located in their garden.

...We are talking of a Sunday school picnic, the Congregational Sabbath School of the Winnebago Agency and the Golden Chain Union of the County Line have united in having a picnic in the Patterson grove on the Little Cobb. We have invited all the Schools within our reach. Expect several to meet with us on the morning of the Fourth of July.

Anyone wishing to see the first steam train over the new road with the picnic excursionist from the Agency must be present on the ground at nine twenty A.M....

Mr. Frank Chase and family are visiting friends in town. Mr. Chase intends buying and settling here permanently.

The years of 1879 and 1880 were noted for their severe storms of wind and hail. On July 2, 1879, such a storm left 2,000 acres of McPherson Township damaged.

Hilton Bridge was built, being 70 feet long and costing $2,918.

-1880-

Janesville Argus - (The following are excerpts from letters to the "Argus" Editor from Winnebago Agency)

Alderman Haynes, who by the way acts in the capacity of both Doctor and Alderman, contemplates the erection of a building the coming summer to be used as a public hall. We are glad to see someone take hold of this matter, for a Town Hall is very much needed, and when built will be appreciated by our people. He was engaged the past week to getting out the timbers and in hauling stone for this purpose. Success to the Doctor.

H. Miller has moved a building from his residence near town onto the lot west of Wills and Murphy store, and has opened a shoe shop.

First to notice of the business interests of our village is the saw and flouring mill of Pfaff & Hilton. This mill company has a reputation of making a superior quality of flour, not excelled by any in the state. Their yard is also well filled with logs to be sawed out this spring while the farmers are seeding and planting. The proprietors contemplate some new improvements on their mill the coming summer. Among which will be a new engine room, two new run of burrs and an addition to the main building. They had sixteen teams on the road last week hauling stone from Mankato. So they really mean business and such improvement is just what we like to see.

In continuation of the business interest of the Agency we will come to the old reliable store of Wills & Murphy where will be found a large assortment of everything kept in a general store. Next we come to the general store of M. Jost who by the way is one of the liveliest men in town. Next we come to the brick store kept by the kind and gentlemanly proprietor, Mr. Charles O'Connor, and next to the variety store of Mr. Charles Young, where will be found everything to meet the demands of the people. And last but by no means least, is the drug store of H. R. King where will be found everything in the drug line.

And another thing we can boast of is three fine saloons, where the weary can while away an hour or two, and find something to refresh the inner man. These saloons are the greatest obstacle that our temperance people have to contend with.

Lubke Wagon & Blacksmith Shop was located just east of where D & D Service Station is presently located. The former blacksmith was Mr. Sack. At that time, Kuske Harness Shop was where the service station is now. A livery was maintained behind the hardware store towards the river. A liquor store was located between the blacksmith shop and the hardware store.

We have also two blacksmith shops, one wagon shop, one cabinet shop, two shoe shops, two hotels, one law and justice office and a newspaper. Come along, someone, and supply this want.

We have four churches and room for more. One Catholic, Congregational, Lutheran and a German Methodist. We have also two good schoolhouses, and as good schools as can be found anywhere, with a daily attendance of about one hundred.

The McPherson Glee Club gave a dramatic entertainment at Foster's Hall February 13 and was a grand success. The speech by "Hans Sauermich" on the benefits of whiskey was well worth the price of admission. The manner in which all acted their parts was really creditable to themselves and their manager, W.R. Gerdes, and should they visit Janesville to entertain your people by all means go and hear them.

Dan Bard's band was over last Friday evening and gave our young folks an opportunity to shake the light fantastic toe at Fosters Hall in commemoration of the birthday of Washington, the father of this country.

The railroad question is the principal topic of the day in this vicinity and the bonus part of the question is that which seems to interest our people the most. Most of them seem to be in favor of good liberal bonus. But we do not intend to bonus this road the way Mankato bonuses the Central and we think that McPherson is able to pay a good liberal bonus for a railroad. But hold your horses and catch your bird before you put the salt on its tail.

Rev. Robert Smith of St. Paul closed a week of revival meetings last Monday evening with about thirty converts.

The winter term of our village school closes today. (This was written in March).

Tomorrow the voters of McPherson vote upon the question of liquor license or in other words, decide which they will have for their future beverage, whiskey or cold water. It is possible that the voters of this town will try to compel those good whole-soled companionable bartenders to take an axe and commence chopping cordwood.

Mr. Harry Hall of Michigan gave three lectures at the church last week on the subject of temperance and the fast young men of the present day. The house was well crowded every night and one hundred and twenty persons donned the red ribbon. Mr. Hall is a fluent speaker, talks from experience and understands the subject that he has to handle.

The farming community is being directed to the cultivation of sugar cane. There seems to be an increasing conviction that the raising and manufacture of sugar are branches of industry to which our climate and soil are well adapted. There will be a good deal of cane planted in this vicinity, and there would be a much larger amount if the people could be assured of abundant manufacturing facilities.

"Nick" (signed)

("Nick's" letter to the Editor stating a need for a "Printing office and newspaper" was dated February 23, 1880. So it had to be after that date that J.H. Barlow started a paper called the "*Messenger*." In the April 20, 1880, issue of the *Janesville Argus* the following item appeared.)

John Barlow having sold out the *Messenger* is now getting up a tent with in "tent" to travel the country over taking photographs and views.

Barnum, the biggest fraud on earth is coming again to Minnesota with his bigger fraud the mammoth circus, the biggest on earth.

A large number of "Prairie Schooners" passed through town the past week bound for the West.

School teachers are getting numerous and complaints are heard of an "overstock." Many are without schools.

We hear the hail storm of Thursday was very severe at Winnebago Agency. That country appears to be unfortunate as it was badly cut up last season. On June 3, 1880, a severe storm of wind and hail struck McPherson Township.

The first load of new wheat was brought in by Nichols of the Agency on Wednesday last. It yielded 21 bushels per acre and Shepard called it No. 1 if cleaned, though it graded No. 2.

In November of 1879 the Minnesota Central Railway, (usually called the Mankato and Wells Railroad) was sold to the Chicago, Milwaukee and St. Paul Railway Company, who assumed charge in January 1880.

During March and April 1880, Harry Hall of Michigan, which did considerable work along Temperance lines, organized Red Ribbon Clubs at the Winnebago Agency.

First Ringling Brothers Show held in Mankato on May 8, 1880.

Population of McPherson Township - 1,023.

-1881-

Excerpts from the *Janesville Argus* -

The School in the Baldwin district (#76-Pestka) in McPherson with Miss Hattie Comstock the teacher is abandoned for the winter on account of diphtheria.

Big ice is being taken out now for the ice houses.

Eggs at Mankato are thirty-five cents per dozen and scarce. A good hen is worth as much as a cow.

The Blue Earth branch railroad was snowed up for nine days.

The town of McPherson in which the Agency is situated, voted no license at the last town meeting by 108 to 100. The officers elected are Supervisors: D. Rasdall,

Chairman, Ami Miely, and J. Bestman, Clerk, D. Cook: Treasurer, J. C. Wells: Assessor, J. B. Hayes: Constables, Grignon and Greener.

D. F. Rasdall of the Agency has purchased the Truman farm at that place upon which is situated the old brick Agency building. Price paid $5,500.

Roads are in a horrible condition. Mud is unfathomable in places, and lots of places.

On June 6, 1881 the farmers of McPherson, Medo, Decoria, and Beauford met at the village of Hilton (Winnebago Agency) and organized a Farmers Mutual Insurance Company. Its first officers were President, J.L. Cook, Sec'y, Char. O'Connor, Directors, E. B. G. Norton, J. D. Hawkins, Char. O'Connor, F. W. Lassow, J. L. Cook and John Bestman. Heretofore fire insurance in the county had been carried by big stock companies like the Fire and Marine of St. Paul, the Continental of Hartford, Conn., and similar corporations, and the insurance man was a familiar figure on our country roads. But the farmer's mutual insurance was the forerunner of a new order of things. In a few years local mutual insurance companies had supplanted the old-line companies.

-1882-

Janesville Argus - excerpts: William Field & Son, of Winnebago Agency have just completed a feed mill and will commence grinding this week. The mill is a 14-inch French burr with a grinding capacity of 300 or 400 bushels per day. They have a sheller of the most approved pattern with a capacity of about 500 bushels per day. The mill is in good shape, complete with elevators, bolts, etc. The machinery was furnished and put up by S.P. Morrison and Co., of Mankato. All kinds of ground feed will be constantly on hand for sale: also oats and corn will be purchased at the highest market price.

The people of Winnebago Agency are affected with mumps and diphtheria.

Duemeland's General Store established December 14, 1882. (The display case was a part of the Duemeland General Store. In 1955, at the time of the St. Clair Centennial, Clair Wolcott is quoted "the case was originally placed in the store when E. A. Duemeland built it back in 1882. It was furnished by the Corticelli Silk Company as an eye-catching display for their threads and other sewing accessories for the women in town.

Turning the rail around its base can turn the shelves, in the case, and thus every item in the case can be seen from one spot. Thin curved glass is fitted into the oak frames, and the center pole is covered with mirrors, which cast multiple light reflections about the store as the shelves are turned. The door would slide easily on a track.)

The 'Lazy Susan' display case which was originally in the E.A. Duemeland Grocery Store when it was built in 1882. It stayed in the store during the time that Wm. Godemann, Wolcott Brothers and then the Hemshrot's had the store. When the Hemshrot's closed the store in 1989, the 'Lazy Susan' was sold to the Earthly Remains antique shop in Mankato where it is now displayed.

(Notation from the 1986 St. Clair All-School Reunion book: "Notes on candy display case."–To stand before this case as a child was to step into a "penny wonderland of sweets." Oh, the wonders it held. You could grab the wooden rail at the bottom of the case and spin it around to survey all the compartments. It was so hard to make a decision, but M. Duemeland had the patience of Job. A penny bought a good handful of candies, but if you were fortunate to have a whole nickel to spend—boy, oh boy! For that you surely needed a sack.)

-1883-

O'Connor Bridge built, 146 feet long, cost $6,345.

-1885-

The building, which will be the location of the Peterson and Perry Meat Market, is taking shape. The business will not only butcher and process your meat but will also buy and ship your livestock.

Population of McPherson Township - 1,149.

-1886-

Reports indicate the gristmill is running day and night, when there is wheat to grind. Mr. H. Miller carries a pretty large stock of boots and shoes at a reasonable price. A.G. Phillips & Co. has had a very prosperous business handling butter and eggs. We have two good hotels—the Union and American houses.

The matter of changing the name of Winnebago Agency post office agitated its patrons for a few weeks during the winter 1885-6. At a meeting held February 6, 1886 the name Hilton was chosen by a close vote, in honor of the proprietor of the main town site, but at another meeting held about March 23, the name St. Clair was adopted on the suggestion of Char. O'Connor. (Some believe St. Clair was chosen after General St. Clair. In 1955 Mrs. Marcella Lange, O'Connor's daughter, who then lived in St. Peter, believed her father took the name from St. Clara. There were about twelve houses in the town.)

February 16 - The drug store under the ownership of Mr. Daigneau is running as good and respectable a store of that class as can be found in a country town and he carries a good fresh stock and keeps it fresh by "loading light and going the oftener."

The Good Templars have elected the following officers for this quarter: W.C.T.-G. T. Wellcome, W.V.T.-Louisa Price, Secretary-Mrs. E. W. Axtelle, Fin. Sec.-Frank Maynard, Treas.-Charlotte Fields, Chaplain-A. D. Actelle, Marshal-Francis Tillotson, Guard-Eliza Andrews and Sentinel-William Brandt.

The Union Sunday school gave an interesting concert Sunday evening, doing a remarkably job being it was their first attempt. There is a good deal of a religious interest now compared with a year ago. Elder Wellcome preaches every Sunday. Rev. Fisk preaches once in two weeks on Sunday evening and Rev Bradley also preaches once in two weeks on Sunday afternoon. So there is no excuse for any one for staying away from church that want to go.

Mr. Daigneau inside the drug store

-1887-

Janesville Argus - Chris Sodeman met with death on the Mankato road to St. Clair. His team ran away and he fell, one of the wheels crushing his head.

Henry Hilton, of St. Clair, sustained the fracture of a collar bone by the run-away of his team recently.

August 6 - District #70, Upper Agency School, and District #73, Lower Agency School, the two school districts that divided the village of St. Clair were united and a new school was built.

Mankato Free Press - November 23 - A collection was taken up in the German Lutheran church of St. Clair for the family of Chris Sodeman, who was recently killed. From $30 to $40 was realized and presented to the family.

-1888-

During 1887, Herman Fitzloff paid a personal property tax of $2.14. By 1888 it went up to $2.48.

Janesville Argus - High license killed two saloons at St. Clair.

St. Clair is to have a new school house to cost $6,000.

Dr. Nutting, of St. Clair, has been appointed one of the county physicians for Blue Earth County.

License carried in St. Clair by a vote of 169 to 83.

Nick Juliar, a prominent farmer of McPherson Township, went to Wisconsin to buy a Norman stallion. He expects to pay in the neighborhood of $2,000.

A gentleman in from McPherson Township informs us that the wind, the night previously was very severe in the vicinity of St. Clair. A log house, a mile and a half from the village, owned by J. O. Koppen was blown down, killing the only occupant, an old man, a bachelor by the name of Reed.

A schoolhouse on the township line between Decoria and McPherson, was blown down, and considerable damage done other ways.

The flouring mill firm at St. Clair has dissolved partnership.

A new schoolhouse has been erected at St. Clair.

Wheat yields 3 and oats 20 bushels to the acre near St. Clair.

A grand Thanksgiving ball will take place at St. Clair.

-1889-

Janesville Argus - McPherson Township, Blue Earth County, has a Farmer's Mutual Insurance Company.

Under the operations of high license the village of St. Clair which for years has supported three saloons, has but one. By a special act of the legislature, St. Clair and Good Thunder, get their saloon license monies applied to district school funds. (The Hintze's Liquor Store was operating at this time.)

Measles are affecting the children of St. Clair to such an extent that the village school has been nearly broken up.

A game of baseball was played at St. Clair between St. Clair and Alma City clubs, with what result we did not learn.

-1890-

February 25 - The recent appointment of Mr. Gebbard as postmaster at St. Clair seems to have aroused the ire of the Democrats in McPherson and a few Republicans have also joined in the protest against Mr. O'Connor's removal. The *Free Press* knows nothing whatever of the local feeling over Mr. Gebbard's selection and has taken no pains to ascertain who or what number of Republicans endorsed his application and urged upon Mr. Lind his appointment; but the fact that Mr. O'Connor has been allowed to serve more than four years and something approaching nine months under a Republican administration, should, in the nature of political changes, be reason enough that friends of the administration be put in charge of the office.

The fact that Mr. Gebbard had formerly been a Democrat may, in the eyes of friends of that party, be sufficient reason why he would be debarred from holding office under a Republican administration. But the Republican Party is a party of progress. When, as it is claimed, Mr. Gebbard saw the folly of his political course and determined reform by joining the Republicans he was entitled to be taken into full fellowship, and it seems that he was. There was nothing, therefore, "disreputable" or questionable about his appointment and the good people of St. Clair should possess themselves. Those who know Mr. Gebbard best believe that he will make a splendid official.

March - Mr. George Caldwell and his wife Bertha expect to move back to St. Paul soon.

Janesville Argus - John Sullivan moved his family last week to St. Clair. He has purchased a farm of 120 acres near that place on the Le Sueur, for $2,300.

The money order system was inaugurated in June 1890 at the St. Clair post office, affording to this community a much-needed convenience.

October - Grignon and Conghoner, butter and egg merchants, have been making improvements in the way of a store house for egg cases and a new coal shed. They have commenced buying poultry. Now the pickers will reap their harvest. Mr. Charles Dumbeck, our new butcher, has his shop and dwelling nearly completed. The blacksmith firm of Wheeler and Levi turned out several new buggies this season. The workmanship is a credit to the firm. Andy Quinn put down a tubular well for N. R. Grignon last week. The water stands 20 feet from the top. Andy is a first-class workman.

November 24 - Our flourmill was broken into and 1,230 lbs. of flour were taken. The thieves broke a window, hauled the sacks downstairs and loaded them over the barbed wire fence to where the team was standing and left leaving a tell tale track in the soft ground, almost to Janesville. The next morning Mr. Rodgers had a search warrant issued to search the premises of a Mr. Rice living some four miles east of here, where half of the flour was found. Mr. Frank Rice, one of the suspected men, was found and arrested and is now in jail at Mankato. The other suspect is still at large and after checking his residence in Janesville the balance of the flour was found at his home.

December 12 - D. F. Rasdall raised a large frame for a windmill. The mill is somewhat larger than those usually put up, for he intends using it for grinding and shelling corn, providing the winds blow just as he calculated. Miss Jessie Rasdall gave a dance in the evening.

The St. Clair fire department held it regular meeting and the company is now out of debt and has a good clear record. They will invest in a windmill soon.

Mr. Ed. Miller is working for Mr. Thomas Ryan in the blacksmith shop.

Would it not be well for our would-be-respectable saloonkeepers to have an eye to the Sunday closing law!

Population of McPherson Township - 1,324.

-1891-

Some of the real smart people (and there are a few of that class) pulled a bolt out of the Fire Co.'s pump and let the plunging rod drop down so far that it cannot be reached. Andy Quinn with his well tools has been at work several days trying to reach it but has been unsuccessful.

The first creamery was started in St. Clair.

Janesville Argus - The village of St. Clair, Blue Earth County, is to have a daily mail hereafter from Mankato. Heretofore mail has been supplied to that point three times a week only.

Dr. Nutting informs us that four windmills were blown down in the vicinity of St. Clair, by the big wind of a week ago Friday.

Several wagon loads of Gypsies are reported encamped near St. Clair.

Mrs. C. Stevens, of Waseca, will be at the hotel in St. Clair, on Monday, October 26th, with a full line of trimmed hats.

A band was started at St. Clair. Independence Day was celebrated.

December 25 - The "Gopher Minstrels" all in black, under the direction of Dr. Nutting performed before an audience of 26. Being it was a bad night and a bad time it will be repeated.

Mrs. Kate Quinn returned from visiting friends in Wisconsin and "Andie" has a twinkle in his eye now that was not seen before in weeks.

-1892-

February - Oysters at 50 cents per dish are pretty high! Storekeepers have finally decided to close their stores at one p.m. Sundays. It is wondered if the saloons will do likewise. It is learned from Prof. Schellbach that the school children are doing very well. Would it not be well for the parents to occasionally visit the school and see how their children are progressing? Dr. Ray has been going night and day for the last two weeks, using up six horses during that time giving treatment to people who are affected with La Grippe. He himself suffered from its effects and had a chance to take a dose of his own medicine. Mel Rasdall made more horse trades in Mankato and St. Clair citizens are thinking of asking him to start a livery in town. Dr. Nutting and family left for their future home in Clarissa City, Todd County, Minnesota.

The Order of the Iron Cross Lodge, with a membership of 25 is holding meetings at Haynes Hall every two weeks. It is rumored that Mrs. Haynes will rearrange the hall into a dwelling place in the spring. If she does We, Us and Co., who use the hall occasionally will have to scheme how to build, as St. Clair must have a hall.

St. Clair has made up her mind not to take a back seat for any village in the county. Why? Firstly, and for all time, it is the healthiest village in Blue Earth County. Secondly, according to the last census this township has a larger population than many who try to put on airs over us. We have a first-class school, a drug store, a grist mill, two general stores and blacksmith shops, a meat market, two hotels, two wheel-right shops, harness shop, a fire company, creamery and dramatic club. The past year has witnessed some building activity. Property has increased in value 200 percent. We have started the idea of building sidewalks in front of dwellings and hope to see a good deal of this work done the coming summer. Let everyone do their best in this line.

It is so healthy here that Dr. Ray thinks of starting a health sanatorium for the treatment of throat lung and nervous diseases. So many already come from a distance to be treated that he thinks it would pay.

The Church of St. Clair of the Winnebago Agency built an addition onto the church and it was renamed the "Church of the Immaculate Conception."

-1893-

Annual meeting of the McPherson Fire Association - At a meeting of the McPherson Mutual Fire Association held in St. Clair on Jan. 4, the following officers were elected: President-Fred Lassow, Secretary-Hubert Bruels, Directors-John Bestman, St. Clair; N. Juliar, Decoria; A. Arnold, Mankato town; Ernest Miller, Alma City; Charles McCarthy, Lyra.

The company is in a very prosperous condition. Up-to-date the total amount of business done reaches $19,996.35. During 1897, $840.15 was paid out on losses sustained through fire and lightning. The total expenditures were $310.55.

Janesville Argus - Rev. J. E. Chase begins a series of revival meetings at St. Clair this week.

Deveraux and Davis are running a meat wagon to St. Clair and the prairie.

Dr. Ray, of St. Clair, has sold his business to Dr. Smith of Waseca. He will visit the World's Fair and seek a location elsewhere.

George B. Caldwell family returns to the area. Because of family bonds and ties, they regard St. Clair to be their home.

The Stanley Steamer was the first automobile in St. Clair. The vehicle was owned by Dr. Smith, one of St. Clair's early physicians. Pictured riding in the car with Dr. Smith is Frank Lassow.

-1895-

In McPherson Township, 12 miles from Mankato and 6 from Eagle Lake, on the Le Sueur River is located the old Winnebago Agency, which until late years has been known as Hilton and now as the village of St. Clair. It has a population of 300 people: daily stage to Mankato: 4 churches - Congregational, Lutheran, German Methodist and Catholic: a graded school: 1 boot and shoe store: 2 blacksmith shops: 1 carpet weaver; 1 wagon maker; 1 druggist; 2 mills; 1 furniture store; 1 harness shop; 1 hotel; 1 livery stable; 1 meat market; 1 physician and three saloons. The daily stage to Mankato cost $.50.

St. Clair Roller Mill
Wood used to heat the building can be seen piled in the lower left corner of the picture. The name Charles Rodgers, the last man to operate the mill, can faintly be seen between the top two windows on the front of the building. At its peak the mill could turn out 10,000 feet of lumber and 100 barrels of flour a day. This picture was taken in 1906. About four years later the mill was torn down.

-1897-

Founding of Pagenkopf general store.

January 15 - The farmers of Decoria, McPherson and vicinity organized the "Farmers United Township Mutual Hail Insurance Company" with Andrew French president, and N. Juliar, treasurer.

William Boswell has bought the "Grandma" Hilton

St. Clair Hotel built in 1895 by George Caldwell.

property for $1,000, and talks some of putting up a new hotel. It is a good location for that purpose and we hope to see something done toward a place to accommodate the public

March 9 - W. J. Ward started a paper called the *St. Clair Star*. Short lived.

Mr. Lindrup is operating a booming business at the creamery. Ex-saloon keeper Charles Pagenkopf has traded his farm for John Murphy's share of interest in a stock of merchandise store known as Murphy and Thielman. The Northwestern Legion of Honor secured the Albert Pagenkopf hall for its meetings. Thielman and Pagenkopf are building a one-story frame structure to be used for McCormick machines and all supplies for the same.

Buttermaking.
To make butter the cream was put into the large cylinder and churned until the butter formed. It was then put into the tubs. The milk separator is at the upper left.

A teacher's examination will occur the 12th of August in St. Clair.

Commander Von Dusko organized a council of the Northwestern Legion of Honor at the residence of Charles Rodgers, with eleven charter members. This is considered a pretty good start for a town that has never paid much attention to orders of any kind.

Janesville Argus - J. W. Chase, who is running a threshing outfit in the vicinity of St. Clair, was in

J.W. Chase's threshing rig. The steam powered engine is followed by the straw wagon (straw was used for fuel for the engine), the threshing machine (which was belt-driven by the steam engine when in operation), bundle and grain wagon and teams. Pictured L to R: William Hall, Thomas Hall, Jake Chase, Henry Gusso, Henry Campbell, Edward Manaige. On the straw wagon is George Caldwell and Frank Mallon.

Wolcott threshing rig and crew

Tuesday and went to Waseca to secure a clover huller.

Fred Gerlich has been appointed postmaster at St. Clair.

Mr. Theodore Kohler now carries the mail from St. Clair to Mankato and will move his family to the latter place for greater convenience.

September - "*Star*" Refuses to "Twinkle."– Mr. W. J. Ward, who had started the *Star*, having agreed to publish a weekly paper for one year, with the financial assistance of local businessmen announced he wanted to remove his plant to some other town. The supporters in St. Clair object to this plan and attached the types, press and all other machinery used in the newspaper office. Mr. Ward immediately began suit to recover his property and Mr. C. J. Pagenkoff, one of the leading merchants and investors retained Attorney William F. Hughes and together they started for the scene of hostilities. The case was to be called at 10 o'clock on September 3.

-1898-

February 18 - Geo. Phillips received a telegram from Baraboo, Wisconsin yesterday announcing the death of the father of the Ringling brothers, the well-known

1897

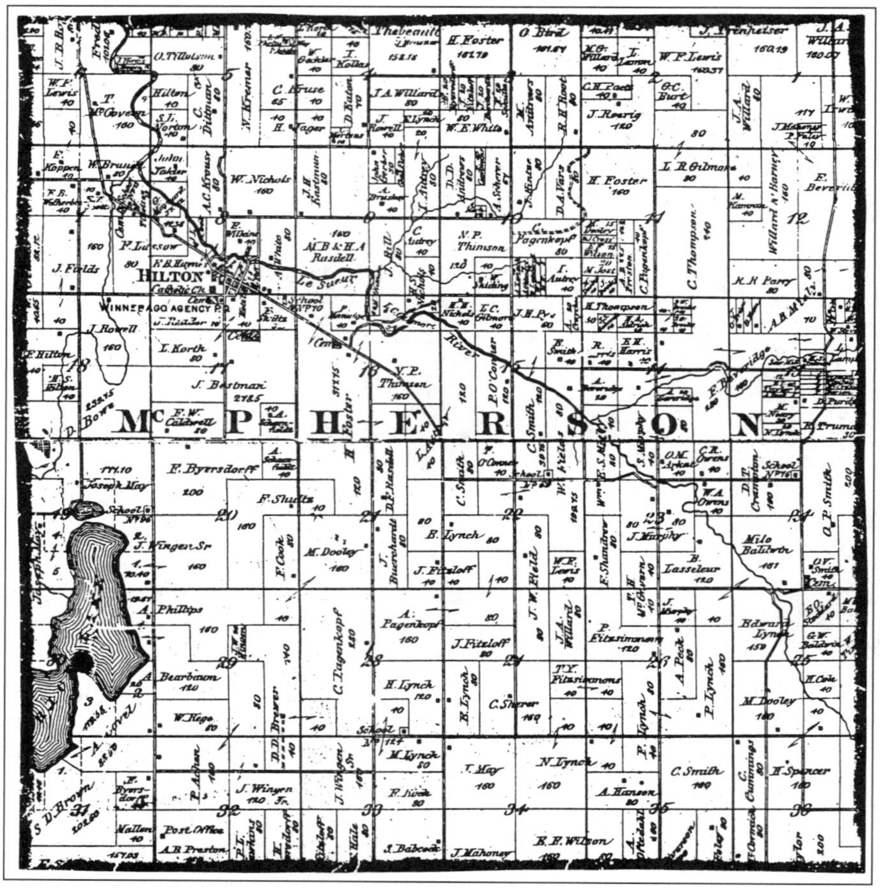

McPherson Township Hall, ca. 1909

showmen. Mr. Ringling was a brother of Mrs. Nick Juliar, of Decoria. Mr. Juliar left for Baraboo today to attend the funeral.

March - Town Directory:

McPherson Township Officers: Board of Supervisors, John Bestman, chairman, John Hintze, P. Lynch; Clerk, Hubert Bruels; Treasurer, Charles Pagenkopf; Justice, Chas. O'Connor - constables, L. F. McGovern, M. Neary.

Churches: Lutheran - Julius Dysterheft, Pastor, Catholic - Father Richards, Pastor, German Methodist - Rev. Itzke, Pastor, and Congregational.

Lodges: Modern Woodmen of America - Jacob Chase, Venerable Consul., Dr. W. S. Smith, Secretary. Northwestern Legion of Honor - Fred Gerlich, Commander; E. A. Duemeland, Secretary.

St. Clair has a historic piece of machinery, in the engine, which operates our flouring mill. It is of an ancient pattern and has been in use for over sixty years. It was first used with a companion of similar make on a steamer operated on the St. Croix and Mississippi Rivers. In 1857, the boat, while on a trip to Mankato with supplies for the Winnebago Indian reservation, parted company with the engine by selling it to the government. When it was taken to the agency, now St. Clair where it was set up to saw wood and grind feed and flour for the Indians. It is a fifty-horse power and notwithstanding its long service is in splendid condition and works to perfection, running the eighty-five barrel mill as smoothly as any of the more modern makes.

The Republican nominee for Sheriff, Fred Gerlich, came to St. Clair in 1883 and operates a saw mill three miles northeast of town. Mr. Gerlich is married and has seven children. He is respected and honored by a host of friends and the whole neighborhood will rejoice at his elevation to the office of Sheriff of Blue Earth County.

Janesville Argus - Mr. Fred Gerlick, of St. Clair, is a candidate for Sheriff, subject to the decision of the Blue Earth County republican convention.

Arthur Axtel and William Hinton, of St. Clair, came over and joined Corporal Cordry's recruits at Waseca.

August 4 - Mrs. Ringling and her daughter and Mrs. Gollmar are visiting Nick Juliar and family. Mrs.

Ringling is the mother of the Ringling brothers and Mrs. Gollmar's family are also show people.

The McPherson town hall was erected.

-1899-

Annual Meeting of McPherson Mutual Insurance Co was held on January 6th. The company has $600 in the treasury with all losses and debts paid.

The *St. Clair Star* suspended.

-1900-

In March the sawmill of Cords & Chase in McPherson burned.

September 24 - Neighborhood News: A reporter of the *Mapleton Enterprise* recently paid a visit to McPherson Township and among the farms visited was that of Mr. Joseph Wingen, where he says, "everything looking so neat and inviting that we were constrained to stop and have a chat with the proprietor. We found the owner busily engaged in working up his apple crop, (the early varieties) into vinegar and cider. Mr. Wingen's orchard consists of over 200 apple trees besides a proportionate amount of all plants and shrubbery adapted to this county and he thinks the ground so occupied worth easily five times as much as if it were allotted to cereals. Necessity arose, Mr. Wingen's ingenuity prevailed, and the result was a cider press. This novel press consists of two separate boxes, one used as a mortar and the other a press. The work accomplished by this rural device proved of equal quality and was as easily secured as if it had cost seven or eight times as much U.S. tender. Mr. Wingen is a courteous and pleasant gentleman to meet and took great pleasure in showing us about his pleasant and well equipped surroundings, which we venture to say are not surpassed for beauty and convenience in this county."

Population of McPherson Township - 1,114.
Population of St. Clair - 150.

-1901-

A law was passed in Minnesota allowing the transportation of pupils. This was of little good because of the lack of vehicles and roads. Dr. Sour is practicing medicine in St. Clair. The Buschena brothers are running the butcher shop. Albert Fitzloff buys 80-acre farm from Alice Lynch for $50 per acre.

Dr. Carl J. Holman purchased the late Dr. Smith's residence and office.

-1902-

April 11 - Harness maker Mr. Frank Ario is seriously ill and near death.

Monday evening at half past nine, our citizens were alarmed by the rapid tap-tap of the fire bell and everybody caught up a pail and ran. The fire proved to be in the bedroom of Mr. Sumner Hilton's little home, and the

Early tractor made in Stillwater, Minnesota, and thought to be owned by Jake Chase.

blaze had nearly consumed the bed and eaten its way outside when discovered. A bucket brigade was quickly formed and with pails of water and vigorous chopping with an axe the firemen soon had it under control. Mr. Hilton's trunk and tools were carried out safely from the front room, which he used for a carpenter shop. During his absence, a lamp is supposed to have exploded. The building was insured in the McPherson Farmers' Mutual Fire Insurance Co. for $300 which will cover the loss.

Mr. Tenish is moving his family into the Dittman house, better known, perhaps, as the Quinn house.

May 16 - Gladys, the little daughter of Mr. Caldwell at the hotel, was severely burned while playing with matches. She set fire to her clothing and before it could be extinguished she was badly burned around the abdomen, thighs and hands.

June 11 - The Catholic Church was legally incorporated in St. Clair.

-1904-

Congregational Church was reorganized and a new church built.

A telephone company was formed: the St. Clair and Belleview Telephone Company was organized with the S. S. Babcock as President, and Henry Thielman, manager.

June - The St. Clair creamery burned to the ground but the engine can probably be repaired. Two hundred tubs of butter and twelve barrels of salt were saved through the efforts of those first on the scene of the fire. The creamery was built over twenty years ago by Henry Grignon and was first used as a cold storage and commission house. The estimated loss being $4,000 to $5,000 with insurance at $2,500 in the Farmers' Co-Operative Creamery Insurance Company. It was rebuilt soon thereafter with brick on a larger and better scale than ever. The estimated cost is $4,000 and the committee in charge is Henry Thielman, Henry Schalow and Frank Brandenberg. (The large brick co-operative creamery was built where the St. Clair City Hall and Fire Department building is currently located.)

James Yellowbank and wife of the Winnebago reservation in Nebraska visited the home of the Louis Tabeau's. Mr. Yellowbank is the son of the old medicine man so well known locally in the days of yore before the reservation was opened for settlement. James is himself a doctor of no mean attainment. He owns over two hundred acres of good land on the present reservation, which he works. Both he and his wife speak English fluently and are otherwise advanced from the standard of life that prevailed when St. Clair was know as "The Agency."

One of the most troublesome matters for anyone who owns stock is the feed question. There have been no oats all winter and now there is no corn in sight. Mr. James Fields, who rode through town Monday en-route from Madison Lake to his farm, three miles south of St. Clair, on a load of the coveted cereal had a narrow escape from being mobbed. He said he had the last load in the market.

August - Monday evening, a gathering of the villagers was much disappointed. It had been noised abroad that Barney, raised on the Maloney farm, was to race against Mr. Treutner's new purchase named Unknown. So the street was well filled with local enthusiasts and spectators, as well as some people from afar. But for some reason, Barney failed to put in an appearance and the first race, it seems, goes to the Treutner pony by default.

St. Clair Creamery built in 1904

HISTORY OF BLUE EARTH COUNTY.

Population of Blue Earth County for Ten Census Years.

	1860	1865	1870	1875	1880	1885	1890	1895	1900	1905
Amboy	....	..	....	....	....	....	215	422	432	490
Beauford	..	105	334	461	598	653	725	774	706	694
Butternut Valley	156	309	590	647	614	631	659	701	661	618
Cambria	.	..	339	337	344	357	356	340	303	319
Ceresco	230	265	313	528	520	497	560	602	588	583
Danville	156	422	557	618	707	690	738	707	681	621
Decoria	....	....	262	413	673	818	1,011	1,007	994	828
Eagle Lake	....		....		....	....		....	...	309
Garden City (Town)	221	689	663	871	817	725	774	827	583	557
Garden City (Village)	173	....	368	....	....	....	....	335	....	263
Good Thunder	..	.	....	....	....	....		421	505	448
Jamestown	230	205	234	417	505	556	861	579	458	460
Judson	2 4	451	661	650	651	611	676	711	695	709
Lake Crystal	..	...	360	320	483	645	824	1,124	1,215	1,231
Le Ray	69	203	448	920	1,170	1,556	1,576	1,595	1,437	929
Lime	234	320	744	565	592	748	610	629	650	575
Lincoln	....	....	495	534	515	4?9	458	566	586	561
Lyra	....	....	433	701	902	1,053	1,159	808	794	694
McPherson	...	506	903	957	1,023	1,149	1,212	1,324	1,114	796
Madison Lake		...	..	....	....		...	366	300	328
Mankato (City)	972	1,973	3,482	5,416	5,550	7,845	8,838	10,173	0,599	10,996
Mankato (Town)	586	565	1,272	1,197	1,284	1,378	1,364	1,434	1,367	1,376
Mapleton (Town)	315	399	583	731	584	516	610	655	543	460
Mapleton (Village)	....	..	....	...	351	447	607	823	1,008	938
Medo	....	385	712	907	850	850	865	866	773	664
Pleasant Mound	....	...	448	536	595	574	688	769	736	757
Rapidan	....	125	449	580	796	801	1,060	1,119	1,075	1,000
Shelby	315	604	728	778	882	881	728	795	819	712
South Bend	452	494	506	504	514	520	547	586	620	571
Sterling	....	462	661	654	704	741	730	714	663	615
St. Clair	....	....	....		....	....	....	....	....	210
Vernon Center (Town)	462	468	665	675	673	669	729	8 8	712	608
Vernon Center (Village)	....	....	....	....	....	....	....	....	311	313
Totals	4,803	9,201	17,302	20,942	22,889	26,462	29,210	32,295	32,263	31,228

John Stroebel Jr. finished threshing on the McPherson farm Tuesday. The yield from 30 acres was 725 bushels of No. 1 wheat.

December - Duane Rasdall returned to St. Clair after taking a bunch of hens to Mankato to sell only to find a couple of roosters in the lot. Putting the roosters into a box he returned to St. Clair and hitched the team and buggy to the hitching post by the Clifton House. One of his roosters got out of the box first entering a grocery store and then to the candy store. The clerk took chase, knocking over $35 worth of candy. The owner wanted Mr. Rasdall to pay $25 for the candy, but Mr. Rasdall refused as he said the clerk not the rooster had done the damage.

The St. Clair State Bank was started in 1906.

Ladies from St. Clair posing in front of the new bank building.

-1905-

Population of McPherson Township - 796.

Population of St. Clair - 210.

-1906-

April - A new restaurant is scheduled to open soon.

June - A new telephone line is being built in this vicinity. Right-of-way secured. Included in the Deeds that were filed were to Alick Oftedahl, $502, Andrew Hanson, $280.50, Theodore F. Heinze, $135, F. A. Meyer estate, $420, John Bestmann, $752.50 and Duane F. Rasdall, $312, all in McPherson Township.

July - The St. Clair State Bank was organized by H. Thielman, N. Juliar, D. F. Rasdell, C. J. Pagenkopf, F.W. Wingen, S. J. Mace, O. O. Juiliar, R. S. Haedt, F. F. Juliar, A. A. Juliar, H. A. Hubmer, Thomas Bowe, F. W. Lassow, F. C. Schultz, S. B. Wilson, George May and John Bestman, with a capital of $12,000. Nick Juliar served as president and Henry Thielman as cashier.

-1907-

April 6 - Doing Good Business-"Alphabet" Road is Carrying the Goods for St. Clairites.

The "Alphabet" railroad may be said to be booming, as it is hauling butter and merchandise for the people of St. Clair, says the *Albert Lea Tribune*. The haul from there to Cream, the present terminus of the railroad, is nine miles, while to the nearest northwestern station it is two or three miles less. That is an example of loyalty pleasant to see. The "Alphabet" brought down 7,000 pounds of butter from the St. Clair creamery and a stock train will be run late Saturday night to connect with the through stock train out of this city early Sunday morning. The people along the line are thus getting the benefit of the road and still it is in poor shape for doing business.

Work completing the grade from Cream

St. Clair's first train. The railroad track was taken up in 1977 after train service was discontinued.

The end of the Alphabet Railroad in St. Clair.

to St. Clair is in progress and thus far the weather conditions have been ideal for this early in the season. A few weeks will see that work completed and when the track is laid St. Clair will be the northwestern terminus of the line during its farther extension. Trains will then have a different schedule and one passenger train will be run each way every day except Sunday, while another train, mixed passenger and freight, will be put on. This will encourage still heavier business and all in all the prospects of the new line are very brilliant, but of course this business is taken from two or three competing lines.

St. Clair Depot. The building was later moved east of St. Clair to the Denn farm.

June 4 - Queer Case at St. Clair - Mrs. Gollmar, Fearing Her Father was Killed, Fainted and is Still Unconscious.

Terrorized with the fear that her father, Hon. N. Juliar of St. Clair, had been killed, Mrs. Sarah Gollmar, swooned last evening and this morning had not regained consciousness.

Mrs. Gollmar conducts a hotel at St. Clair and among the guests of late was Duane Stewart. This man was an undesirable part to have in the hotel. Mr. Juliar says, because he slept with his shoes on. He was ordered to leave about six o'clock last evening and began an altercation with Mr. Juliar. Hearing the loud talk, Mrs. Gollmar was seized with a fear that her father would be killed and she fainted. A physician was summoned but when Mr. Juliar came to the city this morning, his daughter was still unconscious.

Stewart was arrested last night by Sheriff Donahue and Deputy Klugherz and spent the night in the county jail. This afternoon Mr. Juliar consulted County Attorney Plymat and a charge of using abusive language was placed against Stewart pending developments. Stewart will be arraigned before Judge Comstock in the municipal court.

Stewart pleaded guilty to using abusive language when arraigned before Judge Comstock this afternoon and was sent to jail in default of the payment of $15 fine and costs.

Train Into St. Clair - That Village Is Now in Close Touch With the World.

There was something doing at St. Clair last night. The whole population for miles around was on hand to welcome the first train on the Alphabet road, which pulled into the village at 10:30 o'clock. St. Clair is now in touch with the world.

The "Alphabet" road has made good. The first train was operated into the village in accordance with the terms of the contract entered into with the residents of McPherson Township when the bonds in the sum of $13,000 were voted.

The long-cherished hopes of the St. Clairites have been realized. The train that pulled into that village last night was made up of several cars. E. L. Tobie, general manager, and Chief Engineer Cox were aboard. The citizens received the party with cheers and a display of fire works. Hubert Bruels, one of the directors of the road and a resident of McPherson town, was feeling happy over the fact that his promise of a railroad into St. Clair has been fulfilled. Those who have been skeptical, now take off their hats to the new mode of transportation in and out of the town.

The formal celebration of the road entry will occur on July 4.

December 4 - William Funk old resident of St. Clair died from injuries of a fall from a load of hay. He was hauling the load home and fell fracturing his skull and other injuries causing him to lose consciousness.

Train at the St. Clair Depot

July 10 - St. Clairites Had To Go Away From Home To Learn Something - Fred Schostag and daughter and Gottlieb Schostag and daughter, and E.G. Kollos of St. Clair have returned from La Crosse, Wisconsin, where they were visiting relatives.

While in La Crosse the Messrs. Schostag were shown the following article, which was published in a La Crosse newspaper two years ago under a St. Clair date line:

A gigantic bull moose stalked majestically into town yesterday and after sniffing for a moment about the doorstep of William Frantz's saloon, walked through the open door, went up to the bar and examined himself critically in the great looking glass behind it.

Bystanders were for a moment too thunderstruck to move. Then Asa Andrews rushed for his gun and before the animal had left the place sent a bullet through his heart.

Naturally the St. Clairites were very much surprised to read such a story concerning their home town, and they explained that Mr. Franz had mounted a moose head and adorned the wall of his place of business with it. Mighty few moose fool around St. Clair.

Frank Morrell of Janesville, while threshing on the Thissen farm in McPherson Township, near Smith's Mill, had the misfortune to lose his separator by fire. Four stacks of grain were also burned.

September 24 - St. Clair Saloon Man Vanishes - Leaves a Death Note On The Bar Declares He Will Kill Himself - Did Not Assign Reason For Act

A sensation was caused at St. Clair this morning when Tony Fitzloff, bartender at George Schostag's saloon, opened the place and found a note pinned to the bar, saying that he was going to kill himself and bidding good bye to all. It was ascertained that his revolver was gone, and searches for the man at his residence and elsewhere failed to find any trace of him.

Schostag, twenty-eight years of age, and was well liked by all, was known to have a consumption problem.

September 27 - No Trace of George Schostag - Has Vanished Completely: Took Cash And Gun With Him - No trace of George Schostag, the saloonkeeper who disappeared on Monday night.

That in brief is the message from St. Clair. The story of Schostag's disappearance and his threat to commit suicide was told exclusively in *The Free Press* last evening. There are no new developments.

During yesterday afternoon the river was dragged and the surrounding woods were searched, but there was not the slightest trace of Schostag. The hunt in the woods is being kept up, but there are those in St. Clair who express the opinion that the man or his remains will not be found in the timber.

Mrs. Schostag believes that her husband has made away with himself. She can assign no reason for an act of desperation. His home life always was happy. His parents agree with the fact and a number of townspeople are of the opinion that Schostag has sought a secluded spot and there ended his life.

Schostag bought out the John Larson saloon in St. Clair last May. He paid about $3,000 for the building, stock, fixtures and license. He borrowed $1,500 from the bank of St. Clair, his father, Charles Schostag, going on his note. No part of these debts was ever paid. Besides he was indebted to cigar firms and liquor dealers. He claimed however, that these debts did not weigh heavily on his mind. He conducted a farm prior to that time. The saloon has enjoyed a good patronage. Surrounding town's officials have been notified of Schostag's disappearance.

A St. Peter man reported that he observed him seated in one of the coaches on the Omaha train which was headed north to the Twin Cities. It was felt by some of his acquaintance that he is not right in his mind and temporary insane perhaps induced by heavy drinking. In this he is apt to show up again later.

November 29 - Kidnapped, Robbed And Held Captive; Prisoner In A Cave Two Month

Kidnapped, held a prisoner in a dark, damp and gloomy cave, robbed of all his money, beaten and treated like a dog, and turned loose last evening, nearly starved, with locks of hair that Sampson might envy, and whiskers resembling those of a Kansas populist in his best days-that in brief is the story told by George Schostag, the former St. Clair saloon man, who disappeared from that village on the night of Sept. 23, after leaving a suicide note on his bar.

Schostag made his appearance at Frank Mettler's saloon, 209 North Front Street, Mankato, Minnesota, shortly after eight o'clock last evening. He related a story to Mettler that sounded like that which might have originated in the days of romance. Mettler notified Chief of Police Osten that Schostag was at his place, and the chief at once invited the St. Clair man to the police station.

Schostag later related a very detailed story to the newspaperman.

The friends of George regard his story as a "pipe." They are of the opinion that he has been at work in the northern part of the state. The story has been framed up for a purpose, which is apparent.

Schostag stated last evening, that the money stolen

from him by the kidnappers he had intended to deposit in the bank on the following day. He had drawn all but about $7 from the bank on the Wednesday previous.

George had a cigar in his vest pocket last evening that had the appearance of having been there several days. He was quite surprised when his attention was called to it. He could not account for its being there.

He said that the first he knew of the note found on the bar was when Mr. Mettler spoke to him of it. Mr. Mettler did not inform him as to the contents of the note and he knew nothing of what it contained.

It might be said in passing that George looks like a man who has been pretty well fed of late and has not been stinted as he claims.

The building housing the St. Clair State Bank is completed.

December 20 - St. Clair voted to incorporate as a village by a vote of 40 to 9.

-1908-

The Alphabet Railway is a branch of the Milwaukee system from Albert Lea through Medo and McPherson to St. Clair, with the first train arriving at the latter point in the fall of 1907.

January 2 - First election of officers for village of St. Clair. Trustees: Henry Thielman, President, E. A. Duemeland, P. H. Bowe, and J. W. Chase. Recorder: Charles O' Conner: Treasurer: M. C. Dalton: Justices: Charles O'Conner, Christ Acters: Constables: Henry Luedke, A. T. Andrews.

The Huntting Elevator Co. built the grain elevator,

The Botsford Lumber Company was established in St. Clair.

County Line Bridge built, 60 feet, $1,956.

Huntting Elevator (built in 1908) and the St. Clair Depot (built in 1907)

Main Street looking east. ca. 1909

An auction scene in front of the hardware store in St. Clair. ca. 1909.

Street scene on Carnival Day in 1910

A day's catch from the Le Sueur River in 1910
L to R: August Mueller, Jr., Reinhart Westphal, Fred Werth, Walter Westphal, Walter Tolzman, William Grawunder, Paul Westphal, Sr.

Baseball team 1915: Some of the members of the team were Glenn Campbell, Earl Pagenkopf, August Beccue, George Hussey and Elmo Nyquist (back row-far right).

-1910-

Mr. and Mrs. Frank Cords have moved over the bank and will assist Miss Eaton at the telephone office.

Mr. Walter Pagenkopf has sold his house to the Evangelical church for a parsonage.

A bell or a sidewalk? That is the question with the ladies of the Lutheran church.

Mr. Thielman is adding two more dwellings to St. Clair and work has already begun on the basements. These houses are to be north of the depot and on the west side of the street.

Miss Sadie Eaton, who for the past few years has been the patient "hello" girl in the local office, has discontinued her services here and expects to go to Duluth. Everybody is sorry to lose her for Sadie is one of the small few who have learned the winning art of keeping her troubles to herself and giving everyone a pleasant, cordial word and smile. Miss Amy Norton is handling the central.

Population of St. Clair - 210.

-1911-

April - At the council meeting last Saturday evening a motion was made and carried prohibiting dice throwing and the operation of slot machines in the several places of business in town. This marks a new epoch in the regulation of business in this village and should be used as a model by surrounding towns where this custom is still continued.

May 19 - The Huntting Elevator Co. is remodeling their elevator and building another on the south side of the present one.

A serious runaway occurred on Friday when the team of Mr. Anton Lang, became unmanageable and started to run down Main Street, but were stopped after going several blocks. Mr. Herman Fitzloff seeing that Mr. Lang was too old a man to handle the team got into the rig and started for Mr.

Lang's home when the team ran away and threw both occupants out.

Fred Precht is hauling lumber for his new residence and Asa Andrews started to build his new residence.

A hotly contested election was held in the village on May 25, for the purpose of voting on raising $5,000 bonds for a water works system to be installed in the very near future. The bonds were carried by a vote of 16 to 32: The project not to exceed $10,000. Charles O'Connor and Jake Chase were chosen to select a site on which to erect the fire house and water tank. They will endeavor to buy the lot west of the town hall.

June 5 – St. Clair was Hit Hard by a Tornado - Number of Buildings Demolished; Chickens Killed, No Persons Injured.

Wind blew down upon St. Clair Saturday evening and damaged several buildings there and in the country surrounding. It was at about 7:30 when the tornado struck the village. John Bestman's auto shed was picked up and dashed against Henry Thielman's barn. Charles Schostag's barn was demolished, but a horse that stood in a stall was not injured.

The smokestack was blown off the mill and D.P. Miller's chicken house was torn down. Nearly all the chickens were killed. The windmill on Mrs. Augusta McGovern's farm was razed; so were the machine sheds and the chicken house. The windmill on the H. H. Dumbeck farm was demolished.

June 8 - Caesarian Section is Performed Here - Delicate Operation upon Mrs. McGinnis of St. Clair at Local Hospital.

Probably for the first time in local surgery a Caesarian section was performed at a local hospital Sunday morning. Mrs. Emma Dagen McGinnis of St. Clair was the party operated upon. Her pelvis was deformed and contracted, and the infant could not possibly have been taken out alive the natural way. An incision was then made through the abdomen, and the child, a nice little girl, was taken out and the incision closed. Both mother and child are doing nicely and have now passed the critical period and the operation is considered eminently successful.

Dr. C. J. Holman was the operating surgeon, and was assisted by Dr. G.R. Currah, and the local physician was Dr. J.L. Macbeth of St. Clair. The nurses at the hospital are also deserving of great credit for their faithful work.

The physicians have been granted permission by the mother to name the child, and have named her Caesarine. The operation is a very rare one, and attended with a great deal of danger. There is very little in the line of surgery that is not carried out in the local hospitals.

St. Clair State Bank

Inside the St. Clair State Bank, ca. 1911
Ted Penn (left) and George Hubmer (right)

Digging in water lines, ca. 1911

September 26 - Oscar T. Hulseman, popular clerk at Thielman's department store, marries Miss Lydia M. Fitzloff at the Herman Fitzloff home. They will make their home in the rooms over the bank.

October 6 - Depot agent Tuttle has moved his family to Albert Lea. They were unable to find a vacant house in St. Clair and after several months of living in the waiting room of the depot decided to go where they could find a suitable home.

W. O. Lovell & Co. have had considerable difficulty in keeping men at work laying the city water mains on account of the ground caving in. Two men were buried underneath the dirt and almost lost their lives. Quick sand seems to be a big problem. About twenty men came in on the train to offer their services so now they have a new force employed.

Mr. John Bestman, Sr. expects to move in his new house this week.

Ted Penn and George Hubmer are working at the St. Clair Bank. The State Bank Examiner visited the bank the first of the week and found everything in apple pie order.

August - The John Fields family has moved into their fine new residence, which was just completed. Mr. Fields has a home to be proud of and it is a great addition to St. Clair. (This was today's 300 S. County Highway 28.)

Griffith & Walker of Zion City, Illinois, the firm that put in the flowing well in North Mankato, arrived in St. Clair where they have the contract for the sinking of the village well. Work on this will be commenced as soon as the machinery can be placed. This is being done in preparation for the installation of a water works system for the village.

The contract for the erection of the steel tower and water tank to hold 60,000 gallons was awarded to the Des Moines Bridge and Iron Co., at $4,100. As soon as the material can be gotten on the ground the erection of the tower and tank will be commenced. The contract for the excavation for the water pipes was awarded to W. P. Lovell & Co. of St. Paul.

Alphabet Railway formally taken over by the Chicago, Milwaukee and St. Paul Railway, the selling price was $681,540.51. Notice of the deal was served on Julius Schmahl, secretary of state.

During the darkness and heavy rain on Friday night Casper Oftedahl of Pemberton met with a very unfortunate accident. While driving out of town on his way home his horses went into the open water main ditch on Front Street and both horses met their death. Mr. Oftedahl escaped with a slight injury on his right knee. Mr. Dresendorfer, foreman of the lying of the water mains, had his lanterns on the ditch. However, the public in general is of the opinion that the streets were not properly lighted. Mr. Oftedahl took steps to compromise with the city and contractors to make a settlement satisfactory to all parties concerned.

Digging in the water line on Main Street. ca. 1911

November - A special meeting was held in the village council to accept the city well at a depth of 232 feet. A test of 48 hours of steady pumping, throwing 120 gallons per minute did not lower the water. The water is of good quality and comes within 31 feet of the surface. St. Clair water system will be one of the best in the country and will in all probability be completed by December 1.

George Hubmer is giving his handsome new house a coat of paint.

-1912-

January 8 - Today marks the fiftieth or golden anniversary of the marriage of Hon. and Mrs. Nicholas Juliar, old well-known and highly respected residents of St. Clair, this county. The event was fittingly observed today at their fine residence in St. Clair with a family reunion and banquet, which was attended by nine children, thirty-three grandchildren and two great grandchildren.

Those in Attendance.

The children present at today's celebration were Albert and Otto Juliar, farmers of Decoria township; Harry Juliar, a farmer of Mankato township; Dr. R. O. Juliar of Middle River, Minn., Silas Juliar, who is bookkeeper in the Mankato State Bank; Mrs. H. A. Hubmer, Mrs. R. A. Haedt of Decoria, and Mrs. Sarah E. Gillmer of St. Clair. All of the above children together with their children, with the exception of G. F. Juliar of North Yakima, Wash., were with their parents today. The distance being so great and the weather so inclement, the latter and his family were unable to attend.

Held Positions of Trust.

Among the several positions of trust Mr. Juliar has had and is now holding are president of the State Bank of St. Clair, director and one of the organizers of the McPherson Farmers Mutual Fire Insurance Co., treasurer of the Minnesota Hail Insurance Co., and director of the Mankato State Bank in addition to these he has held various town offices.

Thought in no way desirous of the honor, he served in the state legislature on two occasions. In 1895 and 1905, in both cases evidencing his keen insight into the political situation and his knowledge and needs of his townsmen. In politics he is a Republican.

One of Best Known Men in the County.

Mr. Juliar is one of the best and most substantial men in Blue Earth County, and there is perhaps no one now living here that enjoys a larger acquaintance. He is well to do and is now able to enjoy his remaining years in rest and comfort after a hard, vigorous and active life. He is a man whose word is as good as his bond, and that he may live to enjoy many more years is the wish of many friends.

Despite Mrs. Juliar advanced years she is today enjoying the best of health, and happily surrounded by her children and her children's children to the second generation.

Personally, Mr. and Mrs. Juliar have many fine qualities, and it is a great pleasure to meet either on any occasion. Both possess the gift of approachableness and kindly nature, which makes friends at home in their company.

Marriage Performed Again.

At noon today all of the guests and children of Mr. and Mrs. Juliar had assembled at the residence to the number of over a hundred. Mr. and Mrs. Juliar were dressed as bride and groom, and the marriage ceremony gone through again. Rev John Moede of the Evangelical Church of St. Clair, officiating. Mr. and Mrs. Juliar wore yellow roses to symbolize the occasion of their golden anniversary, and despite their years looked young and were very happy. Among the many beautiful presents received by the couple from their children was a fine gold electric clock.

After the marriage ceremony the children and guests sat down to an elegant six-course banquet. At the conclusion of this, Mr. and Mrs. Juliar surprised their children by presenting each with a fifty-dollar gold piece. Several musical numbers were rendered during the banquet, and the children congratulated their parents in many ways. Congratulations by wire and mail were also received. Today's celebration and family reunion was indeed a happy one for Mr. and Mrs. Juliar, and it will be long remembered by them.

At the firemen's meeting the following officers were elected: president, Charles O'Connor; secretary, George Hubmer; vice president, Geo. Hussey; treasurer, Charles Pagenkopf; chief, Henry Lubke; assistant chief, Wm. Boswell; chairman finance committee, Henry Thielman. This organization has a membership of 25.

Dr. A. Wohlrabe of Minneapolis is taking care of Dr. Macbeth's practice during his absence.

July 15 - The St. Clair fire department was called out Thursday afternoon, this being their first experience fighting a fire with their new apparatus since the water works system has been completed. Some children were playing with matches in A. E. Near's barn near the restaurant when a pile of hay caught fire, when the fire was discovered the barn was a mass of flames. Quick work on the part of the fire fighters soon had the fire under control, but the roof and sides of the barn were badly damaged.

The Zion Evangelical Church (later to be the Evangelical United Brethren and then the Zion United Methodist Church) erected the church building. (Special Note: This was used as their church until 2003 when the congregation disbanded.)

-1913-

January 10 - Campbell & Wolcott are making preparations to ship their engine to Kelliher, MN where they intend to start a sawmill.

May 2 - The Kuske Harness, Leather and Hardware Shop was established in the West End of town.

June 20 - Dr. Richard O. Juliar established medical practice in St. Clair. At a special meeting of the fire department it was decided to have the department practice once a week. John Fitzloff has purchased a new Ford Car for his livery and now will be able to take care of his livery in good style, having two cars. Everybody will be able to get to their destination in a hurry. The case of Boswell & Son vs. J. Rinehart in the district court returned a verdict of $108 in favor of the plaintiff. Mr. Rinehart bought a manure spreader of Boswell & Son and after using it for some time wished to return it as being unsatisfactory and would not pay for it. Boswell & Son brought suit to recover the price of the spreader and received full amount.

July 4 - About 9 o'clock in the evening St. Clair was visited by a cyclone which did considerable damage to the buildings and severely injured Mrs. A.M. Quinn. Two white clouds formed and began to dip and twist, the motion of the clouds had no more than started than the general direction of the combined force was directly toward the business portion of St. Clair. The path of the storm was about 300 feet wide and a quarter of a mile long. Plate glass windows and the brick veneer of the Pagenkopf building received the most damage.

Fred Glamm buying harnesses and fly nets.

July 25 - The fire bell arrived and will be installed on the village windmill tower at once.

October 3 - A special school board meeting was held for the purpose of raising an extra $500 for the installation of a new heating plant, the citizens voted the required amount, and the plant will be installed during the Christmas vacation.

Barn built by Henry Schalow on the Charlie Schalow farm. ca. 1915

-1914-

Farmer's Elevator Company of St. Clair purchased the grain elevator from the Huntting Elevator Co.

April 8 - Fire wiped out the Sacred Edifice - Loss Partially Covered By Insurance.

The church building of the Catholic Parish was a wooden structure. The people of the village all turned out to assist in saving the edifice, but the closest hydrant was too far away to be available in getting a water supply. Some of the pictures and the small furnishings of the church were saved, but nothing of special value. The loss is estimated at about $7,000; insurance, $3000.

Pagenkopf's Store - Charles Pagenkopf (left) and Henry Thielman (right)

February 9th, 1915
Louise and Rose Lynch Wedding
Back Row: Rose Wenner, Guy Lynch, Louise Lynch
Front: Rose (Ireland) Lynch

The Church of the Immaculate Conception framed building was destroyed by fire and the present brick building was erected.

July 7 - The annual meeting of the members of the McPherson Farmer's Mutual Fire Insurance Co., was held at the town hall. The polls were open from 9 a.m. to 4 p.m. when the following officers and directors were elected: President-John Bestman, Vice President-Nick Juliar, Secretary-treasurer-Hubert Bruels, Directors-Henry Hodapp, William Boswell, F. W. Wingen and Ernest Miller. The company had in force insurance totaling $4,138,780. A gain of twelve more policies was made during the past year with a gain in money of $138,510.

July 22 - A serious accident marred the visit of the Ringling circus at Mankato yesterday. William Boswell, implement merchant of St. Clair and Miss Margaret Scott of the same village were struck by a falling tent pole, just as they were leaving at the close of the performance. Mr. Boswell was very seriously injured.

-1915-

Henry Thielman built a new store for his mercantile business. (This was later the Pagenkopf Store.)

-1916-

March 3 - A grand ball will be given at the St. Clair town hall. Sandon's Orchestra will furnish music.

Revival meetings were being held at the Evangelical church this week and next week. Everyone is invited to attend.

O'Neal Show company gave two plays at the St. Clair town hall on Tuesday and Wednesday evening.

St. Clair seemed to be very dry last week as the town tank was frozen and the pump and engine were broken. It is repaired again, however, and is in working order.

Tests of clay deposits, which were found in large quantities adjacent to St. Clair are to be made to determine what qualities this clay may have for the making of tile and brick. The matter was brought before the Commercial Club by Nic Juliar who stated that he had been informed by several experienced clay men that the deposits were of a high quality of pottery-clay. William

Gekler who is an experienced brick maker had made baking tests of the clay and said that it is valuable material. Samples were sent to the State Mineralogy bureau.

The "Old Time Dance" given Tuesday evening in the town hall by the "Old Time Boys" where Tangos, Fox Trots, and Hesitations were taboo will long be remembered as the date when the old folks cut loose for a good time. Grand marches, quadrilles, with an occasional lively polka, waltz or schottische was danced to the old melodies of twenty years ago. The veteran, George McComb, was impressed as leader of the orchestra in which the old time instruments were played. Many missed the music of the old dulcimer of which McComb was a master.

Men representing the electric light system were at St. Clair and everyone was in hopes of seeing them put in. Many residents have ordered electric lights installed in their homes as soon as the arrangement can be made for power. The council took up the matter of framing a contract with the Consumers Power and Light Company.

A rumor is current that the businessmen of St. Clair are planning a "Clean up Sale" which will take place soon.

One of the young bachelors, Paul Schuenemann slipped away from friends long enough last week to take the vows and become a benedict. He took Miss Adeline Roemer of Madison Lake as his wife.

The post office was equipped with a night letter box.

The Leo Hardware company is unloading a car of wire and nails this week.

Stephen Foster, Sr., who has been ill for the past month is much improved in health.

The primary room recently had a real tea party at which several of their parents came to drink tea. Matt Pestka with his two little children, Joseph and Marcella, furnished much entertainment. Mr. Pestka brought his phonograph, to the music of which the two children did folk dancing and marching.

Raymond Kruse, George and Carl Fitzloff and Duane Chase made tests of seed corn. They showed that the two-year-old corn was by far the best. Two tests of over 90 to 97 percent were made.

St. Clair's water tower overflows and ices up, ca. 1916

July 5 – Thought Team of Horses were Stolen - Jake Ott of St. Clair Had Experience While Driving to City.

Monday evening Jake Ott of St. Clair, a farm hand, hired a team of horses to John Fitzloff liveryman of that village, to drive to Mankato. When he came after the team to make the start he was accompanied by two strangers, tough in appearance, one of whom accompanied Ott in his buggy, and the other drove his own rig.

While enroute Ott drank whiskey from a bottle given him by his companion and after it took effect says he remembers nothing until he awoke in the rooming house in Mankato yesterday morning. His pockets were rifled of over $25 in money and his team was gone.

Ott immediately informed Sheriff Osten that the team had been stolen and the sheriff notified Mr. Fitzloff, who immediately came to the city.

Later however the local police found the team and buggy standing in the north part of the city and the horses scratched and injured. But the men were nowhere to be found.

-1917-

The St. Clair Chapter of the St. Clair Red Cross was organized on July 26th, 1917, with forty-six members. The officers were chairman, Father O'Connor, vice-chairman, Dr. R. O. Juliar, treasurer, George Hubmer, secretary, Mrs. F. M. Chase, working club, Mrs. R. O. Juliar, captain, and Mrs. H. A. Campbell, assistant.

The National Red Cross awarded those who put in 800 hours service in knitting and sewing. The local branch received two such awards, Mrs. A. H. Matteson and Mrs. Hubert Bruels.

When we first organized our sewing club Mrs. A.H. Matteson said, "I hope the war soon ends, but if it continues I am going to try and knit as many pair of socks as I can, seeing I am old which is 67 years." She knit one hundred and twenty-five pairs. We had ever so many great knitters.

The Junior Red Cross, under Mrs. L. Huggenin, did splendid work. All worked until the Spanish Influenza epidemic broke out in the fall of 1918, then we disbanded for a time.

A "Servicemen Banner" was hung at the St. John's Ev. Lutheran Church, which displayed nine stars, one of which was a gold star. Church members serving in World War I are: John W. Fitzloff, Freidrich Franske, John Freitag, Otto Glamm, William Grams (gold star), Earl Pagenkopf, Theodore Penn, Otto Schmidt and Walter Westphal.

-1918-

April - The flu patients are all making a good recovery and no new cases have been reported.

June 4 - Mr. and Mrs. Tim Sullivan Observe Golden Anniversary of Their Marriage.

Mrs. Sullivan whose maiden name was Ellen Marie Hayes was born in Boston, Massachusetts, August 23, 1850 coming west with her parents while yet a girl and settling on a farm near St. Clair. Timothy Sullivan was born at Mount Morris, New York, on October 23, 1847. Fully realizing that there were greater opportunities for a young man in the great west, he left his home and in 1861 came to Minnesota. Mr. Sullivan tells of a trip he was making by foot to St. Clair. He was slowly making his way over the prairie when a couple of men drove up and offered him a ride. He accepted and rode until near to St. Clair. Here the men camped for lunch, Mr. Sullivan continuing on his way. Afterwards he found out that the men with whom he rode were Frank James and Bob Younger and it was only a few days later that they pulled off their raid on the Northfield bank.

Eddie Franske is assisting John Bestman, Jr. with his farm work.

There were no services at the Lutheran Church Thursday on account of the funeral of the late Chris Grams at the Catholic Church. Mr. Grams was born in 1835 in Germany.

Roy Biggins of Minneapolis will assist R. Schultz at the barbershop. Mr. Biggins comes well recommended having been preparing himself for this work in the barber school at Minneapolis.

Family gathering at the Paul and Anna Westphal home. This photo was taken in 1917 just before Walter Westphal went into the service. Pictured is a 1917 Ford Model T touring car.

Arthur and Walter Westphal in 1917

November - The funeral services for Miss Ethel Murphy, who died at Luverne, ND, of Spanish Influenza, on October 28, were held at the Catholic Church in St. Clair on Wednesday morning at ten o'clock. The death of Miss Murphy is a very sad one and the deepest sympathy of this community where she lived for the greater share of her life, is extended to the bereaved brothers and sisters.

Walter Westphal - Photo taken in 1918 during World War I

November 2 - News has just been received of the death of Mrs. Paul Westphal at Immanuel Hospital on October 30. The message has cast a shadow of sadness over the entire community. Several of Mrs. Westphal's children are very ill with the influenza at their home here, one son, in the service of his country is ill in a hospital in Kansas, and another son is serving with the U. S. Army in France.

November 11 - Mrs. Paul Westphal's remains were laid to rest in the Lutheran cemetery on Sunday afternoon. Her sister Alma Tolzmann of Waldorf, who cared for her during her last illness, and who was recovering from an attack of influenza, suffered a relapse on Sunday and on Tuesday morning, November 4, died of pneumonia at the Westphal home. The children, who have all been ill, are recovering slowly.

Sam McComb, who has been ill with influenza, is able

Henry Schalow built this house on Main Street in 1918. The house still stands today.

World War I service banner displayed at St. John's Evangelical Lutheran Church.

Looking down Main Street from west to east, ca. 1918

to be out again. Several of the children of Mr. and Mrs. Roy McComb are ill with the same disease.

Mayor L. L. Champlin of Mankato has earnestly requested that everyone pause from his or her duties at 11:59 a.m. each day and spend a minute in silent prayer for divine help and comfort during the present crisis through which our country is passing. All Christians, disregarding of creed should devoutly carry out the request.

All of the faculty of the public school have gone to their homes to stay until school will reopen again.

A telegram was received in St. Clair today stating that William H. Grams had died at Camp Grant of Spanish Influenza. The news has cast a deep gloom over the entire community.

News was received this week that Theodore Glaser, formerly know as Ted Glaser, had been severely wounded in action in France, and that he had sustained the loss of his right leg.

The funeral of Roy Smith, who was one of the boys who left here in the last draft call, and who died of influenza while enroute to Camp Cody, was held at the Catholic church in St. Clair.

The village of St. Clair's only doctor, Richard O. Juliar, recalled during the flu epidemic of 1918 & 1920 he had as many as 200 patients a day and used three teams of horses constantly, driving both day and nights.

Oct. 11 - Henry Ringling is Dead in Baraboo, Wis. - Henry Ringling, youngest of the six brothers who in the past 26 years have been prominent in the circus world, died yesterday of heart and other internal disorders. He is survived by the widow, formerly Miss Ida Palmer, and a son, Henry, Jr. 12 years old.

News of peace was received very jubilantly on Thursday noon. For nearly two hours every church bell in town and the fire bell were kept joyously ringing, many guns were fired, and people paraded the streets, waving flags, shouting and singing.

-1919-

February - Sydney Fitzloff, has been serving in the navy and has made two trips to France, has been mustered out and returned to his home.

The St. Clair Ice Company secured their ice to fill the various icehouses in the village from Rice Lake. They put up ice for Mr. Powell, Messieurs Johnson and Schroeder did the packing. They are now hauling ice for the creamery. The ice is about thirteen inches thick.

March - The three month old son of Mr. and Mrs. Harry Phillips was taken, as the other members of the family, with the flu. Everything was done to spare his life, but to no avail, the Angel of Death was hovering near and Thursday she folded him in her arms and took him home. Interment was made in the Catholic cemetery, Saturday.

Another real estate transaction took place in the village. This time Hubert Bruels sold his property in the village to Louis Henzie. Mr. Henzie sold his farm to Louis Nicolai. Mr. Nicolai recently sold his farm to John Hall. The people extend a cordial welcome to Mr. and Mrs. Henzie and family who expect to move into their new home the middle of March. Mr. and Mrs. Bruels returned to Mankato to make their future home. It is with deep

St. Clair School Primary Days in 1919.
Back row (L to R): Mamie Gerlich, Laurence Kruse, John Timmerman, Harold Boswell, unidentified, unidentified.
Center row: Evelyn Schalow, Cel Reichel, Florence Bruels, Odella Lupke, Anna Prescht, Mildred ____, unidentified.
Front row: Leon Fisher, George Miller, Billy Franz, Henry and Elmer Sodeman, ____ Sack, Arthur Flitter and Vera Schostag.

regret that the village had to part with this family, but what was St. Clair's loss was Mankato's gain.

Mr. Chase has started his sawmill in the village and has Messrs. Campbell, Wolcott, Claude McComb and John Roerig assisting him. Will Beccue is doing the teaming for him.

The Botsford Lumber Company received a carload of fencing this week and anyone needing anything in this line will do well to call on the local manager, Mr. Westby, before purchasing elsewhere.

The roads throughout the village were very much improved this week by the means of the road drag. Messrs. Will Dumbeck and Harry Fields did the work.

April - A very pleasing custom, which has generally been observed for a few years past in the two lower rooms of the school, is when one of the members of these grades is fortunate enough to have a birthday during the school year. The indulgent mother prepares a birthday cake and other pleasing dainties, which is greatly enjoyed in the schoolroom by the classmates of the happy child. One of these social events took place in the primary room Monday afternoon. Ervin Schultz, being the honored guest. He was eight years old that day. Mrs. Schultz consisting of ice cream, cake, hermits and candy served refreshments. Ervin was the recipient of several useful gifts.

Home of Henry Schalow built in 1920. This house was next occupied by Bill and Margaret Myers and later by James and Ivadell Hunter.

Easter was appropriately observed by the various churches Sunday, with special service and music. The roads being almost impassable the attendance from the country to the services on Good Friday and Easter was not as large as usual.

July - John Fitzloff returned home from Camp Grant. The boys returned home one by one and are all looking fine. Also returning safely home were John Ario and Robert Sodeman. The hearts of the citizens of this village swelled with pride as the boys come marching home, victorious from the battlefields of France. One could not realize to the fullest extent the dangers these boys had faced or the hardships they had endured for us that

Charlie Schalow's woodcutting machine, ca. 1920

remained at home and kept the home fires burning until they returned. Words could not express the appreciation.

In Blue Earth County agricultural land is worth from $125 to $300 per acre, depending upon its location, though no farm is beyond twelve miles from a railway station and market.

George Hussey and the Farmers' elevator each received a carload of potatoes, which they sold at $1.75 per bushel.

The Congregational Church was disbanded and the property later sold. (The building was moved north across the street and made into a home — later known as the Splinter residence — now a parking lot for the Lutheran Church.)

The 1918-1919 flu epidemic around the world kills estimated 20 million people.

-1920-

Nicholas Juliar is Dead - February 12, 1920 - Former Member of Legislature - He was Well-Known Resident of Blue Earth County for Many Years.

Nicholas Juliar, one of the oldest and best known residents of Blue Earth County, died at his home near St. Clair last night of carcinoma of the liver. Mr. Juliar was one of the pioneer settlers of the county and known to a

Leo Hardware Co.
General Hardware
MARCO LIGHT AND POWER PLANTS, ELECTRIC WIRING, EAGLE TRACTORS, JOHN DEERE IMPLEMENTS
HEATING AND PLUMBING
Heavy Furnaces—Pipe and Pipeless

ST. CLAIR GARAGE
Buick and Chevrolet Cars
SAMSON TRACTORS, SWAN LIGHT PLANTS
We Give Real Service

C. J. PAGENKOPF
General Merchandise
GROCERIES, SHOES, DRY GOODS
Everything to Eat and Wear

ST. CLAIR STATE BANK
A Home Bank for Home People

Driving Distances
ST. CLAIR TO—

Pemberton	8 miles
Waldorf	17 miles
Freeborn	34 miles
Albert Lea	52 miles
Austin	12 miles
Mankato	12 miles
Janesville	11 miles
Waseca	18 miles
Mapleton	16 miles
Good Thunder	18 miles
St. Peter	22 mlea
Owatonna	30 miles
Rochester	70 miles
St. Paul	97 miles

Railway Fares
ST. CLAIR TO—

Pemberton	$ .20
Waldorf	.40
Matawan	.58
Freeborn	.81
Albert Lea	1.20
Winnebago	2.46
Fairmont	2.92
Wells	1.80
Austin	1.94
LaCrosse	6.44
Madison	10.17
Milwaukee	13.13
Cedar Rapids	9.68
Des Moines	13.06
Minneapolis	6.37
Sioux City	12.57

1920. POCKET DIRECTORY —OF— **St. Clair** Minnesota
COMPLIMENTS OF BUSINESS FIRMS ADVERTISED HEREIN

E. G. SACK
General Blacksmithing Woodworking and Repairing

W. J. FRANTZ
Cigars and Tobacco Confectionery and Soft Drinks

St. Clair Drug Store
Dr. R. O. Juliar, Prop.
A Real Drug Store in a Real Town

St. Clair Mercantile Co.
General Merchandise
The Peoples' Store

LEWIS A. HUTTL
Barber Shop, Pool and Billiards
Where You Get Real Service

THE FAIRMONT CREAMERY
Where your cream demands the highest price

BOTSFORD LUMBER COMPANY
Building Materials

The Farmers Elevator Company (Inc.)
Grain, Coal and Machinery
WHERE THE FARMERS GETS A SQUARE DEAL

St. Clair Today

Population 358 — situated on a branch line of the Milwaukee railroad and the Pershing Highway, 53 miles northwest of Albert Lea, and 12 miles south of Mankato, to which city a bus runs every few hours, giving the people of St. Clair a direct line to the Twin Cities. St. Clair has its own water works, light system and sewerage system, and is equal to many cities many times its size in every way. It also has an electric white way which any city could be proud to own. Its streets are wide, and kept in the best of condition and the town has no indebtedness.

Situated in one of Minnesota's best agricultural and dairying regions, the soil being well adapted to raising small grains as well as corn, potatoes and clover seed.

The business men of St. Clair are of wide business acumen and are ready at all times to lend any assistance to any individual or industry looking for a valuable place to locate. They carry heavy stocks, which makes it unnecessary for the farming community to send away for anything.

The room is here for thousands of people, those just starting out in life or desire to change their location, others with capital desiring to get in on the ground floor.

Boost your own town and your own land by buying at home.

County Officials

Evan Hughes	Judge
C. L. Kennedy	Auditor
G. G. Krost	Clerk
P. B. Gabler	Reg. of Deeds
Anton Oates	Sheriff
Henry Spicer	Treasurer
W. H. Datamore	Supt. of Schools
Charles E. Philips	Attorney

City Officials

J. W. Chase	Mayor
Fred Precht	Clerk

Councilmen
Clay Baswell L. W. Hintze
John Fields

Railway Time Table

No. 401 North	11:55 a. m.
No. 408 South	12:30 p. m.

BUS LINE TO MANKATO

Leaves St. Clair	9:00 a. m.
Leaves St. Clair	1:30 p. m.
Arrives St. Clair	12:00 m.
Arrives St. Clair	6:00 p. m.

Church Directory

Catholic	Father O'Connor
Lutheran	Rev. Fritzke
Evangelical	Rev. Georgius
Congregational	

Watch St. Clair Grow

wide circle of friends here and throughout Southern Minnesota.

Throughout the county Mr. Juliar was a well known auctioneer. At the time of his death he was vice president of the McPherson Fire Insurance Company, director of the Mankato State Bank and president of the St. Clair State Bank.

By hard work, perseverance and keen financial foresight, Mr. Juliar accumulated a considerable fortune. He was a member of the Evangelical Association and contributed time, money and energies to the welfare of the church. He was a splendid citizen, a fine neighbor. He was a devoted husband and father and a kind friend.

A Holstein dairy booster meeting was held in the city hall at St. Clair, Tuesday evening, May 2. On account of the rain during the day and evening hardly any from the country were able to attend. However, there was a nice representation from the town and a good meeting was held. Much interest was expressed by those present in building up St. Clair into a strong dairy community.

A committee composed of G.H. Hubmer, C. Boswell, H. Fitzloff and F. Precht had been boosting for the meeting and were confident of a good attendance from the country if good weather had prevailed.

L.E. McMillian, county agent, gave a good talk on the dairy cow, explaining that there was room for much improvement in the class of cows being kept and stating that one-third of the 1,500,000 dairy cows in Minnesota were being kept at a loss. One-third were just barely paying for they're feed, and the other one-third were kept at a profit.

G. Hubmer, cashier of the St. Clair State Bank, chairman of the meeting, gave a good talk and urged cooperation between the town and country.

Action was taken at last night's meeting to hold a big dairy meeting at St. Clair, a week later, on the evening of May 9, at which time a larger crowd is expected to be present.

Population of St. Clair - 398.

1920 St. John's Lutheran Church Confirmation Class
Back row (L to R): Geo. Penn, Ernest Mueller, Henry Flitter, Lester Prail

First Model T car manufactured by Henry Ford using an assembly line. Photo taken in the summer of 1920 of the Wolcott brothers: Ted, Jack, Claire (Pete) and Harold (Chub).

-1921-

June 9 - St. Clair - Baseball team trimmed Janesville. An interesting ball game was played on the local diamond Sunday afternoon. The second team from Janesville played against a rather mixed team of St. Clair. Earl Pagenkopf pitched for the boys and struck out eleven men. Seven of the regular players were laid up and unable to take part in the game. The team is doing fine work and deserves the support of the community. The score of the game was 13 to 7 in favor of St. Clair. The line-up was as follows: H. Beccue-catcher, Williams-center field, Nyquist-second base, Pagenkopf-pitcher, O. Fritzke-shortstop, A. Fritzke-right field, Schmidt-third base, and L. Roerig-left field.

Thielman Grocery Store (left) and Schroeder Mercantile Store (right) in 1921

Hog lot on the Paul Westphal, Sr. farm, ca. 1921

December 27 - Saint Clair Given New Village Hall. The village hall is now completed, but all the rooms have not been furnished as yet. The building is thirty by sixty feet and twenty feet high: heated by a pipeless furnace and supplied with water and electric lights. It is two stories high. The first floor is divided into five apartments. A long room, which extends the full length of the hall on the west side, will be used as a fire station. The room into which you pass as you enter the east door will be used as a rest room. Back of this is a room, which will be furnished for the village officials, where they will hold their meetings and transact such other business as will come before that worthy body. The second floor is all in one large room except a small entry at the head of the stairs, which can be used for various purposes in connection with the hall. This building fills the long felt want of the people of this village. It gives the village council a home, it gives a warm, dry room adequate in size to hold all of the fire implements needed for the village, and the advantages of a rest room for the citizens of the village and community. The band boys practice twice a week in the new hall. Previous to the completion of the hall they met at the depot.

-1922-

June 23 - Laying of Corner Stone in St. Clair. The citizens of the village and vicinity turned out in full force to witness the laying of the corner stone of the new consolidated school building. The program opened with a selection by the St. Clair band, followed by the audience singing "America." Charles O'Connor then gave a few appropriate remarks, after which he read the records that were to be placed into the metal box, which was put in the corner stone for future reference. At the close of Mr. O'Connor's address the choir, consisting of Mrs. Paul Phillips, Esther Schroeder, Mrs. Harold Schwartz and Dr. Macbeth of this place and Carl Pickie of Eagle Lake, with Lena Bestman at the piano, sang a selection. Harry Johnson of Mankato was then introduced who gave a stirring address, which was much appreciated by the audience. Among the many points of interest referred to by the speaker was the relation that the homes, church, and school bear on each other and on our nation. The program closed with a song by the choir, followed by a selection by the St. Clair band. At four o'clock a very interesting and close game of ball was played on the diamond between St. Clair ball team and "Sim's" ball team of Mankato. At the end of the ninth inning the score stood a tie, but during the tenth and last inning the local team succeeded in winning one more score than the visiting team. The game closed in favor of the home team.

St. Clair State Bank - "The Bank that Backs the Farmers" has a capital surplus of $60,000 and pays 5% on deposits.

September 14: St. Clair - Pemberton Road Improved. The graveling of the main road between this place and Pemberton is progressing rapidly. The first of the week they had reached the south line of Charlie Smith's farm, a distance of a little more than two miles from the village. It is reported that they have in the neighborhood of sixty-five teams at work.

A new brick addition was added to the old community school structure, also brick, built in 1888. This enabled the school to expand to twelve grades.

St. Clair baseball team in 1921. Some men in the picture are Elmo Nyquist, Glen Campbell, Earl Pagenkopf, August Beccue and George Hussey.

First boys basketball team hit the floor with not one of the players ever having any previous experience in the game and some had difficulty in attending practice.

-1923-

April 27 - Defeat for Saint Clair Water Bond - Disappointment to Number of People in that Village. During the meeting in the village hall held Tuesday, the water bonds were voted on and resulted in seventeen for and over fifty against. The returns were a surprise as well as a great disappointment to many. It seems no more than right that all the taxpayers of the village should be given the same privilege to enjoy this necessity and have fire protection.

May 10 - The stockholders of the Farmers' elevator held a meeting in the hall Thursday evening. Lawyer Moonan of Waseca was present.

The members of the Lutheran church are having the building, known as the old Congregational church, which they purchased, remodeled. Among the changes being made will be the closing of the north door. An entrance will be made on the south and windows of more modern date will replace the old windows. Mr. Grawunder is doing the work.

Ernest Proechl is having a building constructed on the Fisher property on Main Street, which he will use as a garage. He also rented part of the lower floor of Frank Fisher's building, which he will use in connection with his work.

Paul Westphal farming with horses, ca. 1923

South side of Main Street looking west. Left to right: Dr. R. Juliar, M.D., Drug Store and Post Office. ca. 1923.

Will Gekeler is dealing with the local garage man Jerry Lynch for a Chevrolet coupe. His old car a Maxwell is laid up for repairs at the home of his son Henry.

The Class of 1923 was the first class to graduate from St. Clair having completed 12th Grade. They produced the first school annual and it was called "*The Hojarah*." Hojarah is Indian for "*Echo*." Members of the class were: Nicholas Juliar, president, valedictorian, Oscar Lubke, Secretary, Mabel Juliar (Nisbet), treasurer, Adelle Kruse (Zahn), Lucile Pagenkopf (Dooley) and Kevin O'Brien.

First girls basketball organized and won their first game 4-to-1 against Rapidan.

Enrollment became too large for the school to accommodate the students, the building on the north side of the street, west of the hardware store, which had once been a liquor store, was used for additional classroom space.

A new grain elevator was built.

December 12 - Fred Schultz has sold his property on Front Street to Mr. Prochel. Mr. and Mrs. Schultz will remain in the home until spring, occupying the lower part of the building and Mr. and Mrs. Ernest Prochel will move into the rooms upstairs.

The small elevator (right) was built by Huntting Elevator Company in 1908. The larger elevator (left) was built in 1923.

Mr. Macomber, local depot agent has installed this week a radio set at the depot.

-1924-

Transportation was provided for students. The District owned four wagons: 1 wagon and 1 automobile owned by the driver; 4 routes; heating provided by 18 (charcoal) foot warmers and 8 blankets.

-1925-

May 15 - The Senior class of the St. Clair High School presented its class play "Professor Pepp" on May 12 at the town hall. A very large crowd was in attendance. Following is the cast of characters: Professor Peterkin Pepp-a nervous wreck, Henry Fritzke; Mr. C. B. Buttonbuster-a giddy butterfly of forty-eight, Harold Wolcott; Howard Green, his son who had the court change his name, Kenneth Chase; Sim Batty, the police force of a college town, Harold Juliar; Peddler Benson, working his way through college, Patrick Dooley; Noisy Fleming, just out of high school, Hugh Russell; Pink Hatcher, an athletic sophomore, Milton Juliar; Betty Gardner, the professor's ward, Marcella Pestka; Aunt Minerva Boulder, his housekeeper from Skowhegan, Maine, Louise Frantz; Petunia Muggins, the hired girl, Sylvia Fisher; Olga Stopski, the new teacher of folk-dancing Mildred Heiman; Kitty Clover, a collector of Souvenirs, Monica Thissen; Vivian Drew, a college belle, Beulah Schroeder; Irene Van Hilt, a social leader, Catherine Pestka; Caroline Kay, a happy little freshman, Elzada O'Brien.

Those who had charge of the play were director, Miss Emma Godeman; assistant, Miss Mildred Heiman; songs, Miss Isabel Ogle; music, Community Orchestra.

Peter and Martha Bollmann's first car. ca. 1920.

June 24 - St. Clair Bank Is Model in Equipment - Modern Burglar Proof Vault Has Been Installed By Institution. The bank at St. Clair is among the pioneers in modern bank building for the smaller towns. In past years a bank thought it had fulfilled its mission when it had purchased a reputable burglarproof safe for the protection of its funds. Some few banks realized that they should go farther, among the few being the State Bank of St. Clair, and also provide protection for their depositors and clients. Instead of sending their valuables to the cities, entailing a great inconvenience, they can now rent a deposit box for a small payment, and have their papers and valuables secured and within their reach at all times.

The State Bank of St. Clair has erected a modern burglarproof vault for their new building. Guarding the entrance to this vault is the vault door. This massive door, weighing nearly 14,000 pounds is swung on a crane hinge and is so accurately balanced, a child can swing it. This mass of steel is forced into place by a series of bars termed the compressive system. When the door is forced into place, so that the locking bolts can be locked, it fits so tight that it is impossible to introduce any explosive agent to blow it out.

A vault of this type would be exceptional in a town of twenty times the size of St. Clair, but the bank officials, realized that a bank has another purpose besides the handling of money. It should have the ways and means of taking care of their

Martha Beckmann Bollmann wrote this on the back of this photo: "This is my Wash-Outfit which I received a few weeks back. It runs by it self and the wringer I don't have to turn either. I like it very much and the Outfit cost me $50.00. I also make butter with it. I had washed the day Peter came to get us."

Dairy barn built in 1924 on the William Freitag farm in McPherson Township.

The Ladies Sewing Club
L to R: Ida Schalow, Evelyn Timmerman, Mary Anderson.
The tall lady in the back row is Bertha Alexander.
The rest of the ladies were not identified.

community, the same as the city banks.

The telephone switchboard was located in the upper left-front corner room of the St. Clair Bank. A barber shop was in the basement. Meeting rooms were upstairs. George Hubmer and Ted Penn were working in the bank.

July 4 - Program in St. Clair: Big Crowd - Parade Was Fine Feature; Many took Part - Plenty Events Given - It Was Successful Observance of American Independence Day. Those who had the good fortune to spend Fourth of July at St. Clair all left well pleased with the entertainment afforded them at that village. The businessmen are to be congratulated for the enterprise they showed in staging a fine parade as an opener for the festivities of the day. Other features of the program were a snappy ball game between Waseca and St. Clair, an eloquent Independence Day oration by Judge William Stradtmann of Mankato, horse races, free movies, dancing and music

Preparing for the 50th Anniversary of the Bellview School in McPherson Township, ca. 1924

Ernie Hager and his 1925 Model T Ford

by the Good Thunder band.

A pleasing feature of the day was that every detail of the program was carried out without a hitch, and without an accident. It is estimated that about two thousand people were present at the celebration.

The parade, which was about a half-mile in length, was started at promptly 10:30. This was headed by an elaborately decorated car occupied by Mayor Rudolph Froehlich and wife and Judge Charles O'Connor, one of the pioneer residents of the village. This was followed by the members of the Good Thunder band, which rendered some good music at intervals throughout the day. Herman Godeman, mounted on a large white horse, represented Uncle Sam.

A beautiful float occupied by small children representing Mr. and Mrs. Coolidge and their chauffeur, following the parade took first prize as the prettiest float.

Miss Louise Frantz made a beautiful Goddess of Liberty. Small girls followed her on Shetland ponies. Then came the clowns who kept the crowd merry with their funny antic. Fred Precht drew a great deal of attention with his doll cart drawn by a small dog.

St. Clair creamery's float took first prize as the most unique in the parade. Here one saw butter making in full blast in charge of pretty Miss Viola Precht as milkmaid. On the rig was also a prize cow, a milking machine and butter molder in actual operation. This float was drawn by a large team of horses driven by Paul Phillips, manager of the creamery.

Following this came the St. Clair State Bank float, the St. Clair Mercantile float, followed by Hubert Hodapp and Harry Dumbeck dressed as spinsters driving a shiny horse and buddy, on the back of which was a large place card bearing the inscription, "Husbands Wanted."

Several highly decorated autos, representing the different business houses of the village and private owners followed the Botsford Lumber company's float.

The Huntting Elevator company, the Haugen meat market, Henry Lubke, the blacksmith all had rigs in the parade.

Three small boys drew an imitation pig in an express wagon continually spraying the beast to demonstrate the efficiency of hog dip.

The St. Clair garage had a float and tractor in the procession.

Miss Louise Frantz drew second prize for beauty, "Mrs. Coolidge" beating her just one little point. The clown band carried off the honors for being the most comical.

Zion Evangelical (later Zion United Methodist) added a full basement to the church. The digging was done by manpower and shovels and the dirt elevated out the windows. Walls were added under the original footings to obtain basement heights.

-1926-

St. John's Evangelical Lutheran Church erected a new brick church building.

St. Clair Beet Crop Brings Big Profit - Yield Per Acre Large; Product All Harvested and Shipped. The sugar beet crop has been all gathered and shipped out from the local station. Those raising beets in this vicinity the past season were Earl Carpenter, who had seventeen acres,

Decked out for the 4th of July Parade

Ready for the 4th of July Parade

Decked out for the 4th of July Parade

Rev. Otto K. Netzke and family, the pastor at Trinity Ev. Lutheran Church in Smiths Mill from 1925-1930. He also helped out at St. John's Ev. Lutheran Church in St. Clair. Pastor Netzke was a brother to Mrs. Fred Otto.

Howard Voight, Leona (Schalow) Mace, Adeline (Schalow) Westphal and Charlie Schalow.

John Fitzloff, thirty-one acres, Raymond Fitzloff, twenty-one sixty hundredths acres, Edward Frank, fifteen and thirty-nine hundredths acres, Herman Frank, fifteen and thirty-four hundredths acres, Roy Hubmer, eighteen and fifty hundredths acres, Clem Kollos, eighteen and forty four hundredths and John Kruse, five and fifty hundredths acres, making a total of one hundred and forty-three and forty-five hundredths acres. Forty-six carloads of beets of one million eight hundred and forty thousand pounds were shipped from St. Clair.

-1927-

Transportation for school children is changing rapidly from horse drawn vehicles to the motor bus. One motor bus replaced two horse drawn buses. The bus traveled on the average of 15 miles per hour.

First Marriage Service Held In New Church. The first wedding to be solemnized in the new Lutheran church took place Tuesday, March 1, when Erna Cords, daughter

Ready for winter - Arthur and Walter Westphal

of Mr. and Mrs. Charley Cords, became the bride of Martin Flitter, son of Mr. and Mrs. John Flitter of Smiths Mill. Rev. Fritzke performed the ceremony. Elsa Cords a sister of the bride and the groom's brother Hartwin acted as best man attended the bridal couple.

The bride was neatly attired in a gown of ashes of roses silk crepe and carried a shower bouquet of flowers. The bridesmaid wore a pretty dress of green crepe.

The young couple will make their home on the groom's father's farm near Smiths Mill. Mr. and Mrs. John Flitter are moving this week to Madelia.

-1928-

February 8 - St. Clair Done In Poetry: Ragged Paper Treasured. A ragged, yellow issue of a Mankato newspaper of August 8, 1891, recently unearthed by Rudolph Ario, 109 North Front Street, contains the town of St. Clair done in poetry.

The various poems about different business houses which existed in the town at that time are not signed, but they appear to have been the work of Mrs. A.M. Morrison, wife of the publisher of the paper, which is the *Mankato Journal.*

Probably advertisements, the poems take up the whole front page of the paper.

Among the concerns given poetical treatment are Grignon and Coughanour, butter and egg dealers, of whom it is said. "The golden cream in gallons they take from far and near." The St. Clair Roller Mill "'twas an old government building it stands so well." The American House, a hotel managed by M. St. Cyr, "eat, home-like place with comforts for all." Mrs. J. Nutting a milliner, "a business lady an expert as well." M. B. Rasdall, druggist, who "a prescription will carefully fill if you are ill." Frank Ario, harness dealer "with saddles and whips for riders so gay," and many others.

A poem about the city itself is also printed, which calls the St. Clair people "Good folk all, known to be respected for their hospitality."

February 17 - Rudolph Froehlich, owner of Froehlich Hardware, buys the Elysian Hardware Store.

A saw mill was located next to the south side of the river and a short distance west and back of the brick house presently located on the corner next to the service station. Henry Campbell and John Wolcott worked at the mill.

July 21 - Four elderly Winnebago Indians from the Winnebago agency at Winnebago, Nebraska are in this vicinity today looking up the history of their race here. Only one of them could talk English but each of the group wore up-to-date American clothes.

The father of Twirling Thunder, 70, the oldest of the four had his village on the knoll in Decoria known as the Hog's Back Ridge, said Thomas Hughes, local authority on Indian history. Another of the party going under the name of Lincoln claims to be a descendant of Chief Rogue, a leading chief of the Winnebagoes at the time of the agency here.

Today the four are in St. Clair, one of the tribe's villages, to learn more first hand information pertaining to the seizure of their land. The tribe was driven from this section at the time of the Indian outbreak and was sent to Crow Creek in South Dakota where lack of food caused many of the tribe to starve to death. The Indians had no ammunition to hunt with and the small amount of game in that barren country caused the tribe to move southward along the Missouri river as far as the Omaha reservation in Nebraska where the tribe is now located.

The north side of Main Street looking east, ca. 1928

L to R: Henry Campbell and John Wolcott working at the sawmill.

St. John's Ev. Lutheran Church Confirmation class of 1928. Back row (L to R): Viola Schuldt, Isabella Doss, Diedrich Buesing, Marianna Buesing and Margaret McComb. Front row: Vera Schostag, Frieda Hawker, Pastor Fritzke, Daisy Schroeder and Adeline Schalow.

The tribe is attempting to pass a bill through the United States Congress for retribution for all the sufferings of the Winnebago. The four Indians are in Mankato to gather further evidence of the mistreatment of their tribe.

The Indian will spend several days in this vicinity visiting the village of the tribe in Decoria and St. Clair.

December 18 - Shoot out at the Lynch garage. Bandits who had entered the Lynch Garage at St. Clair may have been frustrated in plans to enter other places, including the bank, when they were put to flight by a fusillade of shots fired at them. Everad O'Brien, operator of the Wm. Frantz soft drink parlor and lunchroom and Maurice O'Connor, his assistant, were sleeping in the buildings upstairs apartment when they heard the squealing of tires and looked out the window. After looking out the window they picked up their guns and fired about 25 shots at the five bandits who then fled. Blue Earth County Sheriff Frank Cords was called at 4 a.m. and he took up search for the thieves.

December 24 - Ten Robberies Admitted By Pair Held As Suspects In St. Clair Garage Looting - Sheriff Frank Cords and County Attorney F. E. Morse Return From Grand Rapids with Sworn Statements.

Elmer A. Jones and Carl Schwitchenberg, two Le Sueur County men confessed to at least ten robberies in Minnesota since the summer of 1927, including the St. Clair garage last Tuesday morning. Together with Percy Duehn, who lives in Rabey Township, Aitkin County, Minnesota, they confessed to forging checks during the summer of 1927 and are being held by Grand Rapids authorities.

On December 18, the pair broke into the St. Clair garage and took a tire, tube and other accessories. It was found that the goods were stored at the home of Duehn. Maurice O'Connor and Everett O'Brien drove them from the garage in a barrage of gunfire, in which Jones was injured, the injury later resulting in his capture. On December 18, Jones and Schwitchenberg returned and told Duehn that he had been shot and asked Duehn to drive him to a hospital. Duehn took him to the Grand Rapids hospital.

Information of the robbery was broadcast over WCCO under the direction of Sheriff Cords, and doctors and hospitals were asked to be on the lookout for men asking treatment for gun shot wounds.

First traces of the robbers were found in Hill City, when they entered a drug store there and Jones asked for treatment. The druggist, having heard the radio report and suspecting that the two were the men wanted, refused to treat him, saying that his wound was so serious as to

Chevrolet Garage owned by Jerry Lynch, John Pint and Lyle Splinter. The garage was later purchased by the school.

Miller's Livery - L to R: Ben ______, Albert King, Lloyd _______, Reube J.________ and Cash Murphy

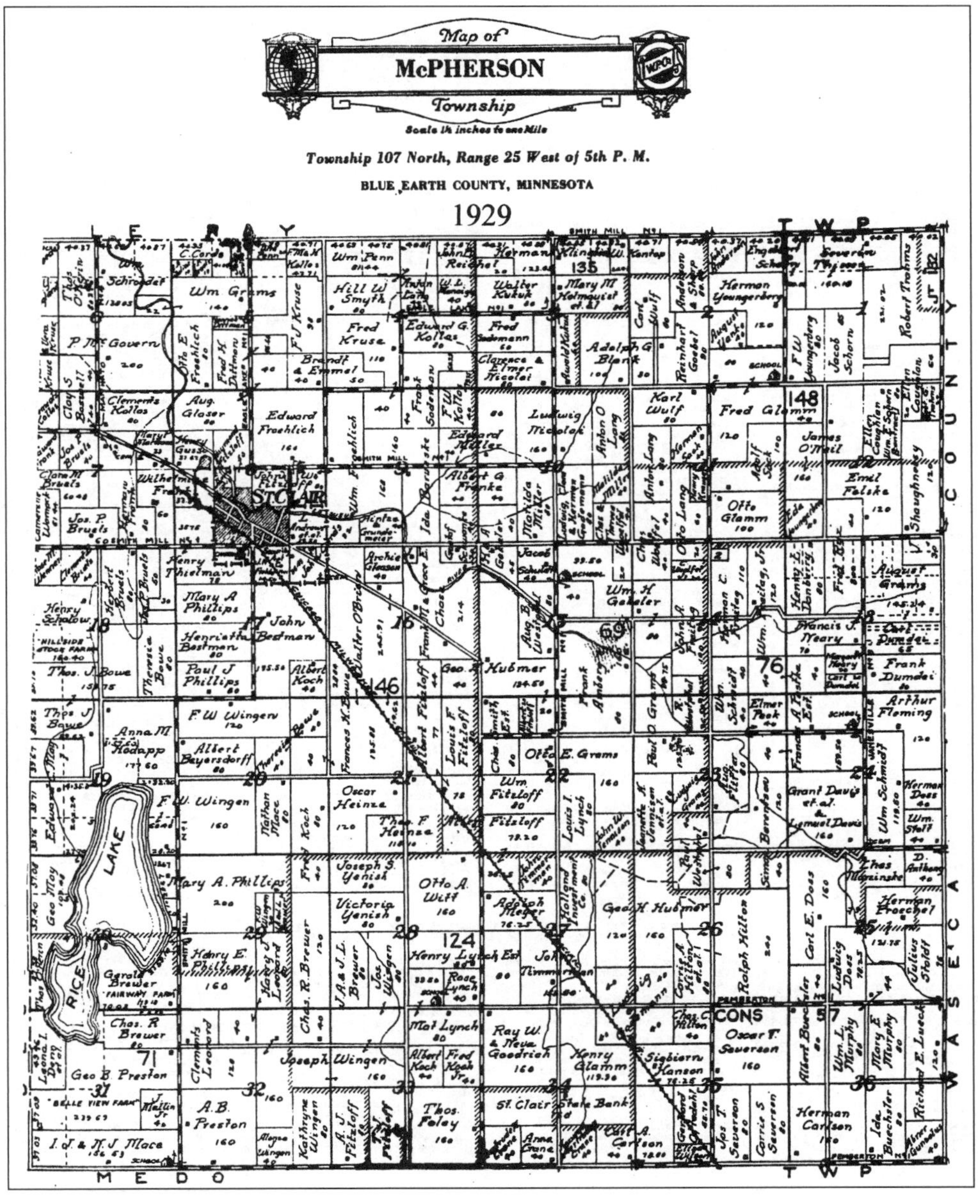

ATLAS AND FARMERS' DIRECTORY OF BLUE EARTH COUNTY, MINNESOTA

Farmers' Directory of McPherson Township 1929

Abbreviations: Sec., *section*; ac., *acres*; wf., *wife*; ch., *children*; ( ) years in county.

Postoffice, Eagle Lake

Anderson, Oscar, Rt 1, wf Mary, ch Harold, Evelyn, R 40 ac, sec 5, R 50 ac, sec 4, O M. A. Brandt, (17).

Dittman, F. H., Rt 1, wf Eliza, ch Arthur, O 87.67 ac, sec 5, (56).

Froehlich, O. E., Rt 1, wf Lydia, ch Donald, Muriel, O 80 ac, sec 5, (30).

Glaser, John A., Rt 1, ch Theodore, Adolph, Emil, Ida, O 80 ac, sec 8, O 40 ac, sec 5, (33).

Godemann, Fred, Rt 1, O 60 ac, sec 3, R 20 ac, sec 3, O Wm. Godemann, (30).

Grams, William, Rt 1, wf Julia, ch Walter, Gertrude, William, Laura, Eva, Carl, Alice, Marion, Robert, O 140 ac, sec, 5, O 22 ac, sec 6, (27).

Klingbiel, H., Rt 1, wf Amelia, ch Anna, Louis, Mata, Edith, Reinhard, Leona, O 200 ac, sec 3, (40).

Kruse, Carl, Rt 1, wf Selma, ch Erwin, Verna, Lester, Esther, Irene, R 110 ac, sec 4, O F. J. Kruse.

Kruse, Fred, Rt 1, wf Bertha, ch Carl, Fred, Lena, O 98 ac, sec 5, O 110 ac, sec 4, O 40 ac, sec 9, (60).

Preston, John, Rt 1, wf Hazel, ch Gerald, R 80 ac, sec 3, O Walter Kukuk, (28).

Reichl, J. L., Rt 1, wf Josephine, ch Bernard, Cecelia, Alene, Donald, O 40 ac, sec 4, O 20 ac, sec 3, (40). Breeder of Holstein Cattle, Spotted Poland China Hogs and White Rock Chickens. "Maple Grove Farm."

Smyth, H. W., Rt 1, wf Tillie, ch Bert, O 120 ac, sec 4, (10). Breeder of Ayrshire Cattle.

Sodemann, Frank, Rt 1, wf Ida, ch Elmer, Henry, Gertrude, O 80 ac, sec 4, O 80 ac, sec 9, (45).

Postoffice, Janesville

Danberry, H., Rt 3, wf Lillie, ch Paul, John, Elmer, O 80 ac, sec 13, (38).

Davis, Grant, Rt 3, wf Margaret, ch Kenneth, Delores, Bernadette, O 80 ac, sec 24, O 1 ac, sec 25, (27).

Davis, Lem., Rt 3, wf Clara, ch Loretta, Ervin, Wilmer, Arline, Irene, Edna, O 80 ac, sec 80, (42).

Dumdei, Frank, Rt 3, wf Augusta, ch Everett, Ruth, Gordon, Marvin, Eugene, O 80 ac, sec 13, (35).

Felske, Emil, Rt 3, wf Mary, O 120 ac, sec 12, (12).

Flemming, Arthur, Rt 3, wf Esther, ch Lester, Ruth, Alvin, O 120 ac, sec 24, (9).

Grams, August, Rt 3, wf Emma, ch Anna, Clara, Otto, Elsie, Leona, O 145 ac, sec 13, (27).

Marzinske, Chas., Rt 3, wf Della, ch Lloyd, Chester, Victor, O 79 ac, sec 25, (43).

Neary, F. J., Rt 3, wf Loretta, ch Irene, Florence, Esther, Helen, Alice, O 70 ac, sec 13, (48).

Pestka, Mary, Rt 3, ch Arthur, Marie, Agnes, Catherine, Rita, Anna, Raymond, Clement, O 160 ac, sec 24, O 40 ac, sec 13, O 40 ac, sec 14, O 40 ac, sec 23, (34).

Proechel, Arthur, Rt 3, wf Catherine, R 121.75 ac, sec 25, O H. Proechel, (27). Breeder of Buff Minorca Chickens and Plymouth Rock Chickens.

Rux, Mrs. Fred, Rt 3, ch Anna, Johanna, Clara, Martha, William, Arthur, Frieda. Alma, Alfred, Luella, O 40 ac, sec 12. O 80 ac, sec 13, (35).

Schmidt, Ernest, Rt 3, R 119.50 ac, sec 24, R 40 ac, sec 23, R 40 ac, sec 14, O Wm. Schmidt, (29).

Schmidt, Leo, Rt 3, wf Gertrude, ch Ellen, R 119.50 ac, sec 24, R 40 ac, sec 23, R 40 ac, sec 14, O Wm. Schmidt, (29).

Schorn, Wm. E., Rt 3, wf Elizabeth, ch Clem, Albinus, Johnnie, O 80 ac, sec 12, R 64 ac, sec 1, R 20 ac, sec 12, O Ellen Coughlan, (44).

Shaughnessy, J., Rt 3, ch Francis, George. Ed. Margaret, O 120 ac, sec 12, O 30 ac, sec 13, (34).

Smith, Lewis, Rt 3, wf Elsie, ch Mabel, R 40 ac, sec 23, O E. Peek, (2).

Stoldt, Albertina, Rt 3, ch Martha, Minnie, Elsie, Will, R 86 ac, sec 25, O Julius Stoldt, (50).

Stoldt, Will, Rt 3, O 40 ac, sec 24, R 76 ac, sec 25, O Julius Stoldt, (40).

Trahms, George, Rt 3, wf Ellen, R 211 ac, sec 1, R 20 ac, sec 12, O Robert Trahms, (24). Breeder of Bronze Turkeys.

Westphal, Paul, Rt 3, ch Reinhardt, Walter, Otto, August, Emil, Willie, John, Paul, Louise, Arthur, O 40 ac, sec 23, O 80 ac, sec 26, (35). Breeder of Poland China Hogs.

Westphal, R. Rt 3, wf Alma, O 36.50 ac, sec 23, O 20.25 ac, sec 14, (36).

Postoffice, Mankato

Kollis, Clements, Rt 4, wf Augusta, ch Mary, Ida, Evelyn, O 120 ac, sec 7, R 42.71 ac, sec 5, O Francisco Kollis, (55).

May, Edward, C. Rt 2, wf Frances, ch Frances, Eugene, O 202.24 ac, sec 19, (34).

Schalow, Paul, Rt 4, wf Lillian, ch Harold, Evelyn, R 200 ac, sec 6, O Henry Schalow, (43).

Schroeder, Wm. Rt 4, wf Grace, ch Beulah, Kenneth, William O, 178.90 ac, sec 6 and in LeRay twp., O 40 ac, sec 31, (46).

Von Helmst, Alfred L., Rt 4, wf Mattie, ch Betty Jane, James, R, 80 ac, sec 6, O Tom O'Herin, (6 months).

Wenner, Harry, Rt 2, wf Rose, ch Ivernie, Robert, Elaine, Edwin, Leland, O 40 ac, sec 18 and in Decoria twp., O 20 ac, sec 12, (42).

Postoffice, Pemberton

Berentson, Fred V., wf Marie, ch Margaret, Verne, Vivian, R 120 ac, sec 23, R 40 ac, sec 26, O Simon Berentson, (14).

Buecksler, Albert, Rt 1, wf Ella, ch Robert, Verna, Leonard, Melvin, Gertrude, Arlene, Ralph, O 80 ac, sec 36, O 40 ac, sec 25, (46). Breeder of Holstein Cattle.

Crane, H. R., Rt 1, wf Ruby, ch Watson, June, O 60 ac, sec 24, (6). Breeder of Percheron Horses.

Doss, Carl E., Rt 1, wf Elsie, ch Deloris, O 160 ac, sec 25, (32).

Doss, Ludwig C., Rt 1, wf Elsie, ch Allen, O 78.25 ac, sec 25, (42).

Erickson, A. H., Rt 1, wf Cora, ch Hildred, Maravine, R 40 ac, sec 34, R 80 ac, sec 35, O Carl Carlson, (18).

Godeman, Sophia, Rt 1, ch William, Martha, Ludwig, Clara, Herman, 40 ac, sec 34, 40 ac, sec 35, 40 ac, sec 27, 40 ac, sec 26, O C. Godeman, (32). Breeder of Shorthorn Cattle and Poland China Hogs.

Hanson, S., Rt 1, O 76.25 ac, sec 35, (50).

Hoffman, Albert, Rt 1, wf Ida, ch Duane, 80 ac, sec 36, O Ida Buecksler, (6).

Lueck, R., Rt 1, wf Edith, ch Mabel, Lewis, Rosella, Leslie, O 120 ac, sec 36. (17). Breeder of Holstein Cattle.

Mattes, Stephen, wf Mary, ch Agnes, Mary, Loretta, Ben, Wilfred, Evan, Cyel, Marcella, Irene, R 240 ac, sec 26, O C Hilton, (22).

Mortensen, L. C., Rt 1, wf Nellie, ch Andrew, Lawrence, Helen R, 160 ac, sec 36, O Herman Carlson, (10).

Murphy, Wm. J., Rt 1, wf Ellene, ch Bonnie, Donald, Bernice, Desmond, O 44 ac, sec 25, O 80 ac, sec 36, (35). Breeder of Shropshire Sheep.

Quam, Selmer, Rt 1, wf Anna, R 160 ac, sec 35, O Oscar, Severson, (35).

Severson, Carrie, Rt 1, O 80 ac, sec 35, (49).

Severson, Joseph, Rt 1, O 80 ac, sec 35, (54).

Severson, Oscar, Rt 1, O 160 ac, sec 35, (47).

Wenner, Ben, Sister Julia Wenner, 80 ac, sec 26 and 40 ac, sec 35 on contract, O C. Hilton, (33).

Postoffice, St. Clair

Bestman, John H., wf Lena, ch Frederick, O 192.50 ac, sec 17, R 80 ac, sec 17, O Henrietta Bestman, (51). Breeder of Shorthorn Cattle and Poland China Hogs.

Bowe, Theresa, ch Theresa, Rose, Jennie, Maggie, Frances, Thomas, 79.62 ac, sec 19.

Bowe, Thos. O 79.62 ac, sec 19, O 240 ac, sec 16, (41).

Cords, John, wf Clara, ch Verna, Arthur, Daisey, Vern, O 36.62 ac, sec 17, O 32 ac, sec 9, (61).

Denn, Aloysius, wf Esther, ch Lowell, Babe, R 120 ac, sec 21, O Oscar Heinge, (25).

Fitzloff, J. W., wf Olga, ch James, O 80 ac, sec 8, (34). Breeder of White Leghorn Chickens, Duroc Jersey Hogs and Holstein Cattle.

Fitzloff, Ray, O 160 ac, sec 9, O 60 ac, sec 8, (27).

Frank, Herman, wf Dorothy, ch Norma, Harland, Hazel, O 80 ac, sec 7, (22).

Gleason, Archie, Rt 1, Brothers, William L. & Henry Menage, O 40 ac, sec 16, (70).

Koch, Albert, wf Ida, ch Esther, Edna, O 40 ac, sec 17, O 40 ac, sec 33, (50).

Koch, Fred, wf Martha, ch Mildred, O 80 ac, sec 20, O 40 ac, sec 29, O 40 ac, sec 33, (60).

Mace, N. J., wf Theresa, ch Jay, Gerald, Clements, Myron, Marvin, O 80 ac, sec 20, R 95.94 ac, sec 21, (37).

Phillips, Mrs. Elise, O 80 ac, sec 17, (45). Breeder of Jersey Cattle and Ancona Chickens.

Schustag, F. C., wf Ida, ch Vera, Walter, Marion, Marie, O 38 ac, sec 7, (49).

Sodeman, Robert, wf Anna, R 39.50 ac, sec 8, O D. R. Andrews Estate, (43).

Timmerman, Louis, wf Evelyn, ch Anetta, R 80 ac, sec 7, R 40 ac, sec 6, O Clay Boswell, (34). Breeder of Shorthorn Cattle and Poland China Hogs.

Yenish, J. S., wf Nellie, ch Charles, Eileen, Loraine, Norbert, Robert, O 160 ac, sec 28, (47).

Postoffice, Smith Mill

Adams, N. H., Rt 1, wf Mary, ch Regina, Frances, Leon, Loraine, Donald, Dorothy, Robert, Ilene, Lawrence, R 160 ac, sec 34, O State Bank of St. Clair, (4).

Beyersdorf, A., Rt 1, wf Florence, ch Edward, O 80 ac, sec 20, (56).

Blank, Adolph, Rt 1, wf Alfreda, ch William, Ella, Luverne, Bernice, Adolph Jr., O 100 ac, sec 3, O 30 ac, sec 2, (7).

Bollman, P. C., Rt 1, wf Martha, ch Lawrence, Edina, Alma, Albert, Marcella, Violetta, William, John, Marie, Valera, Helen, Elsie, 80 ac, sec 2, (8).

Brewer, Chas, R, Rt 1, wf Gertrude, ch Carrie, Esther, Vida, Cyril, Gerald, O 120 ac, sec 29, O 40 ac, sec 32, O 88.50 ac, sec 31, O 59.18 ac, sec 30, (58). Breeder of Red Polled Cattle and Poland China Hogs.

Brewer, Gerald, Rt 1, O 129.98 ac, sec 30, (29). Breeder of Poland China Hogs. "Fairway Farm."

Bruels, Joseph P., Rt 1, wf Rose, ch Raymond, Marcella, Florence, Clotilda, Leon, Herbert, Marion, O 130 ac, sec 18, O 100 ac, sec 7, O 10 ac, sec 5, (47).

Buesing, August, Rt 1, wf Margaret, ch Johanna, Augusta, Herbert, Werner, Charley, Marianna, Dietrich, R 160 ac, sec 33, O Mrs. Hulda Fitzloff, (2).

Carpenter, Earl N., Rt 1, wf Nellie, ch Lucille, Calvin, R 154.50 ac, sec 15, R 40 ac, sec 16, O George Hubmer, (7). Breeder of Holstein Cattle. "St. Clair Holstein Farm."

Chase, F. M., Rt 1, wf Grace, ch Duane, Kenneth, Stanley, O 214 ac, sec 16, Breeder of Shorthorn Cattle.

Fitzloff, Carl, Rt 1, wf Lillie, ch Marion, R 40 ac, sec 21, R 80 ac, sec 22, O A. Fitzloff, (29). Breeder of Poland China Hogs.

Fitzloff, George, Rt 1, wf Ella, O 80 ac, sec 21, O 40 ac, sec 16, (28).

Fitzloff, Louis, Rt 1, wf Minnie, O 80 ac, sec 21, R 40 ac, sec 21, O A. Fitzloff, (33).

Foley, T., Rt 1, wf Rose, ch Mildred, Duane, Marie, Raymond, O 160 ac, sec 33, (63).

Franke, Albert G., Rt 1, wf Amanda, ch Shirley, O 40 ac, sec 9, O 40 ac, sec 10, (14).

Freitag, Herman, Rt 1, wf Esther, O 110 ac, sec 14, (31).

Freitag, John, Rt 1, wf Emma, O 100 ac, sec 14, (35).

Freitag, William, Rt 1, wf Clara, ch Ordella, Kenneth, O 120 ac, sec 14, (39).

Froehlich, E. F., Rt 1, wf Mathilda, ch Oscar, Elmer, Raymond, O 168 ac, sec 9, O 160 ac, sec 8, (45). Breeder of Shorthorn Cattle and White Leghorn Chickens.

Froehlich, William, Rt 1, ch Louisa, Bertha, Herman, Otto, Ed, Rudolph, sec 9.

Gekeler, Henry, Rt 1, wf Emma, ch Violet, Mildred, Harold, Harry, Gladys, O 45.50 ac, sec 15, O 40 ac, sec 10, (45).

Glamm, Fred, Rt 1, wf Bertha, ch Otto, Herman, Martha, Henry, Fritz, Bertha, Richard, Emil, Ella, Lillie, O 80 ac, sec 2, O 120 ac, sec, 11, O 40 ac, sec 12, (44).

Glamm, Henry L., Rt 1, wf Orga, O 120 ac, sec 34, (23).

Glamm, Otto, Rt 1, wf Esther, ch Lorene, Donald, O 100 ac, sec 11, (33).

Goebel, R., Rt 1, wf Mary, ch Joseph, James, Dominic, Mary, O 90 ac, sec 2, (30).

Goodrich, Ray, Rt 1, wf Neva, ch Fae, Elmer, Gladys, Glenn, Emma, O 160 ac, sec 34, (39). Breeder of Poland China Hogs.

Grams, O. E., Rt 1, wf Anna, O 160 ac, sec 22, (30).

Grams, Paul, Rt 1, wf Mabel, ch Bernard, Stella, O 123.50 ac, sec 23, O 39.75 ac, sec 14, (27).

Hawker, William, Rt 1, wf Lizzie, ch Wilby, Alvin, Frieda, Harold, Lyle, R 62 ac, sec 19, R 160 ac, sec 20, O Fred W. Wingen, (48).

Hodapp, H. J., Rt 1, wf Ludgart, ch Phyllis, Bernard, R 40 ac, sec 7, R 60 ac, sec 7, O J. P. Bruels and Clara Lynch, (36).

Kollas, Fred W., Rt 1, wf Bertha, ch Sidney, George, Marvin, O 120 ac, sec 21, (33).

Lang, Anton O., Rt 1, wf Mary, O 10 ac, sec 10, O 40 ac, sec 4, O 80 ac, sec 11, R 20 ac, sec 14, R 60 ac, sec 11, O Otto Lang, (42).

Leonard, Clem, Rt 1, wf Sylvia, O 120 ac, sec 32, (37).

Leonard, Harry, Rt 1, wf Carrie, O 40 ac, sec 32, O 80 ac, sec 29, (30).

Lynch, Geo., Rt 1, wf Cecelia, ch Everett, Marion, O 80 ac, sec 33, (33).

Lynch, Guy P., Rt 1, wf Jennie, ch Bernard, R 80 ac, sec 27, O Henry Lynch Estate, (37).

Lynch, Irenaeus, Rt 1, wf Catherine, ch Lawrence, Agnes, R 80 ac, sec 28, O Henry Lynch Estate, (34).

Lynch, James, Rt 1, wf Sadie, ch Doris, Isabelle, R 97.90 ac, sec 17, R 54 ac, sec 8, O H. Thielman, (40).

Lynch, Linus, Rt 1, wf Rose, R 40 ac, sec 28, O Mrs. Henry Lynch, (31).

Meyer, Adolph, Rt 1, wf Alvina, ch Gladys, O 76.25 ac, sec 27, (38).

Miller, Mathilda, Rt 1, ch Sarah, Alfred, Arthur, O 120 ac, sec 10, (35).

Miller, Ed., Rt 1, wf Anna, ch Charley, Eddie, Verna, Tillie, Ferd, Ben, Celia, Gertrude, Frank, George, Mary, Sadie, O 80 ac, sec 10, (56).

Muellerleile, Edward H., Rt 1, wf Mary, ch Aloysius, Phillip, Bernice, Lucille, Dennis, Robert, Mildred, R 156.80 ac, sec 31, R 40 ac, sec 6, O J. W. Mace, (32).

Nicolai, Clarence & Elmer, Rt 1, O 80 ac, sec 3, (24-22).

Nicolai, Ludwig, Rt 1, wf Pauline, ch Hulda, Arthur, Clarence, Elmer, O 160 ac, sec 10, (40).

O'Brien, Walter, Rt 1, wf Elizabeth, ch Everett, Kevin, Elzada, O 266 ac, sec 16, O 23 ac, sec 21, (49). Breeder of Holstein Cattle.

Phillips, Harry, Rt 1, wf Lucy, ch Eugene, Henry, Clateo, Harold, Adeline, Lester, Genevieve, Nicolas, O 20 ac, sec 30, O 160 ac, sec 29, (46). Breeder of Poland China Hogs and White Leghorn Chickens.

Phillips, Mary, Rt 1, ch Harry, Savallah, O 19 ac, sec 30, O 200 ac, sec 29, (66).

Preston, G. B., Rt 1, wf Carrie, ch Arthur, Clark, Ralph, Grace, Maud, John, Sam, Harold, Chester, O 240 ac, sec 31, (63). "Belle View Farm."

Preston, R. G., Rt 1, wf Nora, ch Glenn, Earl, R 160 ac, sec 32, O A. B. Preston, Estate, (33). Breeder of Duroc Jersey Hogs.

Reichel, J. J., Rt 1, wf Ottelia, R 120 ac, sec 20, O F. W. Wingen, (35).

Sack, Adolf, Rt 1, wf Anna, ch Laura, Erma, Wilfred, Ervine, O 100 ac, sec 11, (41).

(Continued on Page 24)

McPHERSON TOWNSHIP *(Continued)*

(Continued from Page 16)

Sack, Barthold, Rt 1, wf Amanda, ch Ella, Fredie, Ernest, Arthur, Alfred, Richard, Reuben, R 40 ac, sec 11, O Herman Sack.

Schalow, Carl, Rt 1, wf Ida, ch Adeline, Leona, Babe, R 160 ac, sec 18, O Henry Schalow, (42). Breeder of Poland China Hogs and Holstein Cattle. "Hillside Stock Farm."

Schorn, E., Rt 1, wf Anna, ch Tom, Margy, O 40 ac, sec 1, O 40 ac, sec 2, R 85 ac, sec 1, and in LeRay twp. O 20 ac, sec 35, O Jake Schorn, (39).

Schroeder, August F., Rt 1, wf Lena, ch Alfred, Esther, Rosie, Viola, Daisy, R 160 ac, sec 12, O James O'Neil, (36).

Schuldt, Jacob, Rt 1, wf Helen, ch Edna, Viola, Walter, Esther, O 80 ac, sec 15, O 6 ac, sec 14, (9).

Schwanke, Gustave, Rt 1, wf Ida, ch Martha, Clara, Henry, Aaron, Ella, Mabel, O 20 ac, sec 16, O 40.71 ac, sec 9, (17).

Seys, August, Rt 1, wf Emma, ch Henry, Martha, Hector, Oscar, Peter, Jerome, George, Mary, R 160 ac, sec 15, R 80 ac, sec 22, O Frank Amberg, (17).

Smith, Ray, Rt 1, Sister Margaret Smith, R 80 ac, sec 22, O Chas Smith Estate, (34).

Thissen Severin, Rt 1, wf Katie, ch Fred, Mary, Monica, Catherine, Eileen, Severin, Julia, Pat, Celestine, O 160 ac, sec 1, and in Le Ray twp., O 80 ac, sec 36 and in Decoria twp., O 40 ac, sec 36, (41). Breeder of Chester White Hogs and Durham Cattle.

Timmerman, Fred, Rt 1, wf Ida, ch Aris, Leora, R 200 ac, sec 27, O John Timmerman, (36).

Westphal, A. B., Rt 1, wf Lena, O 80 ac, sec 15, (30).

Wingen, Joseph, Rt 1, wf Catherine, ch Lena, Agnes, Belle, Cora, Sophia, Frances, Alonzo, Florence, Marjorie, O 160 ac, sec 32, O 160 ac, sec 33, O 80 ac, sec 28 and in Medo twp., O 74 ac, sec 6, O 201.42 ac, sec 5, O 80 ac, sec 8. Breeder of Purebred Percheron Horses, Hereford Cattle and Poland China Hogs. "Riverview Stock Farm."

Witt, Otto, Rt 1, wf Gertrude, ch Willard, O 160 ac, sec 28, (4).

Wulf, Karl, Rt 1, wf Minnie, ch Emma, O 80 ac, sec 11, O 80 ac, sec 2, (12).

Yanke, August, Rt 1, wf Minnie, ch George, Ellen, O 40 ac, sec 2, (8).

Yungerberg, Eda, Rt 1, ch Sylvester, Lester, O 80 ac, sec 1, O 40 ac, sec 12, (17).

Yungerberg, Herman, Rt 1, wf Martha, ch Harold, Clarence, Reuben, Herbert, O 120 ac, sec 2, (34).

require a doctor's attention. He then advised the two to go to the Grand Rapids Hospital and upon seeing them head for Grand Rapids called authorities there and instructed them as to where the men were.

Sheriff Harmond was then informed and Sheriff Frank Cords along with F. E. Morse left at once for Grand Rapids.

-1929-

The blizzard Tuesday followed by the heavy snowstorm Thursday caused a general blockade and traffic was at a standstill. Our train reached here in safety Friday several hours late but on its return trip went off the track between Freeborn and Albert Lea and we were without train service Saturday. Mr. Hassenfelt rural route mail carrier was unable to make his usual trip Friday and Saturday but Monday he came through in an improvised sleigh which carried him over the snow banks safely. Saturday the blockade on the state road leading to Mankato was lifted by the appearance of the snowplow in the village though old dobbin is still pressed into service on the side roads.

-1930-

January - The farmers are taking advantage of the good sleighing these days by hauling their logs to the Chase sawmill.

The ice harvest is now on. The icehouse at the creamery was filled last week by a number of St. Clair citizens for private use.

A meeting was called at Mankato Monday for the purpose of considering the question of the new bus line through St. Clair to Albert Lea. The meeting opened with a dinner at noon hour at the Saulpaugh Hotel, followed by the business meeting. Mr. Fred Wingen mayor of St. Clair was one of the guests invited to attend.

Esther Schroeder Hager in front of Schroeder's Grocery Store
Schroeder's later became part of Pagenkopf's Grocery

The bus line would solve the problem of a long desired question of the people of our community and will be a boom to the village, providing the schedule is so planned that a visit to Mankato may be made and a return the same day.

August 18 - Case of St. Clair Dance Pavilion May Be Submitted To Supreme Court. Frank Gallagher, Waseca attorney petitioned the Blue Earth Co. Board of Commissioners at their session this morning to release a restraining order prohibiting Jerry J. Lynch and Robert W. Schostag, proprietors of the St. Clair dance pavilion, from giving Sunday night public dances there. They then moved the Pavilion to Kasota, MN.

Westphal hog lot in the 1930s

L to R: Ernie Hager and Herb Buesing

Jack Fitzloff manufactures turkey blankets.

Population of St. Clair - 389.

-1931-

Marvin E. Rohrer purchased the St. Clair Drug Store from Dr. R.O. Juliar. The business contained a complete line of drugs, cosmetics, stationery, gifts, a complete line of painter's supplies, confectioneries, sundries and a soda fountain. It also housed the Post Office.

Elmer and Oscar Froehlich started the Froehlich Brothers Hatchery.

September - A.M. Quinn purchased the Cooperative Oil Company and changed the name to Quinn Oil Company.

The Kuske Hardware and leather goods store was moved from the west end of town to downtown St. Clair. A Webb Oil station was operated in connection with the store.

Sunshine Golf Course is started on the Ray Fitzloff farm (Where Dale and Fran Sargent now live).

-1932-

Sunshine Turkey Farms & Hatchery completed another successful year in the turkey business. About 20,000 poults were hatched in the special turkey hatchery of which 12,000 were sold and delivered over the Northwest and the balance of 8,000 was raised on the farm. Two thousand hens were kept to supply eggs for the new enlarged turkey hatchery. The plans called for an output of nearly 75,000 poults in the spring. Credit is given to Hubbard's Sunshine Turkey Starter Mash.

-1933-

March 6 - All banks in the United States were ordered closed by President Roosevelt.

Prohibition ended - Depression continues.

-1935-

August 14 - Social Security established.

June - Workmen Injured on St. Clair Project. Vernon Lans and Lou Coult, workmen for Lundin Brothers, Mankato contractors, were injured while working on a culvert project on county road No. 172 near St. Clair yesterday.

Mr. Coult was struck on the hand by a sledgehammer when holding a drill for a fellow workman. While Mr. Lans suffered the loss of a great amount of blood when a piece of flying steel from the head of a drill passed under his sleeve, struck his arm and severed an artery. He was taken to St. Clair for treatment and later removed to Mankato.

Henry Thielmann and friends shoveling snow in front of Pagenkopf's Grocery Store.

Ernie Hager inside the Hager Hardware Store. The table in the front of the picture held three glass covered trays containing fishing supplies.

Poster for McRobert and His Troupers

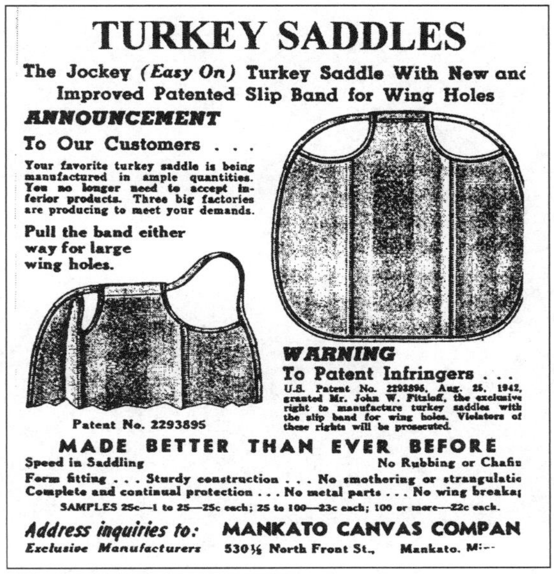

Jack Fitzloff sold the manufacturing and selling rights for his turkey saddles to the Mankato Canvas Company. The manufacturing of this special blanket, used on hens during the breeding season, will necessitate the employment of 40 additional persons at the company. Saddles are being shipped to Portugal and Bolivia as well as throughout the U.S.

-1936-

A liquor store and restaurant opened in the St. Clair Hotel, an 1880's landmark. Originally called the Leary Hotel.

Marvin E. Rohrer was also appointed postmaster.

L to R: Marvin Steel, Lawrence Ireland and Cecelia Gorman

L to R: Stanley Steel and Lawrence Ireland

-1937-

During the summer months, the businessmen of St. Clair are to present free moving pictures to their friends in and around St. Clair. The pictures are to be shown on Saturday nights. (They were shown at an empty lot on which the medical clinic was later built and now houses the McPherson Farmers Insurance Office) Herman Kroenke sold bags of popcorn for 5 cents a bag.

Ted Oftedahl set up a large screen on an empty lot in various towns. The small towns really prospered, as there were cars parked everywhere, some sit-

St. Clair Girls Basketball Team, 1935-36
Back row (L to R): Gertrude Winkelman, Phyllis Sandborn, Leona Mace, Miss Gladys Peik (Coach), Lois Hubmer, Norma Macomber, Keturah Hubmer.
Front row: Marian Boswell, Lucile Carpenter, Virginia Macomber, Helen Schostag, Capitola McComb and Florine Beccue.

St. Clair State Bank (left) and the Leary Hotel.

Schostag Hotel Bar
L to R: Bill Lynch, Tony Fitzloff, three painters who were painting the water tower, Warner Buesing, Sophia Pagenkopf, Anna Schostag and Robert Schostag

ting in their cars and others sitting on the ground. The businessmen in the towns paid him for his services. People would blow their car horns to show their appreciation for the free show. A man from Minnesota Lake also provided this service at times. Mr. Oftedahl in later years operated the bulk tank and gas truck out of Pemberton. Later still, he operated a photo studio in Mankato. He was married to Verna Andrews from Delavan. By Harold Severson.

-1938-

The students of the St. Clair School publish "Student Prints" every six weeks. Subscription rates are 30 cents for the six issues, or 7 cents per copy.

Maxine Seewald, stenographer and assistant bookkeeper at the St. Clair State Bank, where she comes in frequent contact with nearly all of the residents of the St. Clair community, writes the news of her town and vicinity for the *Free Press.*

-1939-

American Eagle Caught at St. Clair, Goes to City Zoo. An American eagle was added to the collection of animals and birds at the Mankato Zoo at Sibley Park this morning. The bird which has a tremendous wingspread was captured by August Westphal of St. Clair who saw the bird alongside a road and ran it down on the ground. The bird appeared to have a wing injury and was unable to take off in flight when pursued by Westphal.

Large Egg Found By Mrs. Otto Witt. When Mrs. Otto Witt, Janesville, Route 3, found an egg measuring seven and one-eighth by seven and three-quarters inches in her hen house recently, she thought that there must be an ostrich in the woodpile. But it was only a progressive White Leghorn with ideas of her own on mass egg production. Instead of being content with laying its quota of one egg, the leghorn got ambitious and produced two at once, one inside the other. Inside the big shell when Mrs. Witt broke it were white and yolk and a second normal egg. The chicken has given no indication as to whether or not it will

St. Clair Boys Basketball team, 1935-36
Back row (L to R): Lewis Downing, Waldemar Gjerde and Mr. Hollister. Middle row: Bill Schroeder, Marvin Steel, Don Meany and Walter Kalbus. Front row: Pershing Hubmer, Lawrence Ireland, Warren Sanborn, Roy Schultz.

St. Clair Baseball Team
Back row (L to R): George Kroenke, Lawrence Ireland, Walter Schuldt, unidentified, unidentified
Front row: Norbert Yenish, Darrell Juliar, Roy Schultz, Charles Yenish, Stan Steel, unidentified, Donald Meany

St. Clair Boys Basketball Team, 1938
Back row (L to R): Sid Kollos, Norb Yenish, Harland Frank, Ralph Ireland, Lawrence Marzinske, Clements "Bud" Mace, Virgil Juliar, Coach Floyd Temple. Front row: Marvin Steel, Roy Schultz, Lawrence Ireland, Warren Sandborn, Donald Meany.

L to R: Marion Haugen, Jim Winkelman, Leland Wenner and Gene May - Taken in the spring of 1940

Louis and Evelyn Timmerman with an early school bus. It was built on the back of a 1930s vintage Chevrolet truck.

continue with its "egg within egg" tactics. The Witt farm is two miles from St. Clair.

December 1 - St. Clair Shades Minnesota Lake in Opener. St. Clair High School opened its basketball season by nosing out Minnesota Lake, 22-20. Nelson of the losers led both teams in scoring with 13 points, while Frank paced St. Clair with seven. Members of the St. Clair team was Harland Frank, Virgil Juliar, Jack Danberry, Lawrence Heminover, Sidney Kollos and Donald Meany. The Minnesota Lake team members were James, Kaus, Latusik, Rohner, Heise, Nelson and Beyer.

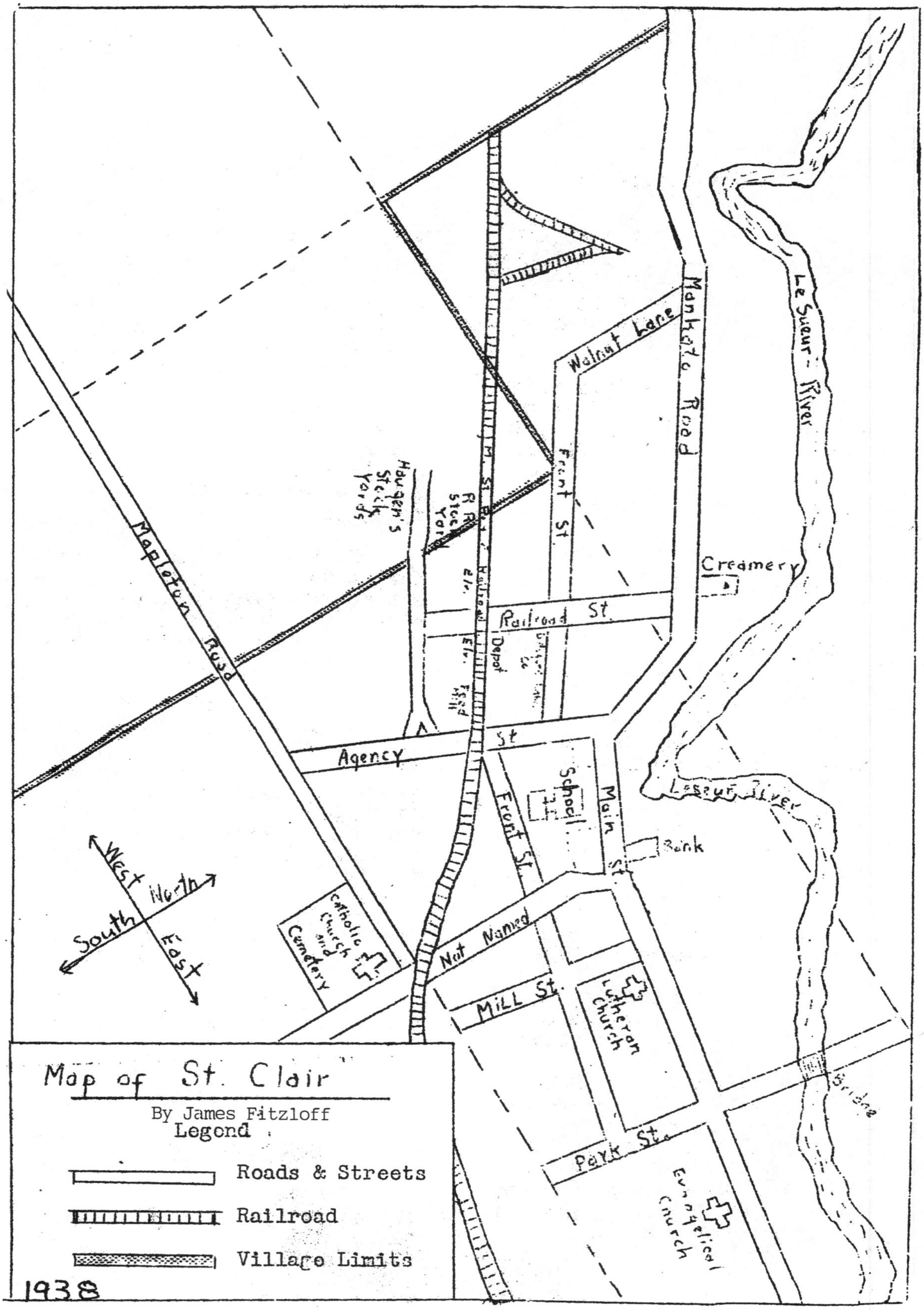
Map of St. Clair
By James Fitzloff
Legend
Roads & Streets
Railroad
Village Limits
1938
Mankato Road
Walnut Lane
Le Sueur River
Front St
Creamery
Railroad St
Depot
Agency St
School
Main St
Bank
Leseur River
Mapleton Road
Haugen's Stock Yards
R.R. Stock Yard
West
North
South
East
Catholic Church and Cemetery
Not Named
Front St.
Mill St.
Lutheran Church
Park St.
Evangelical Church
Bridge

St. Clair ladies on tour of the Watkins plant in Winona, Minnesota. Back row (L to R): Unidentified, unidentified, unidentified, Barbara Maxon, unidentified, Gustie Baer (under the clock), Esther Hager, unidentified, unidentified, Agnes Wingen, unidentified, unidentified Row 3: Mrs. Walter O'Brien, Sr., Clara Macomber, Nona Nyquist, Edie Beccue, unidentified, Helene Schuldt, Emma Gekeler Row 2: Gertrude Witt, Minnie Fitzloff, Kate Quinn, Margaret Schmidt, Hulda Fitzloff, Mrs. Gus Schostag, Cel Lynch, Mrs. Bob Schostag, Jennie Lynch, Toot Schoffman. Front row: Catherine Thissen, Lily Fitzloff, unidentified, Walter Ruethenbeck (local salesman), Vera Bollman, Jennie Winkelman, Lottie Juliar

-1940-

Hubmer With Bank 30 Years. The St. Clair State Bank helps George H. Hubmer celebrate his thirtieth year of service to the bank and to the community. Persons residing in St. Clair and nearby communities are invited to consult with the official staff at the bank regarding financial matters. Regardless of whether you are a businessman, a farmer or a home manager, you will readily appreciate the cordial atmosphere prevailing at this friendly bank.

During the years the St. Clair State Bank has been in operation, it has endeavored to serve the people of this region through a safe, strong and conservative policy. Funds deposited are insured under the Federal Deposit Insurance Corporation plan adopted in 1933.

The officers and directors of the St. Clair State Bank are all local men and fairly understand all phases of the banking business.

The St. Clair State Bank is to be complimented on the protection it affords depositors. An outstanding example of this unusual service is illustrated by the fact that in the fall of 1938, the St. Clair State Bank depositor's trust completed paying depositors off 100%.

For the year ending 1939, this bank had a capital stock of $25,000, a surplus of $10,000, undivided profits, $5,365.38.

Henry Thielman is president of the bank; O.O. Juliar, vice president; George H. Hubmer, cashier; Hugh Russell, assistant cashier; and Joyce Pream, bookkeeper and teller. The directors of the bank are as follows: Henry Thielman, O.O. Juliar, Fred Kruse and George H. Hubmer.

November 11 - Armistice Day storm – the worst blizzard ever to hit Minnesota. A 24 hour, all-time record snowfall from 16.2 to 26.6 inches in various Minnesota locales with 59 people dead within the state and 144 in the nation. Locally, school buses were trapped in the storm and some unsuspecting farm homes had to suddenly put up partial busloads of children. It took several days to get the roads reopened. Many resulting snow banks were as high as the electric power line poles.

December 4 - St. Clair Pays Tribute to Retiring Merchant, Wife. On Sunday evening, the people of the village of St. Clair gathered at the schoolhouse for a farewell party in honor of Mr. and Mrs. Duemeland who are planning to retire from active work in the near future. The St. Clair Commercial Club sponsored the party. Mr. and Mrs. Duemeland have served the village and surrounding area for almost 60 years. He arrived here in 1882, coming from a farm in Limetown Township. A few years later he built the store in which he conducted his business all these years. This is a record of which his friends are proud, and "believe it or not," Mr. Duemeland at the advanced age of 84 is still on the job every day. He clerks, keeps the fires going, and sweeps, just as he has done for years. There is always a cheerful atmosphere about his place of business, old friends dropping in evenings to chat. He and his wife will miss this genial, busy life, and St. Clair will miss them.

Population of St. Clair - 375.

-1941-

January 3 - *Mankato Free Press* - Haugen Sells St. Clair Market, Locker Plant. Elmer Haugen proprietor of a meat market at St. Clair for the past 17½ years has sold

Charlie Schalow farm after the November 11, 1940 blizzard

his market and locker system to Carl Rose who took possession January 1. Rose has been with Haugen for the past 10 years, starting as a driver and later assisting in buying of livestock and meat cutting. Haugen will continue in the livestock business.

March 7 - Death Marks County's First Traffic Accident Fatality for 1941. William Fitzloff, 56, of St. Clair, Minn., passed away at 5:00 Tuesday afternoon of injuries received in a four-car crash at Eagle Lake Friday. He was riding in a car and was thrown out of the machine and sustained a head injury in the accident in which five other persons suffered injury. He never fully regained consciousness.

Mankato Free Press - Ship Named for Former St. Clair Boy. A warship named in memory of a Seattle boy who lived for a time at St. Clair recently was launched at Houston, Texas, with the boy's mother serving as sponsor at the launching.

The youth was Marvin Lee Ramsden, 23-year-old coxswain who served aboard the aircraft carrier Lexington when that ship was sunk in the battle of the Coral Sea a year ago last month. The photo showed Mrs. J. L. Ramsden, Marvin's mother along with Mrs. R. O. Juliar of St. Clair, his aunt who was matron of honor at the launching of the vessel, a destroyer escort, the youth's father J. L. Ramsden, Dr. R. O. Juliar of St. Clair, and Lieut. Con. John McMaster.

Young Ramsden lived at the R. O. Juliar home for a time several years ago and attended St. Clair High School. He was awarded a Silver Star medal posthumously for his action in the Coral Sea battle. He had been in the navy since he was 17.

"Although wounded," the citation stated, "Ramsden courageously remained at his exposed station, in the face of intense strafing and dive-bombing attacks, until he was physically exhausted. By this heroic action he contributed greatly to the destruction of several attacking enemy aircraft."

Mankato Free Press - 49 Draftees to Leave Monday - Local Draft Board No. 2 Men Will Go to Fort Snelling. Blue Earth County Local Draft Board No. 2 this morning released names of 49 rural Blue Earth County men to leave Mankato for induction at Fort Snelling Monday afternoon.

The men are scheduled to leave Mankato 2 p.m. Monday. It was pointed out at the board office that they will be under regulations by which they may request a 10-day leave after their induction to wind up personal affairs. New regulations to go into effect June 16 provide for automatic 24-day furloughs following induction.

The city high school band is to play at send-off ceremonies scheduled at 1:45 p.m. The Mankato Rotary club is providing a speaker for the ceremony.

Lester Allen Wolcott, St. Clair, Eldo Bruno Ewert, McPherson, and Harold William Hawker, McPherson were with the group to leave.

June 5 - Robert Fritzke received an "Industrial Arts" scholarship at Mankato Teachers College.

George Macomber is depot agent.

December 8 - St. Clair Trucker Killed, Strange Mishap. Arthur Flitter, 27, of St. Clair was killed early Monday afternoon in a freak accident on the Clarence Nicolai farm a few miles northeast of St. Clair.

The St. Clair trucker had a blowout in a rear tire of his gravel truck only a few minutes before the accident. Stopping in front of the Nicolai farm he explained to the farmer that he would have to unload to repair the tire and offered to sell the load of gravel.

The deal was made and Flitter started to drive slowly down the farm driveway, standing on the running board of the truck and steering through the cab window as gravel was dumped from the bottom of the truck box.

As he made a right turn off the driveway into the farmyard a front wheel on the truck buckled and the heavy vehicle toppled over. It almost cleared Flitter who was thrown or jumped from the running board, but the edge of the box just caught the top of his head and crushed it as the truck rolled completely over. He was instantly killed.

October - The Blue Earth County corn husking contest is held on the Jack Fitzloff farm. Close to 1,000 people gathered for the event. Durward Irwine of Amboy won the contest, husking 37.87 bushel.

School bus in 1941. On the far left is the bus driver, Ernest Hager, with his son Bill standing in front of him.

-1942-

Population of St. Clair - 386.

With the Surplus Marketing Administration (S.M.A.) supplying the food and the Works Progress Administration (W.P.A.) providing labor and supervision, a hot school lunch was made available at the cost of three cents per day. Meal tickets were sold by the week for fifteen cents. The students lined up in the hall, had their tickets punched, then filed past the Home Economics room door and received a cup filled with hot dish and a spoon. They then filed back to their classrooms and sat at their desks to eat their lunch. The meals were generally served only during the winter months. Clara Hintze started this service.

July 24 - *Mankato Free Press* - Jack's BeanStalk Fitzloff Corn Sets Record. Jack's bean talk or just tall corn? Jack Fitzloff claims it is corn as he brought in some stalks grown on his farm near St. Clair that measure 10 feet, two inches. The corn is DeKalb 607 variety and was planted May 14, Fitzloff said.

Mankato Markets

Winter wheat	.97
Spring wheat	.99
Oats	.35
Barley	.64
Corn	.74
Flax	2.28
Rye	.49

August 31 - 2 Escape Injury in Plane Crash Near St. Clair. James Miller, Albert Lea, and James Kirkey, Minneapolis, escaped serious in jury when their two-passenger light plane crashed near St. Clair yesterday.

Miller, who was piloting the craft, said the plane

L to R: William Myers and William McComb

L to R: Curtis "Leprechaun" McDuff and Ernie Hager

Margie Westphal and her pony "Jerry"

stalled on a steep turn as they were on the outskirts of St. Clair. They were about 300 feet in the air, he said, and as they crashed the plane cut off the tops of several trees.

The plane was demolished. Miller and Kirkey suffered cuts and bruises.

Guy Compton photographed the wreckage of the plane that crashed on the Henry Borgwardt farm at St. Clair.

September 1 - St. Clair Businessmen Help Farmer. When Arthur Dittman, local farmer, found it difficult to finish his grain stacking, due to serious illness of several members of his family, businessmen of St. Clair went out to his farm and finished the job. The men who assisted were Elmer Haugen, Gus Schostag, Geo. F. Juliar, Dick Engelerth, Arthur Dittman, Ted Glaser, Walter O'Brien, Henry Thielman, Albert Franke, Ernie Hager, Nic Juliar, Hugh Russell. Jack Sanborn, Leo Frank, Otto Froehlich, William Beccue and Earl Pagenkopf.

October 2 - Mrs. Jack Fitzloff is appointed as a Blue Earth County Director of the Victory Aides.

-1943-

Enactment of "pay-as-you-go" income tax bill resulting in a 20% withholding tax from wages and salaries.

Corporal Robert Fritzke Writes of Action in Sicily. Corporal Robert P. Fritzke, nephew of Mrs. Jack Fitzloff of St. Clair, who, before he entered the army was a third-year student at the Mankato Teachers College, is somewhere in Sicily with a medical detachment. He writes that he came through the campaign for that island "without a scratch" after seeing action with two different divisions and that the Sicilians "like us, especially our gum and cigarettes." Corporal Fritzke landed with the first American troops in North Africa and went through the Tunisia campaign before going to Sicily.

-1944-

February - The St. Clair American Legion Schmidt-Grams Post 475 is organized.

Victory garden, War Bond drives, rationing stamps and tokens, black markets, scrap drives, black-out drills, leg make-up, "service men's star" window flags, defense work, food shortages, rolling bandages, V-E mail, knitting sweaters and socks, "We regret to inform you" telegrams — all a part of the American life during the war years.

Ration Office at St. Clair Moved. The St. Clair ration application center, now located at the home of Mrs. John Fitzloff, will be moved to the St. Clair Hotel, effective Friday, September 22. The center is open Monday and Fridays from 8 a.m. to 1 p.m.

Rationing Dates:

SUGAR: Stamp No. 14 good for five pounds of sugar until midnight, November 1.

CANNING SUGAR: Stamps No. 15 and 16 in book One good for five pounds each of canning sugar through October 31. Where more than 10 pounds per book holder are needed application should be made to the local board.

MEAT, BUTTER, CHEESE, OILS: Brown stamp "C" from Ration Book Three valid from September 26 through October 30. Brown stamp "D" valid from October 3 through October 30. Brown stamps "E" valid from October 10 through October 30. Brown stamps "F" valid from October 17 through October 30.

CANNED GOODS: Blue stamps "U," "V" and "W" are valid until midnight, October 20. Blue stamps "X," "Y" and "Z" valid from October 1 through November 20.

TIRE INSPECTIONS: "A" drivers must have their next tire inspection by midnight March 31, 1944. "B" drivers must have their next tire inspection by midnight, October 31. "C" drivers must have their next tire inspection by midnight, November 30.

STOVES: Applications for purchase certificates on all gas, oil and wood or coal heating and cooking stoves

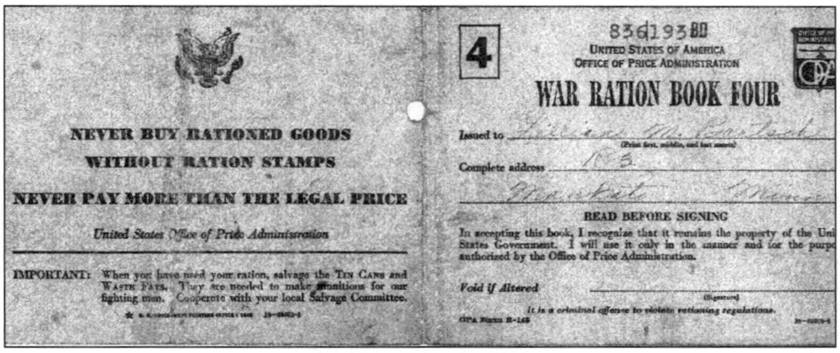

1945 War Ration Book

Ration Stamps

must be made to local war price and ration board.

GASOLINE: "A" coupons No. 8 in new book, good for three gallons each are valid through November 21, Only "B" and "C" new type coupons with words "Mileage Ration" printed on the face are valid for supplemental gasoline purchases at rate of two gallons each.

SHOES: Stamp No. 18 in book one valid for one pair of shoes. Validity date extended indefinitely. Stamp No. 1 on the "airplane" sheet of ration book three good for one pair of shoes beginning November 1, with no expiration date set.

FUEL OIL: Period one unit coupons in new ration books, good for 10 gallons for each unit, valid for deliveries through January 3, 1944. Coupons No. 5 in 1942-43 rations now invalid.

December 11 - Schools Seek Electricity. Efforts are being made to obtain electric lighting for rural schools, Mrs. Elise Phillips, county superintendent of schools, announced today, pointing out that the request for wiring is now pending before the war production board.

At present, Mrs. Phillips said, 25 of the currently open rural schools in Blue Earth County have electric lighting, which is more than two-thirds. Some of the closed little red or white houses also have such lighting.

"The schools with no electricity have to depend upon the day for light," Mrs. Phillips put it, although occasionally when evening meetings are held at the schoolhouses, gas or kerosene lamps are used.

-1944-45-

Harland Frank, seaman second class, son of Mr. and Mrs. Herman Frank of St. Clair, is stationed at the navy training and distribution center at Shoemaker, Calif. He entered the navy in January and received his boot training at Great Lakes. He spent a short leave at his home and then returned to Great Lakes before going to California.

Rapid promotion came recently to Clements T. Mace at Camp Savage, Minnesota when within a short time; he was upped first to private first class and then to corporal. He is a driver of a military police patrol car.

Private Norbert C. Glaser, son of Mr. and Mrs. Theo Glaser, with the infantry, has recently arrived in Italy. He entered the service last November, spent a 14-day furlough with his parents, leaving March 18 for overseas, after finishing his training at Fort McClellan, Alabama. He wrote his parents that he likes Italy, where he has attended musical entertainment and church services making it seem like home.

Seaman first class Gerald J. Preston, son of Mr. and Mrs. John S. Preston, is now stationed at the United States navy's fleet hometown news center at Chicago. He took his naval training at Camp Downs, Great Lakes, Ill., and was later stationed at Hugh Manley High School in Chicago.

David Louise Lynch

Two sons of Mr. and Mrs. Fred Kollos who were recently home on leave at the same time, have returned to their posts of duty. George F. Kollos, fireman second class, has been stationed at St. Louis, Mo. Since the completion of a 16-week course in electrical school at Great Lakes, Ill. He entered the service in December 1944.

His brother, Sidney Kollos, Chief Petty Officer, radio technician, entered the service in October 1942. He was in the pacific nine months, and is now stationed at Capitola, Calif. He also attended school at Stillwater, Oklahoma, and Corpus Christi, Texas, in addition to boot training at Great Lakes.

PTA Hears Talk by Navy Veteran. The St. Clair PTA held its last meeting on April 19, in the school gymnasium. The highlight of the evening was an informal talk by Chief Petty Officer Sidney Kollos, home on leave from the U.S. Navy. He has been stationed on an aircraft carrier in the Pacific.

Private Everett G. Lynch has been presented with the expert infantryman badge. He also has six other medals for his good work in camp. Lynch has been assigned to the infantry replacement-training center at Camp Rucker, Alabama, and is now transferred to Fort Ord, California. He expects to leave for Japan soon. He entered the service in January.

Oscar Seys, technician fifth grade has arrived at La Guardia Field, NY, aboard an air transport command transatlantic plane, after 33 months in the European Theater, where he served as a truck driver with the 10th engineers. He entered the service four years ago. Seys was awarded the European theater ribbon with eight stars, a presidential unit citation, and the French Fourreguerre with palm.

Clements T. Mace has received an honorable discharge at Camp McCoy, Wisconsin, after 38 months of service, 15 of which were spent in the European Theater of operations as a truck driver. He holds the certificate of merit, good driver's badge, good conduct medal, and the European theater ribbon with five battle stars for campaigns in Normandy, northern France, Rhineland, Ardennes, and central Europe.

Private Elroy Wayne Honish has returned to Las Vegas, Nevada, after spending a 14-day furlough with his parents. Honisch is in the ground crew of the Army Air Corps, now awaiting orders for overseas shipment.

Private Lester F. Kruse has gone to Camp Adair, Oregon, after spending a 14-day furlough at his home. He had just completed 17 weeks of basic training at Camp Hood, Texas.

Charles J. Yenish of St. Clair, who enlisted in the Navy Air Corps recently, left Saturday for Worthington to begin his training.

Ivan F. Hurt, a former teacher at St. Clair, has been accepted as an aviation cadet in meteorology and will be sent to one of the army's meteorology schools. At present he is at Chanute Field, Illinois, where he returned after spending a furlough with his wife and daughter in Mankato, MN.

November - The St. John's Lutheran Ladies' Aid presented a two-act comedy "The Strike of the Ladies' Aid." Miss Emma Godeman was the director. The cast included Mmes. Herman Penn, Gerald Brewer, T. Meany, Wm. Myers, Henry Lubke, Wm. McComb, Paul Grams, Herman Kollos, Wm. Hesse, John Westphal, Alvin

DeMars Hotel

Hawker, Harold Cords, A. H. Mackdanz, Otto Witt and Clifford Marzinske. Beverly and Ivadell Myers provided musical comedy and Mrs. Ernest Hager played various piano selections.

-1945-

February 3 - The state department of conservation has sent a letter to John A. Felber, Blue Earth County commissioner from the First District, approving the construction of a temporary dam on Rice Lake south of St. Clair.

The only other steps to be taken in achieving permission to construct the temporary project, Felber said, is to secure an order from District Judge Harry A. Johnson authorizing the award of damages to two farmers living along the lake.

The wartime taboo on construction with concrete and other materials, according to Felber, means that plans for a permanent dam would have to be put off until the armistice. The contemplated temporary dam would consist of plank piling.

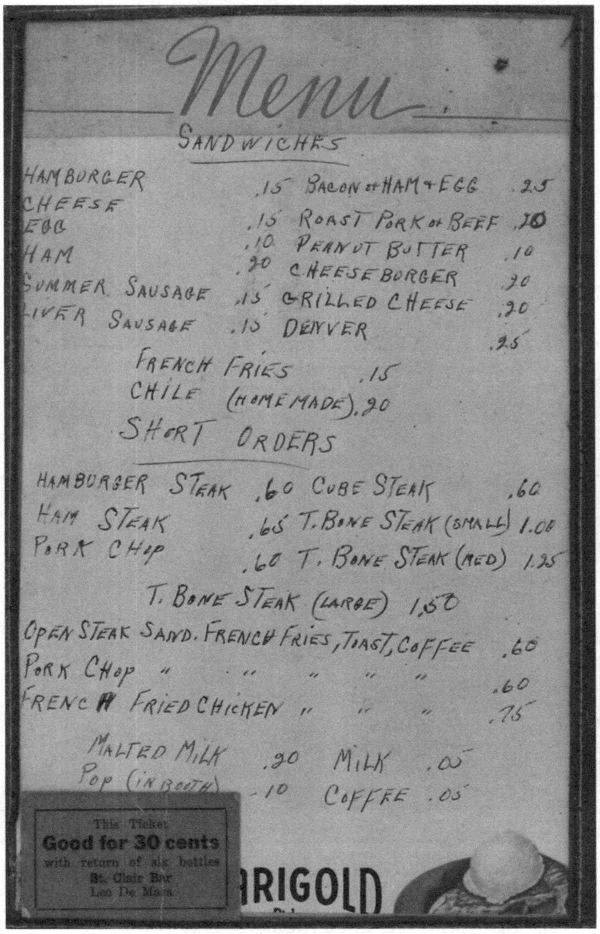

Menu from DeMars - St.Clair Bar

The whole dam project is sought by conservation organizations, which point out that the water level of the lake should be kept at a high enough level to make it a suitable breeding ground for waterfowl.

"Student Prints" - The young people of St. Clair have formed a Youth Center, which has no name as yet. The meetings were scheduled for alternating Wednesday and Thursday evenings from 8 to 11 p.m. allowing for outside activities.

February 10 - *Mankato Free Press* - Pfc. Roy Meany Dies In Action. Private First Class Roy A. Meany, son of Mr. and Mrs. T. E. Meany of St. Clair, was killed in action January 18 in Belgium, his parents have been informed by the war department.

April 27 - The Milwaukee railroad has made a change in its schedule. Formerly they made a run every other day. Now the train comes up from Albert Lea one day, stays at St. Clair over night and returns to Albert Lea the next day. The towns located on this line are Albert Lea, Freeborn, Matawan, Waldorf, Pemberton and St. Clair.

May 14 - St. Clair - W. Gjerde, superintendent of the St. Clair School for the past 10 years, resigns and has accepted an appointment in the Department of Teaching at Iowa State Teachers College at Cedar Falls, Iowa. Superintendent E. J. Erickson of Lester Prairie has been appointed to fill the vacancy caused by Gjerde's resignation.

This Minneapolis Moline Model R was purchased new by Henry Quade in 1945 for $1,000.
At that time he was farming the land now owned by the Winters. In later years he used it to farm the land west of Winters, which at that time was owned by Frank Galler. Rich Winter purchased the tractor in 1984.

REMEMBERING ST. CLAIR VETERANS

Submitted Photo

St. Clair – "A Star For Service" was featured in the January 16, 2002, issue of the *Lake Region Times*. Banners hung in windows of homes and businesses, honoring our soldiers abroad during WWII. St. Clair residents had taken the *Star for Service* one step further with a large *Star for Service Billboard*. Shirley Fitzloff wrote that the billboard was on display just east of Peg's Grocery Store on Main St. when she moved to St. Clair in 1945. The young man shown in the picture was Shirley Fitzloff's husband Jim.

The names were reproduced for clarity.

June 29 - Real hamburger sandwiches will be one of the features of the 4th of July picnic and celebration at St. Clair, sponsored by the Grams-Schmidt American Legion Post No. 475. Jack W. Fitzloff, publicity chairman, said that permission has been given by the office of price administration to butcher a steer for the occasion. There will be a large refreshment stand and entertainment and sports of various kinds.

At 12:30 noon the St. Clair High School band will give a concert with Henri Udelhofen of Mankato as leader. Judge Leslie Morse of Mankato will speak at 2:30 p.m. Following his talk will be community singing of patriotic and army songs, and amateur dance-and-song acts.

A kitten ball game by outstanding teams will be another attraction of the day; also other sports and races with prizes for winners, and a clown band.

In the evening, KYSM will entertain with music and dance acts. There will be a dance at the town hall with music by Pestka's orchestra, to wind up festivities of the "glorious Fourth."

October 9 - James Fitzloff On Ship When Storm Hits. James Fitzloff, seaman second class, quartermaster on a minesweeper, wrote his parents, Mr. and Mrs. Jack Fitzloff of St. Clair, telling them about his hair-raising experience at Okinawa.

"Our ship was lost in the typhoon that struck here about four days ago. I'm telling you, it was an awful thing to go through. I didn't get hurt, except for a few bruises and such, but there were lots of other fellows who have lost their lives.

We were moored in a cave and about five p.m. it struck. There were ships all around us moored only a few hundred yards away and also ships tied along side of us. Our main lines parted when the wind got up to about 100 knots and that was the beginning of things. Ships were tossing around like a bunch of wild broncos, ramming against each other and capsizing.

Our ship turned over on its side and we prepared to abandon ship. None of us would have made it if we would have had to jump because water was swirling all over the place. I judged the waves to be at least 60 feet high. We stuck to our ship and it drifted onto a reef."

He said the camp where he had been stationed was completely demolished. The highest wind velocity recorded on his ship was 135 miles an hour.

November 20 - "His Women Folks," a three-act play is presented by the ladies of St. John's Lutheran. The cast consisted of Margaret Myers, Edna Froehlich, Muriel Froehlich, Hazel Frank, Phyllis Froehlich, Gertrude Marzinske, Gertrude Witt, Beverly Myers and Frieda Westphal. Gertie Froehlich, Ivadell Myers, Joan Froehlich and William Hager provided musical numbers between acts.

The play "His Women Folks" was presented by St. John's Lutheran ladies at the town hall in 1945. Back row (L to R): Margaret Myers, Gert Witt, Phyllis Froehlich, Muriel Froehlich (Mace), Hazel DeMars. Front row: Gert Marzinske, Frieda Westphal, Edna Froehlich, Beverly Born.

-1946-

January - The wedding reception/dance for Gerald Mace and Muriel Froehlich was the last public event held at the St. Clair Town Hall.

April 2 - An application for new unit of the American Legion Auxiliary was organized for the Grams-Schmidt Unit 475 at St. Clair.

-1947-

October 1 - Reception for Leon Bruels - Joan Oftedahl held at Mace's Café.

John Fossum Makes Fast Air Trip From Norway. John Fossum, St. Clair buttermaker, made a record trip on his return from Norway where he had been visiting relatives at his old home when he arrived home Tuesday afternoon. John made the trip by air leaving Oslo, Norway, at 9 o'clock Monday morning and arrived at Minneapolis airport shortly after 2 p.m. Tuesday. He reports conditions quite bad there following the war with retail prices on most commodities very high.

Jack Fitzloff of St. Clair has been named the dealer for Alumni-Drome buildings for the Mankato area and will open offices here when space can be found. The all-aluminum, multi-purpose utility buildings for farm or city use, displayed for the first time in this territory at the Minnesota State Fair, and are made by the Reynolds Metals Company, Louisville, Kentucky.

Duane Schalow hauling grain bundles at the Westphal farm.

October 8 - Janesville Farm has 100-Bushel Yield of Corn. A McPherson Township farmer, Sylvester Youngerberg, has predicted a yield of more than 100 bushels an acre from his 40-acre field of DeKalb hybrid corn. Sylvester reported he "had a stand of three and four stalks in every hill, and there's a good ear on every stalk." To beat the corn borer he tried to get a corn picker equipped with crushers that would grind the stalks so fine that the borers would be killed.

David L. and Selma (Jongbloedt) Lynch, 1947.

Threshing at the Westphal's. L to R: August Westphal, Pastor Mackdanz and Pete Westphal.

Bud Mace unloading grain at the Westphal farm.

Threshing Crew
Back row (L to R): Lyle Hawker, Jack Westphal, Harold Hawker, Pete Westphal, August Westphal, Margie Westphal, Ralph Hilton.
Front row: Deaney Hawker, Bud Mace, Marion Hawker, Bernie Westphal, Dale Hawker, Alvin Hawker, Darlene Hawker.

-1948-

LaVerne Fitzloff is crowned Blue Earth County 4-H Health Queen.

Mankato Free Press - "Cougar-Like" Animal Hunted Near St. Clair. St. Clair townsmen and farmers fearful of the lives of their children and livestock, today beat the countryside for a large, cougar-like animal seen by several persons in that area this week.

One, the eight-year-old son of Wilmar Davis, farmer living a mile and a half northeast of St. Clair, came upon the fawn-colored beast in the Davis farmyard Thursday when he came home from school. No one else was at home at the time.

The beast after snarling at the boy slinked off and before the youth could race to the farm home of Ray Fitzloff, a neighbor, to summon help the animal that had disappeared.

The only loss reported so far in McPherson Township, scene of the animal's latest wanderings, is a sow, found disemboweled on the farm of Ray Fitzloff Thursday.

Today St. Clair garage man Jack Pint again led a search for the animal and reportedly had engaged the assistance of the Ireland brothers in trying to spot the beast from the air.

Reports from the St. Clair community said the animal is about three times the length of a dog, fawn-colored with darker stripes and a long, rope-like tail that doubles over the beast's back when it bursts into long, leaping strides.

Many farmers have now reported seeing the beast. On Monday George Lynch, two miles south of St. Clair, spotted it and on Wednesday it was molesting hogs at night on the Ben Hiniker farm, a mile east of St. Clair. Coon hunters with their dogs were able to pick up the beast and chase it to the Le Sueur River bottoms. At night it has been heard by children of Bob Knutson's and Ray Fitzloff's emitting an eerie howl, mindful of a crying baby. Yesterday Bob Knutson spotted the strange beast while plowing.

At the Froelich turkey farm a special guard was thrown around the 12,000 birds Thursday night as a preventive measure. That farm is on the northeast edge of St. Clair.

This animal is presumed to be the same, which visited Faribault and Watonwan counties during the past three weeks and caused several hundred dollars loss to livestock owners who found remains of calves and hogs in their pastures. It also was reported in the Mapleton area in Blue Earth County.

-1949-

The Rev. Edward F. Brand, pastor of the Evangelical church in St. Clair, dropped dead of a heart attack while shoveling snow in front of his home. He had been in St. Clair for the past year and eight months.

St. Clair Telephone Exchange gets "Modern Touch". Dial telephones have replaced the St. Clair manually operated telephone exchange, affecting 81 village telephones and 88 rural telephones connected to the system.

The Mankato Citizens Telephone Company, which bought the St. Clair Company in 1947, converted the old system to dial operation by constructing an entirely new telephone plant in the village and adjacent rural districts.

A new building, housing the dial switchboard, was

built in St. Clair. Underground cables have replaced former pole lines in the village. All subscribers were given modern dial telephones. Rural lines radiating from the village are newly constructed.

The St. Clair Telephone Company was formerly owned and operated by Gene Fitzloff and his mother, Hulda Fitzloff. Mrs. Fitzloff operated the switchboard while her son maintained the plant. The first call made on the new system was made by St. Clair's Mayor George Hubmer to Mankato's Mayor Rolande F. Johnson.

Jack Fitzloff is named "Nutrena Feed Dealer."

Waiting for at the depot to ship the Fitzloff Turkey Fountains.

-1950-

January 1950 - *Mankato Free Press* – "Eric A. Carlstrom Construction Company was awarded the general contract at $157,000 for construction of an addition to the St. Clair School. The eight classrooms, six for the grades and two for the high school, auditorium-gymnasium will be completed at a later date. E.J. Erickson, St. Clair superintendent, said that enrollment there is 300 in the grades and high school with all classrooms being overcrowded presently."

June - Beginning of Korean War

Population of St. Clair - 318.

L to R: Harvey Kollos, Kenneth Kroenke and Lowell Pagenkopf - January 1951

Removing snow from St. Clair's streets. Raymond Froehlich operated the equipment.

-1952-

St. Clair Hi-Lites - On The Rim by Arboglast (Phil Eager) and Pete (Bill Hager). Arbie's notebook is on its last page and he's been thinking how much fun and the pleasure he's had following the St. Clair teams.

Exams are expected to soon put a lull in the BB season because players will soon lay down the glove and start the cramming, as final exams will soon be here. Diamond hostilities will virtually end on May 23 at St. Clair when they play host to Waldorf, a league leader.

Arbie and Pete have watched the changes from 6's to 5's to 9's upon the courts and fields and now find that this is to be their Last Round Up with sports, soon to be replaced by summer vacation, in second place with a 4-2 record. The five's were and my bet says, will be good next year. Ending in third this year and our nine's who lost only one man from last years and have gained, in my opinion, some good fresh young material this year. They ended in second last year and are going fairly well this year with a 5 and 2 record. So good luck and good winning to future St. Clair teams from A & P.

Last Sports Round-Up: Scots and St. Clair started their rivalry for '52 when St. Clair clipped them 7 to 2 on the home diamond. St. Clair who lost both baseball and football and even in basketball squeezed them out with only two hits. Juliar went all the way for St. Clair with Steffie and Borchert for Mapleton. Rapidan squeezed the "Pottermen" to a 6-7 nerve racking session of non-conference ball. The Raiders who won and lost two, even had Koch and Thompson hurl for them while Jim handled for St. Clair.

With regular Bob Riese now absent from the squad, Chuck Fitzloff and Jim Riese are sharing receiving chores, Jim being our Jack-of-all positions when needed, having played short last year.

Minnesota Lake won over St. Clair on home ground in ten innings on April 30. Score 9-7 favor of Minnies. St. Clair and Minnesota Lake have now a split of games apiece. St. Clair and Minnesota Lake have seven even in the hitting box. Gordie Juliar led St. Clair with three for five.

Pemberton jumped back at St. Clair on May 13, with Jans pitching and held us to a 3-2 victory. St. Clair had five hits for 22 trips and Pemberton three for 24. Jim Riese handling hurling for home team had eleven strike-outs with Jans having nine.

The Janesville Bears growled their way by the Saints in the eight innings of a close game. Gordie who started out had wild pitch fever, but fared well. Riese and Ford shined in the batting box with two apiece. The Bears led till the fifth and then three runs brought her up to four even, both got one even in the sixth and went back to tie the ball games. St. Clair and Janesville stayed tied in the seventh and St. Clair then went poof in the first of the eighth and Janesville won 6-5 on a lucky single with three men on.

The Pottermen have been hard hit by practice absentees being that farm work and senior and junior activities are becoming slightly obnoxious not only to students, but to everyone.

Baseball Leaders — Undecided. The season is expected to end in a scurry and will then be able and only then, to figure out leaders and winners of East District Six.

Herman Kroenke hauled milk for the St. Clair Co-op Creamery, ca. 1952

St. Clair Farmer Hunts Hay Blown Away in Storm. Has anyone seen a bale of hay land in his front yard this week? The Otto Witt's of near St. Clair are wondering what happened to 240 bales, which disappeared during a high wind and rainstorm last Friday afternoon.

Before the storm began there were 509 bales of hay standing in a field on the Witt farm, located three miles southeast of St. Clair along Highway 83, but a few minutes later 240 bales had disappeared.

Not a trace of the bales has been found except for a few straws in a neighbors bean field, according to Mrs. Witt. (An average bale weighs about 75 to 85 pounds.)

A corncrib was tipped over by the wind, and the Witt's had to replant 30 acres of beans, which had been stripped by the wind. Similar reports of wind damage to buildings and crops last Friday have been received in the St. Clair area.

July - Victor and Emma Shaver, Gary, Allene, Craig and Kevin host George Grim writer for the *Minneapolis Tribune* for a Sunday at the farm. Mr. Grim attended church services at the Evangelical United Brethren church, enjoyed breakfast with the family, toured the farm and attended a baseball game with Kilkenny. Mr. Shaver was a school board member and Emma was active with the PTA.

Ernie Hager delivering bottled gas.

Cooks at the wedding of Jim and Rosie (DeMars) Loeffler's wedding. L to R: Marie Juliar and niece, Mrs. C. Phillips, Mrs. Ray Pestka, Mrs. Herman Kroenke.

-1953-

January 20 - March of Dimes Benefit Basketball Game Played. The Pemberton-St. Clair basketball game held on January 20, 1953 for the benefit of the March of Dimes proved to be highly entertaining and profitable. Although St. Clair was victorious in the basketball game, the greatest satisfaction was derived from the knowledge that the benefit was financially successful.

Net receipts from the basketball game were $94.35. The concession stand receipts included a donation of twenty pounds of popcorn from George Macomber and totaled $21.01. Net receipts from the lunch were $10.11 and included cream donated by Mrs. Louis Fitzloff. The grand total was $125.47. This total was donated to the March of Dimes and credited to Pemberton and St. Clair.

The efforts of many people were instrumental in making this project a success. To all of them a special word of thanks is due.

Donkey Basketball Game – Yes, you read right! was held on March 10 in St. Clair. The proceeds from the event will go toward the Pep Club, so the students will not have to pay so much to follow their team to out of town games.

We ask the spectators and the players who come that night to be prepared for some good hearty laughs and lots of fun!

July - End of Korean War.

Kato Loss 1st to "Little" School. St. Clair became the first "little" school since the "1920"s to score a triumph over Mankato in district tourney play by edging the Scarlets 60-59 Friday night at Mankato State for the district consolation crown.

But in recording the unexpected upset, the Saints had to doggedly repel a last minute Mankato bid that whittled a 17-point deficit to one.

Working to perfection on both offense and defense, St. Clair amazed a capacity crowned by blazing to an 19-10 first quarter edge — and then leading the rest of the way by as much as 17 points. Only once in the game did Mankato control the score. That happened halfway through the first

The Charles Grams farm located one-half mile east of St. Clair. The barn was built in 1953 by Everad O'Brien.

quarter when the Scarlets established a short-lived 5-4 edge.

With center Gordy Juliar, forward Bob Fossum and guard Jim Riese linking up offensively, St. Clair swished 16 field goals and 28 free throws.

It wasn't until the final four minutes of play that Mankato made a serious bid for victory. Trailing 56-44, the Scarlets suddenly began to hit. With 1½ minutes to go Paul Moen pocketed two free shots to make it 56-51.

A Moen tip-in and a Brad Hanson lay-up further closed the gap to 58-55. Then at the final gun Hanson hit from the hole, but the Saints held a 60-59 triumph.

Riese probably saved the contest for St. Clair. In the final quarter, Mankato changed defensive tactics to a harassing press in an attempt to iron out difficulties. But the Scarlets couldn't fase Riese whose effective dribbling and passing led St. Clair floor play.

Juliar closes out his prep career with one of his finest contests. He netted 22 points and rebounded consistently. Fossum picked up 15 points, mainly on sweeping drive-ins. (Other players on the team were Kroenke, Hoppe, Buesing and Grams.)

St. Clair went on to win the Sub-District Championship - the first in the school's history.

St. Clair to Erect Building for Doctor and Dentist. The village of St. Clair, like many another Minnesota community, is without a doctor or a dentist, but has decided to do something about the situation.

The village, under the leadership of its Commercial Club and city officers, has begun a campaign to raise funds to put up a building for the practitioners.

A large part of the money already has been raised, but according to Jack Fitzloff, president of the St. Clair Commercial Club, an effort will be made to gain further backing for the project in a public meeting Monday. Fitzloff said that community leaders have already secured a young doctor who will locate in the community of 400 and feels sure that once permanent, adequate quarters are assured there will be little trouble getting a dentist to locate there. A home is now being built for the doctor.

Civic leaders feel that the community has much to offer, stressing the fact it is surrounded by a rich farming community, it has good travel facilities to Mankato where more serious medical cases can be referred.

Among other leaders in the drive and taking care of the legal aspects are Mayor George Hubmer and Atty. Nick Juliar.

Jerome Webster, superintendent at St. Clair, leaves for similar post at Winnebago, Minnesota.

A medical center for both a doctor and a dentist was built in St. Clair for $18,000. Dr. John Wohlrabe, MD was the doctor and Dr. Richard Hall, DDS was the dentist.

Ralph Hilton dies suddenly.

-1954-

Man Confesses St. Clair Thefts. Robert Pfarr, 27, Janesville, who gave himself up to the St. Clair village marshal this morning has been charged with second degree larceny after confessing to three St. Clair break-ins at about 2 a.m. Wednesday.

The charge, which could bring a maximum five-year sentence, was brought on a complaint signed by Deputy Sheriff Harold Childs, Blue Earth County Attorney Carl Peterson reported.

The three establishments broken into were Pagenkopf's General Store, Hager's Hardware and Pint Garage. Total amount of loot taken from the three places amounted to about $15 in cash.

St. Clair Marshal Lester McCollum said he was on the street in the business area of St. Clair at about 8 a.m. today when he heard that Pfarr was in a liquor store and wanted to see him.

When McCollum entered the store, Pfarr said, "Well I'm ready to go," the marshal reported.

McCollum brought Pfarr first to the police station from where he was later transferred to the Blue Earth County Jail. He is being held there today.

Pfarr told authorities that it was the first time he had ever been in trouble. He said he was an unemployed farm

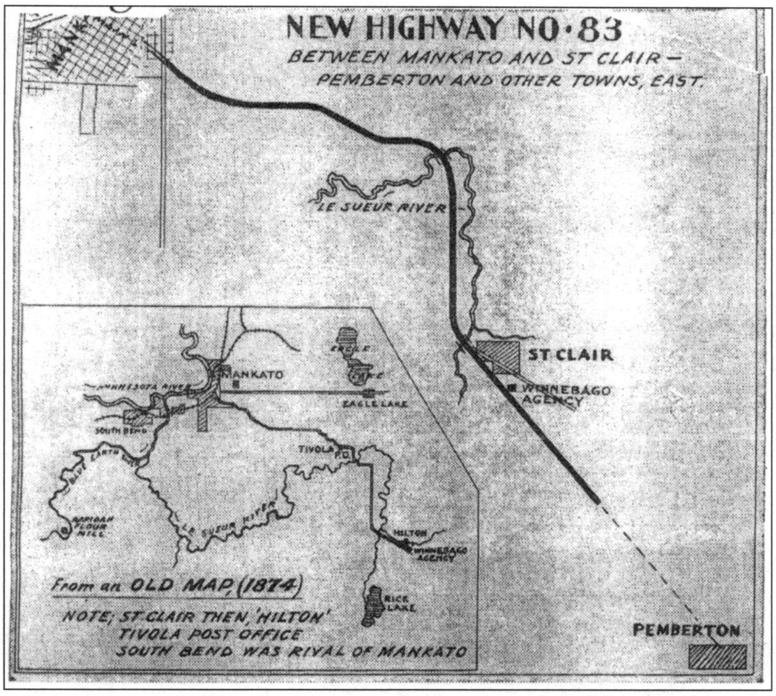

Drawing by Mankato artist A. Anderson showing the new Highway 83 passing on the south side of St. Clair.

laborer and needed money.

St. Clair Gets Doctor - Dr. and Mrs. John Wohlrabe moved to St. Clair in July to take over the practice of Dr. R.O. Juliar who retired. They lived with Mrs. Grace Chase until their new home was completed.

-1955-

St. Clair turns on streetlights for the first time. George Miller serving as mayor.

September 3-5 - St. Clair Celebrates Centennial. Darlene Cords, 15, daughter of Mr. and Mrs. Eddy Cords of St. Clair, is the ruling monarch of the celebration and the St. Clair Centennial Queen. Marilyn Fitzloff was her attendant.

-1956-

Minnesota State Highway #83 is built through McPherson Township.

-1959-

Beginning of Vietnam War.

Marty Winter on his Minneapolis Moline UB tractor in the late 1950s. The tractor was originally purchased new in about 1954 by Ernest Cords, who at the time was farming north of St. Clair. Several years later Marty Winter purchased the tractor and farmed with it until his retirement. The tractor is now owned by Tom Winter.

Albert Fitzloff as Miss St. Clair in 1955

Donavan Schwichtenberg as "Al Jolson" in the 1955 St. Clair Pageant

Albert Fitzloff as Miss St. Clair in the 1955 St. Clair Pageant
Standing behind Albert is Jack Fitzloff

Marvin Steel in the 1955 St. Clair Pageant

L to R: Ed Stagmeir, John Felber, Chub Wolcott, Currier Hubmer, Dr. Williams, Ray Fitzloff, Robert Zavoral, Everad O'Brien

The first night St. Clair turned on the street lights in 1955.
The building on the left is Frank Fisher's service station.

Dean Nyquist hauling pea vines

Louie and Evelyn Timmerman hauling Kingscrost corn from Lake Crystal to Waterville

Dean Nyquist hauling Kingscrost corn

Hager's Our Own Hardware

L to R: Rose's Meat Market (Fret-Frat Foods) and Wolcott Grocery Store, September 1955

Nyquist-Timmerman Enterprise

1956

TRUNK HIGHWAYS
STATE & COUNTY ROADS
TOWNSHIP ROADS
FARM DWELLING LOCATIONS

MC PHERSON TOWNSHIP

TOWNSHIP 107 NORTH RANGE 25 WEST

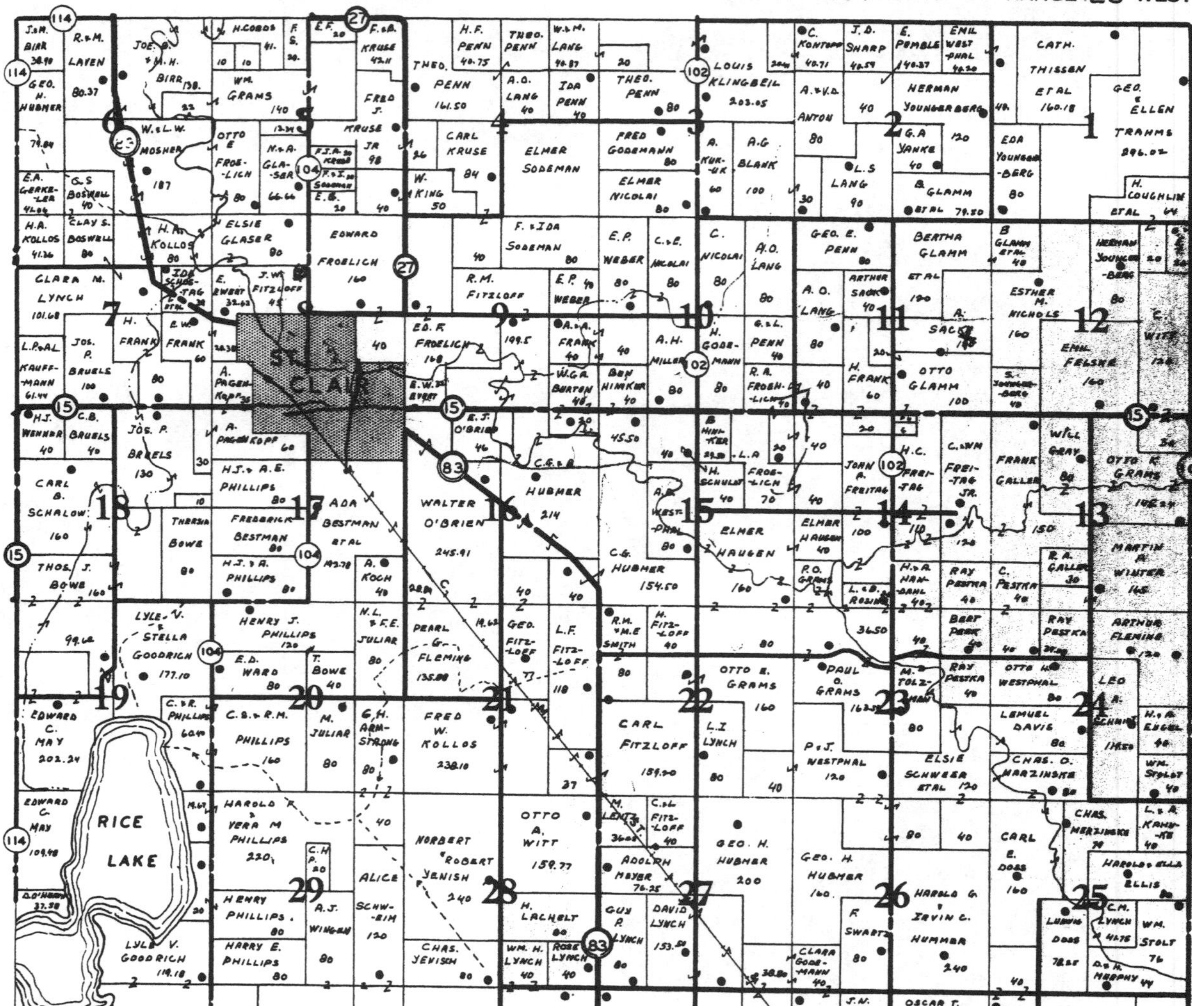

John Fossum in front of the creamery

John Fossum inside the St. Clair Creamery

Farm Bureau Tour (Farmers Union) in 1956
Back row (L to R): Steve Mahowald, Bert Denn, Harold Phillips, Robert Whiting, Henry Phillips, Donald Farm, unidentified, unidentified, Robert Farm, unidentified, Leslie Pietsch, Harry Wenner, Leo Kruse, Pete Westphal, Charlie Schalow, Dan O'Herin, Nick Phillips, Clete Phillips, Allie Trio. Front row: Esther Farm, Hildegard Denn, Vera Phillips, Arlene Phillips, unidentified, Darlene Whiting, Rose Wenner, Rose Pietsch, Adeline Westphal, Edith Kruse, Ruth Phillips

-1960-

Construction of the new elementary wing of the school included 12 elementary rooms, cafeteria and industrial arts shop. Remodeling in the high school building doubled the size of the library, science department, home economics department and commercial department. The new music department is located in the former lunchroom.

Population of St. Clair – 324.

-1961-

October 5 - St. Clair Creamery has $20,000 fire. Fire caused some $20,000 damage to the St. Clair Creamery Thursday night. It burned out the upper story and roof of the brick building built in 1904. Most damage was on the east side of the creamery where the roof and supporting gable caved in. The lower floor where cooling equipment is located did not receive any fire damage but plenty of water.

Cause of the fire was undetermined but manager Donald Burnett believed it might have come from wiring. It started on the upper side of the building near where electrical wires connect.

Mr. and Mrs. Charles Fitzloff of Mankato first spotted the fire, as they came through the village at about 10:15 p.m. They saw what looked like a light coming from the upper floor. They proceeded to the municipal liquor store to report the fire. Constable Herman Loge turned in the alarm for the volunteer fire department and eighteen men answered the call.

At the time of the fire the creamery was functioning as a weighing station collecting milk from farms around the village and stored it in coolers there for bulk hauling to the Le Sueur creamery, at Le Sueur, which owns this operation.

There was one casualty, fireman Herman Born's hand was injured when a ladder banged into it. A doctor checked it immediately and determined no bones were broken.

Two fire trucks and approximately 900

Dean Nyquist with his truck

May Flood of 1960

May flood of 1960
Albert Fitzloff pasture

Bridge east of St. Clair
May flood of 1960

May flood of 1960

1962

MC PHERSON

TOWNSHIP 107 N. RANGE 25 W.

CODE LETTER MC

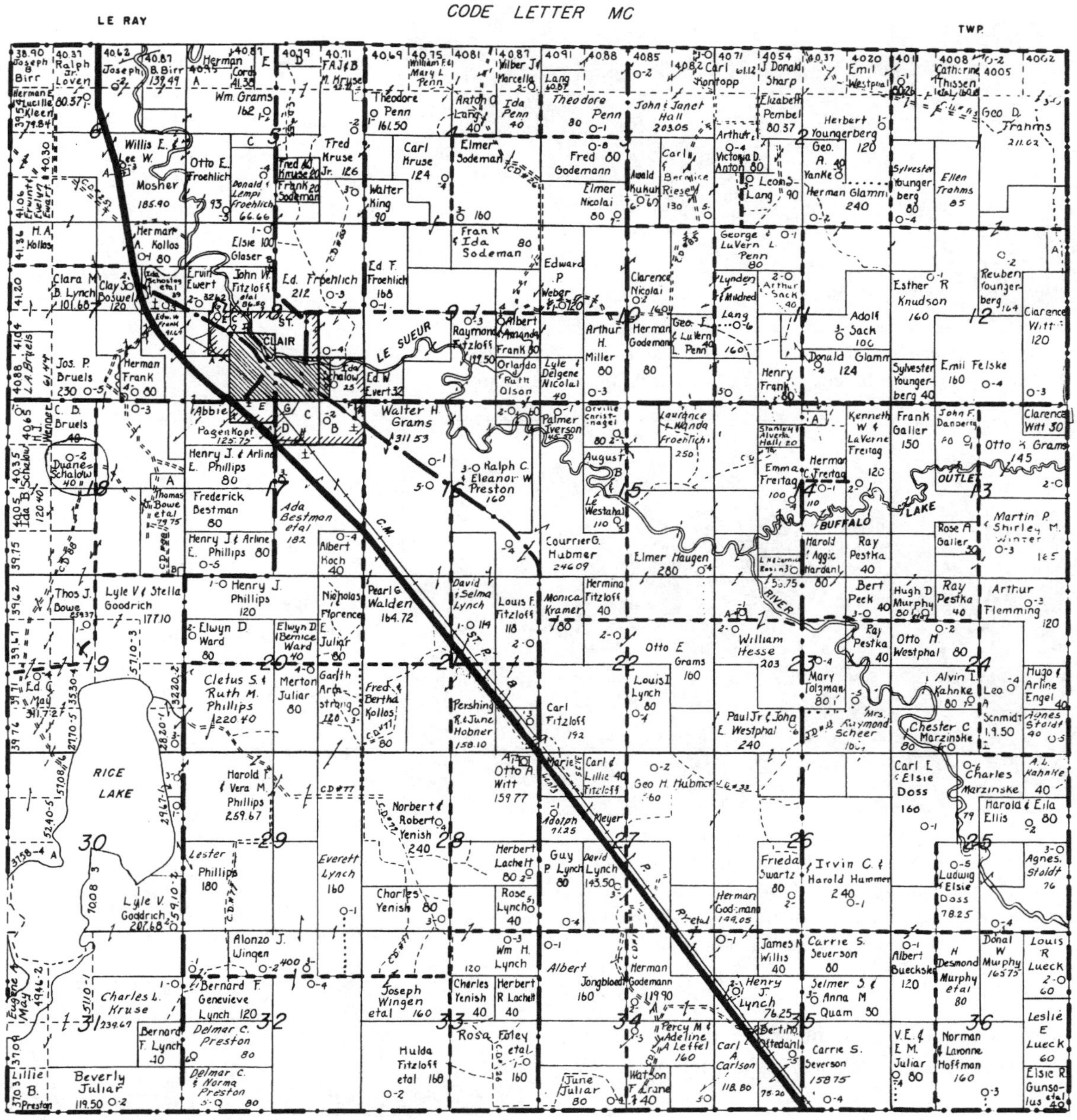

SMALL TRACT OWNERS

SEC	TRACT		ACRES
5	A	Ernest Cords	20.00
6	A	Joe & Clara Mosher	1.10
5	C	Norbert & Ardella Glaser	13.34
5	D	Erna Flitter	20.79
5	E	Frank Smith	20.44
8	A	Goldie Marzinske	1.25
8	B	Lafell J. Dieteman	0.50
8	C	Carl F Rose	5.99
8	D	Stanley W & Jeanette M Drake	.76
8	E	Small Residential Tracts	7.98
12	A	George D. Thrams	20.00
14	A	Aug. B. Westphal	6.00
17	F	Evelyn Timmerman	1.00
18	B	Blue Earth, Nicollet Co-op Elec Ass'n	0.25
17	A	Dean R Nyquist	1.00
17	B	Edward W. Evert	30.56
17	C	Robt. W & Anna Schostag	17.01
17	D	Nona Nyquist	12.62
17	E	Catholic Ch. & School	10.53
23	A	Paul O. Grams	0.44
17	G	Small Tracts Residential	4.74
18	A	E.W. Pagenkopf	10.00
30	A	Danniel C. O'Herin	37.58
17	H	McPhearson Cem.	-
28	A	Willard Witt	0.23

School bus drivers, L to R: Ervin Ewert, Herman Kollos, Gerald Kollos, Dean Nyquist, Bill Myers, Orville Christnagel, Marvin Hemshrot

St. Clair's Elementary School Teachers
Back row (L to R): Marsha Meyer, Margaret Cyphers, James Eaton, Marvin Schubbe, Sivert Olson, Judy Born, Kathy Wingen
Front row: Mary Lou Butzer, Jeanette Drake, Mildred Olson, Vera Lysdale, Harriet Morse, Dorothy Hesse

-1964-

February 1 - The St. Clair American Legion Schmidt Grams Post 475 honored their Charter members and St. Clair Auxiliary Charter members at a banquet and dance in the St. Clair Legion Hall on the occasion of the Post's 20th birthday anniversary. Charter Legion members presented awards were Elmer Haugen, 45 years as a legion member: John Sanborn, 40 years and Theodore Penn, with 20 years. Charter members of the Ladies Auxiliary presented with awards were Sarah Meany, gold star mother, Olga Fitzloff, Lillian Danberry, Mrs. John Sanborn, Mrs. Elmer Haugen, Ada Bestman, Abbie Pagenkopf and Mrs. Theodore Penn.

-1965-

March - First United States ground troop involved in Vietnam War.

-1966-

January 21 - Fire destroys the McPherson Town Hall.

July 1 - Medicare goes into effect.

Harvest States Elevator facility discontinued operation.

-1969-

MSC students have plans for St. Clair. The first community to get a comprehen-

feet of hose were used in fighting the fire. Don Burnett was the operator of the creamery at the time of the fire.

-1963-

June 17 - Bible reading or prayer banned in public schools.

November 22 - President Kennedy assassinated in Dallas, Texas by Lee Harvey Oswald. Lyndon B. Johnson sworn in as 36th President of the United States.

1965 spring flood - new bridge east of St. Clair

1965 spring flood – bridge north of St. Clair

Bumper crop - Lena Westphal with grandsons, Mike and Doug

Mike Westphal sitting on a 1941 B John Deere tractor
Natural corn dryer of the time

Hager Hardware before it was remodeled.

St. Clair State Bank

sive planning study under a new undertaking of the Mankato State College Urban Studies Department is St. Clair. The St. Clair study will go into phases such as land use, utility needs, economic potential, occupation and shopping area, population forecasts, income, education, and age and condition of structures.

The project at St. Clair was an attempt to involve undergraduate and graduate students in productive research on community problems — and to help a community at the same time.

School bus owned by the school district

Unlike many small towns St. Clair wasn't in danger of dying away. Because of its proximity to Mankato, St. Clair is beginning to experience growth. And it wasn't equipped to handle it.

"The town up to now has had no planning," admitted Lyle Goodrich, a village council member.

"We have nobody in this town who has any experience in planning," added Mayor Carl Fitzloff. Top priority is a new sewage system and treatment plant he added.

It was noted it would cost $200,000 to put in a new sewage system and plant. To apply for federal aid, the village needed a comprehensive plan.

Coffee party at the Harlan Frank farm - Myrna Winkelman and children, Norma Bruels and children, Ivadell Hunter and children, the Frank children

St. Clair school bus drivers, L to R: Lyle Splinter, Carl Rose, Marvin Hemshrot, Bill Hager, Orville Christnagel, Herman Kollos, Gerald Kollos, Ervin Ewert

Aaron, Lani and Clay Hager

Main Street looking east in the midst of sewer, curb and gutter project.

Main Street in the midst of sewer, curb and gutter project.

Main Street in the midst of sewer, curb and gutter project.

Hager Hardware after it was remodeled.

Drake's Station starting to take shape.

St. Clair Municipal Liquor Store and Splinter's Garage

Splinter's Garage

This was to be an improvement!
The 300 block of Main Street west

-1970-

Population of St. Clair - 409.

-1971-

Minnesota Elevator Inc. begins as a one-person elevator maintenance company.

-1972-

Mrs. Ralph Buesing is writing the St. Clair News for the *Janesville Argus*.

-1973-

Milwaukee Road filed notice to abandon 41-mile branch line and forget about service to St. Clair.

St. Clair Chapter host the State Holstein Convention on March 3, at Martinka Ballroom, (Kato Entertainment Center) Mankato, MN. Over 700 people attended the banquet.

-1975-

Vietnam War ends.

September 1 - Back In Time. Come this weekend, Ed and Pat Denn and thirteen year old son Mike, will put away the cowboy boots and hats in exchange for riding clothes of a different era-16th Century England. They will be riding at the Minnesota Renaissance Festival near Shakopee, Minnesota. They are members of the Mankato Saddle Club. The Denns are called Sir Ed, Lady Pat and Sir Mike.

-1977-

Since there had been no train service to St. Clair for some time, the tracks were removed and the bed leveled.

Gerald Hicks (Hicks Studio) was the official school photographer for many years, 1976

September - The first annual Scott A. Stolt Golf Tournament is held at the Terrace View Golf Course. This event was begun as a living memorial, a way for the parents, Dale and Mary Ann Stolt, to remember their son they knew for just a short time, and at the same time make a positive contribution to the lives of other children. Scott died of Sudden Infant Death Syndrome in April.

-1978-

If alumni from the St. Clair Public School were to return, they would find that the stark, cavernous halls they once frequented had been transformed into cozy passages lined in lively color. Footsteps are muffled in the halls where the carpeting has been laid and acoustic tiles have lowered the ceiling about three feet. Fluorescent lights replaced the incandescent bulbs. Hallways and classrooms are painted in various pastels, such as soft yellow, pink, mint, pale blue. Some of the students have made contributions to the improved appearance of the hallways by painting murals on the walls. In the elementary wing there are pictures of stories the children may know, such as "The Frog Prince." In the high school, seasonal scenes depict a snow-covered cabin in winter or a trout leaping out of a stream after insects. Other walls are covered by abstract drawings of arrows and angles. A broad, brown stripe that runs parallel to a staircase ends at a picture of an overturned bucket of brown paint.

-1979-

Bill and Janie Hager purchase the café formerly known as the D&L Diner from Lloyd and Dylane McCollum.

L to R: Helen Ward, Alvis More, Rich Ward and Bernie Westphal replaying a ballgame

-1980-

Population of St. Clair - 655.

December 3 - St. Clair Athletic Backers host "The Baldknobbers Jamboree" from Branson, MO. The Baldknobbers have been in existence since 1958, and are the oldest country music show and were known as the best in the business.

-1981-

December 2 - The Baldknobbers return to again perform at St. Clair High School Gym.

Cottonwood's Farewell - Tree is a living reminder of town's history, heritage. To St. Clair, say goodbye to your historic landmark. To the state, say goodbye to what may be your second largest tree.

At precisely 10 a.m. Saturday, the chainsaw will roar. In a few short minutes a historic cottonwood will be reduced to mere second-class firewood.

Taking down a tree this size represents quite a challenge. Due to its location, just a slight miscalculation could result in a flattened home on one side or a smashed garage on the other. If the tree happens to be hollow, as many area residents guess, then the danger of an accident increases.

For the owner, the tree has been a constant source of worry. Even finding a contractor to remove the tree was not an easy job. One was contacted who agreed to do the job until he actually saw the tree. Another was willing for a mere $2,800.

Finally, Thorson Tree Service from Judson and Northside Towing stepped in and agreed to remove the tree for a pittance. Both firms view the tree as a challenge, and if all goes well their public relations image will not suffer either.

To remove this tree they will use a 50-ton wrecker and a special chainsaw with a 60-inch bar imported from Washington State.

Saturday's event is expected to draw a big crowd, and for those interested, it is suggested you arrive early.

By Don Gordon – *Mankato Free Press* - December 1981

St. Clair is quiet, probably typical, southern Minnesota community where few events happen that make the news. Take January, for example. The only newsworthy item on the calendar is the impending wake. The exact date of the wake is not available, only sometime in January, but nevertheless, it is an event that has stirred considerable talk, and almost if not all of the residents are already somewhat saddened. This wake is rather unusual in that it will not be for a person but for — of all things — a cottonwood tree.

This tree is special for several reasons. First, it is probably the largest tree in Blue Earth County. Resident Stan Drake, who measured the tree this week, found it to be 332 inches in circumference at the breast height. This puts it just 33 inches short of matching the state's biggest tree, also a cottonwood, which is located in Rice County. Despite their best efforts, Gwen Peterson's 14-member second grade class of St. Clair just couldn't quite "stretch" completely around the town's landmark.

Second, the tree has become a landmark for the town. Whether it is a grade scholar or an octogenarian, they all know about St. Clair's big cottonwood.

Third, because of its age (estimates range from 200-300 years or more), the tree serves as a living reminder of the history and heritage of the town.

As to why St. Clair's landmark cottonwood is coming down there is no secret – it has become a dangerous liability. The tree owner, Ivernie Galston, discovered that during a recent storm when one branch from the tree demolished a neighbor's garage. After a visit from a tree surgeon her hopes of saving the tree by pruning were dimmed – the tree has a soft center – it must go.

By Don Gordon – *Mankato Free Press* - December 17, 1981

The Diner Crew
L to R: Mary Jane Hager, LaVerne Freitag and Lois Bloemke

The Diner Crew
L to R: Ardis Savick, Lani Hager and Adrienne Verschelde

-1982-

The cutting down of St. Clair's cottonwood tree drew hundreds of spectators and much news coverage. It took one hour and fifteen minutes to fell the second largest tree in the state, which measured more than 27 feet around and stood 110 feet high. It was the largest tree in Blue Earth County and believed to be the second largest tree in Minnesota.

A little bit of history came crashing down in St. Clair on Saturday as the cottonwood tree estimated to be 150 to 200 years old was felled on the Ivernie Galston property. Lowell Thorson of Thorson Tree Service in Judson took the first slice out of the tree. The tree measured more than 27 feet around and 100 feet high. Tree service employee Danny Wilson cut into the heart of a tree that had grown up with Southern Minnesota. The tree is believed to have been the second oldest in Minnesota, but a slice will be taken to Mankato State University to determine the cottonwood's exact age.

Mankato Free Press - February 13, 1982

As Townsfolk Watched, St. Clair's Old Cottonwood Came Down. The Bigger They Are…The Harder They Fall.

One of the oldest trees in Minnesota crashed to the earth Saturday, leaving a huge bare spot in Ivernie Galston's back yard and a hint of emptiness in her heart.

About 300 onlookers stopped by yesterday to watch with Galston as professional tree-cutters brought down the landmark in St. Clair, Minnesota. Old age had doomed

Coffee time at "The Diner"
L to R: Audie Blank, Gene Phillips, Ron Engeleby, George Fitzloff, Bruce Miller, Elroy (Stub) Juliar and Stan Drake

the tree, prompting Galston to part with it, albeit somewhat reluctantly.

"My daughter—she couldn't understand why I was getting so worked up about getting rid of it—she was the first one to start crying when it fell," Galston said last might. "I've got a lot of memories but I just want a little piece to keep for myself."

It took one hour and 15 minutes to fell the tree.

"Ain't too many people that cut trees this size," said Lowell Thorson of Thorson Tree Service, Judson, Minn., which handled yesterday's cutting. "They ain't crazy enough."

Observers had planned to determine the tree's age by counting its growth rings. However, it broke unevenly in the middle when it fell, Galston said, making it difficult to see the number of rings.

Workers used a cable pulled taut by a tow truck to keep the tree from smashing into nearby houses. One neighbor boarded her windows with plywood, but her house suffered no damage.

Minneapolis Tribune - February 13, 1982

March 13 - The Minnesota Vikings football team comes to St. Clair to play basketball.

THE MYSTIC TREE - by Mabel Juliar Nisbet

That cottonwood with singing leaves still guards old building of the town.

Each boarded window, silent, grieves.

That cottonwood with singing leaves once lulled a child, who still believes it friend with white fluff floating down

That cottonwood with singing leaves
Still guards old buildings of the town.
Farmers, keeper of country store, doctor serving rich and poor the same
Are jaunting muddy streets once more.
Farmers, keeper of country store, and over all that big tree's roar
As windstorm, rain and lightning came.
Farmers, keeper of country store, doctor serving rich and poor the same.

The tree, alive with silver leaves while kin are names in burial grounds, and aged witness now perceives the tree, alive with silver leaves.
True witness to the tale time weaver that cottonwood, sturdy, glory crowned.
The tree, alive with silver leaves while kin are names in burial ground.

"This was a prize winning Trio of triolets about the large cottonwood in the front part of Boswell's yard. It tells its own story. However, it was strange that I wrote it the same year that the cottonwood in the Wolcott yard was cut down and received the publicity." — Mabel Juliar

-1983-

The City of St. Clair builds a new building on the location of the former St. Clair Creamery. The building will house the city office, the St. Clair Fire Department and

As the townsfolk watched, St. Clair's old cottonwood tree came down in February 1982.

L to R: Splinter's Garage, Hager's Diner and Hemshrot's Grocery

Combining on the John Danberry farm

John Danberry Sr. raking hay

1953 Homecoming Royalty – Queen Janice (Thrun) Seys and Jim Riese

St. Clair school cooks (L to R): Muriel Mace, Judy Wilder and Ruth Nicolai

Amos Owens
Painted by Marian Anderson

St. Clair school logo – the St. Clair Indians

will also have a social room and a small kitchen. The old city hall building is sold to the Grams-Schmidt American Legion Post 475.

-1985-

March 30 - The Minnesota Vikings return to St. Clair for another evening of fun and games.

-1986-

Winnebago Agency building was burned down because it was beyond repairing or relocating.

August 16 & 17 - The first All-School Reunion of the St. Clair School.

Welcome to St. Clair
"A Community of Excellence"

1989 Minnesota State 9-Man Champions

The Haugen Meat Market/Hager's Diner and Hemshrot's Grocery Store before demolition

-1987-

June 1 - The post for the city's tornado siren was sawed off. Value of the siren and pole was about $2,000.

September 18 - Marian Anderson, national famed area artist started a painting of Amos Owens, a Dakota Indian chief as she enjoys her artist in residence at the St. Clair school.

-1988-

St. Clair school district drops out of pairing talk with the Janesville and Waldorf-Pemberton school districts.

-1989-

Indian Logos: The MCLU and State Education Department notified local school to drop Indian-related nickname.

St. Clair High School Football Team wins 9-man State Championship Title.

Population of St. Clair - 655.

The Haugen Meat Market/Hager's Diner and Hemshrot's Grocery Store before demolition

-1990-

May - The former Hemshrot Grocery and Hendricks (old meat market/café) buildings are demolished.

-1991-

January 16 - Persian Gulf War begins. Permanent cease-fire of this war occurred on April 6.

Demolishing Haugen Meat Market/Hager's Diner and Hemshrot's Grocery Store

The Haugen Meat Market/Hager's Diner and Hemshrot's Grocery Store are demolished

Reunion of the St. Clair Class of 1953
Back row (L to R): James Riese, Gordon Juliar, Robert Linde, William Hager, Barbara (Lotton) Goettl, Bernard Westphal, Gloria (King) Linde, Charlotte (Page) Jongbloedt. Front row: Edward Kroenke, Ivadell (Myers) Hunter, Elvera (Freitag) Hall, Janice (Thrun) Seys, Betty (Mabee) Kruse.

Block by block......

With your help a very special building will take shape in St. Clair's new Memorial Park.

The pavillion is designed to be the focal point of the park. By providing an indoor picnicing area, storage space and restroom facilities the pavillion will be enjoyed by our community and visitors alike.

To achieve our goal of completing the structure by the fall of 1994 we need to raise $25,000. This amount will ensure proper construction of the pavillion and completion of the ball diamond.

Concrete blocks will cost us $1.00 each and the pavillion will need over 3,200 blocks to complete. Then there's the windows, doors, sinks, shingles and much more.

Your donation will help to make the pavillion a reality. Whether it's one dollar, ten dollars or one thousand dollars your contribution will be applied directly to the cost of building the pavillion.

To donate financially simply send a check to:

St. Clair Memorial Park Fund - Pavillion
P.O. Box 262
St. Clair MN 56080

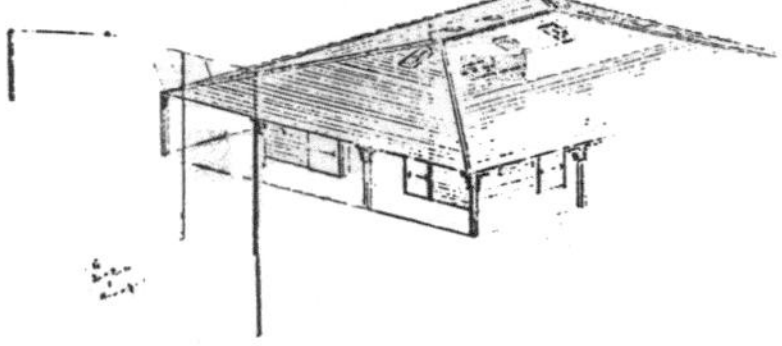

St. Clair Park Board

St. Clair to get new restaurant. The land, owned by the St. Clair American Legion, will be leased to the St. Clair Development Corp., which, in turn, will lease the building to the restaurant's operator. Uncle Albert's Café opened on October 21st.

-1992-

Housing started booming. Phase I of the Goodrich Addition is started with the availability of 37 lots. The subdivision – together with the school project and smaller projects such as the opening of a restaurant last fall, the planned construction of a convenience store this fall and the expansion of the local bank – have people in St. Clair sensing growth in the air.

November 13-14 - Cindy Glamm is awarded the Women of Today Presidential Medallion. At the time Cindy was serving as Secretary of the United States Women of Today. Other St. Clair ladies attending the Women of Today convention held in Willmar were Wanda Coult-District 20 Director, Brenda Phillips-Chapter President, Robin Coult-Chapter Secretary, Sharon Juliar-State Delegate, Debbie Eilrich and Pam Huck.

-1993-

April 14 - Sadie Lynch Celebrates 102 Years. St. Clair native, Sadie Lynch, dismissed with a wave of her hand the fact that she has lived to be 102 years of age. "Nobody wants to hear about that," she said.

Mrs. Lynch was born on April 11, 1891 to Isabelle and John Fields. She went to country school, then St. Clair Public School and went on to become a teacher herself. She married James Lynch on November 19, 1918. They farmed southeast of St. Clair and had two daughters, Doris (Stanley Steel) and Isabelle (Ernest Lorentz).

Cenex C-Store holds "Grand Opening." Goodrich third addition developed for added housing.

Bernard Westphal farm after a tornado in June 1994.

St. Clair new school mascot –
St. Clair Cyclones

August 28 - St. Clair Economic Development Authority Sponsored a Hog Roast. A fundraiser for the city's Memorial Park was held at the Palmer's Bus Service Garages. Approximately five hundred people attended and contributed approximately $1,200. The group served over five hundred adults and children. "D. J. Del" provided entertainment. The hogs were donated by Alvis More and Jerry Phillips.

-1994-

January 5 - Housing Boom is Building in St. Clair. From 1983 to 1992, St. Clair saw the construction of just one residential building – a duplex built in 1988. But from October 1992 through today, 10 new homes have been built, three more are under construction and options have been sighed on six additional lots in a new housing division in the city. Beyond that, an eight-unit apartment complex for seniors has been completed on two other lots.

In conjunction with the Minnesota Valley Action Council, the City Council worked up a plan for a new subdivision and adjacent city-park. When the number reaches 27 to 28, the city will be ready to move to the second phase of the subdivision. Work will then begin on preparing additional 25 lots on the 35-acre plot purchased by the city for the subdivision and eight-acre park.

St. Clair shows off school addition on September 8th, 1994.

-1995-

Darla and Heather Zell lease Uncle Albert's Café.

Wanda Domeier opens Village Bakery.

Ripplinger Hardware closes, ending an era of hardware business for St. Clair.

-1996-

January - The Amberfield Place apartments are built.

April - St. Clair Elevator closed.

St. Clair School Board votes to drop "Indian" nickname on September 17th. It was very depressing to see our Indian mascot that was so proudly presented by our school leave us. By an overwhelming vote on November 6th the new nickname "Cyclones" will be the school mascot.

September - Minnesota Twins player Kirby Puckett visits the St. Clair School.

September 22 - Janesville man's life taken in tragic accident: Steven Dimmel, age 46, from Janesville, Minnesota, died when his plane crashed into a corn field about a mile and a half from St. Clair, in Section 10 of McPherson Township.

-2001-

St. Clair's Kathy's Café closes.

School board shows off plans for its "futuristic school" in February as the district voters had approved a $10.5 million bond referendum in June of 2000. Groundbreaking took place in mid-May.

50th Reunion of the St. Clair Class of 1947
Back row (L to R): Robert Grams, Dale Tachney, Doris (Freitag) Folkerts, Eillen (Hodapp) Goebel, Cecelia Hager, Nicolas Cords, Kenneth Kroenke.
Front row: Virgene (Glamm) Volkmann, Donna (DeMars) Danberry, Vera (Kruse) Sullivan, Beverly (Myers) Born, Delma (O'Brien) Schmahl, Deloris Preston

TJ's Café opens for business in August.

September 11 - A New Day of Infamy - A devastating attack against the people of the United States. Two airplanes are flown into the "Twin Towers" in New York City, destroying them, one plane flown into the United States Pentagon and another plane crash landing in a field. Thousands of people were injured and killed. "Make no mistake, the United States will hunt down and punish those responsible for these cowardly acts," President George W. Bush.

-2002-

May 22 - St. Clair students to be dismissed for the year so the 1922 school building can be demolished by the end of May. The high school section of the new building project has been completed and teachers and students moved into the new area in the middle of May.

May 28 - St. Clair students building a greenhouse learn and show persistence.

November 6 - "A Star for Service" is the theme for the Veterans Day ceremony held at the St. Clair Public School remembering St. Clair veterans.

-2003-

March 20 - President George W. Bush declares war against Iraq.

Dedication for new school building held on June 20, 2003.

Members of the Zion Methodist Church hold last service in June. Jonas and Angie Nissen of Mankato purchase this building and plan for a community dinner theatre and are calling it "Bell Tower Place."

-2004-

March 20 - Annual Meeting of McPherson Farmers Mutual Fire Insurance Company is held. The current officers and directors are James Riese-president, Dale Westphal-vice president, Clarice L. Germo-secretary/treasurer, Jeff Boesch, Russell Christensen, Ronald Marzinske and Todd Stencel-directors. Karon Storjohann is the office manager and Margaret Zabel and Adrienne Verschelde are office secretaries. Douglas Eustice is the fire safety representative. Total Admitted Assets are $1,399,898. Total Liabilities are $564,103. The numbers of policies in force December 31, 2003, were 1,319 with a total of $447,250,635 of coverage.

Southern Valley/Crystal Valley Fertilizer Plant closes, school buys property, Main Street Auto buys buildings.

November - Crystal Valley Co-op sells the Cenex Store to Tweeten's from Hartland, MN.

December 17 - "Tweeten Corner Stop" Convenience

Cenex Gas and Convenience Store

Store opens under the ownership of Arlo and Judy Tweeten. It will provide 24-hour pay-at-the-pump BP brand gasoline, provide a deli and offer a wide variety of goods.

-2005-

June 23-26 - St. Clair celebrates Sesquicentennial.

1948 Chevy Coup owned by Dick Fitzloff. Troy Zabel is taking it out for a joy ride. The house in the background was formerly owned by Art Cords and later Hubert Johnson.

This house was built by Henry Schalow in 1918.
It was the Ludwig Grams house.
This house is one of the few original looking structures in St. Clair.

This chicken house on the old Dewey Andrew's farm is one of the few original looking structures still standing today. Bud and Leona Mace lived on this farm and their son Gary owns the property.

My Hometown

The folks that live in my hometown
Are wonderful and true;
You'll never find more faithful friends
If you look the whole world through.

The spots I cherished as a child
Come back to me, and then,
For just a moment, I relive
Those happy days again.

The hills of home still beckon me,
And oft I do return
To visit scenes and folks I love —
Dear ones for whom I yearn.

There'll always be a cherished spot
Within my heart, 'tis true,
For my hometown and all the folks
Who've been so kind and true.

Eleanor Pederson Hillemann

Little Towns

I love the look of little towns
Where one will always find
The neighbors up and down each street:
The friendly, helpful kind.

I love the sweetness of small towns
With frangrance in the air,
Where flowers bloom in every yard,
With beauty everywhere.

I love the wealth of little towns
Where the folks are able
To grow their gardens fresh and green
For the family table.

I love the hope of little towns
Where everyone, it seems,
Can work so well together there
To realize fond dreams.

Virginia Katherine Oliver

The Charles Pagenkopf family

CHAPTER EIGHT

Our Families

ADAMS, ROBERT

Robert Adams the son of Donald and Lorna (Oldenburg) Adams was born on December 6, 1957. His parents were farmers in the Mapleton area. Robert is a Boiler Serviceman. He married Karma Lang who was born on July 8, 1962. Karma is the daughter of Clyde and Ruth (Thompson) Lang. She is from the Detroit Lakes area and is a social worker at the Mapleton Community Retirement Home, Mapleton, MN. Their children are Molly who was born on July 30, 1988, an eleventh grader, and Sam who was born on February 26, 1990, in the ninth grade at St. Clair Public School.

By Robert Adams

ALEXANDER, JOSEPH

Joseph Leonard Alexander (1806-1904) married Mary Myott (1825-1884) and had fourteen children. Mary was either 50 or 100% Indian. They lived in the Tivoli area near St. Clair. Joseph was a teacher in the Tivoli district and also the U.S. Indian Agent for the Winnebago Indians. One of his daughters, Hannah married Oddo Phelps and lived near Good Thunder. The Phelps family included 11 children, one of the daughters was Hollie Marie and she was my mother.

Another child of Joseph and Mary was Newell. Newell's son, Fred Alexander (1900-1992), married Bertha Timmerman (1903-1997). She was the daughter of John and Anna Timmerman. Fred and Bertha are buried in the St. John's Evangelical Lutheran Cemetery at St. Clair.

Joseph was not a popular man, perhaps because of his religion-Catholic, Scottish heritage, or his kinship with the Indians.

By Phil Forrey

ANDERSON, OSCAR

Oscar Anderson, the son of Christ and Lena Anderson, was born in 1887 in Jackson County, Heron Lake, Minnesota. He was a member of the St. John's Evangelical Lutheran Church Board and was a farmer. On October 8, 1913, Oscar married Mary Kollos, the daughter of Clemens and Augusta Kollos, at St. John's Evangelical Lutheran Church, St. Clair. Mary was born in 1894 in Le Ray Township. Mary belonged to the St. John's Lutheran Ladies Aid. For many years she was a cook at St. Clair Public School. Oscar and Mary lived at 312 Front Street West. They had two children Harold (Verna Herzberg) and Evelyn (Alvin Bjornson). After they retired from farming in the mid 1940's they moved to St. Clair.

Oscar died in 1966 and Mary in 1981. They are buried in the St. John's Evangelical Lutheran Cemetery, St. Clair.

BAER, FREDRICK

Fredrick W. Baer was born on July 11, 1899, in Balaton, MN. On November 27, 1924, he married Augusta Buesing, the daughter of August and Anna (Beckman) Buesing, at Balaton, MN. Augusta was born on July 6, 1903.

Fred and Augusta farmed for several years in that area and in 1934 they moved to St. Clair. Fred worked at the Guaranteed Gravel and Sand Co. in Mankato for 25 years until his retirement. He then helped his brother-in-law Herbert Buesing move buildings. On this job he was moving a grain storage bin and while transporting it became entangled to high voltage wires and was electrocuted.

"Gustie" worked as a cook at the St. Clair School. Fred and Gustie lived at 316 Front Street West.

Fred and Augusta had four children–Lester, Eugene, Marlene and Elwin.

Fred died on October 21, 1971, and Augusta died on April 25, 1988.

BESTMAN, JOHN

From *History of Blue Earth County* by Thomas Hughes-1909

The industrial success of John Bestman is centered around his splendid farm of two hundred and eighty acres in section 17 McPherson township, his connection as director and stockholder in the St. Clair State Bank, and his presidency of the Home Insurance Company. Mr. Bestman has been a resident of Blue Earth County since 1865, and during this time has evidenced the ability to rise above difficulties and discouragement, and from a very small beginning carve his way unaided to comparative wealth and assured influence and position.

Coming to America in 1864, from Holstein, Northern Germany, where he was born in July 20, 1842, Mr. Bestman is one of the three survivors of the seven children of Henry and Anna Bestman, the former of whom was an artisan who spent his entire life in his native land. Arriving in Mankato in 1865, Mr. Bestman had but an imperfect knowledge of the language of the realm, also of its custom and possibilities. He was equipped, however, with a thorough training in blacksmithing, and this he followed in Mankato about four years, and in St. Clair for ten years. He then engaged in farming on the place he now occupies, and has made a decided success of produce and stock raising. He has invested heavily in improvements of all kind, especially high-grade machinery, and his family and stock are comfortably and modernly housed and maintained.

In 1869, Mr. Bestman married Henrietta Beyersdorf, a native also of Germany, and of the union there are three sons and one daughter living, two children being deceased. Of the living children, Charles H. lives in St. Paul, John H. and Helena A., are at home, and Herbert F. is assistant cashier of the New Richland State Bank. Mr. Bestman takes commendable interest in politics, and at the present time is treasurer of the St. Clair School Board. He has been connected with the St. Clair State Bank since 1907 and with the Home Insurance Company since 1881. Both enterprises are a credit to the locality, and an index to the sterling character and public spiritedness of the men directing their destiny. The career of this well known farmer, banker and business man should be an inspiration to the youth struggling against odds, and especially to the stranger from foreign shores who arrives here without money or influence.

John Bestman died in April 1922. Henrietta died in January 1936. Both are buried in the St. John (Bestman) Cemetery in St. Clair, Minnesota.

John H. Bestman was born in 1877 in McPherson Township. He married Helen "Lena" Krause (1876-1931) in 1911 and they had a son Frederick J. After Helen's death he married Ada Fields Dalton (1884-1976), in 1934. Ada was the daughter of John and Isabelle (Larabee) Fields. Ada taught school for 15 years in Blue Earth County. They lived at 210 Front Street East.

John H. died on September 23, 1919, and Ada died on October 28, 1931.

Frederick (Fritz) J. Bestman was born in 1913. He married Eileen Juliar (1914-1963), the daughter of John and Inez (Walters) Juliar. They lived and continued the Bestman family farming operation. They had three sons, David, Steve and Gary. "Fritz" died in 1993.

Helena Bestman was a music teacher in St. Clair. Helena died at age 62 of pneumonia. She was taken ill while preparing for a music recital.

BLANK, ADOLPH

Adolph "Audie" Blank was born in 1912 to Adolph and Elfrieda (Bollman) Blank at Muscatine County, Iowa. He moved to St. Clair in 1923, and attended Schorn's country school in Blue Earth County. He married Charlotte Oftedahl on September 15, 1937, at Medo Lutheran Church, Blue Earth County. Charlotte was born in 1915 and was the daughter of Gerhard and Bertina (Quam)

Audie & Charlotte Blank

Oftedahl in Medo Township.

They farmed in the St. Clair area until 1952, when they moved to St. Clair, living at 109 Front Street South. They were members of St. John's Evangelical Lutheran Church. Audie enjoyed dancing, traveling and fishing. Charlotte was a homemaker, worked as a waitress at the 400 Café in Mankato and at the St. Clair Café. She also worked in the kitchen of the St. Clair School and was a member of the St. John's Evangelical Lutheran Ladies Aid.

Audie and Charlotte had two daughters Beverly (Howard Olson) and Barbara (Walt Masel).

Charlotte died in 1996 and Audie in 2001. They are buried in the St. John's Evangelical Lutheran Cemetery in St. Clair.

BOLLMANN, PETER

Peter Bollman, the son of Juergen and Eliza Bollman, was born in 1880 in Germany. He came to America and received naturalization papers on November 5, 1892, and located in Walcott, Iowa. In 1907 he was married to Martha Beckmann, the daughter of Jacob (1851-1929) and Johanna (1857-1939) Beckman, also farmer in Walcott. Martha was born on October 17, 1890. Peter and Martha first farmed in Iowa, living in a log cabin with their family. In 1917 they were living in Lorraine, Wisconsin, where they farmed, raised a large vegetable garden and operated a sawmill. When the sawmill burned in the early 1920's they moved to a farm north east of St. Clair, Minnesota. (This farm was located in Sec. 2 currently owned by Spencer Wood.) They built all of the buildings with lumber, which was brought from the sawmill in Wisconsin. They later moved to St. Clair and lived in the house just to the west of the former Methodist Church. Peter was very handy at repairing and fixing as well as doing paintings, one of which hung in the liquor store. He was the handyman around town. They lived at 303 Main Street East.

Martha was one of eleven children. Two of her sisters, Anna (August Buesing) and Helene (Jacob Schuldt) also came to the St. Clair area.

Bollmann children at work
L to R: Edna, Alma, Marcella, Lawrence and Albert

Peter Bollmann, Sr. homestead northeast of St. Clair

Peter and Martha Bollmann family in 1943
Back row (L to R): Marcella, William, Albert, Lawrence, John, Edna, Alma, Helen. Front row: Peter, Martha, Violetta, Elsie behind Paul, Marie, Peter, Valera.

Peter and Martha were parents of seventeen children. Lawrence (1908-1978) (Dorothy Maulden), Edna (1910-1978) (Oscar Froehlich), [see separate story], Albert, Alma (1912-1971), Marcella (1914-1957) (Alfred Mullerleile), and twins Martha and Mable (1916-1916). Violetta (1917) (Arlie Fellow), William John (1920) (Janet Pierce). Pearl (1922-1922), Marie (1923) (Ivan Richman), Valera, Helen (1927) (Irven Birdsall), Elsie (1930), Peter and Paul (1933) (Mildred Radford).

Albert (1911-2002) farmed in the St. Clair area for a short time before moving to their farm in Medo Township. He was married to Agatha Oftedahl (1914-2000), the daughter of Gerhard and Bertina (Quam) Oftedahl. They had a daughter Carol (Louie Fitterer).

William (1918-2001) grew up in the St. Clair area. He married Vera Schostag (1914-1996) on April 1, 1941. She was the daughter of Fred and Ida (Frank) Schostag. Bill served in the U.S. Army Medical Corps from 1942-1945. Bill and Vera lived 100 Park Street South in St. Clair. He was a bulk petroleum agent for Standard Oil Company from 1947 until his retirement in 1976. It is remembered that he carried fuel with a five-gallon pail when he first started his business. They had three children, Larry (Bonnie Horazdovsky/Patricia Roberts), twins James (In Suk Yi) and Judith (1948-2004).

Valera (1919) was married to Charles Lindrud and has two stepchildren Charles, Jr. and Cathleen. Valera and Charles were the parents of Robin and Cory. Valera raised her family in St. Clair, living in an apartment above the Pagenkopf Grocery Store.

Peter (1930-1988) was married to Carol Patton and they raised their family living in the Bollman house next to the Methodist church. Their children are Peter (1954) (Janet Maureen), Penny (1950) (Darwin Winter), Donna (1957) (Johnny Martinez), Timothy (1958) (Tammy Enger), Thomas (1959) (Nancy Etta), Terri (1960) (Jeffery Goyne), Charles (1961) (Marry Morrison), Jody (1963) (Larry Hall), Amy (1967) (Tim Danberry) and Douglas (1969-1969). Pete was a lather for Hendley's, owned a green house in Mankato and then worked for Brown Printing in Waseca, Minnesota.

Paul (1933) was a plasterer and carpenter for over 30 years. He worked for Hendley-Artcraft, Craftsman Plastering, Ken Kroenke and Jim Mork. He was married to Mildred Radford of Mankato. Paul has retired and is living in Mankato.

By Paul Bollmann

L to R: Joan Froehlich, Paul, Pete and Helen Bollmann

BORGWARDT, HENRY

Henry Borgwardt was born on April 10, 1890, in Thornton, Illinois. On September 25, 1912, he married Anna Friday (1892), the daughter of Charles and Albertina (Papke) Friday, in Brookings, South Dakota. They moved to St. Clair in 1933. The City of St. Clair employed Henry as constable and he was also in charge of the water department. He also was a custodian at the school. Henry and Anna operated the hotel and café for two years. They lived at 305 Main Street West.

Henry and Anna had four children: Verlyn "Dale" Lola (Eldo Ewert) (1919-1991), Myrtle (Ralph McKibben/Archie Cray), Velma (Richard Friedrichs/Ralph Bunde) and Carl.

Henry died in 1975 and Anna in 1982. They are buried in St. John's Evangelical Lutheran Cemetery, St. Clair.

BORN, ROLAND

Roland Born, the son of George and Martha Born, was born on March 21, 1921. On November 30, 1944, he married Ila Mae Kopke, the daughter of John and Ida (Frey) Kopke. Ila Mae was born on August 2, 1920. When Ila Mae's father retired from farming, Roland and Ila Mae took over the operation. Roland also was a Moorman's Feed salesman.

Roland and Ila Mae have three children, Dean, Karen and Randy. Randy took over the family farm and Roland and Ila Mae moved to St. Clair.

Ila Mae & Roland Born

BOSWELL, JOHN

John H. Boswell was born in England. He came to America with his father-in-law Henry Truman [see separate story], and later the entire Truman family moved to St. Clair, Minnesota, where they operated the Winnebago

Agency farm. John was married to Elizabeth Truman. Elizabeth was born on October 31, 1831, in Lancaster, England. They had seven children Hannah, Julius, Edgar, William [see separate story], Oscar, George and Mary Josephine. George and Mary were born in Minnesota.

Elizabeth died during childbirth in 1870 and John died in 1879. They are buried in the McPherson Union Cemetery, St. Clair, Minnesota

By Marion Boswell Hoffman

BOSWELL, WILLIAM

From *History of Blue Earth County*, by Thomas Hughes-1909

Blue Earth County has no more honored men than those whose active life tasks have been accomplished, and who, from their vantage ground of well earned leisure, look calmly and approvingly upon the struggle for existence being conducted by a later generation. Among these, few have more conscientious labor to recommend them than William Boswell. Only one year the other side of fifty years, he has accomplished much more than the average in a given number of years and there still burns within him the fires of youth and sympathy. He suggests the man, who has lived broadly and usefully, and whose character and attainments benefited their fellow men.

Mr. Boswell was born in Darnestown, Maryland, on January 31, 1857. He was one of the seven children of John H. and Elizabeth Freeman (should be Truman) Boswell, the former of whom was born in England and died in Minnesota in 1879, and the later of whom died in this county in 1895. From Maryland, which long had been the home of the Boswell forefathers; removal was made by John H. Boswell to Washington, D. C. and five years later, in August 1864, they arrived in Blue Earth County. The father at that time took up the quarter section of land, ever the agricultural destiny of which William Boswell, and now his tenant, holds sway. A daughter of John Boswell's, Hannah D. was married to Dr. Joseph Eaton who practiced medicine in Mankato.

In January 1885, Mr. Boswell married Nettie M. Scott, a Wisconsin native. Born to this union was a son, Clay Scott, now twenty years of age, who is engaged in the mercantile business of St. Clair. The Scott family, no less than the Boswell family were early arrivals in Blue Earth County, and took up government land. The grandfather of Mr. Boswell, however, was particularly prominent in the early days, gaining all of the prestige and wide acquaintance, which came of keeping a hotel and post office at the Winnebago Agency for twenty years. Mr. Boswell is fraternally connected with the Woodmen and Masons, having been a member of Lodge No. 12, F. M. and A.M., of Mankato, for the past twenty-three years. During all of the years of his residence in Blue Earth county he has supported movements for the benefit of the people and has been unwearying in his efforts to promote the common good.

[Additional Notations]:

In July of 1914, while leaving a performance of the Ringling Brothers Circus in Mankato, a falling pole injured him. (The circus crew was taking down the tent before the audience had left.) He sustained serious injuries and was paralyzed from the shoulders down. He died a few days later (July 27) during surgery. He was a man highly esteemed in the community in which he lived. He was an active conservationist in bird life. He was also the historian of the St. Clair settlement.

Nettie was born on May 1, 1869, in Wisconsin Dells, Wisconsin. She was the daughter of Edward James Scott. The Scott family moved into St. Clair about 1896. William and Nettie lived at 200 Park Street. She died on August 4, 1917, after she had had an operation. They are buried in the Glenwood Cemetery, Mankato, MN.

Clay Scott Boswell was born on May 16, 1887, on the Scott farm one mile west of St. Clair, in McPherson Township. He attended the St. Clair Public School and in adulthood attended Windom Business College in Windom, MN. He was a landowner, electrician, carpenter, school custodian, volunteer fireman, etc. Clay was known for raising many different kinds of ducks and geese in the backyard of his property in the midst of St. Clair, was a conservationist in bird life, and was historian of the St. Clair settlement.

On December 12, 1912, Clay married Viva Estelle Thielman, the daughter of Henry and Jessie (Rasdall) Thielman (see separate story). Viva was born on February 8, 1893, in McPherson Township and attended St. Clair Public School and the Ladies Seminary in Albert Lea, Minnesota. They lived at 122 Main Street East. They were parents of three children–Harold (see separate story), Marion L. who was born on October 4, 1918, and married Noel Hoffman. Noel was born on September 8, 1915, in Sleepy Eye, MN, and died on January 4, 1973. They have two children–Gary Scott and Karen L. Marion is living in Kingsburg, CA. The third child of Clay and Viva was Jane Ann who married George Kroenke (see separate story).

Viva died on April 15, 1967, and Clay died on April 23, 1976. They are buried in the Glenwood Cemetery, Mankato, MN.

Harold Boswell was born on April 3, 1914, in St. Clair and graduated from St. Clair School in 1932. He was married to Hazel Kenward, the daughter of Robert and

Elsie (Gekler) Kenward, in 1935. Hazel was born on January 17, 1919, in Minnesota Lake, MN. She enjoyed flowers and working in the yard. Harold was a farmer and together the owned and operated Boswell Greenhouse until retiring in 1976 due to ill health. They then sold the business and moved to Lake Washington for ten years and then returned to the farm off MN State Highway #83 near St. Clair. Hazel lived in Mankato after Harold's death. They had one son Robert Clay.

Harold died on March 27, 1986, and Hazel died on June 5, 2001. They are buried in the Glenwood Cemetery, Mankato, MN.

By Marion Boswell Hoffman

BOWE, JOHN

John D. and Margaret (Dumey) Bowe, natives of Ireland, spent seventeen years farming in Illinois. The history of the Bowe family in Blue Earth County dates back to 1870, when John D. Bowe came to Minnesota. He died on October 28, 1884. At the time of John's death Patrick H. was one of three surviving sons of the seven.

Patrick H. Bowe was born in Jacksonville, Illinois, on February 15, 1862. The hardware merchant of St. Clair received his preliminary education in the public schools of Illinois, and all his reasoning life had been a reader of newspapers and good literature, the keeping abreast of the times and in touch with happenings all over the world. For a year he lived at Mankato and then purchased a hardware store at St. Clair, which he operated until 1914. The hardware business in St. Clair had an enterprising and progressive promoter in Patrick Bowe. Progression was the keynote of his career, and it was this which enables him to maintain an up-to-date store, equipped with all kinds of hardware necessities, and which brings him a dependable trade from a large section of country. He took a keen interest in politics, has filled several important offices, and at the present time is promoting the cause of practical education as a member of the school board and served as its clerk for 15 years.

He was employed by the George E. Brett Company in Mankato until his retirement. Patrick was a member of the Modern Woodmen of America for 42 years and of the Ancient Order of Hibernians for 35 years.

Mr. Bowe was united in marriage to Ellen Morris, who was born in the state of New York in 1868. To Mr. and Mrs. Bowe have been born five sons and two daughters, Ada, William, John Emmett, James Leo, Cora, Clemente and Clayton C. Mr. Bowe stands high in the public estimation, both as man and merchant and his contribution to its business and general advancement is to a second and practical nature. Ellen died in 1960.

Thomas Bowe, Sr. was born on July 4, 1863, in Illinois. He was a resident of McPherson Township for fifty-two years.

Thomas married Theresia Huettl, the daughter of Joseph and Maximilian (Magel) Huettl, who was born on September 30, 1866, in Austria. She came to America when she was two years old. They had six children. Theresia (Nathan Mace-see separate story), Thomas John, Jr. (1889), Margaret (Francis Maloney), Jane (Guy Lynch-see separate story), Rose (Linus Lynch-see separate story) and Frances Henry (1905-1940).

Thomas died on February 15, 1920, and Theresia died on October 17, 1960.

Margaret Bowe was born in 1890 and married Francis Maloney, the son of James and Julian (Cotter) Maloney, in 1912. Their children were Mary, Margaret (Walter H. Grams-see separate story), Francis Jr., Catherine, Gertrude, Marcella, Cornelius and James.

Francis Bowe, a 34-year-old farmer living near St. Clair, was taken to a local hospital on December 19, 1939, after he incurred a compound fracture of the left leg in a fall on a St. Clair street. His death resulted from complications. He is buried in the Immaculate Conception Catholic Cemetery.

By Leona Mace

BRANDT, WILLIAM

William Brandt, a native of Germany, was born November 11, 1842. While an infant his parents moved to the United States and settled in Oshkosh, Wisconsin. Here he grew to manhood and in 1862 enlisted in Company B, Third Wisconsin infantry, and served three years. He engaged in the battles of Winchester, Cedar Mountain, Antietam, Chancellorsville and Gettysburg: was also at Lookout Mountain, Chattanooga and Altoona. In 1865 he came to Minnesota and located at McPherson. He was married in 1867 to Etta Borcutt, who bore him two children: William A. and Henry W. who died on November 30, 1873.

BREWER, DANIEL

Daniel Brewer and his wife, Mary Getty came from the state of Massachusetts and homesteaded in McPherson Township, south of St. Clair. Here they were engaged in farming and raised their children Charles, Jennie and Julia. They later moved to Mankato, Minnesota, and their daughters who never married went with them.

By Laura Brewer

BREWER, CHARLES

From *History of Blue Earth County* by Thomas Hughes–1909

The claims to consideration on the part of Charles H. Brewer are founded upon an earnest desire to uphold the merit of a fine old pioneer name. Identified with Blue Earth County for the past forty-five years and representing at all times the best farming element of this part of Minnesota. Mr. Brewer was born on the farm he owned in 1909 and occupied, July 28, 1871, and is one of the three children of Daniel D. and Mary (Getty) Brewer, born in 1833 and 1837, respectively.

Upon leaving his native state to avail himself of the larger opportunities of the less settled west, Daniel Brewer stopped for a time in both Illinois and Wisconsin, arriving in Minnesota in the spring of 1856. Pre-empting a farm in Winona County, he tilled its crude acres for seven years, but failing to realize expectations, came to Blue Earth County and purchased the land now owned by his son. In 1909 he was still living and in the possession of his faculties. He has rendered signal service to this his adopted state, setting a fine example of conscientious and successful farming, and filling with credit the majority of the local offices within the gift of his fellow townsmen.

Charles H. Brewer has known no other home than that where he now lives, or any occupation but farming. At the district school he laid the foundation of his present many sided knowledge, and he has given to the conduct of his farm the best of brain and effort of which he is capable. He has in all two hundred and fifty acres, and thoroughly understanding the science of agriculture, naturally derives a substantial income from this amount of land. He raised stock and general produce, had a fine residence, substantial barns, and ample protection for the result of his harvests. Around him was an interesting family of five children. Carrie (This child was from his first marriage to May Rodgers, who died during child birth.) who married Oscar McCarthy and they lived on a farm near Madelia, Minnesota, Gerald [see separate story], Cyril (Marcella Pestka) lived in Mankato, Esther (Austen Smith) moved to California. Lydia (Harold Childs) lived at Garden City, Minnesota and died when only twenty-three. Before her marriage Mrs. Brewer was E. Gertrude Miller, a native of Rhode Island, and the wedding ceremony was performed September 27, 1897. Mr. Brewer was highly esteemed for his many sterling qualities, for his public spiritedness, thrift, geniality and integrity, and in consequence his friends are many and loyal.

Supplemented by Laura Brewer

GERALD BREWER

Gerald, the son of Charles and E. Gertrude (Miller), took over the family farm in McPherson Township, south of St. Clair. He married Laura Ward, the daughter of George and Rose (Beise) Ward in 1934. Upon Gerald's retirement they moved to St. Clair, living at 204 Park Street North. Laura worked in the St. Clair School District as head of the hot lunch program until she retired in 1978. In 1978 they sold their home and moved into the Schalow Apartments, which had just been built. Gerald died in 1982.

They have two children: James, who married Violet Roeker and they live north east of Waldorf, and Sandra, who married Sidney Nyhusmoen and they live on Lake Scandi near Glenwood, Minnesota. The Brewers have eight grandchildren and eleven great-grandchildren.

By Laura Brewer

BRUELS, HUBERT

Hubert Bruels the son of Johann and Anna Katharina Bruels was born on September 10, 1857. He was five years old at the time of the hanging of the 38 Indians on December 26, 1862, in Mankato.

While Hubert and his brother Nicholas were young men, their father contracted lung fever and it developed into quick consumption. Johann died in 1871 at the age of 48. They were left alone with their mother and a foster sister. The mother married Phillip Hodapp in 1876, and they acquired many step-sisters and brothers of their own age. Anna (Bruels) Hodapp died in 1907.

In January 1881, Hubert Bruels married Elizabeth

Elizabeth & Hubert Bruels

May, the daughter of Joseph and Catherine May. They settled on a rented farm east of St. Clair. On October 16, 1881, their son Joseph, the first of nine children was born. The following year they bought a farm west of St. Clair. While living on this farm, two boys and four girls were born. The second child John died in infancy. When the children were ready to go to school, they attended a one room rural school in the district.

In 1895 when Joseph was fourteen years old, Hubert and Elizabeth sold the farm and bought the one less that a mile from the Village of St. Clair. Another girl and boy were born here. The children then attended a four-room schoolhouse in St. Clair.

The following ten years were good to them. Hubert set up new buildings and acquired new machinery and had nice horses and some livestock.

Hubert was a very civic-minded man. He served as school clerk, township clerk, and always a church trustee. He helped organize the McPherson Insurance Agency. He was a farmer and learned the carpenter trade from his father.

In 1904 Hubert was elected as a Blue Earth County Commissioner.

In 1906 Hubert began working on trying to get a railroad from Albert Lea to St. Clair. In 1907 "The Alphabet" line was established and the farmers no longer had to haul grain by horses and wagons. It served the community for many years.

The oldest child of Hubert and Elizabeth Bruels was Joseph who married Rose Fallenstein [see separate story]. Their second child was John who was born on October 4, 1883 and died on January 28, 1884. Andrew was born on May 25, 1885 and died on April 28, 1908.

Rose Marie (9-16-1888 - 1-5-1945) married Harbert (Harry) Wenner (1-7-1887 - 4-1963). Their children were Ivennie (James Galston), and had two children: William (Linda Oftedahl/Nancy K.), and Rosemary (Fredrick/Bohnert/Ron Rose).

Robert Wenner (8-14-1916) married Agnes Klein, the children Bernard (Victoria McCormick), Harold (Kathy Janssen), Stanley (Debra Eckstein), Rita (Dennis Debough), Gerald (Kristine Kline), Mark and Lester.

Elaine Wenner (3-24-1918 - 3-7-2005) married Merle James and their children are Ramona who married Randy Will and they live in McPherson Township just east of St. Clair on the former Courrier Hubmer farm and have three children, Jamie (Sara More), Kristin and Brian. Mary James is married to Rodney Neher, and Gloria (W. Block/Joseph Winter).

Edwin Wenner (1920-1966) married Elisabeth Brunner (1921-1991), and they had three daughters, Emily (1945-1966) (John Arend), Joyce, and Linda.

Linda Wenner (1951-2000) married Joseph Klaesus and they had a son Steven (1955) (Janet Sue Kruger).

Leland Wenner married Berneil Flores, their children are Leon (Irene Brown), Lois (Bradley Herrig), and Neil (Wendy Sawatzky).

Joan Wenner (1931) married Walter Bunde (1938) and their children are Michael, Cheryl (Kenneth Wiley), Richard (Debbie) and Patricia (William Lincoln).

The last five children of Hubert and Elizabeth were Katherine (4-16-1890 - 11-11-1976) (Gene Womack), Margaret (12-19-1891 - 11-10-1944) (John O'Rielly), Clara (7-10-1894 - 9-27-1984) (Leo Lynch), Anne (10-16-1898 - 12-16-1993) (Walter Desmond) and Clement (3-21-1905 - 3-31-1989) who married Florence Collins. Their son Mark (Judith Fasnacht/Lucia Ross) has two children Nicholas and Christine (Powaser).

Hubert and Elizabeth sold their house in St. Clair in 1919 and moved to their retirement home at 603 North 4th Street in Mankato.

Elizabeth died on December 2, 1927. The following June, Clara and Leo Lynch moved into the house to live with Hubert until his death in May of 1946.

Hubert had acquired many farms and gave each of his children a farm.

Joseph Bruels was born on October 16, 1881, and was the oldest son of Hubert and Elizabeth (May) Bruels. On October 26, 1906, he married Rose Fallenstein. Their first son Raymond was born in rural St. Clair. They moved to the Bruels family farm in 1909, and Hubert and

Rose & Joseph Bruels

Elizabeth moved their remaining family to a house that Joseph and Catherine May had built for themselves on acreage they bought from the original John Bruels estate. Hubert and Elizabeth had bought it at the time of the settling of the May estate. In 1916 they sold the Bruels acreage in Hilltop Mankato and moved to a house they already had in St. Clair on the corner of West Main and Agency Streets.

Joseph and Rose raised eight children on the farm west of St. Clair on County Road #15, and their children attended school in St. Clair. The oldest was Raymond (7-16-1907 - 2-8-1999) who married Arline Cuddy (1915-1981). Marcella (8-6-1909) - Joel Barnes, Florence (9-25-1912 - 7-21-1999) - Carl Rose [see separate story], Clotilda (3-24-1915 - 2-1-2002) - Charles Buesing, Leon (4-4-1918 - 2-19-2000) - Ardella Joan Oftedahl, Herbert (3-15-21 - 10-2-2001) - Norma Kott Moe [see separate story], Marion (5-8-1923) - J. B. Coker/Henry Taylor, and Warren (8-6-1930) who married Patricia Sahli.

Joseph Bruels died on May 2, 1971. Rose died on November 13, 1980.

By Norma Bruels

Joseph & Rose Bruels family
Back row (L to R) Herbert, Clotilda, Raymond, Marcella, Leon. Front row: Florence, Joseph, Warren, Rose, Marion.

BRUMMOUND, ARLYND

Arlynd C. H. Brummound, the son of Arthur and Anna (Urban) Brummound was born on November 15, 1928, in rural Truman, Minnesota. He lived in rural St. Clair with his parents at the time of his death. At 19 he drowned in Lake Emily in July 1948, while his 18-year-old cousin looked on helpless as she sat in a boat a few feet away. Arlynd had a brother Arnold (LaDonna Schwantes) and two sisters Alice (Harold Olsen) and Arvellis (Willmer Broas/William Morrow).

BUECKSLER, FERDINAND - 1990

The Buecksler family began on May 5, 1882 in Pommern, Germany, when Edith Wilhelmina Carolina Ehmke, 23-year-old daughter of Mr. and Mrs. Emil Ehmke of Breitenfield became the bride of Ferdinand Buecksler, 28-year-old son of Mr. and Mrs. Albert Buecksler of Stolp, Germany. Ferdinand had just spent three years of mandatory service in the German army. Ferdinand and Edith left Germany to avoid further confrontations with the advancing Russian Cossack soldiers who came to German farms and took the best of everything the farmers had, including their animals and their sons to take care of the animals. They bid farewell to their loving families and friends and sailed away to America on their honeymoon. They arrived in New Youk June 7, 1882. They took a train directly to Minnesota Lake, arriving with just 11 cents left in their pockets. They slept in a hay barn the first night, and then went looking for their old friends from Germany, Mr. and Mrs. Schultz of Minnesota Lake, who had settled there earlier. Ferdinand found work and they lived in a sod house in Bush Woods near the river. Close by were several Winnebago Indian families who taught them how to grow and prepare local produce and also about the "miracle leaves." These medicinal healing leaves came from the plantine plant, which grows wild and free in the Midwest. Edith washed the leaves carefully, and then either made tea from them for stomachaches or a poultice for bruises, cuts and abrasions. Within 8 to 12 hours the matter and infection would be drawn out of the body. There were no drug stores to run to or a doctor close by — only tried and true home remedy, mostly from Mother Nature's garden.

Ferdinand and Edith worked side by side long, hard hours, and soon the family came to prosper a bit. They moved to the Beise place in McPherson Township, while Ferdinand worked on the Tivoli Bridge project with his friend George Bycees. He walked 7 miles to work each way and made $6 a month from which they saved enough to send money to Germany to help his sister Johanna's family (Mr. and Mrs. Carl Wille) come to America also. The Willie family settled near Mapleton. They lived very frugally but their goals were important to them. Faith in God and hard work helped them accomplish these goals. Their children became good solid citizens, who helped build bridges, roads, do tiling, practice conservation and make America a better place to live in for future generations.

In 1900 they bought the Taylor house and moved it four miles. It took six weeks using just manpower and a dozen big logs. It arrived with nary a crack anywhere. Almost all their food was raised on the farm with lots of home preserving. They only made about four trips a year to Mankato. One treat was bananas which were $1.79 a pound then. They were carefully rationed out. Edith carded and spun wool from their sheep on the spinning wheel, and Ferdinand would knit their hats, mittens, scarves and socks.

They were blessed with ten children. Albert Karl Erdman (4-24-1883 - 6-24-1970; Otto born in 1884 who died from a ruptured appendix at age 17; Clara, born 11-14-1885, married Carl Marquardt, and died in 1913 during an appendectomy; William, born in 1887, died at age 3 from diphtheria; Arthur (3-9-1889 to 5-16-1988) died at age 99+ years; Paul (4-17-1891 to 6-16-1991) died at age 100+ years; Amelia (12-11-1892 to 5-11-1991) died at age 98+ years, Oscar (4-8-1895 to 4-10-1995) died at age 100+ years, Walter (1-10-1898 to 2-4-1996) died at age 98 years; and Ida (4-5-1900 to 11-22-1992) died at age 92+ years. Good work habits and good nutritious food helped many of them attain long life. Ferdinand was one of the signers of the original constitution of St. John's Evangelical Lutheran Church of Alma City when the congregation was formed in 1910.

June 29, 1921. A sad day. Ferdinand passed away from cancer of the stomach after suffering for several years. He left Edith and seven children. The children all remained close and good friends. They helped each other and made a practice of coming back to "the home place" often to see the mother who raised them with a loving strong firm hand. "Mutti" (Mother in German), as she affectionately came to be called by everyone who knew her, was joined on the home place by her daughter, Ida and her husband, Albert Hoffman. They, with their three sons Duane, Norman and Gerald, took excellent care of "Mutti" and the home place. "Mutti" passed away on May 20th, 1950, at the age of 91+ years. She lived long enough to see her family survive and lead happy and successful lives. We are a close knit family who pray, work and play together and love each other very much. We try to get together periodically for happy family reunions.

One of the pleasant memories of grandchildren was of the enormous (or so it seemed to us) apple orchard at Grandma's. In the fall apples would be harvested, put in barrels in the cellar or canned or sulfured. Children were warned to stay away from the sulfur fumes that emitted from the wood-fired cook stove oven when the oven door was opened during the sulfuring process. The finished product made for much good eating in the winter. Another favorite in our household was sauce we called "apples with handles." This was concocted by baking Whitney apples, with stems intact and skin on, in the oven, then canning them in brown sugar syrup. For the large families, they were canned in two-quart jars.

BUECKSLER, ALBERT - 1990

Albert Carl Buecksler, the first child of Edith and Ferdinand Buecksler was born on April 24, 1883, northeast of St. Clair, Minnesota. After completing third grade at St. Clair Country School, he remained at home to help with the farm work. One of the tasks was plowing long hours with a team of horses and a walking plow. At the approximate age of fourteen, he attended "German School" at St. Clair's Lutheran Church for catechism instruction.

Albert & Ella Buecksler family
Back row (L to R): Ralph, Robert, Verna, Leonard, Melvin.
Front row: Gertrude, Ella, Lawrence, Albert, Arlene.

Albert, Adolph Meyers and Sam Lachelt followed the harvest run up into North Dakota, sleeping in barns, straw piles and eating their meals with the farmers they worked for.

Albert met Ella Schroeder at a barn raising and dance. They were married December 2, 1913. They were blessed with eight children, Robert born October 16, 1914 and died September 26, 2003; Verna born April 9, 1916 and died May 12, 1981; Leonard, born January 10, 1919; Melvin born March 6, 1922; Gertrude born December 29, 1924; Arlene, born October 18, 1926; Ralph born October 31. 1928; and Lawerence was born on August 5, 1930 and died October 15, 1969.

In 1916 Albert and Ella purchased 80 acres located 2 miles north of Pemberton from Albert's parents, Ferdinand and Edith (Ida) Buecksler, for the sum of $8,000. Ferdinand had purchased it in 1905 from Nels and Anna Anderson for $4,750. The opportunity was afforded Albert in 1926 to acquire another 40 acres across the road formerly owned by Sigborin Hansen for $3,200. After Albert's death in 1970, the eldest son, Robert, farmed the place along with land he rented until his retirement. Robert owned the land until his death. The farmland was then sold to Mr. and Mrs. Gregory J.

Strobel in early 2004 after having been in the Buecksler name for 99 years.

In July of 1930 Albert was hospitalized at St. Joseph's Hospital in Mankato due to appendicitis. His stay was for 10 days. The receipted bill shows: Room, Board, Care $30; operating Room Service $12; Laboratory Work $3.40; Laundry $.75 totaling $46.15.

During World War II, Leonard served in the army field artillery, Melvin in the army infantry and Lawrence in the Marines.

Albert passed away June 24, 1970, from cancer. Ella died July 2, 1972, from thyroid and heart problems. Verna married Harold Mark Preston in 1939. They farmed on the Preston property their entire married life in McPherson Township. Leonard married Phyllis Roland in 1942. He worked as a Standard Oil bulk agent and Phyllis taught school. Melvin worked at several area farms and eventually purchased the Herman Godemann farm in McPherson Township. Coincidentally, Melvin's great aunt and uncle, Carl and Johanna Wille lived on this same farm, sometime after they emigrated from Germany in the late 1800's. Gertrude married Edgar Stavenau in 1951; they lived and worked in Mankato. Arlene married Paul Manthe. They farmed in the Pemberton area until moving to Belle Plaine, Minnesota, in 1966 where they both worked at the Lutheran Home for many years. Ralph attended Mankato Commercial College, as did Gertrude and Arlene, and he worked in Mankato and Waseca and also as parts man at Hofman Implement in Pemberton. Lawrence married Evelyn Radke and after his stint in the U.S. Marines, they farmed in the St. Clair and Beauford areas until Lawrence's early death.

The home 120-acre farm plus occasional rented acreage, served as the entire source of income for the family of 10 (8 children). Neither parent worked away from the farm; however, the children, as soon as they were old enough, were grateful to "work out," as it was then called, to earn spending money for themselves. Grandchildren of Albert and Ella totaled 14.

By Marjorie J. Ross and Arlene Manthe

BUECKSLER, IDA

Ida Buecksler was born April 5, 1900, in McPherson Township. She arrived into this world as her older sister Clara was being confirmed in the church her father helped built.

Ida met her husband to be (Albert Hoffman) at a church mission festival in Janesville. Al made a statement to a friend when he first met Ida, "This is the lady I am going to marry." After a short courtship they were married on November 2, 1921, four months after Ida's father had passed away. Ida and Albert decided to stay on the Buecksler family farm and help "Mutti." In 1924 they improved the house by doing extensive remodeling. They hired Hank Backhouse to stucco the outside of the house and garage, and he added multi-colored glass chips to the stucco, making the house sparkle in the sunlight. It also was the only house for miles around that had such a beautiful exterior. The glass chips are still on the home place in 2004.

Albert Hoffman started selling Minneapolis Moline machinery off his farmyard. He started by grading township roads with a big steam engine. Neighbors would come to him for corn shellers, threshing machines, plows and general farm machinery. When the business outgrew the farm, Albert and Ida, who was the best business partner a person could ask for, moved the operation to a new building in Pemberton. Ida made many, many trips to Minneapolis for parts and machinery, driving their big truck alone. Their oldest son Duane and his wife Gerda are still operating the business.

The second son Norman and his wife Vonnie took over the family farm operation by raising registered Jersey cows, building a new barn and installing an automatic milking parlor. His grandparents would have been proud of him, if they could have seen all the wonderful improvements they did to the farm they had started from scratch. On March 22, 1963, a horrible accident occurred on the beloved "home place." Duane Oftedahl was helping Norm and Vonnie's son remove feed from one of the new Blue Harvester silos, when the mechanism became clogged. Duane (Buddy) went up and into the silo to see what was wrong. He did not come back. Dennis (Norman's 13 year old son) called and called. He called to his mom, Vonnie, "Get help…something is wrong with Buddy." Then Dennis went up into the silo. Vonnie called Norman's brother Duane, who was the fire chief in Pemberton, to come quick! Then Vonnie went to see why they did not answer. Within a matter of just a few minutes three wonderful people were gone. The gas in the silos was so poisonous; it snuffed out their lives with one deep breath. When Norman came home a short time later his heart almost gave out when he found out what had happened to his beloved wife and son and friend. Norman continued on, he had to, he had four children to care for, and one of which was a small baby son. Norman continued farming until a heart attack claimed his life in 1977. He was 47.

Ida and Albert's third son Gerald was born January 1937 and a multi-talented jack of all trades. He met and married Gloria Kraske, and they had two children. He worked with his brother Duane for four years and then started "Hofman Service" in Pemberton.

Albert passed away in June 1949. Ida helped her sons and their wives until she met and married an old dear friend who had also lost his mate, Louis Krenke. They had a wonderful life together until he passed away. Ida then lived in Alma City.

BUESING, HERBERT

August and Anna (Beckman) Buesing came to the area in the mid 1920's and farmed in the St. Clair area and upon retirement moved to St. Clair. Their son Herbert was married to Violet Gekeler.

The John and Caroline Gekeler family settled in the St. Clair area in the 1860's as farmers. He also was a brick maker and had a brickyard to the west of the Herb Buesing house. Their son William and his wife Caroline were part of the group that founded the Evangelical United Brother Church that became the Zion Methodist Church that has now disbanded. The church is now "The Bell Tower" theater. Their son Henry married Emma Abraham from Smith's Mill (Violet's parents) and farmed in McPherson Township until retirement and then moved to St. Clair.

Herb had several businesses in St. Clair: trucker, garage owner, icehouse owner, and house mover. Herb was a jack of all trades sort of person. In the 1940's they milked six Guernsey cows and bottled the milk in the basement. The milk was delivered to the St. Clair customers. Their second son, Ralph, remembers getting kicked in the head by his favorite cow name "Mooie." The cows were being led out to pasture to be tethered between the three sets of railroad tracks. There was the ice business where Herb would cut ice in the wintertime from the Le Sueur River and Madison Lake. He gave many jobs to the men in the community as his helpers. Almost every winter someone would fall in the ice hole and had to be pulled out and hauled home as soon as possible. Trucks would deliver ice to town and the area farms. Violet's job was at the ice concession when people from the country would come in and buy ice. The ice was stored in a big building and covered with sawdust to keep it from melting. It was the job of many to uncover the sawdust and clean and place the ice into a smaller cooler. The ice blocks were sold by the pound. When needed the customer would ask for 5, 10, or 40 pound blocks. When REA (Rural Electrification Association) ran electricity to the farms, the ice business was abandoned. Later, Violet worked at Birdseye in Waseca for more than twenty years until retirement.

Herb Buesing and partner unloading and sawing logs

Herb had a warehouse between what is now Jeff's Repair (it was Drake's Gas Station, and before that William Myers Oil Company) and Frank's Gas Station (no longer there). The next building was the Black Smith Shop and then Hager Hardware (now Six Flags over Aspen) and then the bank. In the early years, there was a road that crossed the Le Sueur River between the hardware store and the bank. Several wooden bridges were washed out in the spring floods. The sides of the riverbank were cut down and when the water was low you could cross the river. If one looks there today you can still see where the electrical wiring crosses and that is were the road was.

Herb also had Buesing Repair at what was known later as Pint's Garage near where the east corner of the school is now and across from the State Bank and the Up Town Tavern. The trucking business was also going on at this time. Herb hauled cattle to the South St. Paul Stockyards or farmer's grain to Shakopee. On the return trips the truck was full of dry goods for Hager Hardware Store or groceries for Peg's Grocery. Before harvest time on return trips, he drove to the Stillwater Prison to pick up and bring back bailing twine for the Hager Hardware Store. It was 1941 and when lots of items were rationed during World War II, he was in need of a new truck and tires but the government said he wasn't hauling enough, he was unable to obtain new tires and his trucks were worn out.

It was at this time that he started his moving business. The first house he moved was from the Frank T. Ireland farm and that became his own home on Railroad Street. This is now 301 Front Street West. The heaviest house he moved was the Chase house that is now the home of George and Peggy Johannsen on Mill Street. It was so heavy because the walls were insulated with bricks. The floor of the front porch was cement and covered with wood.

Herb moved large barns, small chicken coops, silos, corncribs, houses, etc., etc, for lots of people in southern Minnesota. Ralph remembers a time when a small building was being moved on the back of a truck and they forgot to remove the rollers so the building rolled right off the truck. Another time they lifted Leonard Depuydt's house to put a basement under it. Their oldest son, Orville, still remembers pushing 126 loads of mortar in a wheel barrel to lay the cement block for the basement. He said it was such a boring job you had to do something so he counted the wheel barrel loads.

Herb made his own moving equipment. There were axles, rollers, and trailers but the huge timbers came from Oregon by train to the cities. Herb drove up there to get them and loaded them on each side of his truck. They were about 50 feet long and had to be placed on each side of the truck to haul them home. He had to crawl in and out of the window to drive the truck home.

When an odd job had to be done, Herb was the one that was called. One time he helped get a train back on the tracks near the "Y" turn-around in town. He fixed lawn-mowers, farm machinery and kids bikes. He worked week-ends, Sundays, and some holidays so people would have their item repaired. He removed snow during the winter and never charged the three churches in town. Come to think about it he could have been a rich man but he didn't charge enough. He always had a soft spot for people so he kept his prices down.

Herb was an experienced fisherman and hunter. In retire-ment, Herb and Violet had a huge garden where today there are four homes located. The grandchildren would sell the produce in a stand or by the post office. This land was also used as a go-cart racetrack for the grandchildren. Violet found bean-hoeing jobs for the grandchildren and she showed them how to take care of a garden. They would tell about going to the free movies on Friday night. The screen was back toward the alley. This would be where the McPherson Insurance Company is now. Herman Kroenke would sell popcorn for 5 cents. There were wooden planks to sit on. On Saturday morning the town kids would be at that vacant lot and dig in the sand hoping to find coins or swimming and fishing in the Le Sueur River.

Winnis & Ralph Buesing

Bradley & Roxanne (Buesing) Flowers with sons, Beamer, Brock, Blake and Bryce.

Their oldest son Orville is now living in California. Ralph and Winnis (Renneke) Buesing are living in St. Clair. Their children are Michael and Roxanne. Roxanne and her husband Bradley Flowers along with sons Brandon, Brock, Blake and Bryce are also living in St. Clair.

Herbert died in 1982 and Violet died in 1995.

By Orville, Ralph, and Winnis Buesing.

BUYSSE, JAMES

James P. Buysse was born on March 23, 1950, in Pipestone, MN, to Paul and Dorothy (Priester) Buysse. He graduated from the Jasper High School in 1968 and from Southwest State University in Marshall, MN. He taught elementary education in Jackson, MN, for four years and then obtained his Master's in Education Administration from Mankato State University. In 1977 he came to St. Clair and served as our school principal. He was a member of the National Elementary Principal Association and the MN Elementary Principal Association. He enjoyed fishing and playing rolle bolle ball.

James Buysse

On August 15, 1979, Jim was married to Margie Cordes, the daughter of Elvin and Lois Cordes, in Las Vegas, Nevada. Margie and Jim had two sons, Andy and Brent.

Jim died as a result of an auto accident on October 9, 1996.

One hundred years from now it will not matter
What kind of car I drove,
What kind of house I lived in
How much money I had in my bank account.
Nor what my clothes looked like.
But the world may be a little better
Because I was important in the life of a child.

A Principal Well Remembered: The *St. Clair Senior Cyclone Chronicle*-November 13, 1996

On October 9th of this year, students at St. Clair School experienced the loss of a wonderful friend (also known as our principal). The students were told to stand tall, and we did. We attended classes regularly and also sang at his funeral – but the hurt was still there and everybody felt it in one way or another. Today we have all begun to move on but for many of us the memories of Mr. Buysse (Big Jim) will always linger. He was always willing to lend a helping hand and sometimes even a pair of helping lips. In April of 1996 he puckered up to a piglet to help raise funds during the 2nd Annual Jump Rope for Heart fundraiser. His lips helped to raise over $4,700. As a student at St. Clair it is hard for me to walk by his office and see nobody in his chair or to know that he gave me my kindergarten diploma, but he won't be able to give me my high school diploma. On behalf of the students at St. Clair we would like to send our best regards to his family.

By Mandy Fitzloff

CALDWELL, GEORGE

George Becker Caldwell was one of St. Clair's best-known citizens. He was born in St. Paul, Minnesota Territory, on June 26, 1856. With his parents he moved to the Winnebago Agency, McPherson Township in 1862. Here he spent his boyhood and on December 11, 1888, he entered the bonds of holy matrimony with Bertha Augusta Fitzloff, the daughter of Johan (1827-1912) and Henriette (1830-1905) (Borchardt) Fitzloff, also of Saint Clair. In 1890 they removed to Saint Paul, where for two years he held a position with the first Street Railway Company.

Because of family bonds and ties the young couple returned to Saint Clair in 1893, and in 1895 Mr. Caldwell built the hotel, opening the first Hostelry in the village. Here, for fourteen years, he maintained this inn.

In order to give his children every education facility he took his family to North Mankato in 1907, and accepted a position with the state of Minnesota, as stationery engineer at the old Normal School. They continued to live in North Mankato until 1919.

Shortly after the outbreak of the World War, Mr. Caldwell was tendered a position at the U.S. Naval Training Station at Great Lakes, IL. His sons having already enlisted, he was determined to accept the call of the government, and the family removed to Waukegan, IL. Mr. Caldwell continued in his engineering capacity for the government as Chief Engineer of the Water System, until January of this year (1925) when he requested a furlough that he might have medical attention. He entered Fairview Hospital in Minneapolis where his family lived and he failed to rally from a very serious operation. He died on March 11.

Mr. and Mrs. Caldwell had seven children George James, Donald, Curtis, Howard, George Jr., Gladys and Ruth. They are buried in the Glenwood Cemetery, in Mankato, Minnesota.

CAMPBELL, GLENN

March 4, 1918 – *Mankato Free Press* - Glenn H. Campbell of St. Clair was the first Blue Earth county young man to sacrifice his life on the altar of patriotism and to die fighting for his country. He was killed in action in France. The news of Mr. Campbell's death was received by *The Free Press* from the *Associated Press* shortly before six o'clock Saturday evening. A bulletin posted immediately notified public of the tragic event. A short time before this the parents of the brave, young soldier, Mr. and Mrs. Henry A. Campbell, were informed of their son's death. Naturally, they were shocked but both were borne up by that grand and splendid spirit, which permeates loyal American fathers and mothers who are willing to give their sons to the noble cause of democracy.

Glenn Campbell

Proud of Son's Heroic Death

Both Mr. and Mrs. Henry (Lydia Foster 1873-1939) Campbell were bowed in grief, yet they uttered not a word of complaint and expressed themselves as being proud of the heroic sacrifice that they and their son had made for America for the freedom of the world and the crushing of autocracy and a dangerous and oppressive militarism.

Private Glenn H.

Campbell has laid down his life in a great cause. He has served his country well. His name is enshrined with a wreath of glory whose bright luster never can fade or be destroyed by the ruthless hand of time. He was among the first of the Blue Earth County boys to tender their services to this government, having enlisted at the Mankato recruiting station on May 1, 1917, not many days after congress declared that a state of war existed with Germany and President Wilson called for volunteers. He and several other young men from St. Clair enlisted at the same time and they were sent to training camps where they remained for a brief period.

Was Nineteen When He Enlisted

He was then but twenty years of age. He celebrated his twenty-first birthday January 1. He was lithe, brave, manly, a fine, healthy, true specimen of American young manhood. He had been popular in the old hometown where he had lived practically all his life. Not a mark of discredit had ever been placed against his record. He was true to the best traditions of American institutions and was a credit to the family name. He has gone out of this life as he had lived – true, noble and for a good purpose. Young Campbell had been in action prior to the one in which he met his death. He was wounded in that engagement and for two months was confined in a hospital. All the while he was anxious to return to the firing line and become an active factor in the struggle against autocracy. His last letter to his parents was published not long ago in *The Free Press*. In it he expressed himself optimistically and was glad that he was serving his country.

Will Pay Fitting Tribute

The people of St. Clair are going to pay tribute to Private Campbell on Wednesday afternoon at 2:30 o'clock. The memorial ceremonies will be held in the village hall. Rev. Mr. Zieske, Father T. A. O'Connor and other clergymen will participate in the services.

All business will be suspended, and the whole village and the country adjacent will gather to pay their tribute of respect to the youthful hero who had sacrificed his life for his country.

His father and mother and two brothers, Arleigh and Neal survive Private Campbell. The elder Mr. Campbell is engaged in the milling business in St. Clair.

Henry A (1869-1949), Lydia (1873-1939), and Glenn are buried in the Union Cemetery, St. Clair.

CHASE, JACOB

Jacob W. Chase, born on September 11, 1865, and was a pioneer St. Clair resident. He married Edith Foster (1870-1954) on December 6, 1893. He had a threshing crew, was a carpenter (built the Methodist parsonage, George Ward's house and Louis Grams house) and had a sawmill in St. Clair. They lived at 201 East Main Street. A retired St. Clair contractor, he suffered a stroke in October 1946. He died in February 1947. The Masonic Lodge was in charge of the service at the gravesite in St. Clair. His wife, Edith (Eddie) Foster, two sisters Jeanette (Bemis) and Mary and two brothers George and Frank survived him.

Edith (Foster) & Jacob Chase in 1905

Edith was known for her poem and song writing.

Jake and Eddie are buried in the Union Cemetery, St. Clair.

CHASE, FRANK

Frank M. Chase, a retired farmer, was born in Derby, Vermont, on July 23, 1873. He married Grace E. Rasdall on November 23, 1900, and was the father of three children, two (Duane and Stanley) which preceded him in death. He was a member of the AF & AM No. 24 at Pemberton. He lived in St. Clair, at the corner of Agency and West Main Street most of his life. (In the late 50's and early 60's, Don Trembley, the music teacher, and his family lived in this house. The house was later moved to 229 Mill Street.)

At the time of his death in 1951, his wife, one son Kenneth Chase of Dinuba, California, a brother George of Milltown, Wisconsin and sister, Mrs. Janette Bemis of Lincoln, Nebraska, survived him.

Grace Rasdall Chase was born in 1875 and died in 1954. She was a member of the St. Clair School Board from 1914 until 1954.

Frank and Grace are both buried in the St. Clair Union Cemetery.

Kenneth Chase married Alice Juliar, the daughter of Otto and Louise (Muehlhausen) Juliar. While in St. Clair they lived in the Art Cords/Hubert Johnson home on Main Street. They had a daughter Beverly Jane (Flosi) who now lives in Hemphill, Texas. Beverly remembers, when she was a small girl, of a fire in the attic from the fireplace. Her mother grabbed her out of bed, took her over to the Boswell's and ran back to put out the fire. When leaving St. Clair the Chase family moved to California.

Stanley Chase was born in St. Clair on July 3, 1911, and was educated in the St. Clair School. He attended the Mankato Teachers College from 1929 to 1932 and was captain of the track team and a member of the basketball team. He taught at St. Clair for three years after leaving the college and had secured a teaching position at Westbrook for the next year. He died in 1936 of a self-inflicted gunshot wound at his parent's home. His parents and brothers, Duane and Kenneth, survived him. He is buried in the St. Clair Union Cemetery.

COOK, J. L.

J. L. Cook was born May 5, 1832, in Massachusetts. Removed to Fond du Lac County, Wisconsin, and in 1857 to Freeborn County, Minnesota. During his younger days he learned the shoemaker's trade. In 1866 he located at Winnebago Agency. On his arrival he was appointed postmaster which office, together with that of town clerk and justice of the peace. He enlisted in Company E. 10th Minnesota, and served three years. He participated in many severe battles and served under General Sibley during the Indian campaign. He witnessed the execution of the thirty-eight Sioux Indians at Mankato. On October 30, 1865, he married Jennie A. Stearns. They had one son Frank.

CORDS, FREDERICK

Frederick Cords married Sophia Ehlers and they were both natives of Germany. Frederick first went to Wisconsin about 1855 and for some years operated a lime kiln in that state. In 1868 he came to Minnesota, and followed farming the rest of his active live. They were devoted Lutherans. In 1935 four of their children were living: Frederick, a retired farmer at Mankato, John, a farmer at St. Clair, Henry, of Portland, Oregon, and Blue Earth County Sheriff Frank W. John Cords.

My earliest recollections of my grandfather (b. 4/6/1868) are vague and intermixed with those of many other grown-ups. When I was about 4 years old, however, our family moved from downtown St. Clair to its eastern edge—about two and a-half blocks. My father, Arthur, built a new house there, and it was ready for occupancy.

My whole world seemed to change a great deal as a result of this move. The new house and location were exciting, of course, and there were new people in my life. The most important and memorable of these was my grandfather John. Our new house was located next to his farm's pasture, so I enjoyed much more contact with him than ever before. I spent a lot of time hanging around him and the farm—my mother thought too much. In time, I came to see my presence there as not only fun, but crucial. My role, in my mind, had become that of co-manager.

Grandpa at first seemed to be a large, gruff man who was always in charge of things. He was a member of a fairly large family of boys, orphaned by age 12, and raised by a neighbor and friend. I suspect that had something to do with his independent spirit. I found early on, however, that underneath that gruff exterior he was sensitive and soft-hearted. He could be stern, though. I remember once in the spring, when I was about 8, he stopped his car—a 1929 Model A Ford—downtown and chewed me out for sitting on a cold, wet cement step: "Catch Your Death!" I was embarrassed to be reprimanded in public.

Mostly, it was fun. Grandpa still did some farming and used horses, not having his own tractor. I loved horses, and occasionally he would let me ride with him and even hold the reins. I thought I was driving. Two were black work horses, but the third, Dan, was another story. Dan was brown and sleek with a white diamond in the center of his forehead. Highly spirited, he wasn't a good work horse, but Grandpa used to hitch him between the other two when doing heavy work, like plowing—arguing that once you got Dan going in the right direction, he might just pull a bit. More than a little cussing seemed also to be a necessary ingredient.

I liked Dan so much that I offered to buy him from Grandpa for a nickel I had saved—an immense sum for a young boy during Depression 30's. Grandpa was very touched, and we ultimately struck a deal—I would own Dan, but he would care for him and use him until I was old enough to take over. I got to keep the nickel. Heck of a deal, I thought!

When younger, Grandpa owned a steam engine and a threshing machine (separator) with Jake Chase. They did custom work, following a circuit around the area. The threshing season would last from late July well into fall. Farmers had to wait their turn, so they would "stack" bundles of grain to keep the inward-turned grain heads protected and dry. Weather permitting, they sometimes worked into the winter, doing cleanup. Grandpa told of once threshing in February. Usually, however, they used the steam engine during winters to run a sawmill.

When I was hanging around, Grandpa was farming on shares with the Schwanke brothers, Aaron and Hank. He had been out of the custom business for some time. The Schwankes owned their own threshing machine, but when threshing at John Cords' they let him take over. As I got a little older, he let me handle the spout that poured grain into a box wagon. Did I feel Important! As I write this, I can still hear him shout at me when I wasn't paying attention: "Nicky, dammit, don't let the wheat spill on the ground!"

Grandpa's threshing days were his glory time; he became sort of a legend concerning the management of the rig and crew. One of the old time farmers, by the name of Ireland, liked to tell of the time Grandpa and Jake were scheduled to be at his place on a given day. As the day was actually dawning, Ireland heard a clamor on the road; it was the approaching threshing crew. Also distinguishable was the commanding voice of John Cords, urging the outfit forward with very colorful language. Grandpa's orders to Mr. Ireland were to "get your men on the damm stacks so we can begin threshing a 9 o'clock, as scheduled!"

Grandpa owned another distinction regarding his steam engine. Once, when he was crossing the Le Sueur River just north of St. Clair, the bridge gave way, and the entire outfit crashed to the riverbed below. I understand that it took some doing, and no doubt much swearing, to raise the steam engine. A new bridge had to be built.

Grandpa died on April 13, 1939, when I was 9 years old and in fourth grade. He had been bothered by heart trouble for some time, but I didn't know how serious it was, and I hadn't seen nearly as much of him during wintertime as I did during summer vacation. I dreamed of him the night before he died; you can imagine how this influenced my young, impressionable and superstitious mind. The wake and services were held at the farm home prior to an afternoon burial at the Bestman Cemetery. My father had tried to arrange for services and burial at the Lutheran church and cemetery, but due to an earlier falling-out between a minister and Grandpa—that independent spirit again—that was not to be.

During the wake and amidst commotion in the small farmhouse, I experienced, for the first time in my life, the jolting pain of loss. It was gnawing; it would not go away. I have experienced it many times since, for example, at the deaths of my eldest son, parents and sister, but never more sharply than that first time. It would pass as life went on and I returned to school, but quite frankly, it doesn't take much, even now, to rekindle at least some of that emotion following Grandpa's death.

By the scheduled burial time, a ferocious spring snowstorm had arisen. Chains had to be put on the hearse and a couple of cars in order to negotiate the trip to the cemetery. Very few of the mourners attended the burial; I'm not even sure that Grandma did. It was perhaps a good thing emotionally for me that I was not allowed to go along.

I have Grandpa's favorite rocking chair—the chair in which he spent most of his nonworking waking hours. It sat in the kitchen where most of our chats occurred. It was there where my purchase of Dan transpired. My wife, Maggie, thoughtfully stripped the chair of its many coats of paint (Grandpa was a great painter), varnished it and had it recaned. I spend a lot of time sitting in it reading, and rarely do so without fondly remembering Grandpa John Cords.

<u>Art Cords</u> - "Mr. St. Clair"

On the day of his funeral, April 6, 1963, as all the businesses in town closed, I believe it was Stan Drake who referred to Art Cords as "Mr. St. Clair." In such a small, close-knit town I'm sure many of that generation of businessmen would qualify for the title along with Art: Earl Pagenkopf, Nick Juliar, Jack Pint, Carl Rose, Elmer Haugen, Jack Sanborn, John Fossum, Art Winkelman, Herb Buesing, Jack Fitzloff, Tom Meany, George Macomber, Bob Schostag, just to mention a few of the most prominent, and certainly not to be exclusive. But because he was my father, and given that particular moment in time, I'm sure the reader won't mind if I vigorously endorse Stan's choice for the title. Incidentally, Dad would have accepted and openly supported any of the above-mentioned, along with perhaps several others, as recipients of the honor.

Arthur Oscar Cords was born on June 4, 1898, to John and Clara Cords, who farmed a modest-sized farm at the outskirts of St. Clair. Art, his preferred nickname (as opposed to Artie, his mother's choice), had two older brothers, Ervin and Vernie, and two younger sisters, Daisy and Viva. Ervin, Vernie

Clara Cords

and Viva preceded Art in death.

Art stayed at home to help on the farm, as Vernie, for example, took up a wandering, and sometimes exciting, life. Farming was difficult in those horse-reliant years, and especially under the Teutonic taskmaster that John was. Clara, however, kept the rigors of life from being too strenuous by providing a sensitive buffer between father and son.

Art left school sometime during the seventh grade, arguing that he was needed at home, but that may well have been an excuse, as it was for so many others. About this time, against all the good advice of Professor Harold Hill in The Music Man, he began hanging out at the local pool hall, which was then located in the rear of the barbershop. Soon he was racking balls for the older players, and actually shooting pool in his spare time. Here he found a hidden talent, and soon he was collecting fees and playing for the house. In his late teens, he actually played for the house in the largest public pool hall in St. Paul. Homesickness, however, brought him back to St. Clair to take up another of his interests—barbering.

L to R: Henry Phillips and barber Art Cords
The Barber Shop was on the east side of Main Street

Lauretta (Lynch) & Arthur Cords

During his time at the local pool hall he had started lathering customers' faces prior to the barber shaving them, and then he started to shave, then, under careful tutelage, to cut hair. Subsequently he became a licensed barber himself, and with various partners at first, took over the barbershop, which still included the pool hall.

Another reason Art no doubt returned to St. Clair was his growing interest in Lauretta Lynch, whom he married on October 12, 1922. Three children resulted from the marriage: Betty Marie (1925), Nicholas John (1929) and Joan (1931). He was a devoted husband, father and family man, an exemplary role model at home, as well as becoming a pillar of the community.

During the over forty years of his active business life, the shop became and remained one of the central forums for taking-up and debating the great issues facing St. Clair, and the world for that matter: the other forums being the liquor store(s), where things were perhaps a bit more exciting, but less clear. Dad served the community in many informal and formal capacities: he was President of the Commercial Club for several terms.

Art suffered a major heart attack late in 1951; he couldn't return to work for nearly nine months. He was able to continue at his beloved barbershop for twelve more years, plagued with occasional health setbacks. Fittingly, he died on the streets of St. Clair, suffering a fatal attack on the sidewalk at the border between his and the Quinn properties. The date was April 3, 1963, approximately two months before his 65th birthday and possible retirement. Father Hodapp, a good friend, celebrated the Mass of Christian Burial at the Immaculate Conception Catholic Church; Art lies buried in the adjoining cemetery, now with his wife Lauretta. Along with other deserving past, present and future title contenders, this "Mr. St. Clair," Art Cords, justly remains in cherished memory.

Nick Cords - A Musical Boyhood in St. Clair, Minnesota

My musical life derived no doubt from a certain amount of inherited ability, and, more important, growing up in a musical environment. My mother, Lauretta

(Larie) Cords, emanated maternally from a very musical German family, the Pestkas. Her father, although certainly not as musically oriented, at his wedding reception is said to have danced a jig on a red-hot stove top without charring his shoes (Yes, Nick Lynch was Irish—and a saloon-keeper and wit for good measure).

My father, Arthur (Art) Cords, was not musically talented, certainly in the sense mother was. His claim to any artistic fame was while using only the index finger of each hand, he could play "Peter, Peter, Punkin Eater" on the piano—with gloves on after a few drinks. He was, however, extremely supportive—at times perhaps tolerant—of the rest of the family's musical shenanigans.

Mother, having received lessons from an early age on the organ and piano, was a very good player, and many a joyous, if not perfectly harmonious, evening was spent with the Pestkas and others around the Hallet-Davis piano singing "the old songs." And they all helped people the Catholic Church choir, for a time including mother at the organ, on Sundays.

Although St. Clair (population about 350) wasn't Mozart's Salzburg, or even Louis Armstrong's New Orleans, it was most certainly not lacking in musical opportunities. The author Bill Holm has said, "the heart can be filled anywhere on earth," and that was musically true for me of St. Clair.

By the time I was five, I had embarked on a public music career of sorts as a boy soprano, thanks largely to the gentle urgings of mother. I performed with the McComb Sisters' Acrobatic and Variety Show; my featured "show-stopper" involved singing the current Al Jolson hit, "About a Quarter to Nine." I was supremely devastating, at least according to the McComb sisters (Shirley and Capitola) and mother. My sister Betty, and Jeanette Nyquist performed an acrobatic dance with the show.

Barbara (Bob) Maxon was another producer type, who engineered various entertainment delights in St. Clair. The most personally memorable of these was a couple's performance of "Ma, He's Makin Eyes at Me." At the performance, on cue from Bob and unbeknownst to the girls, the boys kissed their partners—and thus I got to kiss Margie Timmerman! I loved it, I don't know about Margie. (Other probable performers were Donna and Lowell Pagenkopf, Jim Winkelman, Donna Riese, Buddy Schroeder and Corrine Haugen.)

I sang leads in nearly all the school Christmas operettas, as well as continuing my on-again-off-again boy soprano career. My last stand (hurrah?) came in November 1939, following the Nazi and Russian invasions of Poland. At a patriotic rally held in the St. Clair Town Hall I sang Irving Berlin's "God Bless America," incidentally, in about the same key and at the same voice level as Kate Smith.

My high voice was deserting me, but other musical interests had arisen. At age eight, to fill a void left by my utter failure, due mainly to lack of interest, at the piano, I took up the guitar and almost overnight became a singin' cowboy—and yes, a yodeler to boot. This is true: I actually, along with Jimmy Fitzloff, took guitar lessons from "Irv, the Yodeling Cowboy!" In truth, and in defense of Irv, he was a schooled musician, as well as being a very good teacher. He taught me to read the chord symbols so I could wail on the likes of "When It's Lamplightin' Time in the Valley." On Saturday nights my corral was the Grand Ol' Opry, that is when I could ace my older sister Betty out of Your Hit Parade. (I didn't confess this for years.)

In fifth grade, a new wonder appeared in my musical world: the slide trombone. A local, Reed Macomber, directed the St. Clair school's summer band and when he asked what I wanted to play, I moved my right arm out and back, as I'd seen Reed himself do; he was a very good trombone player. The instrument became almost literally the center of my life, aided and abetted by the fact that I was quite good at playing it. Further, it was the Big Band Era, and Tommy Dorsey quickly replaced Roy Acuff as my idol.

Along with playing in the St. Clair school band, and thanks mainly to Harold Boswell, I played my first dance job at age fourteen at Elysian with the Clete Fredericks Orchestra. The World War II manpower shortage no doubt helped me get started that young. After starting out with Reed, I continued to take trombone lessons with Heinie Udelhofen, Ray Saunders and Jack MacKay, Principal Trombone with the Minneapolis Symphony. I played a trombone duet with Heinie, also director of the school band, at my high school graduation in 1947.

Following my high school graduation, I played in an army band and then majored in music and history at Mankato State College. I worked my way through college mainly playing in Spike Haskell's Jolly Millers orchestra, and continued dance work several years beyond that. Following college, I actually taught public school music for a time, until I switched to teaching history, which became my actual permanent profession. I taught history and humanities at Albert Lea High School before moving to Lakewood Community College (now Century College) where I taught American History for twenty-six years.

I continue to play avocationally with the Century College Concert Band and the White Bear Lake Unitarian Society Jazz Ensemble. Our family, including my wife Maggie (Hurley) and sons Jim, John, Nick and

Dan, has been and remains deeply invglved with music; two of my sons Nick and Dan, currently are professional musicians.

Now retired, I enjoy reading, writing, traveling, and playing the trombone.

My life indeed has been highly enriched, even blessed, by music, and it all began and was nurtured during my boyhood in St. Clair, Minnesota—my personal Salzburg, my personal New Orleans.

Frank Cords

Frank wasn't really my uncle—he was my great-uncle, the youngest brother of my grandfather, John. Like John, Frank was orphaned at a very early age and was raised by an aunt. John, some eight years older, looked after Frank, and later Frank lived for a time with John and his wife Clara (Casper). The result of this was the development of a very close bond between these two brothers, a bond that lasted until John's death in 1939. Frank was a large man for the times, standing over six feet tall and weighing approximately 190 pounds. He was outgoing, confident, and extremely adventurous. As you might imagine, he led a very interesting life.

At age 17 he enlisted in the U.S. Army to serve in the Spanish-American War. He liked to tell of the time when his company was stationed at Chattanooga, Tennessee. One day when the order was given to fall out (assemble), only he and one other man appeared—the result of flu and dysentery. Frank said that he didn't feel too sharp either, but he didn't want to miss any possible excitement. I believe the war was over before he got to Cuba, although he did spend about seven weeks there.

After the war he finished high school, traveled, wrestled, worked as a fireman on the railroad, a ranch hand, a farmer, an insurance and car salesman, and construction worker. In 1909 he married Clarissa Nelson, and they had two children—Willard and Verna.

Regarding his on-again-off-again wrestling career, Frank related this story: He was following the county fair and carnival circuit somewhere in Michigan because this was where many wrestling opportunities existed. There was one particularly good wrestler who was beating all challengers.

Rather than challenge him immediately and possibly lose, Frank followed the man on the circuit for awhile and bet on him to win—a profitable enterprise. All the while, Frank was scouting the man and getting to know his strengths and weaknesses. Then came the challenge. Frank beat him and walked away with the prize money. By this time, the two men were acquainted because the other man noticed Frank consistently in the crowds. Evidently Frank's cleverness was recognized, if not totally appreciated.

In 1926, Frank ran for the office of Blue Earth County Sheriff. I don't know the specifics concerning the campaign, except that his wife Clarissa told me about how hard the family worked on it. Even their young son Willard delivered handbills and encouraged all to vote for his dad—"the best dad in the world." Frank won, and served in that capacity for twenty years.

I got to know Frank personally during this period, which was fun and exciting. Because of the bond between Frank and my grandfather John, I'm sure it's safe to say that we saw more of him in St. Clair than we otherwise would have.

He made frequent visits to John at the farm, confiding in him and I think showing off a bit for his older brother, whom he had always admired. Frank got involved in one of the abortive attempts to capture John Dillinger in Minnesota. A result of this was that one of Dillinger's cars, a Hudson, showed up in Mankato. Frank drove the car to St. Clair and up the hill to the farm to show John—horn blaring all the way.

On his visits to St. Clair, he invariably stopped at Dad's barbershop, and sometimes at our house. Once in awhile he would stop to talk to me on the street—did I feel important! Frank represented my encounter with celebrity. He was my hero, and he was my uncle—well, at least, my dad's uncle.

Being a sheriff then was sort of a frontier job. Sheriffs today tend to function in more of an administrative capacity, with multiple deputies to do field (grunt) work. Frank never had more than one or two deputies, one of whom operated the switchboard, so Frank did all the grunt work. If the services of the sheriff were needed, it was invariably Frank who showed up. His life was exciting and sometimes dangerous.

If there was, say, a dangerous fight situation at a barn dance out in the county somewhere, Frank many times showed up alone. He was armed, of course, but firing a gun was a last resort. I asked him once how he handled a situation such as that, and he told me that he quickly tried to focus on the chief troublemaker, isolate him, talk to him and, failing that, take him on!

On one occasion, a dangerous at-large criminal who had made threats about what he physically was going to do to Frank if he ever had the chance, was arrested by police and brought to Frank at the jail. Frank gave him his chance. I don't know the details, but it seems that he made a move, whereupon Frank hit him on the jaw, breaking it in three places.

It wasn't all roughhouse, however. These were the Depression years, and many inmates at the jail received counsel, care, and help finding a job from Frank and his wife. I remember Frank saying to one departing inmate, "Don't let me see you here again! I'll give you all the help I can, but don't ever let me see you here again!"

Probably my happiest memories of Frank Cords involve the times when I stayed with him at the jail and accompanied him on his rounds. He seemed to know everyone and have something to say to each, usually in the form of advice, sometimes developing into a lecture or sermon.

Frank was a fast, some might say reckless driver. The car I particularly remember was a gray 1939 Buick coach, with his stop sign on the fender. He seemed to drive it at top speed all the time. I checked the speedometer as we drove down the alley behind the jail once, and it read 45 M.P.H.!

I accompanied him when he escorted a prisoner to the St. Cloud Reformatory. As we entered the outskirts of Mankato on the way home, I thought he was stopping for some reason and reached for the door handle. He informed me that we were doing 50 m.p.h.—after 85-90 on the highway.

The most exciting event, however, occurred one day about noon in downtown Mankato on the main drag—Front Street. Frank asked me if I wanted to have some fun; I replied in the affirmative. He then ran the entire length of Mankato at 50 M.P.H., with the siren going full blast, and he laughed as cars scurried to get out of the way of this apparent emergency.

Attending the Blue Earth County Fair at Garden City was another spectacular event. As sheriff of the county, Frank had to be there every day, sometimes more than once. This was like heaven on earth for me. He would deposit me at the fair in the morning and pick me up at night, making sure, of course, that I was supplied with enough money. It was a blast! It was so wonderful that not everyone believed I could be so lucky.

One summer there was a wrestler there who took on all comers. I was fascinated and gullible so I frequented the tent quite a bit. During one match, the tent raised behind me and an acquaintance, Joe Stegemeir, entered—without paying, of course. He had been seen slipping in, so the manager and the wrestler accosted him. Since he was talking to me, they assumed that I was Joe's accomplice. I had thrown my ticket away, so all arguments that I was with the sheriff didn't cut much ice.

"With the sheriff, yeah, right!"

The manager told Joe and me to leave and never darken the tent flap again—no problem for me.

Later that day, Frank and I walked past the wrestling tent where the two men were standing out front. They saw us together, and I thought raised their eyebrows a bit, but I'm sorry to say they did not rush to apologize to me.

Frank lost his re-election bid in 1946 to one of his deputies, a younger man and veteran of World War II. He argued that Frank was too old to effectively continue as sheriff. He won and died of a heart attack before completing his first term.

We continued to see a lot of Frank and Clarissa after Frank's retirement. He served on the Mankato City Council for a time, and continued to be an interesting and exciting character. Frank died in 1975 at age 95. I'm sorry I didn't pump him for more personal information; he surely would have been willing. He was a great storyteller. I last saw him about six months before he died, and he didn't recognize me until just before I left. That's not the Frank Cords I choose to remember.

(Additional notations on Frank Cords) from: *Minnesota, the Land of Sky-Tinted Waters*

Frank Cords was born on a farm in Decorah Township on April 15, 1880. He attended school in St. Clair for a brief period of time. Regardless of politics or other considerations the people of Blue Earth County learned respect for his record as a boy and man in struggling through to success and the realization of the best opportunities within his reach. When he was thirteen years old he started earning his own living, grew up in the home of an uncle, and was always an earnest worker and willing to do his patriotic duty. He farmed until 1898 and at the age of eighteen he enlisted for service in the Spanish American War. He was with the twelfth MN Regiment, which spent most of its time in Minnesota or in southern training camps, and did´not get to the front.

After his military service Mr. Cords took up carpenter work. He was also in the railway service as a fireman for the Northwestern Railway for four years. Frank became sheriff of Blue Earth County in 1926.

In 1907 he married Clarissa Nelson, a native of Minnesota. Her father Elias Nelson came to the states in 1870 and was a substantial and well to do farmer. Mr. and Mrs. Cords had two children: Verna L. and Willard E. Frank was a member of the Bethlehem Lutheran Church of Mankato, was a York Rite Mason and Shriner, a member of the B. P. O. Elks, Independent Order of Odd Fellows, Fraternal Order of Eagles, and Ancient order of United Workmen. He was a Republican in his political affiliation. He enjoyed outdoor activities of all kinds, and was a member of a gun club. While on the farm he served as township treasurer and was a member of the Creamery Board and School Board.

Frank Cords died on May 11, 1975.

By Nicholas John Cords

COVEL, ALPHEUS

Alpheus Covel and his wife Eliza Jane Nash came to McPherson Township from Beaver Dam, Wisconsin, in 1866. Alpheus was born in 1821 and Eliza in 1820. They had the following children, Martha, David, Albert, Charles, Benjamin, George, Mary, Harriet, Cordelia and William.

Alpheus died in 1893 and Eliza in 1904.

George Covel was born in 1852, took over the family farm. He married Ella Reynolds who was born in 1863. Their children were Lottie (George Goodrich), Eunice (Bennett), Harvey, Orin, Edna, Bernice (Kotz). Harvey and Orin worked for the Railroad Company.

George died in 1932 and Ella died in 1931.

Lottie was born in 1879 and married George Goodrich who was born in 1888. They then took over the family farm. Their children were Allan (Gertrude Grams), Lyle (see separate story), Dean (Everilda Anton), Keith (LaVera Dallman), Rowena (Arthur Scherger), and Lila (Eldon Remington).

By Lyle and Stella Goodrich

DANBERRY, HENRY

Henry and Lillian Danberry were farmers, 3½ miles east of St. Clair in McPherson Township, for 25 years. They raised three sons, Paul, Elmer and John.

John Danberry graduated from St. Clair School and helped his parents with the farming. He met a senior gal by the name of Donna DeMars, the daughter of Leo and Tony DeMars (see separate story) and they were married in 1948. Jack's parents then left the farm and Jack and Donna took over the operation. Jack loved to raise feeder cattle along with his general farming.

Jack and Donna raised five children: John Jr. (Marie), Michael (Wendy), Nancy (Rick Prahl), Joan, who is married to Peter Preston, [see separate story] and Jane (Jody Klint).

The entire family graduated from St. Clair Public School and they were members of Immaculate Conception Catholic Church in St. Clair.

Jack and Donna farmed for 53 years. Their son Michael farmed with his dad until November of 1993. Jack died on November 13, 1999. Donna is now living in Mankato.

By Donna Danberry

DELING, KEVIN

Kevin and Diane Deling are first generation residents of McPherson Township. The family moved to the former Emil Westphal farm site in the northeastern part of the township in January of 1987.

Kevin Jon was born on July 9, 1963, at Waseca, Minnesota, to John and Judy Deling. He has one sister and two brothers. Kevin has worked for RDO Equipment in North Mankato since 1996 and is a Diesel Service Field Technician. In March 2005 he was elected as a supervisor on the McPherson Township Board.

Diane Ruby was born on August 3, 1962, in Owatonna, Minnesota, to Don and Audrey Parker. She has one brother and two sisters. Diane works for the J.C. Penney Company in Mankato. She is a Senior Customer Service Specialist for the Home and the Ladies Intimate Department.

Kevin and Diane have two children, Derek Allan born on January 7, 1990, and Kelly Jean born on December 21, 1992, both at Mankato, Minnesota. Both of the children attend school at the St. Clair Public School.

The members of the Deling Family are active members of the St. John's Evangelical Lutheran Church in St. Clair.

By Diane R. Deling

Kevin & Diane Deling
with children Kelly and Derek.

DEMARS, LEO

Leo and Antonia DeMars came from Elk River, Minnesota, in 1945. In St. Clair they operated the St. Clair Hotel where they also lived. Food was also served at the hotel. A lot of the students from the school would come during the noon hour. A lot of hamburgers and chip steaks were served. People would also come in after ball games and after the free movies. Sister's Donna, Rose and I would have to take turns working for dad. Dad was remembered for playing jokes on the kids. Hamburgers sold for 15 cents, T-bone Steak were from $1.25-$1.50, depending on its size and a pork chop was 60 cents.

Leo and Tonie had ten children: LaVerne (Hazel Frank), Joyce (Ernest Hill), Donna (John Danberry), Shirley (James Fitzloff - see separate story), Rose (James Loeffler), Darlene (Robert Kulseth), Jackie (Mark Healy), Janice (Lowell Ellis), Kathy (Thomas Wright) and Patricia (Tony Staloch).

By Shirley Halberg

Tonie & Leo DeMars

The DeMars Family
Back (L to R): Shirley, Rose, Joyce, LaVerne, Kathy and Donna. Front: Jackie, Pat and Jan.

DICKINSON, CLARK

Clark Dickinson, the father of Huldah Dickinson Hilton, was born in Vermont circa 1792. He was still living in Vermont in 1810 but by 1833 had moved to Green Bay, Wisconsin. He was one of the founding settlers of Oshkosh, Wisconsin. He served as a lay preacher in the Methodist Episcopal Church for over 60 years. Clark and his wife, Sally (last name unknown) had five children. He died in Oshkosh in 1872.

DITTMAN, FREDERICK

Frederick Dittman was 69 at the time of his death. He was a life long resident of McPherson Township. He had a son Arthur and sister Hannah. He is buried in St. Clair.

DITTMAN, HANNAH

Hannah Dittman died on July 2, 1947, at the age of 77. She was one of St. Clair's memorable residents. An individualist who never changed with the times. She lived in the house at 333 Main Street East, which later was the home of the Robert Zavoral family. Milton Juliar wrote the following tribute to her on February 9, 1927, as an English assignment.

The Home Town Washerwoman

What is a town without its washerwoman? Every up-to-date, modern town has one or more and so has a certain little town in Minnesota. There are probably two types or two different classes of washerwomen. One is the kind that was lucky or rather unlucky enough to secure a lowdown, good-for-nothing husband to call for and deliver the washing. You have probably seen a husband of this nature slowly making his way along the sidewalk pulling a little wagon which contains a basket of clothes neatly covered over with a white sheet. The second is that class that has managed to escape cupid's arrows, or probably I should say that they have failed to get in the path of cupid's arrows. Anyway this is the kind that I am speaking of. The kind that travel from one home to the other with a bar of soap under one arm and a washboard under the other.

If you should ever pass through this little town and should happen to see Hannah (for Hannah is her name) on the street, I am sure you would recognize her at once. She is just one of those good old fashion girls. She does not use lip stick, rouge, and all the other vile flapperish things. Hannah is tall and slender. Her beautiful straight, gray hair is put up in a knot on the back part of her head. Her face is narrow and of a charming color. Near the end of her nose is perched a pair of brass rimmed glasses. She wears dresses that would probably contain enough material for two or three of the dresses that are commonly worn in this age. Her feet are enclosed in what might be a pair of number nine or ten shoes and are most likely that kind that are about ten inches in length. However I have never seen the tops of them, because her dress extends about to her ankles.

Hannah has a very peculiar habit that one could not help but notice if one should happen to see her. She never walks on the sidewalk but always down the center of the street. I do not know why she does it unless she thinks that she can make better time on the street than she could dodging between the people on the sidewalk. It is a very common thing to hear some young woman say: "Well, Hannah, Do you think we will have any snow today?" And after searching the clear June sky for any trace of snow cloud, determining the direction of the wind and a few other things she would probably say, "No, I don't hardly think we'll get any snow today. We might have a little rain tomorrow though." She is always in earnest about every thing she says and does not realize that the other person is only joking. If you should happen to see her near her home on the edge of town you would probably see her out trying to mow off her lawn with a hoe. But there is one thing about her that you cannot help but like and that is her love of flowers and her ability to grow flowers. In that section of the country where the winters are long and cold it is very hard to grow certain kinds of flowers. But she has the most beautiful beds of tulips that one could wish to see. I rather think that old man fate was very unkind to have her pass through this world as a washerwoman instead of a florist of great renown.

DOLAND, GEORGE

George E. Doland was born in New Hampshire, in 1832. He lived in the city of Manchester until he was eleven years old and then remained on a farm until 1855. In 1855 he moved to McPherson. In 1864 he enlisted in the 11th Minnesota and served through the remainder of the war. He married Ann Farmer on December 5, 1852. Their children were Mary, Eliza, Carrie, Ellen, George, John, Lizzie, Nettie and Annie.

DRAKE, STANLEY

Stanley Drake was born in 1920 to Merton and Mary (Delaney) Drake in St. Paul, MN. After his mother's death in 1922, he and his two sisters were placed in the MN State School/Orphanage in Owatonna, MN (1923-1931). As a ward of the state, he attended country school and worked for families in the Waseca area from 1931-1939.

Enlisting in the army in 1939, he served three years as surgical technician in Panama. In 1944, President Roosevelt asking for volunteers with previous jungle service to undertake an unspecified & dangerous and hazardous mission issued a bulletin. Stan was one of the 3,000 volunteers who became known as Merrill's Marauders and later Mars Task Force serving in the China-Burma-India Theater. In 1945 after receiving an honorable discharge as Tech 3rd Gr. Med Det 2nd BN 475th Inf, he was awarded several medals, including the Purple Heart and one from each of the three Asian countries in which the 475th Infantry had fought.

On June 16, 1947, he married Jeanette Nyquist the daughter of Elmo and Nona (Fields) Nyquist at the Evangelical United Brethren Church in St. Clair. They lived at 324 Main Street West in the house built by Dr. R. Juliar.

After completing the two-year automotive program at Dunwoody Institute (1945-47), he purchased the St. Clair Service Station, from Bill and Margaret Myers, which was located directly across from the St. Clair School.

Not only were Stan and his wife, Jeanette, owners of St. Clair Service, but forty years as auto mechanic, towing service and gas station attendant deserves recognition for Stan as one of St. Clair's businessmen providing the most years of service to the community. With the assistance of Stan and Jeanette's children a successful business existed in St. Clair. A sincere thank you is extended from the family to the many customers who faithfully supported Drake's St. Clair Service.

He retired in 1988 to enjoy fishing, golf and bowling. He sold the station to Leo Ripplinger.

He was a member of Zion United Methodist Church, American Legion Post #475, and lifetime member of Merrill's Marauders Association, Ranger Regiment Association, China-Burma-India Veterans Association and Muskies, Inc.

Jeanette graduated from St. Clair High School and then attended Mankato Normal College and got an education degree. She taught many years at St. Clair, touching the lives of many students. She is now living in Winona with her daughter Nancy.

Stan and Jeanette's children are Scott (Sue), Michael (Vonna) and Nancy (Dwight Nelson).

Stan was the foster son of Bill and Margaret Myers. He died on February 27, 2001.

By Jeanette Drake

DUEMELAND, ERNEST

The general merchandising business of Ernest A. Duemeland, parallel with the history of St. Clair and Blue Earth County, was established in 1882. In obedience to the scientific law of supply and demand it kept pace with the enlarging community, and through fair and dependable methods filled a many sided public need. The

E. A. Duemeland Drygoods & Groceries

quality which insured successful merchandising was possessed in large measure by the owner, and not the least of these were a thorough understanding of the tastes and inclinations of his patrons, an unfailing courtesy, and a genuine desire to please. Mr. Duemeland came with sterling German stock, and the first ten years of his life were spent in Hanover, Germany, where he was born January 5, 1856. With his parents, Henry and Dorothea (Gibbons) Duemeland, he came to America in a sailing vessel in 1866, being six weeks on the ocean and settling soon after the arrival in New York in St. Peter, Minnesota. The next year the father took up a homestead in Le Sueur County, where they engaged in farming many years, the father dying in 1879 at the age of seventy-two years, and the mother in 1891 at the age of sixty years. They reared a family of sixteen children, eight sons and eight daughters, giving them such educational and other opportunities as were possible from their meager earning.

The popular merchant of St. Clair was the twelfth oldest in his father's large family. He was educated in the district schools, and lived on the home farm until embarking in his merchandising business. In 1880 he was united in marriage to Mary Lane, a native of Wisconsin, and of German descent. Of the union there were two sons, Henry J., engaged in the wholesale grocery business at Bismarck and George A. with the Patterson Land Company of St. Paul. Mr. Duemeland was interested in Republican politics to the extent of sustaining the interest of the party by his vote, but had no party aspirations. Fraternally he was connected with Lodge No. 29, I.O.O.F. The family lived in the apartment of the grocery store and was members of the Lutheran Church.

Ernest Duemeland died in 1947 in Bismarck, North Dakota.

From the *History of Blue Earth County* by Thomas Hughes-1909

DYER, LUCIUS

Lucius Dyer was an Indian farmer, but when the Indians left in 1863, he purchased the land and home of the Indian agents. He made the home into a hotel. The first town meeting of Rice Lake was held in this home on September 19, 1863. In March 1865, he sold this hotel to Josiah Truman.

FIELDS, JOHN H.

John H. (1858-1940) and Isabelle Fields (1862-1959) lived on a farm southeast of St. Clair until 1910. They then moved into town and lived at 300 South County Road 28. Their children: Harry C., Ada (John Bestman), May (H. E. Seewald), Sadie (James Lynch) and Alma (Elmo Nyquist).

FISHER, FRANK

Frank Fisher lived in St. Clair and operated a small service station between the Quinn Oil Co. and the Hager Hardware businesses. He was the son of August Fisher who was born in Germany and immigrated to America. Frank was married to Anna Pietsch. They had two son Harry and Leon and two daughters Sylvia (Art Peterson) and Delores (Bert Smyth).

Harry Fisher was born on November 16, 1911, and was married to Mildred Juliar, the daughter of Otto and Louise (Muehlhausen) Juliar. Harry attended school in St. Clair and they farmed south of St. Clair for many years. He served on the Pemberton School Board, Pemberton Lumber Yard Board and the McPherson Fire Insurance Board. When they retired they moved to St. Clair and lived at 318 County Road #28. Harry died on May 9, 2002. Mildred is living with her son Roger in Shakopee, MN.

Leon Fisher was born on December 11, 1915, and on April 3, 1941 he married Joyce Priem (1916-1981), the daughter of George and Nellie Priem. Leon was employed by the Cities Service Oil Company in St. Clair for 34 years. He retired in 1978. He was a life long member of the United Methodist Church in St. Clair. They lived at 201 Park Street North. Leon died on October 3, 1993, suffering from a heart attack while duck hunting. Joyce worked at the St. Clair State Bank and was secretary for the United Fund in St. Clair. She was a member of St. John's Evangelical Lutheran Church in St. Clair.

FISHER, CHARLES

Charles Fisher was born around 1849 in Prussia and moved to Wisconsin. Here he married Lena Gerber, the daughter of John and Louisa Gerber, in 1877. Their first two children George and Emma were born in Wisconsin. Around 1879 they moved to Minnesota and settled in McPherson Township.

Charles and Lena's children were George, Emma, William (Amanda Johnson/Lillian Haack), Matilda, Ida, Bertha, Alfred, Alma (Johnson), Gertrude, and Carl.

In February of 1903, Charles died from self-inflicted wounds. He was fifty-three years of age and had lived near St. Clair for a number of years. He owned a forty-acre tract and was free from debt. He was a quiet, inoffensive citizen and was well liked by everybody. For years he had suffered from a nervous disease, but was not in such a serious condition as he himself believed he was. He is buried in the Union (Boswell) Cemetery in St. Clair.

Lena married Charles Mohr in 1905 who was a widower and they lived south of the Sodeman farm on the next road.

Alfred, the son of Charles and Lena Fisher, was born on July 18, 1891, and died on March 9, 1903, shortly after his father's death, from heart failure. He is also buried in the Union Cemetery under the name of Fisher.

FITZLOFF, JOHAN

Johan Ludwig Fitzloff was born in Pommerania, Germany, on January 22, 1827. He was raised on a farm and came to America in 1863. He married Henrietta Borchardt (b.1830) in 1854 in Germany. They immigrated to America with their three sons, Albert, Herman, and Otto, arriving in Milwaukee in 1863. By 1865 they were farming near St. Clair, Minnesota in McPherson Township. Three more children were born there, Bertha, John and Charles. Johan L. was a bricklayer by trade and reportedly made the first bricks in the county. He also was one of the founders of St. John's Evangelical Lutheran Church along with August Barneke and August Kopke in 1869. He and his wife celebrated their 50th wedding anniversary in 1904. Henrietta died May 2, 1905. John L. then retired from farming and lived with his son Johan Carl and his wife Emma in St. Clair until his death on February 11, 1912.

Albert Fitzloff married Mary Kruse and farmed near St. Clair until his death on June 6, 1929. They had six children: Sophia (Albert Brandenburg), William H., Carl (Lilly Prange), Louis (Minnie Niebauer), George (Ella Jans) and Marie (Elmer Lentz).

Carl & Lilly Fitzloff

Carl W. Fitzloff was born February 12, 1899, in McPherson Township to Mary and Albert Fitzloff. He was a lifetime resident of McPherson Township where he farmed until retirement and then moved to St. Clair. They lived at 205 Park Street North, which had been the home of Dr. John Wohlrabe, MD.

Carl and his wife Lilly (nee Prange) of Beauford were married June 10, 1925, in Mapleton. Lilly E. Prange was born September 11, 1896. They were the parents of five children. Marion (Donald Drescher deceased), Donna (Donald Watson) both deceased, LaVerne (Burton Williams), Albert deceased (Arlene Witt), and Charles (Beverly Best).

Carl was a lifelong member of St. John's Evangelical Lutheran Church, St. Clair, where he also served as chair-

Children of Carl & Lilly Fitzloff
Standing (L to R): Marion, Donna and LaVerne.
Seated: Charles and Albert

man of the church council for many years. Carl was a dedicated community leader. He was a board member of County School District 124 (Lynch School) on the McPherson Township board, member of the Minnesota Farm Bureau and the Agricultural Service Center. Carl also enjoyed hunting, fishing, and sharing his garden produce with many relatives and friends.

Carl served as mayor (1966-1969) being one of the residents developing the plan for the St. Clair Sewage System. He was a member of the Sportsman Club, St. Clair Booster's Club, Red Cross Volunteer and the Senior Citizens Groups.

Lilly Fitzloff was a homemaker and caring mother. She is remembered for the songs and nursery rhymes she taught to her children. She enjoyed a large garden, raising chickens, and was admired for her sewing, canning vegetables, fruits and meat raised on the farm, and her hospitality. Carl and Lilly had a welcoming home for relatives and friends. Lilly was a member of St. John's Lutheran Church, St. Clair, honorary member of the St. John's Ladies Aid, American Legion Auxiliary Post 475, the St. Clair Neighborhood Home Extension, 500 Card Club, involved in many St. Clair School district activities and the Senior Citizen's Group. She was a life long resident of Blue Earth County.

Carl W. Fitzloff passed away on April 10, 1978, and Lilly E. Fitzloff passed away December 10, 1973, they are buried in the St. John's Evangelical Lutheran Cemetery.

By Marion Fitzloff Drescher

FITZLOFF, ALBERT H.

Albert H. Fitzloff was born on January 4, 1935 to Carl and Lilly (Prange) Fitzloff in Blue Earth County. He graduated from St. Clair High School in 1954 and served in the U.S. Army 1955-57. He married Arlene Witt the daughter of Erick and Lotie Witt on June 10, 1958, in Rapidan.

Albert and Arlene farmed in the St. Clair area. They were also employed by Dean Foods, formerly Bird's Eye, in Waseca for more than 20 years. They moved to Mankato in 1987. Albert served on the church board of St. John's Evangelical Lutheran Church and he was a 39-year member of the St. Clair American Legion Post 475. He enjoyed collecting toy tractors and they enjoyed caring for their yard.

They were the parents of Debbie, Ken and Mary.

In 1987 Ken died as a result of injuries he sustained in a car accident. Albert died in 1997. They are buried in the St. John's Evangelical Lutheran Cemetery, St. Clair.

Arlene is living in North Mankato.

FITZLOFF, HOWARD

Howard Fitzloff was the son of George and Ella (Jans) Fitzloff who were farmers. (When they retired they lived at 105 Agency Road.) He was born in 1930 and graduated from St. Clair High School. He had one sister Marilyn (Alvin Walton). He studied accounting at the Mankato Commercial College and then worked as an accountant at Grand Forks, ND before he entered the U.S. Army. He served in the Korean Conflict from 1952 until December of 1953. He then worked at Hegstrom Painting in Janesville. He then lived in St. Louis, MO, for two years, working in sales. He returned to Janesville and started working for the Harvest States (GTA) Elevator in Janesville. In 1960 he came to the Harvest States Elevator in St. Clair. He retired in 1989. He then worked part-time for Warren Riese driving truck and worked for Southern Valley Co-op in St. Clair. He was a member of

Arlene & Albert Fitzloff

Eileen & Howard Fitzloff

the St. Clair America Legion. He enjoyed fishing and working around his home.

On July 29, 1955, Howard married Eileen Krause at the Little Brown Church in Nashua, Iowa. Eileen, the daughter of William and Gertrude (Popham) Krause was born in 1934, in LeRay Township, Blue Earth Co. She graduated as valedictorian of her 1952 Janesville High School graduating class. After high school she worked at the E. F. Johnson Co. in Waseca. They moved to St. Clair in 1960, where she worked at the St. Clair State Bank, was a bookkeeper at the St. Clair Public School and was a bookkeeper for Harvest States Cooperative Elevator. Howard and Eileen lived at 229 Main Street West and then built a new home at 50 Fitzloff Avenue. They were members of St. John's Evangelical Lutheran Church.

Howard and Eileen had two sons Jeffrey (Lois) and Daniel (Virginia Reynolds).

Howard died in July of 1996 and Eileen died four months later in November. They are buried in the St. John's Evangelical Lutheran Cemetery, St. Clair.

Herman Henry Fitzloff was the second son of Johan Fitzloff. He came to the United States with his parents at the age of seven. His father was a brick maker and brick-layer. He married Ottelia Barueske, the daughter of a carpenter and builder, who came to America at the age of three. They were married on July 13, 1883 in the Winnebago Agency (now St. Clair, Minnesota) and were among the earlier residents of St. Clair and McPherson Township, where they farmed just north of town which later became part of the city and raised eight children. The children were Lydia Marie (1855-1960) (Oscar Hulseman), Antonius "Tony" (1887-1927) (Hulda Frank), Dorthea "Dora" (1889-1954) (Herman Frank), Hedwig "Hattie" Ida (1893-?) (Fred Kruse), John "Jack" Wilhelm (1895-1960) (Olga Fritzke) [see separate story], Leilah Clara (1899-1924) (never married), Raymond "Ray" William (1901-1979) (Anna McNamara) [see separate story], and Ellen Emma Anne (1905-1973) (George Trahms).

They were proud of the fact that their grandfathers John Fitzloff and August Barueske were not only elders of the first St. John's Evangelical Lutheran Church of the Winnebago Agency, but were instrumental in building the church in 1876. They were all quite musical. They sang, played the piano, violin and the fiddle. Many lived all their lives in and around St. Clair. They were active in church and community activities, enjoying entertaining.

By Shirley Fitzloff Halberg and Colleen Fitzloff Roberts

Eugene Fitzloff was born in 1924 and was the son of Antony and Hulda (Frank) Fitzloff who at one time lived at 313 West Main Street. He was a life long resident of the St. Clair area and graduated from St. Clair High School. He was a master electrician, and was the president of Fitzloff and Sons Electric in St. Clair from 1953 until his death. He was a member of St. John's Evangelical Lutheran Church and a retired member of the St. Clair Fire Department. He married Ramona "Monie" Hager, the daughter of Raymond and Marie (Baynes) Hager on November 27, 1957.

Monie was born in 1925 and graduated from Waterville High School, Waterville, MN. She worked as a nurse's aid at St. Joseph's Hospital in Mankato and St. Olaf Hospital in Austin. She worked for 12 years at Hardeggers Resort on Lake Jefferson near rural Cleveland. After her marriage she managed Fitzloff Mobile Home Court and Laundromat and helped her husband run Fitzloff Electric. In 1976, she became one of the first female mayors in Minnesota when she was elected mayor of St. Clair.

Eugene and Monie had four children Eugene Jr. "Tony," Bill, Harold and Ellen.

Eugene had a sister Leona (Harlen Ulman). He died in 1981 and his sons Bill and Harold have taken over the Fitzloff Electric business. Monie died in 2003. Both are buried at St. Johns (Bestman) Cemetery, St. Clair.

John "Jack" William Fitzloff was born to Herman and Ottelia (Brueske) Fitzloff on April 10, 1895 in St. Clair. He married Olga "Olie" Louise Fritzke on August 18, 1922 at St. John's Lutheran Church in St. Clair. Olie was born to Rev. Gustav E. and Bertha (Otto) Fritzke on May 31, 1893 in Clark, South Dakota. Olie's father Rev. Fritzke married them.

Jack & Olie (Fritzke) Fitzloff

John attended agriculture school and Olga attended nursing school, both in Minneapolis. They had one son James "Jim" Aurthur [see separate story]. John farmed for a few years, was a DeKalb Seed Corn distributor, realtor at St. Clair Land Co., distributor of Aluminum Drome and Crown Metal Buildings, and he and his wife ran the St. Clair Drug Store for many years. At one time Jack was a candidate for Sheriff of Blue Earth County.

Jack had three patents on inventions including the turkey saddle (some of which were sent to Oporto), Portugal, turkey fountains and slip band for wing holes. Jack enjoyed singing and playing violin for the St. Clair School PTA. Jack and Esther Hager sang for weddings and funerals at St. John's Evangelical Lutheran Church.

Olie was a nurse, teacher, an organist at St. John's Lutheran Church for many years, helped run the Fitzloff Drug Store and later after Jack passed away moved to St. Paul and ran the gift shop at a hospital. Olie kept active with scrapbooks galore, (many memories of St. Clair which are being used for this publication.), playing her piano and organ for all to enjoy, and loved playing Bridge.

Jack passed away on January 26, 1960. Olga passed away on June 24, 1983. They are buried in the St. John's Evangelical Lutheran Cemetery, St. Clair, Minnesota.

By Shirley Fitzloff Halberg

James Arthur Fitzloff, the son of John "Jack" and Olga (Fritzke) Fitzloff was born on February 5, 1926, at the family home in St. Clair, Minnesota. The home is located next to the Le Sueur River Bridge at 204 Park Street North. Jim attended St. Clair School and graduated in 1943. He went directly into the Navy and was stationed in Japan and Okinawa during World War II. After his return home, he attended the University of Minnesota for two years and then attended the Radio and Telegraphy School in Minneapolis. He was a station agent and telegrapher on the railroad for many years. He retired from Mankato State College where he worked as Purchasing Agent. Retirement came early because of ill health. Jim loved music, especially playing guitar and occasionally the piano. (He played by ear.) He loved refinishing furniture, especially caning.

Shirley (DeMars) & James Fitzloff

On June 11, 1949, Jim married Shirley Ann DeMars, the daughter of Leo and Antonia (Iverson) DeMars, at St. John's Evangelical Lutheran Church in St. Clair. Shirley was born on July 16, 1932, in Rockford, Illinois. Shirley was a nursing assistant for many years, at the Immanuel Hospital in Mankato and also did home-health care. She worked for 21 years at Midtex in Mankato until the company moved. She was active in the Ladies Aid at St. John's Evangelical Lutheran Church, St. Clair. She has made a lot of videos and taken many pictures for a number of people for various occasions and many of these pictures include history of St. Clair and memories of her children and grandchildren in sports or school activities. She has made scrapbooks for her grandchildren, which is still an ongoing hobby. Shirley assisted with the publication of *Years of Memories*.

Seated (L to R): Dick, Shirley (DeMars), Greg
Standing: Roxanne and Jackie, James Lee Fitzloff

They had six children, Lee James (1951-1951), Greg (1952) (Pamela Johnson) their children are Jason and Stacey, Roxanne (1954) (Robert Loeffler), their children are Heather, who has a son Dominic, and Stephanie, who has a son Logan. Roxanne is now married to Jeffrey Seys. James Lee (1956-1987),

James Lee Fitzloff

Dick (1957) (Melody Weir), their children are Mandy, who has two children Brandon and Alexander Fitzloff, and Ryan, who has a son Riley. Dick is now married to Cheryl Fredenburg. Jim and Shirley's youngest daughter is Jackie (1960).

Jim passed away on February 3, 1990, and is buried at St. John's Evangelical Lutheran Church Cemetery, St. Clair.

Shirley remarried on November 6, 1998 to Lyle Halberg. They bought a town-home in Mankato and enjoy their winter home in Pharr, Texas.

By Shirley Fitzloff Halberg

Shirley (DeMars Fitzloff) & Lyle Halberg

Raymond "Ray" William Fitzloff, the son of Herman and Otilla (Brueske) Fitzloff, was born in 1901 and for decades was involved with farming of field crops, raising hundreds of thousands of turkeys and chickens and many different farm animals, which kept him on a very busy and exciting lifetime adventure. His Sunshine Turkey Farm even had a nine-hole Sunshine Golf Club in the early years.

In the late 1920's, he and George Trahms owned turkey hatcheries, managed by Louie Kunz, for their choice mammoth bronze turkeys. The Sunshine Turkey Farm and Hatchery went from 2,700 poults in 1929 to 75,000 in 1933. Their feed supplier, Hubbard Mill in Mankato noted them as the largest and most successful turkey raisers in southern Minnesota. The Chicago market couldn't get enough of their premium turkeys. The need for housing the birds was ever increasing over the years and in the early 1940's, Ray designed and built a huge rectangular three story plus a basement building with four big cupolas on top. There were six huge rooms with very large feed bins. It was covered with galvanized metal (shining silver look). He designed and built a feed manufacturing system where he could grind his corn, etc. and auger it into a gigantic commercial mixer along with other ingredients to create a very nutritious feed for his turkeys, chickens and other farm animals. The feed was then automatically moved through a shaft from this building "the granary" to the bins in the six rooms in the three-story building next to it. He spent a lot of time studying and researching nutritional needs and other needs of his turkeys, chickens and farm animals. The formulas Ray created worked very well and were a cost cutting measure by making much of it himself.

He built brooder houses for the turkeys and had them out in the yards with their new smaller homes when they got bigger. After a lot of research and planning, Ray designed and built an automatic watering fountain. This innovation was a real miracle for saving 90% labor time in making sure the turkeys had fresh water all of the time with nothing plugging up or overflowing. These fountains were sold nationwide and in foreign countries. He also was concerned about the "complexion" of the center of attraction on the Thanksgiving dinner table. Turkeys tend to get a little vicious with each other so he again came up with a design and creation of a canvas protective covering on the turkeys' backs. He designed a Turkey Saddle to protect the birds from injury. The Mankato Canvas Co. manufactured them and in 1935 he shipped 25,000 all over the USA.

Time for some recreation. The same Canvas Company, which also had paid Ray a $5,000 Royalty for the Turkey Saddle patent in 1946, produced Ray's design for a canvas ice-fishing house, which fit over an aluminum frame. It was very easy to transport and included a heater. He caught the "big ones" in comfort! Ray, throughout the years was known as "Mr. Fisherman in Minnesota."

Always venturing out and trying something new, Ray decided to raise sugar beets in the 1950's. He had big fields of them as sugar was being rationed. This required more building for the housing of the workers that the county agent brought from Mexico. He and his hired men built one bigger house, which was more permanent for them and they also had three smaller trailers. "Little Mexico" was exciting as the farm grew to a small town from spring to fall. There were many cookouts and a lot of guitar music and singing. One dear family came back and stayed for 25 years. (This was the Marcelle Duenes Family.) Ten pounds of sugar was a great gift to friends during the rationing and Christmas baking season. Sugar beet raisers got a lot more than the minimum allowed. Ray and Anne were generous people.

Ray had many different enterprises and unusual types

of crops over the years. One year he had a big field of sunflowers for a sunflower seed company. During World War II, he raised hemp to have rope made for the warships. He raised popcorn and supplied the popcorn wagons in Mankato and Minneapolis and shipped it by railroad cars all over the mid-west. He raised peas for the Birdseye Company in Waseca. The list goes on and on.

In Ray's later years, he and his son Ray Jr. worked together farming the land in a very tapered down version from earlier years. Ray retired in the 1970's and did some traveling. He went to the Olympics in Munich, Germany, with his nephew and also had many trips to visit daughter Colleen's family when they moved to different cities in the U.S. He loved Atlanta, Georgia.

Back in 1931 Ray Fitzloff who already had his farm going strong for several years then, married Anne Francis McNamara, daughter of Robert and Agnes Collins McNamara of Belmont, Iowa. Anne had a background of having been a telephone operator and then a beauty shop operator. Now as a farmers wife, she found herself doing a lot of cooking and baking and also feeding the 2-4 hired men that lived in the other four bedroom house on the farm. As their family grew, she engaged the help of an assistant cook and housekeeper. Anne was famous for her wonderful turkey dinners and heavenly baked products of bread, rolls, cakes and pies. Her "never fail" recipes were mouth watering good!! She was known to be the friend to have for a "friend in need," always there. She was a most gracious hostess. Their home was a favorite gathering place for family and friends on special occasions and holidays. Great food, music and fun. Ray and Anne had four children. There was Carol Ann, born in 1933, Colleen Rae in 1935, Edith Anne in 1937 and Raymond Herman in 1940. Carol Ann lived only four days. Ray's wife Anne passed away in 1972.

Colleen Rae still carries the "Sunshine Turkey Farm" in her nickname "Turk" since 1953. She brought Mankato State College friends home and they saw the turkey farm sign and gave her the nickname, which she's carried proudly for years. She married Dean Roberts, a college boyfriend from Mankato on April 10, 1955 and joined this soldier in Germany three months later. They had two children, Bruce Dean born in 1957 and Julie Ann in 1960. They also have two grandchildren, Meredith 19 and David 16. Colleen's favorite career position was in the employment business in Minneapolis, Minnesota. She also enjoyed welcoming many, many U.S. and foreign Mayo Clinic doctors wives as a Welcome Wagon Hostess in Rochester, Minnesota, and being a receptionist and medical secretary at a seven man law firm in Rochester. Dean retired from Equifax (formerly Retail Credit Co.) in 1998 in Atlanta, Georgia, after almost 40 years of service. After Germany they've lived in nine different cities in the U.S., but all the family has lived in Atlanta, Georgia, since 1976.

Back (L to R): Ray and Anne Fitzloff
Front: Colleen, Ray Jr., Edith (1957)

Edith Ann married William "Bill" Mettler from Mankato in 1956 while he was in the Air Force at San Antonio, Texas. From Texas they went to Guam and then to Mankato where they operated the Mettler Insurance Agency for many years until Bill's passing in 1977. They had one child, Lisa Ann born in 1958. Edith and Lisa moved to Denver, Colorado, late in 1977. Edith was a hostess at the Simms Landing Restaurant and also did public relations for Simms Landing and four other major restaurants in the Denver area for many years. Edith and Lisa Sprague lived in Atlanta from 1993 to 1996 and then moved to Marco Island, Florida, where they currently reside.

Raymond Herman married Mathia "Mae" Thisted in 1964 in Albert Lea, Minnesota. They had four children, Dawn, Cheryl, Carl and Mark. They lived on his dad's farm for many years doing farm work and sometimes working outside of the farm. Mae worked at Midtex in Mankato. After his fathers passing in 1979, he operated the farm for a few years. There was a major fire that destroyed the big buildings on the farm. He later sold the farm and the family moved to Watertown, South Dakota, where Mae was able to transfer. Ray worked at a casino in the area. There hasn't been any Ray and Anne Fitzloff family members living in the St. Clair area since the 1980's.

There are recorded tapes of Raymond William Martin Fitzloff, a farmer, designer, builder and inventor leaving his special life's motto behind

"I would rather be thought of as an honest man than to

be a millionaire" and "St. Clair is the nicest place in the world because it's full of nice people."

By Colleen Fitzloff Roberts

Otto Fitzloff lived in Janesville and married Lydia Proechel. The only daughter Bertha married George Becker Caldwell. The fourth son John Carl married Emma Gerlich and lived in St. Clair until 1919. The youngest son Charles married Martha Schiek.

FITZSIMMONS, THOMAS

Thomas Fitzsimmons was born in Marquette County, Wisconsin, in 1854. He remained with his parents, Patrick and Sarah, and came with them to Minnesota in 1864. They settled in McPherson where he farmed fourteen years and then moved to Mankato where he had a saloon for two years. While in Mankato he married a Miss L. Richards on July 6, 1881. He then moved back to McPherson and operated a saloon and billiard hall at the Winnebago Agency and also had a farm of 200 acres about three and one-half miles from the village.

FOSSUM, JOHN

John Fossum operated the St. Clair Creamery, which was built in 1904, for many years. John was born in Trondheim, Norway, in 1904 and came by himself to the United States in 1918. He worked on the ship for his passage and also

John & Sadie Fossum

worked in New York on the piers until he could afford to travel west to Michigan, where he worked in the lumber industry. He left Michigan and traveled to St. Paul, Minnesota, where he worked at the St. Paul Hotel as an elevator operator. One day while working he struck up a conversation with a guest who was a butter-buyer from Philadelphia, who after meetings talked Dad into going to the University of Minnesota Agricultural School where he enrolled in the butter making program.

Upon graduating from the University in 1925 or 1926, Dad's first and only creamery job was at St. Clair Creamery. He was a helper for a few years after which he became the manager-buttermaker and continued until 1956 at which time the creamery closed, as did many small creameries throughout Minnesota.

Dad met a local girl, Sadie Miller, who was the daughter of Edward and Anna Miller (see separate story) who farmed approximately two miles north of St. Clair. They married in 1931 and had two sons, Lowell and myself Robert. After my parent's marriage, mother became the creamery helper until its closure. They lived at 229 Main Street West.

During most of these years, Dad would sell and ship his butter to Philadelphia, and yes it was to this same person who befriended my Dad in St. Paul. Although I don't recall his name, I remember him well, as each summer he would visit and stay at our home for a few years. Maybe the reason I remember him was when I was young he would always bring my brother and myself a present.

After the creamery closed, John and Sadie built and operated a drive-in in Red Wing, Minnesota and later in Waseca until their retirements in 1970. Dad and mother continued to live in Waseca until Dad passed away in 1988, and mother in 1989. Both of my parents came from families of eleven children.

FOSSUM, ROBERT

I was born in St. Clair on February 1, 1937, to John and Sadie (Miller) Fossum. I had one brother, Lowell (5-27-1932) who was a depot agent and later an auditor for the Milwaukee Road Railroad. During his career he worked at the depots in Minneapolis, Milwaukee, and Cedar Rapid, Iowa, until he passed away in 1999.

I attended St. Clair Public School from 1943 to 1955, when I graduated and enrolled at Mankato State University. I also served a stint in the U.S. Army.

During my high school years I always loved sports, playing football, basketball and baseball. I was fortunate enough to play on some exceptionally good teams which enabled me to set, which at the time was a career high scoring record of 1,410 points in basketball with a single

Robert Fossum, 1964

game high of 42 points. (Dennis Moe, who scored a game high of 48 points in 1986, later broke the single game high.)

Mary Lou Hoppe, the daughter of Merrill and Monica (Hodapp) Hoppe, also a 1955 graduate of St. Clair and I were married in 1957 and we plan on celebrating our 50th anniversary in the near future.

We have three daughters, Christine (Mike) Thompson of St. Peter and their children, Rachael and Claire, Karen (Randy) Gibson and their children, Cole, Chad, and Taylor of LaCrescent, Minnesota, and Tamie (Tim) Collins and their children, Betsie, Danni and Abby of Waseca.

When I graduated from Mankato State in 1959, I taught mathematics at St. Clair High School and coached football, basketball and track for seven years. After teaching seven years at my alma mater, I became High School Principal and Athletic Director and continued as football coach for an additional two years. In 1967, I applied for and obtained the Superintendent of Schools position at Henderson Public School. Later as Henderson and Le Sueur Public Schools consolidated, I continued as superintendent of these two communities until I retired twenty-six years later in 1993.

Currently Mary Lou and I have moved to Mankato, where we reside at 211 Ridgewood Street.

I consider myself very fortunate for having been a resident of St. Clair for nearly thirty years, especially during a person's formative years from which a person's life values are formed.

By Robert Fossum

FOSTER

Two sons of the Foster family ended up at some time in St. Clair. It is noted that Henry B. Foster came to St. Clair in 1855 with the Winnebago Indians, and Stephen Foster, Sr. also lived in St. Clair. A brother, S. Jackson Foster lived in Huron, SD.

March 27, 1883 - Death of Mrs. Henry B. Foster

Mrs. Henry Foster, of Winnebago Agency, who has been ill for some months, died at her home, on Thursday morning last, in the 60th years of her age. Mrs. Foster had resided in this county for nearly twenty-one years. She came here before the removal of the Winnebago Indians, and when they were taken to the Missouri River country and their reservation opened to settlement and sale she preempted what is now a valuable farm at the village and upon which the Indian school house had been located. Subsequently she was married to Henry Foster, Esq., and their home has been at the agency ever since. Mrs. Foster was an estimable lady, foremost in every good work; kind to the poor and unfortunate; and the generous hospitality of her home is proverbial. Mrs. Foster is a sister of Mr. O. Pitcher, of this city; and mother of Messier. Duane F., and Melvin B. Rasdall of McPherson also of Hobart and Blanche Rasdall. The funeral on Saturday was very largely attended by sympathizing friends.

Notes from the *Review*: June 8-July 20, 1906

Henry B. Foster was born on April 22, 1825, in Trumbull County, Ohio. In 1837 the family moved to the Prairie du Chien, Wisconsin, area and in 1840 they moved to Iowa. It was here that he obtained a government position of assistant blacksmith for the Winnebago tribe of Indians. He came to St. Clair, then the Winnebago Agency, in June of 1855, with the tribe of Indians, they having been removed by the government to that agency from Long Prairie, Minnesota. Mr. Foster held the position of assistant blacksmith with the tribe, in which he continued for a year when he formed a co-partnership with Charles H. Mix, purchased a stock of goods and

Henry Foster, interpreter, trader and first township clerk

engaged in the mercantile business until the removal of the tribe in 1863. He was appointed the first postmaster of Winnebago Agency in 1856; he was elected county commissioner in 1860 and in 1872 a member of the state legislature from this county. He also held numerous town offices.

When the First National Bank was organized in Mankato, he was one of the original stockholders and since 1879 had served continuously on its board of directors, serving for thirty-nine years and was very well to do. He at one time owned 720 acres of land.

In 1864 Henry married Mrs. Lydia A. Rasdall, the widow of Abel Rasdall, [see separate story]. She was the daughter of Orrin Pitcher [see separate story] and the sister of the late Judge L.O. Pitcher of Mankato. Lydia died on March 23, 1883. Henry and Lydia adopted a daughter Blanch Estelle.

Mr. Foster was numbered among the substantial citizens of the county, and through industry and frugality had acquired sufficient of this world's good to enjoy life. He was the soul of honor, an exemplary citizen, a good friend and neighbor. He was modest and unassuming, yet drew around him a large circle of friends and acquaintances that loved and respected him.

On June 8th, 1906, Henry suffered a stroke from which he never recovered, dying on July 7th. A large number of Masons and citizens drove out to St. Clair to attend the funeral. Services were conducted by Mankato Lodge A.F. and A.M., of which the deceased was a member. The Masons from Janesville, Alma City and other neighboring towns attended in large numbers, as did also friends and acquaintances from the surrounding country. Three stepsons survived him, Duane F., Melvin B. and Hubert Rasdall [see separate stories] and an adopted daughter Blanche Estelle Stevenson of Iowa.

The board of county commissioners which had been in regular session since the day before the funeral adjourned at noon to attend the funeral. The county commissioners made the following resolution and it was unanimously adopted. "Whereas, Henry Foster of McPherson, one of the oldest and most prominent and respected residents of this county, died Saturday, July 7th, and whose funeral is to take place Tuesday, at 8 o'clock, at St. Clair" thus be it "resolved that this board adjourn in respect to his memory and to attend the funeral in a body."

Henry and Lydia are buried in the Union Cemetery, St. Clair.

Funeral notations made in the July 10th edition of the *Mankato Review* stated that the funeral was largely attended and notable among sad occasions of this kind in St. Clair. A large number of Mankato people attended the funeral in respect to their respected friend. They went in wagonettes and carriages and automobiles and those who rode in the autos had rather unpleasant experiences. Two rigs fared especially badly. M. D. Fancher's auto was disabled by the explosion of a tire, and the car belonging to B. Bangerter, Jr., overheated and went out of commission. The heavy rain and poor roads made traveling in the country very disagreeable and caused the mishaps above mentioned. The parties in the autos were compelled to ride to the city with farmers.

July 19 - From Thursday's Daily: A petition was filed with Judge Hughes today for the administration of the estate of the late Henry Foster of St. Clair, who left no will. The estate is estimated at $7,000 personal and $25,000 real estate. There is but one heir, the adopted daughter, Mrs. Blanche E. Stevenson of Shellrock, Iowa, who is the petitioner and asks that Duane F. Rasdall of St. Clair be appointed administration.

July 20 - From Friday's Daily: A document purported to be the last will of Henry Foster, late of St. Clair, was filed late yesterday afternoon together with the petition of Stephen Foster, Jr., one of the heirs mentioned in the will, asking for the appointment of D. F. Rasdall as executor in compliance with the codicil attached to the will.

The will and petition were filed after Mr. Foster's adopted daughter, Blanche E. Stevenson, of Shell Rock, Iowa, had filed her petition naming herself as the sole heir, and asking that letters testamentary be issued to D. F. Rasdall. Special letters were issued as prayed and a date of hearing set on the petition. It is said that the fact that a will existed was known until yesterday by but few.

The document was executed March 28, 1902, and

witnessed by C. J. Pagenkopf and E. A. Duemeland and it appointed F. W. Lassow executor. The bequests were as follows:

To his brother, Stephen Foster, Sr. of St. Clair, acreage in section 16 of McPherson Township. To his adopted daughter, Blanche E. Stevenson, of Shell Rock, Iowa acreage in section 16, of McPherson and lots 11 and 12, block 1, in the Lakeview addition to North Mankato. To his nephew Henry P. Foster, 21 acres in section 3. To his nephew Stephen Foster, Jr. 300 acres in section 16.

The estate included 53⅓ shares of the capital stock of the First National bank of this city. Of this 23⅓ shares were set aside and reserved to be sold by the executor, and from the proceeds the debts and funeral expenses and administrative expenses were to be paid. The residue was to go to Blanche Stevenson, and the other thirty shares in equal proportion to the brother and testator, Stephen Sr., and the nephews and nieces, Stephen Jr., Henry P., Minnie O. Wolcott, Edith Chase, Lydia Campbell, May Hall, and Blanche Stevenson. This made 3¾ shares to each.

To Blanche Stevenson he left the life insurance policy in the Equitable Life association, for $600, and the testator's right, title and interest for $2,000 in the Mutual Benefit Life Insurance company of New Jersey.

To his brother S. Jackson Foster of Huron, SD, he left a "large easy spring rocking chair."

To his nephew Stephen Foster, Jr., he left all horses, cattle, hogs, poultry, wagons, carriages, sleighs, harness, tackle, farm implements, tools, and machinery. Also household furniture, books, wearing apparel, and all articles of ornament or value and all of the rest of the estate and also the balance of the residue of the estate.

A codicil, dated July 16, 1903, revoked the appointment of Mr. F. W. Lassow as executor and appointed D. F. Rasdall executor.

The schedule of property in the petition gave the personal property at $12,185 and the real estate at $31,400.

Stephen Foster, Sr. was born on July 28, 1831 in Bordman, Ohio. He was one of the pioneer settlers of this county. Mr. Foster was a man widely known and universally liked by all that knew him. In August of 1858, in Grant County, Wisconsin, he married Missouri Emeline Adkins who was born on October 1, 1833. Missouri died on March 27, 1911, from uremic poisoning. Stephen died on October 7, 1917, from the effects of a general breakdown, due to old age. They, as well as several of their children and spouses, are buried in the Union Cemetery, St. Clair.

The Fosters children were Henry P., May (1862-1944), Amine (1865-1865), Minnie (John Wolcott - see separate

The Foster Sisters
In back at the top of the picture is Minnie Foster Wolcott, center left is Edith Foster Chase, center right is Mary Foster Hall, and in front is Lydia Foster Campbell

Standing (L to R): Minnie Foster Wolcott and Mary Foster Hall
Seated: Lydia Foster Campbell, Mrs. Stephen Foster, Edith Foster Chase - Children are unidentified.

story), Edith (Jacob Chase - see separate story), Abbe (1871-1873), Lydia (Henry Campbell - see separate story) Stephen Jr. and May (Thomas Willie Hall).

Henry P. Foster, the son of Stephen and Elizabeth (Adkins) Foster, Sr. was born in September 1859 in Iowa County, Wisconsin. He came to Minnesota with his parent in 1869. On September 8, 1880, he married Sarah Campbell (1862) of Potosi County, Wisconsin. He resided on a farm northeast of St. Clair until he moved to a farm east of St. Clair where he lived until his death. Mr. Foster was a man of rare character, being strictly temperate, exceedingly intelligent, outspoken and always wearing a glad smile that won him into the hearts of all his fellow men. He had a wide acquaintance and was much respected. He was known as a friend to all who enjoyed his acquaintance. He was devoted to his family in every respect and his one great ambition was to love and provide for them in every possible way.

Henry and Sarah had eight children: Earl, Ethel (Edward Peterson), Goldie Mae (John Schostag), Pearl E. (1880-1911) who was married to a Ward, George (1884-1915), Winnefred Fay (1887-1913) who was married to Robert Schostag, Raymond (1888-1901) and Hazel O. (1895-1903).

Henry died on May 20, 1911, suffering from rectal cancer causing with peritonitis. His remains were laid to rest in the cemetery on the Tilliston Hill. Sarah, Pearl, Raymond and Hazel are also buried in the Union Cemetery, St. Clair.

FRANK, GUSTAV

Gustav and Wilhelmina (Monthey) Frank came to the St. Clair area from Janesville-Iosco area. They lived on the western end of St. Clair where they farmed.

They had eight children, Mathilda "Tillie" (Edward Froehlich), Eda (Fred Schostag), Hulda (Tony Fitzloff), Martha, Herman [see separate story], Ernestine "Tina" (Joseph Wolf), Leo (Letha Tenny) and Edward.

The children all grew up and lived most of their lives in the St. Clair area. They were all farmers except Martha who worked in Mankato. Many of the children and grandchildren of these families still live in the St. Clair area.

Herman Frank and his wife Dorothy (Fitzloff) farmed just west of St. Clair. They had four children, Harland [see separate story], Norma (Carl Wobschall), Hazel (LaVerne DeMars), and Alice (Charles Warner)

By Hazel Frank DeMars

Harland H. Frank was the only son of his parents, Herman and Dorothy (Fitzloff) Frank. He attended school in St. Clair where he played baseball and trumpet in the school band. After he graduated, he joined the U.S. Navy and spent some of the time in Honolulu, Hawaii. When he returned home, he joined his father on the farm. He built almost all of the buildings on the farm site, and together they raised dairy cattle and raised the calves as beef cattle. They also had hogs, ducks and chickens.

On December 5, 1953, he married Betty M. Palmer of Frazee, Minnesota, at the St. John's Evangelical Lutheran Church in St. Clair.

Betty was in charge of the 400 hens each year, and had a good egg business. They also had 15 apple trees.

They became parents of three children, of whom they were very proud. They all were confirmed at St. John's church, and graduated from St. Clair High School. Each one was recipient of the John Phillip Sousa awards when they were in band.

Jane M. Frank, born March 9, 1958, graduated from St. Clair High School and Mankato State College. She taught band at Echo-Wood Lake for 2 years. She then went on to Martin Luther College in New Ulm and taught school at the Minnesota Valley Lutheran High School. She met Fred W. Holasek and they were married in St. John's church on June 20, 1987.

They live in Lester Prairie, Minnesota, and own 20 green houses there, "The Fred Holasek and Son Greenhouses." They have 2 sons, Alan, born June 2, 1991, and Jay, born August 4, 1995.

Robert J. Frank, born November 13, 1961, graduated from St. Clair High School and Mankato State College. He received his Masters and Doctorate at North Texas State University in Denton, Texas. He is tenured, teaching Music Theory and Composition at Southern Methodist University in Dallas, Texas. He married Kathy Strawn in Kauai, Hawaii, on July 10, 2004. Kathy is a Paralegal.

Diane E. Frank, born February 5, 1966, graduated from St. Clair High School and Mankato State College. She received her Doctorate at University of Wisconsin in Madison, Wisconsin. She is living in Seattle, Washington, doing research at the Fred Hutchinson Cancer Research Center there.

By Betty Frank

FRANZ, W. J.

W. J. Franz came to the United States at the age of eight, lived in the St. Clair vicinity for many years, and later moved to Austin, Minnesota and lived with his daughter Mrs. Arnold (Louise) Bloomfield. On June 6, 1898 he married Rosaie Proehl (1879-1928). Their children were Louise, Virginia, Lydia and William, Jr. One of

Saloon owned by W. Franz (now the UpTown Tavern)

O'Connor's and Wm Franz's Saloon, The Commercial Club held their meetings in the social hall upstairs. This building is now the UpTown Tavern.

his sisters was Mrs. August Schroeder. (Virginia and Lydia died when very young.) William operated the soft drink parlor and lunchroom that was located where the UpTown Tavern is currently located. In October of 1928 he sold this business to Walter O'Brien. He died in 1943.

FREITAG, WILLIAM

The Freitag Farm - 100 plus years of History

William Freitag was born in Germany in 1862. He came to America at a young age (he did remember the ride over) with his parents and sister. They settled near Milwaukee, Wisconsin. Later they moved to Minnesota. William married Fredericka Kruse (1863-1907). In 1891 they purchased the Freitag home place in McPherson Township. It was 100 acres in section 14. Reike died in 1907 and William in 1943. They are buried in the St. John's Evangelical Lutheran Cemetery, St. Clair. They had five children, Lena, William, John, Herman and Lydia.

Lena Freitag was born in 1887 and was married to Henry Frank. They did not have any children.

William Freitag was born in 1889 and married Clara Grams in 1915. Clara was born in 1898 and was the daughter of August and Emma (Jeseritz) Grams. They had two children, Ordella and Kenneth.

William died in 1960 and Clara in 1990. They are buried in the St. John's Evangelical Lutheran Cemetery, St. Clair.

<u>Ordella Freitag</u>, who was born in 1919, married Donald Bennett and had a daughter Tammy. After Don's death she married Robert Scholljergerdes and they are living in Waseca, Minnesota.

LaVErne & Kenneth Freitag

Kenneth Freitag was born in 1925 and in 1948 he married Laverne Borneke, the daughter of Clarence and Anna (Johnson) Borneke. They took over the farming operation. Kenneth was a McPherson Township supervisor for many years. (Kenny remembers walking over the bridge behind the bank in St. Clair. He also noted that the WPA program built the bridge over the creek by the Freitag farms and that his dad mixed all of the cement and Frank Heminover wheeled the mixed concrete to the bridge site.) They have three children. Steven who married Lisa Long and they live at Becker, Minnesota, Thomas and Zandra. Zandra married Duane Jindra and lives in Hutchinson, Minnesota.

Thomas Freitag married Luann Thorsen and they are now living on the farm where his dad was born. They have five children. William, Dustin, Charles (who has two sons, Brandon and Alexander Fitzloff), Christopher and Sarah.

Thomas & Luann Freitag family
Back row (L to R): William, Charles, Dustin.
Front: Thomas, Luann, Sarah, Christopher

Joan & Ervin Freitag

John Freitag was born in 1893 and he served his country during WWI. Upon his return home he purchased the farm from William in 1923. In 1924 he was married to Emma Risto who was born in 1900. They had three children. Ervin was born in 1929 and is married to Joan Nelson. Ervin farmed and then had a TV sales and service business in Janesville. Joan worked for Dr. M. C. Florine, MD, for many years and is now working for Dr. Kelly McCoy, DC. Erv has retired and they are living in Janesville. Lorraine was born in 1930 and was married in 1953 to Anton Throdahl. They have seven children, James, Karen, Susan, Judy, Eric, Amy and David. Lorraine and Anton are presently living in Mankato, MN. Elvera was born in 1935 and was married to Stanley Hall [see separate story]. (Their son Jon presently owns the Freitag Farm.) John died in 1955 and Emma in 1987. They are buried in the St. John's Evangelical Lutheran Cemetery, St. Clair.

Herman Freitag was born in 1897 and married Esther Doering. They had one daughter Doris who was born in 1929 and is married to Wendell Folkerts. They have three children and presently live in Phoenix, AZ. Herman died in 1967 and Esther in 1970. They are buried in the St. John's Evangelical Lutheran Cemetery, St. Clair.

Lydia Freitag was born in 1902 and never married. When the mother died in 1907, William moved off the farm into Janesville and Lydia moved with him and kept house. Upon William's death Lydia lived with Lena and Henry.

The brothers William, Herman and John all lived within one mile of each other from the home place. They shared labor at haying and harvest times until tractors and combines took the place of horses and manual labor.

By Elvera Hall

FRITZKE, REV. GUSTAV

Rev. Gustav E. Fritzke was born in Germany and came to America when eight years old. The family settled near New Ulm and later moved to Nicollet where he attended school. He was ordained in the ministry in 1890. He was married on August 5, 1892 to Bertha Otto of Nicollet, Minnesota.

His first charge was a missionary in Clark, S.D., and surrounding territory. Later he went to Litchfield and Ellsworth townships. He was at Hutchinson 23 years and at St. Clair for 15 years from 1920 until 1935.

In 1935 he retired and moved to Minneapolis, and in 1943 came to Mankato, residing at the Security Apartments.

They were parents of five children, Olga (Jack

Fitzloff), Marie (Carl Weppler), Otto W. (Naomi Anna Kimm), Arthur (Lenore Paulson, parents of Robert), and Henry (Alice Harms).

They are buried at Crystal Lake Cemetery, Minneapolis, Minnesota.

FRITZKE, ROBERT

Robert was the son of Arthur and Lenora (Paulsen) Fritzke. He graduated from the Marshall High School, Minneapolis in 1937 and then attended Mankato Teachers College before entering the service 1941-1945. After the service he attended and graduated from the University of Minnesota. He married Gertrude Winkelman the daughter of Arthur and JoHanna (Apple) Winkelman on June 27, 1947, at St. John's Lutheran Church, St Clair. At one time they lived at 324 West Front Street.

Gertrude also graduated from St. Clair, attended Mankato State Teachers College, and was a postal clerk with Robert for 22 years. She retired in 1972.

Robert and Gertrude have two children, Nancy and Steve; both graduated from St. Clair School and Mankato State College. They both are living and working in Minneapolis.

Robert was postmaster at St. Clair from 1949 until his retirement in 1977 after 31 years of services. Robert and Gertrude are members of St. John's Evangelical Lutheran Church, St. Clair, where Robert's grandfather Gustav E. Fritzke served as pastor from 1920-1935. They are living in St. Clair.

Gertrude & Robert Fritzke

By Robert Fritzke

FROEHLICH, WILLIAM

William Froehlich was born in Letschin, Germany, on March 13, 1843, and fought in the Franco-Prussian War of 1871. He worked as an apprentice mason. As he wanted to avoid any more fighting in a war, he decided to come to America. A lot of the foreigners had the same idea in fighting the wars, so thought they would look for a new land. Everyone had heard so much about America being a lot better place to live. America was thought of as the land of gold or as the saying goes a land of milk and honey. It was also told that this land had more freedom and better living conditions. When the Froehlich's arrived they found that it was not as good as had been thought. When William had decided to come to America he went to the port and was eating in a restaurant, where he met this waitress Amelia Radke (10-14-1843). He proposed marriage and they were married within a week. They left Germany by sailboat on October 14, 1871, and arrived in New York on Christmas Eve with only $5 and a wooden chest containing their possessions. Amelia's father did not approve of the marriage and that is why he gave them a wooden chest. He told her she could be buried in it.

William and Amelia found this land was an answer to their prayers and were happy to be here. If things had not worked out for them here they would have returned to Germany. They first settled in Pennsylvania, then moved to Michigan and then they traveled to Mayville, Wisconsin, where Martin Froehlich lived. William worked for a pastor cementing a well where he received a ham and home made soap as his pay. After seven years they moved to Smith's Mill, Minnesota. They then moved to St. Clair. William cleared the trees off the land and being a mason built houses out of soft bricks. He built several of the old red brick houses in the St. Clair area.

The children born to William and Amelia were Louise (1872-1956), who married Albert Nicolai, Jr., was born in Wisconsin and after her marriage in 1892, moved to Hector, New Ulm and Minneapolis, Minnesota. They had nine children. Bertha (1873-1964) was married to John Kamrath from Minnesota Lake, was born in Wisconsin and moved to Minneapolis, Minnesota. Emma (1874-1882) was born in Wisconsin and died when she was 8 years old, and Edna, (1877-1882) who was born in Smith's Mill, died when 5, both from diphtheria. They are buried in St. John (Bestman) Cemetery. Herman (1880-1937) (Winifred Grout) was born in Smith's Mill, graduated from Mankato College and Hamline University. He did post-graduate study in Chicago, New York City and Vienna. He was one of the founders of the

Physicians Hospital in Thief River Falls, Minnesota, was the doctor on the Red Lake Indian Reservation and was county coroner for many years. Dr. Herman was elected a Fellow of American College of Surgeons and was a captain in the Medical Officers Reserve Corps. They lived in Thief River Falls and Minneapolis. Their children were Edward [see separate story], Otto [see separate story] and Rudolph [see separate story].

William, one of the oldest residents of Blue Earth County, died on March 10, 1938, and Amalia died on November 9, 1913, in Blue Earth County. They are buried in the St. John's Evangelical Lutheran Cemetery, St. Clair.

By Faye Johnson and Muriel Mace

FROEHLICH, EDWARD

Edward was born on October 12, 1881, on a farm between St. Clair and Smith's Mill and moved to St. Clair with the family in 1883. He married Mathilde Frank (7-11-1883) on March 20, 1906, in St. Clair. They farmed just north of St. Clair in Sections 8 and 9. Their children were Elmer (1910-1938) who died as a young man, Oscar (Edna Bollman) [see separate story], and Raymond (1919-1972) (Phyllis Hodapp). Ray and Phyllis had three children a daughter who was born and died in 1953, Thomas (1954) (Sara Ayes) who live in Good Thunder and Mark (1955) who lives in Mapleton. He was a farmer just north of St. Clair and they lived in the red brick house that William Froehlich built. Edward and Raymond were both chairmen of the St. John's Lutheran Church Council at various times in their lives.

Edward died on June 12, 1965, and Mathilde died on June 26, 1958. They are buried in the St. John's Evangelical Lutheran Cemetery, St. Clair.

By Faye Johnson and Muriel Mace

FROEHLICH, OSCAR

Oscar W. Froehlich was born on March 3, 1909, to Ed and Mathilda (Frank) Froehlich. He grew up in the St. Clair area and in 1937 he married Edna Bollman (2-4-1910), the daughter of Peter C. and Martha (Beckmann) Bollmann. They had three children - Margaret Joan who married Lowell Pagenkopf [see separate story], Dale (Maria Garduno) whose children are John, Anthony, Linda and Raymond, and Daniel (Connie Buecksler), whose children are Kyle, Paul, and Kelsey.

Oscar lived his entire life in McPherson Township. He farmed with his father and brothers and in 1931 along with his brother Elmer started the chicken and turkey hatching business. From a 1972 article in the *Janesville Argus*, it is noted that every year the family operation ran 80,000 hen and tom turkeys through their huge 76 X 220 building and the rangeland on the farm. They used 26 circular propane heaters to keep the floor temperature close to 75 degrees in the building. The birds were sold to Swift & Company, in Montevideo and were sold under the name "Butterball."

When a flock was sold, the barns were cleaned out and things were gotten ready for a new batch. Over 200 tons of wood shavings were hauled to the field in the cleaning operation.

In 1982 it is noted that they were raising nearly 100,000 turkeys a year. Flocks numbering 27,000 were raised on the range during the summer months.

Dale & Maria Froehlich family
Back (L to R): John, Tony, Ray.
Front: Dale, Maria, Linda

Daniel & Connie Froehlich family
Back (L to R): Daniel, Kyle
Front: Connie, Kelsey, Paul

Another 12,000 spent 17 weeks growing inside. The birds were hatched in Marshall, Minnesota and trucked to St. Clair to be raised. When ready to be shipped back they averaged about 15 pounds.

In his later years, he continued operating his turkey farm with his sons and grandsons.

Oscar and Edna were members of St. John's Evangelical Lutheran Church, St. Clair. Oscar greatly enjoyed time spent with his grandchildren and great-grandchildren.

Edna died in 1978 and Oscar in 1996. They are buried in the St. John's Evangelical Lutheran Cemetery, St. Clair.

FROEHLICH, OTTO

Otto Froehlich was born on December 22, 1883, on a farm between St. Clair and Smith's Mill, Minnesota, in LeRay Township. He married Lydia Jenrich (May 12, 1888) from Mapleton, in 1911. He went to Webster, North Dakota, and with his brother Rudolph, worked for Peder Sorenson and operated a meat market. He later returned to St. Clair and became a farmer and farmed 80 acres northwest of St. Clair, in Section 6. Otto died on March 15, 1980, and Lydia on August 11, 1939. They are buried in the St. John's Evangelical Lutheran Cemetery, St. Clair.

Their son was Donald (1911-1975), who married Lempi Niemela (1917-1998) of Cokato. They lived with Otto and helped run the farm in Section 6 and Donald also did carpentry work. Their children are Jerry (Beverly Linde) who lives in rural Janesville, Maurice (Frances Mosher-Ann Peterson), who lives on the home place and Marcella (Allan Taber-James Collman), who lives north of St. Clair.

Donald and Lempi are buried in the St. John's Evangelical Lutheran Cemetery.

Their daughter Muriel Ruth (10-8-1924) married Gerald Mace and they ran the St. Clair Café for awhile. Later Gerald worked for the Blue Earth County Highway Department and Ruth worked at the school for many years.

Gerald was born on February 16, 1918, and was the son of Nathan and Theresia (Bowe) Mace. He died on February 6, 1990, and is buried in the Medo McPherson Cemetery.

Gerald and Muriel had four children. Bonnie (1946) who is married to Ronald Roalson (1942) and their children are James (1972) and Andrew (1975). Geraldine (1947) who is married to David Sonday (1947) and their children are Jeremy (1974), Jennifer (1976) and Daniel (1978). Nathan (1960) who married Shawn Kawell and their children are Tanner (1987) and Brandon (1990), all living in St. Clair. Geneva (1949) who married Paul Mueller and they live in Mankato, their children are Gretchen (1982), Heidi (1984) and Joseph (1986).

By Faye Johnson and Muriel Mace

Rudolph Froehlich in his company truck.

FROEHLICH, RUDOLPH

Rudolph Froehlich was born on September 29, 1895, when the family lived in the red brick house north of St. Clair in McPherson Township Section 9, where Dale and Maria Froehlich are living today. He along with his brother Otto, went to Webster, North Dakota, and operated a meat market. He then moved to Paynesville, Minnesota, where he again operated a butcher shop and was mayor for one term. He then returned to Webster where he married Gertie Sorenson (2-12-1888). He worked for Peder Sorensen, Gertie's father, who was a large landowner in the Devil's Lake area. He later returned to the St. Clair area and ran the hardware store. He then managed a hardware store in Le Sueur, managed a grocery store in the cities, before moving south of Waseca to farm. He later bought the farm just east of St. Clair in Sections 11 and 15. Rudolph and Gertie moved to St. Clair and lived at 117 North Park Street. He was mayor of St. Clair in 1925 and the chairman of the church council in 1926, when the St. John's Lutheran Church was built. Their children, both born in North Dakota but graduated from St. Clair, were Dorothy (1911-1998) (Harvey Amlund) who had two sons, Dale and David, and Laurance.

Rudolph died on January 29, 1957 and Gertie died on April 21, 1975. They are buried in the St. John's Evangelical Lutheran Cemetery, St. Clair.

By Faye Johnson and Muriel Mace

Laurance A. Froehlich was born on March 11, 1914, in North Dakota and he graduated from the St. Clair Public School. He married Wanda Andrews, of Merrillan, Wisconsin on September 5, 1936, in Litchfield, Minnesota. Wanda graduated from Merrillan High School in 1932 and attended Abbott School of Nursing. After their marriage they lived in Minneapolis, Waseca and St. Clair. Larry worked on the Canol Project for Bectel, Price, Callahan in Canada in 1943-44, was in the SeaBees in WWII, farmed, was a field man for Bird's Eye, managed the Janesville Green Products and later the Great Western Sugar plant just west of Waseca. Wanda worked at the Waseca Medical Center and Lake Shore Inn Nursing Home in Waseca.

Wanda & Laurence Froehlich

Larry and Wanda lived on the farm in Section 5 and 11 for many years before moving into St. Clair, living at 113 Schalow Drive. They were members of the St. John's Evangelical Lutheran Church, St. Clair American Legion, and Wanda served as a leader in the Husky Helpers 4-H Club. They had three children, Andrea (1940) who married Curtis Roessler and lives on a farm near Minnesota Lake, Gail (1945-1964) and Faye (1953) who is married to Ken Johnson of Eagle Lake and they live in Forest Lake, MN.

By Faye Johnson

GERBER, JOHN

In November 1879 several families bought land in McPherson Township two miles north east of St. Clair. They came from Prussia and lived several years in Franklin, Wisconsin. Among them was John Gerber and his wife, Louisa, and their three children, Mary (Christian Sodeman), Lena (Charles Fisher) and Fredericka (Carl Schostag).

It is known that John was born about 1816 in Mecklenberg, Prussia. Louise was born about 1824 in Prussia. It is believed that they died in McPherson Township and are buried in the St. John's/Bestman Cemetery, St. Clair.

By Verna Sodeman

GJERDE, DOUGLAS

Douglas Gjerde grew up in Elmore, Minnesota. He is a carpenter and is a cabinet installer for Steven Cabinets, Inc. Doug married Denise Lloyd who is from Ledyard, Iowa, just nine miles from Elmore. The first years of their marriage they lived in Elmore with their children Holly, Bridget and Lacey. They also lived in Waseca for six years and after Lacey's graduation from high school in June 2000 they moved to St. Clair. Denise had been the Officer-in-Charge at the St. Clair Post Office since

Johann & Hannah Glamm

John & Bertha Glamm

Otto & Esther Glamm

December of 1997 and was promoted to Postmaster in March of 1998.

Holly is married to Michael Kreig and they have a daughter Kelsey, and live in Prior Lake, Minnesota. Bridget lives in Shakopee and Lacey is in Minneapolis.

By Denise Gjerde

GLAMM, JOHANN FRIEDERICH LUDWIG

Johann Friederich Ludwig Glamm was born in September 1825 in Pomerania, Deutschland (Germany). He died in December 1902. Hannah L. Wilhelmina Borchardt was born in May 1821 in Pomerania, Deutschland (Germany). She died in August 1900. Both immigrated to the United States in 1883 and settled in McPherson Township. The first tombstone in St. John's Evangelical Lutheran Cemetery marks their graves.

John Frederich Ludwig Glamm was born on October 5, 1858, in Pomerania, Deutschland (Germany), and came to the United States in 1876. He died on May 31, 1931. Bertha C. Krause was born on June 2, 1871, and came to the United States in 1889. She died on April 30, 1959. Bertha's family's farm only had 24 acres.

Known as Fred, he and Bertha were married December 2, 1892, and first farmed forty acres on the north end of the Art Miller farm and later purchased two hundred forty acres two miles northeast. Judy Miller now owns this farm. They had six boys, Otto, Herman, Fred, Henry (Orga Strauss), Richard, (Julia Riese Flitter) and Emil (Albena and Chris Wendt) and four girls, Martha (Herman Youngerberg), Bertha (Fred Kollos), Ella (Fred Miller - see separate story) and Lilly (Hans Bohnhof). They farmed, milked cows, and raised hogs and chickens. Fred and Ella Miller lived with her parents and later Herman Glamm. Ella Miller was the last of the Fred Glamm family.

Otto Robert Henry Glamm was born in 1893 in McPherson Township. He served in World War I and was wounded in France. Esther Rosalia Sophie Schroeder was born in September 1903 in McPherson Township the daughter of August and Caroline (Frantz) Schroeder. They purchased one hundred acres from Fred Glamm one

Marcella & Donald Glamm

mile south of the home place. Fred Glamm purchased a farm for each boy and when they married, he sold it to them so he could buy for the next son. Later Otto and Esther purchased the twenty-four acres of the Henry Krause farm. They farmed, milked cows, raised chickens, and had a purebred spotted hog herd. The children were Lorene (Lester Flemming), Donald (Marcella Bartlett), Virgene (Alvin Volkmann), and Carolyn (Curtis Hall). After Otto's death Esther moved to 328 West Main Street.

Donald Eugene Glamm was born on June 13, 1927, in McPherson Township, the second child of Otto and Esther (Schroeder). He married Marcella Mae Bartlett who was born on November 14, 1929, in Portland Township, Kossuth Co., Iowa. Marcella taught school in Comfrey, North Mankato, and St. Clair. They purchased and farmed the one hundred twenty-four acres plus rented land. They later purchased the Orville Christnagel and Adolph Sack farms. They bred a high producing herd of Registered Holstein cattle. Donald was awarded the two highest awards from the Minnesota Holstein Association: "The Person of the Year," and "Longtime Meritorious Service." Marcella received "The Good People Award" for her dedicated work as Guardian ad Litem for the court systems and as a volunteer at St. John's Evangelical Lutheran Church Office. Marcella received "The Roger Wolfe Achievement Award."

Donald and Marcella Glamm have two children. Joanne is a radio newsperson in Le Mars, Iowa, and David. Donald and Marcella Glamm moved to St. Clair in 1996 purchasing the Sylvester Youngerberg home.

David Glamm (Cindy Little) purchased the home farm and is continuing with the Registered Holsteins with production of 25,000 milk and 1050-butter fat. David Glamm has three children, Tammy, John and Terry.

By Donald Glamm

Ardella & Norbert Glaser

GLASER, AUGUST

August John Glaser was born on July 3, 1860, in Raditz Province, Posen, Germany. His parents were Michael and Wilhelmine (Jeske) Glaser. He married Maria Schwanke who was born on September 22, 1869, in Potash, Poland, which was near Germany. They immigrated to the United States in 1876 and were farmers in McPherson Township.

The children born to August and Marie were Theodore Henry [see separate story], Ida Adlinde [see separate story], Gustav Adolph [see separate story] and Emil A. who was born on October 16, 1899, and married Mary Bradley who was born on May 1, 1909. Emil died on June 11, 1982 and Mary on July 1, 1958.

August died on April 7, 1947 and Maria on March 8, 1907.

By Verna Sodeman

GLASER, THEODORE

The Glaser farm has been in the Glaser family for over 100 years. August and Maria were the first owners and purchased the farmland in 1902. They brought their four children with them, Theodore, Ida (Karl Sodeman) Adolph (Ruth Anderson) and Emil (Mary Bradley).

Theodore Henry Glaser was born in Iosco Township on January 16, 1892. During World War I, early in 1918, Mr. Glaser was drafted into the army and served in the infantry in France. On October 5, 1918, he was wounded by shrapnel fire in Flanders, the after-effects of which troubled him most of his life.

On July 18, 1923, he was married to Elsie Kohlhoff of Elysian. Approximately around 1931 Ted and Elsie purchased the 120-acre farm from his father. Ted and Elsie then built the present house on the homestead. While building the house, they lived in the granary.

This union was blessed with two sons - Norbert and Wesley of Minneapolis. The Glaser's spent their first 15 years of married life at Mankato. Thereafter they moved to the farm north of St. Clair.

Mr. Glaser died in 1950. At the time of his death he was also survived by a brother, Emil and sister, Ida (Frank Sodeman). A brother Adolph preceded him in death.

Mrs. Glaser died in 1969 and both are buried in the St. John's Evangelical Lutheran Cemetery, St. Clair.

Norbert Glaser

In the fall of 1944 Norbert Glaser met Ardella Stanke, who was born on June 1, 1925, at a wedding dance in Elysian. Her parents were Fred and Lena Stanke. They lived on a farm near Smith's Mill. She had four older brothers and one younger sister. Norbert and Ardella became engaged in November 1944. Shortly after that Norbert was called into service for his country. He was in the Army and served in Italy and in the states for two years. He returned home in July 1946. Ardella and Norbert were married in the Eagle Lake Lutheran Church on September 4, 1946.

Norbert and Ardella started farming on the Glaser farm and also purchased the Art Dietman farm that adjoined the Glaser home place. This was where Ardella and Norbert lived until they bought the Glaser farm place and land from his mother in the early 1950's. They then moved to the Glaser home place and still reside there.

Norbert worked at the State Hospital in St. Peter for over 25 years and also farmed. When he retired from those two jobs he went on the road buying furs and also started his own mink ranch fur business on the home place. He worked many 18-hour days to dress and stretch coon, beaver and mink for the young trappers in the area. His fur building was a hub for all the local trappers for a chat.

Ardella was a practical nurse for over 20 years at the Immanuel Hospital and also did private home nursing. She also worked as a cashier at the old Madsen's restaurant in Mankato. Ardella and Norbert had their home open to about 30 young children through the "foster care" program over a ten years period in the 1970's. Their children are:

Ardella Lynn (Ardie) Glaser was born on July 14, 1947, and attended St. Clair School until the ninth grade. She then attended DMLC in New Ulm, MN, and graduated from there in 1965. She graduated from Cosmetologist School and had her own shop in Madison Lake for several years and also was a Cosmetologist

Sue & Allan Glaser with their son Jesse

Instructor in Virginia, MN. She married Phil Pemble on August 28, 1965. They lived near Eagle Lake for about ten years and then purchased a farm near Kelsey, MN. They have three sons:

Theodore (Ted) was born on January 27, 1968. He married Coral Jarbi on December 14, 2001, and they have a daughter Alexis who was born on June 26, 2003. He is a foreman on road construction and lives near Kelsey, MN.

Trent was born on January 14, 1976 and was married to Jessica Boyer on June 6, 1998. They have a son Colton who was born on December 12, 2003. Trent is a Chemical Engineer and they live in Sidney, Ohio.

Travis was born on May 21, 1980, is a heavy equipment operator and lives in Floodwood, MN.

James & Melinda Rollings family
Back (L to R): Melinda, James, Danielle
Front: Lucas and Kate

Allan Theodore (Ted) Glaser was born on February 6, 1948, and attended St. Clair School and served in the Army during the Vietnam War. He received bronze and purple medals for bravery. He married Sue Freyberg on April 28, 1980. They have a son Jesse Theodore who was born on May 28, 1982. Ted retired from ADM in Mankato. Jesse and Sue are employed by Valley News in Mankato.

Melinda Lou Glaser was born on October 16, 1953. She attended St. Clair School and the Mankato Vocational School. She married James (Fred) Rollings on April 12, 1975. He worked at Tire Associates in Mankato before retiring. Melinda worked at the *Free Press* and at Shopko in the accounting department. They are living in St. Clair in a house that was a Spec Home built by Doctor George Penn. Her great-uncle Willie Koholoff helped build this house. Melinda and Fred have three children

Danielle, Katie and Lucas.

Danielle was born on February 29, 1976, and graduated from St. Clair High School. She married Sean Laird on August 22, 1998. They are living in Minneapolis where she works as a buyer for the Target Corp. They have a son Ean Joseph who was born on August 21, 2003.

Katie was born on May 22, 1979. She married Korey VanErdwyk on June 19, 2004, and they are living in Pemberton, MN. She works in financial planning.

Lucas was born on December 22, 1983. He is attending Minnesota State University, Mankato, MN, and is planning a career in banking.

The Glaser Farm has and will remain the Glaser Farm for many years to come.

By Ardella Glaser and Ardella Glaser Pemble

GODEMANN, CHRISTIAN

Christian Godemann was born in 1845 in Germany. He married Sophia Hagge (born in 1853 in Satow, Germany), in 1875. They came to America in 1893 with the listed destination as Mankato. When they arrived in McPherson Township shortly before midnight, they spent their first night at the farm, which became their home for thirty-five years. Christian died on Christmas Day, 1924 and Sophia died on January 16, 1939.

Minnie (Dimmel) and William Godemann

The children were William J., Martha (Emil Guse), Ludwig (1887-1952), Alvina (1888-1896), Clara and Herman F. (1900-1981). Ella Jeddloh - (1911-1961) and later Elma Louise Oftedahl McComb (1917-1990). Herman and Louise lived at 225 Mill Street.

Christian and Sophia are buried at St. John's Evangelical Lutheran Cemetery, St. Clair, Minnesota.

William J. Godemann (1878-1965) and his wife Louise Dimmel (1884-1956), the daughter of Frederick and Sophie Dimmel, owned the former Duemeland Grocery

Emma Godemann

Store and lived at 301 Main Street West. They are buried in the St. John's Evangelical Lutheran Cemetery, St. Clair.

GODEMANN, FRIEDERICH

Friederich (1843-1907) and Marie Godemann had five children: Carl (1880-1942), Fred (1881-1967), Ida (Theodore Penn - see separate story), Emma and William R.

Friederich is buried in the St. John's Evangelical Lutheran Cemetery.

William R. Godemann, was born on May 27, 1894, in Germany. He was married to Hattie Schumacker.

Emma Godemann was born in 1892 in Germany. She was a schoolteacher and principal at St. Clair in 1923 as the yearbook was dedicated to her. She lived with her sis-

Stella & Lyle Goodrich

ter, Ida. She was a very short lady and was very hunched back when she walked. She died on February 22, 1954.

Carl, Fred, Emma, William and Hattie are buried in the St. Johns (Bestman) Cemetery.

GOODRICH, LYLE

Lyle Vernon Goodrich was born in McPherson Township and was the second child of George and Lottie Goodrich. He married Stella Marie Grams.

Lyle was a farmer and also worked for Gulf Oil Company for three years selling fertilizer. He retired in 1978. Stella is a housewife.

Lyle started the first Blue Earth County Mounted Sheriff's Posse in the fall of 1975. Lyle and Stella had two children, Merlin (Elmay Geyer) and Linda (Larry Gerber). Merlin and Elmay took over the family farm and had three children, James, Jon and Joyce. In August 2004 they moved to California. Linda worked for Mankato State University as a secretary in the Division of Nursing for ten years. She now works at the Mankato Post Office. Linda is married to Larry Gerber and they live in Mankato, Minnesota.

Lyle, Stella, Linda and Larry are all members of St. John's Evangelical Lutheran Church, St. Clair

By Lyle and Stella Goodrich

Linda & Larry Gerber

GRAMS, CHRISTOPHER

Christopher Grams was born in 1835 in Germany. He was married to Amelia Doege and in 1886 they came to America. Christopher was one of the oldest residents of the McPherson-St. Clair area when he died in April of 1919. They engaged in the pursuits of farming and by hard and persistent work they soon succeeded in developing for themselves and family a good home. In 1910 they retired from the farm and bought a home on the hill next to the Methodist Church, in St. Clair.

Mr. and Mrs. Grams had eight children. The oldest daughter Minnie (Gherke) died in 1913. The surviving children were Otillie (William George), Ludwig, Chris, August, Pauline (Copham), William and Auguste (Jeseritz)

When Christopfer and Amelia moved to town their son August purchased the farm and continued farming. Amelia died in 1924.

By Holly Walechka

GRAMS, LUDWIG

Ludwig Grams was born in 1862 in Germany and his wife Marie Westphal was also born in Germany in 1861. In 1886, they came to the United States with their two children, Emma and Anna, Ludwig's parents, Christopher and Amelia and his brothers, William and August.

After arriving in America, Ludwig, Marie and children moved in with Ludwig's sister, Minnie Gherke and her husband, Ferdinand, who had come to America earlier and were living in rural Janesville. After several moves they rented 80 acres and buildings in McPherson Township. They later purchased the land here and lived on the farm until they moved to St. Clair in the spring of 1919 living at 200 Main Street West. Ludwig and Marie passed away 13 days apart on December 8th and 21st, 1945. Ludwig died of lobar pneumonia and arterial sclerotic heart disease. Marie also suffered from arteriosclerosis and was living with her son Paul at the time of her death. They are buried in the St. John's Evangelical Lutheran Cemetery, St. Clair, Minnesota.

Ludwig, Marie and Ludwig's sister Gusty and her husband Rudolph Jeseritz celebrated their double Golden Wedding at St. John's Lutheran Church, St. Clair, Minnesota, on March 7th, 1936.

Marie and Ludwig Grams had seven children:

Emma married Reinhold Lachelt, lived in McPherson Township, their children Gertrude (Otto Witt) and Herbert (Luella Priebe).

Anna who was only six weeks old when the family came to America and did not travel well, getting so sea sick, she died shortly after arriving in Janesville.

Elsa married John O'Brien.

Paul married Mabel Prechel, they who farmed in McPherson Township and later moved to St. Clair where they lived at 205 East Main Street. They had a daughter Stella (Lyle Goodrich) [see separate story], Bernard and foster son William Hesse [see separate story].

William Heinrich grew up in the St. Clair area and died while in the armed service during the flu epidemic. The American Legion Post in St. Clair is named after him.

Eric was born and died as a small child of diphtheria.

Otto married Hannah Koopman, farmed next to his parents in McPherson Township and upon retirement moved to St. Clair. They had a daughter Marcella who lives in St. Clair.

William Heinrick Grams

Taps were sounded over the grave of another soldier boy at St. Clair yesterday afternoon when Private William H. Grams, son of (Ludwig) Louis and Marie (Westphal) was laid to rest with military honors, in the German Lutheran cemetery of that place.

Private Grams was the victim of Spanish influenza. He left here with a contingent of Blue Earth County boys, August 26th for Camp Grant, Illinois.

While the casket was not carried into the church, Rev. Mueller of the German Lutheran church held services there which relatives and friends of the deceased very largely attended. In the funeral sermon Rev. Mueller paid high tribute to the young man, and extended sympathy to the bereaved parents.

Local members of the National Guard, consisting of Sergt. Stefty, Sergt. Sanborn, Private H. R. and Claud Huettl, H. Luei Johnson made up a firing squad and took charge of the services at the grave. Chief of Police Edward Ario acted as bugler and sounded taps over the grave.

Private Grams was born in Lyon Township, Waseca County on October 12th 1894. He died on October 4, 1918.

By Stella Goodrich

GRAMS, AUGUST

August Grams came to America with his parents and two brothers. He was married to Emma Jeseritz and they took over the family farm. Their children were Anna (Albert Priem), Clara (William Freitag), Otto, son (twin to Otto), Leona (Evert Doss) and Elsie (Walter Witt) the parents of Lyle Witt.

Otto Karl Grams was born on August 10, 1899. He, being the only surviving son, took over the family farm from his father August. Otto had a twin brother who died at an early age.

Otto married Gertrude Mittelsteadt. They had one daughter Anieta (Marvin Meyer). Gertrude died in childbirth. Otto later married Edna Schoenfeld. They had four children, Karl (Carol Lee), Ruth (Melvin Meyer, a brother to Marvin), Dorothy (Eddie Rutt) and Alvin (Barbara Hunt).

Upon their retirement they moved to Janesville, Minnesota. Otto died on November 21, 1990, and Edna died in 1999. They are both buried in the St. John's Lutheran Cemetery, St. Clair, Minnesota. Their son Karl purchased the family farm in the 1970's. He married Carol Lee and they raised five daughters, Karen, Nadine, Holly (Kevin Kubista/L. Rick Walechka), Carolyn (Wayne Gottschalk) and Marlene. Karl was killed in a farming accident in 1983. Carol remarried Lyle Witt and they continue to live on the family farm.

In 2004 Holly, Rick and their children Collin, Jordan, Austin, Aaron and Benjamin are building a new home on the Grams farm. This will be the fifth generation of family on this farm.

Six generations of the Grams family have resided in and around the town of St. Clair.

By Holly Walechka

GRAMS, WALTER E.

Walter E. Grams was born on May 30, 1905, in LeRay Township to Emil and Dora (Santo) Grams. As a boy he lived near Erie and later moved to Duluth where he worked at a steel plant. He worked for various farmers in Southern Minnesota until 1935 and then moved to the Brainerd, MN, area where he operated a farm. In 1926, he married Irene Vierguts, the daughter of William and Ida (Kruger) Vierguts, at St. Paul's Lutheran Church in West Duluth. Dora was born on September 15, 1905, in Becker, MN. She attended school in Becker and Sylvan, enjoyed needlework, playing cards, fishing and reading.

Irene & Walter E. Grams, Sr.

In 1949 they moved to a farm near St. Clair where they lived for two years and they moved to St. Clair. Here Walter was employed at the St. Clair School for sixteen and a half years. After he retired he worked for Harold and Hazel Boswell in the greenhouse and helped with the farming.

Walter and Irene had two sons Donald (Jodell) and Walter, Jr.

Walter died on May 1, 1996 and Irene on September 25, 1999.

Walter Grams, Jr. was born on December 19, 1926, and attended school in Pillager, MN. He served in the U.S. Air Force from May 1946 until May 1949. He spent 9 months in Germany. He was married to Wilma M. Shutt on July 19, 1947 in Pillager. After the service he farmed for a short time at Pillager before he moved to Mapleton where they farmed for twelve years. In 1965 they moved to St. Clair, and he worked for Kato Engineering for 28 years, retiring in 1992. He was a member of the American Legion Post #475 and they were members of St. John's Lutheran Church in St. Clair. He enjoyed fishing and woodworking.

Walter and Wilma's children are Raymond (Norma), Wayne (Darlene Seys), Kathleen "Cookie" (Randy Shaw) and Diane (Eugene Goettl, Jr./Steve Cords/Michael Fitter).

Walter Grams, Jr. died on September 5, 1996. Wilma is living in now living in Mankato.

GRAMS, WALTER H.

Walter H. Grams was born to William and Julia (Hoehn) Grams. His home place was where the

Five Generations
Front: Great-great grandmother
Margaret Grams
Standing: Great grandfather Charles Grams,
Grandfather Michael Grams,
Mother Chantel Grams Medina holding
daughter Jaidence Medina (April 2004)

Minnesota Elevator Company is located today. He had three brothers and five sisters. Walter was the oldest. His brothers and sisters were Gertrude (Allen Goodrich), William Jr. (Evelyn Leifermann), Laura (Jay Myers), Eva (Alfred Hodapp), Carl (Marie Cuddy), Alice (Edmund Hodapp), Marion (Guy Hinton), and Robert (Helen Hirte).

On November 12, 1935, Walter was married to Margaret Maloney, the daughter of Francis and Margaret (Bowe) Maloney. Walter farmed in the St. Clair and Pemberton area. They moved to the Everad O'Brien farm east of St. Clair in 1959. Margaret's grandparents, James and Julian (Cotter) Maloney, were the owners of the land where the Immaculate Conception Church property is today. They donated this ground to the parish when it was established. Walter served on the St. Clair School Board from 1955 until 1972. Walter and Margaret's children are Charles (Chuck), Dorothy (Dennis Novotny)

Carol and Charles Grams

who live in Bloomington, MN, Mary Lou (Patrick Gulden), Olympia, Washington, Monica (Terry Schmidt), Cleveland, MN and Bill (Jane Salstrom) who lives in Winthrop, MN.

Charles Grams took over the operation of the family farm in 1959. He was married to Carol Schubbe, the daughter of Elwin and Melinda (Benz) Schubbe, on September 13, 1958. Chuck and Carol's children are Michael (Julie Hagen) who live in Cottage Grove, MN, Jane (Tim Manthei), Mankato, MN, Jerry (Renee Fick), North Mankato, Sara (Bill Phelps), Mankato, Mark (Pam Torborg), Mankato, Cathy (Patrick Buse), Eden Prairie, MN and Douglas who is living in the original brick house that was built in the pioneer days.

By Carol and Margaret Grams

GRAWUNDER, WILLIAM

William Grawunder was born in August 1874 in Watertown, Wisconsin. He married Ida Mueller, the daughter of August and Ernestine (Manthe) Mueller, on June 3, 1897. After their marriage they farmed in Freedom Township, Waseca County. William also was a carpenter and in 1916 he built a house for them at 329 West Main Street in St. Clair. They had a daughter Lydia who married Fred Silkey and after his death, Louis Klingbeil [see separate story]. Ida died in October of 1944. William died in October 1962.

GRIGNON, H. R.

H. R. Grignon was born in 1850 in Iowa. He moved to Long Prairie, Minnesota, and then in 1856 to Prairie du Chien, Wisconsin. Two years later he went to the Winnebago Agency in Minnesota. In 1860 he moved to Mendota for two years. He went to Wisconsin to attend school but returned to Minnesota from 1866 to 1870, living in Rice County. For a time he was in the mercantile trade and was also employed as a clerk and traveling salesman. He then was engaged in buying and selling butter. In 1870 he married Jennie Phillips. Their children were Virginia H. and Belle.

Esther & Ernie Hager

Standing (L to R): Ernie & Esther Hager
Seated: Curtis & Lena McDuff

HAGER, ERNEST

Ernest F. Hager, the son of Joseph and Katherine (Yaeger), was born on November 22, 1903, on a farm southwest of St. Clair. He moved into St. Clair in 1920 and worked for Jerry Lynch in the Chevy garage (Pints) as a mechanic. On June 4, 1929, he married Esther D. Schroeder, the daughter of Frank and Mary (Matthies) Schroeder {see separate story]. Esther was born on October 11, 1898, in Wells, MN. Esther taught in a rural school for 1 year (1916-1917) and then moved with her family to Mankato in May of 1917, where she worked at the Woolworth's Store. When the family moved to St. Clair, Esther worked with her father, Frank, in the Mercantile Store.

Mary Jane & William Hager

After the closing of the Mercantile in the fall of 1933, Esther and Ernest Hager purchased the building that came to be known as Hager Hardware. The building has an adjoining apartment where the four of them lived. In 1939 Ernie and Esther built a new home at 113 Park Street North which cost $5,000 at the time.

Ernie and Esther operated the business for almost 30 years, which included not only hardware but also International Harvesters and Minnesota farm

L to R: Clay, Bill, Mary Jane, Aaron and Loni Hager

implements, bottled gas, and Ernest also drove school bus from 1937-1954. In 1963 they sold the business to their son Bill.

William "Bill" Hager was born on December 8, 1935. On September 23, 1958, Bill married Mary Jane Verschelde, the daughter of Herman and Mary (Hollobusch) Verschelde, in St. Clair. Mary Jane was born on April 24, 1939, in Illinois and grew up in Minneota, Minnesota. They lived in the apartment above the hardware store. Mary Jane was a beautician with a beauty shop in Mankato and operated the Mary Jane Hager Salon in St. Clair. She was a beautician for 40 years. The hardware business had changed through the years. The implement line had been dropped and home appliances, lawn mowers, small appliance repairs etc. were added to the business. Bill also drove school bus from 1954-1968. In 1978 Bill and Mary Jane sold the business to Cal and Anne (Massop) Gamble, building a new home at 312 Main Street West.

Bill and Mary Jane Hager, owners of "The Diner"

Bill and Mary Jane have 3 children, Clay, born January 15, 1963, Lani, born August 15, 1965 and Aaron, born January 9, 1967. Clay is married to Linda Stevens, born on May 5, 1964. They live on Lake Miltona, Miltona, Minnesota, with their children Collin, born February 27, 1991 and Amelia, born July 14, 1995. Loni is married to Paul Latusek, born August 4, 1959. They live in Minnesota Lake, MN with their children Timothy, born February 5, 1998, and Jared, born September 20, 2001. Aaron is married to Rachel Rudisill, born December 9, 1970. They live in Eagle Lake with their daughter, Makayla, born April 1. 1998.

After a period of 2 years Bill and Mary Jane bought the former Rose's Meat Market building, which was the D&L Diner from DeLane McCollum and named it "The Diner." It was a home style Ma and Pa café where the whole family worked together. Not only with the café in the front part of the building, in the back was a room used for Feed and Seed meetings, confirmations, miscellaneous parties, club meetings and ladies day out gatherings. Many high school students worked for Bill and Mary Jane. Many high school ball games were replayed in this back room.

Bill and Mary Jane sold The Diner in May of 1985. Bill operated the "Master Plan Hearing Center" in Mankato doing hearing test, evaluations, sales and repairs. Mary Jane continued with her beauty shop and tanning salon until 1992 when she then went to work for Taylor Corporation in purchasing until 1997.

Bill retired in 1995 and Mary Jane retired in 1997 and now they are living on the north shore of Lake Miltona just north of Alexandria, Minnesota.

By William (Bill) Hager

HALL, STANLEY

Stanley Hall was born in 1932 to Harold and Inga (Finstad) Hall in Mankato, MN. He graduated in 1950 from St. Clair High School. He married Elvera Freitag in June 1951. They farmed for many years in LeRay Township, Blue Earth County and later moved to east of St. Clair. He earned a Bachelor of Arts and Master Degree's from Mankato State University. From 1974 to 1977 he taught at MSU. He then was employed at St. Peter Security Hospital, St. Peter, MN. In 1982, he received a specialist degree in curriculum from MSU. He was the director of education at St. Peter Security Hospital until 1987. He was employed by Palmer Bus Service in St. Clair, and in 1977 he retired from MBW in New Ulm. For many years, he served at tri-state and national levels of Dakota-Minnesota Columbia Sheep Breeders Association boards. He had served as chairman of the St. Clair School Board. In April 1985 Stan and Elvera purchased the Freitag home place from the estate. They were members of St. John's Evangelical Lutheran Church, and he was completing his first term as the president of the church.

Elvera was the daughter of John and Emma (Risto) Freitag and was born in 1935. She graduated from the St. Clair High School in 1953 and worked in Owatonna for a year before she was married and at Waseca Mutual Insurance Company in Waseca, MN for two years after her marriage. In 1968 she started working at the Brown Printing Company in Waseca. She retired in April of 1999, after working for 30 years. After Stan's sudden death, she started working at Corporate Graphics Commercial, North Mankato, MN.

Stan and Elvera had five children. Timothy (1958-1958), Jerome (1959) who lives in Duluth and has one child. Kristine (1960) is living in Crystal and has two children, Marcus (1963) is married to Daphne Schmidt and is living in Duluth, Jon (1965) is married to Jeanette Lang, the daughter of Jerry and Mary (Glynn) Lang. They have three children.

Elvera & Stanley Hall

Stanley died on December 5, 1999 at St. Mary's Hospital, Rochester, Minnesota. He is buried in the St. John's Evangelical Lutheran Cemetery, St. Clair.

HAWKER, WILLIAM

William Hawker, the son of John Hawker, was born in 1881 in Germany. On December 18, 1907 he married Eliza Birr, the daughter of Carl and Johanna (Weizig) Birr, in Redeemer Lutheran Church, Decoria. Eliza was born on July 4,1887, in Le Sueur county, Minnesota. Bill and Eliza farmed near Mapleton and St. Clair. Their children were Wilbur, Alvin, Frieda (John Westphal - see separate story), Harold (1920-1975)(Rosella Drummer), and Lyle (1922) (Lillia Rudolph). The boys at one time were all farmers in McPherson Township.

William died in 1951 and Eliza died in 1980 and they are buried in the St. John's Evangelical Lutheran Cemetery, St. Clair.

The William Hawker family
Standing (L to R): Alvin, Wilbur, Lyle, Harold
Seated: Eliza, Frieda, William

Wilbur L. Hawker was born on January 26, 1909, at Mapleton. On April 24, 1931, he married Mildred Flitter (1913-1976), the daughter of Robert and Martha (Kopke) Flitter. He was employed at Land O'Lakes in Lake Crystal for 15 years and then was custodian at the Martin Building in Mankato. They lived in Lake Crystal and after Wilbur's death on January 17, 1955, Mildred moved to St. Clair and live at 301 Main Street West.

The children of Wilbur and Mildred are Judy

Elenora & Alvin Hawker

(1943-1949), Wayne, Marvin and Phyllis.

Wilbur, Mildred and Judy are buried in the St. John's Evangelical Lutheran Cemetery, St. Clair

Alvin Hawker was born on December 11, 1910, in Mapleton, Minnesota. In June 1937 he married Elenora Maass, the daughter of Frank and Marie (Holtz) Maass at Medo Lutheran Church, Medo Township, Blue Earth County. He farmed in McPherson Township and then worked for Vetter Stone Co., from 1961 until 1986 when he retired.

Elenora was born in 1918 and attend school in Pemberton, Minnesota. After they moved to St. Clair, living at 345 Main Street West, Elenora worked at St. Clair School in the cafeteria.

Alvin and Elenora have four children, Marion (Ronald Flo/Jerry Westphal), Darlene (David Terhurne), Dale (Susan Bruels) and Laurie (Randall Cords). They also had an infant daughter that is buried in the Medo Lutheran Cemetery.

Alvin and Elenora were members of St. John's Evangelical Lutheran Church where he served on the church council and Elenora is an honorary member of the Ladies Aid. Alvin died in 2001 and he is buried in the St. John's Evangelical Lutheran Cemetery, St. Clair.

HAWKINS, HONORABLE J. D.

Honorable J. D. Hawkins was a native of Vermont and was born December 9, 1836. When he was eight years old the family moved to Wisconsin and then to Dodge County, Minnesota, in 1862. One and one-half years later he came to McPherson Township. He enlisted in 1864 in Company D, 11th Minnesota and served until the close of the war. In the fall of 1880 he was elected to the legislature. At Fond du Lac, Wisconsin, in 1861, he married Paulina L. Hill.

Dr. E.B. Haynes, the first doctor in St. Clair. He also served as an alderman.

HAYNES, DR. E. B.

Dr. E. B. Haynes was born in Greene, Chenango County, New York, in 1818. He was engaged in the manufacture of lumber and in connection ran a gristmill. He went to Lycoming County, Pennsylvania, in 1846 and there continued the lumber business. For several years he practiced medicine. He located in McPherson in 1864, where he devoted his time to the practice of medicine and to farming. He married Celia Rogers in 1830. She died in 1844 and then in 1853 he married Elizabeth Camp. They had one daughter, Elizabeth, who married H. Eastman.

Dr. Haynes died on September 6, 1887, and is buried in the St. Clair Union Cemetery.

HEINBAUGH, PHILLIP

Phillip and Tracy Heinbaugh live in St. Clair. They have two children, Cole born on March 18, 1998 and Hunter born on December 29, 2001. Tracy was the daughter of Clifford and Linda Vaske. Her brothers and sisters are Candy (Hoehn), Clint, Amber (May 31, 1980-May l, 1996), Maribeth and Gabrielle.

By Phillip Heinbaugh

HEMSHROT, MARVIN

Marvin Hemshrot, the son of George and Anna (Gekler) Hemshrot, was born on July 25, 1915, in Rochester, MN. He married Lucille Hall, the daughter of

Lucille & Marvin "Murph" Hemshrot

Edwin and Bessie (Russell) Hall, on January 18, 1941, at Zion Methodist Church in St. Clair. He served in the U.S. Army during World War II before working a portable feed mill for 36 years and owning and operating the Hemshrot's Grocery Store in St. Clair and lived in the apartment in the building.

In 1989 after selling groceries in St. Clair for 34 years, "Murph" and Lucille received an offer from the St. Clair School District to buy the property. With the small-town economics and big-city competition they did decide to call it quits. The idea to shut down and retire wasn't a voluntary one — but the future did not look promising. The building had been in business for a century being established on December 14, 1882, by Gus Duemeland. It was then sold to Wm. Godeman who in turn sold it to Harold and Clair Wolcott, who in 1956 sold it to the Hemshrots. At times it also housed the St. Clair Post Office as well as the city library.

Over the years the grocery business changed. Along with a dwindling clientele the dwindling of suppliers changed. Earlier times saw the ice cream, meat, milk and bread trucks stopped by several times a week. Towards the end it was hard to get them to deliver such small amounts even once a week. This forced them to buy supplies for their store from some of the big Mankato grocers.

The Hemshrots closed the doors and then held a public auction on April 29, 1989, to sell off the remaining stock

Their lives saw some changes even though they both operated the store they often worked separately, staggering hours. Lucille had to adjust to running a household kitchen, as she was used to just taking home what she need and never really shopped for food. Lucille did find time over the years to do some paintings, which adorned the walls of the grocery store.

Marvin and Lucille had three children: Jean (1941-2001) (Larry Teff), Judy (Gary Miller - see separate story), and Kent (Deborah).

Dorothy & William Hesse

Marvin died on October 8, 2002 and is buried in Woodland Hills Memorial Park, Mankato. Lucille is still living in St. Clair.

HESSE, WILLIAM

William Hesse was born in Elm Dale Township, Morrison County, Minnesota, to Paul and Franzska Hesse. He grew up as the foster child of Paul and Mabel (Prechel) Grams in McPherson Township. William married Dorothy Berentson, the daughter of Simon and Kate Berentson, on June 16, 1937. They farmed in McPherson Township, later moved across the road when semi-retired and later moved to the Schalow Apartments is St. Clair. William died in May of 1998. Dorothy is now living at the Mankato Lutheran Home, Mankato, Minnesota.

Norlas Hesse

Bill and Dorothy had five children. **Norla** is a Registered Nurse and has now retired after 30 years of working at Immanuel-St. Joseph's-Mayo Health System in Mankato and assisted with the publication of *Years of Memories*, **Harvey**, **Ada** died as an infant of pneumonia and **Sylvia** who is now retired after working as a Library/Media Specialist in the North St. Paul/Maplewood District and lives in White Bear Lake Township. **Jeffrey** who married Lea Giles in the Philippines while in the Peace Corps and they have two children. He works for the United States Agricultural

Sylvia Hesse

Beverly & Harvey Hesse

L to R: Tate, Vicki (Hesse), Megan Rose
Standing: Gerald Rose

Back (L to R): Larry & Londa (Hesse) Lillo
Front: Jason, Joni, Jennifer

Department in Washington, D.C. As part of this department he has served in Canada, Malaysia and recently returned from Russia to continue his career in D.C.

Harvey Hesse, the son of William and Dorothy (Berentson) Hesse, took over the family farm and is still living there. He married Beverly Bartelt, the daughter of Herb and Elsie (Schnoor) Bartelt of Waldorf, Minnesota. They have three children. Vicki who married Gerald Rose, the son of Dean and Ardys (Stoltzman) Rose, and they have two children Tayton and Megan and live in Mankato. Michael who is married to Susan Prange and they have three children Kristina, Keri, and Kile and they live in Colorado Springs, Colorado. Londa who is married to Larry Lillo and they have four children Jessica, Jennifer, Joni, and Jason and they live in St. Clair.

By Norla Hesse

HILTON, AARON

Aaron Hilton II was one of 11 children of Aaron Hilton and Lydia Webb. He was born in Maine in 1808, where his family had lived for nearly 200 years, but chose to leave it for Wisconsin in 1849. He married Jane Bailey Gould. He died in August of 1875 in St. Clair, Minnesota, the town that he had founded on August 11, 1865, by laying out a portion of McPherson Township. He named his town Hilton. By 1866 the village was booming, containing three general stores, a dozen other stores, two saloons, a hotel and a mill. The mill was built by Aaron Hilton in 1864. The Hiltons are one of the oldest families in America. The brothers William and Edward Hilton came to the New World in 1623 on the *Fortune*, and are credited with being the first white settlers in New Hampshire. Aaron's mother, Lydia Webb, was descended from Ruth Alden, daughter of John Alden and Priscilla

Aaron Hilton II

Jane Bailey Gould Hilton

Mullens, who came to the New World on the *Mayflower*. His wife, Jane Bailey Gould, was born in 1812, also in Maine. Jane's ancestor William Furbish was transported to the New World on the *Unity* after being captured at the Battle of Dunbar. Her ancestor Quinton Pray arrived on the *Ann Cleve*.

HILTON, SUMNER CHARLES

Sumner "Sum" Charles Hilton was born in Lincoln County, Maine, in 1833 to Aaron Hilton II and Jane Bailey Gould Hilton. He learned the trades of miller and engineer. In 1849 he moved to Wisconsin and settled about eight miles from Oshkosh. For three years he was a river pilot in Wisconsin, and then engaged in building mills. In 1854 he married Hulda C. Dickinson, the daughter of Clark Dickinson, a Wisconsin minister and one of the founders of Green Bay, Wisconsin. He worked at a lumber mill at Mankato, Minnesota, from 1858 to 1860 and then enlisted in the 9th Minnesota Union forces and fought at many battles. In 1864 he was captured and sent to Andersonville, serving until the war ceased. He then came to the Winnebago Agency and built a sawmill and a flourmill. Sum taught himself milling engineering, and apparently became quite an expert at it. He visited California in 1868 and again in 1872. Alice J. (Melvin Rasdall-see separate story) and Harriet A'Della were their children.

Alice J. and Harriet A'Della Hilton

Sumner Charles Hilton, the second son of Aaron and Jane's five children

Huldah (Dickinson) Hilton

HILTON, HENRY

The gifts of industry, perseverance, good judgment, integrity and patriotism which found convincing expression in the life of Henry S. Hilton, inevitably won him permanent place among the up builders of Blue Earth County, who labored for its welfare from before the Civil War until the dawn of a new century. January 22, 1901, this able miller, farmer, civil engineer and soldier passed beyond the ken of those who had known and honored him, and whose memories are fragrant with the sense of his upright and noble nature.

Born in far off Maine, January 7, 1842, Mr. Hilton was a son of Joseph and Sarah (Smith) Hilton, the former of whom died in Maine and the latter in Boston, Massachusetts. He was one in a family of seven children, and he was reared in comparative poverty and obliged to assume early responsibility. He acquired the rudiments of education in the country schools of Maine, but by nature a student, he later availed himself of every possible opportunity of acquiring knowledge. Seeking a larger opportunity for his powers than seemed to present itself in his native state, he moved from Maine in very early manhood, and after a short sojourn in Wisconsin took up his residence in Mankato where he became interested in saw-milling until the outbreak of the Civil War. He later settled on the farm in McPherson township later owned by his family and here he devoted his energies to general agriculture and stock raising with excellent financial results. (Note: The farm was located just south of the Lutheran Church where Mill Street is today.) He also practiced civil engineering to a considerable extent. His farm, however, was his chief source of profit and delight, and he improved it continually, adding each year to its effectiveness as a place of residence, and it facilities as a money making proposition. He was a lover of trees and the beautiful things of nature, and was very orderly in his methods and habits.

On August 17,1866, Mr. Hilton married Katherine Donahue, a native of Illinois, and of the union there were seven children, four sons and three daughters. The children were: Even, a resident of St. Clair; Charley, a painter; William, a civil engineer; Georgina, wife of Thomas McCarty, a farmer of Northern Dakota; Libby of Portland, Oregon; Margaret; and Ralph, the last two living on the home farm. Mr. Hilton was a Republican in politics, and his religion was Congregationalist.

In 1861 Mr. Hilton enlisted in Company H, Second, Minnesota.

From *History of Blue Earth County* by Thomas Hughes-1909

(Additional note: The Hilton farm was located just south of where the Lyle Goodrich house is today. The Hilton house was the first house in St. Clair - Bill Hager.)

HINTZE, JOHN

John Hintze came to America and settled in Wisconsin where he met and married Marie and they came to Mankato, Minnesota, in 1866 and in 1876 they moved to a farm in the vicinity of St. Clair. They lived on the farm for ten years and then moved to St. Clair, living at 330 East Main Street. Marie was born on June 20, 1842 in the province of Hanover, Germany. She came to America in 1866 and first settled in the state of Wisconsin where she married. She always enjoyed the love and respect of all that knew her. She belonged to that type of pioneers who built up Blue Earth County to what it became in the early days. Her life was a very active and useful one. Through her earnest belief in Christianity, she did many loving deeds of kindness, which will be long remembered by her many friends.

John died in 1919 and Marie in May of 1921. They had the following children Mrs. Albert Jenrich, John, Robert, Marie, Clara, Louis and Charles.

HODAPP, HERBERT

Herbert R. Hodapp was born in 1938 to Hubert and Ludgart (Baumgartner) Hodapp in Mankato. A Class of 1956 graduate of St. Clair High School, Herbert studied electronics at DeVry Institute in Chicago. He was self employed, working in RCA-TV sales and service for many years. Herbert also worked for Associated Engineering and Midwest Electric in Mankato. He enjoyed flea markets, swap meets, and steam engine exhibitions and made his own spark plugs.

The Hodapp family lived on the Schostag farm which was located on the hill where Custom Woodworking and Lone Pine Treasures is currently located. Herbert later lived at 502 Main Street West.

Herbert died on May 6, 2003, at his home in St. Clair and is buried at Immaculate Conception Catholic Church Cemetery in St. Clair.

HOLTZ, HENRY E.

Henry Edward Holtz was born on May 12, 1915, to Frederick and Augusta Holtz. On August 28, 1953, he married Viona Sohre at St. John's Lutheran Church, Good Thunder, MN. Viona was born on May 27, 1921, to Arthur and Martha Sohre.

Henry served in WWII from 1942 until 1946. He earned the rank of Sgt. and numerous medals including the Purple Heart.

After their marriage they originally lived on the O'Brien property east of St. Clair. The couple moved to St. Clair in January 1955 where Viona is still living today.

Henry worked for Carl Fitzloff assisting with the farming and at the George Miller produce as well at the Jim Hunter Produce. He then was the manager of the St. Clair Municipal Liquor Store in St. Clair for seventeen years.

Henry and Viona had two children:

Larry was born on June 19, 1955, and married Julie Hoffmann on April 3, 1982. Their children are Kristin, born on April 13, 1984, Andria, born on March 9, 1987, and Matthew, born on December 18, 1989.

Connie was born on July 15, 1958 and married to Roger Depuydt on March 28, 1981. Roger was born on April 30, 1958 and died on March 27, 1988. They have two children: Daniel, born on September 27, 1985, and Kimberly, who was born on August 24, 1987.

Henry died on April 29, 1980, and is buried in the St. John's Evangelical Lutheran Cemetery, St. Clair.

By Viona Holtz

Duane & Gloria Hubmer family with
Great Grandmothers Thorn and Hubmer.

HUBMER, HERMAN

Herman A. Hubmer was born in 1862 in Wisconsin and came with his parents to Danville Township as a child. He grew to manhood there and then moved to Decoria Township. He lived there until 1921 when he retired from farming and moved to St. Clair. He served for a time as a village councilman and was a trustee of the Evangelical church.

Herman married Mary Juliar (1867-1933), the daughter of Nicholas and Catharine (Stevens) Juliar. They were parents of sons Clarence (Norma Oelke), George, Otto, (Irma Ott) and Roy (Dora Hoffman), and daughters Mrs. Sterling Morrisson and Alma.

Herman died in 1943.

George H. Hubmer was raised on a farm near St. Clair, Minnesota. He attended the St. Clair School and then Mankato Commercial College. Upon completing his courses in 1910, he secured employment as a bookkeeper and teller at the St. Clair State Bank, later being appointed cashier of the bank.

In 1940 he celebrated his thirtieth year of service with the bank organization and during the long period of years, since he was first employed as bookkeeper and teller, he had made many friends throughout the St. Clair district.

In commenting on the service rendered to the residents of St. Clair and vicinity, he stated that the St. Clair State Bank was established in November 1906. All through the years that have passed it has been noted for its strength and is an example of the steady and substantial progress made in St. Clair during the past 34 years. This bank today is noted for its complete banking facilities and the sound judgment of it officers.

Mr. Hubmer added that the entire personnel at the St. Clair State Bank are anxious to make customers feel at home. All employees realized that good service is something very much desired by banking customers and with this factor constantly in mind they endeavor to operate the bank on this basis.

George married Lydia Courrier on December 14, 1911. They lived at 300 East Main Street and later built a new home at 100 Schalow Drive. Their children were: Courrier G. (Beryl Cornell), Valera (Leo Weyrauch), Florence (Robert Zavoral - came to St. Clair from the Twin Cities around 1950 driving a 1948 Olds-pretty sporty for St. Clair) and Keturah (Fred Doescher).

Roy R. Hubmer was married to Dora Hoffman and lived at 109 Park Street North at one time. They had two children, Pershing and Lois (Hugh Rosania).

Pershing Hubmer was married to June (Mohlke) and they had four sons, Duane, David, Bruce and Roger.

Duane Arnold Hubmer was born on April 29, 1944. On June 18, 1966, he married Gloria Louise Thorn at the First Lutheran Church, St. Peter, Minnesota. She was born on July 27, 1946, and is the daughter of Ray and Lillian Thorn. Duane farmed in McPherson Township and is now working in Mankato. Gloria is working at the Mankato Clinic. They are still living on the farm.

Duane and Gloria had three children, Michelle, Melissa and Marcus.

Michelle was born on April 14, 1970. On September 7, 1996 she married Kevin Richard Larsen (2-19-1969) at the Zion United Methodist Church, St. Clair. They have a daughter Allison Marie who was born on February 11, 2001. They are living in Rochester, Minnesota.

Melissa was born on October 14, 1973. On September 20, 1997, she married Thomas William Herman (12-30-1974) at St. Casmir's Catholic Church, Wells, Minnesota. They have two children: Nathan Thomas (9-15-1998) and Elizabeth Michelle (2-17-2004). They are living in Dubuque, Iowa.

Marcus was born on May 29, 1979 and is living in Burnsville, Minnesota.

By Duane and Gloria Hubmer

HUBMER, MARLIN B.

Marlin was the fifth child of Edward and Hattie (Kohlhaff) Hubmer, born on his grandfather, Martin Hubmer's, homestead in Danville Township near Minnesota Lake.

The Hubmer family moved to Raymondville, Texas, when Marlin was two years old, and they later came back to Minnesota, moving numerous times before settling on a farm near St. Clair, Minnesota. All this moving disrupted Marlin's elementary education and to pursue his high school education, he used a horse and buggy or rode horseback the five miles to the St. Clair High School from which he graduated and was awarded the medal of "Best All Around Boy." He then attended two years of college.

Baseball, softball, and basketball were the sports Marlin loved and participated in, and these experiences gave him determination, confidence, and the ability to compete, cooperate, win, and lose without being discouraged. These attributes reflected in his life and community work.

Marlin and Ruth farmed and fattened over 1,000 head of feeding lambs each year. They started operating his father's St. Clair farm and when that was sold, purchased a small farm in South Bend Township near Minneopa State Park and later farmed in Oshawa Township near St. Peter, Minnesota.

A decay of law and order in the United States prompted Marlin and Ruth to do something about this problem by presenting the St. Clair School "The Freedom Shrine" (27 documents forming our United States Constitution and Government) which was secured through the Mankato Exchange Club, because children need to learn about their heritage.

By Marlin Hubmer

Additional notes: Marlin married Ruth Oliver on May 17, 1941, in Sioux Falls, SD. He was a Red Cross First Aid and Civil Defense instructor, served as a delegate to farm and political conventions and was active in environmental and agricultural organizations. He was a member of Centenary United Methodist Church, Kiwanis Golden K, the Farm Bureau, the Mankato Chamber of Commerce and Summit Center. He enjoyed traveling, sports and reading. Marlon died on June 6, 2002, at the Hillcrest Health Care Center, Mankato, Minnesota. Ruth died on January 20, 2005 at the Janesville Nursing Home, Janesville, Minnesota. They are buried in the Danville Township Cemetery, Blue Earth County.

HUNTER, JAMES

James E. Hunter was born on October 3, 1931, in Roanoke, Virginia to James and Alyce (Coverstone) Hunter. He graduated from Jefferson High School in Roanoke, served two years in the Marine Guards and four years in the U.S. Air Force. He married Ivadell Myers on June 20, 1954, in St. Clair.

Ivadell, the daughter of William and Margaret (Kleeman) Myers, graduated from St. Clair High School attended Gale Institute in Minneapolis and then went to work at Northwest Airlines in the office until her marriage, when they moved to Sacramento, California, as Jim was stationed in the service there. Upon his discharge they returned to Roanoke and in July 1956 they returned to St. Clair and purchased Miller Produce. The name was changed to Hunter's Produce. Jim and Ivadell had an egg truck that went out five days a week to pick up the

Ivadell & Jim Hunter, owners of Hunter Produce

Jim Hunter in front of the Hunter Produce building (formerly the Town Hall)

Hunter Produce egg truck

Jim Hunter loading egg cases

farmer's eggs. Jim was on the route for about the first month. He wanted to meet the customers and also to find out where the routes were. Jim, being from Roanoke, was lost one mile out of St. Clair so this proved to really get interesting but with the help of Ivadell's sister, Beverly Born, riding with him they were able to find the routes and meet the customers. Ivadell stayed at the produce and waited on the door customers and also helped the women candling the eggs. There were three to five women working most of the time. They were Ruth Nyquist, Muriel Mace, Elsie Phillips, Gladys Dagen, Esther Christnagel and Agatha Bollmann. They hired a man to drive the egg truck route. Heinie Holtz was the first driver. Donald Dagan and Cy Woites also worked for them on the egg route. Jim also would pick up flocks of chickens at night and take them to Wells - the days were long and the nights short. They also sold Funks and Pioneer Seed Corn. They worked Saturday and Sunday in order to keep things going for the next week. Making up the egg cases was always a big job. They needed extra hands for this so their children Vivian and Keith as well as their nieces Cindy and Melanie Born would help. The Hunters owned the business almost ten years. The large companies came into the area and paid more than the small town business could pay so the business was sold. James later sold insurance, worked at Kato Engineering and then for Jones Metal products as a purchasing agent, in Mankato. He retired in 1993.

They enjoyed traveling, spending time at their trailer up north and winter vacations in the Gulf Shores of Alabama, fishing, watching sports, hunting and woodworking.

While in St. Clair they lived at 230 Main Street West and in 1978 they left St. Clair and moved into there new home in the Ralph Ireland addition. In 1991 after Jim suffered a heart attack, they downsized and moved to a smaller house in Mankato.

Ivadell went to work at the St. Clair State Bank, retiring in 1995 but still helps out when needed.

Jim and Ivadell's children are Vivian (Dan Stelter/Ben Lyons) and Keith (Joleen Rathai/Lisa). They have two grandchildren, Lindsey Stelter and Tanner Hunter.

Jim died on January 4, 2004 and is buried at the St. John's Evangelical Lutheran Cemetery in St. Clair. Ivadell is still living in Mankato.

By Ivadell Hunter

JOHNSON, HUBERT

Hubert Johnson, the son of Andrew Johnson who was from the Mapleton area, is married to Marlys Juliar, the daughter of Elroy and Viola (Schroeder) Juliar. Elroy and Viola were farmers in Decoria Township before moving to St. Clair upon retirement. Hubert and Marlys, who have been married for 56 years, have had relatives living in this area for several generations.

Hubert worked at the Continental Can Company in Mankato and Marlys worked at the St. Clair State Bank before they retired.

They have three children: Gregory (54 years), Joel (51 years) and Pamela (49 years). They have six grandchildren and one step-grandson.

Hubert and Marlys at one time lived in the Cords house at 200 East Main St. in St. Clair.

By Marlys Johnson

JOST, MATHIAS

Mathias Jost, a native of Prussia, was born May 20, 1842. He immigrated to Wisconsin in 1852 with his parents, living in Milwaukee County until coming to Minnesota in 1861. He enlisted that year in Company I, 9th Minnesota and served three years. He participated in many battles. On October 20, 1865 he married Margaret Lang. He was engaged in mercantile trade in Mankato for three years and then for six years was in farming. He then moved to the Winnebago Agency and carried on in mercantile trading. They had five children.

JULIAR, HON. NICHOLAS

None of the human agencies which have paved the way for the present prosperity of Blue Earth County have risen superior in judgement and attainment to those of our citizens who claim Teutonic lineage. The thrifty, economical and persevering qualities instilled into the youth of the Fatherland lost little when transferred to this side of the water, and their alliance without less conservative and more venturesome business methods produce naught save the most practical and substantial of results. Many individual instances abound in this part of the state which attests the fact that the wellborn and representative German rarely is the victim of unauthorized aggrandizement, but on the contrary moves with certainty of direction and definiteness of purpose that the speculate or uncertain element is also entirely eliminated from his transactions. Offered in confirmation of this assumption is the career of Hon. Nicholas Juliar. He is president of the St. Clair State Bank, director in the Farmer's Fire Insurance Company and treasurer of the Union Minnesota Hail Insurance Company. The holder of practically all of the offices within the gift of his fellow townsmen, and the owner, besides his splendidly appointed town home, of twenty-one hundred acres of land in Blue Earth County.

Mr. Juliar is the son of a weaver, Nicholas Juliar (1798-1882), and he was two and a half years old when brought to this country from Alsace-Strasburg, Germany, where he was born December 28, 1841. His mother was Magdalen (Eidling 1807-1889), and she had, besides Nicholas Jr., ten other children, one daughter, Salome, the mother of Al Ringling, (Ringling Brothers and Barnum & Bailey Circus), the world's greatest showmen, and one daughter, Mary, the mother of Gollmar Brothers (Gollmar Brothers Show). The family set sail from Haver in the spring of 1845, arriving at Castle Garden, New York, after seven weeks of buffeting with storm and calm. In the vicinity of Milwaukee, Wisconsin, the father bought a farm, and 15 years later moved to Baraboo, the same state, where he died in 1882, and his wife surviving him until 1889. Nicholas Jr. was educated in the public schools of Milwaukee County and when old enough learned the harness trade, which he followed in Milwaukee for seven years. He then returned to the old homestead nine miles out in the country, and four years later sold out his interest and moved to Blue Earth County, where he purchased a section of land. He was successful in general farming and stock-raising, conducted both on a gigantic scale, and, adding to his possessions as his business grew, owned in time his present tract of twenty-one hundred acres. His land is among the best in this northern section, and is admirably adapted to the various products known to flourish with extremes of weather. As a natural consequence he established a reputation for important undertakings, his word was recognized as better than his bond and his advice and council in all that pertains to the lands man's occupation was eagerly sought and as implicitly followed.

As banking is the outgrowth of the need of its facilities, and as the property and income of Mr. Juliar transcended in immediate needs, his position as head of that eminently popular and reliable banking institution, the St. Clair State Bank, seems natural and fitting on. His connection with the insurance companies had added to their strength and standing in the community, and various other concerns have learned the worth of his good name and reputation for worthwhile accomplishment. He was one of those invaluable men who recognize a personal obligation in local undertakings generally, and who willingly sacrifices business chances to further the well being of the community. Though in no way desirous of honor, he served in the state legislature on two occasions, in 1895 and 1905, in both instances evidencing his keen insight into the political situation, and his knowledge of the needs and possibilities of his townsmen. He was an ardent Republican, a conscientious voter, but withal sufficiently liberal and far sighted to follow the dictates of conscience rather than the arbitrary dictates of any particular party.

The union of Mr. Juliar and Catherine Stevens, a native of Wisconsin, occurred in 1862. Mr. and Mrs. Juliar had ten children. Albert and George are farmers in Blue Earth County and Richard is following the medical profession in Mountain Lake, this state. Otto and Harry are farmers in the county and Silas is connected with the State Bank of Mankato. Mary is the wife of H. Hubmer, a farmer; Emma is the wife of R. Haedt, and Sarah, Mrs. E. G. Gollmar of St. Clair. In addition to all of his other lines of business, Mr. Juliar for twenty-eight years was a public auctioneer. In religion he was a member of the Evangelical Association. Personally he is a man of many fine qualities, one whom it is a pleasure to meet, either in a social or business way. He has the great gift of approachableness, and the kind of tact and consideration which makes everyone at home in his environment.

Nicholas was an uncle to Al Ringling who came to this area in 1872 as a member of the Chamber Bros. Musical Company called the New Palace Show. Al along with his brothers who originally lived in Baraboo, Wisconsin, had learned the harness and saddler trade. The brothers were all athletes, and very proficient on the horizontal bars. Every evening after their work at the William B. Walker Harness and Saddlery Co., in Mankato they would keep up their athletic practice. After a time they decided to go into the circus business. From the beginning success crowned their efforts. The show left here in two lumber wagons and teams of horses, which had to negotiate miles and miles of muddy roads. (Special Note: Harold Severson made a note in his "The Early Days" that his great grandfather and his neighbor, Jim Faley, were hired by Ringling Brothers to use their teams of horses to pull the circus wagons to the next stop, which he believed was Alma City. The Ringling Circus set up for their first performance in Jim Faley's farm, which was in Medo Township and he was the first violin player for the Ringling Circus.) Despite those difficulties, the boys overcame all obstacles, and the determination to win has gained for them a brilliant and lasting renown. (It is noted in 1948 that the Blue Earth County Historical Society some time ago started a movement to encourage placing of a monument at the YMCA corner in Mankato to mark the spot where the great show originated.)

Children of Nicholas Juliar and Catherine (Stevens) Juliar were: Henry (1863-1882), Albert A., Mary (1867 - 1933) (see Herman A. Hubmer story), George, Emma (1873 - Robert A. Haedt), Richard O., Otto (1870 - Louise Muehlhausen), Sarah (1882 - Edward G. Gollmar), Harry H. and Silas (1887 - Genevieve Hernlundt).

From *Blue Earth County History,* by Thomas Hughes-1909

JULIAR, ALBERT

Albert A. Juliar was born on February 8, 1865 in Milwaukee, Wisconsin. He came to Blue Earth County with his parents in 1877. On December 22, 1886 he married Charlotte Muelhausen and in 1919 moved from Decoria to St. Clair, Minnesota. He was a director and secretary-treasurer of the McPherson Insurance Company for seventeen years. Their children were Wilmar, George, Aaron, John, Lawrence, Cora, and Nicholas L.

JULIAR, AARON

The Land - January 3, 1980 – "From the 19 to 20 Century/Juliars Found Farm Life "For the Best"

St. Clair - If a 19th century farmer appeared on the 20th-century agricultural scene, he would be wise to go to Aaron Juliar for advice on how farming has changed. Juliar, 91, was once a 19th-century farmer himself.

"We planted corn by hand when I was a boy," Juliar said. "We had horses that pulled boards with pieces nailed onto the boards to make rows. The rows crossed, and then we planted where the cross met, dropping in the corn by hand. We used corn binders at harvest, but we cultivated between each row with one horse and a little plow."

But by 1911, when he married his uncle's hired girl, Rose Hagemeister, Juliar was using more modern farm equipment. Rose Juliar, 90, said she remembers her husband plowing with a sulky plow the autumn after their marriage.

Mrs. Juliar also remembers modernizing their home. "We had to do painting in this house," she said, "and he (her husband) built two closets. The house is over 100 years old."

Proud of this home she has had for the past 68 years, Mrs. Juliar pointed out a sturdy, wooden rocking chair that was a wedding present from another uncle of the groom. And in the large, farm kitchen is the heavy, wooden table and chairs around which the Juliar's seated six children. Son Darrell, who now farms the "home place" said, Dad and Mother have nearly 60 children, grandchildren and great-grandchildren now.

Darrell, an agricultural chemical salesman during slow farm seasons, enjoys the conveniences of modern life, as do his parents, but that hasn't always been so.

Mrs. Juliar remembered, "We had an ice-box – no refrigerator – no electricity, no telephone, no indoor plumbing and no fences. We put up the fences and planted box elders around the house and several orchards."

Born in Beauford Township, Mrs. Juliar gave up a salary of $2.50 a week and room and board when she married.

"That was good wages in that time," she explained.

Her husband had grown up on the farm adjoining the one they bought in 1911. He remembers being the first farmer in the neighborhood to get a two-row cultivator.

The 1920's saw more progress made in farm modernization. Darrell remembers playing in the old log barn before it was torn down.

"The folks built a new barn of milled lumber about five times as big as the old one and went from five or six cows to about 20." Darrell said.

Mrs. Juliar said, "We had pigs, chickens, white Peking ducks, and about 300 geese one year. We sold our poultry to market. A big truck pulled up to the barn, we drove the geese into the barn and then into the truck."

By the time the Depression cast a pall over the 1930's, the Juliar's were established farmers, but they had to borrow money from the Federal Land Bank to use for mortgage payments, according to Juliar.

"But we didn't have too much hardship," he said. "We had one severe drought and then one bad hail-out." Mrs. Juliar added, "it didn't take much to live on. We had our own food – with butchering and canning – and we had wood heat, and we used horses for farming. We were almost self-sufficient. One neighbor had to run only $3 through his checking account in one month.

By the late 30's, improved farm commodity prices brought better fortune to farmers, according to Darrell.

"Then prices were frozen for a few years during World War II," Darrell remembered. "We got a new tractor and car just before the freeze."

Because factories were geared to war-machinery production, farm machinery replacement parts were scarce, according to Darrell.

"Old welding shops did quite a business, and by the 40's prices accelerated quite a bit for three or four years, but not only grain and livestock prices – costs too, like machinery prices, though not as much as the income. And energy was very cheap."

During World War II, the Juliar's bought a new truck and a grain drill, according to Darrell. The Agricultural Adjustment Act office issued the Juliar's a permit to buy the scarce machinery, which was sold only to farmers who could prove a need for the equipment.

The early 50's were good years for farmers. People upgraded equipment, and a lot of new machinery was purchased and new silos, too. His folks put up a new Quonset building.

Although government farm programs began to flourish before World War II, the Juliar's waited until 1949 to benefit from acreage allotments and price supports, according to Darrell who bought the farm.

Aaron and Rose (Hagemeister) had the following children: Adelyne (Harry Horowitz), Cora (Walter Schultz/Herbert Sjostrom), Velma (Roy Schultz - Blue Earth County State Representative for many years.), Darrell (June Crane), Vernon (Grace Larsen), and Gordon (Barbara Lewis/Joan Toogood).

John Juliar was married to Inez Walters and they were the parents of Melbourne, Russell, Eileen (John Bestman - see separate story) and Bernice (Elwyn Ward - see separate story).

George A. Juliar was married to Emma Ewart and their children were Earl, Delmar, Iona and Charlotte.

Lawrence Juliar married Lydia Hagemeister and their children were Merle, Mary (Francis Page), Lila (Albert J. Jongbloedt-children Susan, Charles, Ronald, Denise, Thomas and Julie live in McPherson Township), and Albert, Sr. (1936-2005) (Beverly LeBrun-children James, Janet, Jerome, Jeanne, Nick, Joe, John, Judy, Joyce, Jeff, Albert, Jr. and Dean).

Cora Juliar married Henry Steckelberg and their children were Harry and Marion.

Nicholas Juliar married Florence Coleman.

L to R: Elzada (Juliar) and her husband John Howley, Verna (Ramsden) and Dr. Richard Juliar Celebrating their 50th wedding anniversary in 1952

George F. Juliar was born in 1870 and married Bertha Schostag (1874) in 1904. Their children were Elroy, Ralph, Esther, Clara, Irving and Merton.

Elroy was married to Viola Schroeder and their daughters were Marlys (Hubert Johnson - see separate story) and Ardyce (Duane Swan).

Ralph was married to Rosalie Schroeder (a sister to Viola) and their children were Elaine, LaMarr and Terry.

Esther married Edward Evert and the children are Elvira and Ruth.

Irving married Clara Oelke and their children are Lorin, Virgil and Orvis.

Merton married Myrtle McWhorter and they were the parents of Donovan, Dennis and Betty Lou (Lawrence Kruse).

JULIAR, RICHARD O.

Richard O. Juliar not only was the doctor of the community of St. Clair for many years, but also had been a leader in practically every form of community activity. Among other relationships that made him a very busy

Inside the St. Clair Drug Store

man there he was also the postmaster.

Dr. Juliar was born at Milwaukee, Wisconsin, September 13, 1876, and in the following year his parents came to southern Minnesota and located at what was called the Winnebago Agency. He grew up at St. Clair. The district schools supplied his early education and in 1897 he was graduated from the Mankato State Normal. His professional training in the University of Minnesota where he graduated in medicine in 1903 followed this. Doctor Juliar first practiced at Little River, remaining there four years, and during 1907-08 he attended the New York Post Graduate Hospital Medical College for special training. In 1909 he returned to his old home community to the daily calls to duty in his profession.

On September 3,1902, he married Verna J. Ramsden, daughter of William and Naomi Ramsden. Her father was born in Canada and her mother in Chicago.

Dr. and Mrs. Juliar had two children Elzada Frances, born September 14, 1903, and Mabel Lillian, born January 21, 1905. Elzada married John Howley, (whose parents at one time operated the St. Clair Hotel) and who was employed by Street Railway Company in Los Angeles, California. (They had a son Mark.) Mabel married Dean Price who operated an oil station at Le Sueur, Minnesota.

President Wilson first appointed Dr. Juliar postmaster of St. Clair in 1914, and his services were retained after 1935. Another service he gave to the community was a drug store, which he conducted from 1909 until 1931. He was also the health officer. While at the University of Minnesota he took a course in pharmacy as well as medicine. He was a member of the Blue Earth County, Minnesota State and American Medical Associations, the Masonic Fraternity, Modern Woodmen of America, and the Evangelical Church. In politics he voted an independent ticket. His recreation was hunting and fishing.

JULIAR, HARRY

Harry Juliar (1884-1971) was married to Nettie Mehlhouse and they had two sons, Milton and Harold. Milton was married to Alma Knutson with children Marvin and Darlene. (Lived at 209 Front Street East.) Harold married Lila Schull and their children are Dale (Helen Raves) and Donald (Constance Hussey).

JULIAR, NICHOLAS

Nicholas Juliar was born on July 14, 1906, and grew up in St. Clair. Nicholas was a member of the first class to graduate in 1923 at St. Clair. After his high school graduation he attended the University of Minnesota, Minneapolis, and graduated with a law degree from William Mitchell University. It was while he was in Minneapolis that he met and married Florence Coleman, the daughter of George and Grace (Nicholson) Coleman. Florence was born in 1903 in Ashton, SD. She also lived in Iowa and California before settling in Minnesota. It was during this time that she met and double-dated along with Lita Grey, who later went on to marry Charlie Chaplin. She worked at the Mayo Clinic in Rochester before finally moving to Minneapolis. After his graduation Nick returned to St. Clair and was a lawyer and also operated real estate and insurance businesses in the area from their home at 301 East Main Street. Nick also worked as campaign manager for Harold "Red" Stassen during one of the former governor's presidential bids. Nick was very involved in politics and in his community. He died on July 1, 1972, and is buried in the St. John (Bestman) Cemetery in St. Clair.

Nicholas "Nick" Juliar, 1923

Florence continued to live in St. Clair after her husband's death until she moved to Fountain Hills, Arizona, to be closer to her family. She celebrated her 100th birth-

Nick & Florence Juliar

day at Fountain View Village, Fountain Hills, Arizona. She was still taking exercise classes every day, regularly getting a manicure, attending chapel and going out to lunch with her friends at this time. She contributed her long life to a "fast and furious" lifestyle.

By Clarice Germo

KARELS, THOMAS

Tom Karels, Sr. along with his wife Mary (Hawker) and their three sons Tom Jr., Billy and Stacey, moved to St. Clair on April 1, 1976. They moved to 305 Main Street West, and from day one we have done remodeling, added onto or built something new to the house or the property it is on. Changes are good but they take a long time to complete!!

Our mailing address has changed at least four times since we moved in. It started with R4-Box 97, then R4-Box 87, then when 911 changed the numbering systems we were R4-305 West Main St. and now it is 305 Main St. West, Mankato, MN, 56001. Because we have a mail box on the road edge and not uptown, it now is Mankato and not St. Clair.

Tom and his sons were very active in St. Clair. They belonged to Cub Scouts, Boy Scouts, J.C's, The Actioneers, and Tom Sr. has been on the Volunteer Fire Department since July 1977. Tom, Sr. was also a member of the Athletic Backers at St. Clair High School. Tom, Sr. worked building construction until June 1987 when he became a Union Representative for the Construction Laborers Local 132 in Mankato. Tom Sr. retired from this position on February 1, 2003.

Mary along with daily work of taking care of four sons found time to work at the *Mankato Free Press*, then the Merry Maids Cleaning Service, Carlson Craft Enterprises and is now working as a dietary aid at Good Council for the School Sisters of Notre Dame in Mankato.

Thomas Jr. was born on February 21, 1968, in Lake Crystal, MN. He was a member Boy Scouts Troop 130 and played a little basketball while in school. He worked construction for numerous contractors in Labors Local 132. He married Regina Jobe in April 1989. Regina had a daughter Elizabeth who was three years old at that time. Their son Andrew was born on June 5, 1990. Tom and Regina were divorced three years later. In 1995 Tom Jr. purchased the Carl Rose house and moved to St. Clair. On June 1, 1996, Tom, Jr. was married to Sheila Bohm of Mankato. Jordon was born on June 20, 1997, Morgan on August 28, 2000, and Brandon on October 11, 2004. During all this time Tom Jr. has worked for North Town Auto in Mankato or B & R Auto in Beauford. His wife Sheila has worked for Royal Stationary, a part of Carlson Craft Enterprises, along with raising their children.

William (Billy) was born on January 30, 1972, in Good Thunder. He was a member of the Cub Scouts and Boy Scouts. Whenever he could he would go with his Dad on the glass recycling runs, collecting glass for the Actioneers Fundraisers, helping on special projects, filling Santa Bags, doing the Sand Box Fills, helping with the Easter Bunny, working with St. Clair Days and wrestling for St. Clair High School. Then on June 12, 1990, Billy drowned in a tragic accident east of St. Clair.

Stacey was born on October 8, 1975. He started wrestling at a young age and progressed very well through his school years receiving many, many, 1st place trophies. His football skills led him to serve as Captain of both the football team and wrestling team his senior years. He was a Cub Scout and Boy Scout and also worked with the Actioneers Club. Stacey graduated in 1994 and joined Laborers Local 132.

On June 14, 1997, Stacey married Sarah Melby. Sarah worked for Taylor Cop until their first son Billy was born on May 9, 2000. Since then she has been a stay at home mom. They had their second son Michael on February 14, 2004.

Stacey worked for numerous contractors and is currently employed by Kellington Construction from the Twin Cities Area as a Laborer Foreman, working mostly in the Metro Area. He lives in Good Thunder, MN, in a home he keeps on remodeling to fit their needs.

Christopher was born on July 31, 1977, after the family had moved to St. Clair. He was the most athletic of all our boys. He started wrestling in pre-school and wrestled every year. When he joined the varsity squad in 7th grade he suffered his first loss ever. He took that loss and went on to improve himself despite a crippling left knee injury, a torn ACL, during wrestling practice. After an operation and therapy Chris was able to play football the next fall and get Athlete of the Week, Honorable Mention and was on KEYC-TV Channel 12. His wrestling skills excelled and he became part of the All-State Wrestling Team of 1996. He achieved 4th Place at #189 and had a total of 100 wins.

Chris was also active in the Cub Scouts and Boy Scouts, the Actioneers, St. Clair Days Celebrations and in 1996 he graduated and joined Laborers Local 132 in Mankato. He worked for numerous contractors and is currently working for Hollenback & Nelson Construction. He is also a member of the Operating Engineers Local 49.

Chris met his wife, Carrie Mangen at his brother Stacey's wedding, He was "Best Man" and Carrie was Sarah's "Maid of Honor." They were married on July 17, 1999, and purchased a home in the Lakeville-Farmington area. Chris had a daughter Allie who was born on March 8, 1997. They now have Madison, born in April 2000 and Maci, born in March 2003. Carrie works as a Dental Hygienist in Inver Grove Heights, MN, and is raising those girls to be Grandma and Grandpa's pride and joy. All in all we have ten grandchildren and are proud as peacocks of all of them.

St. Clair has been our home for 28+ years and we have never regretted moving here.

By Thomas Karels, Sr.

KING, H. R.

H. R. King was born in Greene, Chenango County, New York, on January 9th, 1854. When he was three years old accompanied his parents to Sterling, Minnesota. In 1862 they moved to Mankato and seven years later to Waseca County, Minnesota. On January 1st 1879 they settled in the Winnebago Agency. He then formed a partnership with W. E. Kenyon in the drug trade and later was sole proprietor of the business. On April 23, 1881, he married Maggie J. Geddes.

KING, WALTER

Walter Ernest Christian King, the son of Nichlaus and Bertha (Schoettler) King, was born on February 22, 1903, in Mankato, MN.

Helen Elsie Menk, the daughter of Henry and Elsie (Krueger) Menk, was born on February 11, 1911, in Mankato, MN. Walter and Helen were married on October 7, 1931, in Mankato, MN.

Walter & Helen King celebrating their 50th wedding anniversary in 1981.

L to R: Judith, Walter, Helen and Gloria King

The couple lived on a 90-acre farm about 1½ miles north of St. Clair in McPherson Township raising dairy cows, pigs, chickens and ducks along with growing corn, wheat, oats and soybeans over the years. They retired from farming in 1968 and moved to Mankato.

They had two daughters, Gloria Ann (Harold Linde) and Judith Helen (Marvin Metzler), both living in Mankato. Four grandchildren and eight great grandchildren survived them at the time of their deaths. One grandson preceded them in death and one great granddaughter died following their deaths.

Walter and Helen were active members of St. John's Evangelical Lutheran Church in St. Clair. Walter was the church secretary for about 25 years Helen was a member of the Ladies Aid. Walter, along with Earl Carpenter, Art Wilson, Roy Hubmer and Emil Nyquist was on a bowling team for over 18 years, first being sponsored by the St. Clair Creamery and later the St. Clair State Bank. Walter and Helen were also members of the Farm Bureau, the Conservation Club and the St. Clair Senior Citizen's Club.

Walter died on March 5, 1988 and Helen on February 12, 1989. They are buried in the St. John's Evangelical Lutheran Cemetery.

By Gloria Linde

KLINGBEIL, HERMAN

Herman Klingbeil was born in German in 1865. He married Emilie Burmeister who was born in 1873 in Slettin, Germany. Their children were Edith (Neuton Pritchard), Anna (Robert Schostag - see separate story), Louis, Meta (William Kasch), Sophia, Reinhart, Leona and Eva (1918/1918).

Louis H. Klingbeil was born in February 1897 in

McPherson Township, Blue Earth County. On December 12, 1931, he married Lydia Grawunder Silkey. He was a farmer most of his life, running the Pea Vinery north of where Dale Froehlich now lives. He had also worked seven years for the Bird's Eye canning company in Waseca. When they retired they moved to St. Clair, living at 329 Main Street West.

Louis died on November 18. 1970, and Lydia died on October 1. 1975. They are buried in the St. John's Evangelical Lutheran Cemetery, St. Clair.

They had two children Donald (Joan Hudson) and Lois (Donald Newell). They lived in the Grawunder house.

Donald Klingbeil was born in September 1936 to Louis and Lydia Grawunder Klingbeil. He graduated from St. Clair High School in 1954, and attended Mankato State College; Dunwoody Institute, Minneapolis; and later, the Mankato Area Vocational Technical Institute. He married Joan Hudson in August 1958. He was employed as an electrician and worked part time for TV Signal Co., and Mankato Mobile Radio Co. He died at work on July 12, 1983, in a 210-foot fall from the Green Giant Tower in Le Sueur, Minnesota. Joan was a schoolteacher.

They had two children: Julie (Steve Wolner) and Alan (1964-1988)

Donald and Alan are buried in the Minneopa Cemetery, rural Mankato, Minnesota.

KOENTOP, WILHELM

Wilhelm Frederick Koentop (Kontop) was born in 1869. He was married to Minnie Sodeman, the daughter of Christian and Marie (Gerber) Sodeman, in 1894. They were farmers in McPherson Township.

The children of Wilhelm and Minnie were Ida (Awald Kukuk (3-16-1891/1-13-1981) who was born on September 5, 1894, and died on August 26, 1978. August (1897-1911), Ella (3-18-1899/6-30-1961). Marie, known as Mary, was born on September 7, 1901 and married William Borchert. Wilhelm (9-18-1903/12-26-1903), twins Emil (1-16-1905/4-30-1905) and Edward (1-16-1905/3-13-1905). Alma (12-21-1906/8-31-1999) who

Emilie Klingbeil with three of her children

The log cabin home of Herman and Emilie Klingbeil, ca. 1900

The home of Herman & Emilie Klingbeil

The 30th wedding anniversary of Lydia and Louis Klingbeil in 1961, L to R: Joan and Donald Klingbeil, Lydia and Louis Klingbeil, Lois and Don Newell

married Peter Schmitt and later Ben Rathman, Karl (Carl) (11-5-1911/4-9-1981), Agnes (11-5-1913/1913) and John, who died in 1919.

By Verna Sodeman

KOLLOS, CLEMENTS

Clements Kollos was born in 1869 in Austria and came to America when he was four years old. In 1892 he married Augusta Schroeder, the daughter of August and Johanna Schroeder, who was born in 1871 in Germany. She attended school in Germany and came to the United States with her family at 21 years of age. Clements was a farmer near St. Clair until he retired and moved into St. Clair. He was a resident of the St. Clair vicinity for 54 years.

The children born to this union were Mary (Oscar Anderson), Evelyn (Louis Timmerman - see separate story), Herman (Anita Grams) and Ida (Fred Timmerman).

Clements Kollos died in 1947 and Augusta died in 1971. They are buried at St. John's Evangelical Lutheran Cemetery.

Herman Kollos, the son of Clement and Augusta (Schroeder) Kollos, was born on November 15, 1907. On November 11, 1930, he was married to Anita Grams at St. John's Lutheran Church in St. Clair. Anita, the daughter of Emil and Dora (Santo) Grams was born on September 14, 1911. Herman and Anita farmed north of St. Clair until 1964 when they moved into St. Clair, living at 309 Main Street West. Anita enjoyed working at the Boswell Greenhouse, gardening and working on the farm. They were members of St. John's Evangelical Lutheran Church where Anita was a member of the Ladies Aid.

Herman and Anita had two children Dorothy (Robert Kurtzbein/Kahn) and Gerald. Gerald is married to Dee Bjornson of Pemberton, Minnesota. Gerald and Dee took over the family farm and have now moved to St. James, Minnesota, where they operate the Kollos Feed Store. Their children are Kevin, Jeffrey, Jodi, Michael and Jamie. Jodi is married to Richard Arndt. They have a daughter Bailey and live in St. Clair.

KOPKE, AUGUST

March 16, 1934 - *Janesville Argus*

August C. Kopke (originally Koepke) was born in the province of Breslau, Schlasin in Germany, February 1, 1846. He received his education in Germany and served a term in the German army, leaving the army when 24 years old. He also learned the miller's trade under a very thorough miller.

He left Germany in 1870 and came to America. He remained in New York for one day then took a train to Milwaukee. Unable to find work in the city he worked on a farm for a short while. Leaving there he arrived in Mankato on the first train ever to run into the city on October 27, 1870.

His first job in Blue Earth County was helping in the unloading of a steamboat at the Mankato levee for which he received 30 cents an hour. A few days later he obtained work cutting logs for a log home on the Henry Hoffman farm near Mankato.

Mr. Kopke worked at various jobs until 1872 when the miller of St. Clair, then the Winnebago Agency, was killed. Those in charge of the mill in St. Clair came to Mankato and hired Mr. Kopke to run the mill. After working there for some time he obtained an interest in the mill and remained there for 16 years.

On January 16, 1874, he married Anna Lubke, the daughter of Henry Lubke, in Mankato at the home of the bride's sister, Mrs. William Siebert. Anna was born at Stettin, Germany, and came to the United States in 1872 with her sister. She was only seventeen years old at the time of her marriage.

In 1887 he traded his interest in the mill for 60 acres of timberland north of St. Clair which he cleared and started farming. (This parcel of land was located west of where Carl Riese lived in 1986 and ran north along road 49 starting from the intersection. At one time it was in the name of A. Kukuk.) In 1907 he exchanged it in a deal for a farm of 160 acres south of St. Clair. In 1875 August helped build the first German Lutheran Church. He was a life long member of this church. August and Anna farmed in the St. Clair area until 1919, when they moved to the family home on Railroad Street in St. Clair and turned the farming over to their son, John.

The children of the Kopke's were:

Selma (1875-1956) married Henry Lubke - see separate story. **Martha** (1877-1965) who married Robert Flitter (1877-1914) in 1900 and on May 26, 1923, married Fred Koch (died in 1944). **Anna** (1878-1952) married Charles Luthultz on May 19, 1910, **Alma** (1882-1966) [see separate story], **Amalia** (1884-1961) married Henry Medaris, **Emma** (see separate story), **Johnnas** (1891-1959) [see separate story], and **Karl** (1893-1893).

August and Anna celebrated their 60th wedding anniversary in 1934.

August died in November of 1939 and Anna in January of 1940. They are buried in the Glenwood Cemetery, Mankato, Minnesota. Several other members of this family are also buried at the Glenwood Cemetery.

By Wayne Ganzel & Kathleen Wood

Alma Kopke was born on January 3, 1882, and on December 31, 1918, married Harv Gordon (1880-1939). They were owners of the Gordon Funeral Home in Mankato, MN. When Harv died Alma's sister, Emma went into partnership in the Funeral Home. Alma and Emma were some of the first female morticians and funeral directors licensed in the state of Minnesota.

Alma died on April 11, 1966. They are buried in the Glenwood Cemetery, Mankato, MN.

Emma Kopke was the daughter of August and Anna (Lubke) Kopke. She was born on August 18, 1888, and grew up in the St. Clair area. On January 29, 1909 she married Ralph Wood who died about 1923. Emma and Ralph had three children. Dale, John (Kathleen's father), and Delores (Kathleen's beloved Aunt/Mentor) who was born on July 14, 1910.

She then married Arnold Sauer who died in 1940. In 1947 she married Ben Winslow. Emma and Ben lived in the St. Clair family house at 118 Railroad Street. She along with her sister Alma owned the Gordon-Wood Funeral home in Mankato, MN.

After retiring from teaching in Ely, MN, Delores returned to St. Clair and lived with her mother and step-father Ben in the family house on Railroad Street. She continued to live here until illness forced the sale of the home.

Emma died on March 14, 1981.

[Please accept this history in the loving memory of the Kopke/Wood family (mostly Delores Wood, who would love that her family history is being shared), who loved the St. Clair people and the quiet, safe life it afforded them.]

By Kathleen Wood

Johnnas (John) Kopke was born on January 7, 1891, and took over the family farm in 1919. He married Ida Frey on October 15, 1919, at the Frey home in Beauford, MN. Ida was born on October 20, 1897, and was the daughter of Fred and Barbara (Nagel) Frey.

Lita (Kopke) & Merlin Schonrock

After their retirement from the farm they moved to St. Clair, living at 332 Main Street West. John died on January 11, 1959 and Ida died on June 3, 1980. They are buried in the St. John's Evangelical Lutheran Cemetery, St. Clair.

John and Ida had two daughters. Ila Mae (Roland Born-see separate story) and Lita who was born on December 15, 1924, and on June 14, 1945, married Merlin Schonrock (1922), the son of Herman and Ida (Nitschke) Schonrock. Merlin and Lita had two daughters, Marlys and Janice.

Lita died on March 26, 2003, and is buried in the St. John's Evangelical Lutheran Cemetery, St. Clair.

KRAUSE, HENRY

Aged Farmer Killed by Dog. (1942)

The body of a 74-year-old bachelor, who had been killed and partly eaten by his shepherd dog, was found in a farmhouse three miles southeast of St. Clair Sunday morning. The victim lived alone at the farm.

He was found in a room of the farm home by a nephew who had come to take him to church.

The animal, a young shepherd dog, was ugly when the coroner went to inspect the body and was removed from the room only with great difficulty.

Henry was born in 1866 in Germany and came to this country when he was about 25 years old.

His sister, Mrs. Bertha Glamm, survived Henry.

KROENKE, HERMAN

Herman Kroenke was one of the nine children of Michael and Amelia (Zellmer) Kroenke. In 1926 he married Kathleen Kremer. In 1929 he worked as a farm hand around the Minnesota Lake, Minnesota area. Their son George Robert was born in 1927, Kenneth Herman in 1929, Edward Dale, on a farm east of Minnesota Lake, in 1935, and David Thomas in 1941, in Mankato.

Herman was employed by the city as town marshal from 1935 to 1947. During that time he had a small herd of milk cows that he would milk, bottle and deliver locally morning and evening. During the war years in the 40's the town would show outdoor movies in the empty lot where the McPherson Insurance Co. now is located. Herman bought a popcorn popper and sold popcorn for five cents a bag on those evening. His later years were spent as custodian at the St. Clair Public School.

The family lived in four houses in St. Clair. The first

was the big house across the street from the Methodist Church. In 1937 they rented for $10 a month the large eight-room house north of the water tower and later moved to the south side of the water tower. Son Kenneth recalls the rent here to be $15 a month and it had fifteen rooms. They then bought a home that was located on Minnesota State Highway #83 about three miles north of town. They moved this house into town on the lot at 212 Park Street South. They lived there for the remainder of their lives.

By Kenneth Kroenke

Herman Kroenke in 1920

The Herman Kroenke family in 1952
Standing (L to R): George & Jane (Boswell) Kroenke, Kenneth, David, Edward
Seated: Herman & Kathleen Kroenke

George Robert Kroenke was born on December 4, 1927 and was the son of Herman and Kathleen (Kremer) Kroenke. He graduated from St. Clair High School and enlisted in the U.S. Army on April 25, 1946. He served in Japan until his 1947 discharge. He married Jane Ann Boswell on June 14, 1952, at Immaculate Conception Catholic Church. They lived at 122 Main Street East. He worked as a butcher at Wiste's Meat Market in Janesville, and later at Hilltop Meat Market in Mankato, which he owned for 10 years. After his semi-retirement, he did some plaster work with his brother. He was a member of Immaculate Conception Catholic Church and a former member of the American Legion Post 475 of St. Clair. He enjoyed entertaining people, fishing, hunting, bird watching, flowers, nature, and gardening. George and Jane were parents of Mary, Thomas, Michael, Patrick and Clay.

Kenneth Herman Kroenke was born to Herman and Kathleen (Kremer) in 1929 in the Minnesota Lake, Minnesota area. I attended school in St. Clair, Minnesota, graduating in 1947 I worked at various farm jobs during my school years. During World War II the older boys in the community were all in service thus giving the younger group a chance for the local jobs. At the age of 15, I obtained my drivers license by simply paying thirty-five cents at the courthouse. I then got asked to drive a brand new 1942 Ford truck hauling peas to a pea vinery. During the time I hauled pea vines I met lots of new people. Some of them were local boys but later we had Bahamans and Jamaicans and even some German war prisoners. All this at age fifteen was very educational to

The Kenneth Kroenke family in 1986
L to R: Ramona, Angela and Daniel
In back: Kenneth

say the least. After high school I took a job working for Henry Seys on his farm. They had seven children and the oldest was only nine, not quite old enough to drive a John Deere all day long.

By the time January 1951 rolled around Uncle Sam wanted me to come to his aid during the Korean War. Some of the local boys decided we should enlist in the Air Force instead. Lowell Pagenkopf, Harvey Kollos, and I signed up. The enlistment was for four years. Lowell and I stayed together until we finished Basic Training in Wichita, Texas. I served eighteen months in Okinawa.

Returning home in 1955 I began as an apprentice with Hendley Plastering Company in Mankato, Minnesota. I was a plasterer most of my working years.

In 1959 I met my wife Ramona in Texas and we married in 1961. We bought the William Beccue place north of the Le Sueur River on the north east of St. Clair where we are still living. We adopted two children, Angela Lynn in 1966 and Daniel Kenneth in 1969.

The last few years before retirement in 1992, I worked at the St. Clair School as a custodian.

St. Clair has always been a great place to grow up, settle down, raise a family and grow old. It has been a caring, friendly and a safe place.

By Kenneth Herman Kroenke

Edward Dale Kroenke was the son of Herman and Kathleen (Kremer) Kroenke. He was born in 1935 in Minnesota Lake, Minnesota. He graduated from St. Clair High School, St. Clair, Minnesota, in 1953. He served in the Army from 1955 to 1958, and received a bachelor's degree in elementary education in 1964. He married Ralene Schaub in 1956 in Madison Lake, Minnesota. He taught in California from 1964-65, taught sixth grade in St. Clair from 1963-1966, and was the principal at Nicollet, Minnesota, from 1966-1968. He received a master's degree in school administration from Mankato State University, Mankato, Minnesota, in 1968, and received a specialist in school administration from Mankato State University in 1977. He was the principal at Truman, Minnesota, from 1968-1978, superintendent at Kensington from 1978-1988, and was elementary principal and superintendent of Red Lake Schools from 1988 until he retired in 1994.

When Ed and Ralene lived in St. Clair they moved the Chase house to 229 Mill Street.

Ed and Ralene had two sons, James and Dale and two daughters Kathleen and Lori. At the time of his death in 1996 at Laughlin, Nevada, he had ten grandchildren.

KRUSE, FREDRICK JOHN

Fredrick John Kruse was born in 1868 and on December 6, 1894, he married Bertha Frank (July 19, 1874) at St. John's Evangelical Lutheran Church in St. Clair. Fredrick's father cleared some of the land and had the original claim. They raised their family on this farm. Fredrick died on November 6, 1955, and Bertha on October 10, 1965. They are buried in the St. John's Evangelical Lutheran Cemetery St. Clair.

Fred and Bertha had three children, Carl Frederik, Fredrick Albert and Lena Sophie (3-11-1907) who was married on April 22, 1926, to Walter Dimmel and they had a son Melvin.

Carl Frederik was born in 1896 and was married to Selma Rosenthal (1897). Their children are Ervin, Verna, Carl (Mary Armstrong), Esther (John Velin), Irene (Jerry Stoffel), LaJune (Elroy Honisch) and Lawrence who married Betty Mabee. Their son Robert is living in St. Clair and is employed at the St. Clair State Bank. When Carl and Selma retired they lived at 108 North Park Street. Carl died in 1986 and Selma in 1973 and they are buried in the St. John's Evangelical Lutheran Cemetery in St. Clair.

Fredrick was born in 1903 and on June 5, 1932, he married Bertha King (1912-2004), the daughter of Nichlaus and Bertha (Schoettler) King of Mankato. They lived on the farm until they retired and moved to Mankato. They had one daughter Barbara (Merlyn Blume) who lives in St. Paul Park, MN, and has a son Paul.

Fred died in 1981 and Bertha died in 2004. They are buried in the St. John's Evangelical Lutheran Cemetery, St. Clair.

By Barbara Blume

LACHELT, HERBERT

Herbert Lachelt, the son of Reinhold and Emma (Grams) Lachelt, was born on January 24, 1917 in McPherson Township. (The elder Lachelt's lived at 200 Main Street when they retired.) He graduated from the St. Clair High School and worked on the home farm and also with his brother-in-law Otto Witt. On April 10, 1951 he married Luella Priebe at St. Paul's Lutheran Church in Waseca, MN. Luella was born on August 8, 1921 in Otisco Township. Waseca Co., MN. They farmed in McPherson Township. Herbert was the treasurer of McPherson Township from 1961 until the time of his death. He was also on the St. John's Evangelical Lutheran Church board and served as secretary and treasurer of the church Cemetery Board.

Anton Lang farm

Herbert and Luella had a foster son Jimmy Brown who married Linda Ulwelling. They have two children Sarah (Nathan Brown) and William.

Herbert died on April 12, 1990, and Luella died on April 29, 1991. They are buried in the St. John's Evangelical Lutheran Cemetery.

LANG, ANTON

Anton Lang was born on December 5, 1883, the son of Otto Lang. He was married to a Sophia and then married Agnus Soukup. He was a farmer and she was a homemaker. They had five children, Violet (Johnny Banta) who moved to Oregon, Stella (Erv Smelling) who moved to Michigan, Leon (Dorothy Rudenick), who farmed and lives in McPherson Township. He also worked for a gas company and the Continental Can Company in Mankato. Wilbur (Marcella Willard) lived and farmed in McPherson Township. The youngest was Lynden. Anton died in 1966.

Lynden Lang was born on November 8, 1919, and on February 23, 1939, he married Mildred Rudenick. They continued the farming operation. Mildred was born on August 28, 1922, and she was a homemaker. Lynden died in 1992.

Lynden and Mildred had four children: Jerome Lynden, Sharon (Rodney Benning), Thomas (Kathy Gens) who all live in McPherson Township, and Marian who lives in Apple Valley, Minnesota.

Jerome Lynden was born on September 23, 1941, and he continued the family farming operation and also worked for the Blue Earth County Highway Department. On November 16, 1963, he married Mary Alice Glynn, the daughter of Eugene and Mary Alice (Conway) Glynn, who was born on June 19, 1942. Mary Alice was an elementary school teacher at the St. Clair School for many years. They purchased the Edward B. Weber farm northeast of St. Clair in 1969, and have farmed in McPherson Township for 35 years. Jerry has lived in McPherson Township most of his life. Jerry and Mary raised their children here and have enjoyed the closeness of the family.

Jerome and Mary Alice had four children. Jeanette was born on June 5, 1965, and on July 12, 1985, married to Jon Hall, the son of Stanley and Elvera (Freitag) Hall, who was born on August 12, 1965. Jeanette is working for the Sprint Company and Jon works for Culligan. Their children are Katrina (1990-1993), Keri Anne (March 2, 1992) and Samuel (January 28, 1994).

Jerome Anton was born on January 26, 1967, and on July 18, 1992, he married Kristine Majeres, who is the daughter of Maynard and Patricia (Larson) Majeres, former St. Clair residents and now is living on Reeds Lake near Waterville, Minnesota. Jerome and Kristine purchased the home where Lynden and Mildred raised their family in 1992. The unexpected and sad death of Jerome's grandpa, Lynden in April of 1992, led grandma to the decision that she didn't want to live in such a large

Jerry and Mary Alice Lang farm

Mildred Lang with her son Jerome and his family

home alone. Although she did want to continue living on the farm, she purchased a trailer home and moved it to the front of the property. She sold 9 acres and the farmhouse. Jerome is helping his father Jerry with the farming and also works for the Pepsi Company in Mankato. Kristine, who was born on September 18, 1968, is a homemaker. They have three children, Neal Todd Lynden (August 26, 1993), Clair Marie (February 11, 1996) and Paul Anton (January 16, 1998).

Todd was born on November 7, 1970, and died in 1992 as a result of an auto accident.

Mary Kay was born on December 4, 1974, and was married to Richard King, (December 28, 1973) who is the son of James and Terry King of Waterville, Minnesota, on August 24, 1996. She has a business degree and Richard is self-employed. They have two children, Alexander (May 14, 1996) and Julia MaKenzie (December 18, 2000).

In the summer of 2003 Mildred, Jerry and Mary, and Jerome and Kristine sent in the paperwork for having the farm officially declared a century farm. It has been in the Lang name since 1892. Jerome and Kristine are so grateful to have their family grow up with so many loving grandparents so close by.

By Mary and Kristine Lang

LEWIS, ROY

Roy Lewis, the son of William and Laura (Jones) Lewis was born on September 30, 1901, in Judson Township, Blue Earth County. Roy lived in the Lake Crystal and Garden City area. He was married to Nadine Robertson on February 18, 1925, in Garden City, Minnesota.

Nadine was born on September 27, 1906 in Colfax, Iowa, and was the daughter of Robert and Viola (Hurst) Robertson. The family moved to Minnesota and in 1924 she graduated from the Garden City High School. After their marriage they lived in Mankato where Roy worked for the Lundin Construction Co. Nadine worked at the Geo. E. Brett Company until 1938 when they moved to St. Clair. Roy worked for the Blue Earth County Highway Department from 1938-1965 and was a member of the Fire Department and the Commercial Club. Music was Nadine's "world" and she taught piano lessons in her home until 1966, was church organist at the Zion Methodist Church, as well as a choir member. She was also a 4-H leader and a member of the Woman of the Moose Lodge. She also did many paintings.

Roy and Nadine had three children, Donald (Molly Stockstad), Jarrett "Jerry" (Patricia Thrun) and Barbara (Gordon Juliar/Jerry Horsager). They lived at 113 Railroad Street and later moved to 217 Main Street West.

Roy died on January 28, 1990 and Nadine died on February 3, 1988. They are buried in Woodland Hills Memorial Park, Mankato, MN

LINDLOFF, REV. DONALD

Donald W. Lindloff, the son of Rev. William and Elsie (Grimm) Lindloff, was born on June 13, 1929, at Elkton, SD. He attended Dr. Martin Luther College in New Ulm, Northwestern College in Watertown, WI and Concordia Lutheran Seminary in Springfield, Ill. After he graduated from Wisconsin Lutheran Seminary in Mequon, WI in 1954, he was ordained and installed in his first congregation at Mound, SD. In 1966 he accepted the call from St. John's Evangelical Lutheran Church in St. Clair where he served until 1994.

Pastor and Mrs. Lindloff, who assisted with the duties for the congregation, had two daughters: Linda (Delbert Draeger) and Lyless (Rev. Ronald Winter). After their retirement Pastor and Mrs. Lindloff moved to North Mankato. Pastor Lindloff died on February 23, 2002, and is buried in the Evangelical Lutheran Cemetery, Watertown, WI. Mrs. Lindloff is now living in Wisconsin.

By Myrtle Westphal

Rev. & Mrs. Donald Lindloff

LINNELL, RICK

Rick Linnell was born on December 16, 1954, the son of Oswald and Donna Linnell in Grand Marais, Minnesota. He graduated from Cook County High School, Grand Marais and received his BS degree from the University of Minnesota, Duluth, MN. He then went on to earn his Master's Degree from the University of St. Thomas in Curriculum Development and Design. He received an Administrative Degree from Tri-College

University, Moorhead, MN. He came to St. Clair in 1996 and was the school principal. Since 1997 he has been the Superintendent of the St. Clair Public School.

On July 30, 1983, he was married to Anne Remington. They have two children, Eric James who was born on November 22, 1989, and Kelsey Anne who was born on January 23, 1995.

Anne is on the faculty at St. Clair and the children are students at the school.

By Rick Linnell

LOEFFLER, HAROLD

Harold Loeffler, the son of Harry and Elenora Loeffler, was born on January 20, 1945. On December 16, 1967, he married Corine Frank, the daughter of Raymond and Irene (Frase) Loeffler, at Salem Lutheran Church, Eagle Lake, MN. Corine was born on December 10, 1946, and died on August 12, 2004. Both Harold and Corine grew up in neighboring LeRay Township, were McPherson Township farmers and great sports fans of the St. Clair Athletic Programs. They have three sons, Brian, Bradley and Bruce. Corine's mother, Irene, is currently living in St. Clair.

Brian Harold Loeffler was born on March 19, 1970. On February 8, 1997, Brian married Shelly Boehler and they are living at 61313 187th St. in McPherson Township. This was the Raymond Fitzloff farm at one time. Brian is farming with his father and brother and Shelly is working at the St. Clair State Bank. They have three children: Jessica (May 31, 1997), David (March 8, 2000) and Courtney (May 31, 2004).

Bradley Loeffler married Stephanie Bergan on December 16, 2000, and they have a son Thomas who was born on November 12, 2003. Bradley farms with his father and brother Brian, they live in LeRay Township and he is the head wrestling coach at St. Clair High School. Stephanie is working at ISJ Hospital in Mankato.

Bruce resides in Chaska, MN.

By Brian Loeffler

LOGE, HERMAN

Herman Loge brought his family to St. Clair when he was hired as the City Constable and was also in charge of city maintenance. When first coming to St. Clair they lived in the former medical building and later moved to 212 Park Street South. Herman married Florence Klatt in 1940 in Elmore. Their children were Donna (Carlyle Matheson), Hermina (Donald Folven), Sandra (Gerald Urban), Lynette (Juel Merseth), Loren and Marlyn who married Katharine Beyer. Marlyn and Kathy live in St. Clair and have two sons, Michael and Matthew.

L to R: Eric, Lorelee, Linda and Loren (standing) Loge

Loren "Chet" Loge was born on January 20, 1944, in Wells, Minnesota. He married Linda Zawacki on September 7, 1974. Chet worked for Archer Daniels Midland in Mankato for 24 years. He enjoyed restoring old automobiles. He died on October 28, 1995.

Linda graduated from Bethany Lutheran College and after her husband died she moved to Mankato and is now working at Bethany as the Associate Dean of Admissions.

They have two children, Lorelee and Eric.

LUBKE, ERNEST

Ernest Lubke was born in 1855 in Stettin, Germany, and emigrated to America in 1872, settling in Missouri where he served his apprenticeship as a blacksmith for several years before engaging in that business for himself. Later he went to Iowa and in 1901 came to St. Clair and stayed until 1910 when he moved to Dickinson North Dakota. While in St. Clair he had a blacksmith shop with his son, Henry.

Ernest was first married to Mary Tress who died in 1889 in Missouri from pneumonia. She had gotten sick after hanging out laundry in the winter. They had four

Lubke Blacksmith Shop

Henry Lubke in the blacksmith shop he established in August 1898.

children, Henry, Edward, Dorothy and John. He later married Hulda Dahlem and they had ten children with the last four Helena, William, Annetta and Arlin being born in St. Clair.

Hulda died in 1914 in Halliday, ND, and Ernest died on January 26, 1983 in Oakdale, ND. They are buried in Oakdale, ND

Henry F. Lubke was born on September 30, 1878 in Mexico, Audrain County, Missouri, and came to St. Clair in 1898. Here he established a blacksmith shop with his father on Main Street. (The shop was located between the Drake Gas Station and Hager's Hardware with the Fisher Station right next to Hager's.) He later moved the business (after the building burned down) to a side street into a building he purchased from Frank Fisher. He did general blacksmithing as well as all kinds of plow work, wagon work, electric welding and miscellaneous repairing. He later sold the business to Clements (Bud) and Leona Mace.

Henry was elected mayor of St. Clair at the annual village election in 1936. He was also a school board member for 12 consecutive years before he was elected mayor.

In 1902 he married Selma Charlotte Kopke, the daughter of August Kopke and Anna Lubke, his first cousin. They had four children, Ruth, Oscar (Genevieve Feipel), Delois and Adella (Harold G. Brenner).

Ruth and Delois both died in Faribault, Minnesota. They lived at 118 Railroad Street.

Henry died on July 7, 1942, in Mankato and Selma died on September 18, 1956, also in Mankato. They are buried in St. Clair, Minnesota.

By Wayne Ganzel

LYNCH, HENRY

Henry Lynch was born in September 1848 in Cedarburg, Wisconsin. On April 7, 1875, he married Mary Fields, the daughter of William Fields. Mary who was born on December 8, 1855, in New York, grew up on what was later the Ludwig Grams farm. Henry died in June 1925 and Mary died in October 1930.

The children were Joseph, William, Clements, Guy, Irenus, Linus, Louise Ignatius and a daughter Rosella who died when she was nine years old.

Guy Lynch was born in 1892 and lived as well as farmed in McPherson Township. He was married to Jane Bowe, the daughter of Thomas and Theresia (Huettl) Bowe, who was born in 1898. They had a son Bernard Lynch, Sr. Guy died in 1978 and Jane in 1996.

Bernard Lynch, Sr. was born in 1921 and also lived and farmed in McPherson Township. He married Genevieve Phillips, the daughter of Harry and Lucy (Hodapp) Phillips, who was born in 1924. They had three children, Bernard, Jr., Robert and Raymond. Bernard and Genevieve are still living on the farm.

Bernard Lynch, Jr. was born in 1943 and is living and farming in McPherson Township. He married Karen Tacheny, the daughter of Nicholas and Agnes (Goettl) Tacheny, who was born in 1944. Karen is the manager of the St. Clair Convenience Store. Bernie and Karen have two children. Brian (1964) is living in St. Clair and is its current mayor and works at KatoLite in Mankato. He is married to Linda Kruse (1967) and they have three children, Nicole (1994), Marcus (1997) and Danielle (2000). Linda is the publisher of *The Country Register*. Their daughter Julie (1966) is an executive assistant and is married to Matt Klages who is a Martin County Deputy. Their children are Jenna (1997) and Kylie (1999).

Robert (1948) is married to Sandra Burt, the daughter of Charles and Doris (Kittleson) Burt, who also grew up in St. Clair. They are living in Eagan, Minnesota, and have one child Kim (1977).

Raymond (1961) is married to Shari Hodapp, the daughter of Lyle and Louise (Frederick) Hodapp, who is also a graduate of the St. Clair High School. They are living in rural Mankato.

By Karen Lynch

Louise Ignatius Lynch

Irenus Lynch married Katherine Thissen, the daughter of Gerhart and Frances (Fredrickson) Thissen. They took over the family farm. Their children were Agnes,

Lawrence, Nicholas, Lorraine and Joanne.

Linus Lynch married Rose Elizabeth Bowe, the daughter of Thomas and Theresia (Huettl) Bowe. Rose was born on June 26, 1902, in McPherson Township. They were farmers in McPherson Township. She died on January 27, 1977.

Louise Ignatius Lynch was born on July 11, 1883, in McPherson Township. On February 9, 1915, he married Rose E. Ireland, the daughter of John and Mary (Foley) Ireland. Rose was born on September 12, 1894. They were farmers in McPherson Township.

Louise died on January 25, 1969, and Rose died on September 16, 1981.

The children of Louise and Rose were Gertrude, David, Henry (Viola) and Eileen. Gertrude married Edward Miller, Jr., the son of Edward and Anna (Woefel) Miller. Their children were Rose, Leo, Ann, Mary and Helen.

David Louis Lynch was born on March 16, 1919, and grew up in McPherson Township. He served his country during WWII and was stationed in India. On November 12, 1947, he married Selma Jongbloedt at St. Peter and Paul's Catholic Church, Mankato. Selma was born on September 13, 1918, and is the daughter of Alois and Pharilda (Willaert) Jongbloedt. They were farmers in McPherson Township and continued to live on the farm after retirement. David is now a resident of the Mankato House in Mankato.

The Louise Lynch family in 1953
Standing (L to R): David, Gertrude, Henry
Front: Rose, Eileen, Louise

The 50th wedding anniversary of
Louise and Rose Lynch in 1965

The 40th wedding anniversary of Selma and David Lynch
in 1987, L to R: Albert & Lila Jongbloedt,
Selma & David Lynch

The David L. Lynch family in 1958
Back (L to R): Selma and David L.
Middle row: Rita, David J., Mary, Bonnie
Front: Linda and Allan

Their children are Allan, Rita (3-4-1950 - O'Neil) is living in Florida, Bonnie (2-24-1952 - Oddy) is living in Brooklyn Center, MN, Linda, David Jr. and Mary.

Allan (8-20-1948) Lynch married Ella Lindeberg on September 5, 1970. Allan is a farmer in rural Mapleton and owns a construction and tiling business. Ella works at the Janesville-Waldorf-Pemberton school system in their library. They have four children: (Todd (Shelly), Scott (Collette), Matthew and Sally.

Linda (10-16-1953) Lynch is living with her mother on the family farm and is working at Brown Printing in Waseca, Minnesota.

Mary (2-18-1955 - Jeff Miller) is living on her grandparents building site and works at FarmAmerica near Waseca and at the St. Clair Public School. She has two sons Patrick (2-5-1990) and Jason (July 3, 1991). Both are students at the St. Clair School.

David J. (10-7-1956) Lynch graduated from the St. Clair Public School and has taken over the family farm. On August 30, 1980, he married Marilyn Manthey at the Trinity Lutheran Church, Janesville. Marilyn is the daughter of C. Raymond and Doris (Braun) Manthey. David is a hog farmer and sells DeKalb. He is a supervisor on the McPherson Township Board and is on the Region 9 Board of Commission. Marilyn graduated from the Janesville Public High School and the Lakeland Medical/Dental College. Minneapolis. She interned at the Mankato Clinic and was hired upon graduation. She is currently doing home health care. David and Marilyn have three children, Michael (4-14-1985) a student at South Dakota State University, Brookings, SD, and twins Mark and Heather (12-25-1989) both students at St. Clair High School.

By Marilyn Lynch

L to R: Michael, Heather, Mark, Marilyn and David J. Lynch

LYNCH, MATTHEW

Matthew Lynch was born in Cederburg, Wisconsin, and came to Blue Earth County in 1879 and had farmed ever since near St. Clair. He was a member of the school trustees, having served on the board for some years. He was well liked by all that knew him, and his death brought sorrow to numerous homes.

At the time of his death his wife, five sons, William (Ann Dooley), James (Sadie Fields), Jerome (Grace Biggins), George (Cecelia Thissen) and Thomas (Lauretta Schalow) on the home farm, and two daughters, Agnes and Lillian (Clark Jones) survived him.

William Lynch was a painter.

Jerome (Jerry) Lynch married Grace Biggins and at one time owned the ballroom that was located east of St. Clair by the Le Sueur River.

George Lynch (1895-1991) took over the family farm. He married Cecilia Thissen, the daughter of Gerhart and Frances (Fredrickson) Thissen, and their children were Everett (Audrey Goettl) and Marion (Donald Goettl).

Matt Lynch farm

MACBETH, GEORGE

George Macbeth married Lola May Pressnall, the daughter of Alexander Pressnall, on February 17, 1892. They had three children, Lyle, Kenneth and a daughter who married Sidney Fields. The Macbeth's were members of the Methodist church.

MACBETH, JESSE LYNN, M.D.

Dr. Jesse Macbeth, M.D. a practicing physician and surgeon for over a quarter of a century, was a resident of St. Clair, Blue Earth County. He was of Scotch and English ancestry and was a member of a well-known family of southern Minnesota.

He was born in Tivoli Township, Blue Earth County June 20, 1880. His father, Charles C. Macbeth, was born in Glasgow, Scotland, in 1827, son of Colin Macbeth, who spent all his life in Glasgow and was a landscape gardener by profession. Charles C. Macbeth came to the United States when young man, and was also a landscape architect and gardener. He practiced his profession in Canada and later in New York. He married at Buffalo, New York, December 18, 1852, Ann Herniman. She was born in London, England, in 1827, daughter of John Herniman, who brought his family to the United States and for many years followed the business of contracting and building at Buffalo. For a number of years the Macbeth family lived on a farm at Grand Island, New York, also lived for a time in Michigan and Wisconsin and about 1866 came to Minnesota and settled on a farm in Blue Earth County. Charles C. Macbeth died in 1915 and his wife in 1921. They were members of the Methodist Church and Republicans in polities. Charles C. Macbeth was always a student and a man of wide information. There were eleven children in the family. Charles, born in Canada, June 18, 1854, a grocer at Minneapolis; William, born December 25, 1855, at Buffalo, died March 23, 1931; Walter, born in May, 1857, at Grand Island, New York; Matilda and Mary, twins, born October 7, 1859, at Grand Island, later residence of Mankato; Albert, born in May, 1862, at Buffalo, a physician at Fort Wayne, Indiana; Nellie, born April 3, 1864, at Buffalo, lived in California; James, born December 31, 1867, a dentist at St. Paul; George, born December 31, 1869, was in the stock business at St. Clair; Carrie, born December 19, 1872, lived on a farm in Blue Earth County; and Jesse Lynn.

Dr. Jesse L. Macbeth was born in Tivoli Township and was educated in the grammar and high schools at Mankato. For his professional training he went to Fort Wayne College at Fort Wayne, Indiana, where he graduated in 1905. After an internship in St. Joseph's Hospital he located at St. Clair in 1906, and steadily practiced there. He was a member of the Blue Earth County, Southern Minnesota, Minnesota State and American Medical associations.

Doctor Macbeth married May 8, 1920, Sadie Eaton. She was born at Benson, Minnesota, daughter of Dr. J. S. and Hanna (Boswell) Eaton, her father a native of Vermont, and her mother of Washington, D.C. Dr. J. S. Eaton practiced medicine for many years at Benson, Minnesota. He served three years as a captain in the Union army during the Civil War. Mrs. Macbeth attended school at Benson. She was a member of the Auxiliary of the Blue Earth County Medical Society and sustained an active interest in church and social affairs of St. Clair. They lived at 111 North Park Street. Doctor Macbeth died on November 19, 1946.

MACE, JACOB

Jacob W. Mace was born September 24, 1859, in West Virginia. (There is a county in Virginia which is called "Mace County.") He came to Minnesota with his parents when he was but four years of age. He lived for a time at St. Charles, Minnesota, and then moved to McPherson Township, where he lived on a farm up to six months before his death, when he took up his residence in St. Clair. He married Isabelle J. Todd who was born on June 26, 1864. Their children were Nathan Jacob, Claud H. and Willis.

Jacob died on May 15, 1921, and Isabelle died on April 29, 1932.

Nathan Jacob Mace was born on June 14, 1891, in Medo Township. On November 24, 1915 he married Theresia Gertrude Bowe, the daughter of Thomas and Theresia (Huettl) Bowe. Theresia was born on September 12, 1894. Their children were: Jay N. (B: 1916 - Mary Gilronan), Gerald, Clements, Myron (B: 1922 - Mary Faltersack) and Marvin (1929)

Nathan died on December 4, 1953.

By Leona Mace

Seated (L to R): Theresia Bowe and Nathan Mace on their wedding day, November 24, 1915
Standing: Rose Bowe and Thomas Bowe, Jr.

Gerald G. Mace was born on February 16, 1918, in McPherson Township. He married Muriel Ruth Froehlich, the daughter of Otto Froehlich (see separate story) in 1946. They operated the St. Clair Café (currently "UpTown Tavern") for three years. In 1951 they moved into the house at 338 Main Street East, St. Clair. Gerald then worked for the Blue Earth County Highway Department for twenty-seven years. Muriel had various jobs and then was the head cook at the St. Clair School from 1972-1990. She is active at St. John's Evangelical Lutheran Church, sells Avon Products and works for Carlson Craft.

Their children are Bonnie (Ronald Roalson - sons James & Andrew), Geraldine (David Sonday - children Jeremy, Jennifer & Daniel), Geneva (Paul Mueller - children Gretchen, Heidi & Joseph) and Nathan (Shawn Kawell - sons Tanner & Brandon).

By Muriel Mace

Standing (L to R): Carl, Gary, Suzanne
Seated: Clements and Leona Mace

Clements "Bud" Mace was born on July 6, 1920, in St. Clair. He attended school in St. Clair and then attended the Dunwoody Institute in Minneapolis learning the blacksmith trade. He married Leona Schalow, the daughter of Henry Schalow (see separate story) on June 11, 1941, at St. John's Evangelical Lutheran Church in St. Clair. Bud and Leona bought the Lubke Blacksmith shop, which they operated until he was drafted, serving his country in WWII. They closed the shop and then Lial and Nettie Ward operated it for them until Bud returned from service. They then operated it for 2 or 3 years. It was at this time that they lived in the Andrews brick house on the east edge of St. Clair, raising cattle and selling the milk on a milk route. This is where the Schalow Apartments are now located. They then bought the trucks and started the trucking business. He was working for the Harvest States Elevator in St. Clair when he became ill with lung cancer. He was a member of the American Legion Post 475.

Leona was born on July 17, 1921, in St. Clair. She graduated from St. Clair High School. She helped Bud with their early businesses and later took nursing classes in Rochester, Minnesota, and at the Vocational College and Mankato State University in Mankato. She worked as a LPN in both Immanuel and St. Joseph's Hospital in Mankato. She is a member of St. John's Evangelical Lutheran Church, where she was one of the first Sunday school teachers and also helped to start the first choir in the late 1930's. She also belongs to the Ladies Aid. She does a lot of volunteering for the American Legion Club in St. Clair.

Leona and Bud had three children, Carl, Suzanne and Gary.

Bud died on November 22, 1987, and is buried in the St. John's Evangelical Lutheran Cemetery, St. Clair.

Carl Clements Mace was born on March 9, 1943. Carl graduated from St. Clair High School and Mankato State University, Mankato, with a B.S. degree in accounting. He married Betty Smith on December 12, 1964. They moved to Casa Grande, Arizona, in 1971 where he owned his own office, working for the Henry and Horn Accounting Firm. He earned his CPA in 1972. Carl died on October 6, 1992, suffering from lung cancer.

Suzanne Lynn Mace was born on August 15, 1952, in Mankato. She graduated from St. Clair High School and later from Mankato State University with a B.S. degree in accounting. She worked for Arthur Young of the "Big & 7" in Minneapolis, Minnesota. She went on to earn her CPA. She came back to St. Clair to help care for her ill father. She is working at Brown Printing in Waseca, Minnesota, where she is a supervisor in the invoicing and billing department. She married Harold Lanz, Jr. on June 16, 1984. They purchased the building site of George and Cecelia Lynch southeast of St. Clair, and built a new home where Suzanne is currently living.

Gary Nathan Mace was born on July 4, 1948. He grad-

Home of Suzanne Mace Lanz which is located
on the former Matt Lynch farmstead

uated from St. Clair High School and Mankato State University with a B.S. degree in accounting. He earned his CPA and now owns his own accounting business in Mankato. He is member of the American Legion Post #475 and held the office as District 2 Commander and Vice Commander for the State of Minnesota.

By Leona Mace

MACOMBER, GEORGE

George Macomber's early years began in the Rapidan area. I don't know much about George's (my Dad) early years. I know his mother died when he was quite young. Mostly his father, Andrew Hamlin Macomber (1860-1951), raised him. My mother, Clara Evelyn Reedstrom, was born in Rapidan to Swedish immigrants named Charles Reedstrom and Eva Nelson. Charles worked on the railroad between Rapidan and Mankato and built a log cabin close to the tracks. He used to feed and house some of his crew (he was foreman) and hired a young Swedish girl named Eva Nelson who lived nearby to do the cooking and housework and they were married and lived in the same house. My mother was the oldest of six children, and after going to "teacher's college" a couple years she taught school in a l-room school house in the Rapidan area, where she had kids from grades 1 to 8. In due time she met and married young George Macomber in 1914, and they moved into a small house George had built located across the street from the school. He went to work in St. Clair as the depot agent, driving over Monday mornings and coming home to Rapidan Friday evening. That was a long commute in those days so he bought 4 acres of land on the west edge of St. Clair and built a Dutch Colonial type house while living in the depot (was at 117 Front Street South.) The family, which now consisted of George Reed, Geneva Grace, Virginia Shirley, and Norma Winfred, moved in 1927. One of the first things we girls did was decide to give ourselves a grand address. We chose "999 Walnut Avenue." We thought it sounded pretty fancy when we answered ads in magazines to get a sample (free) of Tangee lipstick or a sample of Ponds' cream!

We all became active in our little community as well as helping "work" the farm. We picked strawberries, raspberries and potato bugs that we then put in cans of kerosene that we carried up and down the rows, and helped harvest both pumpkins and potatoes. Mother loved flowers so Dad planted lots, and if the sweet pea crop was prolific, sometimes we took bouquets uptown and sold them to the merchants for 10 cents! Sometimes we sold sweet corn, too.

Dad helped form a little golf club out east of town - he and Hugh Russell, were active in that also the Catholic priest. It was built in someone's pasture and I think they dubbed it "St. Clair Sunshine Golf Club." According to a diary I kept in the early 30's, Dad hit a "hole-in-one" in January! Must have been a mild winter!

Dad played the clarinet and got involved in conducting the school band at one time and also a church band at the Evangelical Church, and both Reed and he played in various Elks' bands in the area. Reed later played baritone and slide trombone and played in a dance band of the Pestka boys. Mother conducted the choir at the Evangelical Church and we all sang at one time or another. I played the piano for Sunday school and later for church.

Some of my fondest memories of growing up are the times we kids put cans, nails, etc. on the train track and retrieved them after having been smashed by the train as it turned around and headed back to Pemberton etc. St. Clair was the end of the line. I remember Mother feeding hobos who hitched rides not realizing the train only ran three days a week, so it left them stranded and hungry for a couple of days.

I also fondly remember many times spending a day or night with my friend Marion Boswell at the old Winnebago Agency, guests of Grace Chase (Aunt Grace to Marion) who lived there. She entertained us by teaching us songs and poems, which sometimes we "performed" at the Boswell home in St. Clair. In the summer we would sleep in the big upstairs porch. We also enjoyed the Caylor Players - a group of vaudevillians who put on a show at the Town Hall on Saturday nights. If we got tickets from the merchants we got in for 10 cents

A passing thought - our graduating class of 1936 consisted of five seniors! The two boys, William Schroeder and Pershing Hubmer, are deceased, but the three girls, Helen Schostag Kenward, Marion Boswell Hoffman, and Virginia (Tooty) Macomber DeMars, are all in their mid-eighties, and still the best of friends. We phone and write each other often, and have lots of great memories of being raised in a small town!

By Virginia Macomber (Mrs. Martin) DeMars

MANAIGE, FRANK

Frank Manaige was born in 1857 and was one of the early settlers in St. Clair. He died in November 1941 in York, Nebraska, at the age of 84. At the time of his death he was survived by a half-brother Louis.

Mrs. Manaige had died very suddenly on March 13, 1891. She was very well known and her death was sad news. She left behind her husband and two bright little children, one scarcely a year old, the other only seven.

MANAIGE, PETER

Peter Manaige was born in Broome County, New York, in 1819. His father Louis Manaige, a native of Canada, served in the Revolutionary War and died at Leroy, Minnesota, in 1870, at the age of ninety-nine years. Peter moved with his parents to Portage, Wisconsin, in 1830. In 1840 he married Miss A. Decorah and two years after this he moved to Clinton County, Iowa, where he engaged in merchandising. In 1846 he was appointed interpreter for the Winnebago Indians. In that capacity he came to Minnesota in 1848 and located at Long Prairie. In 1855 he came to McPherson Township. Their children were Archie, Margaret, Charles, Paul, Josephine, Angeline, Teressa, William L., Edward and Henry.

Paul P. Manaige was born at Long Prairie, Minnesota, on March 13, 1850. In 1855 he came to St. Clair where he lived until his death on December 12, 1923. He married Hattie Stocker in St. Clair. Six children born to this couple of which Andrew and Richard survived their father. His brothers surviving him were Charley, Edward, Louis and Henry.

Richard Manaige: A memorable town character was Richard Manaige (Zik), a half-breed Indian. The first (Pete) Manaige was brought to the Winnebago Agency to act as interpreter and was of Canadian descent. Richard was of this lineage. Though he had many and varies jobs around town, Richard was reported to be one of the best double-headed axe men in the area. When he put his mind to it, he was a good worker. He also had a love for the "fire-water" and though he was not allowed to buy it, he found that vanilla and lemon extracts were a fair substitute and available—until his secret was uncovered.

Richard was 68 when he died on December 14, 1948, from extensive burns to his body and exposure to the elements. It is believed that he may have spilled kerosene on his clothes while trying to start a fire in the stove in the shack where he lived alone. Richard lived in a chicken coup, which was located behind the DeMars Hotel. His clothing ignited and he ran about a block to the faucet outside of the City Hall to drench the flames. That is where William Lynch, who lived nearby, discovered him early the next morning. He was alive, but died in the ambulance on the way to the hospital.

The only other Indians in the town, Henry and Louis Maneige, kin of Richard's had moved away. Henry Dotson, a close friend of Richard's had died the previous year. A niece, Mrs. Harold (Marni) Gwilt of Mankato, survived him. His brother Andrew died in 1946.

Angeline Manaige Dotson was born in 1856 in Long Prairie, Minnesota, and was the daughter of Minnesota pioneers who had lived in St. Clair for many years. She died in St. Clair in January 1942 at the age of 86. A son, Henry and a daughter, Mrs. Edward Mountain, as well as two brothers Henry and Edward survived her. She is buried in St. Clair.

William Lewis Manaige was born in 1861 in St. Clair. He was the son of pioneer parents and a former assessor of McPherson Township. He was a farmer and lived in this vicinity his entire life serving as tax assessor for the township for six years. He died in March 1939 and was survived by brothers Henry and Edward E. and a sister Angeline Dotson.

MARZINSKE, CARL

Carl Marzinske was born on December 17, 1841, in Nadelitz, Pommern, Preussen (Prussia). In 1869 he married Wilhelmine Krueger, born on October 1, 1843, also in Nadelitz.

Wilhelmine came to America when she was 29 years of age, settling in Milwaukee. They moved to Minnesota in 1880, living at St. Clair until the death of her husband. She then moved to the home of her daughter, Louise Ganzel.

In 1885 they are listed in the McPherson Township Census, having five children, Louise (Wilhelm Ganzel), Augusta (Joseph Reed), Robert (Goldie Putsch), William (Amanda Schmidt) and Charles (Della Lade).

Carl died in February 1914 and Wilhelmine in July 1935. They are buried in the St. Johns (Bestman) Cemetery in St. Clair. On their gravestone is the following verse, (in German) "I have a belief, that I am wearing, the crown of righteousness."

By Wayne Ganzel

Chester Marzinske, the son of Charles and Della (Lade) Marzinske, was born on October 1, 1916, in McPherson Township. On June 22, 1946, he married Marjorie Kowles in Elysian, MN. Chester was a farmer and was a custodian at Mankato State University, Mankato from 1961-1980.

Chester and Marie had six children: Penny (Steven Cattnach), Vickie (Terry Fry), Jill, Jerry, Charles (Wendy Reed) and Richard.

MAY, JOSEPH

The May family in the McPherson-Decoria Township area is one of Blue Earth County's pioneer families. Today the Jack and Lisa May family live on the original farm in the original brick farm house in McPherson Township. Every generation of the May family in Minnesota has now lived in the brick house. Gene and

Patricia (Sexton) May live on a nearby farm across the township line in Decoria Township which is part of the May farm.

The first May to settle in Blue Earth County was Joseph May and his wife Katherine (Trout) May. Both had been born in Bavaria (South Germany) in the 1820's. Joseph had lived in Dodge County, Wisconsin, since the late 1840's wherein a town called Mayville, which had been founded by a Chester and Stephen P. May. Mayville, Wisconsin, still thrives today.

In 1864 Joseph moved his family to Mankato via covered wagon and oxen. The family still has the ox yoke from that trip. In May 1865, just a few weeks after President Lincoln's assassination, Joseph moved to the farm near St. Clair where Jack May now lives. Part of the present home was already standing at the time.

Thomas Hughes, in his *History of Blue Earth County*, writes in George May's biography that part of the house had been built by the government for a "deposed Indian chief." This would presumably refer to the Winnebago Agency era of Blue Earth County.

It has been recorded in several places, including Thomas Hughes' *History of Blue Earth County*, that Joseph May became one of the largest farmers in the state. He owned approximately 1800 acres in Blue Earth County at one time.

The Joseph May family consisted of seven children, five of whom eventually married into pioneer families of the area. They were: George who married Mary Hodapp, Anna married Wendal Hodapp, John who married Katherine Robel, Elizabeth who married Hubert Bruels, Stephen who married Viola Ireland and sons Andrew and Joseph who married in Oregon.

MAY, GEORGE

George May, the oldest son of Joseph and Katherine May was born in Dodge County, Wisconsin. When he was 10 years old, the family moved to Mankato in 1864. Eventually he took over the farm and he was also a large and progressive farmer in his own right as described by Thomas Hughes. In recent times an older neighbor indeed marveled at hearing stories as a boy about the May's 20 teams of horses in the barn which still stands today (since 1866). George was a founder of the McPherson Farmers' Mutual Insurance Co. and was for some years Vice President of the St. Clair State Bank. He was also active in community affairs and held various offices, which helped to promote and improve the village of St. Clair.

George and Mary (Hodapp) May were married in 1874. They had ten children: Phillip, George S., Katherine, Edward, Marie, Ottilia, Joseph, Aloysius, Karl and Anna. In 1909 George moved his family to Mount Angel, Oregon, and much of his land was sold. The home farm was rented until 1918 when Edward C. May moved back to his Minnesota home and married Frances Wingen. George returned many times to visit his sons, family and other relatives. He passed away in 1944.

Edward C. May was raised on the family farm in McPherson Township near St. Clair. His father and grandfather were pioneer farmers in the area since 1894. In 1918 Edward returned from Oregon, where he had lived for about eight years, to marry Frances Wingen. They settled in the family's farm home that he had been raised in. Frances Wingen was the daughter of another McPherson Township pioneer, Joseph Wingen. It is an interesting coincidence that Edward's grandfather Joseph had decades before helped look after a young Joseph Wingen while hauling grain on overnight trips to Owatonna. Joseph Wingen had taken over the farm at 14 years of age in 1865 when his father Jacob Wingen was killed in a mowing accident.

Edward and Frances had two sons, Gene and Francis, while struggling through the depression. They raised both milk cows and beef cattle. To sell cattle from the area, before trucks were available, one would have to drive them to St. Clair, put them on the train to Albert Lea and from there to the market in South St. Paul. In the 1930's on some occasions Edward took them to Chicago on the train, as market prices were better there. In the early years cream from the milk was transported to St. Clair Creamery by team and wagon at least three days a week. Later years a truck from Model Dairy in Mankato came on a route to pick up cream from the farms. Edward owned and operated a thresher in the 1920's. This meant cutting, shocking and staking grain bundles. He helped relatives and neighbors get grain threshed.

From the 30's to the 50's farming changed from horses and threshers to combines and tractors. Edward and sons Gene and Francis continued to improve with new methods of farming. As youngsters they were thrilled to operate a row crop tractor which planted and cultivated corn. Later, one of Gene's hobbies was to maintain and display this same tractor at pioneer power shows.

The elder brother Francis passed away in 1950. Gene and his father Edward continued to farm together until 1954 when Gene took over the entire operation. Edward passed away in 1965 at the age of 82 years.

In Thomas Hughes in his *History of Blue Earth County* described the May family as "having stood for the strength and morality of the community since its establishment in McPherson Township during the last year of the Civil War. He describes Gene May's grandfather

George May as one who won the approval of all that knew him. Gene May has filled these shoes nicely in this half of the 20th Century. He, too, is respected in the community in much the same way, with a reputation of honesty, patience and levelheaded thinking. During Gene May's tenure with the family farm it has undergone extensive improvement. Most of the farmland has been "system tiled" to provide the drainage needed in Blue Earth County soils for maximum crop production.

Jack May, the son of Eugene and Patricia (Sexton) May, always enjoyed being with his father around the farm as a young child. Helping with chores and other work often involved being around the homestead where his grandmother Frances lived. Always being a nostalgic person from his childhood to present, he usually would ask to hear stories about the "old days," or "about when you were little," when visiting with his "Grandma Franc" (Frances had always been known as "Franc"). When she was born in 1887 a neighbor suggested to her mother naming her after President Grover Cleveland's wife, Franc. Having graduated from Mankato State Normal School in 1911, and having taught at several schools including St. Clair, and having been a homemaker in the community for 60 years, she was more than able to accommodated Jack's insatiable appetite for history. Jack cherishes the memories he has of his grandmother and of her stories of the past. Frances passed away in 1983.

Having spent a great deal of time on the historic homestead as a boy and appreciating its history, Jack is more than happy to have the opportunity to raise another generation of Mays on it. He married Lisa Keepers in 1980. They graduated from Mankato State University in 1980 and 1982 respectively. Their children are Kathleen, Michelle, Colleen and Thomas (1988-2001). Jack has been involved in farming with Gene since 1978. Jack and Lisa's children represent the sixth generation to live in the original brick home on the original homestead.

By Jack May

MC COLLUM, LESTER

Lester and Lena (Widmen) moved to St. Clair in 1948. Lester built a sawmill on the home place. In 1954 he was serving as the St. Clair Marshal. Lester and Lena raised five children: Delphin Mason of Mankato, Bernard, Le Roy (Marlyn) of Cleveland, Lloyd, and Deloris (Dean Mosher, daughters Dawn & Debbie) of St. Clair.

Bernard McCollum (1937-2004) graduated from St. Clair High School in 1956. He married Carol Jane Hiller on June 4, 1956. He worked for Hodgman & Sons Construction, was a janitor at the St. Clair High School for about 10 years and worked for the Minnesota Highway Department for over 26 years, retiring in 1999. Bernie and Carol lived at 201 Park Street South and have a daughter Connie (Bradley Danberry) and three grandchildren, Jared, Nicholas and Megan who lives in Janesville. After Bernie's death Carol moved to Janesville.

Lloyd McCollum (Dylane Miller/Ginger) owned and operated the D&L Diner in St. Clair from 1978 until 1983. He also took over the family sawmill at 204 Main Street West. In 2005 they moved into rural McPherson Township.

The children of Lloyd McCollum are Steve, Denise, Jeff, Tim (Tammy Gary, children Caleb, Tonia and Desiree) lives at Byron, Justin (Jesse, children Katelyn and Brendan) lives in Good Thunder, and Mike (daughter Victoria) lives in Mankato.

Steve McCollum married Deborah Riemann who also grew up in St. Clair. They are living in St. Clair and have two children, Amanda and Eric. Amanda has a son, Trenton.

Denise McCollum married Brandt Baker also a St. Clair native, has two sons Timothy and Thomas and lives in Brainerd, Minnesota.

Jeffery McCollum married Connie Goettl who grew up in Eagle Lake, Minnesota. They live in rural St. Clair and have two children, Joshua and Kristen. Jeff worked for Leo Ripplinger at Rips Service (Leo also owned the hardware store.) from 1990 until he purchased the shop and business on October 1, 1993. (This was formerly known as Drake's Station, Myers Oil Co., and Quinn Oil Company.) Jeff is an auto and truck mechanic.

By Jeff and Connie McCollum

MC COMB, JOHN

The John McComb family came to this area in the 1870s and bought farmland in Medo Township near the Medo-McPherson Cemetery. Over time some of his family would become residents of St. Clair. John (1818-1894) was born in Ireland and came to America as a young man in the late 1830's. He lived in Pennsylvania until 1845 and then moved west to farm near Madison, Wisconsin. It was there that he married Agnes Frasier (1843-1915), who was born in Montreal, Canada. They had six children: Lincoln (Cora Neller), Kathryn (Andy Quinn - see separate story), George (Elizabeth), Samuel, Frank, and Roy (Anna Kroenke). All of the sons had farms in Medo Township. John and Agnes are buried at Medo-McPherson Cemetery.

Frank (1876-1955) and Ida (Andrews) (1894-1990) were married on January 15, 1918, in St. Clair and farmed in Medo Township, but eventually moved to St.

L to R: Capitola McComb (age 6) and Shirley McComb (age 7)

Clair, living at 317 Main Street West. Ida was born in St. Clair to Asa and Fannie (Wheeler) Andrews. They had 2 daughters: Shirley (Ralph Conway) and Capitola (Andrew Stevenson). Ida taught the girls how to perform acrobatic, tumbling, ring and trapeze acts when they were very young. They became known as the "McComb Sisters" and performed at many fairs and community celebrations in Minnesota, Iowa and the Dakotas during the 1920s and 1930s. Ida also made all of their beautiful costumes. Shirley and Capitola graduated from St. Clair High School in 1937.

L to R: Anna McComb, Ida and John Kopke, Roy McComb

Frank and Ida are buried at Medo-McPherson Cemetery.

Roy (1878-1973) and Anna (1886-1963) moved to 309 Main Street West in the 1940s after selling their farm to their son William. Anna was born in Green Bay, Wisconsin, to Michael and Emilia (Zellmer) Kroenke and was a sister to Herman Kroenke. Both the Kroenke and Zellmer families emigrated from Prussia in the late 1870s to Wisconsin. Michael and Emilia met there married and eventually moved west to the Mapleton area. Roy and Anna had five children: Stella (Wilbur Yackel), William, Dorothy (Francis Waldera/Ruben Jager), Margaret (Donald Guddal) and Alvin.

Roy and Anna are buried at Medo-McPherson Cemetery.

William McComb (1908-1961) married Louise Oftedahl (1917-1990). Louise was the daughter of Peter J. and Ovidia (Holm) Oftedahl of Pemberton. They farmed and in 1956 decided to sell the farm to Nick and Florence Juliar, and move the family to St. Clair. After William left the farm he worked with Hodgkin's Construction, building roads.

Louise had attended Cosmetology School after graduating from Pemberton High School and decided to open a beauty shop in St. Clair. In 1956 "Louise's Beauty Shop" was opened in the basement of the home of Roy and Anna McComb located across the street from the creamery. In 1959 William and Louise purchased a house from George Hubmer, at 300 Main Street East, and

Louise and Bill McComb

the beauty shop was relocated to that house. Louise sold the house in 1964 and moved to an apartment above the barbershop. The beauty shop was relocated to the back half of the barbershop. In 1966 Louise purchased the old town hall with the intention of building two apartments upstairs and an apartment for herself and a beauty shop downstairs. The project was close to completion when a fire on January 21, 1966, destroyed everything. In 1969 Louise closed her beauty shop. It was also this year, that she married Herman Godemann of McPherson Township. They built a new house on Mill Street, which was eventually sold to Steve and Cindy Olson.

William and Louise had three children, who all graduated from St. Clair High School. Their children are William (Jeanne Ellis), Joanne (Robert Nahlovsky) and Mary. Mary taught at St. James Public Schools for many years until her retirement. In 2001 she moved to Mankato. Mary assisted with the publication of *Years of Memories* and is a volunteer at the Blue Earth County Historical Society.

William and Louise are buried at Medo-McPherson Cemetery.

By Mary McComb

MC LAUGHLIN, DR. RAYMOND

Dr. McLaughlin, the son of Mark and Nova (Donovan) McLaughlin, was born on December 16, 1900, in Sleepy Eye, Minnesota. The family moved to Appleton, WI, where he graduated from high school. He then attended Marquette University, Milwaukee and graduated from the University of Minnesota Dental School. In 1926 he started a dental practice in Madison Lake, Minnesota. He also had offices in St. Clair at the hotel and in Mankato. He retired in 1975.

He was married to Alice Carrigan in 1927 at Madison Lake. He enjoyed hunting, fishing and they were members of the All Saints Catholic Church. He was a member of the Knights of Columbus, the American Dental Association, a volunteer fireman, 2-term mayor of Madison Lake in the 1940's and a board member of the Peoples State Bank in Madison Lake.

The McLaughlin's had two children Mary (Wallace Johnson) and Thomas who died in 1970.

Dr. McLaughlin died on July 9, 1989 at the Hillcrest Health Care Center, Mankato, MN.

MC PHERSON, GEN. JAMES B.

Gen. James B. McPherson was born in Sandusky, Ohio, on November 14, 1828. He graduated from West Point in 1853 and was appointed a major general in 1862. He served with distinction in the siege and capture of Vicksburg. He became commander of the Army of the Tennessee in the spring of 1864. He was killed near Atlanta, Georgia, on July 22, 1864. McPherson Township, formerly known as Rice Lake Township and then McClellan Township was named after him.

MEANY, THOMAS

Thomas was born on August 22, 1877, in Rose Creek, Mower County, Minnesota, to Mr. and Mrs. William Meany. In 1920 he was married to Sarah (1891-1965) Bluhm of Waldorf, Minnesota. He was the manager and grain buyer at the local elevator. They lived at 205 Main Street West. Thomas died in June 1945 and is buried in Immaculate Conception Catholic Cemetery. Sarah is buried in St. John's Evangelical Lutheran Cemetery. They had two sons, Roy and Donald.

MEANY, ROY

Mankato Free Press:

Pfc. Roy Meany received his elementary and secondary school training at the St. Clair Public School. He was graduated from high school in 1941, as valedictorian of his class. While in high school he was very active in all school activities. In 1941 he participated in speech work, and was awarded the highest rating given in his division at the regional speech contest. He also was a member of the basketball team, editor-in-chief of the school paper, and a member of the school band.

After he graduated from high school, he attended Mankato State Teachers College for almost two years, then enlisted in the Army Reserve. On March 25, 1943, he left for Fort Snelling, where he was assigned to the coast artillery at Camp McQuaide, California. He was transferred to Stanford University for testing purposes, then to the University of Oregon where he was stationed from June l, 1943 to December 4, 1943. Here he received a certificate in recognition of completion of three terms in the army specialized unit. The military graduation on December 4 was the first ever held at the University of Oregon. He was then assigned to combat duty.

From December 11, 1943, to February 7, 1944, Pfc. Meany received his training at Camp Van Dorn, Mississippi. He was then transferred to Camp Breckenridge, Kentucky. From this camp he left for overseas duty. His last furlough was February 28, 1944.

He arrived with the 83rd division in France. This division launched the hard-punching drive on St. Malo and Denard bottling up 12,000 Germans in one of the most heavily fortified areas in France. Many of the 83rd

Thundering Herds were from Minnesota.

Pfc. Meany was a member of the 83rd infantry division platoon who marched the 20,000 Nazis in mass surrender at Beaugency, France. 24 enlisted men of a 83rd infantry division platoon had effected the mass surrender.

Pfc. Meany was a volunteer member of the famous bazooka team headed by Lt. George Partenan of L'Anse, Michigan, which sunk a Nazi launch.

He was awarded the good conduct medal for exemplary behavior, efficiency and fidelity. On May 11, 1944, he was awarded the combat infantry badge for displaying exemplary conduct in action against the enemy in France.

Pfc. Meany was killed in action January 18, 1945, in Belgium.

MIELY, A. B.

A. B. Miely was born in Augusta County, Virginia, in 1847. When he was fifteen years old he moved with his parents to McDonough County, Illinois, and then came to Minnesota in 1864 and settled in McPherson Township. In connection with farming he also operated a sawmill. His parents, Louis and Amanda Miely resided in Jefferson County, Kansas, where they farmed and raised livestock. He married Anne E. Crabbe on October 1, 1872. Their children were Mabel L., Fred L., and Ray B.

MILLER, ARTHUR

Arthur Miller was born on March 26, 1902, in McPherson Township. He was the son of William and Mathilda (Block) Miller who were farmers in the township. Arthur's father died when he was an infant and when old enough he assisted his mother with the farming. He was also a lineman with the Co-op Telephone Company. He retired in 1967 and continued living on the farm one mile east of St. Clair, until 1983 when he moved to the Delgene Nicolai home. In 1988 he moved to the Mankato House. He died on August 22, 1990.

MILLER, EDWARD

Edward Miller, the son of John and Margaret Miller, was born on August 15, 1870, and grew up in the Wabasha, Minnesota area. He was the eleventh of 12 children. On May 28, 1895, he married Anna Woefel, the daughter of Charles and Philomena (Bolnig) Woefel. (see separate story) Anna was born on October 26, 1872, in Austria.

Edward and Anna settled in the St. Clair area as this was where her parents were living. Here they raised 13 children: Charles (Kate Klebel), Edward Jr. (Gertrude Lynch), Iverna (Adolf Fasnacht), and Fred (see separate story). Mathilda, Ben, Cecelia (Raymond Reichel), Gertrude (Edward Bolte), Anne who died when only about eleven years old, Helene "Sadie" (John Fossum - see separate story). Frank, George (see separate story), and Marion (Francis Madigan)

Edward Miller died on July 3, 1944 and Anna died on June 13, 1931.

By Sondra Von Arb

Fred Miller was born on May 24, 1900, and married Ella Glamm, the daughter of Fred and Bertha Glamm. Fred and Ella lived with Herman Glamm in McPherson Township. Fred worked at Hilltop Greenhouse in Mankato. They had one son Gary.

Fred died on March 8, 1976 Ella remained on the farm until she moved to the Janesville Nursing Home in Janesville, Minnesota. Ella died on April 10, 2005. They are buried in the St. John's Evangelical Lutheran Cemetery in St. Clair.

Gary F. Miller was born on July 18, 1942 in Mankato, Minnesota. He graduated from St. Clair High School in 1960. He married Judy Hemshrot, the daughter of Marvin and Lucille (Hall) Hemshrot in March 1963. They lived on the Glamm farm in McPherson Township. He was a member of the St. John's Evangelical Lutheran Church Council and besides farming enjoyed ice fishing, deer hunting and woodworking. Judy graduated from St. Clair High School in 1960 and helped Gary with the farm operation.

Gary and Judy had three children, Jodi (Steve Dieteman), Julie (Kevin Timm), and Greg (Janice).

Gary died on November 30, 2000 and is buried in the

Judy & Gary Miller

St. John's Evangelical Lutheran Cemetery, St. Clair. Judy is still living on the family farm.

George Miller was born on October 8, 1914. He graduated in 1933 from the St. Clair High School and attended college in Mankato. While living in Mankato he worked for the Coca-Cola Company. He owned and operated the St. Clair Produce from 1945 until 1956, where he bought, candled and sold eggs. He also culled and resold chickens as well as chicken feed and seeds to farmers. In 1956 he sold the produce building and business to Jim and Ivadell Hunter. He then was the manager of the Good Thunder Liquor Store until his retirement in 1981. He was the mayor of St. Clair from 1954-1957, during this time the town turned on the streetlights for the first time. He was an avid gardener and fisherman. He also enjoyed playing baseball, playing on the St. Clair team and later for the Madison Lake team. He was an active member of the Mankato Farmers Market and the Mankato Moose Lodge.

On May 7, 1938, George married Corrine Pickel in Mankato. Corrine, the daughter of Henry C. and Bergene (Oftedahl) Pickel, was born on October 5, 1917. She graduated from the Pemberton High School in 1935. She was a homemaker and enjoyed cooking, reading, crossword puzzles and gardening. They were members of Immaculate Conception Catholic Church in St. Clair and she served on the altar society. The family lived at 117 Front Street North.

George and Corrine were the parents of eight children: Sondra (Ronald Von Arb), Jerilynn (Jerry Wilking); Bruce (see separate story), Thomas (Nancy Wilder), John R. (Sue Manthe), Joan (Jerry Stalberger), Daniel (Val) and Douglas. It is remembered that one year there were so many Millers on the football team that first names were included on the football shirts.

George died on May 24, 1991, and Corrine on March 16, 2003. They are buried in the Immaculate Conception Catholic Cemetery, St. Clair.

Bruce George Miller, the son of George and Corrine (Pickel) Miller, was born on April 2, 1943, in Mankato. He graduated from the St. Clair High School in 1961 and served in the U.S. Army from 1962 until 1964. He attended Mankato State University and graduated from the University of Minnesota in 1971 with a law degree. He worked for Joseph Paris and was in private practice with James Hulwi for a short time before joining the McLean Peterson Law Firm of Mankato in 1987 and also had an office at the St. Clair State Bank. He married Sharon Huseman on July 24, 1971, in St. Paul. He was a member of the Minnesota Bar Association, the St. Clair American Legion, Fraternal Order of Eagles, Nicollet County Public Defenders, and the Worthington Community College Backers. He was an avid golfer.

Sharon has been with the St. Clair School System for many years as an elementary education teacher.

Bruce and Sharon are the parents of four sons: William, Ben, Sam and Tony.

Bruce died suddenly on March 9, 1992, at the Immanuel-St. Joseph's Hospital, Mankato. He is buried in the Immaculate Conception Catholic Church Cemetery in St. Clair.

By Sondra Von Arb

MOE, EMIL

Emil Moe was first married to Agnes Larsen. They had four children. Evelyn (10-23-1915) was married to Ervin Ewert, a farmer on the west edge of St. Clair and also a school bus driver. They had a daughter Delores who was married to Conrad Steck (1934-2004).

The second child was Mildred (1-24-1917 - 12-23-1993) who married Melvin Drager. Donald (see separate story) and Vernon who was born on June 12, 1920, and was married to Vernell Oftedahl.

Emil later married Mayme Burgess, a widow with six children, Evelyn, Mildred, Maurice, Milton, Vaughn and Lowell.

Donald Moe, the son of Emil and Agnes (Larsen) Moe of St. Clair, was born on February 6, 1918. On February 14, 1956 he married Norma Kott the daughter of Ernest and Wanda Kott, at S.S. Peter & Paul's Parish House in Mankato.

In February 1956 they moved into their new 2-bedroom rambler at 326 Main Street East. Delmer and Elmer Rudolph built their home.

Donald worked for the Blue Earth County Highway Department (the county shop at this time was where Lloyd McCollum's sawmill is located) and was a volunteer St. Clair Fireman.

Two sons were born to Norma and Donald, Darryl (11-29-1956) and Dennis (2-8-1958).

Donald passed away on September 11, 1961, from complications of asthma at the age forty-three.

After Donald's death, friends, neighbors and relatives helped Norma in many ways.

On February 20, 1965, Norma married Herbert Bruels at the Immaculate Conception Catholic Church in St. Clair. Herbert, Norma and the boys continued to live in the St. Clair house for five years. In September 1970 they moved to the Bruels farm about a mile west of St. Clair. After the death of Joseph Bruels, Rose his wife, lived in a mobile home on the farm before retiring to Hillcrest Nursing Home in Mankato, where she passed away in 1980.

While growing up and going to school the Moe boys helped Herbert with the farm work and chores. Herbert was a good dad to the boys. He was a farmer, worked for Carney Insulation and was a volunteer St. Clair fireman.

Herbert passed away on October 2, 2001.

After Herbert's death, Darryl Moe took over Norma's land and also is working for the Minnesota State Highway Department. He is now living in the Moe house in St. Clair.

Dennis Moe married Susan Kruckeberg, the daughter of Merville and Marge Kruckeberg of St. Clair, and they have two daughters, Bridgette and Cassie. Dennis has worked for Tire Associates in Mankato for twenty-five years.

By Norma Moe Bruels

MORE, ALVIS

Alvis More, the 8th of eleven children of Fay and Helen (Burnell) More, was born on January 16, 1934. He grew up on a farm south of Pemberton, Minnesota. He helped his father farm, worked for his brother-in-law doing carpenter work, and drove truck for Nordass American Homes in Minnesota Lake. In 1954 he entered the U.S. Army and spent his time in Alaska and was discharged in June 1956. On September 24, 1956, he was married to Carol Schull at the St. John's Lutheran Church in St. Clair.

Carol Jean Schull, the daughter of Richard (1902-1986) and Edna (Fesselt) (1906-1995) Schull, was born on October 29, 1936. She grew up on a farm in Medo Township, six miles south of St. Clair. She was the 2nd of five daughters: Ida (Conley Birr), Carol, Joan (Eldon Preis/Dean Lavitzke), twins Janelle (John Imm) and Janice (Willis Westphal). The girls were all married at St. John's Evangelical Lutheran Church.

Carol & Alvis More

The family did most of their business in St. Clair. Richard and Edna, members of St. John's since 1950, are both buried in the St. John's Evangelical Lutheran Cemetery, St. Clair.

Carol went to the Perch Lake country school and graduated from the Mapleton High School in 1954 and attended Mankato Commercial College. She worked at Greens Five and Dime and at Southern Minnesota Supply Company in Mankato as a secretary and receptionist. Alvis and Carol lived south of Pemberton from 1956 until 1961 when they moved to rural Waldorf for three years and then moved to the George Hubmer farm, southeast of St. Clair, in 1965. They farmed there for 28 years. They have six children all who graduated from the St. Clair High School.

In 1989 they moved to the More home farm south of Pemberton. Alvis served as Fifth District Blue Earth County Commissioner for fourteen years. He has served on various boards and committees including the ASCS Board, Blue Earth County Pork Producers, Farmers Union, St. Clair Community Ed., PTA, and Boosters Club. He also enjoys playing cards. Carol enjoyed crafts of all kinds and has done extensive geneology with her sisters. Most of all she was kept busy keeping Alvis organized and to his appointments at the right time with the right papers. Alvis and Carol's children are Steven, Jeffrey, Debra, Lynda, Marvin and Larry.

Steven More married to Noreen Pfeffer and they now own and farm the George Hubmer farm. Steven is the treasurer of the McPherson Township Board and is a school bus driver in addition to farming. Noreen is a registered nurse at the Mayo-ISJ Hospital in Mankato. They have three children Sara (Jamie Will), Melissa, a student at Minnesota State University-Mankato, and Brian.

Jeffrey More married to Julie Kietzer and they live on the former Richard Schull farm south of St. Clair. Jeff is farming and also sells a variety of farm seeds. Julie is working at the Mankato Clinic. They have five children, Jennifer, a student at the Minnesota State University-Mankato, Joshua, Justin, Jessica and Jodi.

Debra More married Carl Fugleberg and they are living in Byron, Minnesota. Debra is a registered nurse at the Mayo Clinic in Rochester and Carl is a sub-contractor in the painting business. Their children are Tim, Stephanie, Colleen, Natalie and Amanda.

Lynda More married Steven Kruse, the son of Charles and Jeanette Kruse, McPherson Township residents. Steven is farming south of St. Clair, has a hog operation and is a supervisor on the McPherson Township Board. Lynda is working at the UC Laboratory, a soil and water testing business in Janesville. Their children are Bradley,

Kendra, Derek and Maria. They are very active with activities at the St. Clair School.

Marvin More married Alicia Dauk and they live in St. Clair and have two sons Matthew and Andrew. Marvin is working for the Blue Earth County Highway Department. Alicia is a para-legal in Mankato.

Larry More married Lori Rieser and they are living in Byron, Minnesota. Larry and Lori are social workers; Larry works for Senior Linkage and Lori is at the Mayo Clinic in Rochester, Minnesota. They have a daughter Allison.

By Carol More

MYERS, WILLIAM

William Myers, the son of William and Emma (Rick) Myers, was born on January 26, 1904. He attended St. Mary's Township rural school and Immanuel Lutheran School in Freedom Township. On September 22, 1926 he married Margaret Kleeman, the daughter of Charles and Minnie (Koplen) Kleeman, at the Freedom Lutheran Church, Freedom Township. Margaret, born on July 28, 1905, was a homemaker and helped with the family farming and later the family businesses.

Bill and Margaret had three children, Wallace (Irene Snyder), Beverly (Wayne Born) and Ivadell (James Hunter) {see separate story]. In 1941 the family moved to St. Clair, living at 230 Main Street West. Bill bought a portable hammer (feed) mill and went out to the farms in the country to grind feed. In 1943 he purchased a gasoline bulk plant and filling station (The Home Oil Co.), which had been closed up. The new business was called Myers Oil Company. He then signed up to work on the Alaska Highway with three other St. Clair men. This left Margaret and the three children to run the oil business. The first March station receipts were $69.69 and in April they were $246.13. Elmo Nyquist ran the bulk oil truck and those March sales were $58.10, April $403.20. Being new in town and starting a business that had been closed was hard. After 2 years in Alaska Bill returned to operate the oil truck himself. He added on the station and hired a mechanic to operate the station. Bill and Margaret's foster son Stanley Drake (see separate story) later bought the station. In 1955, Beverly's husband, Wayne Born (1930-1970), the son of George and Martha Born, took

Myers "Deep Rock" Filling Station

Myers Home Oil Company
Margaret Myers with her children Wallace and Beverly

Home Oil Company, home of Kelly Tires,
Deep Rock Gas and Prize Oil

Myers "Phillips 66" Bulk Gas Truck

Myers Oil Company Bulk Gas Truck

Bill Myers Bulk Storage tanks with the elevator in the background

St. Clair school bus driver Bill Myers

Bill Myers "Prompt Service" portable feed mill

over the Myers Oil Co. bulk oil truck. Beverly and Wayne had two daughters, Lucinda (Lennie Davis) and Melanie (Alan Esser).

Bill then bought a school bus, driving for ten years, and a fuel -transport truck, so he was still a busy man. The Myers Oil Co. was sold to Southern Valley Co-op in 1971. (Special Note: This property was sold to the school in 2004 and all has been cleared away and the ground will be part of the athletic complex.)

In 1958 Bill and Margaret moved to Lake Washington for the summer and spent winters in Cape Coral and Fort Meyers, Florida. They moved back to St. Clair in 1982.

Bill died in 1988 and Margaret continued living in the Schalow apartments in St. Clair. She was a member of St. John's Lutheran Ladies Aid, the American Legion Auxiliary and enjoyed quilting, playing cards and watching the Minnesota Twins. She died on March 4, 2002. They were members of St. John's Evangelical Lutheran Church and are buried in the church cemetery.

By Ivadell Hunter

NICOLAI, LUDWIG

Ludwig Nicolai (1869-1937) was the youngest son of August (1828-1915) and Florentina (1835-1922) Nicolai, Sr. He married Pauline Krueger (1878-1962) and they had four children, Hulda (Erich C. Ewert), Arthur (Emma Heinze), Clarence and Elmer.

August, Florentina, Ludwig and Pauline are buried in the St. John's Evangelical Lutheran Cemetery, in St. Clair.

Clarence Nicolai was born on September 30, 1903. Clarence married Edna Anna J. Schuldt on September 4, 1930 at St. John's Evangelical Lutheran Church, St. Clair, Minnesota. Edna, the daughter of Jacob and Helene (Beckmann) Schuldt was born on November 10, 1911, in Lyon Co. Iowa.

Clarence attended Riese Country School in Blue Earth County and then began farming. They farmed in McPherson Township, Blue Earth County, until retiring in 1968, when they moved to St. Clair, living at 101 Front Street North. Edna later moved to the Schalow Apartments.

Clarence and Edna had two sons, Lyle Clarence (see separate story) and Delgene Louis who was born on December 14, 1938, at Immanuel Hospital, Mankato, Minnesota.

Clarence died on November 1, 1993 and Edna on November 22, 2002. They are buried in the St. John's Evangelical Lutheran Cemetery in St. Clair.

Lyle Nicolai was born on January 1, 1934, in McPherson Township. He graduated from St. Clair High

School and then entered the army for two years. On May 2, 1959, he married Ruth Martha Kiecker, the daughter of Elmer John and Gertrude (Seehusen) Kiecker of Fairfax, Minnesota. Ruth was born on November 11, 1938. Lyle worked for the Blue Earth County Highway Department for 33 years as a blade operator. He also was an electrician and worked part-time for Steel Electric of St. Clair for many years. Ruth was a homemaker and enjoyed baking. She worked at the St. Clair School for 22 years and has retired as head of the Food Service Department. She is still helping them out occasionally.

Lyle and Ruth's children all graduated from St. Clair High School. Julie (Randy Spear) has graduated from Concordia College, St. Paul, Minnesota, and is working at Atlantis Plastic, Mankato, Minnesota. Their daughter Nicole graduated from St. Clair High School and then Minnesota State University, Mankato, and is working at the Minnesota Elevator Company, Mankato, Minnesota. Jordan graduated from St. Clair High School and is attending Minnesota State University, Mankato, Minnesota.

Steven, after graduation, entered the U.S. Air Force serving his country in Korea where he met Yun Yim whom he later married. Their children are Theresa, Jennifer, and both graduates of St. Clair High School and attending Minnesota State University, Mankato, Minnesota, and Jeremiah, a student at St. Clair School. In February 1998, he married LaVonne Holteen. Steve is still active in the U.S. Air Force Reserve and he and LaVonne are both employed by the Minnesota Department of Transportation, Mankato, Minnesota. They are living in St. Clair, Minnesota.

The family of Lyle and Ruth Nicolai
Standing (L to R): Steve, Mark, Elizabeth, James, Thomas
Seated: Laura, Ruth, Lyle and Julie

Mark entered the U.S. Air Force after graduating and served his country for nine years. He is now living in St. Clair and is working at the Minnesota Elevator Company, Mankato, Minnesota.

Elizabeth is married to Myron Schweim and they are living and farming in rural Mankato, Minnesota. Elizabeth is attending South Central Technical College, Mankato, Minnesota, and is working at the Minnesota Elevator Company, Mankato, Minnesota. Their children Andrew, Ryan, Mallory and Chelsea are all attending St. Clair High School.

James entered the U.S. Air Force after graduating and served his country for four years. He then started helping his uncle in the wood crafting business. He is now working at Woodcraft Interiors in Edina, Minnesota. He is married to Sherry Kreft who graduated from Wabasso High School and then graduated and worked in the cosmetology field. They have two sons, Kendall and Marshall, and they are living in St. Peter, Minnesota.

Thomas is self-employed and is the owner of "Nicolai Masonry." He is married to Katherine Arnoldt who graduated from the Janesville-Waldorf-Pemberton High School and South Central Technicoal College. She is employed at the Minnesota Elevator Company, Mankato, Minnesota. They have two children, Abigail, who is attending St. John's Pre-school, St. Clair, and Joseph. They are living in rural St. Clair.

Laura went to New York after graduation and was a "nanny" while she attended college. She has graduated with a Master's Degree in K-12 special education from Manhattanville College in Purchase, New York. She is teaching in Wrappingers Falls, New York. She is married to James Scampoli who graduated from Mercy College in New York with a degree in occupational therapy. They have two sons, James Jr., and Jonathan and live in Wrappingers Falls, New York.

By Ruth Nicolai

Elmer L. Nicolai was born in 1906. On November 12, 1929 he married Helen Ward the daughter of Charles and Millie (Brazier) Ward. He was a lifelong farmer and salesman for Moorman's Feeds until he retired in 1960. After retirement he sold real estate for a few years. They were members of St. John's Evangelical Lutheran Church and served on the Church Board for many years.

Elmer and Helen had four children: Everett (1930-1933), Marvin (Patricia Daubler), Donna Jean (Ivan Borchardt) and Judy (Richard Wilder).

Elmer died on September 7, 1983 and Helen who was born in 1912, died in September 2003 and they are both buried in the St. John's Evangelical Lutheran Cemetery, St. Clair.

NYQUIST, DEAN

My father, Dean Richard Nyquist (born in 1924), was the son of Elmo and Nona (Fields) Nyquist from St. Clair. They also have a daughter Jeanette (Stan Drake - see separate story). They lived in the big square house just across the road to the east of the Catholic Church. My great-grandmother, Isabelle Fields, lived with them. She and her husband John had raised their children, Sadie (James Lynch), Ada (John Bestman), Harry, May (H. E. Seewald) and Nona, in that same house. My grandfather owned a small acreage south and east of their farmstead. Many houses eventually sprung up along Highway 83 (Nyquist Addition today) on the land that they owned.

My grandmother took Jeanette to the Methodist Church in St. Clair, while my grandfather and my father, Dean Richard Nyquist, was born in 1924. His parents were Elmo and Nona (Fields) Dad went to church at the Lutheran Church. While going to school in St. Clair my Dad played the bass drum in the band. He told us more than once about the time that he tried out for the chorus, and the director told him that he was the worst singer he had ever heard!

It was in the late 1940's that my Dad swept my Mom off her feet when he gave her a ride on his Harley Davidson motorcycle. Dean Nyquist and Marjorie Timmerman, the daughter of Louie and Evelyn (Kollos) Timmerman, were married on September 27, 1948, at St. John's Lutheran Church, St. Clair. Dean and Marjorie lived at 506 Main Street East and had two daughters. Mary Lee, who is married to David Schenk, lives in Owatonna, MN. They have three children and four grandchildren. Judy Ann is married to Richard Winter, they live in rural Janesville and have three children and two grandchildren.

My mother and father lived in the small house across the street from Roy and Nadine Lewis for a few years. They then decided to move an old country school building into town, right next to Louis and Evelyn Timmerman, my maternal grandparents, and fix it up as their new home. My Dad and my Grandpa Timmerman both drove school buses for St. Clair School and they had a custom trucking business, hauling grain and gravel for farmers in the surrounding area, as well as peas, sweet corn and sugar beets.

Tragedy struck in 1957, when my mother passed away from cancer. I was 7 and my sister was 4 years old. My Dad was a bit lost for a few years. He continued to live next to my Grandparents, and they became the primary caregivers for my sister and I, as Dad continued to put in long hours away from home with the trucking business. As time went on he eventually sold the house to August and Lena Westphal, and moved back home with his parents. In 1966 he started working for the Blue Earth County Highway Department after my Grandpa Timmerman retired from trucking. He retired in 1987.

On November 23, 1966, Dean was married to Ruth (Lamont) Schwichtenberg, the widow of Paul Schwichtenberg (see separate story). They built a home in the Nyquist addition along Highway 83 on the south edge of St. Clair. They spent many happy years together, living in St Clair their entire married life, until 2001 when my Dad passed away suddenly at the age of seventy-two. Ruth worked for Dr. Niles Batdorf, M.D. in Mankato, MN, for many years.

Ruth & Dean Nyquist

My Dad was well known and respected in the community. He was an active member of St. John's Lutheran Church, where he served as an usher and church treasurer, and a member of the Church Council. He also spent many years on the volunteer St. Clair Fire Department, the city council, United Fund and a board member of St. John (Bestman) Cemetery in St. Clair. He enjoyed bowling, watching basketball, eating popcorn, going to dances, fishing, and anything that involved transportation: including trains, airplanes, trucks, cars, road graders and motorcycles. He enjoyed spending time with his family and being a part of life in his hometown.

Dean passed away in March 2001, and along with Marjorie, is buried in the St. John's Evangelical Lutheran Cemetery, St. Clair. Ruth is still living in St. Clair.

By Mary Nyquist Schenk

O'BRIEN, EVERAD J.

Everad J. O'Brien, the son of Walter and Elizabeth (Pestka) O'Brien, was born on November 11, 1903, in St. Clair. He married Lucile Conway, the daughter of Mr. and Mrs. John Conway. They had two daughters, Mary Lou (Robert Sahli) and Audrey (Richard Murphy). The family lived on the farm one half-mile east of St. Clair. Everad was Blue Earth County Agricultural inspector from 1959-1971. When he retired from farming they moved to St. Clair, living at 304 East Main Street.

After Lucille's death in 1962, Everad married Ragina

(Fitzgerald) Sandick. Her children were Robert, Ronald, Terrance and Valeria (Eugene Vogel).

Everad died in 1972 and they are buried in Immaculate Conception Catholic Cemetery.

O'CONNOR, PASCHAL J. "PAT"

Mankato Free Press - Former St. Clair Man Among Six Hunting Casualties. Paschal J. "Pat" O'Connor Fatally Injured as He Dresses Deer near Tenstrike, North of Bemidji. A former St. Clair resident was counted among six dead in Minnesota's three-day-old deer hunting season today.

Paschal J. "Pat" O'Connor, 37, who was born at St. Clair, was fatally shot Saturday a short distance from a roadside near Tenstrike, Minn., north of Bemidji. He lived about an hour after being shot, and was able to give a description of a man who ran away after firing the fatal bullet from a distance reported not more than 75 or 100 feet distant.

O'Connor, a veteran of World War II, in which he served with an army medical unit, told his brother, Fergus O'Connor that he was bending over dressing a deer when he was hit. Fergus, who was nearby, heard him yell as he was struck and ran to his aid. The injured hunter said he was able to turn around after being struck and told his brother that the man who fired the bullet was of stocky build. Other hunters reported they saw a man running away but were unaware of the accident at that time. Beltrami county authorities acting on O'Connor's description launched a search for the man who fired the fatal bullet.

The stricken hunter, who was struck just above the hip, with the bullet following an upward path through his body, told his brother that, from his medical experience in the war, he knew his injury would be fatal. A physician was called and O'Connor was treated at the scene of the shooting. He was conscious until his death.

O'Connor was clothed in red, his brother said, and was unable to explain why the fatal shot was fired, inasmuch as the other hunter was nearby and, he reported was not in a position to see the deer O'Connor was dressing without also seeing O'Connor.

Paschal O'Connor was a linotype operator for the *Free Press* while in the area and was superintendent of the shops at the Hamilton Manufacturing Company in Minneapolis. His parents were Mr. and Mrs. Arthur O'Connor of St. Clair.

O'CONNOR, PATRICK R.

Patrick O'Connor and family came to St. Clair, Minnesota in 1864. He was born in Sligo, Ireland. March 17, 1810. He learned the stone mason trade before departing for Albany, New York in 1838. The following year he married Margaret McDermott of Dublin, Ireland. In Albany he was first sergeant of the Emmett Guards and took part in the suppression of the anti-rent revolt in New York State and also served in the Mexican War of 1846 with them.

After the war the family moved to Chicago where Patrick, with his brother, was engaged in the building and masonry contracting business. He was associated with the Chicago Emmett Guards and served as their captain. He was often referred to as "Captain O'Connor" because of his military career.

In 1855 Mr. and Mrs. O'Connor moved to Wisconsin and started farming but when the Civil War broke out in 1861 he received a commission from the governor of Wisconsin and enlisted and organized a full company of 103 men and served with the Seventh Wisconsin Infantry under Gen. Grant. They took part in the battles of Pittsburg Landing and Corrinth.

He returned to Wisconsin after the war in 1863 and shortly afterwards moved to Winnebago Agency near St. Clair where he preempted a farm and lived the rest of his life about four miles southeast of St. Clair (now the home of Bernard and Myrtle Westphal). The brick house remained as a landmark for many years, testimony to his fine workmanship. He made the bricks right on the farm. Mr. and Mrs. O'Connor raised five sons and five daughters:

John who lived in the parental home and never married.

Charles married Susan Goodwin, a Canadian and had three sons and one daughter. Arthur was in the freighting

Homestead of Captain Patrick O'Connor (1810-1905) and Margaret (McDermott) O'Connor (1818-1904), located in McPherson Township

business in St. Clair. Charles, William E. and Laura Lang spent their younger days in St. Clair.

Alice married James Kelly, police officer at Mankato for many years. Once, while a special policeman he had charge of the Younger brothers after their capture following the Northfield robbery. They had five children, Laura Conway, Alice, Susan Fields, Clara and John.

Charlotte Autrey, wife of Isaac Autrey who was a scout friend of Buffalo Bill. They had ten children: James, Charles, John, Thomas, Paul, Felix, Alice Petit, Mollie Fox, Rella Bohan and Lauretta Maloney.

Thomas married Mary Ann Sheeran. They had two children: George and Margaret. Mary Ann died in 1897 and later Thomas married Martha Tracey. They had Laura O'Connor Whetstone. Thomas farmed and taught school in Redwood County. Margaret O'Connor McGinn, who taught school in St. Clair in 1917 and later moved to Canada, often spoke of the kindness of her grandparents and uncles and aunts. They always welcomed her to their homes after her mother Mary Ann died in 1897 and later when her father Thomas passed away.

Edward married Emma Laflin and two boys Edward and Charles were born to them.

Francis – unmarried.

Margaret Jane married Steve Murphy and they had two girls. Catherine Gallagher who lived at Janesville and Eleanor Joyce, mother of Roderick, Joe, Bernard and Sabinus who all lived on the farm at Janesville as young boys.

Agnes married Stephen Murphy and they lived at Eagle Lake for many years. The children Eulalia taught school in Minneapolis for a long time and Francis drove a school bus into the city from Lake Minnetonka. Francis lives in St. Paul and still drives around the city.

Jennie married Joe Pettit and they had one girl, Lurene, who died accidentally in 1905. Patrick reached the age of 95 and passed away about a year after Margaret. They are both buried at the Catholic Cemetery in St. Clair.

By Aimee McGinn Karst

CHARLES O'CONNOR

Charles O'Connor suggested the town be named St. Clair in 1886

The family represented by this well-known citizen of St. Clair traces its lineage to Ireland, where many successive generations lived and labored. It was not until near the middle of the nineteenth century that this branch of the family established a home in the United States. The original immigrant having been Patrick O'Connor, a native of Sligo, Ireland, and a man of versatile ability and unquestioned loyalty to the country of his adoption. To him belongs the distinction of having been the first man to sign as a volunteer for the Mexican War. When he crossed the Atlantic to the New World in 1838 his wife, who bore the maiden name of Margaret McDermott and was a native of Dublin, accompanied him. After they had established a home in Albany, New York, there was born to them a son Charles, December 10, 1843. The family left Albany in 1847 and journeyed to Chicago in the primitive fashion preceding the introduction of railways. For nine years they remained in Chicago, where the son attended school and where it was his privilege to study in the famous university, St. Mary's of the Lake.

A later place of residence was at Fond du Lac, Wisconsin, where the family made their home for nine years. From there they came to Minnesota in 1864 and settled in Blue Earth County, where they pre-empted a claim of one hundred and sixty acres. Both in Wisconsin, where he had secured government land, and subsequently in Minnesota, the father conducted general farming and earned a livelihood by tilling the soil. His last years were passed in retirement from agricultural cares and he passed away at St. Clair in 1905 one year after the demise of his devoted wife. Among the pioneers of his part of the county he is remembered as a farmer of ability, a kindhearted neighbor, generous to all in need, and solicitous to promote the welfare of his community. It was by his suggestion that the name of Hilton was changed to St. Clair.

The marriage of Charles O'Connor was solemnized in January of 1874 and united him with Miss Susan Goodwin, a native of Canada. Three sons and one daughter blessed their union. Arthur who was engaged in the freighting business, Charles, William E. and Laura. The family was faithful members of the Roman Catholic Church and contributed generously to religious movements under charge of that denomination. In politics Mr. O'Connor has been a believer in Democratic principles all of his life, and has voted that ticket ever since attaining his majority. For eight years he held the office of postmaster of St. Clair, to which office he was appointed upon the solicitation of prominent members of his part. For twenty years he has officiated in the capacity of town clerk and for a quarter of a century he has been justice of the peace. His qualifications for the latter office, as indeed for all positions held by him, are increased by his knowledge of the law, which he studied in early manhood for a considerable period, thus familiarizing himself with jurisprudence to a degree very useful to him in subsequent affairs. As an attorney his counsel often has been sought by the people of the village and surrounding country and his advice upon disputed legal points is considered authoritative by his clients. As a citizen he has shown a constant interest in all measures for the up building of the town and has contributed of time and influence to aid important projects.

From *History of Blue Earth County*-1909

O'CONNOR, FRANCIS - 1909

An inquiring mind, constant progression and well-applied industry are responsible for the success of Francis O'Connor, who with his brother, Charles O'Connor, farmed the old O'Connor homestead. Francis O'Connor was the son of Patrick and Margaret McDermott O'Connor, the former of whom died April 9, 1905, in St. Clair, and the later died January 24, 1904.

Mr. O'Connor was educated in the public schools, and has had the average advantages of the country-reared youth. He is a natural farmer, interested in his work, and a believer in its dignity and usefulness. Politically he was a Democrat, but aside from the normality of casting his vote; he was not interested in local political undertakings. In religion he was a Roman Catholic. Mr. O'Connor enjoyed an enviable reputation in his township, and is a promoter of all that tends to the greater enlightenment and happiness of the community in which he lives.

OLSON, FREDERICK J.

In August of 1955, Frederick J. "Fritz" (1914-1986) and Mildred (1912-2001) Olson and their four children moved from Mankato to St. Clair (201 Front Street West), where Fritz began his duties as depot agent for the Chicago, Milwaukee, St. Paul and Pacific Railroad, familiarly known as the Milwaukee Road. He had previously served as depot agent in Albert Lea and Good Thunder, then worked at the interlocking plant (known as "the tower"), located behind Hubbard Milling in downtown Mankato. The tower was where switches were pulled to change the tracks to accommodate trains entering and leaving the yard in Mankato.

Fritz was a member of the Order of Railroad Telegraphers. In 1955 the telegraph was still sometimes used to communicate between stations on the railroad line, but shortly thereafter agents relied almost completely on the telephone.

In September of 1955, Mildred began teaching 2nd grade in the St. Clair public school, where their three oldest children were enrolled: Karen in 8th grade, Howard in 6th grade, and Jean in 4th grade. Mildred taught 2nd grade for several years, transferring to 1st grade when the new elementary school addition was completed in 1960.

The youngest Olson child, Steve, who was not yet three, went with Fritz to the depot every day, and thus became acquainted at an early age with the St. Clair people who did business with the railroad.

In the 1950's and 60's, when products were still largely shipped by railroad, trains came through St. Clair every Tuesday and Friday, perhaps more often during harvest season when grain was carried by train. The duties of a depot agent were to fill out bills of lading, make a daily yard check of the cars that were waiting to be unloaded or transferred elsewhere, notify businesses or individuals that whatever they had ordered had arrived on the train, and other miscellaneous details of paperwork.

A typical depot consisted of three main sections. The office contained telephone, telegraph, typewriter, and other usual office equipment and supplies. The waiting room was where passengers would wait for their train to arrive, but since the Milwaukee Road no longer carried passengers by the late 50's, the room was just a big space, empty of everything except a few benches and a pot-bellied stove. The freight house was the largest section of the depot, where freight was stored until the recipient came to pick it up.

The Olsons lived in a house previously owned by Alma Hubmer and located just across the street to the west of the school. From the home's backyard it was less than a block to the depot. Fritz and Mildred bought the house for $10,000. Some of the neighbors on the block were Aloysius Jongbloedt, Sarah Meany, Mr. and Mrs. Ted Penn, and Paul and Ruth Schwichtenberg and their three sons.

Besides working as depot agent, Fritz played trumpet in several bands. At various times he was a member of

Norm Wilke's Little Fisherman, Ernie Coopman's Jolly Brewers, and the Elks Band in Mankato. The Elks Band used to present a concert every Wednesday evening in the summer, at the old band shell in Sibley Park. Fritz, as a member of the American Legion Post in St. Clair, also played Taps every Memorial Day at area cemeteries.

Fritz was a member of the United States Army throughout his adult life. His active duty was spent at the Naval School of Music in Washington, D.C. He was in both the National Guard and the Army Reserves. During the strike at the Wilson meatpacking plant in Albert Lea in the late 1950's, his National Guard unit was called to help maintain order. Each summer he spent two weeks at either Camp Ripley, Minnesota, or Camp McCoy, Wisconsin. Fritz attained the rank of Master Sergeant.

Fritz had a heart attack in 1974 at age 60. Shortly thereafter he retired from the railroad and moved to Bonita Springs, Florida, where he remained until his death from a second heart attack on July 13, 1986.

Mildred's teaching career began in rural schools in the early 1930's, after two years of Normal Training in Austin, Minnesota. Her first few teaching jobs were in rural schools in the Austin-Albert Lea area. Her first teaching job paid $50 a month. In the late 40's and early 50's she taught in the rural school at Vernon Center, Minnesota, where her duties included not only teaching students in six grades, but also doing such janitorial duties as starting the fire in the schoolroom stove each morning. If the roads were bad after a snowstorm, she was the one to decide whether or not to call off school for the day. She often told of driving the car with one side on the shoulder for traction when the roads were slippery.

In 1951 she taught at Bear Creek (Mower County) rural school, and when the Olsons moved to Mankato in 1952, she worked as a substitute teacher in the Mankato Public Schools, most often at Union School on North Broad Street. Mildred retired from teaching in 1977 after 33 years of teaching. The next year she moved into an apartment in the new building at the east edge of St. Clair, where she lived until 1999. In February of that year she moved to the Mankato Lutheran Home. She died there in 2001, just short of her 89th birthday. Fritz and Mildred are both buried at St. John (Bestman) Cemetery in St. Clair.

The four children of Fritz and Mildred all live in southern Minnesota. Karen and her husband, Vern Ferch, live in Waseca. Howard married Beverly Blank, also from St. Clair, and they live in Byron. Jean lives in Arlington and is a retired teacher. Steve and his wife, Cindy (Parkins) also from St. Clair, still reside in St. Clair.

By Jean Olson

Ruth & Orlando Olson

OLSON, ORLANDO

Orlando Olson married Ruth Bartsch on October 14, 1947. They moved to the Schwanke farm, located on County Road 15 about one mile east of St. Clair, on November 1, 1952.

Orlando served aboard the USS Clemson destroyer from 1942 to 1946 and was also on the underwater demolition team, which destroyed coral reefs so that other ships holding soldiers could dock on the islands. He was stationed in the Panama Canal and many South Pacific Islands.

He was honored upon discharge with the Presidential Unit Citation with one bronze star, Philippine Liberation medal with two bronze stars, American Theater medal with one bronze star, European African medal with two bronze stars, Asiatic Pacific medal with four bronze stars and the Good Conduct medal.

Orlando graduated from high school and went on to attend four years of Agricultural College. He was employed at the Continental Can Company, Mankato, for 30 years and he also farmed.

Ruth graduated from Mankato High School and prior to marriage she did secretarial work at the Hubbard Milling Company, Mankato. She was then employed by Mankato State University and in 1971 transferred to the Drivers License Division. In 1976 she transferred to the State Highway Patrol District Office in Mankato where she was employed for 25 years.

Ruth and Orlando had four children: Orlando Jr. (Lenny), Diane, Judy and Terry.

Lenny Olson has a Master's Degree in education and is employed by the St. Clair Public School. Donna (Sieberg) is a nurse at the School Sisters of Notre Dame, Mankato. Their children both graduated from St. Clair

The Orlando Olson, Sr. family in 1997
L to R: Judy, Diane, Ruth, Orlando,
Orlando Jr. (Lenny) and Terry

Public School and are attending Minnesota State University, Mankato. Jennifer is a senior and Joshua is a sophomore.

Diane Olson married Jerry Schwartz and they own a resort in Northern Minnesota and Jerry is also a State land-surveying engineer. They have three children Greg, Brian and Jen. Greg is also a land — surveyor and his wife Diane is a registered nurse in Rochester, Minnesota. They have two children Trevor and McKayla. Brian is an international business and economics professor in Beijing, China. Jen is a junior at Hillsdale College in Hillsdale, Michigan.

Judy Olson is supervisor of the Advising Center of Students at Minnesota State University. Her husband James Passer owns Buck's Motors in Mankato, Minnesota.

Terry Olson is a chiropractor and owns Olson Family Chiropractic in Eagle Lake, Minnesota. His wife, Terese (Sontag), is also a chiropractor and is employed at Immanuel-St. Joseph's Hospital, Mankato, as a medical technologist. They have two children. Kelsey is in fifth grade and Nick is in the second grade.

Orlando and Ruth were seasoned travelers who have been to all of the fifty states, and have had many memorable vacations. Just a few places they have traveled to include Michigan's Upper Peninsula and Mackinaw Island, Alaska and Mt. McKinley, Eskimo Olympic and Arctic Circle, Denali National Park, Jasper National Park in Canada and Glacier National Park. Ruth has also been to Puerto Rico, New Zealand and Australia.

Orlando and Ruth moved to St. Clair in August of 1990 after living in the country for almost 43 years. Orlando passed away July 24, 1998. Their son Lenny took over the family farm and converted the farmland to CRP acres.

By Ruth Olson

The Charles Pagenkopf family

L to R: Earl and Abbie Pagenkopf with Ernie Hager

PAGENKOPF, CHARLES

Charles J. Pagenkopf was a pioneer St. Clair merchant. He was born in Watertown, Wisconsin, on December 5, 1856. He came to Minnesota with his parents when still a boy and settled on a Medo township farm where he grew to manhood. In 1878 he married Mary Krueger. Mary was born on a ship in the Atlantic Ocean when her parents crossed from Germany. In 1897, he entered the general mercantile business at St. Clair. He retired in 1932.

The children were sons Walter C. (Belle Wingen), Carl (Lillian Rusch) and Earl (Abbie Thielman) and the daughters were Rosa (Ed Guyer), Sophie, and Lucille (Pat Dooley).

Charles died on April 16, 1937 and Mary on October 26, 1938. They are buried in the St. John (Bestman) Cemetery, St. Clair.

Earl Pagenkopf was born on February 23, 1896, and grew up in St. Clair. He took over the Pagenkopf Grocery Store in St. Clair from his parents. On June 9, 1923, he was married to Abbie Thielman, the daughter of Henry and Jessie (Rasdall) Thielman. Abbie attended school in St. Clair and graduated from the Mankato High School and Mankato Normal School. She taught in St. Clair for one year and then worked at the St. Clair State Bank for five years. After they purchased the Pagenkopf store in 1932, she assisted her husband at the store until 1958, at which time they sold the store to their son Lowell and his wife Joan (see separate story). They also had a daughter Donna who married Jess Kunkel and their children are Kathleen and Scott. At the time of her death she was the last charter member of the America Legion Auxiliary in St. Clair. Abbie was a member of the Mapleton Eastern Star Lodge. Earl and Abbie lived at 213 Main Street East.

Earl died in 1956 and Abbie died on April 14, 1986,

Lowell Earl Pagenkopf was born on April 10, 1930. He graduated from St. Clair High School and in 1951 entered military service in the U.S. Air Force. On September 10, 1951 Lowell married Margaret Joan Froehlich the daughter of Oscar and Edna (Bollman) Froehlich. Joan also graduated from St. Clair High School. Upon his honorable discharge from the U.S. Air Force in 1953, Lowell returned home and farmed the family land. He later purchased the family grocery store, making him the third generation proprietor. For 30 years, Lowell and Joan operated Pagenkopf's Grocery (Peg's) in St. Clair until their retirement in 1996 when they moved to Reed's Lake in rural Elysian.

Joan & Lowell Pagenkopf

Lowell and Joan were members of St. John's Evangelical Lutheran Church where Joan played the organ for many years. Lowell was a member of St. Clair American Legion Post #475 (48 Years), and the St. Clair Volunteer Fire Department (42 Years), serving many years as Fire Chief. Lowell and Joan were active, devoted member of the St. Clair community, volunteering there time to many organizations over the years.

Lowell and Joan have one daughter Rebecca (Becky) who married Tom Thompson, the son of Donald and Dorothy Thompson. Becky and Tom both graduated from St. Clair High School and both work in Mankato, Minnesota. They have two sons, Slade who lives in St. Paul and Blake lives in Mankato, Minnesota.

Lowell died on February 8, 2005, and is buried in the St. John's Evangelical Lutheran Cemetery.

By Joan Pagenkopf

PALMER, FLOYD

Palmer Bus Service, Inc.

It was August 1974 when St. Clair School District #75 was considering the sale of their school buses. Floyd Palmer learned of this information through a Blue Bird salesman named Marley Kittleson and a brother-in-law Kenneth Lenz. The sale would consist of eleven school buses, one van, and three acres of land with a steel building. The asking price was $81,500 and the contract included eight routes, one special education route and all the extra curricular trips.

Harold Walton was superintendent at the time. The school board consisted of Marvin Preston, Marcella Glamm, Glen Schostag, Stan Hall, Dale Sargent and Lawrence Ireland. During negotiations, when we were at somewhat of a standstill I told the board, "If you sell me the buses I will be like the old oak tree, I will be here forever." The turning point seemed to come after that statement because it was then that I was sold the buses.

Speaking for my family and myself we would like to make a personal statement. The Palmer family will forever be grateful to the superintendent and the school board of 1974 for selling us the buses. We have been in business in St. Clair for the past thirty years and we will continue like the old oak tree. Lois and I raised our family in St. Clair with Hollie (Rick Johnson) graduating in 1987, our daughter Leah dying in 1985, our daughter Jenna (Corey Fromm) in 1995, and our daughter Amber in 2001. Lois was the daughter of Alvin and Dorothy (Schweim) Maurer.

Here is a little history on Palmer Bus Service, Inc. today. We now operate in sixteen school districts within Minnesota and Wisconsin and we have Palmer Charter Services in Little Falls and North Mankato. In St. Clair today we operate seven bus routes and preschool and special education routes. Totally the bus-company consists of 375 school buses and fourteen charter coaches.

On a personal note, St. Clair will always be in my heart because they gave me my start. I thank God every day for the opportunity they gave a young kid and his family

By Floyd D. Palmer

PENN, WILLIAM

Karl Fredirk Wilhelm "William" Penn (1860-1929) was the son of Gottlieb and Wilhelmina (Ruda) Penn. On July 3, 1890, he married Marie Frank (1871-1933) who was the daughter of Christoph and Wilhelmine Frank. They were farmers north east of St. Clair in Sec. 4. Their children were an infant son, Theodore, Herman and George.

Wilhelm and Marie are buried in St. John's Evangelical Lutheran Cemetery, St. Clair.

Theodore G. Penn was born in 1891 and grew up in St. Clair, Minnesota. Ted was employed by the St. Clair State Bank and the Blue Earth County Farm Bureau. He married the former Ida Godeman (1884), the daughter of Fred and Marie Godemann on November 10, 1923. They lived at 205 Front Street West. He died in 1967 and Ida in 1983.

Theodore and Ida are buried in St. John's Evangelical Lutheran Cemetery, St. Clair.

Herman Penn (1893-1951) married Alvina Boettcher (1900-1987), the daughter of Herman and Louise (Mueller) Boettcher. Herman took over the family farm. They had two children William and Mary.

Herman built a new house in St. Clair on 331 Main Street West and the family moved to town. Herman continued to operate the farm as well as raising sheep in the pasture across the street in town. (This was in the area of where the sewer-plant road - and the Kopke, Sodeman, Baer houses later were built.) In 1951 Herman became suddenly ill.

Herman and Alvina are buried in St. John's Evangelical Lutheran Cemetery, St. Clair.

Mankato Free Press–1951 - A St. Clair Man, the victim of polio, died early this morning, October 8, in Minneapolis.

Herman Penn, 57, became ill Thursday afternoon. When his brother, Dr. George Penn of Mankato, visited him that day, Herman told him of his sickness. Dr. Penn brought him to Immanuel Hospital that night. On Friday a consultation of several physicians was held. The illness was diagnosed as polio. Herman Penn was sent to the Kenny Institute in Minneapolis that night.

Mr. Penn died at 12:45 a.m. today as a result of the disease.

After Herman's death, Alvina who was a registered nurse, rented out the farm to Elmo Nyquist, Henry Linde and possible others. She later sold the farm to a Mr. Howley from the Good Thunder area. In 1957 Alvina took her children William (1938-2004) and Mary and moved to Swiss Street in Mankato.

Alvina died in 1987 in Colorado. William married a girl he met while going to high school in Mankato, packed up the car and headed for Colorado. He was a chronic asthma patient and the air was much more tolerable their. William Penn died on November 23, 2004, in Loveland, CO.

Dr. George Penn graduated from St. Clair High School, Carlton College, and the University of Minnesota Medical School. He completed his internship and residency at Browdlawns Hospital, Des Moines, Iowa, from 1932-1934. Dr. Penn practiced obstetrics/gynecology in Mankato from 1934-1972. He delivered over 8,000 babies. At the time of his retirement he was on his second generation of patients-babies, who grew up, married, and like their parents, became his patients. He received only $5 for the first 20 deliveries he performed. It is noted that Dr. Penn never sent out a bill. He expected patients to find out what they owed and pay it on their own. He felt people were basically honest and believed in a maxim by Benjamin Franklin: Keep your shop – and your shop will keep you.

Since there was no pediatrician in town when Dr. Penn arrived, he studied pediatrics as a hobby, then offered the service to his patients.

He married LuVern Steinke in 1934 and they had two children, Carolyn and John (Jack). LuVern died in 1965. Carolyn married David Maki, lives in Edina and has two sons, Jason and John. Jack and his wife Nancy live in St. Peter and have two daughters, Lindsey and Emily. In 1968 Dr. Penn married Bess Ellison who died in 1995.

Many Mankato State University alumni remember Dr. George Penn as he demonstrated his support of the School of Nursing in many ways. In the early years of the School of Nursing, he lectured in the nursing courses. He taught nursing students in the maternal-child clinical experiences. In later years he supported the school through the endowed scholarship fund in memory of LuVern Penn and Bess Ellison Penn. The School of Nursing was very fortunate to have this scholarship continuing as a living legacy of the Penn family's support to nursing students today and tomorrow and of continued excellence in nursing education.

PHELPS, SILAS

Silas Phelps was the son of Ephraim and Sallie (Spike) Phelps. He was born in New York State. He moved to Monroe County, Michigan, where he married Jane Candee, the daughter of Asa and Mary (McAlpine) Candee. Their children were Mary, Erica, Oddo, Emily,

Asa, Daniel, Amy and Ephraim. They first came to Minnesota in 1855 and settled in Saratoga Township in Winona County. They came to Blue Earth County about 1865 and lived in McPherson Township. The family, except Oddo, moved to Ottertail County in 1878. Oddo married Maria Alexander, the daughter of Joseph and Mary (Myott) Alexander. Their children were Louisa, Silas, Luella, John, Francis, Charlotte, Claud, Myron, Byron, Glenn, Ruth and Hollie. They lived in McPherson, Mankato, Decoria, and Lyra Townships.

PHILLIPS, EUGENE

Eugene Phillips was born on May 19, 1910, in McPherson Township to Harry and Lucy (Hodapp) Phillips. On September 1, 1931, he married Elsie Hager in Madison Lake, Minnesota. They farmed until 1950 and he was the manager of the St. Clair Municipal Liquor Store for 25 years, retiring in 1975. He also was clerk of the City of St. Clair for many years. They were members of the Immaculate Conception Parish in St. Clair where he served as secretary-treasurer and sexton for the church cemetery. He was also a member of the St. Clair Fire Department. Elsie was the church organist for 35 years and a cook at the St. Clair School. They lived at 401 Main Street West.

Eugene and Elsie had five children, Clarice (John Germo), Mary (Pete Wolff), Carol (William Webb), Audrey (Don Varpness) and Paul "Pete" (Joanne O'Herin).

Eugene died on June 19, 1988 and Elsie died on November 29, 1977. They are buried in the Immaculate Conception Catholic Cemetery, St. Clair.

PHILLIPS, NICHOLAS

Nicholas Phillips, son of Anthony and Anna Phillips was born on February 22, 1861 in Danville Township. He married Mary Wingen (1862-1934) on February 14, 1882. She was the daughter of Jacob and Sophia (Dorweiler) Wingen. Their children were Harry, Paul and Savallah (David Steel).

Nicholas Phillips was one of the splendid types of rugged pioneers who are so surely one by one passing on to their eternal rest. He was honest and upright in word and deed, hard working, home loving and always thoughtful of his family's welfare. He leaves behind him the record of a stainless character and a life full of honest endeavor, which is the highest tribute that can be paid to any man. He was taken very seriously ill on Saturday, March 13, 1926, and removed to St. Joseph's Hospital in Mankato on Sunday afternoon. An operation was performed on Sunday evening in the hopes of saving his life. In spite of all that medical skill and good nursing could do he passed into the Great Beyond on Tuesday morning, March 16, 1926.

Paul Phillips was born in McPherson Township in 1885 to the late Nicholas and Mary (Wingen) Phillips. He was an esteemed citizen in his community and at the time of his death held the position of town clerk. He served as manager of the St. Clair co-operative creamery. He was a very industrious worker and his farm was always kept in the best of condition. He was a resident of McPherson Township all his life and died in April 1929 of pneumonia after only a few days illness.

Paul was married to Elise Gerlach of Good Thunder who for a number of years taught in the Mapleton Public School. Paul is buried at the Glenwood Cemetery.

PHILLIPS, NORMAN

Norman H. Phillips, the son of Henry and Arline (Menton) Phillips, was born on March 24, 1940, in Mankato, MN. He graduated from St. Clair High School. On June 3, 1961, he married Sandra Lee Nolan in Mankato. They lived in Mankato until 1967, when they moved to rural St. Clair. He worked at Continental Can in Mankato for many years and farmed in the St. Clair area. After retirement they moved into Mankato. He was a member of St. John's Lutheran Church and enjoyed fishing, camping and playing cards. Sandra worked at Goldfines until the store closed, then at the Janesville Nursing Home, sold Avon Products and later worked in the kitchen at the St. Clair School.

Norman and Sandra had four children, Brenda Lee (Tim Phillips), Debbie (Jeff Schweim), Cindi (Darrin Groskreutz) and Todd. He had one sister Judy (Harlan Witt).

Sandi & Norman Phillips

Norman died on January 2, 2002, and is buried in the St. John's Evangelical Lutheran Cemetery, St. Clair.

PINT, JACK

Jack Pint was the owner and operator of the Allis Chalmers/Chevrolet/G E Appliance Store for many years. He was the brother of Johanna (Mrs. Arthur Winkelman). He was married to Edna Appel, the daughter of Conrad and Anna (Schwartz) Appel. Edna was born

Pint's Garage. Located on the corner across from the UpTown Tavern.

on July 12, 1902, in Springfield, Minnesota. She worked at the Brett's Department Store in Mankato and was the secretary for the family business. They lived at 301 Main Street West.

Jack died in 1958 and Edna on May 6, 1999. They are buried in Springfield, Minnesota.

PITCHER, ORRIN

Orrin Pitcher was born in 1776 in Norwich, Massachusetts. He moved to the wilds of upstate New York in 1807. In 1813 he began clearing land and building a cabin in the area that became Ellicottville, New York. (He is credited with having founded that town.) He died in 1867 in Iowa. He married Miranda Woodruff, born in 1790 in Litchfield, Connecticut, to one of the oldest families in Connecticut. (Her ancestor, Matthew Woodruff, had settled in the area that became Farmington, Connecticut in the 1630/1640s.) Miranda died in Iowa in 1878. Their daughter Lydia was the wife of Abel Rasdall, parents of Duane, Melvin and Hubert, early settlers in McPherson Township. Lydia later married Henry Foster.

PRESCHER, ROBERT

Robert Prescher, the son of Julius and Ernestine (Pockrandt) Prescher, was one of thirteen children. He grew up in the Mapleton area married Lorrie Neubert. They came to St. Clair in 1968 and he was the manager of the lumberyard. In 1978 they built at new home at 505 Main Street East. When the St. Clair Lumber Yard closed, he continued working for the Pemberton Lumber Company in Pemberton. While in St. Clair he served for six years on the village council and was the church treasurer of St. John's Evangelical Lutheran Church. They have two daughters who attended school in St. Clair, Julie and Lisa. Robert served for three years on the University of Minnesota-Waseca Vocational Technical College Advisory Board for building trades. He started Maple Edge Building Center in Mapleton having the Grand Opening on November 20, 1976. Robert has now retired.

PRESTON, ASAHEL

Asahel Brewster Preston came to Blue Earth County in the spring of 1864 taking up land in McPherson Township that had been a part of the Winnebago Indian Reservation which the U.S. Government was selling as the Indians were being moved from the Reservation to Nebraska and South Dakota.

Asahel Preston's parents were Samuel and Elizabeth Preston, who had lived in South Hadley, Mass. and moved to Bureau Co., Illinois, in 1835 via the Great Lakes landing in Chicago and going on to Princeton, Illinois. Asahel was born August 25, 1835, in Princeton. He was the youngest of eleven children and the only one coming to live in Blue Earth County. They moved to Caroll Co., Illinois, when he was a year old and he grew to manhood there.

He married Hannah Jarman in Winona County, Minnesota, on December 21, 1859, and they celebrated their 65th wedding anniversary in 1924 having lived on their original homestead for 60 years. They had five children namely Mary, George, Samuel, Howard, and Maude. He died May 1, 1925, and is buried in the Medo-McPherson Cemetery. Asahel was always proud that he had voted for Abraham Lincoln in 1860 and 1864. He became a staunch prohibitionist and always voted that ticket though his was the lone such vote in that precinct. He was a Bible student and had family worship morning and night for 50 years.

Asahel purchased 160 acres from the U.S. Government in 1866 at $10 to $15 per acre. This became a century farm in 1966. During those one hundred years, the farm has been owned and lived on by Asahel, George, Clark, and Delmar Preston and at the present time is farmed by Asahel's great-great grandson Scott Preston.

Asahel's wife Hannah lived her last days at her daughter's in Denver, Colorado. She died July 7, 1935.

Their Children: **Mary**, the first born, died at the age of 18 from diphtheria, George, Samuel, Howard and Maude.

George Preston married Mary Fox in 1886 and they had a son Arthur who was born in 1887 (his mother Mary died two weeks later. Arthur married Tillie Beck and their children were Evelyn Yackley and William Preston.

After the death of his first wife, George married Carrie Stroebel in 1891. Their children are

Clark Howard Preston married Lillie Frey, their children - Delmar, Delores, and Donnave Bartsch.

Ralph George Preston married Nora Albrecht, their children - Glenn, Earl, Marvin and LaVerne.

Grace Elizabeth Preston taught school in Minnesota and Oregon then lived in Mapleton, Minnesota.

Maude Charlotte Preston married Gustave Wolff.

John Sidney Preston, Sr. married Hazel Danner, their children - Gerald, Dale, Lila Mae, and John Jr.

Samuel Merritt Preston married Rosella McMahan their children - Sharon and Robert.

Harold Mark Preston married Verna Buecksler - daughter Janet (lived at 329 Main East Street).

Chester Asahel Preston married Dorothy DeRemer- daughter: Darlene Simpson.

Samuel married Susie St. John their children - Leslie, and Guy. They moved to Alexandria, Minnesota

Howard married Mary McCarthy their children - Leona Escott and Derward. They moved to Montana.

Maude married Merritt Babcock - moved to Denver, Colorado. They had a foster son, Alvin Hilks.

Many of the Prestons who are deceased are buried in the Medo-McPherson Cemetery in Blue Earth County, Minnesota.

By Grace Preston

PRESTON, MARVIN

Marvin Preston was born on July 4, 1930, in McPherson Township and was the son of Ralph and Eleanore (Albrecht) Preston. He attended the Medo School and graduated from the Pemberton High School. He then attended Dunwoody Institute in the Twin Cities. He was married to Patricia Rahbeck, the daughter of John and Pearl (Brubaken), on February 23, 1952, in Mapleton, MN. They farmed in McPherson Township, on the former Winnebago Agency homestead. When the Agency House had deteriorated to the point of "no hope," they built a new home at 509 Main Street East. He was forced into retirement in 1987 due to failing health. He died on February 6, 1988, and is buried in the St. John's Evangelical Lutheran Cemetery, St. Clair. He was a member of the St. Clair School Board from 1960 until 1975, and a member of the St. Clair Boosters Club. They were members of the St. John's Evangelical Lutheran Church.

Patricia graduated from the Mapleton High School in 1951 and then attended the Mankato Commercial College, Mankato, MN. After her marriage she was a homemaker and they raised five sons. Gary (7-8-1953), Joel (10-14-1955), twins John (5-15-1957) and James (5-15-1957), and Peter (April 30, 1959). John took over the family farming operation and Peter (Joan Danberry) and their children Daniel, Jacob and Alicia are living in the new home they built on the Winnebago Agency Site. Joel is married to Phyllis Jongbloedt and they are living in St. Clair.

The Peter and Joan Preston family
L to R: Joan, Alica, Jacob and Daniel, Standing: Peter

After Marvin's death Pat worked at the YMCA in Mankato for seven years. On February 16, 1991, she married James Keller (1933-2000) of Mapleton, Minnesota. They lived on the Keller Farm just south of Mapleton until his sudden death. Pat is now living in Mankato.

PURDY, DANIEL

Daniel Purdy was born in Hardin County, Ohio, in 1843. When he was ten years old he went with his parents to Black Hawk County, Iowa. After a residence of three years they moved to Blue Earth County, Minnesota In 1875 he settled in his new home in McPherson

Township, Section 13. On June 21, 1870, he married Miss E. Owen who borne him four children: Walter L., Dana L., Winfred L., and Addie L.

QUINN, ANDY

Andy M. Quinn was born in 1866, the son of James and Hannah Quinn who were early pioneers in Medo Township. He married Kathryn McComb (1866-1959) the daughter of John and Agnes McComb of Medo Town. They moved to St. Clair, living at 212 Main Street East, after their marriage and for many years Andy owned and operated a well digging machine. After he sold that he went into the oil business, "Quinn Oil Company," in St. Clair. When he died in January 1947 his wife, one brother James (Sarah Annis), and sisters Eliza McWhorter, Jennie (Thomas McGovern), Mrs. John Jenkins and Mrs. William Smith survived him.

Andy and Kathryn are buried in Medo-McPherson Cemetery.

By Mary McComb

This organ belonged to Kathryn Quinn.
It was donated to the Blue Earth Historical Society by her grand-niece Mary McComb.

Quinn Oil Company, 1931

L to R: Betty Cords and Kathryn Quinn in the late 1920s

L to R: Kathryn Quinn, Capitola McComb, Betty Cords (baby) and Mrs. Jesse Macbeth, 1925

RASDALL, ROBERT

Robert Rasdall was born in 1779 in either Virginia or Kentucky. His father was William Ragsdale, but Robert at some point changed his surname to "Rasdall." The great majority of people who bear that surname today are descended from Robert Rasdall. Robert married Elizabeth Wright (b. in South Carolina in 1784.) They raised their nine children in Warren County, Kentucky, and died there (Robert in 1849 and Elizabeth in 1858). They were small farmers and owned slaves. (The conflict between their strong Southern heritage and their son Abel's strong Union leanings are reflected in the fact that Robert's grandson, Melvin, named his sons "Lee" and "Grant".) Robert's ancestor, Godfrey Ragsdale, was the only survivor of the Poechancanough massacre at Jamestown in 1644. (His mother hid the infant Godfrey and the Powhatans failed to find him: he was found on the next day by his aunt and uncle, who adopted him and made him their heir.)

Abel Rasdall's story is worthy of a biography or a film. Born August 15, 1803 in Barren County, Kentucky (the oldest of 9 children of Robert Rasdall and Elizabeth Wright), he is — according to family myth — supposed to have come from a family that tracked with Daniel Boone. Certainly Abel became the classic "mountain man;" after serving in the Black Hawk War, he became a trapper and fur trader. In fact, his first two wives were Native Americans and he had children with both. There is no record of the fate of either wife or children. Abel moved into the Wisconsin territory around 1832. He became the first white settler of the area. After other European families settled the area, there were references to the fact that Abel lived in "a tent" by a lake many miles outside of town. He came into town occasionally to barter with the settlers. He became a cabin builder in Wisconsin while still the wigwam and trail were pre-dominating features of the landscape. However, by 1838 he seems to have decided to join the European settlement, and soon moved into town and built himself a frame house (which may have served as the first tavern to Madison). He built the first lodge house in Madison, thus becoming the unconscious civic father of the now flourishing metropolis. In this house his son Melvin B. Rasdall was born on November 13, 1848. He also erected the City Hotel of Madison, in 1849 and he built the gristmill twelve miles north of the village. He married Lydia Pitcher on May 24, 1845, in Madison, Dane County, Wisconsin. Lydia's father, Orrin Pitcher, had also been a frontiersman of sorts, so perhaps Abel's way of life didn't daunt her – but it's fascinating to think of a New York-born woman moving to the wilds of Wisconsin and marrying a frontiersman 21 years her senior. Two children came along (Duane and Melvin), and then tragedy befell the family. Abel was killed in an accident at his sawmill on June 6, 1855, before the birth of his third son Hubert. He is buried in Burke Township, Dane County, Wisconsin. The next record of the family appears in the Wisconsin Supreme Court case of Rasdall vs. Rasdall, in which it is revealed that before Abel married, he got involved in a scrape in which he shot a man and thought he'd have to flee to Canada. He signed over title on all his property to his younger brother William Rasdall. When the scrape blew over and Abel realized he could remain in Madison, he failed to take back his title. This legal technicality didn't cause trouble until Abel's death, when apparently William claimed ownership of all Abel's property, leaving Lydia and the children destitute. The Supreme Court had to consider the issue, and decided that legally they could not force William to give the property back to Abel's widow (although the Court exhorted William to listen to his conscience and do the right thing by his brother's family). There is no record of what William chose to do — we only know that William grew and prospered and that Lydia took her children to Minnesota and remarried. Lydia later married Henry Foster

Rasdall, Duane

So earnest and painstaking an exponent of scientific farming and rational, intelligent country life as Duane F. Rasdall, could find no more satisfying opportunity for the exercise of his ability than the old Rasdall farm in section 16, McPherson Township, where he owned two hundred and ninety-six acres of fine land, all of it under cultivation. This farm, a part of the old Winnebago Reservation, is eloquent with reminders of a tribe of Redmen now but sparsely represented, and chief of these evidences of early occupation is the old brick house built for the Indians by the United States government. The efforts of the late owner of the property are distinctly modern in character and the old and new shoulder each other in comparative harmony of action. Mr. Rasdall was engaged in general farming and stock raising, and he was past master of the science, which has outstripped the slow and laborious methods of his forefathers.

Born in Madison, Wisconsin, December 4, 1846, Mr. Rasdall was the son of Abel and Lydia Ann (Pitcher) Rasdall. Mr. Rasdall had the usual advantages of the boys of his time and place, and while working hard on the home farm in the summer, welcomed the diversion of attending the district schools during the leisure of the winter. He came to Minnesota in 1863. On April 19, 1869, he was united in marriage to Alice Jane Faley. In 1880 they purchased the Winnebago Agency farm from Henry Truman, as they already owned the property next to the Agency. To this union there were two sons and two daughters: Jessie, wife of H. Thielman (see separate story); Charles (1872-1909) a farmer in McPherson township, Grace Estelle, wife of Frank Chase (see separate story), of St. Clair; and Mark, engaged in the transfer business in Montevideo.

Mr. Rasdall passed away October 17, 1909. Mrs. Rasdall died in July 1921.

In political affiliations Mr. Rasdall was a Democrat, and among other offices held by him was that of chairman of the town board for eighteen years. He was a director in the Farmer's Fire Insurance Company, a director of the St. Clair State Bank, and was otherwise connected with local undertakings. Religiously he was connected with the Congregational church. He was ever ready to help in all good works, and has ever held out a helping hand to those whose fortunes were less happily placed than his own.

[Additional Notation: Duane and his brothers lived on the Henry Foster farmstead (later owned by Walter O'Brien, Everad O'Brien, then Walter Grams, where Douglas Grams, Walt and Margaret's grandson now lives) until Duane's marriage when the brothers moved out. In 1893 Duane and Alice Rasdall's granddaughter Viva Thielman Boswell, was born in this house.]

By Marion Boswell Hoffman/Thomas Hughes

Melvin B. Rasdall was born on November 13, 1848, in Madison, Wisconsin. The family resided at and near Madison until 1863, when he came to the St. Clair area with his mother and brothers. Melvin attended the public schools and then went to Mankato to attend school. He worked for John C. Wise, Sr. on the old *Mankato Record*, putting in jokes and setting type while attending Normal School. He was only fifteen when he ran away to the Civil War. In 1864 he enlisted in Company F, First Minnesota Heavy Artillery, under Captain Owens and thereafter did garrison duty until the re-establishment of peace in 1865. After the War he returned to Mankato and attended Mankato Normal School, Mankato. During these five years he was variously employed as a wage earner, thus paying his way through school and graduated with the first class. There were only six members of this class. They were required to teach two years upon receiving a diploma, so he dropped out two days before graduation. He then engaged in general merchandising for about three years and then went to Colorado for a year. The ambitious young man learned to be a druggist and in 1877 established himself into the druggist business and as long as he lived, he owned the drug store at St. Clair, Minnesota. He was the Postmaster, had various connections with local enterprises, and was a Republican. He was also the township assessor for six years. He was a prominent member of the Independent Order of Odd Fellows, of which he was at one time Past Master, and was at one time affiliated with the Masons. He was also a member of the Grand Army of the Republic.

During the winter and summer he began his day at five o'clock in the morning, whistling. He was the most popular man in St. Clair, happy, helpful, and an excellent conversationalist, being well versed in history and politics. He loved books and people. "Mell" as Mr. Rasdall was familiarly known, was a genial, whole-soled gentleman who always had a pleasant word and cheerful greeting for his friends and acquaintances. His hearty, good-natured laugh was an excellent antidote for the blues and it was a pleasure to meet him at all times. His friends were limited only by his acquaintance, than which probably no man's in this county was more extensive, and among whom the announcement of his death was cause for genuine regret.

Melvin was the second son of Abel Rasdall and Lydia Ann Pitcher. He died on September 8, 1909.

Mankato Record

"Another old settler has gone to a well earned rest-another genial, kind and helpful neighbor has passed from this earth, another active and energetic member of the community has laid aside his arms and retired to await the call of the last trumpet. Another sturdy marcher has dropped from the ranks and lain down to rest along the path that marks the onward march of the great brotherhood of man."

Melvin married Alice Jane Hilton (1857), the oldest daughter of Sumner and Hulda C. (Dickinson) Hilton of Weyauwega, Wisconsin, in 1877. They had six children: Lee S., Grant Arthur (1891-1951), Frank, Lulu (Charles Hamilton), Effie (Robert Brown) and Stella (William Hall). She was an open, sociable, good-hearted woman. She ran the family homestead, and maintained close ties with her sister and her sister's family.

Alice Hilton Rasdall with her youngest, Grant Arthur Rasdall. This was taken on the family property in St. Clair, Minnesota, ca. 1903.

Melvin B. Rasdall, ca. 1903.

The photo below shows Melvin and Alice Rasdall's youngest son, Grant, sitting with a group of friends in St. Clair, eating watermelon in the summertime. (If you look at their feet, you'll see the piles of watermelon seeds.) Grant is the second from right, about to take a bite.

Here are the four remaining children of Melvin and Alice Rasdall, seen at Grant Rasdall's home in Los Angeles, probably in the 1930s.
From the left: Lulu Pearl Rasdall, Lee Sumner Rasdall, Effie A'Dell Rasdall, and Grant Arthur Rasdall.
Lulu was the last to pass on, dying in Los Angeles in 1960.
Lulu and Lee left no children, but Grant and Effie did.

After Melvin's death the family fell apart and they quickly moved out of town. They appear to have moved to Idaho where Alice and some of the children worked on the railroad. Alice died in 1912, in St. Maries, Idaho.

Grant Arthur Rasdall, Sr. was born in 1891 in St. Clair, Minnesota, and died in 1951 in Los Angeles, California. He graduated on the honor roll from Mankato High School at age 15 and went on to the University of Minnesota. He was required to commit to three years of teaching when he received his diploma and so dropped out of school a few weeks before graduation. He enlisted in the Army in World War I and served as a commissioned officer in France. After marrying Jean Fisher Hutchinson in Salt Lake City, he moved to Los Angeles, California, where he worked for General Telephone until his death in 1951 (with a two-year hiatus during which he worked for Paramount Studios). Grant was the second son of Melvin B. Rasdall and Alice J. Hilton.

RASMUSSEN, DEAN

Dean V. Rasmussen was born on January 16, 1946, at Deaconess Hospital, Minneapolis, Minnesota. He graduated from Eden Prairie High School in 1964. He then attended Worthington Community College, graduating in 1966. His future plans were to secure a high school teaching position in Health/Physical Education with involvement as a Head Football Coach and assistant coach in another sport. To obtain this goal he continued his education at Mankato State University, Mankato, MN. In June 1969 he graduated with a Major in Health/Physical Education, Minnesota Teacher Licensure, Grades K-12, Project Quest Certification and a Coaching Certificate.

He started his teaching career at St. Clair Public School

Dean Rasmussen speaking at the St. Clair Veteran's Day activities. Dean was recognized for his years of dedicated service to the St. Clair School and its students. He was also recognized for his service to his country.

in 1969. He taught for one year and then in 1970 received his draft notice. He joined the U.S. Air Force, serving until 1974. On March 1974 he received his Honorable Discharge. On July 1970 he was awarded the American Spirit Honor Medal.

Dean then returned to teach in St. Clair and continued his teaching and coaching career. He has taught K-12 Physical Education and Health classes over the years. He filled various varsity coaching positions: Head Football for 12 years (1981-1992), Assistant Football 8 years (1969, 1974-1980), Head Boys Basketball 3 years (1969, 1974-1976), Head Girls Basketball 2 years (1977-1979), Head Girls Track 2 years (1975 & 1976) and Assistant Boys Track 2 years (1988 & 1989). From 2000 until 2002 he served as an Assistant Boys Basketball at Loyola High School, Mankato, and is currently an Assistant Football Coach at Mankato West High School. He started this position in 2002, the year this team won the Minnesota 4A State Championship.

The record as head football coach at St. Clair stands at 88-35. This was with the 11-man team from 1981-1888 and then 9-man from 1989-1992. The team honors for his career included 1 State Title (1989), 1 Academic State Title, 1 Academic Section Championship, 4 State Tournament Appearance, 4 Section Championships, 2 Section Runner-up, 9 years of playoff appearances, three conference championships and four conference runner-ups.

Individual honors include the 1989 State 9-Man Coach of the Year, 1989 Toyota State 9-Man Coach of the Year, 1982, 1988, 1989, 1992 Conference Coach of the Year, 1990 Assistant Coach of the All-Star Game and 1987 Worthington Football Program-Alumni of the Year Award.

He has been a member of the Minnesota State High School Football Coaches Association for 21 years, Minnesota State High School League Football Advisory Committee for 2 years, and the Minnesota State High School Football Coaches Academic All-State Team Committee for 2 years.

By Dean Rasmussen

Dean Rasmussen retired from full-time teaching in November of 2004, having taught three generations of some families. Dean was recognized at the 2004 Veterans Day activities held at the St. Clair School for his 31 years of dedicated service to the district. He plans to continue as a substitute teacher for the school.

Mr. Rasmussen could have taken a teaching deferment but chose to do his duty to his country and enlisted in the U.S. Air Force. He served two years in Japan and was then assigned to work in the Pentagon in Washington, D.C.

Mr. Rasmussen has truly been a dedicated educator in every aspect of his involvement with his students. He has enjoyed hearing from his former students and how things, he has taught them, has helped them in life. He always demanded respect and felt that teaching respect was primary to a good education to prepare students for the real world. His philosophy was "that part of coaching taught him to expect students to come with appropriate haircuts for under a helmet, to say "please" and "thank you" and to show respect. Teaching isn't only about grades but about helping students become better people. The closing comment from Mr. Rasmussen at the presentation was "Teaching has been a great 35 years. It was like going to school, not going to work, I wouldn't trade it for anything."

By Jerry Groebner, *Lake Region Times* Editor

RIPPLINGER, LEO

Leo and Jo Ann Ripplinger purchased the hardware store about 1982 from Calvin Gamble. His formula for success in the hardscrabble world of small town business was a simple one: "you gotta satisfy the customer." Living upstairs over the store allowed him to open the doors whenever a customer called for an emergency fix as well as the regular business hours, which started at 7:00 a.m.

The surroundings at the store were a comfortable blend

of the old and the new. Heavily varnished hardwood floors and an ornately stamped metal ceiling are reminders of how the store, built in the late 1880's, looked.

Leo stocked the usual hardware store items either in bulk or individually packaged, as well as house ware items. He also replaced windowpanes, did repair work on appliances, bicycles and small engines. Leo treated his customers like people, not like crooks. He never had security guards at all the gates. He cared for his customers. He knew he couldn't compete with the big conglomerates in Mankato, so he focused on the service aspect, which was what he really was selling. The convenience of a small town business was important to his customers.

Leo also was the owner of the former Drake's Station next door until he sold that business to Jeff McCollum in 1993.

ROHRER, M. E.

St. Clair Drug, M. E. Rohrer, prop.

That's what the sign said that hung in front of the store. When I was little I wondered what "prop." was.

My Father graduated from the University of Minnesota College of Pharmacy in 1925. My Mother graduated from Winona Teachers College. In 1931 they bought the St. Clair Drug Store from Dr. Juliar and moved from Minneapolis to St. Clair. I'm not sure if the soda fountain was in the store when they bought it, or was a later addition. Whichever, it was probably the most popular spot in the store and also in the town. The St. Clair Post Office was at the back of the store. My Dad and Mother were the Postmaster and Postmistress. I remember my Dad studying to take the Civil Service exam, and memorizing the capitals of all the states, etc.

The first day they opened for business and tallied up the profit at the end of the day they had made five cents!

M.E. Rohrer in the Rohrer Drug Store.

There were only two doctors in town, Dr. Juliar and Dr. Macbeth. The prescription business wasn't exactly thriving. My Dad added many sidelines to make ends meet. He had a large veterinary medicine department; he sold wallpaper; he would even go out and measure the rooms. A big paint department was also added. He carried lots of school supplies when school started. Come December a good selection of Christmas gifts including toys were added, and I learned how to gift-wrap. Of course, all the regular drug store items were stocked. There was also a small lending library, and a big magazine rack.

Above the drugstore was a large three-bedroom apartment where we lived. It had a wonderful screen porch at the back. My sister Judy (Thielscher) and I slept out there until the first snow flakes arrived. Cold! Mother didn't make many desserts. She's say "Go downstairs and get some ice cream." Ice cream is not one of my favorites to this day!

When I was in Jr. High I was excused shortly before noon to go back to the store and get the soda fountain ready for the noon rush. Malts were 15 cents; milkshakes 10 cents; sodas 10 cents (with two scoops of ice cream!). We made fountain cokes and root beer (in frozen mugs) and made our own syrups. During the war we had extra coupons for sugar to make the simple syrup. Another really busy night for the soda fountain was the free outdoor movie night. We would be swamped! Lots of work, but fun, too. Our soda fountain was the only one in a radius of 25-40 miles.

Labor Day was another big event in our lives. The drug store was closed but we set up a hamburger stand right next door. My Uncle Donald (Mother's way younger brother) who was in high school in Stillwater, came every summer to work at the drug store. He was the fry cook at the Labor Day hamburger stand. Uncle Donald is now 88 years young. He lives in Tempe, Arizona, with his son. He dated Marion Boswell, among others while in St. Clair.

In 1945 my Dad, who was 40 years old, had serious surgery (gall bladder) at the Mankato hospital. Things went from bad to worse. His brother, Chris Rohrer, was a doctor in Waterville. He finally took him to Mayo Clinic where they literally saved his life. In January 1946 (the war finally over) we had enough gas again and went to Prescott, Arizona, to stay with my Mother's sister, while my Dad recuperated, and he did!

During all the years in St. Clair one or another of the Bollman girls worked at the drug store. I'm sure there were seven or eight sisters but at the time we were in Arizona I think it was Marie Bollman. She held it together with a pharmacy buddy of my Dad's from Waterville who came a few days a week.

While in Prescott my Dad became interested in a much bigger store. My Mother always wanted to move to Arizona, but I think that once she got here she really missed St. Clair. With the help of a brother-in-law, my Dad bought the store. My Uncle Donald had just gotten out of the service, went to USC, and graduated in Pharmacy and joined my Dad. They formed the Rohrer-Bloom Drug Store, and it was a perfect partnership! My Dad got into politics and loved it. He was the Chairman of the Yavapai County Board of Supervisors for 20 years.

My brother, sister and I all graduated from Prescott High School. I went on to the U of A at Tucson and graduated in Pharmacy. I couldn't get that drug store business out of my sister. Judy graduated in Nursing at Boulder, Colorado. She went on to be a stewardess for United Airlines, flying to Hawaii when they had to have a nurse for overseas flights. Marvin got his Ph.D. in psychology.

I don't know too much about what happened to St. Clair Drug. I don't think it remained a drug store for too many years longer.

By Dorothy Rohrer Schnackenberg

ROSE, CARL

Carl Rose was born on December 15, 1909, and was the son of Frederick (1864-1945) and Elizabeth (Jaeger) Rose. (She was a sister to Ernie Hager's mother.) He was married to Florence Bruels, the daughter of Joseph and Rose (Fallenstein) Bruels, who was born on September 25, 1912. Carl took over the former Haugen Meat Market in the 1940's. It was a butcher shop and meat market with freezer lockers to rent. It was a vital part of the community until the mid-1960's, when it closed. It later became a restaurant.

Carl then became an employee of the city of St. Clair as the sole maintenance man and also was the only police officer for many years.

Carl and his wife Florence were life long residents of St. Clair, living at 340 Main Street West, and raised a family of eight children, who all attended the St. Clair Public School. Their children are Shirley (1934) (William Hardie), Dale (4-28-1936) who is married to Janice Pufahl, Dean (4-28-1936) who is married to Ardis Stoltzman and their children are Patrick and Gerald who is married to Vicki Hesse, the daughter of Harvey and Beverly (Bartelt) Hesse. Gary was born in 1938, Terrance in 1941 (Judy Spiess/Dorothy Hanson), Sharon (1950) (Thomas Dauk), Cynthia (1954) (Lawrence Sterle), and Kimberley (1959) (James Seys).

By Sharon Dauk and Norma Bruels

ROWELL, MARY

Miss Mary Olive Rowell was a pioneer resident of St. Clair. She was born in Maine in 1852 and lived in St. Clair since early girlhood. She died at age 91 on August 29, 1943, and is buried in the Union Cemetery in St. Clair.

RUSSELL, HUGH

Hugh Russell, the son of Charles and Annie (Nesbitt) Russell, was born on February 3, 1906, at Eagle Lake, MN. On June 7, 1940, he married Mae Westmack in Minneapolis, MN. Hugh graduated from St. Clair High School and attended business-college for one year. He worked at the St. Clair State Bank for many years. In 1952 he started the Russell Insurance Agency and did income tax preparations, out of their home at 108 Front Street South.

He was on the St. Clair School Board and was a member of the Boosters Club and the St. Clair Fire Department. He was one of the organizers of the St. Clair United Fund and served on its board of directors for many years.

Hugh and Mae had three children Sandra, Darla and Steve.

Mae helped her husband with his business and was a teacher at the St. Clair School. Hugh died in June 1981. Mae is now living in the Schalow Apartments in St. Clair

SADER, BRIAN

Brian and Mary Sader are originally from the Wells, Minnesota area and met in school. While in school Brian was a wrestler and Mary fell in love with him. After graduation from high school Brian enlisted in the Navy so they married and moved to San Diego, California. They lived there fifteen years and then got transferred to Memphis, Tennessee; Kingsville, Texas; back to San Diego, California; Guam; and again back to San Diego. Brian retired after over 20 years of service to his country.

While in San Diego Mary started working with crafts. She had thought it would be fun to have a business where she could combine her interest in crafts.

Brian had taken some shop courses in high school, did some 4-H woodworking projects and thought he would enjoy woodworking after his retirement from the service. Upon the encouragement of his brother Jerry, they moved to St. Clair in 1993. They built a new home in the Goodrich Addition.

Brian started his business in his garage, then moved

into the old Ripplinger Hardware building and outgrew the facility.

Mary started working at Mankato West High School and then for a local transportation company. When the craft store next to Brian's business was closing she saw her chance to fulfill her dreams.

Together, the Sader's decided to build a facility that would house both of their businesses, located just west of St. Clair.

SARGENT, DALE

Dale Sargent, the son of Johnathan and Eleanore (Schumacker) Sargent was married to Frances L. Ritter the daughter of John P and Mary C. (Horvat) Ritter on November 21, 1959.

Children born to this marriage are Terrence P., Kevin John, Cheryl Ann and Douglas Scott.

Terry Sargent married Mary Reichwald on June 26, 1987, in Mankato. They welcomed Calvin James on December 22, 1989, and Patrick Jacob on May 10, 2001. Mary passed away on July 15, 1994. Terry remarried JoAnn Frissel on May 1, 1999, in Minneapolis.

Kevin John Sargent married Catherine Anderson on August 12, 1995, in Forest Lake, Minnesota. They welcomed Cassidy Marie on February 4, 1995, and Robert John on October 30, 1998.

Cheryl Ann Sargent married Terrance F. Lindberg on May 22, 1993. They welcomed into their home Carrie Lea on April 11, 1995, and Nathan Dale on June 22, 1999.

Douglas Scott Sargent married Julie L. Amundson on May 14, 1988 in North Mankato. They welcomed Angela Lynn into their home on December 23, 1993, and Amanda Rae on April 12, 1995.

In April of 1994 Dale and Fran moved into their present home in McPherson Township. (This ground is where the Sunshine Golf Course was years ago.) Kevin and Doug also live in McPherson Township.

By Fran Sargent

SAVICK, RICHARD

Richard and Ardyth (Pogatchnik) Savick grew up in Frost, Minnesota, and moved to St. Clair in 1957. Dick worked at the St. Clair State Bank for eight years. (They at one time lived in the Andy Quinn house at 312 Main Street East.) They then moved to Mankato, returning to St. Clair in 1968 when. Dick started his carpenter business. Ardyth work at both the D&L Diner and The Diner. She is now a bartender at the St. Clair American Legion. They have two daughters, Vicki and Kimberly, both attended St. Clair Public School.

Vicki Savick married Dominic Tortorella, owns Calico Creek General Store in Mankato and they live in McPherson Township. They have two children, Dominic who is working at Champs in Mankato, and Mario who works for the Taylor Corporation in Mankato.

Kimberly Savick married James Jannike and they live in Winthrop, Minnesota. They have two children, Jennie a student at Rasmuessen College, Mankato, and Cole a grade school student.

By Richard Savick

SCHALOW, HEINRICH

Heinrich (Henry) Schalow was born on November 25, 1852, in Stettin, Germany, and came to America as a young man. He lived in Shakopee for some time before moving to Decoria Township and then to St. Clair. He was a carpenter by trade. He built the house at 230 Main Street West where they lived. He married Emilie Hoppe who was born in 1854. Emilie died in 1922. In 1930 he rented the house to Art Winkelman's and moved to St. Paul to live with his son Ben. The Winkelman's later bought the house. He also built several other homes in St. Clair. He built the house, which is still standing today directly north of Agency Street on Main Street. This house presently still looks almost like it did in 1918, when it was built. Heinrich never owned a car. He walked everywhere he went. Henry died on August 13, 1947.

Henry and Emilie had nine children. Emma, Paul (Malizabeth Harris), Anna (Sumcoe), Carl (Ida Voight),

Henry and Emilie (Hoppe) Schalow

Four Generations
Standing (L to R): Carl Schalow and Adeline Schalow Westphal
Front: Paul Schalow and Margie Westphal Fritz

Carl & Ida Schalow family.
Standing (L to R): Adeline, Duane, Leona
Seated: Carl and Ida

Carl (Charlie) and Ida (Voight) Schalow on their wedding day, June 11, 1913

Elizabeth (Harry Dumbeck), Edith "Edie" (Ben Zenzen), Henry "Hank" Jr., Lillian (Crown), Ben (Sadie).

Carl "Charlie" B. Schalow was born on July 17, 1887, in Decoria Township. He married Ida M. Voight, the daughter of Franz and Wilhemena (Ehrenberg) Voight, on June 11, 1913, at St. John's Ev. Lutheran Church, St. Clair. Ida was born on July 1, 1889, in Glencoe, Minnesota. Carl and Ida first lived just north of where the Dennis and Mark Kruse building site is and then moved to the Schalow farm, which is located south-

Standing (L to R): Clements Mace, Adeline, Margie and husband Paul Westphal
Seated: Carl Mace, Duane Schalow, Ida and Carl Schalow, Leona Schalow Mace holding Suzanne Mace, Gary Mace.

west of St. Clair. Carl's father built the house and other buildings on this farm site. When their son Duane married they built a house at 108 Schalow Drive in St. Clair.

Carl died on November 8, 1959 and Ida died on May 30, 1963. They are buried in the St. John's Evangelical Lutheran Cemetery, St. Clair.

Carl and Ida's children were Carl (1916-1916), Adeline (Paul Westphal - see separate story), Leona (Clements Mace - see separate story) and Duane.

Duane Schalow was born on April 20, 1929. On December 22, 1956, he married Leona Buhr (1929-2005) who was from Mankato. Duane took over the family farm where he met his accidental death, getting caught in a corn chopper, on September 21, 1975. Duane and Leona had five children, Julie, Georgia, Charles, Sharon and Leonard.

By Leona Mace

SCHMIDT, AUGUST

August Schmidt was born August 9, 1850, in Germany. He married Wilhelmina (Minnie) Hiller in 1872. Minnie Hiller was born March 7, 1852, in the Province of Posen, Germany, and was the daughter of William and Elnora (Hadel) Hiller.

August and Minnie Schmidt came to America in 1875 and settled on a 40 acre farm in Blue Earth County, near St. Clair. Minnies brother's Johann, William and August also settled in Blue Earth County, where they raised a family of nine children: Emma, John, Ida, Minnie, Alma, Amanda, Mary, Otto and Henry.

August Schmidt died June 2, 1899. In 1907 Minnie married August Riese. August Riese died in 1928 and Minnie died June 23, 1935, at the home of her daughter, Mrs. Herman Doss, in Janesville. August and Minnie Schmidt are buried in St. John's Evangelical Lutheran Cemetery in St. Clair.

Emma Emilie Schmidt was born (3-17-1875/7-16-1947) in Orandorff, Germany. She was six months old when her parents immigrated to America. Emma married Albert Gottlieb Wille (1862-1945) on November 20, 1890. Their children: Emil, Otto, Elsie (Charles Doss) and Ida Frieda Bertha (born 1-18-1902). Emma and Albert are buried in the Rosehill Cemetery, Wells, Minnesota.

August and Minnie (Hiller Schmidt) Riese

John Schmidt married Augusta Veigel. Their children: Emma (1905-1905), Leona (Born 1906-Harry Frantum), Martha (Born 1908-Sylvester Besser), Lydia, (1908), John (1901), Sadie (Lawrence Waugh), Lester, Esther, Syvella, Carl, Irene, Genevieve, Oscar and Mildred.

Minnie Schmidt (11-7-1881/7-7-1913) married John H. Williams (Died: 10-15-1916) in 1898. They had one son, Ralph. Minnie and John are buried in Pilgrim's Rest Cemetery, Mankato, MN.

Ida A. Schmidt (2-7-1883/5-5-1968) married Albert Koch (1879-1960) in 1906. Their children: Esther (Aloysius Denn), Edna (Delmar O'Brien) and Albert (1911-1911). Ida and Albert are buried in St. John's Evangelical Lutheran Cemetery, St. Clair.

Alma Martha Schmidt (6-25-1885/7-4-1960) married Herman Ludwig Carl Doss (8-18-1878/1-12-1960) on May 20, 1903, at St. John's Evangelical Lutheran Church, St. Clair. Their children: Carl (1904-1971) married Rose Manthe, Arline (1906-2004) married Hugo Engel (1907-1971) on May 27, 1931, Helen (1908-1909), Evert (1910-1963) married Leona Grams (1911-2001) on November 26, 1931, Isabella (1-9-1914) married Sylvester Youngerberg on September 30, 1933, and Marie (7-22-1916) married Leslie Lueck on February 16, 1933. Alma and Herman are buried in St. John's Evangelical Lutheran Cemetery, St. Clair.

Amanda Louise Schmidt (8-3-1887/7-10-1974) married William Marzinske (1881-1955) on October 27, 1904. Their children: Robert (1905-1966) married Marie Klampe on June 4, 1931, Lila (Viola Lilly Wilhelmine - 1908-1993) married Louis Lueck (1904-1986) on July 9, 1930. Walter (1906-1963) married Evelyn (1911-1988) Dumdei on June 8, 1932, Marie (1912-1984) married Lyall Berg on January 2, 1936, Hazel (1915-1986) married Ervin Doss on October 24, 1934, Elnora (1-16-1917) married Dallas Doss on July 11, 1946 and Edwin (3-13-1918). Amanda and William are buried in Alma City Cemetery, Waseca County.

Mary Louise Schmidt (1889-1984) married August Carl Beccue (1890-1982) on December 4, 1913, in St. Clair. Their children Farleigh (1915-1967) married Marcella Weber and David (1918-1988) married Beverly Penhiter. Mary and August are buried in St. John's Evangelical Lutheran Cemetery, St. Clair.

Otto Schmidt married Rose (maiden name unknown). Their children: Virginia, Milton and Clifford.

Henry William Schmidt (5-5-1897) married Caroline Emma Ratzloff (1903-1949) on January 23, 1923 in St. Paul, Minnesota. Their children: Harry (12-5-1925) married Mildred Zechek on July 11, 1947, Mary Lou (5-9-1927), Geraldine (12-21-1928) married Richard Dougherty on July 10, 1948, and Carol (7-8-1940) married John Svien. Henry and Caroline are buried in Union Cemetery, St. Paul, Minnesota.

By Julie Schrader

SCHMIDT, PASTOR DANIEL

It was on August 20, 2000, that the Lord led the Voters' of St. John's Evangelical Lutheran Church to extend a Divine Call to Pastor Daniel Schmidt to serve the congregation as their Pastor. Pastor Schmidt accepted the Call in September. He and his family moved to St. Clair from Menomonie, Wisconsin, in October. Pastor Schmidt was installed as the Pastor of St. John's on Sunday, October 22nd. Some highlights of Pastor Schmidt's ministry at St. John's are the dedication of the new entryway in April of 2001, the celebration of the 135th Anniversary of St. John's in 2004 and the beginning of "Follow Me" Preschool in September of 2004, with an initial enrollment of 11 students. During his ministry Pastor Schmidt has had the opportunity to serve the members of St. John's and the community with the Word of God, including a number of Baptisms, Confirmations, Weddings and Funerals. Pastor Schmidt and Elizabeth, the daughter of William and Naomi Schimmel of North Mankato, Minnesota, were married on August 28, 1993 at St. Paul's Lutheran Church in North Mankato, MN. During their marriage, the Lord Jesus, the Lord of the home has blessed them with five children: Daniel Jr., Emily, Jacob, Benjamin and Grace.

By Pastor Daniel Schmidt

SCHMIDT, ROY

Private Schmidt dies at Camp Cody.

William Schmidt of McPherson Township, Blue Earth County, received a telegram announcing the death of his son, Roy Theodore, at Camp Cody, New Mexico.

The young man died of pneumonia following influenza.

The case is peculiarly sad from the fact that death occurred just a week from the day he left Mankato. In a talk with his father we learned at that time the boy appeared all right and was in a happy frame of mind. The father is of the opinion that he contracted the disease at Mankato before he left.

Many who were in the courthouse at the time were subsequently taken ill; several of the boys on the train, at the same time as Roy, were also taken ill. At first the telegrams were encouraging, but later they took a different character and finally the sad news of his death was received.

The deceased was twenty-two years of age. He was born and brought up on the Blue Earth County farm just over the line, where he resided when he entered the service. He was a favorite with his companions, a bright, genial, lovable boy. His sudden death was a very sad affliction to his parents.

His father, mother Mary (Lambrecht), one sister Regina (Sib. Kahnke) and brothers Ernest, a soldier in France, Leo, and Frank survive him. His Uncle Emil Dieudonne also survived him.

A private funeral service was held and the remains were laid to rest in the Catholic Cemetery in St. Clair.

SCHNEIDER, CLIFFORD

Cliff, Monica, Dan, Joan and Ed Schneider moved to St. Clair in 1973. Dan graduated in 1983, Joan in 1984 and Ed in 1986 from St. Clair High School.

Dan joined the Marines in 1983. He married Pam Howe, who was from Austin, MN, in 1987. Dan is now a Correctional Sargent at the Arizona State Prison Complex. Pam works as a program manager at the Valley of the Sun School.

Joan married Brad Meyer, the son of Marvin and Anieta (Grams) Meyer from Janesville in 1988. Joan is a registered nurse and is a Heart-Lung Transplant Coordinator at the Mayo Clinic, Rochester, MN. Brad is a driver for U.P.S. in Rochester. They have two children; Jessica ages 13, and Adam 10. The Meyer family lives outside of Dodge Center, MN.

Their youngest son, Ed, married Tami Heller from Minot, ND, in 1992. Ed is a Pediatric Respiratory Transport Therapist, and Tami is a MRI technologist at the Mayo Clinic. They have a seven-year-old daughter, Justine. They now live in Bryon, MN. In December 2004 Edward went to New Orleans to present his paper on Transport & Aerial Therapy for which he won a National Award.

By Clifford Schneider

SCHOSTAG, CARL

Carl Schostag, the youngest son of Christian and Juliane (Kindler) Schostag, was born on October 8, 1852, in Eichdorf, Posen, Preussen (Prussia). Carl also known

The Charles Schostag home north of St. Clair

Robert and Annie Schostag home

L to R: Helen and Annie Schostag

Helen Schostag Kenward sitting in front of the St. Clair Hotel

as Charlie came with his parents to America in 1853. He became a citizen of the USA on October 2, 1897.

In about 1880 he married Frederika (also known as Raka) Gerber, the daughter of John and Louisa Gerber. She was born in 1860. They lived in the St. Clair area and had six children. George (Helena Youngerberg/Clara Strutz), Albert (Dorothy Lubke), Baby son, Robert (Winnefred Foster/Anna Klingbeil), Alvina and Alma (John Kapinski).

Carl died in 1937 and Raka in October of 1951. Carl, Raka and Alma are buried in the Pilgrim's Rest Cemetery, Mankato, Minnesota.

George Schostag was the oldest son of Carl and Raka (Gerber) Schostag, was born on September 21, 1880 in Mankato Township. He lived in McPherson Township with his family and in November of 1903 he married Helena Youngerberg, the daughter of Gottlieb and Hulda (Meyer) Youngerberg, who was born on February 9, 1883. They had two children Everett (Ida Gensmer) and Mabel (Hugo Roemhildt). George and Helena later divorced. Helena then married Robert Berndt and he adopted Helena's two children.

George moved to Crookston, Minnesota, following the divorce in 1909. (An article on George from 1907 was given earlier in this publication.). George was then married to Clara Strutz and they had three children Theodore, and twins Myrtle and Merle.

George died in 1918 during a flu epidemic in Crookston where he is buried.

Albert William Schostag, Sr. was the second son of

Carl and Raka (Gerber) Schostag and was born on March 25, 1882, in Blue Earth Co., MN. He married Dorothy Lubke, the third child of Ernest and Marie (Tress) Lubke who was born on July 23, 1885, in Mexico, MO. Albert and "Dora" had six children, Alfred (Lucy Kastner), Alvina (Hallie DeRemer/Ivor Jones/Robert Callis), Hilda (Lyle Noyes Coult), Louise (George Ganzel), Viola (Francis McMullen) and Albert (Ellen Anderson).

Albert died in March of 1965 and Dorothy died in 1966. They are buried in the Pilgrim's Rest Cemetery, Mankato, Minnesota.

Robert Schostag was the fourth child of Carl and Raka (Gerber) and was born on December 21, 1885. He married Winnefred Foster, who was born in 1887 and was the daughter of Henry P. and Sarah (Campbell) Foster. They had an adopted daughter, Hazel (Herbert Kahn). Winnefred was the sister of Goldie (John Schostag). After the death of Winnefred on January 11, 1913, Robert married Anna Klingbeil, the daughter of Herman and Emilie (Burmeister) Klingbeil, on November 13, 1913. Robert and Anna had a daughter Helen (1919-2005), who married Howard Kenward, and lived in Mankato.

Robert and Annie lived at 128 County Road 28 South. (Additional note: Robert had a farm lot, raising pigs, and pasture, which were located in the area of today's Memorial Park.)

Robert died on November 16, 1969, and Anna on September 21, 1969. They are both buried in the St. John's Evangelical Lutheran Cemetery, St. Clair.

SCHROEDER, AUGUST FREDERICK

August Frederick Schroeder was born in 1875 in Germany. At the age of 17 he came to the United States and on September 19, 1899, he married Caroline Frantz. She was born in 1878 and died in 1951. The couple lived on a farm near St. Clair until they retired to St. Clair. He died in 1949.

They were the parents of six children: Alfred, Esther (Otto Glamm - see separate story), Rosalia (Ralph Juliar), Viola (Elroy Juliar), Leona (Ray Holthus) and Daisy (Robert Wagner.). He had two sisters Augusta (Clement Kollos) and Anna Polchow as well as a brother Albert.

August and Caroline are buried in the St. John's Evangelical Lutheran Cemetery in St. Clair.

SCHROEDER, CHARLES

Charles Schroeder was born in 1837. At the age of fourteen he commenced learning the trade of wheelwright and blacksmith. When fifteen years old he left Prussia, his native country, and settled on a farm in Dodge County, Wisconsin, where he remained until 1881. He then bought a farm in McPherson Township. In 1858 he married Ernestine Bocholtz. They were the parents of six children: Minnie, Charles, Florentina, Louisa, William and Robert.

SCHROEDER, FRANK

Frank H. Schroeder was born on June 26, 1872, and he was married to Mary T. Matthies who was born on February 25, 1879. They had a daughter Esther D. (Ernest Hager - see separate story), who was born in

Frank Schroeder, owner of Schroeder Grocery, in 1930

Frank and Esther Schroeder in the store
This store was the Farmer's Mercantile Store
before the Schroeder's came to town

L to R: Frank, Esther (Hager) and Mary Schroeder

Wells, MN. The family moved to Mankato, where Frank worked for the Mankato Produce Company and had a route through St. Clair, so he was known in the area. Frank was asked to move to St. Clair and manage the St. Clair Mercantile Store, which was farmer owned. In May 1921 the Schroeder family moved to St. Clair and lived in an apartment above the Mercantile Store.

Frank died on February 8, 1938, and Mary died on April 9, 1979, at the age of 100.

By William Hager

SCHULDT, JACOB

Jacob Schuldt was born on May 17, 1880, in Schleswig-Holstein, Germany, and came to this country at the age of one year. On March 23, 1910, he was joined in wedlock with Helene Beckman the daughter of Jacob and Johanna (Shoeder) Beckman at Rock Rapids where they lived until 1920. Helene was born in 1885. In 1920 they moved to a farm near St. Clair, residing there until his death in 1948. Helene moved to town living just east of the Lutheran Church. (This house has been moved to 316 Main Street East.) Helene died in 1971. They are buried in the St. John's Evangelical Lutheran Cemetery, St. Clair.

Jacob and Helene's children were Edna (Clarence Nicolai - see separate story), Walter, Esther (Orville Christnagel) and Viola (Willard Miller).

SCHULTZ, FREDERICK

Frederick C. Schultz was born in Watertown, Wisconsin. He married Amelia Splinter at St. Clair on June 15, 1882. They lived on a farm near St. Clair for a number of years, and later moved into the village where he operated a store. He was assessor in St. Clair for two years. They then moved to Elysian.

Fred and Amelia had three children, Fred A., Mrs. Theodore Heinze and Mrs. Forrest Biggins.

Both of the Schultz's are buried in the St. John (Bestman) Cemetery, St. Clair

SCHWANKE, GUSTOF

Gustof Schwanke was born on March 10, 1867, in Germany and he came to the United States when he was nine years old in 1876. He was accompanied by his 6 or 7 year old sister Maria (August Glaser). They were sent to the United States to live with their aunt, a Mrs. Wentland, who lived near Elysian, MN, after their mother died in Potash, Poland (near Germany). It was said they had their names sewed on their clothes to identify them as they traveled alone. He married Ida Schreyer who was born on March 24, 1865. They farmed and raised their family in McPherson Township one and a half-mile east of St. Clair.

Gustof and Ida had six children. Martha born on September 17, 1895, and died on March 3, 1986, was a nurse and was married to Holger Anderson. Clara was born on June 21, 1897, and died on July 30, 1985, was married to Paul Polinska and later to Corba Babbit. Henry was born on September 14, 1899, was a farmer until 1950, never married and died on November 21, 1989, in New Ulm. Aaron was born on August 29, 1901, married Ruth Gomsrud, was a farmer and died on October 17, 1976. Ellen was born on May 25, 1904, and married Henry Hoffman. Mabel was born on October 26, 1906, married Oscar Burtness and died on March 29, 1999.

Gustof died on January 21, 1941, from a long heart illness and Ida died on May 15, 1945, they are buried in St. John's Evangelical Lutheran Cemetery, St. Clair.

By Verna Sodeman

SCHWICHTENBERG, PAUL

Paul Schwichtenberg was born on July 14, 1916, and was raised on a farm at Waterville, MN. He married Ruth Lamont and they farmed in the Waterville area until 1948. In 1951 he moved with his family to St. Clair, living 212 Main Street West, and he was manager of the

Commander Elevator for many years.

He was active in the community being the St. Clair City Clerk for many years and was a volunteer fireman. He enjoyed fishing, bowling, curling, dancing, and having fun with his friends and family.

Paul and Ruth had three sons. Donovan married Myrna Rixman and they have two children. They live in Edina and he is presently the President of St. Paul Technical College in St. Paul, MN. Dennis was married to Jeanne Wrightson (1942-2004) and they had three sons. One of their sons died of cancer at the age of 27. Dennis has been Martin County Court Reporter for 30 years. He lives in Welcome, MN, and has seven grandchildren. Leon married Marlene Pawlicki and they have three children and one grandchild. They live in Bloomington where he is an electrician.

Paul died on June 22, 1962, at the age of 45, of a heart attack. He is buried in the Sakatah Cemetery, Waterville, MN. His family continued to live in St. Clair and the boys graduated from St. Clair High School.

By Ruth Schwichtenberg Nyquist

SMESTAD, STEPHEN

Stephen Smestad is the son of Leonard and Esther Smestad of Dawson, MN. Leonard was a Lutheran Church of America (and then Evangelical Lutheran Church of America) minister. He was born on August 23, 1913, and died on September 3, 1982. Esther, who was a homemaker, was born on July 7, 1913, and died on March 15, 1980. Stephen is a nuclear medicine technologist who works for Aureus Medical.

Stephen married Deloris Stine the daughter of Leonard and Lee Stine of Carlton, MN. Leonard, who worked as an electrician, was born on April 22, 1920. Lee, who was born on February 25, 1923, was the head cook at Carlton High School. Deloris is an educational speech clinician for the St. Clair Public Schools.

Stephen and Deloris moved to St. Clair in June 1977. They have two children, Zachary Stephen, who was born on November 23, 1978. He is a student at Minnesota State University, Mankato, and is majoring in Computer Informational Science and a minor in Scandinavian Studies. He will graduate in May 2005. He works in "technical support" at Carlson Craft, North Mankato, MN.

Jacob Daniel was born on May 27, 1980. He graduated from the University of St. Thomas in St. Paul, MN, in December of 2002 with a degree in geography/minors in biology and business. Currently he is a student at the University of Minnesota working towards acceptance to dental school.

By Deloris Smestad

SODEMAN, CHRISTIAN

Christian Sodeman was born in 1842 in Prussia. He married Mary Gerber, the daughter of John and Louisa Gerber, who was born on July 6, 1849 in Mecklenburg, Prussia, in 1871 at Franklin, Wisconsin. In November 1879, they came to McPherson Township, being neighbors to the John Gerber family.

They had heard of the bright prospects farther west so they came to this area.

The first three children Friederice (Ernst Franske), Minnie (Wilheim Koentop), Anna (Albert Flitter) - born to Christian and Mary were born in Wisconsin. Carl (Elizabeth Strobel), Emma (Peter Roerig), Frank (Ida Glaser), and Robert (Anna Andrews/Abbie Gleason) were born in McPherson Township. Three sons died in infancy.

On November 1887 Christian was killed when he and another man were hauling quarry rock from Mankato to build an open well on his farm, where a "stone bee" was being given him. He fell asleep on the way home and fell off the wagon and the wagon ran over him.

It left Mary to raise her family alone on 40 acres of land, the youngest only a year and half old. In 1897 Mary built a new house to replace her log house. The Elmer Sodeman family later lived in it. She lived on the farm the rest of her life except for a short time when she lived with her son, Robert, in St. Clair until he was married. Her son, Frank and his wife when they were married, rented her land until 1919 when they bought it from her. She was 70 years old, lived with them until her health failed and then she went to live with her daughter Emma Roerig and family in St. Clair.

Mary died in 1923. Mary was noted as one of sterling quality, a considerate neighbor, and a loving and kind mother. Her presence will be greatly missed in her home circle. They are buried in St. Johns (Bestman) Cemetery, St. Clair, Minnesota. After Mary died Emma's husband moved Christian's grave from the east part of the Cemetery to the central part.

Frank Sodeman was born on April 19, 1884. On September 5, 1912, he married Ida Glaser, the daughter of August and Maria (Schwanke) Glaser, who was born on April 26, 1895. They took over the family farm.

Frank and Ida had four children. Elmer (see separate story), Henry (Margaret Bradley 12-17-1915/3-27-2004) was born on November 22, 1914, and died on November 27, 1984, they farmed in LeRay Township, Gertrude (5-11-1919) (Arnold Larson 11-30-1911/3-2-1990), and Helen (Jerome Michels 10-8-1912/10-9-1987) was born on February 4, 1930, and died on August 9, 1979. While in St. Clair they lived at 320 Main Street West.

Frank died on December 14, 1966, and Ida died on February 4, 1984. They are buried in the St. John's Evangelical Lutheran Cemetery, St. Clair.

Elmer Sodeman was born on July 31, 1913, in McPherson Township to Frank and Ida (Glaser) Sodeman. On November 30, 1945, he was married to Verna Lucile Hohenstein, the daughter of Otto and Carrie Hohenstein, at Salem Lutheran Church, Eagle Lake, MN. Verna was born on October 27, 1923. They resided on the Sodeman family farm in McPherson Township their entire married life. He was a lifetime member of St. John's Evangelical Lutheran Church. He was also a 23-year member of the McPherson Township Board. He enjoyed old farm machinery and his annual trip to Pioneer Power in Le Sueur, MN.

Elmer and Verna are the parents of Carol (Thomas Suddendorf - born on November 5, 1945) who was born on October 24, 1946, and who is a secretary, and Dennis who was born on August 22, 1953. Dennis is the fourth generation of Sodeman's to operate the family farm.

Elmer died on November 17, 2001, and is buried in the St. John's Evangelical Lutheran Cemetery, St. Clair.

By Verna Sodeman

Verna & Elmer Sodeman

SPEAR, WILLIAM

William J. Spear was born in 1927 in Mankato to Clifford and Clara (Guenther) Spear. He served in the U.S. Navy from 1945-1946. In July 1952 he was married to Betty Drager in Mankato. They lived at 212 Park Street South. Bill worked for the City of Mankato, the Blue Earth County Highway Department and various contractors around Mankato. He was a member of the Eagle Lake American Legion.

Bill and Betty had five children Rick (Cathy Depuydt), Randy (Julie Nicolai), Rhonda (Bruce Frank), Robin (Andy Reichard) and Rochell (Bart Routh).

SPLINTER, LYLE

Lyle Splinter was born on December 19, 1910, to Frank and Katherine (Pollei) Splinter. He attended school in Ceresco Township, Blue Earth County, Minnesota. He was an auto mechanic from 1961-1977, owning and operating the St. Clair Garage in St. Clair. He drove school bus from 1966-1977 and served as the chief of the St. Clair Fire Department for 25 years and served on the city council for 20 years. He was a member of the Immaculate Conception Church in St. Clair and of the Loyal Order of the Moose in Mankato. The house where they lived was on the lot which is now the parking lot for the Lutheran Church.

On August 22, 1938, he married Agnes Kortuem, the daughter of John and Rose (Mach) Kortuem at All Saint's Catholic Church, Madison Lake, MN. Agnes was born on November 27, 1915. She enjoyed crocheting, gardening, cooking and traveling. She was a member of the Immaculate Conception Altar Society and the Women of the Moose.

Lyle and Agnes had five children: Lorraine, Barbara, John, Dennis and Raymond.

Lyle died on November 6, 1986, and Agnes died on September 10, 2000.

STEEL, MARVIN

Marvin, the son of David and Savallah (Phillips) is a lifelong resident of the St. Clair area growing up on a farm. He brought his bride Ardis Seifert from the Springfield area to St. Clair in October 1957. Together they farmed in rural St. Clair and in 1960 started Steel Electric. In 1986 the business was sold to Steve Seys.

Ardis has worked as a social worker for the St. Peter Regional Treatment Center, Blue Earth County, volunteer on several Immaculate Conception Catholic Church committees and volunteer coordinator for the American Red Cross Bloodmobile for St. Clair.

Marv and Ardis have retired and are living in St. Clair. In 2003 they were named St. Clair's Grand Marshals for the annual parade.

By Marvin Steel

STOLT, DALE

Dale Stolt started working at the St. Clair State Bank in the spring of 1971 and he has continued working there for the past thirty-four years. In 1973 Dale and Mary Ann built a home at 105 Willow Lane in the Nyquist Addition. In 1975 their daughter Kelly was born. Kelly, her husband Todd Miller and one-year old son Jaden are living in Hanska, MN. Kelly is working at the St. Clair State Bank as a Loan Clerk. In 1977 their son Scott was born and died from Sudden Death Syndrome. Their second daughter Amy was born in 1979. Amy, her husband Seth Becker and one-year old daughter Cadence are living in Fairmont, MN. Amy is working as a social worker for Faribault and Martin Counties.

What an absolutely perfect setting to work, and own a business, and to live and raise a family.

By Dale Stolt

STORJOHANN, HENRY

Henry "Hank" Storjohann was born on November 1, 1934, in Janesville Township, Waseca County, MN, to Fredrick John and Ida (Berndt) Storjohann. He graduated from Janesville High School and the Agricultural School in Waseca. He served in the U.S. Army from 1957 to 1959. He was united in marriage to Karon O'Donnell on August 6, 1965, in Janesville. He was employed at Southern Valley Coop for 39 years and at the time of his retirement was Agri Product Manager. They lived at 400 Hilltop Drive, St. Clair, before moving to Eagle Lake, MN. They were members of St. John's Evangelical Lutheran Church of St. Clair. He enjoyed golfing, landscaping, carpentry around his home and was a Vikings fan. Karon is the manager of the McPherson Farmers Mutual Fire Insurance Company in St. Clair after working as an office secretary for many years.

Hank and Karon's children are Heidi (Perry Hoekstra) and Jerry (Bethany Smith) and they are both St. Clair graduates.

Hank died on December 8, 2003, and is buried in the St. John's Evangelical Lutheran Cemetery, St. Clair.

Karon & Henry Storjohann

THIELMAN, HENRY

Henry Thielman was born near St. Clair on August 13, 1869, to Peter (1825-1886) and Sophia (Dorweiler/Wingen) Thielman. He was married to Jessie Rasdall on September 31, 1891. They had two daughters, Viva (Clay Boswell) and Abbie (Earl Pagenkopf). Henry was an enterprising businessman: worked in and operated a general store with John Murphy, traveled as a representative for McCormick Harvester Company, and later managed the St. Clair Creamery for six years. From 1906 until 1939 he operated a general merchandise business in St. Clair. He was President of the St. Clair Bank and a Director of First National Bank in Mankato. Henry was the mayor of St. Clair from 1900 until 1915 and was a member of the school board from 1915 until 1917. He enjoyed big game hunting, gardening, whittling and fishing. They lived at 212 Front Street West. Henry died in 1951, Jessie in 1953. Both are buried in Glenwood Cemetery in Mankato.

The family of Henry and Jessie (Rasdall) Thielman
Standing (L-R): Abbie Thielman Pagenkopf holding son Lowell, Earl Pagenkopf holding daughter Donna, Clay, Marion and Harold Boswell.
Seated: Viva Thielman Boswell holding daughter Jane, Henry and Jessie Thielman.

TIMMERMAN, JOHN

John Timmerman was born on August 11, 1860 in Mecklenburg, Germany. In 1889 he married Anna Gerlach who was born in 1870 in Mankato Township to Mr. and Mrs. Herman Gerlach. The couple lived on a farm in McPherson Township until 1914 when they moved to St. Clair. Mr. Timmerman passed away in 1931 and Anna in 1948. Their children were Ella (Louis Priem) Herman, Fred (Ida Kollos), Louis (see separate story), Walter, Bertha (Fred Alexander - see separate story), Raymond and John (Mildred Gekeler).

TIMMERMAN, LOUIS

Janesville Argus – April 28, 1976

Louis Timmerman retired in 1955 after 25 years of bus driving. He recalled when his school bus was "a cracker box behind a team of horses."

He drove teams from 1924-30, alternating the box from wheels to a sled in the winter. "One Thanksgiving I put the sled under the box and didn't take it off for three months," he said.

Before fall freeze-up. Louis would put never-slip shoes on his teams so they could go on ice. He had to replace the shoes a couple times a year. His bus routes took about an hour when he drove a team, but when he got a motorized bus his route began to grow. When Louie retired in 1955 at the age of 60, he was traveling 24 miles on the route. During the 25-year stint of bus driving he was to cover over 140,000 miles without having a single accident even though he had plenty of experiences.

Louie said the weather and bad roads were the bus driver's biggest headaches in those days. "I remember when we used a charcoal heater to keep the kids warm in the bus," he said. "When the weather was good I drove a Baby Grand Chevrolet in place of the horses."

Louie Timmerman

Louis married Evelyn Kollos on November 20, 1917. When in St. Clair they lived at 504 Main Street East. They had two daughters. Unetta was born in 1921 on a farm near St. Clair. She attended rural school in Waseca and Pemberton high school. She was employed at the St. Clair telephone exchange until she had to give it up because of poor health. She died in 1939 at the University of Minnesota Hospital. Daughter Marjorie (Dean Nyquist) who was born in 1930 and died in 1957. Dean and Marjorie had two daughters Mary (David Schenk) and Judy (Richard Winter).

TRUMAN, HENRY

Henry Truman was born on May 30, 1801, in Lancaster, England. Sometime before 1863 he came to America. While living in Washington D.C. he purchased the Winnebago Agency property from the United States Government. In the autumn 1863, after the purchase, he brought his second wife, Mary Smith, son Josiah, daughter Elizabeth, their spouses and their families to St. Clair. They traveled by train from Washington D.C. to Chicago and then they traveled over land by ox-cart. Lucius Dyer was in charge of the Agency at this time and refused to move from the location until all the business connected with the Agency was in order. Thus the Truman family could not move in until the spring of 1864. The Truman family, all thirteen of them, sought shelter in an abandoned, log house. While living in the Agency House the entire family helped operate the Agency, which was also serving as a hotel.

Josiah Truman was born in Lancaster, England, on October 1, 1825. He was married to Susan (maiden name unknown) and they had two children Hannah and Edward.

Elizabeth Truman was also born in Lancaster, England, on October 10, 1831. She was married to John Boswell (see separate story).

Between 1867 and 1879, the wives of Henry (Mary 1786-1867) and Josiah (Susan) and well as Elizabeth (Truman) Boswell all died, one from illness due to old age and two during childbirth. Josiah then returned to Baltimore, Maryland. Henry and John continued to operate the agency. In 1880 Henry Truman sold the Agency and also returned to Baltimore, Maryland, where he died in 1881. He is buried at the Congo Church Cemetery in Darnestown, Maryland.

By Marion Boswell Hoffman

WALTON, HAROLD

Harold Walton was born to Birdie and Lewis Walton in Pine River, Minnesota, on December 7, 1917. An only child, he lived on a farm and attended Pine River schools where he met Elaine Phillips, the daughter of Mable and Nick Phillips who also were farmers. They graduated from Pine River High School and Harold obtained a Normal School Training Certificate. He began teaching in rural Cass County, MN.

Harold and Elaine married June 22, 1937. Their first daughter, Connie, was born and Harold accepted a teaching position in Hillman, Minnesota, a rural two-room schoolhouse that had an apartment. Harold also attended St. Cloud Teachers College and the University of Minnesota. Elaine had contracted polio and was hospitalized many times during this period of their marriage. She used crutches and in later life a wheelchair but neither slowed her down!

In 1944 Harold accepted a teaching position in the Pequot Lakes School District, the same year their second daughter, Patricia, was born. While living in Pequot Lakes, their son, Michael, and daughter, Wendie, were born. Harold also served as principal and superintendent at Pequot Lakes prior to accepting the Superintendent position in St. Clair in 1957. He served the St. Clair School District for twenty years before his health forced him into early retirement.

Harold loved his job. He knew every student, their parents and became good friends with teachers, custodians, cooks, bus drivers and school board members. Each year Harold and Elaine drove through the entire school district to take the census. He was proud of St. Clair and the St. Clair School system. He was an outstanding role model and many of the teachers that worked with him went into administration.

The Harold Walton family.
Back (L to R): Michael, Patricia, Connie
Front: Elaine, Wendie, Harold

The Walton's were active members of the Methodist Church. Harold organized a Boy Scout Troop and every year took the scouts to the Walton cabin in the Pequot Lakes area.

After retirement, Harold and Elaine lived in Lake City and southern Texas. Harold died in 1988 and Elaine in 1997. A scholarship was presented in Harold's name to the St. Clair School District in 1989.

Their children have many fond memories of growing up in St. Clair and of the St. Clair School District and enjoy returning to St. Clair for class reunions. Connie (Gary) West graduated from Pequot Lakes the year the Walton's moved to St. Clair but lived in St. Clair with two of her sons while her husband was in flight training for Northwest Airlines. She was a computer data input specialist. They are retired and live in Phoenix, AZ, and Wabasha, MN. Pat (Lowell) Mohn graduated from Mankato State and the University of Minnesota. She taught and coached in St. Clair for seven years. She became a school administrator and served as Superintendent of the Amboy-Good Thunder School District from 1983-1989. Dr. Mohn and her husband, also a retired school administrator, live in Green Valley, AZ, and Kamp Dells, Waterville, MN. Dr. Michael Walton (Nancy) lives in Bloomer, WI. After the Mayo Clinic purchased his practice in Wabasha, MN, he accepted a position as the lead doctor and administrator for the ER facility for the Chippewa Falls, WI, Hospital. Wendie (Toby) Clement, a former Housing Inspector in Aurora, Co, married Toby, a high school friend from Beauford, MN. Now retired, he was an owner of Gannon Jewelry in Phoenix, AZ. Luci (Tom) Bowen, became a member of the family during her high school years. Luci is a child support officer for Waseca County and Tom is a supervisor at Archer Daniels Midland, Mankato, MN. They live in Madison Lake, MN.

A former St. Clair student once told Harold's granddaughter, Tricia Denn, that when the gymnasium was full of students and Mr. Walton would whistle to get their attention, the gym would become silenced and even basketballs would freeze in mid-air. Although he was a strong disciplinarian, the students respected him.

While in St. Clair the family lived at 217 Mill Street and at 513 East Main Street.

By Pat (Walton) Mohn

WARD, ELWYN

Elwyn Ward (1900-1998) was the son of Charles H. and Millie (Brazier) Ward, Sr. He married Bernice Juliar, the daughter of John R. and Inez (Walters) Juliar. They were farmers in McPherson Township south of St. Clair.

They had two children Richard and Sharon (Larry Hanson).

Richard Ward graduated from St. Clair Public School and then went into farming with his father. He married Helen Glynn, the daughter of Eugene and Mary Alice (Conway) Glynn. Richard and Helen raised their family on a farm northeast of St. Clair. They have five children: Kelly is married to Jeffrey Johnson and they have three children, Dustin, Dylan and Kourtney. They are living in Shakopee, MN. Michael is married to Tara Krautbauer, they have a son Mason and are living on his grandparents, Elwyn and Bernice Ward's, homestead. Colleen is married to Bradley Reich of St. Clair and they have three sons, Joshua, Caleb and Kaden and live in Waconia, MN. Daniel is married to Kristi Tolman and they have a son Jalen and live in Shakopee. Sara is living in Mankato.

Helen and Richard are now living in Mankato and Richard commutes to help with the farming.

By Helen Ward

The Richard and Helen Ward family

L to R: Bill and Louise McComb, Annette and Lial Ward

WARD, LIAL LEE

Lial Lee Ward, eldest son of William and Clara (Mann) Ward, was born in Sterling Township, Blue Earth County, Minnesota. He went to the Johnson School through the eighth grade. He started high school in Mapleton but had to quit when he tipped the old car he was driving over. He worked on farms, became a blacksmith, and later went into construction. He owned his own blacksmith shop in St. Clair. They lived at 213 Main Street West.

Lial married Annette Manthey, the daughter of Herman and Maggie (Carpenter) Manthey. They were parents of four children.

Merle Norman who married Patricia O'Herin. They had two children. Merle was killed in an accident near Mapleton on September 23, 1955.

Norman Lee, married Doris Armes and they had three children.

Juanita Jane married Richard Brunz. He was killed in a truck-train accident on April 15, 1969 in Clarion, Iowa. She has four children. Juanita then married Herman Speck and lives in Good Thunder, Minnesota.

Raymond Lial married Sue Wilder and has two children.

Lial and Annette lived in the Wolcott house while living in St. Clair and later built a home in Good Thunder and moved there. Annette worked at Midtex for years. While working construction, Lial was hit on the head, rupturing a blood vessel, suffering blackouts. He died January12, 1976, and is buried at St. Clair.

Annette married Paul Chamberlain, who died a few years later. She then married John Hoffman.

WENNER, HARBERT

Harbert (Harry) Wenner (1-7-1887/4-1963) married Rose Bruels (9-16-1888), the daughter of Herbert Bruels. The couple moved to St. Clair in 1917. The couple had the following children, Ivennie (James Galston) whose children are William (Linda Oftedahl/Nancy) and Rosemary (Fredrick/Bohnert/Ron Rose). Robert (Agnes Klein) whose children are Bernard (Victoria (McCormick), Harold (Kathy Janssen), Stanley (Debra Eckstein), Rita (Dennis Debough), Gerald (Kristine Kline), Mark and Lester. Elaine married Merle James and their children are Ramona (Randy Will), Mary (Rodney Neher) and Gloria (Wayne Block/Joseph Winter). Edwin married Elizabeth Brunner and their children are Emily (John Arend), Joyce, Linda (Joseph Klaesus), Steven (Janet Kruger). Leland married Berneil Flores and their children are Leon (Irene Brown), Lois (Bradley Herring) and Neil (Wendy Sawatzky). Joan married Walter Bunde and their children are Michael, Cheryl (Kenneth Wiley), Richard (Debbie) and Patricia (William Lincoln). Mrs. Wenner died in 1945.

By Norma Bruels

WERDIN, EDWARD

Edward Werdin bought an oil station in St. Clair in the early thirties. He was married to the former Clara Koplen, the daughter of William and Amelia Koplen. She was born on a farm in Freedom Township on March 18, 1886. Edward and Clara were married on October 18, 1903. They had a son Wilfred. She died in 1940. In May 1942 Ed married Hazel Abraham and they had a daughter Faith. Ed died on December 30, 1972.

WESTPHAL, PAUL MARION

Paul Marion Westphal was born on July 13, 1866, in Budsin, Kreis Kolmar, Germany. In 1890 his sister Marie and her husband Ludwig Grams sent a total of $77 to Paul in Germany so he could come to America. Coming to this country at the age of 24 he started farming on a farm next to his sister which he homesteaded on September 10, 1901. He married Anna Mueller, born on March 29, 1874, the daughter of August Mueller and Ernestine Manthe, on December 5, 1893, and in 1915 built a large farm home for their ten children. Anna was not able to enjoy her family very long as she died at the age of 44 in 1918. Paul continued farming with his sons and died at the home in 1942. His great grandson Dale is still farming this ground and it became a Century farm in 2003. Paul and Anna are buried in the St. John's Evangelical Lutheran Cemetery in St. Clair.

Paul and Anna's children were Reinhardt, who married Alma Kriesh and farmed in McPherson Township, Walter who married Edna Dimmel and farmed in Waseca County, Arthur who married Florence Bluhm and lived in Waseca, August (see separate story), Otto (see separate story), Emil, who married Leona Drager, farmed in McPherson Township. William who married Leona Santo and farmed in Waseca County, daughter Louise who moved to California in 1927 and married Paul Young, John and Paul. (see separate stories)

The Paul Westphal family in 1917
Standing (L to R): Reinhardt, Walter, Emil, Arthur, William, August, Otto
Seated: Paul (Pete), Paul, Louise, Anna, John (Jack)

Walter Westphal during WWI
Images of his parents Anna and Paul in the background

August Westphal was born on August 20, 1898 in McPherson Township where he also attended school. He worked as a farm hand for several farmers and helped his father tile. He was working on the Michael Silkey Purebred Poland China Hog Farm in LeRay Township when he met his future wife, Lena Silkey. Lena was born on February 21, 1904, to Ludwig and Ottilie (Santo) in

August and Lena Westphal, March 1926

LeRay Township. They were married on March 16, 1926, and later moved to a farm in McPherson Township, which they bought in 1927. This farm had been part of the Winnebago Indian Reservation. August and Lena retired in St. Clair in 1963 and lived at 506 Main Street East. August was a resident of the Janesville Nursing Home when he died. August and Lena had three children. Mavis graduated from the St. Clair High School and worked at Green's 5 and 10 cent store in Mankato until her marriage to Elmer Rosin and then moved to the Nicollet area. Bernard (Myrtle Krause) (see separate story) and Arlene (1937-1973) graduated from St. Clair High School and married Stanley Carlson and lived in the LaSalle area.

Lena died on March 28, 1978, in a Mankato Hospital and August died on April 16, 1984 at the Janesville Nursing Home. They are buried in the St. John's Evangelical Lutheran Cemetery, St. Clair.

Bernard Westphal, the son of August and Lena (Silkey) Westphal, was born on December 31, 1935, and attended country school and graduated from St. Clair High School. He farmed with his father and now with his son, Dale. He served as an elder of St. John's Evangelical Lutheran Church, St. Clair, and has been the clerk for McPherson Township for 40 years. He served as a director for the Blue Earth County Township Association and served on the Blue Earth County Agricultural Board and the Blue Earth County Variance Board. In April 1992 he was the 34th heart transplant recipient at Mayo Clinic, Rochester, Minnesota. He married Myrtle Krause who was born on April 2, 1939, the daughter of Alvin and Esther (Vandrey) Krause of Willow Creek, Minnesota. She graduated from Garden City High School and Mankato State University with a B.S. degree in nursing and worked at the hospitals in Mankato, Minnesota. She later worked for Dr. Thomas F. Kiner, DDS, in Janesville, Minnesota, for twenty-four years. She enjoys gardening, genealogy and coordinating the *Years of Memories* publication. They have four sons who all graduated from St. Clair High School.

Michael, born on November 23, 1961, attended the University of Minnesota, Waseca, and graduated from South Dakota State University, Brookings, South Dakota. He is currently working for the Cargill Company, Nutrena Feed division and is living in Owatonna, Minnesota. He married Marilyn Hoechst the daughter of Woodrow and Margaret Hoechst of Minnesota Lake, Minnesota. Marilyn graduated from the Minnesota Lake High School and the University of Minnesota, Waseca. She is employed at their church in Owatonna. They have two sons, Joshua and Aaron, who are attending the Owatonna Public School. The family is active in the music activities in their church.

Douglas, born on January 22, 1963, attended University of Minnesota, Waseca, Minnesota, and graduated from Mankato State University, Mankato,

The Bernard Westphal family in 2000
Back row (L to R): Linda, Douglas, Dale, Mike, Marilyn, Donald, Beth. Center row: Thomas, Bernard, Myrtle, Aaron. Front row: Laura, Megan, Eric, Joshua

Minnesota. He is serving as the Blue Earth County Farm Service Agency Director, Mankato, Minnesota. He is on the St. Clair City Council and has served on the St. John's Evangelical Lutheran Church Council. He married Linda Danner, the daughter of John and Rita Danner of Litchfield, Minnesota. Linda graduated from the Watertown Sr. High School, Watertown, South Dakota. Linda works at the Hilltop HyVee Grocery Store, Mankato, Minnesota. They are living in St. Clair and have two children, Thomas and Laura, who both attend St. Clair Public School. Doug and Linda enjoy working at school activities.

Donald, born on January 25, 1967, graduated from Bethany Lutheran College, Mankato, the University of Minnesota, Minneapolis, and has a Master's Degree from Minnesota State University, Mankato. He is currently the Dean of Admissions at Bethany Lutheran College, Mankato, is a writer for the *Viking Update* Paper, and broadcasts the MSU hockey games for the local cable television. He is married to Beth Jones, the daughter of Loren and Hazel Jones of Belle Plaine, Minnesota. Beth is a graduate of the Belle Plaine High School and the University of Minnesota, Minneapolis, Minnesota. She is a registered nurse at Immanuel-St. Joseph's Hospital. They live in North Mankato and have two children, Eric and Megan, who attend Mt. Olive Lutheran School in Mankato.

Dale, born on September 14, 1968, graduated from the University of Minnesota, Waseca, and is presently operating the family farm. He has served on the St. Clair School Board, is a director of the McPherson Mutual Insurance Company and was on the St. John's Evangelical Lutheran Church Council. He is operating the road grader and snowplow for McPherson Township.

Otto Westphal was born in McPherson Township, in February 1900. He attended rural school and farmed in McPherson Township. On April 2, 1929, he married Kathryn "Sadie" McGannon, the daughter of Mr. and Mrs. James McGannon, at St. Paul. He was a member of the McPherson Township board for several years. Sadie was born in 1899, in Janesville Township, Waseca Co. She had lived in Ellendale, ND, for about 25 years before coming back to this area. Otto entered the Janesville Nursing Home in 1965.

Sadie died in 1962 and Otto died in July 1969. They are buried in the Immaculate Conception Cemetery, St. Clair.

Otto and Sadie were foster parents to their niece Kay, who graduated from St. Clair High School and married George Seys. They farmed in the rural St. Clair area. Kay and George had six children: Debra (Wayne Baumgartner), George Jr. (Colleen Preston), John (Marlee Winkelman), Chris (Kim Baumgartner), Donna and Angela (Brent Thoreson).

John "Jack" Westphal was born on May 26, 1908, in McPherson Township, Blue Earth County. He attended country school and married Frieda Hawker on August 28, 1935, in St. Clair. Frieda was born on October 24, 1913, and was the daughter of William and Eliza (Birr) Hawker. They farmed in the Pemberton area with his father and brother and continued living on the farm after his retirement until his death. Jack was an active member of St. John's Evangelical Lutheran Church serving as a trustee and conference delegate for many years. He also served as an officer for the local branch of Aid Association for Lutheran insurance and as a member of the Agricultural Stabilization and Conservation Board for several years. Frieda moved to Mankato after her husband's death. She was active in the church Ladies Aid, AAL and now enjoys doing volunteer work at ISJ hospital and the MRCI Thrift Shop in Mankato.

Jack died on November 12, 1996, and is buried in the St. John's Evangelical Lutheran Cemetery, St. Clair.

John & Frieda Westphal wedding, August 28, 1935
Back (L to R): Alvin Hawker, John (Jack) Westphal, Frieda Hawker Westphal, Louise Westphal
Children in front: Wayne Hawker, Betty Lou Westphal, Mavis Westphal

Frieda and John Westphal

Paul (Pete), Margie and Adeline Westphal.

Paul "Pete" Westphal was born on July 13, 1910, in McPherson Township, Blue Earth County. Paul attended country school and on June 28, 1934, married Adeline Schalow of St. Clair. Adeline was born on March 26, 1914, and was the daughter of Carl and Ida (Voight) Schalow. They farmed in the Pemberton area with his father and brother until his death on August 29, 1970. He is buried in the St. John's Evangelical Lutheran Cemetery, St. Clair.

Adeline continued living on the farm until relocation to Mankato in 1987. Their daughter Margie graduated from St. Clair Public School and Mankato State College. After graduation she did graduate work in several different colleges and received her Master's Degree in Biology from St. Mary's College in Winona with a National Grant. Margie taught Biology and Chemistry in West Concord and at John Marshall High School in Rochester, Minnesota. Always having a special love for horses, she is living with her husband Scott Fritz on a farm in the Rochester area. Marge has retired from her teaching duties. They spend the winter at their home in Chapala, Jalisco, Mexico.

By Myrtle Westphal

WILKINS, FRANK

Frank Wilkins was born in Allegany County, New York, on June 6, 1841. At the age of thirteen he moved with his parents to Columbia County, Wisconsin, and in 1868 came to Minnesota and settled at the Winnebago Agency. He finished his education at the Normal School at Mankato. He then taught eighteen terms. He had a farm of 200 acres of which forty acres were in McPherson Township. He enlisted in Company H, Second Wisconsin infantry and served two and one-half years. He was engaged in many battles and was wounded once. On April 15, 1865, he married Matilda S. Abbott and they had three children: Clara L., William E., and Grace E.

WILLS, J.C.

J.C. Wills was born in Chicago, Illinois, on October 3, 1852. His father, a sea captain, was drowned when his son was an infant. The mother with her family located near Milwaukee, Wisconsin. At the age of fourteen he moved to Mankato. He was a clerk in Mankato and then at Shelbyville. In 1870 he attended one term of school at Milwaukee and then became teller of the First National Bank at Mankato. He then clerked at the Winnebago Agency Bank. He finally established himself in the mercantile trade with W. H. Harrison, forming a partnership in June 1879. On October 17, 1877, he married Eva Crick and they had two children, one was Charles W.

WINGEN, JACOB

Jacob (1824-1865) and his wife Sophia (Dorweiler) (1827-1897) were born and reared in Prussia. On crossing the ocean to the United States proceeded direct to Clayton County, Iowa, where the father took up land and improved a farm. Later he removed to Minnesota and settled in McPherson Township, where he remained until his death in 1865.

Jacob and Sophia had nine children: Joseph J., Fred W., Anthony J., Sophia (Ulrich), Augusta (McGovern), Anna (Lang), Lena (Ulrich), Mary (Phillips) and Jacob.

Joseph J. Wingen was a landmark to the community. Mr. Wingen was born on November 18, 1850, in Rhine Province, Cologne, Germany and came to the United States with his parents when he was 15 months old. The journey from New York to Milwaukee was made partly by train and partly by stagecoach. Here a yoke of oxen was purchased and a wagon was made for the trip overland on planked roads to Guttenberg, Iowa, where his mother's parents lived. Here they lived in a log cabin for four or five years. In 1864 his family started in a covered wagon for Long Prairie, Minnesota. The trip took about three weeks. Not satisfied with the land there, they journeyed on to Mankato and finding too much woodland, they came on to Winnebago Agency, now known as St. Clair where they bought the Oscar Wayner place. In 1865 his father died, leaving his mother with nine children. Joseph J. was the oldest and so managed the farm and helped his mother bring up the children.

Coming here in the pioneer days of Southern Minnesota, he grew up with the country and developed with it, becoming one of the most prosperous farmers in this area. Articles concerning his life, which he took great delight in writing for the newspapers, and especially in his autobiography *From the Cradle to the Grave* were written in 1937 for his family, who treasure them highly.

In 1872, Mr. Wingen was united in marriage with Katherine Phillips (1854-1933) and in 1873 they located on the farm which has been the Wingen homestead ever since. They celebrated their 60th wedding anniversary just two months before Mrs. Wingen passed away on January 27, 1933.

During his long years of residence here, Mr. Wingen was recognized for his stability of character, his neighborly kindness, his generosity and thoughtfulness for others. He took into his home two orphan boys, John and Andrew Kanuck. For many years Mr. Wingen was a director of the St. Clair Bank and also of the town and school boards.

Their children were Leona (Henry Denn), Agnes (Matthias Pestka), Frances (Edward May), Marjorie (George Gahl), Belle (Walter Pagenkopf), Florence (Ernest Gahl), Sophia (Schoffman), Cora (LaPointe), Alonzo J. (1890-1961) (Erna Schonrock), and Jacob.

Joseph died in June 1939. He and Katherine are buried in the Immaculate Conception Catholic Cemetery in St. Clair.

Fred W. Wingen lived at St. Clair and in its vicinity for 75 years. He was born in 1856, at Guttenberg, Iowa, and came to Minnesota by covered wagon when he was eight years of age. He married Mary Phillips (1867-1942) in 1880. The couple celebrated their sixtieth wedding anniversary before his death. They lived for many years on the Wingen homestead south of St. Clair until 1917 when they moved to town. Mr. Wingen served as mayor of St. Clair for three years and was a director of the St. Clair Bank. They were the parents of three children: Laura (John Schneiderhan), Josephine (Louis Huettl) and Mrs. Lewis Merrill.

Fred W. died in 1940 and he and Mary are buried in the Immaculate Conception Catholic Cemetery in St. Clair.

Anthony J. Wingen was born in Clayton County, Iowa, September 13, 1854, and attended the country schools near the farm. Arriving at man's estate, he took up agricultural pursuits for himself, and remained on the homestead in McPherson township until 1897, when he removed to the farm he later owned and occupied.

In 1879 A.J. was united in marriage to Minnie Schutz (1859-1920), the daughter of Frederick and Minnie (Kurth) Schutz, natives of Prussia, Germany, but pioneers of McPherson Township. The children in this family were Jacob, who died at an early age, Frederick (Louise Burscke) the eldest son, who farmed at Vernon Center, Minnesota, the second son Edward, was employed as a bookkeeper in the Bank of Commerce at Mankato, Minnesota. The only daughter, Leona, was a schoolteacher.

In former years Mr. Wingen filled school offices and he maintained a deep interest in all measures for the development of the schools and the county. Lodges did not receive his support, nor did he prevail upon to take any but an independent attitude in politics. Through unwea-

The Winkelman Family.
Bottom left: Art, Jennie, James and Myrna Winkelman.
Center: the James Winkelman family.
Center left: Marlee Winkelman.
Top left: Jeff Winkelman. Center right: Thomas Winkelman.

ried labors he accumulated a competency and attained a position among the large landowners of the county.

Anthony died in 1945. He and Minnie are buried in the Glenwood Cemetery, Mankato.

WINKELMAN, ARTHUR

Arthur Winkelman was born in 1893. He married JoHanna "Jennie" Apple on August 17, 1917, in Springfield, Minnesota. JoHanna was born in 1897. They moved to St. Clair in 1930 and they lived in the house, which later was the Lyle Splinter home. They then moved to the Henry Schalow house, which later was the Bill Myers home. Here they rented out rooms to Herbert Ahl and John Fossum when they worked in the creamery. When Jennie's sister and brother-in-law, the Jack Pint's, came to St. Clair they also lived with Art and JoHanna. The later moved to 117 Railroad Street. Art started the St. Clair Feed Mill. He managed his business until he passed away in 1969. JoHanna continued to live in St. Clair until her death in 1991. They are buried in the St. John's Evangelical Lutheran Cemetery, St. Clair.

Art and JoHanna had three children: Gretchen, who married Frank Groebner and moved to Faribault, Minnesota, and had two children Ann Marie and David, Gertrude (Robert Fritzke - see separate story) and James.

James Winkelman is the son of Arthur and JoHanna (Apple) Winkelman. He attended St. Clair School and graduated from Bethany Lutheran College, Mankato, Minnesota. He met his wife Myrna in 1952 and they were married in 1953. She was working at the Bell Telephone Company in Mankato at the time they met. Myrna is the daughter of Ben Otto and Marvel (Jessup) Daby from Mankato, Minnesota.

James took over the Winkelman Feed Mill after his father's death in 1969 and retired in 2001.

James and Myrna have three children. Jeffrey James graduated from St. Clair School and is married to Mary Oachs, the daughter of Roger and Gloria (Rosin) Oachs of Mankato. Jeff works for Fine Impressions and enjoys restoring antique toys. Mary enjoys working at Oaklawn Nursing Home. They are living in Mankato, Minnesota.

Thomas Mark graduated from St. Clair School and is married to Melody West, the daughter of Ronald and Dodie West of Granite Falls, Minnesota. Thomas works for the City of Mankato in the Water Department. Melody is the program coordinator for Horizon Homes in Mankato. They live in Mankato.

Marlee Jo also graduated from St. Clair and is married to Ronald Kramer, the son of Francis F. and Elaine (Gehring) Kramer of Waseca. Marlee Jo operates a photography business, is on the board of directors for the W. I.S.H. Modeling Agency and sells Avon products. Ronald works for the City of Waseca and has a "Hosta" greenhouse. They live in Waseca, Minnesoda.

Myrna, James, Jeff and Thomas are members of St. John's Lutheran Church, St. Clair.

"God Bless Our Town of St. Clair."

By Myrna Winkelman

WINTER, MARTIN

Martin P. (Marty) Winter was born in 1922 and was the son of Martin E. and Frieda (Schulz) Winter. His father (1899-1987) was a farmer and rural mail carrier and his mother (1898-1995) was a housewife and a nurse's aid. Marty was a lifelong farmer (dairy), loved hunting and raised many dogs from Terriers and Beagles to Coonhounds and Airedales. In 1948 he was married to Shirley Reedstrom (1927), the daughter of Frank and Lydia (Kriel) Reedstrom from Rapidan, MN. Frank (1902-2003) was a farmer and "Jack of all trades." Lydia (1904-1996) was a homemaker and assistant post-mistress. Shirley graduated from Rapidan High School and attended Mankato Commercial College. She worked in the County Extension Offices in Waseca and Mankato. Later she worked for thirty years as an accountant in Janesville and Waseca.

On March 1, 1951, they moved to the farm in McPherson Township where they raised their family of five sons. Marty died on August 13, 1993. Shirley is still living on the family farm and is now married to Herman Guse.

Richard D. Winter was born in 1949 and attended Trinity Parochial School in Janesville and graduated from St. Clair High School. Rich served his country in the U.S. Army from 1970-1972. He attended Mankato State College and South Central Vocational-Technical College graduating as a draftsman. He is presently a rural mail carrier working out of the Janesville Post Office. In 1972 he married Judy Nyquist, the daughter of Dean and Marjorie (Timmerman) Nyquist. They have three children Tricia (John Giesche), Michelle (Shawn Bingham) and Brent, and two grandsons.

Robert M. Winter was born in 1952. He also attended school in Janesville and graduated from St. Clair High School. He worked in construction and worked at Hiniker Manufacturing Co., rural Mankato, for over 30 years, as traffic and shipping manager. He married Linda Faltersack and they have two children, Connie (Matt Bartz) and Cheryl (Chad Bleess) and three grandsons and a granddaughter.

Ronald L. Winter was born in 1953, attended school in Janesville and graduated from the St. Clair High

School. He was a welder at the Hiniker Company until he started his own welding shop and also does custom tilling and seeding. He married Beth Frazen and they have two daughters, Susan and Christine.

Ray A. Winter was born in 1956, attended school in Janesville and graduated from St. Clair High School. He farmed with his dad, lives on the family farm and has now taken over the farming operation. He is a crop farmer and has expanded into a vineyard and nursery business. He married Lisa Barnes and they have a son Thomas and a daughter Angela.

Russell J. Winter was born in 1960, attended school in Janesville and graduated from the St. Clair High School. He enlisted in the National Guard, is farming in partnership with his brother and works at the St. Peter Treatment Center, St. Peter, MN, in security. He married Cathryn Anderson and together they own and Cathryn operates "The Coffee House" in the River Hills Mall, Mankato, MN. They have two sons Tyler and Eric.

By Shirley Winter

WITT, CLARENCE

Clarence Witt was born on February 22, 1915, and was the son of Robert and Bertha (Rost) Witt. He grew up on the family farm by Buffalo Lake, Alton Township, and Waseca County. He married Lenora Possin on June 30, 1938 at Freedom Lutheran Church. Lenora was the daughter of Otto and Bertha (Schendel) Possin, who was born on September 30, 1916, and grew up in Freedom Township, Waseca County.

Clarence and Lenora moved to McPherson Township in 1944. There was no running water, no telephone, no electricity but an outdoor toilet. The drinking water in the house was in a white porcelain pail with a dipper. Electricity was installed about 1947 at which time we got a radio and telephone. The bathroom and pressure water system was installed in the early 1950's. Our first television was bought in 1955. Dad's first car with a radio was a 1953 Chevrolet. In the 1940's and before, water was carried in pails to the chickens and pigs. The cows were left out of the barn into the cow yard where there was a large water tank. When it was dark the cows were milked by lantern light.

Lenora & Clarence Witt

The children of Clarence and Lenora were: **Bonnie** (Merlyn Proechel) who lives by Waseca, Minnesota, and worked as a Technical Clerk at the Waseca County License Bureau and is now retired. Merlyn is a farmer.

Harlan (Judy Phillips) lives on a farm near St. Clair. Judy is a homemaker.

Sharon (Robert Wilder-deceased) lives in Mankato and works at General Electric near Mankato.

Linda (Richard Maxson) lives in Maple Grove. She is an insurance accountant in Minneapolis and Richard is director of engineering in Minneapolis.

Daryl (Lisa Linn) lives in Mankato and is a farm equipment mechanic at John Deere Implement in Mankato. Lisa works with adult day care in Mankato.

Clarence and Lenora retired and moved to St. Clair where they lived at 102 Willow Lane. He died on November 5, 2001, and Lenora died on April 22, 2005. They are buried in St. John's Evangelical Lutheran Cemetery, St. Clair.

By Bonnie and Merlyn Proechel

WOELFEL, CHARLES

Charles Woelfel was born in 1845 in Bain, Austria. He married Philomena Bolnig, an orphan, who was born on March 8, 1845, also in Austria. She was very happy to be married and to be part of a family. Their first two children, Joseph and Anna, were born in Austria. Because their living conditions were not the best, they decided to come to America. They traveled with another couple who knew some people who had come to St. Clair earlier. When they arrived to their destination they cleared trees and settled on a farm and lived the rest of their lives here. When they came to America they left behind Charles' brother, Anton but sent for him when the mother died.

Six children were born to this marriage: Joseph (1870) married Christina Troske and they had nine children. Anna (1872-1931) married Edward Miller (see separate story). Maria was born on November 1, 1874, shortly after the family arrived in America. She was a Priest housekeeper for 35 years. She died on September 6,

1944. Francis Charles, known as Carl (1879-1944) married Helen Gales and they had ten children, Teresa Marie (1882-1971) and Charles Carl (1884-1959).

Charles Woelfel died in 1912 and Philomena died in 1921.

By Sondra Von Arb

WOLCOTT, JOHN FREMONT

John F. Wolcott was born on July 16, 1866, in St. Clair to John Solomon and Phoebe Melissa (Graham) Wolcott.

The Wolcott house (after it was remodeled) next to the large cottonwood tree

Angeline Fisk (left) and Tutie Grignon Rasdall Boswell standing next to the cottonwood tree in Wolcott's yard

On September 15, 1886, he married Minnie Olive Foster, the daughter of Stephen and Missouri (Adkins) Foster. Minnie was born on September 17, 1866, in Miflin, Wisconsin.

John lived in St. Clair all his life except for about one and a half years that he spent homesteading in South Dakota. While in St. Clair they lived at 213 West Main Street West. He was employed as a farmer, thresher and carpenter. John was the last of the well-known threshing and lumber mill crew under the management of Jake Chase and Henry Campbell.

The children born to this couple were: John Henry (1887-1888), Dolly Mae (1889) married William Warwick and lived in San Francisco, California, Foster Fernley "Jack" (1892-1921), married Cora Head, Lloyd Earl (1894), married Ruth Swart and lived in Tacoma, Washington, Olive Ione (1897-1976), married John Aura and lived in Hibbing, Minnesota, Theodore (1900-1920), Harold "Chub" (1906-2000), and Claire "Pete" (1908-1972).

John died on January 10, 1951, and Minnie died on June 27, 1947. They are buried in the Union Cemetery along with six of their children.

Harold Stephen "Chub" and **Claire Allen "Pete" Wolcott** were born in 1906 and 1908 respectively in McPherson Township. They both graduated from St. Clair High School in 1924 and were veterans of WWII. Harold served in the U.S. Army Air Corp and Clair in the U.S. Army. From 1951 until 1956 the brothers operated the Wolcott Brothers Grocery Store. They later lived at 330 Main Street East. Chub died in 2000 and Clair in 1972.

Harold (Chub) Wolcott in front of Wolcott's Grocery Store

Pete and Harold Wolcott in Wolcott's Grocery

Pete Wolcott in Wolcott's Grocery

ZABEL, DENNIS

Dennis Zabel, the son of Donald and Edie (Guise) Zabel married Margaret "Muggs" Evan, the daughter of Edward and Thelma (More) Evan. The families are from the Minnesota Lake area. Dennis works for Tow Distributing Corporation in Mankato and was the mayor of St. Clair from March 1995 until March 2003. Muggs works at the McPherson Farmers Mutual Insurance Company in St. Clair. Their children are Troy, Jill married Michael Kroc, they have a child Riley and live in Mankato, Tracy married Chris Songe and lives in Little Canada, Minnesota, and Katie (2-6-1981/12-13-1997).

Troy Zabel married Kelly Seys, the daughter of Jerome and Janice (Thrun) Seys. They purchased the former St. Clair Municipal Liquor Store in 1995. Kelly works in the business office at the St. Clair Public School. They have three children, Haley, Shaya and Peyton.

By Troy Zabel

Standing - (L to R): Katie, Tracy, Michael & Jill (Zabel) Kroc, Margaret (Evan) Zabel, Kelly (Seys) & Troy Zabel
Seated: Dennis Zabel

The photo below shows Melvin and Alice Rasdall's youngest son, Grant, sitting with a group of friends in St. Clair, eating watermelon in the summertime. (If you look at their feet, you'll see the piles of watermelon seeds.) Grant is the second from right, about to take a bite.

CHAPTER NINE

Memoirs

THE WINNEBAGO INDIAN AGENCY

The Post Office was called the Winnebago Agency and Lucius Dyer was appointed Postmaster. He had been the Indian farmer under the Republican Administration, but on the departure of the Winnebago Indians, he purchased the land, on which the large brick residence of the Indian Agent stood, and occupied it as a hotel.

In March 1865, he sold the place to Josiah C. Truman, who about the same time succeeded him as Postmaster.

The house and land were sold to Duane Franklin Rasdall (my great grandfather). Sometime in the late 1890's or early 1900's the house and land were sold to my grandparents Frank Madison Chase and Grace Estelle Rasdall Chase. They sold the house and land to the Preston's sometime in the 1940's and moved to town.

While Grandpa and Grandma were farming the agency land there were still a few Indians living on the banks of the river, halfway down the hill from where the barn now stands. There was one widow squaw who lived there, who kept opening a hole in grandpa's cornfield and letting her cow in to eat. He caught her opening the fence one-day and went down to stop her, but she chased him up the hill to the barn with an Indian Billy club. It was a smooth oval stone (about the size of an egg), wrapped with leather and then wrapped unto the leather handle. I don't know what happened to this club when they moved into town, I hope it was given to the museum in Mankato as they did not have it in town when I visited. I played with it and lived in the agency house; first while I was still in Minnesota and then when I visited up to the time they sold the place. I have many fond memories of the house and barnyard.

When they moved to town they lived in the two-story house that was on the front corner of the school grounds until their deaths. The school bought the property, selling the house, which was moved to the street that runs between the Nick & Florence Juliar and the Thielman/Pagenkopf house.

I still have relatives in St. Clair and the area. Through the Chases and especially through the Juliar's, in fact the Preston's who bought the house are related on the Juliar side.

I realize I didn't spend a lot of time in St. Clair and most of my memories are from 1934 to 1938, and then the many summers I spent in St. Clair and on the farms of both grandparents. A lot of them are the same as Louann Fisher's on my mother's side and Lowell Pagenkopf on my father's side.

You all do know that the old O'Brien house without additions is the last standing of the three agency buildings. Richard Manaige burned down the one that was on one tip of the triangle on a cold winter night, when he was drinking and set a fire to stay warm. Some of the bricks were still there when I was a girl and played with Audrey O'Brien.

by Beverly Jane Chase Flosi

Reminiscence of the Winnebago Agency House

The Winnebago Agency House was a very special

place for my family as the Agency Farm has been the home of my father's paternal ancestors, the Henry Trumans and the John Boswells, from 1864 to 1876. Later it became the home of my mother's maternal ancestors, the Duane Rasdalls from 1882 to 1924 and the Frank Chases from 1924 to 1941.

Many happy hours of our childhood and youth, my brother's and mine, were spent at the farm. No matter the season, we always found plenty of things to do: chasing butterflies in the meadow or riding the haying wagons or the shock wagons during harvest were summer time activities, and sliding down the granary roof on scoop shovels was a winter favorite.

The Agency was never my home, but the home of our Aunt Grace and Uncle Frank Chase. The house was unusual in several ways. There were two parlors; one was less formal and had a floor about five inches higher than the other. This room was technically the bar during the hotel days. The story is that "loggers," men who logged the timbers on the Le Sueur River nearby, wore out the floors with their spiked boots and another floor would be laid over the worn one.

There was an auxiliary-heating stove in the dining room during the winter months and Aunt Grace's raps on the stovepipe signaled time to rise. Chores were hastily accomplished for the tempting breakfasts that awaited everyone. The kitchen was a large room, twenty-two feet long and fifteen feet wide, and it accommodated a number of people. A favorite breakfast menu included homemade sausages and buckwheat cakes made from a "starter," with real maple syrup.

Christmas was a wonderful event at the Agency: the big dinner and the warmth of sharing this festive season were deeply felt. If the weather was inclement and the road snow-blocked, we knew that Uncle Frank would call for all of us with his horses and sleigh. That was a real bonus. Frequently we went prepared to stay an extra day or two, though our father would return home to attend to the furnace. Most often the crowd included other than family, friends who were unable to go to their own families, or who had no family. I recall the year the phonograph records "Three O'Clock in the Morning" and "Barney Goggle" were so popular. Someone had received the records as a gift and those selections were played on the Victrola and danced to all night long. The central hallway provided an ideal dance floor.

One could while away many hours exploring the farmyard. There was the barn and a number of other essential buildings a farm needed in those days, but my greatest fascination was the windmill. I well recall being daunted several times as I attempted to ascend the windmill ladder. One time I achieved success. I reached the topmost platform and there I surveyed the surrounding countryside. Oh, I felt as though I was on top of the world!

Harvest time was very exciting, it demanded hard work but allowed for social time as well. Mother and father responded to the call for auxiliary help, and my brother and I were included for we ran errands. The threshing crew would come down the lane like a procession, the big engine, the separator, the bunkhouse for the crew, and Mother assisted with the food preparation, and our Father would usually join the field men in forking the bundles of grain on the "shock" wagons. It was then hauled to the separator. I enjoyed the rides on the wagons and remember the feeling of getting "stuck" with the barley beards. It was a treat to be allowed to ride the farm wagonloads of grain as it was taken to the elevator. Sometimes the person in charge would permit me to hold the reins, which guided the horses.

Aunt Grace had a subtle way of convincing us to work with her. She would tell us that we must complete the necessary daily tasks in the morning, promising that after the noon dishes were finished the afternoon was reserved for amusement. This resulted in memorable times such as picking wild flowers or berrying in the timberland, or swimming in the Le Sueur River. If the wild grapes were in season, we picked them; the reward was a wild grape pie. My mouth "puckers" at the thought of it.

Near the timber toward the northwest was what we called the "reservation." It was so called because the Manaige's, a Winnebago Indian family, had chosen to accept their eighty-acre land allocation in 1863 and had remained there. I had two young friends who were descendants of them. Our mothers had been schoolmates and had continued their friendship. I would go there when the girls were visiting their grandmother. Their great Aunt Archie was about ninety years old and very wrinkled and wizened. I firmly believed she was made of leather.

by Marion Boswell Hoffman-
The Heritage of Blue Earth County, MN - 1990

Clay's Memories from St. Clair - 1976

Clay Boswell related his memories of St. Clair to his daughter Marion Boswell Hoffman in 1976, shortly before he died.

Charlie Rogers ran the flourmill next door to our (Boswell) house. Rogers' lived where Mrs. Gertie Froelich lived. Blanche and Hazel were the Rogers' daughters (Viva's friend Blanche). The flour was sold to the Scheerschmidt Bakery in Mankato located across from Hubbard Mill. Scheerschmidt's and Wiggins Meat Market were connected. The mill was behind Frank

Amberg's (Hubie Johnson's) barn. The river formed an ox-bow which provided power for the mill, which was originally a sawmill and shingle factory for the Agency-it was government owned.

Sarah Quinn Ryan, sister to Andy Quinn, lived where school playground is located today (currently the northwest corner of the school). She had two children…Jim and Dora

Frank Ario lived where the Ed Frank home now stands. His son, Victor's first wife died, he remarried and had six children – Ed, Lena, Frank, John and Rudolf. Rudy lived in the Fred Baer house.

Asa White, Boswell House, Dr. Haynes and Agency house were the first houses in St. Clair or rather Hilton town site. Gustav Hilton built and lived in the old Boswell house initially John Lindrup lived in the house next – for one year. Grandfather William Boswell bought the house in 1893 and added a large addition which was completed in 1896

Josette Store located where the Hardware Store now stands (currently Four Flags Over Aspen). Mr. Gus Duemeland worked here. Rudolph Froelich owned it in the 20's and 30's.

Jim Nesbitt lived in a house where George Hubmer home now stands. Mrs. Nesbitt was a sister to Charles Russell (Hugh Russell's father).

Asa White married a Winnebago-native American woman. They lived in a home now owned by Schalow's; (where Schalow Apartment North is located today) it was constructed of brick made in St. Clair. The brick yard was located by the "Old Forde" Road (next to the Fisher, later Harry and Mary Miller home) - took in the area where Mary Anderson, Halls and Otto Witts had homes. It was run by Jake Chase and Henry Campbell. Asa White died and his wife remarried an Andrews who was a carpenter by trade. They had 3 children, Dewey (Dwight), Asa and ??. Dewey later continued living in the old white home-he married Anna Schalow and had one son, Dewey II.

Asa Andrews married Fanny Wheeler (Tivoli Wheelers) – they had 6 children – Ida, Mame, Jim, Genevieve, Una and Thelma. They lived in the home later owned by Nora O'Leary (next to where Hugh Russell lived).

Asa later built the home (where George Fitzloff's lived) and the family lived there for awhile. Clay's Aunt Mae Rowell lived next door.

Fred Dittman and wife Anna lived in the old Dittman brick house near Glaser's. They had two children, Hannah and Fred.

Klingbeil farm was below the hill north of Elmer Nicolai's (Michael Peters) on the same side of the road.

August Kopke farm was across from Elmer Nicolai's farm.

Robert and Frank Sodeman had a sister Emma who married Peter Roerig. The Roerig's built the house where Gus Schostag lived.

Andy Glasgow lived where the Ralph Ireland's live. Children were Phil, Andy, Grace and ? Bill Brandt married Grace Glasgow and lived at the Gerald Kollos place (first place north out on Hwy #83 on east side of road). Some of the original house is still there.

Arch McCollum and wife Lidianne lived behind the former Ken Cords farm on the shores of McCollum Lake (located west of St. Clair on today's Blue Earth Co. Road 90).

Bear Lake was located on the Leo Kruse farm. Clay Boswell's mother told of 25 Indian families that would spend several summer months camped by Bear Lake shores. The county ditch drained both McCollum Lake and Bear Lake to the Le Sueur River.

Chris McGovern, brother of Peter, lived where the Ray Kruse family lived. The children were Frank, Mike, Jim, Jane, Kate and Sadie. Peter McGovern's children were Lawrence (Larry) and Jack. Peter later lived in a house right by the St. Clair water tower.

Frank Bushine married Bertha Scheiding. They lived at the Hookemeyer Hotel. They had 2 daughters Bertha and Kate. This was the Schostag Hotel in the 1930's and later.

Meinsingerr (Munsinger?) Liquor Store was located on the Stanley Drake lot. It later was Kuske's harness-shoe repair shop.

The old Fields family lived on the Leon Bruels farm. Children were John, William, Jim and a daughter who married Harry Lynch.

John Fields lived on the former Norman Phillips farm. Later they lived across the street from the Catholic Church.

Romacks ran a store in Tivoli (where Qualsets live).

Henry Hilton (cousin to Gus and Sumner Hilton) was a Civil War Veteran and suffered from tuberculosis. His wife acted as a doctor in the area. Children were Charlie, Bill, Ebenezer, Ralph, Georgia (now a McCarthy), Libby and Margaret. Charlie married Grace Buckholz (a teacher). Georgia McCarthy lived in North Dakota. Ebenezer married a Krause, worked for the railroad and lived at Albert Lea, MN. He found a small girl abandoned in a railroad depot and raised her. Ebenezer lived in St. Clair where Ada Bestman's garage stands. The Hiltons lived across from the German Lutheran Church and the house was still standing in the 1920's.

Jim Wheeler married Savallah Rowell. They lived in a house where the Wilson home (formerly Louie Grams house - just west of Jeff's Repair - former Stan Drakes) now stands. Later Mel Rasdall bought and lived in the Wheeler house.

Rowell's lived where Herb Bruels lives (Norma lives today). Children were Charlie, Savallah, George (later lived in North Branch), Nell, May and Lillian. May moved to St. Clair and died there.

Ira Nixon lived by Bear Lake.

Felix Purde lived by Lower farm (southeast corner of Mankato Township). He had a relation in Good Thunder named Lige Phelps.

Ike Autry family lived on the Courrier Hubmer farm. Later moved to the land later owned by Tony and Hulda Fitzloff. Sons were Scott and Doc.

Valentine and Vinsante St. Cyr were sons of a French father and a Winnebago Native American mother. Lived in the house now owned by Borchert's.

Ed Manaige had a beautiful daughter Rose. They first lived in a home located near the Precht home, where Meyer's garden is located. Later moved to a home where Kenneth Kroenke lives. Still later moved to Tomah, Wisconsin. Kenneth Kroenke lives along the Le Sueur River.

Plete Manaige (real name Peter Paul) lived below and behind where Chuck Grams lives, the old O'Brien place, flat land near Le Sueur River. His wife was the daughter of Lash Apelle (who lived right below the Nelson's house). Children were Richard, Andrew and Margaret (who married a Kelly). The Kelly's lived where Lang's are living – children were Ira, Lawrence (who later lived in California) and Josie. Josie married a Reichel. (The O'Brien farm was before Chuck Grams).

Margaret Manaige, sister to Plete married Louie Thebow and lived at the end of Carl Kruse road.

Peter Manaige family lived on the same 80 acres where Plete lived. Children were Josie, Louie, Angeline, Henry, Margaret, Ed and Plete. Angeline Manaige married a Dotson - also lived with Peter Manaige on the 80 acres and had three children Sybil, Henry (who was a streetcar conductor in St. Paul), and John. Sybil married Ed Mountain from Good Thunder. They had 4 children - Charlotte, Jean, Jim and Bobby.

Joe Alexander married a Winnebago Native American woman - they lived near the Nick Tachney farm. (Fred Alexander of Madison Lake was a descendant.) A Winnebago by the name of Chapman lived with the Alexander's. He was an area handy man.

Gustav and Sumner Hilton operated the government sawmill located along the Le Sueur River. The mill was behind the Amberg (Hubie Johnson/Doug Gjerde) property.

William Tillotson lived near the McPherson Union Cemetery - on top of the rise (Lone Pine Treasures). He gave 40 acres of the Fred Schostag farm and 40 acres of the new Boswell farm to his son Oliver Tillotson. Oliver bought timber at the St. Anthony, Minnesota, sawmill and picked it up in Mankato and hauled it via oxen and wagon to the later Boswell farm. He built the house where Clay Boswell was born. Oliver Tillotson married a Winnebago Native American woman - their children were Scott, Doc and Mabel. They later lived on the William Grams' farm. Fred Schostag's lived there.

Wetherbee's (relatives of Hiltons) lived on 40 acres between Boswell's and Bruels' farms. Had a wood framed house. He was a Civil War veteran.

Wilking's lived kitty-corner from Wenners - also had a wood frame house.

Symion Payr lived across from Dennis Kruse (Jeanie and Mark Kruse), later sold to Klimpton (wood framed house).

Joe Koppen lived on peat-land (later Clay Boswell's 80 acres) - barn, house, shed, were log buildings.

Schroeder family lived where Orin Birr lives. The children were William, Charlie, Robert, Lizzie and Flora. Flora married Albert Byersdorf and had one son Eddie - lived where Curly Ward lives.

Otts lived on highway 83 near Dickenson School. Log building now is in Sibley Park.

Englerth family lived across the windmill on the Depuydt farm.

John Bestman married Henrietta, sister of Albert Byersdorf. They lived on the Bestman farm. Children were John (married Lena Krause), Charlie, Herbert and Lena.

John Murphy owned store (Harrison store - which Harrison built when he left partnership with Henry Foster), Jim Nesbitt and Charlie Pagenkopf bought the store from Murphy. Then Harrison and Thielman started their general store.

Grandpa Bestman and Wheeler operated blacksmith shop. Located next to Duemeland Store (now the school property).

Grandpa Krause was a wagon-maker. He had a house with a lean-to next to the blacksmith shop, which was located in front of the old gym.

Jim Wheeler and Jim Ryan had a blacksmith shop located on the Stan Drake (Jeff's Repair) lot. Previously that area had accommodated a livery stable, which was owned by Mel Rasdall.

Lassow farm located on the Edward Frank place. The children were Albert, George, Irna and Frank. Grandfather Thielman paid for Albert's law-degree education.

Sylvester Wills lived where Eldo Ewert lived.

Josie Bushine married Arthur O'Connor (son of Judge Chase O'Connor). Children were Cyril, Paschel, Maurice, and Margaret. Lived in old Hemshrot house.

Arnold and Frank Bushine had meat market across

Le Sueur Road where the park was later located.

Lumberg married Jessie Ira and lived where Joe Hodapp lived.

St. Clair Doctors:

Dr. E. B. Haynes - lived in Wolcott house
Dr. Joseph Eaton
Dr. Ray
Dr. Nutting
Dr. Insley
Dr. W. S. Smith - lived in the later Nick Juliar home
Dr. Davis - also lived in Nick Juliar home
Dr. Carl J. Holman-appendix surgeon
Dr. Jesse Macbeth
Dr. Richard Juliar - built the drug-store building which had an apartment above for his family, pharmacy, post office, and medical office on the first floor.
Dr. John Wohlrabe

St. Clair Today vs. St. Clair Yesteryears

I am standing looking up the Main Street in St. Clair — I see an Ice Cream and Beer Warehouse, American Legion Hall, Insurance Building, Liquor Store, Restaurant, 2 Grocery Stores, Bank, Hardware Store, Gas Station with car repair shop, an Elevator, Feed Mill, 3 churches, City Hall, Fire Station, Post Office and a Fine School Building.

Now my mind goes back to yesteryears when St. Clair was a bustling, industrious town with a Roller Mill, where people brought in their wheat to be made into flour. This Mill was down by the river near where the bridge is and across from the present Post Office — also there were 3 Grocery Stores, Hardware Store, Livery Stables, Blacksmith Shop, Harness Shop, Drug Store, Barber Shop, 3 or more Saloons, Creamery, a Cream Station, Poultry and Egg Business, Restaurant, Bank, Telephone Exchange Office, Garage and Gas Stations, Meat Market, Town Hall, Fire Station, Churches, 2 Medical Doctors, Lumber Yard, Elevator, Depot, School, and the "Turn Around" for the train to do its switching as this was the end of the railroad and the train had to turn around and go back to Albert Lea.

Laura Ward Brewer

Saturday nights the farm families would come to town bringing the eggs in and getting the weeks groceries, possibly the men would be getting haircuts. Every store had a bench in front of their building and the people would sit and have a good visit before going home.

It is told that at one time the river was so wide that a ferry line went from Quinn's corner (presently Mrs. Patricia Panzram home) over to the hill north of where Oscar Froehlich's residence was.

At one time there was a butcher house and meat market located on the north side of the river and west of the North Bridge. At a later time this area was to become the City Park.

Then there was the "Free" Outdoor Movies once a week on the empty lot where the McPherson Insurance building now is, and how the people thronged into town those nights to see the movie!

Then in cooler weather there was the "Old Medicine Shows" in the old Town Hall; this cost 10 cents per person, and what a crowd would gather in there. The Tonic that was sold was a "Cure All.!!!" Some very good programs were put on by the Caylor Co. and the Alger Co.

The churches would have Ice Cream Socials on the empty lot between the Mercantile Store and the old Pagenkopf Store.

The old Town Hall was the place where all the dances were held, and there were lots of them.

Yes, St. Clair was once a very lively town, but times do change. People now go farther for their pleasures, food and clothing and that is due to the modes of transportation, I suppose.

Our town has grown in population though, and this is because people seem to like living in smaller towns. We first had the Nyquist Addition with many new homes on the south edge of town: then the Denn Addition and more new homes on the east edge of town. Next came the Frank Addition and again more new homes on the west edge of town. We also have a Trailer Court in town, and last but surely not least are the 2 Schalow Apartment Buildings where there are 20 apartments with mostly Senior Citizens as renters that are very happy living there—as one person said, "We're just like one big family helping one another."

My, what a difference 100 years – 75 years, yes - even 50 years can make in a community. They say it's progress: I suppose it is: but sometimes we wonder.

by Laura Ward Brewer - 1986

Additional Memories: The North Bridge. At a later time this area was to become the City Park.

East of town, taking road #15 out towards the bridge, there was a pavilion called The Crystal located south of the road and west of the river. Jerry Lynch was the owner. Dances with live music and roller-skating to calliope music was held there with reports of both "good times" and "rough times." The pavilion was eventually moved to the Mankato-Kasota area and became The Crystal Ball Room.

On this same road, but a little farther east, there was a golf course located on the north side of the road (across from where Elvera Hall now lives). This was one of Ray Fitzloff's enterprises.

When St. Clair's nom de plume was "Podunk"' its social classes included the "River Rats." Honored citizens bore distinguished titles such as "High Pockets" (Harry Fisher), "Irish" (Laurance Froehlich), "Iggy" (Fritz Bestmann), "Buzz" (Harold Boswell), "Pretty" (Chester Preston) "Slippery Liz" (Everad O'Brien). This heritage of titles was handed down through the years... "Jughead" (Marvin Juliar)," Bubbles" (Warren Bruels) and many more too numerous to list.

Husky Helper – Clever Clovers 4-H Club

4-H (Head, Heart, Hands, & Health) is an organization dedicated to helping young people see their potential and develop skills that make a positive difference in their lives.

My 4-H story began in 1952 when I became a member of the Husky Helpers 4-H Club. Members were kids who lived in the St. Clair area. The club was open to all – those who lived in the country or in town. Having an animal to show at the county fair was a big part of this experience. Almost everyone had a pig, a lamb, or a calf (dairy or beef), even if they were a "town kid." There were a number of other projects one could take such as Food Preparation, Food Preservation, Clothing, Bread, Garden, Home Improvement, Home Beautification, Mechanics, Safety, Tractor and Poultry.

I graduated from 4-H in 1959. Some of the leaders (all volunteers) that I had during that time were: Mrs. Milton Juliar, Mrs. Dorothy Hesse, Mrs. Dan O'Herin, Harry Fisher, Mrs. Paul Schwichtenberg, Mrs. Otto Witt, Mr. and Mrs. Stanley Steel, and Mrs. Laurence Froehlich.

Highlights of a 4-H year included participation in the Blue Earth County Fair and the Tri-County Fair. Some lucky kids won trips to the State Fair and the Junior Livestock Show. The annual County Achievement Banquet was something to look forward to – the menu never varied (roast beef, corn, coleslaw and ice cream) but it was good. Perhaps it didn't taste as good if you suspected it was the beef you had spent a lot of time with during the year! Some of the more stressful events were getting your records completed on time, training an animal to do what you wanted them to do, and cleaning up a weed-infested garden before everyone in the club came to view your project on Tour Day.

The opportunity to have fun at monthly meetings, meeting kids from all over the county at the fair, winning prizes (and a modest amount of prize money), and to play softball kept a lot of us coming back year after year. I earned enough money from the sales of my 4-H animals to pay for all the tuition at three years of nursing school.

I've been involved in 4-H to some degree for many years, my own years as a member and many more years of helping nieces, nephews, grandnieces and grandnephews with some of their projects, especially the clothing project.

Lots of changes have occurred over the years such as the proliferation of projects available for almost everyone's interest and skills. Judging has gone from product review to today where the interview of the 4-Her is at least as important as the product. This has been a good move as it encourages the 4-Her to become a lot more involved and knowledgeable about their project. (O.K., I hate to say it but there were times in the past when someone other than the 4-Her completed the project!)

All volunteer organizations seem to have their ups and downs over the years. Husky Helpers was no different, sometimes the largest club in the county to evolving to a time when another club began in the area (Clever Clovers) and finally Husky Helpers disappeared into history.

The thing that has not changed is the opportunity for young people to develop new skills while having lots of fun!

by Norla Hesse

Memoirs of Dorothy and William Hesse Family

Dorothy, a teacher in a McPherson Township rural school, met William and married him in 1937. William, or as he was commonly known as Bill, came to the Paul and Mabel Grams' farm as a nine year old from the State Orphanage in Owatonna, Minnesota. Bill was born in Morrison County; his mother died of tuberculosis and his father was unable to care for his four children. Bill could have left this home at the age of 18 but chose to stay and work for Paul Grams on his farm. Later Bill and Dorothy purchased the farm from the Grams' and raised their family of four children. (Norla, Harvey, Sylvia and Jeff) 4-H was a big part of the children's growing years. They showed pigs at the county fair for a number of years. Showing pigs is not as easy as it sounds – they need to be worked with daily to get them to move in the direction desired. That direction should be always in front of the judge, not running wildly around the ring or knocking some kid off his feet by running between his legs. They also need to be washed and powdered (if they are white pigs) and that is another whole story of how to get the job done and not to end up with you dirtier than the pig ever was. Even in those days kids had lots of distractions and the daily workout didn't happen very regularly. Getting the pigs fed, and kids to the Fair required a lot of planning and cooperation. Every year Dad would threaten "to never do this again!" But then we would win a trip to the State Fair or the Junior Livestock Show, in addition to having a lot of fun at the County Fair, and he would relent for "one more year if we kept our part of the bargain."

One family highlight was the year Harvey won the prize for Grand Champion gilt and Grand Champion angel food cake. Winning the cake award, over his sister and a lot of other girls, kind of went to his head. An article and picture of Harvey and his winning cake made the *Mankato Free Press*. This article was picked up by the Twin City papers, prompting a lot of messages from out-of-town friends and relatives.

That the cake even made it to the fair had much to do with the support of our mother. Harvey, of course, baked the cake at the very last minute the night before the fair. Oh my, when the cake came out of the pan there was a mixing spoon baked right into the cake! (That is what happens when you prop the spoon against the side of the cake pan, turn your back to put the mixing bowl into the sink, the spoon quietly slips into the batter, and the baker is too tired to remember the spoon.) The truck hauling the 4-H animals was coming at 3:00 a.m. to pick up the pigs and Harvey was going to ride along. Mom got Harvey up at 2:00 a.m. and he mixed up another cake. He took that cake out of the oven just as the truck pulled into the yard. The cake was brought to the fair in the baking pan, removed and entered. (I think it won because it was the freshest cake at the fair!)

Now many years later, after being reminded of his accomplishments on various occasions, I have challenged him to another match. So far he has resisted but I think his daughters and my sister are beginning to practice making angel food cakes. They will have to do their best; I won the Grand Champion in Open Class for that angel food cake in 2004 at the Blue Earth County Fair.

by Norla Hesse

Life near St. Clair

Living near St. Clair and going to St. Clair school when I was young was a happy time for me. We could always find something interesting to do and we didn't have T.V. or speedy cars like now.

We had lots of cousins to play with and many aunts and uncles that helped entertain us. Grandma Frank had a big house and lovely yard. It was a place the family gathered to visit, play games, eat, and socialize. We never had to worry about where to spend holidays; we all went to Grandma Frank's for a big "potluck" dinner.

I enjoyed going to St. Clair School for twelve years. In high school, I took part in plays, speech contests, and cheerleading for the basketball team. We only had basketball and baseball for sports and really enjoyed beating the Pemberton teams.

I played snare drums in the school band. During the summer, we had band concerts on Saturday nights. We also had outdoor movies that were free but we had to fight off the mosquitoes. Some times we had shows at the town hall. A group called the "Kahler Players" put on a variety show that cost a whole 10 cents which was a lot of money at the time.

Life was good and we thought it was exciting.

by Hazel Frank DeMars

Growing Up Near St. Clair
Frank sisters have many memories

We grew up about two and a half miles north of St. Clair going north of the Post Office on County Road 28. Our dad, Raymond Frank (Irene Frase), always had tales of the "olden days."

While walking beans or picking rocks across the road from where Stanley and Delores Wilmes (once the farm of Charles and Matilda (Frank) Cords), live we found shards of pottery. Dad said there had once been a sawmill there. We also found arrowheads there.

We often went fishing in the Le Sueur River, with our dad, behind the Cords and Russell places on County Road 28. Dad showed us where he had cut cottonwood logs and dragged them out of the river bottoms to build the then "state of the art" hog barn that still is standing. A lot of people also fished under the bridge at Mineral Springs just three miles north of St. Clair. Our father often talked about the Indians believing that the water at this springs had medicinal powers. This was used by the

Winnebago Indian medicine man.

Dad told us about a large hill, which was located about two and three-fourths mile north and one-fourth mile east of St. Clair. It overlooked a pasture. It was called "Dunn's Hill" because a peddler named Dunn lived in a cave there. This hill has since been leveled for better farming.

Corine Frank married Harold Loeffler and they raised their family on the farm that was owned by Fred and Bertha (Frank) Kruse. Bertha would tell she would give the Indians the leftovers from her garden in the fall when they would walk through the farm.

Carol Frank married Jerome Johnson and they live east of the Raymond Frank farm. Their son Michael and Lisa (Dorland) and family now live on this Frank farm. As a child I remember going to the Creamery (where the fire hall now stands) with my father, then perhaps to Buesing's for an ice chunk for the icebox. We had electricity but my folks couldn't find a refrigerator to buy because of World War II rationing. Then we might go to the lumberyard (where the trailer park is). We might buy coal to supplement our wood furnace. We also might stop at Rose's Meat Market to pick up frozen meat or vegetables from a locker, which had been rented by my folks. On some of the trips to town we would stop at Hager's Hardware and Pagenkopf's Store for supplies. I remember taking eggs to George Miller's Produce and going to Art Cords' Barber Shop so dad could get a haircut.

by Carol Frank Johnson

Memories of Catechism

As young kids we attended summer catechism classes at the Catholic Church in St. Clair for three weeks every summer. (As soon as school left out! You can imagine how thrilled some kids were.) I loved it - my first contact with the dear nuns. During recesses these days we often played around the edges of the cemetery. I love cemeteries to this day. Later in my life I taught school with some dear nuns at a private school in St. Cloud.

My parents were Clifford and Anna (Schultz) Hager. They were married at the Immaculate Conception Church in St. Clair in 1927. My grandparents were Joseph and Catherine Hager. We still come to St. Clair to visit the cemetery.

by Cecilia Hager Biggins

St. Clair Reminiscence

I started school in St. Clair in 1936 with Dorothy (Berentson) Hesse for a teacher. There were two grades in each room up to eighth grade. From noon to 1 p.m. we ate lunch and then walked west past the creamery to Carl Rose's house, which was at the end of town.

Sometimes we walked up town to Godemann's Grocery Store. It had a round glass circular shelf that held lots of penny candy.

I can see the stores up and down the street. Rose's Meat Market was next to Jack Pint's Garage and was the Chevrolet dealership. Where the municipal bar now stands was Mace's restaurant and then the vacant lot where free shows were held every Friday night. That was always a big evening when everyone turned out and people stocked up on their week's groceries.

The drug store located in a large stone building was a popular place. We all liked the soda fountain. In the back was the post office. Marvin Rohrer and family lived upstairs and ran the business.

There was a smaller building attached to the drug store where Dr. Juliar had his office. He was a typical family doctor who made many house calls, especially when a new baby was expected.

East of the drug store was a town hall where many couples had their wedding dances. Across the street was Miller's Produce and Pagenkopf's Grocery. When the produce company left town, the building housed a restaurant for awhile.

In the vacant lot by Pagenkopf's was the hotel owned and operated by Robert and Anna (Klingbeil) Schostag. After that the De Mars family ran the hotel and bar. The bank was managed by George Hubmer and later was operated by his son-in-law, Robert Zavoral. Ernie and Esther (Schroeder) Hager owned and operated the hardware store and later his son Bill took over.

On the northwest corner of the school lot was a yellow house with lots of shrubs around it and a garden. Many of our balls went in that direction during recess and playtime. Sometimes they broke a window. Fred Bestman and his wife lived there. He was on the school board (also the Chase house).

Every spring our family went to Froehlich's Hatchery to buy baby chicks. It was on the north side of town by the river and was owned and operated by Oscar Froehlich and his wife.

The town constable was Herman Kroenke. He fit the job very well and was respected by all. Bill Myers, later Stanley Drake, ran the gas station. I don't want to forget Mrs. Roy Lewis who gave many piano lessons in her home.

There was a train that came to St.Clair from Albert Lea and then went back again. It seems it made the run about once a week when I was younger.

St. Clair Days were a big event every Labor Day weekend. School started the following day.

by Anieta Grams Meyers - 1993

A Little Girl Growing Up

I lived on a farm about two miles from St. Clair. I had no one to play with because my brother was deaf and attended the School for the Deaf at Faribault, Minnesota. I entertained myself playing with my dolls and in the summer making mud pies.

In the evening while mom and dad were milking cows by hand, I would play store with my crew of cats. I pretended the weeds around the barn were flowers and I would sell them to my cats. I dearly loved my cats.

I had to help with chores after school such as feeding the chickens and ducks, picking eggs and filling the wood box with wood from the woodshed.

I remember the harvest season. The men would cut the grain with machines called "binders." Then they shocked the grain in the field. The next step was to thresh the grain with a threshing machine. The women and children looked forward to this because the threshing was done as a neighborhood project.

Muriel Froehlich Mace

Morning and afternoon lunch was always served out by the threshing machine. Dinner was a big thing and usually between 13 to 20 people were fed a full course meal. When my father and brother were helping the neighbors, mom and I did all the evening chores including milking the cows by hand.

I attended St. Clair Public School for all 12 grades and started in the old section of the building for grades 1 through 6. A new elementary wing replaced it later.

My first grade teacher was Marcella Pestka Brewer and my first bus driver was Bob Schostag. At that time there were no school lunch programs so we carried a dinner pail with cold lunches.

We occasionally brought pennies to spend on candy at E.A. Duemeland's General Store during noon hour. This was fun because it had a rail at the bottom of the case and you could spin it around to get a look at all sorts of candy.

We also liked to go to the store to tease the older woman who did the scrubbing and cleaning. She always pulled her mop and pail with her as she walked down the street.

Her name was Hannah Dietman. She lived on the east end of town in a big house that had a hole in the screen door. She had a great number of cats that went in and out of the house through the hole. It was said the cats ate with her at the table. We were all very curious to get into her house to see what it was like inside, but we were never invited in.

During these years the roads were dirt and often turned to mud during wet weather. Gravel or paved roads were unheard of. My father would drive me to school with a horse and buggy. We had to cross the old bridge over the Le Sueur River and I was frightened almost to death to cross the bridge.

Transportation in the winter was by horse and bobsled. We wrapped up in blankets and foot warmers to go to the neighbors. Entertainment was mostly card playing and visiting. We had no television or radio at this time and didn't get electricity at our house until 1939.

Dad had previously operated a butcher shop in North Dakota. When he moved to the farm, he did all his own slaughtering of pork and beef. He and mom made their own sausage and canned meat. This was always used for lunch after playing cards and when company came to the house.

One of the card games I remember well was called "Norwegian Whist." This was so much fun when neighbors came or we went to their homes.

Saturday night was bath night. We used the old round wash tub that was placed beside the kitchen range. Water was heated on the stove and poured into the tub. After baths, we played rummy with cards and in later years listened to the Hit Parade top ten tunes on the radio.

Sunday afternoons were spent going to my grandparent's house. In the spring we'd often spend the afternoon sitting on the riverbank fishing. Oh what fun!

Dad hauled cream to the creamery in St. Clair by horse and wagon and later with a truck.

As to communication by telephone, the main switchboard was located in St. Clair above the bank. Since the people in the country were all on one line and everyone knew the rings of their neighbors, there was a lot of listening to other people's conversations. A lot of news was spread by the telephone!!

I remember an older man named Cassidy who lived in

a shack behind the hardware store and bank building. Later he moved his shack out to Mayflower Hill, which was about a half mile north of St. Clair. Our school picnics were held at Mayflower Hill and we were apprehensive about going to the picnics because Cassidy lived out there.

During the summer months, free shows were held once a week on Friday nights. This was a great time to see friends and neighbors and to do our grocery shopping.

St. Clair had three churches, three grocery stores, a meat market, drug store, blacksmith ship, hotel and liquor store with a dentist's office upstairs, a barbershop, harness shop, hardware store, railway depot, gas station, an elevator and feed mill and a lumber yard.

Then there was the town hall, city hall and two doctor offices. In its day St. Clair was a thriving town. When I was married, our wedding dance was the last event held at the town hall. Later a produce firm used the building.

by Muriel Ruth Froehlich Mace – 1993

St. Clair Reminiscence

I don't know a lot about the early days of St. Clair, but I do have recollections of the late 1930's and 40's.

My parents Dick and Edna Schull and my four sisters and I lived on a farm not far from town. My parents always banked in St. Clair and did a lot of business there. My father would sell his market hogs and cattle to Elmer Haugen. Ole Schroeder was the trucker that did all the hauling.

We traded our eggs at Miller's Produce, which was located on the north side of the street next to Pagenkopf's Grocery and Mercantile store. We would stop at St. Clair with eggs on Fridays on our way to Mankato.

Dad would tell us if we worked hard during the week, he would take us to the free show at St. Clair on Friday night. We knew he would do it anyway because he enjoyed it as much as we did, but we would hurry and help, especially on Friday.

The shows were held on the lawn under the big huge shade trees on the south side of the street. The drug store was on the left and the liquor store on the right located where the Medo-McPherson Insurance building stands today.

Many of the movies were western with stars like Roy Rogers, Gene Autrey and Hopalong Cassidy. The intermission gave everyone time to visit with their friends and neighbors or have a treat. Herman Kroenke would have a popcorn stand at the corner of the drug store.

After the movie, mother would do her trading at Rose's Meat Market, Wolcott's Store and sometimes at Hager's Hardware and Pagenkopf's. At times, she visited all of them. We kids would beg her for money to buy treats, comic books and paper dolls. Occasionally my folk's friends would give us a nickel or quarter to buy a treat. It was often very hot so it was refreshing to sit outside at the movie with a cool breeze blowing. We kids would be very tired on the way home!

When we were sick, the folk's took us to see Dr. Juliar who had a small office beside the drug store. He always seemed to have the medicine on hand that we needed.

The Rohrers, who had some lovely daughters, operated the drug store. My aunt took my sister and myself to one of their weddings. It was a beautiful affair.

Later Olga Fitzloff ran the store. It had a soda fountain and two booths. I remember Mace's Café. It stood on the corner, with the DeMars Hotel and Restaurant across the street next to the bank.

We were members of St. John's Lutheran Church and went to catechism on Wednesday afternoons and Saturday mornings. Rev. A. Mackdanz and Rev. Arthur Kell were two pastors I remember.

On Wednesday afternoons, my parents would pick us up at the Perch Lake country school and take us to St. Clair for catechism. We would ride home on the school bus as far as Pestka's and then walk from there. Louie Timmerman was our bus driver and he was very, very strict.

On Saturdays, mom and dad would take us to church and pick us up at noon. Sometimes we would have to wait in the drug store.

My older sister attended high school at St. Clair during her freshman year. After that our country school consolidated and we went to Mapleton.

When our country school had a day off, I would visit the St. Clair School. I met many nice children who are still our friends today.

I vaguely remember that St. Clair had Labor Day celebrations each year.

In 1965 my husband and I moved back into the St. Clair area. All of our children graduated from St. Clair High School.

I hope my reminiscing brings back memories for you too!

by Carol Schull More – 1993

St. Clair history as I remember it

My Grandpa, August Kopke, had the Kopke Flour Mill which was located on the north bank of the Le Sueur River; the cement abutments are there yet on the bank of the river about 300 feet west of the bridge. Our son Dean Born owns that property now. Dean lives in Slidell, LA, with his family.

My uncle, Henry Lubke, was the blacksmith in St. Clair. He sharpened plowshares and shoed horses. I can remember going to the blacksmith shop and watching him and hoping he wasn't hurting the horse. To me, horses were the next thing to humans. When I was growing up I had a horse we called Jane. She was like a member of our family. I rode her every day. We went to the pasture and brought the cows' home for milking. Our mailbox was a half-mile north of our home so I'd ride after the mail.

The school I attended was half a mile north and half a mile west of our home so I'd ride my horse to school, then tell her to go home and away she would go.

by Ila Mae Kopke Born

Kate Quinn: A St. Clair "Woman of Mystery"

At the outset I should explain that in this article I shall refer to her variously as Kate and Mrs. Quinn. Actually, I never knew her by any other name than Mrs. Quinn. My older sister Betty agrees with me, although in her case there was one exception, to be mentioned later. And finally, Betty and I both agree that we never heard our mother, Lauretta Cords, call her anything but Mrs. Quinn, and they were by all standards the very best of friends! So hopefully, the reader if necessary will forgive me.

It is interesting how names, nicknames and titles are applied and at times misapplied to relatives, friends and acquaintances, and how they so often control our thoughts and images concerning the recipient. Kate Quinn provides a good, if sometimes complicated, example.

A "woman of mystery" was a title applied to Kate by my father, Art Cords, not because she was necessarily a mysterious, scary type of person, but because of a particularly delicious piece of cake she sent over from one of her Ladies' Aids. She periodically held these in her home which was immediately adjacent to ours in St. Clair. Dr. Macbeth, who lived to the north of Quinn's, and Dad did not like to attend these aids: Dr. said he was too busy, and Dad wasn't overly excited about attending an aid right after work. For these two then Kate would prepare special servings, with a few added amenities, as she really liked them both. One night while eating an accompanying piece of cake, Dad wondered aloud concerning where she got all the marvelously delicious ingredients; this was mysterious to him, and thus Kate became a "woman of mystery." It was a friendly label.

Unwittingly, Dad's title hit a much broader, unintended and sometimes negative mark concerning Kate. Indeed, for many townspeople, including some relatives, she actually was a "woman of mystery." Some even called her reclusive; a few, eccentric. Her front yard seemed heavily overgrown and forbidding, which to some gave her house an unwelcome appearance. (The darkness of her front yard was offset by the boulevard in front of her house, which she covered with Moss Roses.) Her rather large garden, in which she spent huge amounts of time, was indeed imposing. As a young boy it reminded me of a jungle; I can't recall ever being in it, although many times I watched her sunbonnet bobbing around in there.

Not a lot of people were visitors to her house; I spent most of my time there in the kitchen and dining room. I only entered the parlor on one or two occasions, for example when it was opened for the aids. Further, Mrs. Quinn occasionally seemed to act on impulse. Sometime during the early 1920's, she left, unannounced I understand even at first to her husband Andy, to serve in a nurse's capacity in the oil fields of Oklahoma. After a fairly short stay, the "*St. Clair News*" in the *Mankato Free Press* announced her return. (I don't suppose there was a connection with Andy managing the Skelly Oil Company, do you?) Also, she had certain personal dislikes which she frequently verbalized, and these no doubt fostered return feelings, and may have added to her negative image.

All right, Mrs. Quinn had her mysterious, reclusive, and perhaps even eccentric side, but for our family all that was far over-balanced by a view of her as a warm, friendly, caring neighbor. Mother was raised by Frank and Frances Amberg, who built their house next to Quinn's in 1913. Mrs. Quinn and Frances early became close friends, and this extended to mother who was a teenager at the time. Shortly after Frances died in the fall of 1925, Mother and Dad, who had married in 1922, moved back to the Amberg house to take care of Frank. My older sister Betty had already been born in March of that year.

It is easy to say that Mrs. (Kate) Quinn became a surrogate mother to Betty, less so to me I suppose because I was a boy, and also less so to Joan who was only three when we moved away from the Amberg house to the east end of town. Betty recalls as a young girl running over to Quinn's on many a morning, entering the house, heading for the bedroom and calling "Antie Quinn! Antie Quinn! where are you?" Antie Quinn would be waiting for her in the center of a big featherbed into which Betty bounded and then they would play games such as "Burrow Hole, Burrow Hole" which basically involved Antie Quinn tickling Betty unmercifully. This fun-and-games activity would be followed by a fried egg sandwich, occasionally after a visit to the henhouse to secure the eggs. Teeth were then brushed. The toothpaste was produced by scratching a wet toothbrush over a bar of Palmolive soap. The taste, according to Betty, still lingers; it was awful!

It wasn't all pleasant, at least for Kate: On one occasion Betty and Jimmy Fitzloff filled Mrs. Quinn's bathtub with her clothes and turned on the water. They were both reprimanded and sent from the house, but the exile didn't last long, and Kate never tattled to mother. The closeness continued through school and beyond. Betty recalls somewhere around the age twelve she and Bernice Sanborn sang an early (November) Christmas carol, "Silent Night," to Kate, Clara Hintze, Annie Sodeman and Lou Bucholtz. (It was the only song they knew in two parts.) Later, Betty, with some urging from mother, showed her engagement ring to Antie Quinn; at the wedding dinner held at our house Mrs. Quinn bedecked the place with goldenrod. There was so much of it that mother put the overflow in the basement, worried that some of the guests might be allergic.

Betty also lovingly recalls Mrs. Quinn's beautiful paintings; a favorite involved three kittens, peering over a bowl of milk; the bowl contained a small mouse. Cats and other animals, nature, and still life were favorite subjects. Mrs. Quinn taught Betty to play Peter, Peter, Pumpkin-Eater on her organ in the parlor. Betty was able to play that selection again last year (over seventy years later) on that same organ, now in the Blue Earth County Historical Society Museum. One of Kate's grandnieces, Mary McComb, donated it to the museum.

Although I had fewer personal contacts with Mrs. Quinn, those I had were positive and memorable. Her husband Andy was a jovial guy, whom I always enjoyed seeing; I don't recall his dog Jack, but Betty notes that it was a constant companion to him. He once gave me a Skelly Oil-sponsored Jimmie Allen model airplane—too difficult for me to build at age ten (the propeller had to be carved out of a solid block of balsa wood), but Jimmy Fitzloff came to the rescue and did it right.

My apprehension about the garden was lessened when I partook of some of its produce. Most memorable here was the delicious root beer she concocted, from scratch, using actual roots out of her garden. As I grew older, my personal contacts with her lessened, but I always enjoyed seeing her and, if however briefly, talking with her; she never failed to show a sincere interest in what I was about. Upon high school graduation she gave me a tie, a very gaudy tie with a jungle scene on it. At center was a yellow lion, among other wild beasts. Mother, naturally, said that I should wear it—preferably when Mrs. Quinn could see it; I failed on that one. However, I must admit that it wasn't long before gaudy ties of that type became popular, at least in some quarters. Was she ahead of her time? And as I write this, I'm wondering if she may have painted the scene. But mother would have known—I think. One of the people I visited first, again with some mild urging from mother, on my first army furlough was Mrs. Quinn, who continued to display an honest interest in that exciting (?) phase of my existence.

Mrs. Quinn (Kate) was public-minded too. I don't think she missed a single public function in St. Clair. This included PTA meetings, basketball games, operettas, class nights, graduations, and proms—until the magic time the "spectators" were to leave. St. Clair Creamery and Commander Elevator programs in the Town Hall were rarely if ever without her presence. I played for a St. Clair prom about 1957-58, and I recall seeing her there; she died not too long after. And she attended nearly every dance at the St. Clair Town Hall. She, with a friend or two, invariably sat on the bench on the east side of the hall—right in the dead center (which meant that we young blades avoided that area as we performed our dance-hall shenanigans—that is mostly made fools of ourselves). Stated another way, I didn't want to appear in the next day's conversation with mother. She and her friends left at intermission, which then gave us free run of the entire hall.

Her detractors no doubt attributed this behavior to her simply being nosey, there to gather questionable gossip tidbits about the citizenry. Her friends, including me, accepted it; she certainly wasn't the only one to ever watch and tell—then or now. As a matter of fact, I would have been surprised not to see her at these events. Perhaps her presence gave me some sense of security. I remember once at a basketball game, held in our old "cracker-box" gym, with Mrs. Quinn sitting at her chosen place directly in front of the boiler-room door. She, as all the other spectators, sat on the foul line—the ball was out-of-bounds if it hit a fan. It was before the game and we were warming up. For no apparent reason, I threw the ball as hard as I could at one of the other players, probably Dale Tacheny, Don Lewis or Lowell Pagenkopf. My aim was as usual faulty and I hit Mrs. Quinn dead center on her forehead, bending, but not breaking her glasses. She was stunned; I was horrified. I ran over to her and apologized profusely, feeling I had without doubt committed some heinous crime. After a few seconds of near-blackout, she feebly responded that she was all right, and that she forgave me, realizing that I hadn't tried to do it. (In all likelihood, if I had aimed, I would have missed—it was that bad.) I steered clear of her for a while, but nothing was ever said about it again.

I saw much less of her during and after college; I was teaching in Albert Lea when she died in 1959 at age 93. She did, even to her friends, become less visible in those later years; she and mother however continued their long relationship. I'm pleased, even honored, to have been asked to write this brief memory of Mrs. (Kate) Quinn. She certainly deserves prominent inclusion in a St. Clair anniversary publication such as this. The project also gave me and my sister Betty a chance lovingly to rekindle personal memories of a wonderful neighbor, babysitter and friend. Also, it provides an opportunity to introduce, or perhaps reintroduce to the reader a St. Clair "Woman of Mystery."

by Nick Cords - Assisted by Betty (Cords) Van De Mark

(Additional note: Helen Schostag Kenward remembers Mrs. Quinn as the maker of the best outdoor "Sun Pickles" she ever tasted.)

Paintings by Kathryn Quinn

Paintings by Kathryn Quinn

Painting by Kathryn Quinn

Memories of an Enchanted Minnesota Farm Childhood

Introduction

I'm writing this with the idea of recording information and vivid recollections of my childhood. Included are the events that shaped those years on the farm—all the joys and disappointments that I experienced in that part of my growing up years. Many of these things I write about were told to me by my aunt and other relatives; these, plus my own experiences, amount to memories that I greatly treasure.

So as I write this, if you could stand with me in the present and look out into the past, and try to visualize this reminiscence of an enchanted childhood that was lived on a farm in the early 1900's with Aunt Frances and Uncle Frank Amberg. Their farm lay about three and one-half miles northeast of St. Clair, and nine miles west of Janesville, Minnesota.

Picture of My Childhood

The picture of my childhood that comes to mind is one of peace and nostalgia— long winter evenings at home, dimly lit rooms, kerosene lamps, telephones on walls, coffee grinders, horse drawn carriages, corn husk mattresses to sleep on, and the windmill which stood just outside one corner of the house. A black rooster weather vane stood on top of the windmill, and just under it the wheel squeaked when the wind blew hard and made it turn real fast. There was the vegetable garden in front of the house, the fields and the meadows that stretched out beyond the farm buildings which were built near the edge of a steep, wooded hill that sloped down toward the Le Sueur River. There, on the river's wooded shores and flats, I found companionship in nature; it became my playground.

My Childhood Paradise

The woods, the cliff-like hills with cow paths winding down, the flats and, last but not least, the Le Sueur River that wound its way through the pasturelands—all this represented my childhood paradise. Spring usually arrived early in March and then I began to roam through what was known as the "flat," a large low bottomland next to the river. It was surrounded by hills and covered by tall trees that grew high to reach the sunlight. Its floor was literally covered with wild flowers the whole summer for me to enjoy and pick. The first to appear was the "snow drop" which was truly the harbinger of spring. It was a lovely white long-toothed flower that grew up between the dead leaves, pushing itself up through the ridges of remaining snow. Then when the warmer days arrived there were the violets to greet you, beautiful blue and yellow ones; and never, ever, to my mind at least, were there to be found such large violets as those down on this flat. These little wild flowers that grew in the shadows, half hidden by their green leaves, made, so to speak, a carpet for my happy childhood feet. They were mine to watch and gather and I kept fresh bouquets in my aunt's home daily. Later, there appeared the dog-toothed violet, the jack-in-the-pulpits, the wild phlox (a lavender flower that grew in crowd-like clusters), wild honey suckle, blue-eyed Susan's, to say nothing of the wild ferns. It was truly my very own greenhouse, and I controlled it all—a veritable Shangri-la.

Always during the month of May I kept a "May Altar" in my room. My aunt let me use a high pedestal-type table, covered with a white linen cloth, and she would loan me the beautiful "Blessed Virgin Mary" statue that usually sat on a bureau in her own bedroom. Placing this statue on the table, I would keep fresh flowers in vases around the Blessed Mother all during the month of May. There of course were many other uses for flowers in the month of May, one of these having to do with May baskets. On May 1, young grownups would prepare and "hang" baskets containing flowers and other pleasant things on selected members of the opposite sex. They would rap on the door and call out. "May basket for so-and-so," and then run so the intended couldn't catch and kiss them. The deliverer usually was caught and kissed (much to their delight and no one's surprise) in front of an appreciative audience, as this event usually took place in early evening when it was still light.

I spent lots of time just wading in the river, and of course my faithful dog Tippy was always at my side. I made playhouses in every nook and cranny of the woods, and along the river. I had a port in every bend and turn of the river, a place to stop and rest as it were. Once I found a whole nest of round white eggs in the sand along the riverbank. I ran home, got a pail, gathered them all up (almost a pailfull), and lugged them all the way up the hill. My aunt said she didn't know what kind of eggs they were, but I think she had a pretty good idea. She told me to place them on top of the woodpile and to wait and see what would happen. One day about a week later I went to look and it seemed as if the whole woodpile was crawling with little baby mud turtles. I was sure excited and a little frightened, but soon they were gone. I was told they all headed back to the river, at least I hope that's what happened to them.

There was always the opportunity to fish; I loved to fish during those early years. One year it was extremely wet, one heavy rain followed another; the river overflowed and flooded the entire flat, even part way up the hills. This spoiled much of my summer fun, but I could still fish below the hill just back of the barn in spite of the high water.

In September the woods began to take on the shades of fall and there were other things to do. The elderberries would ripen and be ready for picking. Wild grapes were gathered by my aunt and uncle to be made into wine. There were wild gooseberries to be picked and my Grandmother Amberg would come and join me in this venture. We also picked wild cherries and chokecherries. I had a real pal in her and I will write more about her later. The butternut trees would be loaded with nuts, and as they dropped I picked many a bushel and put them into sacks. The hired men then would come down after their work, carry the nuts up to the granary and spread them on the floor. One day the sacks were forgotten and by the next day the nuts were gone. Squirrels had eaten holes in the bottoms of the sacks and had taken the nuts to hollow trees where they stored them for the winter.

Friends sometimes came to play and often we went through the woods and down by the river to pick up butternuts or go fishing. A special neighbor friend, Nona Fields, used to come at least once a week and we'd sit for hours on the riverbank and fish. We didn't usually catch much, once in awhile perhaps a big carp, which wasn't too tasty. In summer they weren't to be eaten at all. But Nona would always take a carp that she caught home, and I think that it, like mine, usually ended up somewhere else than on the dinner table. Finally, we just threw them back into the river. Nevertheless it was a treat for her and others to come and play by the river, as most didn't have one running through their property. Among others that came were: Annie Gekler, Rosie Gekler, Hazel Hintze, Marie Pestka, and Mary Neary.

Sometimes my friends and I waded in the river and dug up clams. I brought them home by the dozens, where I opened them and hoped to find pearls. The hardest thing was to open then; they lived up to their name for they "clammed up" tight when you tried. At first I didn't know about pouring hot water on them to make them open, so I used a hammer. I did find three white pearls that were not perfectly round, and one black one. They were ultimately lost—perhaps during our move to town, but it didn't much matter to me as long as I could search for more. We didn't always play in the woods or on the riverbank; we also played house, school, put on long dresses and it seemed as though we bothered no one. I could visit the Geklers only once during the summer, but I visited Nona, Marie, and Mary often.

School Days, 1904-1912

I started school when I was six years old. I went to what was known as the O'Connor School; it was nearly one and one-half miles away. My aunt generally kept the teacher, which meant room and board, so my first teacher, a Miss Reed from Mankato, stayed at our house. When the weather was bad—too cold, stormy, or too much snow—we were taken to school by a wagon or sleigh and team, which also came for us when school was out. I liked school and all my teachers, and now I somehow feel privileged to have been able to attend a one-room country school. I have many pleasant memories of it.

On cold winter mornings the teacher always had to get to the school house early to start a fire in the old pot-bellied stove, unless she could hire some neighborhood boy to take the job. We sang every morning before the teacher called us to order. The classes were always called up front to recite.

Then there were the Christmas programs. These programs involved the singing of Christmas songs, everyone got a piece to recite by heart, and maybe there was a short play with Santa Claus in it. Sometimes they ended with a box social. My aunt and uncle were not much on attending these programs, but they would see that I got there and had a way home with some neighbors.

Among some of the other teachers I had were: Miss Burns from Mapleton, Miss Presnall from Eagle Lake, Miss Sullivan from Mapleton, and Miss Suess from Janesville. Ethel Foster from St. Clair was my favorite, I guess because she liked to come home with me and stay overnight. Laura Kurth was my last teacher at country school; I liked her very much also.

One job that I wasn't too fond of was cleaning the erasers. It was done either at recess time or after school. It involved cleaning off the blackboard and taking the erasers outside and clapping them together—two at a time. This really made a lot of chalk dust that used to cling to our clothes. We all had to take our turn at cleaning the erasers.

How can I ever forget the morning in May when a thundershower came up and a bolt of lightning struck the schoolhouse? I have never heard such a deafening sound since. At first we were just numbed and couldn't move. But suddenly we recovered, got up and ran out of the schoolhouse and over to Charlie Gekler's place across the road. The Gekler family was watching and they claimed there were splinters from the strike falling all around us as we ran, but none hit us. The splinters came as a result of the lightning striking the roof of the schoolhouse, and also the bell tower. The entry actually was moved inches away from the school itself. The children's tin lunch boxes that sat on the floor of the entry were melted away—doughnuts, sandwiches, etc., burned and charred black. Needless to say, school was dismissed for the rest of the day.

The games we played during nice weather were: "Anty Over" the woodshed, baseball (I never was a hard hitter, but I could run real fast). hide and seek, and drop the handkerchief. The teacher almost always played with us. I also remember the picnics at the end of the school year, which were generally held in a woods next to the schoolyard. There would be potato salad, sandwiches, beans, cake, cookies and lemonade; and the inevitable ants, flies and mosquitoes (they didn't know of any sprays in those days). And so it was that we said "good-bye" to our teacher and friends until the fall when, in September, the term started again.

The walk to and from school itself holds many pleasant memories. The school was about a mile and a-half away. I followed a long crooked road that skirted the woods until I reached the main road, and then I turned and walked north. The O'Connor place, after which the school was named, was just to my left. Then I crossed the bridge that spanned the LeSueur River and on about a quarter mile to the school. The bridge provided a place to gather, talk, and play on the way home. The Freitags, Nearys and Annie Gekler would walk with us to the bridge before they turned off toward their homes. It was especially exciting at the bridge in the spring of the year when the ice started to melt and the river got high, sometimes almost reaching the floor of the bridge. We'd throw sticks and branches into the water and watch how fast the current would carry them away. We often met John O'Connor at the bridge and talked to him awhile before moving on. Those that went my way were the Fields' and Louie Grams. In the winter months it was at times hard trudging through the heavy snow. I was always wrapped up pretty well—heavy underclothes, wool dresses and leggings buttoned on to my overshoes. A big white fascinator was wrapped around my head and face.

The John Fields Family (Nona Nyquist)

Now this would not be a complete story of my childhood on the farm if I didn't devote considerable time and space to the John Fields family. They lived just to the right of us across a road; then you would turn off that road to the left into their place. Approaching the Fields, you walked down a beautiful shaded lane with a row of high cottonwood trees bordering it on the west. It was a very refreshing walk of a hot summer's afternoon, particularly after you reached the shaded lane where the rustling leaves produced a chattering-like sound that made you feel as if they were welcoming you. It was fun to visit the Fields, a family of six girls and one boy. Millie was the oldest, and I remember her usually sitting in a captain's chair by the cook stove in the kitchen. She was in poor health, but she was always cheerful and never complained. Next followed Ada, Sadie, Jenny, Nona and May; Harry, who was my age, was the only boy. Nona was my special friend and I've already talked about her visits to our farm. At Fields, where there were so many girls, we used to put on long skirts—there were plenty there—and play. Once I was given two skirts to take home and I thought I was blessed. Jenny was a happy-go-lucky girl and she played the organ. Sometimes she would come over to our farm and play and sing for us.

One early fall Jenny was to start school in Waseca and Nona was assigned to take her to Janesville where she would board the train. Nona asked me along so she wouldn't have to return home alone. The famous "Gip" was hitched to the buggy and we started for Janesville early on Sunday afternoon. "Gip," to quote a phrase, was "as slow as molasses in January," you literally had to beg him to move every inch of the way. Sometimes he would just stop, and you'd think about maybe giving up and walking. We finally got to Janesville and saw Jenny off on the train, but all the while the sky was getting darker and darker. It looked as though a serious storm was coming. I wanted to stay in town for awhile until maybe it would blow over, but Nona thought we should get home, so we started. About one hour later and, thanks to "Gip," about two miles out of town, it started to pour. Plenty of lightning and thunder followed, and the horse stopped dead still. It was very dark, but we did have a big rain umbrella and a blanket to wrap ourselves in; and we prayed that "Gip," having started again, would get us through. The roads started getting muddy and very slippery–remember, no gravel—and we had no lantern so we had to depend on the lightning and old "Gip" to guide us through. Once, an enclosed surrey passed us with two lanterns on the front. These lanterns were very dimly lit, which made it all seem extremely mysterious. There were two possible roads that we could take out of Janesville; we took the one which would take us past the Louie Hintze farm, which was close to the Fields place. Before the Hintze place we passed the Brock farm; I had been there once with my uncle. We saw some men crossing the yard with lanterns, probably coming in from doing the chores. I suggested stopping here, hoping they would recognize our names and loan us a lantern; Nona agreed. I tracked across the muddy yard, and two men held up lanterns to see who in the world I was. They were very nice and asked us to stay the night; they would even take care of old "Gip." But Nona insisted on getting home, so they filled a lantern with kerosene and we were on our way again. As we passed the Hintze place we could see a lantern approaching us in the distance; it was Mr. Fields, walking to meet us. We were all relieved. The Ambergs, of course, were worried too, and were about to start out on the other road to look for us. This was about 9 o'clock in the evening and we were very tired and hungry—"Gip" too. We also were scared! We ate at the Fields and then the Ambergs brought me home. This all remained a vivid memory.

Music and its Importance in My Life

When I was about eight my aunt decided that I should begin taking music lessons on the piano and organ. Jenny Fields, whose music talents and abilities I've already spoken of, and I started taking lessons from a Miss Lennox who was teaching school in St. Clair at the time. People by the name of O'Leary were running the hotel in St. Clair at the time and they offered to let us use the hotel parlor, which contained a piano, for our lessons on Saturdays. We divided up the driving; we did it one week, the Fields the next. At first Jenny would hitch up our old friend "Gip" to a buggy and we'd ride to our lessons. One day we scraped a telephone pole and tore a wheel off the wagon; after that Mr. Fields drove us when it was their turn. Jenny's lessons with Miss Lennox ended as a result of an incident one winter's day. At the time of her lesson a young man about town, Freddie Schultz, asked Miss Lennox to go for a ride with him in his flashy cutter, drawn by a beautiful team. She accepted, and Jenny waited and waited, while Mr. Fields, somewhat short-tempered anyway, got angrier and angrier. Finally after about a half hour's wait, Mr. Fields took Jenny home and that finished that arrangement. I was allowed to continue; however, Miss Lennox apparently learned a lesson—no more cutter rides with students waiting.

After moving to St. Clair, at age fourteen, I began asking for a new piano of my own. The folks bought me a beautiful Hallet and Davis piano, and I started taking lessons from Josie Wingen again. Since our earlier encounter she had studied music in the Twin Cities for a year, and had become a very good teacher. I now liked her very much, and was saddened when she decided to quit teaching, leaving me out in the cold again. However, it wasn't all bad news. Josie continued, on occasion, to come to the house and play duets with me; she had a lot of fine music, and these sessions were just like lessons for me. If it could be possible for me to relive moments from my past, some of my first choices would involve the times I spent at the piano playing duets with Josie Wingen. She was such a wonderful player, and as she played the upper part of the duet I seemed to be able to capture her marvelous touch and feel for the music as I played the lower part.

Josie was also an accomplished singer, having studied voice while she was away. My aunt talked me into some voice lessons from her, but after about three lessons involving all those exercises I decided to stick with the piano. Our duet sessions, however, continued on after she got married, and even after my marriage. She was the church organist at Immaculate Conception Catholic Church and she talked me into substituting for her, and then taking over. She argued that she didn't like to accompany herself when she sang solos. When she left the area I remained as the church organist for some time.

First Communion, Confirmation and the "Pledge"

We loved going to catechism at Immaculate Conception Catholic Church in St. Clair. The pastor, Father Kiley, taught us well, making our religion clear and interesting. As we approached first holy communion we were instructed not to be thinking of the pretty clothes we were wearing, but of the occasion. The boys wore knee-length pants and white shirts with ties; the girls wore white dresses, white veils and a wreath of waxed flowers on our heads. With all this finery on we had a lot not to think about. We also were told not to talk a lot, laugh, or act in a frivolous manner that morning, or even all that day. I tried very hard to carry out these instructions from the moment I got up on that first communion day of mine, August 15, 1910. My father had sent me a lovely communion dress made out of white albatross material which was popular at the time, making it difficult not to look at it once in awhile or maybe even to feel a little vain or to admire myself. This may have happened to some of the others too, but at least the effort was there, and I think that the Lord generally looked upon us with favor.

About a year later we were confirmed, so that meant another summer of extended instructions. The lessons now were longer and much harder, involving much serious study; Father Kiley wanted us to be ready to answer any question the Bishop might ask. My aunt bought my confirmation dress, made of a very pretty voile material with wide insertions of lace. At this time it was just beginning to be possible to buy some quite nice ready-to-wear clothes.

Our class was very concerned about confirmation day, particularly what questions would be asked and by whom. Everyone was not questioned by the Bishop himself, although Bishop Heffron was a very kind man: May God Rest His Soul. The Bishop stood behind the altar railing and was flanked by two priests on either side. We formed a line of about ten in front of this group and each received a question from one of them, after which another line would move up. We were especially afraid of Father Trainor from Waseca because if you didn't answer him correctly he was liable to bawl you out in front of everybody. So when my line came up the first thing I did was to figure out who would question me; it came out Father Coleman of St. Mary's. When it came my turn this priest must have sensed this shy little girl, looking scared and hoping and praying I could have the strength to answer—if I knew the answer, of course. So this kindly priest leaned forward and, putting one hand on the altar railing, asked me confidentially-like and in a low, clear voice, "What is sanctifying grace?" I leaned forward and answered very confidentially-like and in a low and perhaps not so clear voice, "sanctifying grace is that grace which makes the soul holy and pleasing to God." I remember he smiled at me and nodded "yes," and said, "good girl." Father Kiley was very helpful that day too. He stood back on the altar and tried to remind some class members of answers they did know, and inform a few of answers they didn't. For example, if the question called for the number of commandments he would hold up ten fingers, on more difficult ones he would form the answers with his lips.

Now when you were confirmed you had to take the "Pledge." You raised your right hand and repeated after the Bishop that no liquor of any kind would pass your lips until you came of age. This was serious business and I raised my hand somewhat reluctantly as it meant no tasting of the good grape wine that my aunt made, to say nothing of the more potent dandelion wine. Also ruled out was the small glass of beer I enjoyed on a hot summer's day when my uncle bought a pony of it to serve to the hired men on special work occasions. That summer of my confirmation my father came to get me for a visit and thinking I was too thin, prescribed a glass of beer a day to increase my appetite. If you recall, he owned a saloon so he had plenty of beer. Well, I had to tell him about the "Pledge," and when I did he about hit the ceiling, saying, "I guess it won't hurt you to have a little beer; the "Pledge" is for older people who can't stop drinking." This was a real problem for me because I was instructed that I'd surely go to hell if I broke the "Pledge." But I did have some beer at my Dad's; I'm sure others may have broken the "Pledge" too. Then there was a delicious beer soup that auntie made for me when I was sick with La Grippe (the flu), which supposedly had special healing properties—another problem. After all these years I still occasionally feel guilty for having broken the "Pledge," and that I'll have to answer for it in the next world. I wish with all my heart that my father will be there to help bail me out, and that auntie will also be there to offer a big bowl of her beer soup to St. Peter.

Red-Buttoned Shoes and Peg's Store

When I was about four years old I got my eyes on a pair of high red-buttoned shoes in Pagenkopf's store in St. Clair—I just had to have them. Pagenkopf's was a typical general store of the times. It had groceries, a yardage goods department, dishware, shoes and other footgear, men's work clothes and many other items. About once a year a barrel would be set out in the shoe department, filled with shoes that were on sale. The red-buttoned shoes were on top of this barrel and I spied them on a fateful day that I came shopping with my aunt. I wanted them desperately, never mind whether they fit or not. They were tried on and I said they fit fine—actually they were too short. They only cost $1.50, and seeing how badly I wanted them (I was clutching them for dear life), my aunt bought them. From then on I was determined to wear them every day, and did until my aunt spirited them away and hid them. In later years it was thought that at least some of my foot problems could be traced to these much-loved, but ill-fitting shoes.

Charlie Pagenkopf, the proprietor of the store, was aided by his good wife who called everyone "Dearie." They had a daughter, Sophia, and three sons: Walt, Carl and Earl. This family ran a family type store where people, beyond purchasing goods, could gather and talk things over. This was especially true on long, cold winter evenings when many townspeople and farmers, would go to "Peg's store," gather around the big old heater that stood at the back which was periodically fed by a couple of chunks of wood which crackled and popped for minutes after, and discuss issues of mutual interest. For example, once someone from the country reported that a cougar was seen stalking the riverbottom at night. Shortly, about a dozen men went out to find this animal, although as they searched it appeared that it had left the area.

Charlie was always good to the kids. He had one of these large, round glassed-in candy cases that revolved on sort of a turntable. I loved to buy a sack of candy from him. He would blow open a paper sack, and then very carefully begin to select pieces with which to fill it. There were slices of candy made from sugar and coconut, colored to look like bologna; chocolate covered pigs with marshmallow centers, containing a silver-colored ring as a prize; licorice sticks; all the different colored mint and peppermint candies; horehound sticks (supposed to be good for colds), and many other varieties. Charlie would slowly fill the sack and when it would be almost full he would act as though he was ready to close it, but then he would stop, stroke his moustache and say, "Oh well, I guess I can get another piece in." And so this wonderful man never did hand a sack of candy to me or any other child that was closed at the top, never sent a child away disappointed or unhappy. Thank you, Charlie, from all of us.

An End and a Beginning

During my early religious training I was taught that I had a Guardian Angel who always watched over me, and never to forget to thank him at the end of each day. I believed that God is everywhere and sees me always. If I do something wrong I can't hide it from him—he sees it. And everything I do is put down in the great recording book up there, and I will be judged according to the good and bad deeds I have performed here on earth. When I arrive at the Pearly Gates this great book will be flung open by St. Peter for the whole heavenly court to see, and I shall be judged. Bolstered and somewhat frightened by these beliefs, I grew up with my enchanted childhood relationships and experiences, admittedly taking my time about it, savoring every enjoyable moment. To me, childhood mirrors a peace of mind that is rarely, if ever, found in later life. I believe this is especially true today when everything seems to be moving at such a fast pace that there isn't time to stop and smell the roses (or daisies, if you like).

And so I conclude this journal of my enchanted childhood on the farm. My aunt and uncle have long since passed away, and so have most of the other people that I've written about here that touched my life in one way or another. I hope to have, in some small way, succeeded in helping to keep their memory alive.

Written by Lauretta Lynch Cords – 1977
Submitted by Nick Cords

Memories

These "Memories" were originally begun with the thought that some knowledge of my family background would be of interest to my family. The comments evolved into a mixture of my early life in a small town and life during the depression. I have made no attempt to make the scenes flowery, not to exaggerate and to be as factual as possible. Some detail could have made the incidents more interesting. Whole stories could be woven around some of the incidents. Most of this was written while, Jan and I were on vacation in March 2000.

Grandfather Ole Haugen born 3/17/1861, died 5/31/1931, came to America in about 1885 at the age of 24. He was born in Vaga Gulbrandsdal Norway, father Iver Haugen, born 7/27/1832, died 9/18/1911, mother Ingeborg Haugen, born 1/6/1834, died 3/7/1921. Ole was second of seven children. Ole's father and mother immigrated and are buried in the cemetery at Hanska.

Ole was about 5'10", light hair, and blue eyes and wore a mustache. He could read and write Norwegian and English. He played the violin, but could not read music. His work was all unskilled. He worked for the railroad for many years on the rails in Minnesota. At Hanska and nearby yards he loaded boxcars and unloaded coal. My dad told of the time that he and Oscar, dad's older brother, helped their dad unload a car of coal, all by hand with scoop shovels, for $1 a day. This must have been about 1912.

Ole married Kari Wiste. Kari born May 2, 1868, died July 23, 1907, came to America with her parents Ole and Anne when she was two years old. Both of my parents spoke Norwegian and Dad spoke some German. Ole died in 1931.

Years ago I examined the title to the house that grandfather Ole owned and found several mortgages of $500 each. I later learned that these mortgages helped start three small businesses. Dad borrowed $500 using the house as collateral in 1923 when my mother and dad were married. They bought a meat market in St. Clair, Minnesota. They lived in the residence on the second floor. Dad's Uncle, Oliver Wiste, helped dad get started.

Elmer Haugen, my dad was the second of five children of Ole and Kari Haugen. My mother was Julia Braaten, the youngest daughter of Rungnild (Rose) Braaten, who never married. (They lived at 201 Front Street East.) Grandma Rose came to America in about 1890 at the age of 19. She had an uncle who had purchased passage and became ill so Grandma took his ticket. She left home with clothes she wore and a trunk of clothes and blankets her family put together. She never saw her parents or home again. She worked as a housemaid for two years to pay the price of the ticket. She lived in Mankato, never learned to drive so would walk everywhere. When she walked home from her jobs she walked by the offices of the local Power Company. At some point she started buying 1 share of stock in the Power Company each week. Her daughters did not know this. Just before she died at age 94, with a quite clear mind, she told them of the stock. The shares bought at $0.25 to $0.50 each were then worth over $25,000.

Grandma always worked and when visiting felt out of place unless she was washing dishes or doing something. She sewed, crocheted, and made small carpets and quilts. She spoke English, but with a heavy Norwegian accent. She became an U.S. citizen during WWII, in order to obtain full ration stamps. This was a help to me when I was in the Navy, in radar and electronics and required a "secret" clearance. The report came back to the Navy command in which I was serving that Grandma was a foreign national, of a friendly country and just recently naturalized. I was allowed to stay in my work with secret clearance. My sister Corrine and I tutored Grandma to pass the test for citizenship. She had to know basic structure of our government, some history and how to vote. Grandma then qualified for social security. I remember that when the benefits began the check was for $34 per month.

In 1940 an incident occurred which I will never forget. The Germans (nobody called them Nazi's) invaded Norway. When the news started coming in of the landings, the Lutheran minister, my Dad, and his uncle, Oliver Wiste, came to the meat marked in St. Clair and listened to the news. For three days and nights they stayed there, drinking beer, eating home made bologna (Dad and Oliver were experts), telling stories in Norwegian and singing Norwegian songs. Dad sang in a Norwegian men's chorus, though not often. They would cheer for any fighting and shed many tears when any new landing took place.

The British tried to oppose the Germans but were thrown back. We learned later that the British sent men and large guns to Norway, but the ammunition sent did not fit the guns!

Life in St. Clair in the 30's

Life in St. Clair in the 1930's was quiet and largely uneventful. I was born January 22, 1928, and in 1940, when twelve years old, I tried to join Boy Scouts. Because the German Lutheran Church, St. John's of the Missouri Synod, opposed any organization outside of the church, there weren't enough boys in St. Clair to form a troop. I bought the Boy Scout Handbook and practically memorized it.

Mankato was 12 miles away and we went there about 1 time per week to shop. On Sunday we went to visit Grandma quite regularly. I could not go there for scouts.

Our family, Dad, Mother, Corrine and I would go somewhere almost every Sunday. We visited Dad's relatives in Hanska, sometimes Mother's relatives there, Dad's Uncle Oliver in Janesville, Mother's cousins in Byron (near Rochester) and Mother's sister Rikka, Otto and their daughter Helen Lange in Elmore. Helen was 2 years older than I was. They occasionally would come to St. Clair.

One of Helen's classmates was Walter Mondale, then called "Fritz" because of his custom of wearing his hair short. It is also called a "Heine" (German) and also called a crew cut. He later became an U.S. Senator and then Vice President. He failed in his presidential bid. His father was a Methodist minister in Elmore.

St. Clair had 3 saloons and 3 churches. All were equally popular in their set times. At many times Dad did his share of the drinking. Saturday nights the saloons were full. Beer was 5 and 10 cents a glass. Two women from the Salvation Army in Mankato would come to St. Clair to solicit donations, walking through each liquor store and standing outside for a time. They were always received with respect and donations.

Many, many times our minister was paid with farm produce and animals. He could at times sell these for cash. He and his family were very poorly paid. Although Dad never became a member, he always gave some money, monthly, to the minister.

Dad ran a meat market with butchering room in a separate building out back. He would bring in a hog and shoot it in the head with a .22 rifle. It was an old stained rifle then and I still have it. He would then stick a knife in the throat of the animal to allow all the blood to come out. If the blood stayed in the animal the meat would be bad.

He would kill large animals, like a cow or bull, by hitting them (knocking them) in the head with an axe or sledgehammer. This would stun the animal and allow Dad only a short time to stick the animal and allow the bleeding. Occasionally we would catch the beef blood in a pan or bucket and Dad would make blood sausage (Blut Wurst). This was very popular with the German farmers.

Dad made many kinds of sausage and stuffed mostly natural casings for the long bologna and also ring bologna. He learned much of this from his uncle, Oliver Wiste, who made a great variety of bologna and summer sausages. (Oliver Wiste was the owner of "Wiste's" in Janesville.)

From about 1920-1923 Dad worked in Mankato for a man named Kopolovitch, a Polish Jew, who taught him to make many more varieties of sausages. Dad sold his

Pig ready for slaughter

sausages both locally and also in other towns including Minneapolis. Dad at times, was the only businessman in St. Clair who made much money during the depression. In one day, about 1930, Dad by himself butchered 40 veal calves loaded them in a railroad car with ice and they were then shipped to Albert Lea to Swift Packing Company for processing.

Farms went into depression in about 1925. The farms in Europe had little or no production during WWI and at that times American farm products were in great demand. The European farms caught up with production about 1924, and American farmers lost their market. U.S. farm products dropped in value.

Dad butchered veal (calves) and sent them to Albert Lea for processing. He also bought Jack Rabbits shot by local farmers in the winter and then sent them to Chicago for the Jewish Market. In 1938 Dad had saved enough money, estimate $10,000 to buy the Amberg Farm of 240 acres. He paid the price in full in cash with no mortgage.

Dad never had a mortgage on his house or farm. He paid cash for the meat market using $500 borrowed on the Haugen home in Hanska and paid this off in about 2 years.

Dad's best days to sell meat were Saturday and Sunday after church services. Most farmers didn't come into town from Sunday to the following Friday or Saturday. Catholics ate no meat on Friday. Dad often said they were his best meat customers on Saturday and Sunday.

Many people, including farmers, had no money to buy meat during the depression. Dad never turned down a local person who wanted or who needed meat for food. He would either give it to them or tell them "I'll put it on the bill."

Dad knew Father Byron of the Church of the Immaculate Conception. Father sometimes called Dad and Dad would prepare a beef roast or other meat and Father would pick it up to give to a needy family. Dad never charged for this meat and never knew who received it.

When Dad sold his shop in about 1948 he wrote off over $25,000 in past due or old accounts with customers.

I had a job to do after school for as long as I can remember. I had to keep the fire and smoke going in the smokehouse. The sausages would be hung on long iron rods together with hams, fish and anything else being cooked and cured in the smokehouse. We used clean wood, flavored sometimes with special wood chips.

For a boy my age, I think I had the best of all worlds growing up in St. Clair. I knew the family who owned the drug store and soda fountain. I bought many sundaes and ice cream sodas there for a few cents. The general store was across the street with its great variety of dry goods, canned goods, fruits and vegetables in season. Dad had an agreement with the general store, Peg (Pagenkopf). They would sell no meat and Dad would sell only meat.

The hardware store also was across the street and was a constant source of amazement to me. I still could spend much time in a hardware store.

The blacksmith shop was behind our butcher building. The smithy, Mr. Lubke, was a big man and unusual, as in that very dirty business he wore a white shirt everyday! He wore a large leather apron with leather cuffs to protect the arms. He was one of only a few smithies that would sharpen plow shares. He was strong enough to hold the plowshare in his hands against the grinding wheel to sharpen it. When sharp he would put it in the fire on the forge (very hot) and when red hot dip it in a barrel of cold water. This would "temper" the steel and the plow would stay sharp longer.

He also sharpened discs, hay cutters and did general welding. I recall one job I helped him for which I felt a great level of accomplishment. We made a hay bucker, like a front-end loader, to be mounted on a tractor, using the power take-off to raise and lower the forks of the hay bucker.

This was during the war and we could buy no new iron or steel. All repairs and new equipment were made from junk parts. We made the tines of the hayfork from old automobile drive shafts. The shafts are tempered, very strong and we would sharpen one end. They were used to get under and lift the hay.

I helped design and lay out the tines, to weld them and also to design and lay out the lift mechanism with steel cable. The finished product was a thing of beauty and great pride. I don't know of anything else I've ever made or created which gave me greater pleasure. I was about 14 years old.

I raised pigeons in a hand built pigeon roost behind the meat market. We would find young pigeons by climbing up after them in barns. We, Jim Fitzloff and I, would raise them, try to train them and let them go. Occasionally we would eat them as squab.

Guns were a part of my life. I had a BB gun at about age 5 or when I was strong enough to cock it. I had a .22 rifle at about age 9. I would shoot gophers in the field, cut off their 2 front feet and turned them in at the Blue Earth County Extension Office for 2 cents a pair. I paid 18 cents for a box of 50 bullets, 22 shorts and made money. Longs and long rifle bullets were also available but I didn't buy them. They traveled too far, about 1 mile, I was told and were no more effective than shorts. They were too dangerous to use in my opinion.

We had foxhunts where men were dropped off a vehicle every 2 telephone or power poles and then walked to the center of a section (1 square mile). We used shotguns. No one was allowed to use a rifle. We usually shot some fox.

To shoot gophers, I would whistle as calling a dog. The gopher would sit way up on his back legs and I could hit him in the head.

I became quite a good shot. I could hit black birds on the fly. Crows were a snap as they flew slower. I could hit coal briquettes thrown in the air. I tried hitting a spinning quarter tossed in the air but was never very successful.

When I was about 12, Dad bought me a new 22-bolt action repeater which held about a dozen shorts and which had a telescope to be attached as a sight. I still have the gun. I could hit literally almost anything.

The bridge on the east end of St. Clair over the LeSueur River, which ran along the north side of St. Clair, was an important location. After we made model airplanes of balsa wood and very thin tissue paper, we would sometimes fly the planes off the bridge. We also attached ropes to the bridge and used them to swing out over the water and then drop. I learned how to swim there.

We couldn't swim on the west side of the bridge because that was where the sewage from St. Clair emptied into the river. There was no sewer plant and the sewage was raw. We always thought that the fish we caught down stream from the sewage tasted better. We would catch bullheads, catfish, suckers, carp and occasionally a game fish like Walleye or Northern Pike. We fished there from the earliest day I can remember.

The same river ran through Dad's farm, which was 4 miles east of St. Clair. It was a slow shallow river most of the years, except in the spring when it carried perhaps 4 times as much water.

On the farm were 4 gravesites of a woman and her 3 children. They drowned trying to cross the river sometime about 1900 or earlier. There were several family graves on the farm, but they were unmarked and I never knew who they were. Southerners had a practice of burying their dead on their farms. The County Commissioners had and still have responsibility to preserve and protect old gravesites. I never knew of anywhere that they exercised that obligation.

The farm was initially claimed as a homestead in about 1865 or right after the Civil War. A major homestead law was established by Congress in about 1863 and signed by then President Lincoln. All homestead claims had to be signed or initialed by the President. Many in Minnesota contained the signature of "A. Lincoln."

During the 1930's activities were very simple. We had no television and radio stations broadcast only at limited times. After school I listened to Jack Armstrong, the All-American Boy and others.

We had Parent Teacher Association meeting, P.T.A., monthly in the school gym. They were always well attended. There were sing-alongs and then someone with talent would sing or play. Corrine played the piano many times. She and I sang duets on a couple of occasions. I still remember "There's A Long Long Trail Winding" and several others. Very simple songs but as I remember we had fun singing and playing.

In the winter we skated. The rink was just behind my house and I recall turning on and off the big lights many times. Several of the boys, myself and others, played hockey on the "dead river" ice areas. We had no regular sticks and made our own. School was near by where we played running games in the evening.

We rode our bicycles all over. Mankato was 12 miles west. One day Jim Fitzloff and myself (age 10?) rode to Mankato to visit Grandma. We neglected to tell our parents and there was some concern until Dad called Grandma and there we were. He drove to Mankato and brought us home. The roads all were gravel. Our bikes had large balloon tires with inner tubes. This may have made the ride smoother but it was hard to "pump" on the gravel.

Friday night in St. Clair was a big night. The town paid the cost of putting on free outdoor movies. We sat on benches. The stores were open and farmers flocked in. News was passed from person to person.

We played cards and also board games. We had some games of Monopoly, which went on for 3 or 4 days.

Rationing hit our family during WWII when gas, sugar, catsup, canned goods of various kinds, meat and other items were rationed. We were issued books of coupons good for various items for various times. I still have some coupon books.

Gas was short and an average person received a "C" book. This allowed perhaps 3 gallons of gas per week, which would get you nowhere. The national speed limit was 35 MPH, which was in effect from 1942 through the early part of 1946. This saved on gas and also on tires, which were largely made of rubber. The Japanese held all our resources of rubber.

Businessmen and farmers would receive a "B" book, which allowed perhaps 20 gallons of gas per week. Farmers were usually able to get any amount of gas for farm tractors, and were not limited.

Dad had a fleet of trucks, including 1 or 2 semi-tractors and trailers, 2 or more straight trucks of 1½ tons or more and several pick-ups. We never lacked gas as his was called essential business of hauling livestock.

We made wine and stored it in bottles in a hog shed on the Fitzloff place. One day Jack, Jim's father, found it. The puzzle was solved, where the sugar went. We divided the wine, all had some and we had a good laugh.

Sugar was in high demand and short supply. We raised sugar beets on the farm. Dad had equipped 2 buildings to provide housing for Mexican workers on our farm. They would cultivate the beets by hand. After the plows dug them up they would cut the tops off by hand. Whole families would work including the very young and very old.

My dad was called up with the Minnesota National Guard in 1917 and was sent first to Fort Snelling and then to Fort Dodge near Ames, Iowa. Here he was in an accident and was sent to Lutheran Deaconess Hospital in Minneapolis where he spent 3 months. During this time he learned the basics of typing and also about investing in corn and other grain markets. From this time on he played the markets, making several thousand dollars a year. He was also very good with mathematics, thus making meat pricing quite accurate. He also got to know George Hormel, who started the Hormel Meat Packing Company in Austin, Minnesota, and was an honorary pallbearer at his funeral.

In 1936 the temperatures were at 0 degrees or below for 6 weeks. The trucks were cold and to get more heat out of the engine, the drivers would cover the radiator with cardboard or a large thick blanket. Many times the engine would over heat and crack the engine block. Dad replaced many blocks that year. Snow was heavy; farmers had to tunnel out of the house to reach the barn or to just get out. Some farmers froze when they became disorientated and lost in the snowstorms or big drifts in their own farmyards. Farmers soon adopted the practice of running a rope or twine from the house to the barn or elsewhere. The barn was almost always warm with the heat generated by the cattle.

Dad was a catcher on the town baseball team. He often said that the catcher has the best opportunity to judge the opposing hitters and also the opposing pitcher. He became an umpire at one time but never liked it. Dad was a very strong man and as a butcher he regularly carried quarters of beef weighing 250 pounds or more. My mother was in good health until she was about 72 years old. At that time, on Halloween, she was giving children treats for Halloween when she fell in her kitchen and broke her hip. He never recovered and spent the next 10 years in a wheelchair. She had severe osteoporosis, which is basically a lack of calcium in the bones and precluded the bones from mending.

Leadership was something I fell into from time to time. In 2nd grade we had a "rhythm" band and I was chosen the leader. I seemed to be a leader in many games we played after school. In my junior year I was president of our class, 12 boys and 5 girls. At our junior-senior prom I was the M.C. for the program. Talking before crowds has never been a problem for me. We had an active declamation or speech program. I competed in extemporaneous speaking and won 1st place in a contest in Mankato. I also took part in a class play.

I was a member of the "Husky Helpers" 4-H Club from age 10 to about 14. I still remember the 4-H pledge - "I pledge my head for clearer thinking, my hands for greater service, my health for better living and my heart for greater loyalty." I raised a Holstein calf, a pig and some white chickens. The calf got too big for the pen so I gave it up, the chickens were disqualified as they said I had washed the chicken's feet. Not true as I raised the chickens in a wire coop I built, off the ground, and they never walked in the droppings or on the ground. I was disappointed because I thought they would win a prize.

We lived across the street from St. John's Lutheran Church and every Sunday and many other days when they had food for a church activity they would bring the excess or the garbage and throw it into the pigpen. The pig did pretty well. That August at the county fair I won a prize for the size of the pig. Mr. Carpenter was our leader and we thought very highly of him. He even helped us start a German or old time band.

During the 1930's a play troop, the Caylors came to St. Clair and put on a play every Friday or Saturday night. They tried to get local kids involved.

The train that came from Albert Lea would come as far as St. Clair and the tracks were laid so it could switch cars, to turn the engine to point back east and to pick up other cars. We had a station, a station agent, George Macomber, and could receive telegraphs. Telegrams from the War Department were very feared. Mr. Macomber had a son Reed who was serving in the area of fighting and almost couldn't complete a telegram for fear it was for him. A telegram came in for Tom Meaney who was very well liked and who managed the Farmers Elevator. He had 2 sons in the Army, Donald and Roy His son Roy had just graduated from high school and was in the army about 6 weeks before he was killed. When the telegram came in reporting that Roy was killed, George could not deliver it to his friend Tom. He called Dad who in turn called Jack Sanborn. Together the three men delivered the telegram to Tom and his wife.

There was a high wooden water tower where the train switched and turned around. The engine used water to make steam to power the engines and had to replace the water when it was low. I climbed the side of the tower but would never go over the top. Some boys thought it was great sport to hang a rope inside the tank and go for a swim on a hot day. In the winter the train could usually get through the snowdrifts. A large plow was mounted on the front end. I recall only one time when the train couldn't get through. The drifts were over the height of the engine.

I got my driver's license when I turned 14. I paid $0.35 and took no test. I haven't taken a test to this day. I still have my first license. We could get a chauffeur's license to drive a truck at age 16, with only a short test on how to change a tire and back up a truck or semi. Again I obtained my chauffeur's license without any more test than this.

Dad's trucks, mostly the semi's, went into Hormel Packing at Austin, MN, every day. This was about 75 miles one way and usually took 5 hours. Ole Schroeder worked for Dad and was the principal driver.

Other men would drive for $5 per trip. At busy times the trucks would go 24 hours a day. Some drivers, wanting to make money, would ask to take 3 or 4 loads a day. Dad set a limit of 2 loads per day per man.

I started driving the semi truck to Austin at about age 14. I had only a license to drive cars but no one ever asked to see a chauffeur's license, I was short and had to sit on a Sears catalog to see over the steering wheel. I did not grow taller until I went in the Navy at age 17.

Through the 30's and until 1945 when I went in the Navy we had band concerts every Friday evening in the summer in a bandstand, before the free movie. I played the snare drum and occasionally the base drum. We always considered it great fun. I played the drum in the Navy when in boot camp at Great Lakes.

War bonds were sold regularly in St. Clair. A young woman, I believe from Mankato, got up and sang without accompaniment, "Remember Pearl Harbor" and other war songs. Bonds were sold that day.

Gold star mothers were a phenomenon of the war. When a son, brother, father or husband went into service a family would exhibit a blue star in a window or front door. If the man was wounded they exhibited a Silver Star. In the event of a death a gold star would be shown as symbol of that extreme sacrifice. There were a few gold stars in St. Clair, a village of about 300 people.

Christmas at home included setting up a fresh balsam tree about 5 ft. tall in our living room. We had strings of colored paper rope. We hung decorations mostly handmade and strings of popcorn. We had no electric lights until after the war.

At the Evangelical church a large tree was put up, about 12 feet tall or more. This had lights. We had a Christmas service where brown paper bags were given out to everyone and delivered to all we knew who were elderly, shut-ins or small children who didn't attend regularly. I recall delivering many bags. The bags contained about 2 apples, 2 oranges, some candy and cookies. They were all a great treat.

We exchanged small gifts between the young people. I remember giving Marlys Juliar a small $0.10 bottle of perfume. That was a big deal then!

At age 14, in 1942, I started to attend night training class at the Mankato Teachers College with Jim Fitzloff. We drove into Mankato about 6:00 p.m. and returned home after class ended at 9:00 p.m. 3 or 4 days per week. We always tried to get an ice-cream sundae before going home.

L to R: Marlin Haugen, Lowell Pagenkopf, Dean Schroeder.
Truck owned by Elmer Haugen.

My first car was a 1928 Studebaker 2 door car. I paid $25 for it in 1942. I had been saving for a bicycle but this had greater appeal. The car had not been driven for a year or two so I had to repair some tires, replace the battery, change the oil and spark plugs and other service. It then ran fine. The car had some rust so I sanded it and painted the car. I painted it light blue with yellow trim. I thought it was a sharp looking car.

I recall we paid $0.12 per gallon for gas when I bought the car. When I returned from the Navy in July 1946 gas was about $0.25 per gallon. The depression was very deep and long. Farmers received only $2 per hundred weight for hogs, $0.10 a dozen for eggs, $0.10 for a peck of potatoes and similar prices. They couldn't pay their taxes or afford new clothes or other things. An old law in Minnesota allowed a man to replace tax payments if he would work 4 days on roads or bridges, supplying a team of horses. Some farmers did this, but the counties couldn't keep it up. They needed the tax money more than they needed the roadwork.

My mother had completed two years of Commercial College in Mankato. She then worked in the office of Registrar of Deeds in the Blue Earth County Courthouse. She never worked outside the home during their marriage except as a salesperson in the meat market. We lived above the market where mother and dad worked long hours, opening at 6:00 a.m. and closing at 10:00 p.m.

I was born at home in St. Clair during a snowstorm, January 22, 1928. A friend and neighbor, Jack Sanborn came over and together the two men brought me into the world. Later that day or the next, Dr. R. O. Juliar, who lived in St. Clair, attended Mother and me. Dr. Juliar said there was little for him to do, as the two men did a good job.

In about August 1944 I opened and started a shop to repair radios. I had studied electronics and radio at Mankato College when I went to night school and had worked in electronics in the defense work. I also worked a few weeks for a man who repaired radios for Mahowald's, a large hardware store and radio sales and repair shop in Mankato. There I learned some short cuts in repair and pricing.

I bought a used tube tester which was in small self-contained box and with which I could test all the tubes then in use. They were all vacuum tubes. Solid state electronics and transistors had been invented but were not known to the public for another 6 or 7 years to 1950 or 1951. Earl Pagenkopf had urged me to do this. I paid $40 for the tester and some inventory of parts and tubes.

Most farms had no electricity. They had wind powered generators to produce 6 or 12 volt direct current, D.C. Alternating current, A.C., cannot be stored but D.C. can be stored in batteries. Some farms had large banks of batteries, 6 volt each, and were very heavy. I did some work with these systems. I climbed a couple of tall windmills to service the wind generators. This was in winter and I didn't like climbing icy metal ladders. There was no other radio repair shop in our area and I soon had a shop full of radios. If I had a problem I could not figure out I went to the repairman at Mahowald's and he was always willing to help me. Today we would call him a "mentor." In May 1945 when I went into the Navy I sold the assets of the shop including the hard to find tester. Earl wanted to keep this in St. Clair but we couldn't find anyone able to do or understand the work.

I had a sister Corrine who was two years younger. At school she had the nickname "Corky." (Mine was "Butch" because of the butcher shop). Corrine was married to Marvin Dimmel who was a farmer from Janesville. They had three children Steve (Marcia Schatzke), Caroline and David. (Steve and Marcia's son Andy is now operating the Haugen family farm southeast of St. Clair.)

Dad had a stroke at about age 78, which left him partially paralyzed on his left side. He could walk with a cane or walker. He couldn't talk, which was a terrible limitation and had difficulty swallowing. He spent the first year at home where they had a young man, Charles Marzinske, living with them. Mother had fallen, had a broken hip, which never healed, and was in bed or in a wheelchair. My parents moved into the Janesville Nursing Home where dad lived for five years and mother for 10 years.

Thoughts on Memories

Life in the 20's in the farm country encountered a depression about five years before the market crash of 1929 and the Nation wide depression in the 30's. The depression ended with WWII December 7, 1941. Wartime life ended about 1946 with the end of rationing, boys coming home and good jobs became plentiful. Life in the 50's and thereafter have been building years. Today we live in a period of luxury and plenty, never known before anywhere in the world. Having lived in the depression, I can still advise my children and grandchildren who I love very much to act like the squirrels and prepare for winters, all the while enjoying every minute of this wonderful world.

My love to all,
Marlon O. Haugen - May 2000

All in a Day's Work - At Pagenkopf's Grocery in St. Clair

A blend of tradition, work, and family.

Tradition and charm are hallmarks found in abundance at Peg's Grocery nestled in the heart of downtown

St. Clair. Located in a two-story building on Main Street near the bank and across from the municipal, this store has a personality and deep roots you won't find at the huge grocery super stores in Mankato.

Everyone in St. Clair knows that "Peg's" Grocery stands for Pagenkopf's - Lowell and Joan, that is. It's the same nickname that was "pegged" on Lowell's dad, Earl, who also ran the family grocery. In fact, you can go back one more generation to Grandfather Charles (Mary Krueger) Pagenkopf and you'll still find a St. Clair grocer.

But don't stop there. Lowell's mother, Abby, was from the family of Henry and Jessie Thielman, proprietors of the St. Clair Mercantile. And on the other side of the fence, Lowell's wife Joan hails from the Oscar Froehlich family who ran Froehlich Brother's Hatchery of St. Clair.

Beautiful wooden floors and decorative, sculptured, tinned walls and ceilings echo of an elegant by-gone era. The original counter top features a circular hole with a spool of string below. It dates back to a time when people brought in and traded eggs for groceries. The grocer would use the string to bundle up the box for the return trip home. And still today at Peg's Grocery, children enjoy the opportunity to pick candy from two Penny Candy jars.

Lowell virtually grew up in the family grocery store. As a young boy, he helped fill shelves, candled eggs, fired up the coal furnace, and was chief floor sweeper and shelf duster - a job he still holds. His parents taught him the value of work. He had to earn money for candy just like everyone else. And his mother taught him how to properly make change for the customers by counting up to the amount - not like today's cash registers, which just compute it. The Pagenkopf's still figure your change the traditional way.

Joan Pagenkopf inside Pagenkopf's Grocery

A star athlete at St. Clair High School, Lowell married his high school sweetheart, Joan Froehlich, in 1951. He went on to serve in the United States Air Force and they lived away from St. Clair for a few years. In 1956, his father died unexpectedly from a heart attack, and Lowell returned to run the grocery business for two years for his mother.

Lowell and Joan Pagenkopf

In 1958 he and Joan bought Peg's Grocery on their own. Ten years later, they modernized and moved the store location next door as they expanded bringing in self-serve shopping carts. "Up until that time, the customers would tell us what they wanted and we at Peg's would get it for them - whether it was a can of corn or a box of cereal," Joan relates. "We had bulk meats and cheese too. We sliced it off and wrapped it up for them. Most everything used to be bulk. Now it is packaged." Today the store gets merchandise from Gateway Foods in Blooming Prairie and features a variety of groceries, greeting cards, wrapping paper, videos, scratch-off lottery tickets, and a wide assortment of drug store items like toothpaste and aspirin. "With the changes in the way people buy, we've pretty much become a convenience store," Lowell said. "We have a grocery salesman who comes around every two weeks. He's always telling us about someone else who is closing up. So far we've been able to keep paying our bills. We don't know what the future holds, but one of the things we like is being independent. We cater to the public of course - but you don't have someone telling you what to do.'

The flip side of working for yourself is the long hours. Open six days a week from 8 a.m. – 6 p.m. Lowell and Joan share duties for running the store. They have no part-time help, and often find time for extra projects like fixing a cooler's condenser on a Sunday, taking inventory, or whatever needs to be done. "Sometimes it's hard when you get tired," Lowell said. They time-share too so Lowell can make his annual fishing trip to Wisconsin - and he fills in when Joan needs to shop or play golf.

This past year their daughter Becky Thompson of Mankato gave then a special Christmas present. The gift was her working at the store for a week so that her parents could have much needed vacation. Becky, Firm Administrator for Abdo, Abdo, and Eick Accounting, had to take a week of her own vacation to do so. "It was really nice of her," Joan said. "Becky's job involves a lot of responsibility and her ability to work with people is important. The experience she got working with the public at our store helped. She worked to earn her candy money. I remember the thing she hated the most was sorting out potatoes. When she'd stick her finger into a rotten one, she'd let out a scream."

Becky and her husband, Tom, have two sons, Slade and Blake, and you can be sure Joan and Lowell never miss an event the boys participate in. Often just one can go while the other runs the store-but they love to follow what their grandchildren do.

Lowell and Joan are proud of the good relationship they have had over the years with the school kids. Peg's Grocery was and still is a favorite noon hangout and the smell of pizza is in the air from 11:30 a.m. until about 1:00 p.m. Kids sit on the carpeted bench by the window and talk about stuff. Not long ago, the Pagenkopf's were invited to a 25th-year class reunion. "They said that we were such a big part of their school years that they couldn't have a reunion without us," Joan said. "Lowell had some fun with them. He made up a bogus bill for a broken window and door latch and for peanuts consumed, etc. It was something like $60 and then he added on 25 years of interest and came up with $4,000. We all had a good laugh!"

"We still think that a small community is the place to raise kids," Lowell said. "You know everyone and 99 % of the people get along real good." The community obviously feels the same way about the Pagenkopf's as they were selected to serve as Grand Marshall for the St. Clair parade this summer. Joan related that in December 1987 when Lowell had a stroke and spent time in Rochester, "People were so good. They offered to shovel snow and unload trucks and help out. The nurses remarked that Lowell got so much mail he must really be popular."

Lowell and Joan have been actively involved in the community of St. Clair. He drove school bus for 25 years and has belonged to the volunteer fire department for nearly 40 years, having served as chief. He has been a long-time member of the local Legion, and other organizations. Joan, active at St. John's Evangelical Lutheran Church, was organist for 30 years, taught Sunday school for 25 years and chaperoned the youth group at church for a number of years. She also belonged to the PTA, Home Extension and other groups.

Lowell enjoys gardening and pheasant hunting with his son-in-law and grandchildren. Joan loves music, adding to her Snow Village, and working on family history projects. Following St. Clair sports has been great fun, too. "We especially like football," Joan said. "There's always something to go to."

Life at Peg's Grocery is a blend of tradition, work, and family. It seems somehow only natural that Lowell and

Joan occupy the upstairs of the same building, in what was once a Woodsmen's Lodge. The ceiling here too features the beautiful sculptured tin designs. Downstairs, at the back of the store hangs a beautiful scenic painting by Joan's grandfather, Peter Bollman, nearby is the hum of the family clothes dryer. Joan offers advice, which has been food for generations. She says, "Keep smiling."

Lake Region Times by Helen Peterson – July 21, 1993

"The Rest of the Story" - 2004

Two years later in 1995, the Pagenkopf's daughter Becky and her husband, Tom Thompson, decided to build a new home on Reed's Lake. They asked Jo and Lowell to move to the lower level and after much thought they decided to do that. The following year an auction was held to dissolve the store inventory and some personal items. The store was sold to a developer to be remodeled into an apartment building. In October 1996, they moved to their new home. The current St. Clair Athletic Field is located on the land the Pagenkopf's sold to the school in 2002.

by Joan Pagenkopf

The sweetest gift that life can hold
Is "time" more precious far than gold?
And yet, we often throw away
Those precious hours that make today.
Author unknown
(Submitted by Joan Pagenkopf)

Memories of Grandpa Louie

My Grandfather, Louis William Timmerman (better known as "Louie"), was born in 1894. He was raised on a farm just south of where Highway 83 now goes, between St. Clair and Pemberton. (Today the Lynch family owns the farmstead.) He had two sisters and four brothers, however two of his brothers died at a young age. I don't know very much about my Grandpa's early upbringing, only that his family was of German heritage and his father's first wife died in childbirth. He was a lifelong member of the Lutheran Church in St. Clair.

My grandmother, Evelyn Kollos, grew up on a farm just north of St. Clair. At the tender age of 17 she ran away from home. She and my Grandpa took the train to Wisconsin, where they were married. For their honeymoon they rode the train to Hancock, Minnesota, and stayed with Grandpa's cousin for a week. My Grandparents tried their best to farm just west of St. Clair, but they were not very successful. They had a daughter, Unetta, born in 1921. They moved to a farm near Waseca for a few years, but times were hard during the depression years, and they ended up returning to St. Clair. My mother, Marjorie Nyquist, was born in 1930.

Louie was quite the musician in his day. He could play the fiddle and the button accordion. He and Grandma would entertain at what they called "house parties." Grandma would play chords on the piano, while Grandpa played the old, familiar melodies. They passed their love of music down to my mother, who passed it along to my sister and myself.

Grandpa built a house that is still nestled between the split in the road at the east edge of St. Clair. He drove school bus for St. Clair School and had a custom trucking business. Later my father, Dean Nyquist, would go into business with him. He also drove truck for the Mankato Rendering Works and would tell us stories about picking up dead farm animals from as far away as New Ulm. We did not enjoy hearing those stories as much as he enjoyed telling them.

I never met my Aunt Unetta as she passed away from leukemia at the age of 18. Seventeen years later my mom also succumbed to cancer. She was only 26 years old. Needless to say this left an impact on my Grandparent's lives. They had to go on, but it was difficult, at times. My sister and I came to live with our grandparents when we were seven and four years old.

Living with Grandparents presented some challenges for us, but we managed okay. Grandpa kept a few sheep and chickens around and we usually had a cat or two. Grandpa and Grandma would take my sister and me with them to visit relatives and friends, and of course Grandpa's favorite pastime, fishing. I remember one year when we got so much rain that the sheep pasture became a small lake, so Grandpa launched his boat and took us for a ride around the pond. Every summer we would all take a trip to Northern Minnesota and fish some more and play cards.

My Grandfather also loved to hunt deer. When he was in his early seventies I remember my Grandmother hiding his gun in an old foldout couch they had, because she told him he was just too old to hunt anymore. When my Grandmother passed away Grandpa reclaimed his gun and went deer hunting every year until he was nearly ninety. He shot a deer when he was 87 years old! I know that he made lots of people nervous with his passion for hunting, but once he was determined to do something it was almost impossible to stop him.

After his retirement from trucking, Grandpa took on the job of mowing the Lutheran Church cemetery on the east side of St. Clair. He did that job many, many years, with a little help from the neighbor kids and his great-grandson, Brian.

Getting older and being left alone when Grandma passed away were things that Grandpa seemed to take in stride. He was always going visiting or fishing. He would give the nice big fish to his neighbors and save the little ones for his family. He really enjoyed a good home-cooked meal, especially if it included meat and potatoes.

Grandpa went into his nineties and was still living in his house, driving, fishing, and watching Twins baseball on TV. One day there was a township meeting going on near his house when Grandpa came home and he drove his pickup into his garage, only he hit the gas pedal instead of the brake. He drove right through the end of his garage, up the ditch, onto the road and back to his driveway. The men who were at the Township Shed at the meeting came out to investigate the commotion. By then Grandpa was parking his vehicle back into his garage, except that now the back wall was lying on the ground. Grandpa couldn't understand what the fuss was all about! My sister and I were finally forced with the task of auctioning off Grandpa's things and selling his house. He went to live in Janesville the last few years of his life, eventually spending 1.5 years in the Janesville Nursing Home.

My Grandpa did not have the opportunity to get much formal education, but he was a unique member of our family, even if he did make us worry a lot about him as he got older. I can't member him ever being crabby. He loved life and always had a plan. He planned to celebrate his 100th birthday with a big party, but passed away 6 months short of fulfilling that goal. I like to think of him as a St. Clair icon.

by Mary L. Schenk

Poem written by Edith Foster Chase for the 50th wedding anniversary of Rev. and Mrs. G. E. Fritzke - August 5, 1942

Going Down the Years–
Wedded lovers, hand in hand, going down life's lane
Weaving hours of loveliness into memory's chain,
Through the fields of springtime – in the morning sun -
Going on together, hearts that beat as one.

Joy and sorrow, here and there, braided in the chain-
Just a little sunshine - just a little rain -
Just so much of happiness-just so much of tears,
Hand in hand together - going down the years.

Going on together, toward the setting sun,
Holding fast to memories, gathered one by one,
Faith and understanding, woven in with tears,
Hand and hand together going down the years.

The same old wish from the same old friends,
Jake and Edith Chase

Poems by Mrs. Chase Are Published in the *World Fair Anthology* - 1941

Edith Foster Chase (1870 - 1954) whose poems have appeared from time to time in the papers of the *Mankato Free Press* has just received a copy of *The World's Fair Anthology*, which contains two of her selections. Mrs. Chase has been writing poetry for about nine years. She received her first recognition when she entered an international contest writing a poem entitled "Power." Edwin Markham won the first prize ($1,500) in the contest. Mrs. Chase's poem received honorable mention, and she received a letter of congratulation from the London Poetry Society. This encouraged her to the extent that her poems have appeared in *The North American Book of Verse, The Michigan Verseland Anthology, The Minnesota Journal of Education, The Minneapolis Tribune,* and *The Country Home*. Her poems have also appeared in the following verse magazines: *Better Verse, Poetry Caravan*, and *The Country Bard.*

During the Roosevelt-Landon presidential election (1901) she wrote a campaign song for Landon which was sung over WNAX every day during the entire campaign. For the last few years several of her poems have been read over WTCN, the last one appearing about three weeks ago on a Sunday afternoon in connection with The St. Paul Poet Seminar program. As a result some of these poems have appeared in the *WCTN Radio Anthology*, a recent one being in "The Meadows of the Moon." Edith Foster Chase is the wife of Mr. Jake Chase of St. Clair. She is now busy planning a book of verse to be published sometime in the future. Her father, Stephen Foster and uncle, Henry Foster, were first cousins of Stephen Collins Foster, the songwriter, a direct descendant of Alexander Foster, the first of this Foster family to come to America.

'LONG IN FEBRUARY

Forty below and still a snowin'
Nobody comin' and nobody goin'.
Nobody goin' and nobody comin'-
Old teakettle keeps right on a hummin',
Fire in the cook stove-furnace, too,
Pokin, the fire's 'bout all I kin do,
Old round oak keeps a 'crackin' and snappin', -
Kids kind a itchin' to do some scrappin', -
Maw's over there on the lounge a nappin',-
Keeps me a 'wonderin' jest what's goin' to happen.
House all shut up tighter'n a drum,
Dog-gone if I don't wish spring'd come.
Bein' shut in makes a feller's bones ache,
It's time for the backbone of winter to break,
Ev'r day's getting' me madder 'n madder,
All that old woodchuck and his shadder. -

- Edith Foster Chase, St. Clair

Glamour Girls of Easter Parade 1941
Just Two Years Old

At our house we're hoarding - a million in gold
An armful of loveliness - just two years old;
So innocent - so winsome-so mischievous-so wise
With a face like an angel come down from the skies,

When she smiles she's all dimples - when she laughs she's so dear,
When she pouts she's so darling that we spoil her, I fear,
She's so kissable and tender - so naughty and bold -
But Oh, she's so precious and just two years old!

So demure in wee dresses beruffled and pretty
She plays at keep - house with her dolls and her kitty,
With gay ribbon bow in a tangle of curls
She enmeshes our hears - this wee girl of girls,
She's so cuddly - so marvelous, in our arms just to hold
And Oh so adorable and just two years old.

She drives us with reins held in two dimpled hands,
Her fetters are sweet though as strong as steel bands.
With tears and with kisses she shackles us down
We are slaves to her notions - she rules with a frown.

Sometimes we must spank her - sometimes we must scold
But oh, how it hurts us - she's just two years old!

- Edith Foster Chase, St. Clair, Minn.

These Poems Won Honors - 1942

In the recent Thanksgiving poem contest conducted by the National Thanksgiving Association two St. Clair women, Emma Marie Godemann and Edith Foster Chase won honorable mention in competition with more than 900 writers. Their Thanksgiving poems appear below.

I Thank Thee

Dear Father of mankind,
On this Thanksgiving Day
I thank Thee
For a land where Freedom's flag
Still waves on high,
Under a sky whose stars shine steadily,
Not blotted out by droning planes of war.
The light is not blacked out for us at night,
Our home is not a target for a bomber's thrust;
The boys and girls in this great land
Are free from gas masks and from air alarms-
Please keep our country thus!
For eyes that still see peace,
For hands raised in salute to Freedom's flag.
For hearts attuned to a democracy—
I thank Thee

by Emma Marie Godemann

Our Heritage

This day of days - Thanksgiving Day
A nation kneels to Thee
To render thanks, Almighty God,
For a homeland that is free;
To thank Thee for America,
A land of rich increase
Where floats, today, Old Glory
Above a world at peace.
To thank Thee, God, for pioneers
Of earth and sky and sea,
Safe-guarding this, our heritage
Of home and sanctity'
Safe-guarding this, our country's flag-
A sacrificial trust,
The emblem of our liberty,
Nor shall it trail in dust.
To thank Thee, this Thanksgiving Day
For a homeland, tried and true,
For freedom's gift of worship
And the faith our fathers knew.

by Edith Foster Chase

Poem written by Jack Fitzloff in response to a postal card sent by his niece who had moved to Texas:

Snow That Comes Over The Knees

The card you sent sounds good to me
About eating oranges right off the tree
Basking in sunshine, sprawled on the ground
In January with birds all around.
Throwing away my long woolen tights
Sleeping bare thru warm winter nights.
I'm one of those guys that likes to fish
Not like a president, that's not my wish
Like to sit in the sun on a riverbank
Hang onto a pole and wait for a yank
Or paddle out on a nice little lake
To fish and sleep and let the sun bake
Dreaming of home - no thank you please
This beats snow that comes over the knees.
Now to get packed-What'll I need?
Wifie for one thing-she's a good old keed
My rod and reel, the shotgun too
And Sandy, my dog — no that wouldn't do,
The guitar and fiddle — by the Rio Grande
Maybe I can join some Mexican band

By gosh I can feel that warm winter breeze
To heck with snow that comes over the knees.
Well, here we go now all full of smiles
Each day we make a few hundred miles
The housing shortage is getting bad
We think of something that makes us sad
After we drive way across the nation
No room 'cause we have no reservation,
We'll live under a tree with the birds and the bees,
Rather than snow that comes over the knees.

One day, I think it was the second week in February.
For cold it was, a fellow wouldn't travel far.
The telephone she ring so Loud "Who is it did I say"
It's for you, my Dear OLD Jack I think its P.T.A.
The kids up there want's you to do a little act.
It would'nt be the first time, and that's a galldurn fact.
So Ole up and out, scratch just like a hen.
I'm Looking for a book, they call Sven. Svenson. Sven.
She found the book, and said we better practice now
I said, "All right we will," but Let's hurry "Frau."
So we drove up town and parked our car, right by the butcher shop
I say's to myself agin now don't you be a flop
We walked in the school and "Boy" this is a dandy
But on second thought it would'nt hurt to have a little brandy.
I took one swig and just another, small one more.
Because the way it feels my throat, is just a little sore.
The kidd's they clap and call me Uncle "Jackie"
"Oh" this is fun, I'll be sonafdgun by "Crackey"
I took my fiddle out and "Ma" sit's by the Piano
I tuned up G and A and D and then "I sing soprano."
But all at once, out of the sky there was an awful pain.
I tried to Laugh, I tried to sing but it was, all in vain.
"Ma" Looked at me, half white in face "you in a trance"
"No, no" I said, "I do not care," just call the ambulance.
They Load me up feet first or not, don't remember which
I heard one guy remark, "he's "sickly looking peech"
I thougt of Ole, I tought of Jim
I think surely, I was on the rim, Of what they call eternity!
But as I lay here, seem.s I hear a tune. "Oh no",
It's just ma that feeds me with a spoon.
So, here I am in hospital, they surely treat me swell
The nurses come tiptoeng in when, er I ring the bell
I know I,ll get well, "Oh yes I will", so that,ll be just Okay.
It must be so, that's all I know, the Swede's were here today.
Good Luck! Hungry Hollow

Poem written by Jack Fitzloff

Recollection of Growing up in St. Clair, Minnesota

-Catching frogs so we could go fishing - then catching the big ones!

-Making tents out of blankets across the river.

-Sledding and tobogganing on Mayflower hill (the hill north of fire station across the river).

-Ice skating behind Pint's Garage (Mr. Gjerde would flood the playground and build a fire in the warming house.)

-Free shows and popcorn on Friday nights. Lots of people in town.

-Labor Day celebrations - Rococo's Carnival - (This tradition was dropped in 1947 or 1948 and then restarted in 1955 for the Centennial Celebration.

-Annie Schostag burgers and eggnog (best in the world) and coke. Annie made the eggnog for the liquor store.

-Blue Earth County Highway Department shop was located where Lester McCollum had saw mill-we played "king-of-the-hill on sand and gravel piles (spent a lot of time here). Joe Mosher, Sr. helped Lester operate the mill.

-Going out to the city dump by Ray Fitzloff's with the 22 and shooting bottles and rats. Also went to Haugen's Stockyard and shot rats. They would scatter all over town. Yuck!

-Summer baseball - east end of town against west end. The make shift ball diamond was by the railroad track.

-Herb Buesing's Ice House - organic Popsicle for kids. Building is still on the lot two-story building. Herb went to various lakes to get ice, wherever it was the clearest. He packed the ice in sawdust and would have ice all summer. When he delivered it to the various homes he would have to chip the block to fit the iceboxes and the kids would flock around him to get the ice.

-My dad, Ernie Hager built his house in 1939 for less than $5,000.

-The "Hilton" house was behind where Lyle and Stella Goodrich now live. This was the first house in town. Robert Schostag had a yard where he raised pigs and Herman Kroenke had his cows.

-"Texaco Night" at the town hall - would have a talent show and then run specials on oil. Other business did different promotional events. Also had wedding dances at this hall.

-Swimming nude behind Froehlich's Hatchery.

-Bill Beccue's mules in pasture behind "Margie's" Beauty Shop.

-Bill Beccue cutting hay all over town on empty lots. He lived where Kenneth Kroenke now lives. He also delivered coal. The coal would come to the elevator who then sold it and it had to be shoveled off the train car by hand into the coal shed, which was by the railroad tracks. It was then shoveled back onto a old four wheel cut down wagon, taken to who ever had ordered it and then shoveled to where ever it was kept for future use.

-Grandma Lottie Juliar (Nick's mother) living upstairs at Nick's house.

by William "Bill" Hager

Remembering My Childhood

My home was the corner (white) house, behind what is now "The UpTown Tavern." I was born there on February 12, 1919. There was an icehouse, which stored ice chunks that were packed in sawdust to last until spring. A big elm tree in our yard had a great tire swing, and I'd watch for Father O'Connor to come down to get the mail. He would give me some good pushes. We had two lots and on one corner was a barn for Dad's horses. Across the alley was a storage barn for school buses that were set on trailers with tires. In winter, they were set on sleighs. Eventually there were motorized ones. My dad had a great supply of handkerchiefs and chocolate covered cherries every Christmas.

My dad, Robert Schostag, also was called on to take the doctors (MacBeth and Juliar) to answer calls from farmers when a baby was due and also to take them to the hospital in Mankato. He did dray work, bringing crates of bread and canned goods to stores from the train depot.

There wasn't a problem, even in winter, for me to get to school, just hurry across the play yard. Of course, in winter it was a big skating rink, no warming house, so I'd walk home with skates on, warm up and go back.

Oh, for the good ol' years in grade school. Not a care in the world! Easter couldn't come soon enough so long underwear could be forgotten. Decide to have a "picnic" down by the river and buy 2 wieners for 5 cents at the meat market; get a can of pork and beans and 2 small potatoes for each, and then build a small bonfire. Bury the potatoes under the ashes, punch holes in top of bean can so it could heat in the coals. It was a bit tricky getting the hot can out and open. Greatest meal!!

There was a lovely park by the red bridge north of town across from Jack Fitzloff's. I believe the Commercial Club was responsible for it. There were arched wooden bridges spanning the creek and there were some picnic tables. It succumbed to vandalism and neglect.

There were live evergreens in the schoolrooms and churches, with candles burning during the Christmas program. Children each got a sack with an apple or orange, some hard candy and nuts.

When you were grown up, gloves and hats were worn to church and dresses. No shorts or mini-skirts! Respect was the rule in God's house.

In grade school, we had Valentine parties. What an honor to be chosen to decorate the box and everyone brought valentines and mothers took turns furnishing heart cookies and red punch. Then when we were in the third and fourth grade, with Lucille Pagenkopf as our teacher, we had "peanut showers." Of course, the floor would be covered with shucks, much to the chagrin of the janitor. It was soon banned!

Oh how we "grew up" when we could walk into the high school section from the elementary part. There were operettas. My Mom made me a pink and rose crepe paper costume for Miss Spring. Walter Schostag was winter and Virginia Macomber was fall. Someone was summer in red flannel! The first and second graders had a band! We wore white pants (probably pajama bottoms) and black jackets made by our moms. I had a tin drum and there were triangles to ring and kazoos! Games we played were Cricket, Kick the Can, and Fox and Goose.

We had lots of fun, sliding on hills in winter, and in summer picnics with little planning. Clay Boswell iced the hill behind their home and we kids would toboggan to the river. It was a tough haul back up the hill. We'd go in the house basement and warm up with hot chocolate. Of course, there were always music lessons to interfere! For Mother's Day we girls would walk about half a mile to the woods and pick beautiful purple and yellow violets, Dutchman Britches, buttercups, and some white flowers. Those bouquets were more meaningful than a dozen red roses.

"Podunk" was a busy town. It had grocery stores, hardware, barbershop with pool hall, garage for repairs, gaso-

St. Clair Elementary School band – 1st and 2nd grades circa 1928

line, and storage, creamery to take a stone butter crock to get fresh butter, blacksmith where you could see horses being shod, Kuske shoe repair where your shoes got new soles only to be fascinated by his ability. The St. Clair Drug Store had magazines, soda fountain, school supplies, gifts, jewelry, cosmetics, post office, and Dr. Juliar's office and exam room, beside their living quarters upstairs. When ladies or girls came to get a "trim" at the barbershop, Art Cords would warn the males to watch their language! The telephone switchboard was above the St. Clair Bank. My folk's number was 35, I believe. When they lived in their home (retired from the hotel) and I would call from Mankato, if I got no answer, Hulda Fitzloff would glance out the window and say, "Oh, she is just coming across town, try later."

My parents bought the St. Clair Hotel and Café in 1928 or '29. By that time there were very few "drummers" (salesmen who came by train and rented a room), they had cars by then.

The big deal was the Labor Day celebration. Hundreds of people came, every business had a float in the parade, kids decorated bikes and doll buggies, all led by the school band. A carnival set up a ferris wheel and other rides. Mother roasted at least 5 or 6 huge beef roasts to be sliced and it was never enough.

There were free outdoor movies on weekends to bring in the surrounding farmers. There were also the Caylor Players who were a troupe from Wells that acted in the Town Hall along with old time dances. The high school gymnasium was so small, when there were basketball games; the players could end up on spectator's laps. Graduation was also held at the Town Hall.

There was the Crystal Ballroom, owned by my dad and Jerry Lynch, out near the Black Iron Bridge (Hwy. 15) east of town where the Manaiges lived. They had roller-skating and dancing, but Blue Earth County outlawed Sunday night dances. The Crystal was moved in two parts to Nicollet County near Kasota on Highway 169. They had great bands from Fairmont, Iowa and even Lawrence Welk. It had a huge rotating crystal ball illuminated. It was dubbed "The Sheep Shed" by some because of the size.

My dad farmed some acreage behind the water tower, raising pigs, chickens, and several cows. He rotated soybeans, corn and small grain. The park is located near there now. In fall or spring, a beef and a couple of pigs would be butchered, cut up and stored at Rose's Meat Market (formerly Haugen) in a locker there. My mother was often called upon by the sportsmen club to roast raccoon! She was also noted for her Tom & Jerry mix for holidays. I can visualize her breaking eggs in a stone mixing bowl and whipping them to froth with a wire whip. The "coon and nog" was served at the liquor store (now Uptown Tavern).

I recall one Halloween, an outhouse was pulled out in front of the Hotel, and somebody's cow was tied to it. We woke in the morning and it had snowed, and there stood the poor cow. It was not kids that pulled that off!

On summer evenings, when we were freshman and sophomores, five or six of us girls would get together and walk from one end of St. Clair to the other. Probably purloining an apple or two, if the branch hung over a fence. It wasn't scary, and we sorta hoped a car of boys would drive by and whistle. Shameful hussies!! We were never afraid to walk home alone from a friend's house, unless we listened to "Behind the Squeaking Green Door" on the radio, no television then.

Birthday parties were fun. When we lived in the hotel, my mother invited my teachers, too. Salad was a "candle," pineapple ring with half a banana stuck in the circle and a cherry for the "flame," setting on a lettuce leaf no doubt.

Not to be forgotten - the candy carousel in Duemeland's store. It had 3 or 4 shelves to choose from for your nickel or pennies, jawbreakers, licorice babies, etc.

When my parents were retired and my children were at their house in the summer, the trucks full of pea vines stopped near their house, as the drivers went to get a beer before driving east of town to the venery. My children ran to the trucks and pulled vines off and sat in the yard shucking peas for their stomachs. Grandma ended up with some pods for creamed peas and little potatoes!

I also remember "Hobo Jerry." He would come to town in the spring on the train. He would do odd jobs around the hotel and around town. I think he may have slept in the shack behind the hotel. In the fall he would get back on the train and we did not see him again till spring.

by Helen Schostag Kenward

St. Clair Memories

-First and foremost – the pungent, delicious scent of lilac bushes in front of the school

-The wonderful smell before it rained – the wonderful smell after it rained

-Picking violets on Mayflower Hill for Mother's Day

-Swimming at Lake Washington

-Going to the movies in Mankato

-Fireworks on the 4th of July

-Fireflies

-Mosquitoes

-Sleeping on the screened porch in the summer

-The smell of sauerkraut being cooked in the Town Hall kitchen for Labor Day

-Saving money all summer for the Labor Day celebration

-Decorating our bikes for the Labor Day Parade – lots of crepe paper

-Gorgeous fall leaves (who needs New England?)

-Running and jumping in piles of leaves

-The smell of bonfires

-A huge early snowstorm, late 1930's so many of the turkeys at Froehlich Hatchery died, huddled together, just a few weeks before Thanksgiving

-Skiing and sliding on Mayflower Hill

-The smell of wet wool in the skate house – heated by a pot bellied stove

-Christmas Eve at our beautiful Lutheran Church – a huge Christmas tree, bags of nuts, candy, apples, oranges!

-Catechism class every Wednesday p.m. (we were excused from school) and Saturday a.m. – for two years

-Peg's Grocery Store; Pint's Garage; Haugen's Meat Market; (Mother would give me a dollar and say, "go get meat for supper!") Cord's Barber Shop; Hager's Hardware; Schostag's Hotel

-Miss Gorman telling us ghost stories

-And the smell of lilacs in the schoolyard

by Dorothy Rohrer Schnackenberg

Rambling Reflections

My connection to St. Clair began on a rainy Saturday morning in May 1954 when I arrived for an interview for a teacher-librarian position with Supt. Robert Kafka. After being interviewed in his office, he took me out to meet Courrier Hubmer who was chairman of the school board. He happened to be in the barn so we "slogged" through mud, which was a rather "rare" experience for me. I was hired and began my duties in the fall of 1954.

The St. Clair community celebrated its centennial (100 Years) the summer of 1955. At that time there were several businesses, including a drug store, a lumber yard, a garage, a hotel which later became apartments, a beauty shop, a bank, a couple of grocery stores and gas stations, plumbing and electrical business, a tavern, and a feed store and a grain elevator.

I was living in Mankato and car-pooled with Harriet Morse (3rd grade teacher), Mary Steel (4th grade), Irma Brooks (elementary principal and 1st grade), and Dagny Gullerud (Home Economics). It took about 45 minutes around town to pick up everyone plus about 30 minutes to St. Clair on the old winding road, including driving across the wooden Tivoli Bridge.

On August 27, 1960, I married George Panzram (a former St. Clair teacher and coach) who moved on to the Waldorf school district. I commuted to St. Clair for five years. In 1965 we bought the old Quinn house, which was then owned by Dick Savick who happened to be George's former student at Frost, MN. The house located in the corner of Park and Main Streets became available so we decided to move to St. Clair where I presently reside. It was George's turn to commute for about twenty years. Several residents of the town were retired farmers who turned their farms over to sons and daughters.

The activities of the school were an integral part of the community. There was 6-man football (later 9-man, and presently 11). The farmers, business people, and residents took "time off" to come and cheer for the team. There were no lights on the field so games were played on Friday afternoons much to the delight of students and faculty. Teachers were assigned to chaperone the fan bus. Homecoming was celebrated by crowning the queen on top of a hay wagon. (A king was added a few years later.) A pep fest was held around the blazing bonfire. The cheerleaders led the student body around town, even winding through the liquor store.

The junior class was assigned to decorate the gym for the prom and their mothers prepared food for the banquet and other functions. Members of the class managed to

Patricia Panzram

sneak into the cafeteria and "borrow" a few cookies while they were "working" on their projects. Most of the juniors and seniors participated in their class plays, which provided opportunities for them to be out on school nights. The principal and superintendent checked regularly to see if they returned home by curfew time.

Teaching an English class in the "upper room" of the original school building was somewhat challenging. During wintertime we wore coats, as it was cold and drafty. Occasionally a pigeon feather would float lazily down to our amusement. Band practice was held in the lower room.

Supt. Walton assigned teachers to take the school census in order to familiarize us with the families in the district. We were at times greeted by some growling dogs as well. Farmers and gardeners donated many vegetables and some fruits, which were prepared for lunch by the cooks. Students could have as many sandwiches (mostly peanut butter) and as much milk as they wanted.

The library was housed in a single room on the 3rd floor. It later doubled in size when a wall of the next room was removed. Elementary students came to the library once a week to check out books. Reading stories to them and teaching library skills was very satisfying and enjoyable.

The superintendent and principals also taught classes. Teachers had 3 to 4 different class preparations. Because we had no foreign language, I suggested that I could teach German. In 1957 it was added to the curriculum. Surprisingly, there were about 20 students consisting of juniors and seniors. Thereafter a second year was added. It was somewhat unique for a small school.

Competitive athletics for girls was nonexistent until the 1970's, which included full court basketball and gymnastics. Previously girl's sports consisted of G.A.A., an after school club for those who enjoyed physical activities. Equality was not an issue. It took many years to evolve because such sports were considered too strenuous and "unladylike." Girls will remember those "snazzy" one-piece maroon gym suits.

Somehow 50 years have passed and the "city" of St. Clair will celebrate its sesquicentennial in 2005 (150 years of existence). Former students range in age from the 60's to the 40's. I have had the privilege of attending graduations, weddings and sadly some funerals plus other events of their children and even grandchildren. I have especially enjoyed attending class reunions and reminiscing about the "way we were."

Time marches on and the population has tripled in size with new housing developments and a first class new school.

by Pat (Antonson) Panzram

E. A. Duemeland Drygoods & Groceries

CHAPTER TEN

St. Clair of the Past

PAST BUSINESSES & ORGANIZATIONS

St. Clair Commercial Club

On March 13, 1909, the citizens of St. Clair met at the Char. O'Connor building for the purpose of organizing a Commercial Club and was called to order by Charles O'Connor. Motions were made, seconded and passed to elect O. P. Miller as president, Nick Juliar as vice-president, F.W. Seaman as secretary and M. C. Dalton as treasurer. In the book of minutes it also states that Char. O'Connor, M. C. Dalton and F. W. Seaman are to be the committee to draw up the Constitution and By-Laws of the organization. A motion was made, seconded and approved that the organization be called "St. Clair Commercial Club." It was also decided that the membership fee should not be less than fifty cents. Thirty-one members signed the membership list paying fees of $.50 to $5. At the following meeting on March 23, a three-member committee be appointed by the president to arrange and take charge of all Auctions Sales with full power to conduct same according to their own best judgment. Mr. J. Leary, H. Lubke and F.W. Seaman were appointed to this committee. At the April 19 meeting it was reported that $211.13 was taken in at the "auction." On September 4, 1909, a motion was made, seconded and carried to have a "Street Fair" to run for two days, Sept. 24 and 25. A special meeting was held on September 14 and the committee reported that the $102 raised was not enough for the Fair so they were instructed to check with the 4th of July committee about adding those funds otherwise the baseball team would be excluded. The next minutes in the secretary's book were for September 1913 when a letter of protest was drawn up and sent to the Home Rule League of Minneapolis, Minnesota. It was in regard of the Governor of Minnesota calling a special session in order to create a state public utilities commission, composed of three members to be appointed by the Governor. The group deemed it unwise, unnecessary and an uncalled for burden upon the people of the state.

At the February 16, 1916, meeting it was decided to help the St. Clair Consolidated School project to the amount of $50 and designated $135.61 to the citizens 4th of July celebration. In reading through the minutes it is noted that the Commercial Club made several payments to Dr. R. O. Juliar for treatment to various patients. In September it was reported that the committee had conferred with the McPherson Township Board on acquiring some financial assistance for improvement of the Bellview Avenue to Bruels Hill. The board instructed it would be necessary to procure from the county some financial assistance for such improvements. In November it was voted to go to the city council to remove all hitching posts. In June 1917 it was ordered to pay H.A. Hubmer for 155 loads of gravel at 10 cents a load for $15.50 and to Ed Coggershall for 122 loads of gravel at ten cents a load. On January 16 it was voted to solicit donations and also sell chances on a hog with all proceeds to be given to the St. Clair Chapter of the Red

Cross. In the March 1919 minutes it was noted that a total $1,348.94 was turned over to the local Red Cross Chapter. It was then noted that the St. Clair Commercial Club be relieved of further responsibilities regarding the Community Red Cross Sale. It is also noted that the secretary of the Commercial Club communicated with the Northern States Power Company of Minnesota Division regarding the rates and service of light and power for the village in general. In March 1921 it was voted upon to buy three bass horns and a base drum for the band. A benefit was held to pay for same. In May of the same year it was approved to adjust membership fee to a minimum of $1. It was also decided to contribute $138 for the Rice Lake Road improvements. In the February 1928 meeting it was voted to take over the Farmers Institute from the Community Club and then form an advertising committee, an entertainment committee and a refreshment committee. George Macomber requested that the Commercial Club help boost a Livestock Shipping Association. In May of this year it was decided to support the band concert and to erect a bandstand with lights.

1935 is the last year of notes in the secretary's book. In March election of officers was held. Those elected were President Hugh Russell, Vice President Marvin Rohrer, Secretary Fred Erickson, and Treasurer Ernest Hager. It was also decided to support the school band through the summer (3 months). The bandmaster was to give lessons to the pupils and give a concert each Saturday night for June, July and August. In May the bills paid were $7.62 for music and $71.70 for the bandstand. Mr. Erickson was to wire the stand and Hager Hardware was to furnish the material and turn all bills in to the Commercial Club treasurer. On June 6 it was decided to have a sign made for the RNA convention which was to be held in St. Clair on June 12th. They also voted to be more diligent in enforcing the water rent ordinance and recommended that the rent collected every three months and if not paid within 30 days after the quarterly bill is rendered, that the Marshall be instructed to turn off the water. It is hereby recommended that if the water rent is not paid within 10 days after the bill is reordered that the Marshall take such unpaid bills and try to collect same.

The club apparently became inactive for a time and then reorganized with the group calling itself the "Sportsman Club" and later the "St. Clair Boosters Club." This group sponsored several events including the annual "feather party," which accommodated capacity crowds and were held in the American Legion Social Hall or the school cafeteria. Bingo and raffle tickets were the game and turkeys, ducks and chickens were the prizes. The big event of the evening was the drawing of the "door prize," for which most held their breath hoping not to win. The prize being the live "Big Tom" which was in a pen and had made his presence known throughout the evening. Lunch was always available.

This organization supported many youth programs including purchases of 4-H steers. When the local snowmobile club disbanded $2,500 was given to the Boosters Club.

Over the year's membership dwindled as members got older. The St. Clair Jaycees and Jaycee Women had been organized with the younger generation. In 1989 after the St. Clair Football Team won the State Nine-man title the members decided to disband. They purchased the "Welcome to St. Clair Sign" and divided the balance of their monies between the St. Clair Actioneers and the St. Clair Women of Today as a 4-year CD.

St. Clair Drug Store

Dr. Richard O. Juliar built the St. Clair Drug Store in 1909. At various times it also housed the St. Clair Post Office. Dr. Juliar also had his medical practice in this building. The Juliar's operated the store until 1931 when the Rohrer family took over. They operated it until 1945. Sometime around 1948-1949 Elzada (Juliar) and John Howley returned from California with the intention of operating the drug store as well as the post office. This however did not work out so they returned to California. John and Olga Fitzloff took over the operation and owned it until John's death in 1960. William and Iola Bjorklund then purchased it. They lived in the back of the store and Iola had a gift shop in the front. Bill taught science at the high school and also repaired televisions. It was then remodeled and made into apartment with various owners over the years. In 2004 it was purchased and still has apartments. The front of the lower level is now the home of Marquardt's Cowlectables.

St. Clair Hotel

The first notation of hotels appeared in 1880 and 1886 where listings of the business in St. Clair shows having two hotels, the Union and American Houses. The fate of these hotels is unclear.

The St. Clair Hotel appears in 1895 when it was built by George B. Caldwell. The Caldwell family operated it for fourteen years. At one time Joseph Meurer, the parents of former Blue Earth County Sheriff Emil Meurer, the hotel was owned by. The establishment was known as the St. Clair Hotel. It had a kitchen, restaurant, bar and eight rooms. In 1929 during the depression, Robert and Anna Schostag purchased it and operated it along with the restaurant and bar until 1945 when they sold it to Leo and Tonnie DeMars. In 1953 the DeMars sold it and it was owned and operated by John Delya, Percy Nissan and Glen Thompson. Glen Thompson then took possession of the building. (Glen had worked with Robert Schmidt at the liquor store, which was located in the old Mercantile adjacent to Pagenkopf's Grocery. This establishment was closed by the city that had purchased it and made it a Municipal Liquor Store. It was closed when the Municipal moved across the street.) Archie Cray and Henry Borgwardt later operated the bar portion of the hotel business. In 1954 Gene Baer bought the building and he along with his wife Bonnie, operated the hotel, restaurant and bar until 1956. It was then purchased by Robert Zavoral of the St. Clair State Bank, moved further to the north and remodeled into apartments. It has now been torn down thus the end of the St. Clair Hotel.

St. Clair Area Jaycees
St. Clair Area Actioneers

In 1971 a group of young, energetic men decided there were several ways in which they, as a group, could work together and contribute in making the community a better place. They felt the best way to do this was to join a national group called the "Jaycees." This group continued as the Jaycees until 1983 when they felt it was costing them too much money just to belong to the association. They then disbanded their affiliation with this group and continued their "good deeds" for the community independently. The name Actioneers was suggested by Karen Grams a member of the Jaycee Women. The commitment of the group was to be men of action not auctioneers who talk fast to sell something

Charter members of this organization were Darcy Johnson, President, Ralph Buesing, Dave Frantum, Tom Freitag, Dave Glamm, Tom Jennings, Tom Karels, Sr., Jerry Marzinske, Alan Miller, Jerry Phillips, Dan Stelter, Sam Veroven, Steve Wilmes and Daryl Witt. The group held its meetings at Hager's Diner.

A "Home Commitment" project, which was completed by the group, was the washing and painting of the Herb Buesing home. In 1982 they assisted in the cutting down of state famed Cottonwood Tree on Main Street.

The group continued doing the programs for the youth of St. Clair, filling sand boxes, Easter egg hunts, Santa Claus Day, the school's "Run, Punt and Pass" Program, free throw contest, volleyball serving contest, wrestling tournaments. They also provided skating rinks in Frank Park. The group constructed the wooden playground equipment, on the former school grounds.

General community projects included citywide cleanups using farm trucks for collection and glass recycling. This was a first in Blue Earth County. The "glass sheds" were constructed by the group with lumber from the Lamberts and United Building Center facilities. Sheds were located not only in St. Clair but also in Beauford, Eagle Lake, Good Thunder, Madison Lake, Mapleton, Pemberton and Rapidan. The Mankato Locations were Bel Mar Mall, Circle Inn, Cub Foods, HyVee Downtown, Mankato Iron & Metal, Morson-Ario VFW, South Street Tavern, Square Deal Bar and Susan's. Jean Lundquist, who at the time was working for the KTOE Radio Station, gave great publicity assistance to the group. From 1985 until 1991, the group collected over 900 tons of glass. January 21, 1992, was declared "St. Clair Area Actioneers Day" by the Blue Earth County Commissioners. The glass-recycling project became too large for proper commitment and contamination was also a problem. Blue Earth County then started a "recycling" program and the Actioneers distributed recycling bins throughout St. Clair.

Recycling of paper was another project for the Actioneers. Papers were collected on the first Saturday of the month and then an attempt was made to chop and bail the papers. The recycled paper was then taken monthly to Carlson Craft in North Mankato. Aluminum cans were collected, stored in the Phillips barn and then sold.

In 1984 the group, working with the St. Clair Jaycee Women, started the "St. Clair Day's" celebration. The Area Actioneers initiated and designed the first St. Clair Days Button, organized the Medallion Hunt and lined up tents for the Municipal Liquor Store Beer Garden. The 1991 Button commemorated the Desert Storm Conflict. They also have sponsored the Christmas Lighting Contests.

Providing recreational facilities seems to be an endless task. They built the first shelter at Frank Park and helped build the first concession stand on the St. Clair School Athletic Field. Later they dismantled this building, recycling blocks and used its roof for the open shelter at Memorial Park. The recycled blocks were used for the foundation for the current pavilion building also at Memorial Park. The group has built and installed new playground equipment at the same location. In 1990 they bought the first recycled plastic picnic tables.

The last major project for this group was helping sod the new softball field at Memorial Park, not once but twice! The results of the first attempt did not satisfy the group so they re-rolled the sod, re-graded the whole field and relaid it for the second time.

The projects of this group were totally funded from glass recycling. On September 1, 1999, the organized group decided to disband. They enjoyed an evening out as a group at the Chateau in Cleveland, Minnesota, which was their last outing as a group. The balance of the cash on hand was divided evenly and donated to the St. Clair School for improvements to the gymnasium acoustics system and the city for use at Memorial Park.

Additional members over the years include: Kevin Allen, Butch Anderson, Randy Born, Rick Britton, Jim Buysse, Larry Carlson, Cy Denn, Russell Faye, Bradley Flowers, Bruce Goodrich, Dan and Frank Ireland, Jeff and Jim Juliar, Bill, Chris, Stacey and Tom Karels, Jr., Rich Lebens, Jeff Ludvig, Gary Mace, Jerry Marzinske, Doug Miller, Allen Olson, Floyd Palmer, Tom Pepper, Delbert Point, Leo Ripplinger, Brian Sader, Randy and James Schaub, Kevin Schroeder, Dennis Cox-Townsend, Stacey Veroven, Brian Wall, and James Williams.

by Tom Freitag, Dave Glamm and Tom Karels, Sr.

St. Clair Lumber Yard

The Botsford lumberyard was located next to the train depot where the trailer court is today. It was operated by Jack Sanborn and then by Robert Loeffler. It was eventually sold to the Pemberton Lumber Company of Pemberton, Minnesota. Robert Prescher was the manager when it closed. After it was closed for business it was dismantled.

Sunshine Golf Course

In the early 1930's George Macomber came up with the idea of developing a golf course. George, Ray Fitzloff, Hugh Russell, Jack Sanborn, Art Winkelman along with Father Byron organized the development of this project. The course was located on land owned by Ray Fitzloff along what is now Blue Earth Co. Highway #15 (where Dale and Fran Sargent currently live). This ground also served as a pasture so they were not concerned about mowing the grass. It was a nine-hole course and the only handicap being the "cow pies" which were located any and everywhere. There were fences and sand around the holes with 3x4 runs with sand. The sand was smoothed out with their hands. Robert Fritzke, James Winkelman and Jimmy Fitzloff were the caddies. Father Byron would pick up the boys and transport them to the course. There were no fees for using the course and it was still in existence in 1935.

by Robert Fritzke

Modified by Local Rules.

LOCAL RULES

1. WINTER RULES PERMITTED—(Ball may be lifted on Fairways and played within club length, not nearer the hole without penalty.) Fairways are designated by numbered stakes. Beyond stakes in rear of green is rough.
2. In the rough, ball must be played as it lies.
3. Any ball driven over fence is out of bounds. Replace on Fairway and lose one stroke.
4. Players must not drive from tee until party preceding is out of range.
5. Players must not play up to any putting green until match preceding has holed out and moved away.
6. Players who have holed out must move away promptly and not obstruct the putting greens.
7. Ball in river; another ball may be dropped on opposite bank. Penalty one stroke.
8. Bushes and trees in Fairways and around greens are considered natural hazards.
9. High heeled shoes will not be allowed on putting greens; they ruin greens.
10. Players may omit holes No. 3 and No. 4, going from second green to bridge head, to play No. 5, if timid about river.
11. Lost ball, drop another where lost; penalty one stroke.
12. REMEMBER THE PLAYER BEHIND. If ball be lost, let players following go through. Do not be unnecessarily deliberate either in walking or playing. Either keep going or let the faster play-

SUNSHINE GOLF CLUB

ST. CLAIR, MINN.

On Fitzloff's Sunshine Turkey Farm

Additional Past Businesses

Barber Shop, Pool and Billiards: Lewis A. Huettle
Bill's Athletic Supply: William D. Hager
Blower's Produce
Carpenter LP Gas Service
City Service Products: Leon & Frank Fisher
Commander Elevator Company: Roy Meany, Paul Schwichtenberg, F. J. Sahli, Charles Moser, managers
Denn's Construction: Edward Denn/David Kruse
DeRemer Implement
Dr. J. L. MacBeth, MD
Edward Ewert Milk Delivery
Farmer's Elevator Company, Inc. Grain, Coal and Machinery
Gambles OK Hardware: Calvin Gamble
Gem Theatre
General Blacksmithing, Woodworking and Repairing: E. G. Sack
Hintze & Grundmeier Hardware Company
Hi-Way Meats: Marvin Schull & Robert Blace
Hoppe's Barber Shop, Mike Hoppe
Leo Frank Electrician
Leo Frank Hardware
L. Hugunin General Merchandising
Louise's Beauty Shop: Louise McComb
Moore Mobil Oil Company: Chuck Moore
Nissan's Cafe
Standard Oil Division: Doug Mathiason - Crop/Guide Manager
St. Clair Bar: Glen H. Thompson, propietor
St. Clair Barber Shop: Steven Bickel
St. Clair Country Gardens
St. Clair Land Company
St. Clair Sanitation: Tom Hoeft & Robert Huber
Stelter Electric: Dan Stelter
Stransky Meat Market: Marvin Stansky
TJ's Café
Town'N Country Salon: Vicki Mosser, Manager
Uncle Albert's Cafe

Sharing

There isn't much that I can do, but I can share my bread with you, and I can share my joy with you, and sometimes share a sorrow, too, as on our way we go.

There isn't much that I can do, but I can sit an hour with you, and I can share a joke with you, and sometimes share reverses, too, as on our way we go.

There isn't much that I can do, but I can share my flowers with you, and I can share my books with you and sometimes share your burdens, too, as on our way we go.

There isn't much that I can do, but I can share my songs with you, and I can share my mirth with you, and sometimes come and laugh with you as on our way we go.

There isn't much that I can do, but I can share my hopes with you, and I can share my fears with you, and sometimes shed sometimes shed some tears with you as on our way we go.

There isn't much that I can do, but I can share my friends with you, and I can share my life with you, and ofttimes share a prayer with you as on our way we go.

Maude V. Preston

Coffee time at "The Diner"
L to R: Audie Blank, Gene Phillips, Ron Engeleby, George Fitzloff, Bruce Miller, Elroy (Stub) Juliar and Stan Drake

CHAPTER ELEVEN

St. Clair 2005

ORGANIZATIONS

St. Clair American Legion Post #475

The Grams-Schmidt American Legion Post 475 was formed on February 4th, 1944. The Post is named after two local veterans who died during World War I - William Henrick Grams, the son of Ludwig and Marie (Westphal) Grams and Roy Schmidt, the son of William Schmidt. The original charter lists nineteen individuals: John P. Sanborn, John W. Fitzloff, John A. Freitag, Lloyd E. Russell, William Groll, Henry Seys, Theodore Penn, Clark Preston, Roy Hodapp, Earl Pagenkopf, Elmer Haugen, Theodore Tillman, Robert Sodeman, Edward Kroenke, Hubert Hodapp, Otto Glamm, John Tacheny, H. J. Ireland and Elmo Nyquist. The first twelve individuals signed the original charter.

These men recognized that a local American Legion Post would be beneficial to veterans returning and soon to return from service in World War II.

The city allowed the Legion the use of the second floor of the city hall for its meetings and events.

One of the first activities for the Post was conducting military funerals for local servicemen who had given their lives serving in World War II. Since the Post did not yet have ceremonial rifles, Post members used their own shotguns for rifle salutes. In order to achieve a perfect volley of fire – only one of the members used live ammunition.

St. Clair American Legion

Gene Goettl, a 1971 graduate of St. Clair School and the Commander of the St. Clair American Legion Post

Local veterans and their wives and school children watching the folding of the American flag.

Post membership grew to eighty-seven members in 1962 and declined to twenty-seven members in 1981. In 1982 the Post reorganized, and membership has grown steadily to our present membership of 107.

In 1983 the Legion purchased the old city hall building, renovated and remodeled it to serve as our present Post home.

We invite any veteran of wartime service to join us in our service to fellow veterans and their families.

by Gary Mace

St. Clair American Legion members carefully and respectfully folding the American flag while the purpose of the fold was being explained. Legion members (L to R): Harold Holmgren, Delmar Preston, Hubert Johnson, and Dobie Painter.

St. Clair American Legion Post 475 Ladies Auxiliary

The Grams-Schmidt - St. Clair American Legion Post 475 Ladies Auxiliary was officially granted its charter status on October 11, 1946. Olga Fitzloff was elected its first president. Phyllis Froehlich, vice-president, Florence Juliar, treasurer, Leona Mace, secretary, Mrs. Jack Sanborn, chaplain, Mrs. Edwin Hall, sergeant-at-arms and Sarah Meany, historian were the remaining officers. Other charter members were Ida Penn, Ada Bestman, Lillian Danberry, Clara Freitag, Helen Schuldt, Julia Haugen, Harriet Day, Abbie Pagenkopf, Mildred Twedten, Edna Froehlich, Augusta Baer, Bea Buesing, Ruth Buesing, Hulda Fitzloff, Dorothy Frank and Alma Cords. Two of the charter members, Florence Juliar and Leona Mace are still living today.

There are presently 67 members today. The group who applied for the charter was known as the "Moms." The ladies corresponded with the servicemen during WWII, sent packages of treats to the boys and made bandages and cancer pads. The unit is very active in service to those serving our country and also the veterans in nursing homes and shut-ins.

by Leona Mace

St. Clair Volunteer Fire Department

The first notation regarding an organized fire department was on December 12, 1890, when a newspaper stated that "the St. Clair fire department held it's regular meeting and the company is now out of debt and has a good clear record. They will invest in a windmill soon." In March 1891 there is a notation that "Some of the real smart people (and there are a few of that class) pulled a bolt out of the Fire Co.'s pump and let the plunging rod drop down so far that it cannot be reached. Andy Quinn with his well tools has been at work several days trying to reach it but has been unsuccessful." On a Monday evening in 1902, at half past nine, the rapid "tap-tap" of the fire bell alarmed the citizens of St. Clair. Everybody caught up a pail and ran. A bucket brigade was quickly formed and with pails of water and vigorous chopping with an axe the firemen soon had the fire at the home of Sumner Hilton under control.

In May 1911, Charles O'Connor and Jake Chase were chosen to select a site on which to erect the fire house and water tank. They endeavored to buy the lot west of the McPherson Town Hall. In August 1911 Griffith & Walker of Zion City, Illinois, arrived in St. Clair. They had the contract for the sinking of the village well. The contract for the erection of the steel tower and water tank to hold 60,000 gallons was awarded to the Des Moines Bridge and Iron Co., at $4,100. The contract for the excavation for the water pipes was awarded to W. P. Lovell & Co. of St. Paul. In November a special meeting was held of the village council to accept the city well at a depth of 232 feet. At test of 48 hours of steady pumping, throwing 120 gallons per minute it did not lower the water. The water was of good quality and came within 31 feet of the surface. It was felt the St. Clair water system would be one of the best in the country and would in all probability be completed by December 1, 1911. It has served us well!

No longer used but still useable are the two pieces for fire fighting equipment shown above. The hose cart and pressure tank cart were part of the first fire fighting apparatus acquired by St. Clair's volunteer fire department. The artifacts are still stored in the municipal building.

At the firemen's meeting held in the spring of 1912, the following officers were elected: president, Charles O'Connor; secretary, George Hubmer; vice president, George Hussey; treasurer, Charles Pagenkopf; chief, Henry Lubke; assistant chief, William Boswell and chairman finance committee, Henry Thielman. The organization had a membership of 25. On July 15, 1912, the St. Clair fire department was called out and this was their first experience fighting a fire with their new apparatus since the water works system had been completed. Quick work on the part of the fire fighters soon had the fire at A. E. Near's barn under control. At a special meeting in June 1913, the fire department decided to have the department practice once a week. On July 25 of the same year the fire bell arrived and was installed on the village windmill tower immediately!

On April 8, 1914, the Catholic Church, which was a wooden structure, burned. As the fire hydrants were too far away, the fire department could do little to save the building.

St. Clair was given the new "Village Hall" on December 27, 1921. The building was thirty by sixty feet and twenty feet high; heated by a pipeless furnace and supplied with water and electric lights. It was two stories high. The first floor had five apartments. A long room, which extended the full length of the hall on the west side, was used as the fire station. It gave a warm, dry room to hold all of the fire implements.

In April 1923, a vote for a "water bond" was defeated thus the availability of fire protection was still limited to only a few residences of the city.

Over the years the fire department has served the community well. A new Chevrolet fire truck was purchased in 1955 and in 1973 they purchased another new truck at the cost of $10,500. The truck was an all-purpose vehicle with a 1,500-gallon tank on it plus many other types of equipment. Lyle Splinter was the fire chief at this time. The annual "Fireman's Dance" was a huge fund raising event for many years and helped purchase equipment for the department.

St. Clair City Hall and Fire Station

In front: 1940 Chevrolet Pumper Truck
In back: 1978 International Tanker Truck

In 1974 the city built a new city hall and a fire hall was included in the project. This complex was built on the lot, which formerly was the location of the creamery, at 304 Main Street West.

Today the St. Clair Fire Department consists of twenty-six fire fighters and one reserve-fighter. The qualifications to become a fireman are:

Be a United States citizen and legally able to work in the United States.

Complete 110 hours of "Basic Firefighters" classes.

Complete 40 hours of "First Responder" classes

Attend one hour of training per month.

Live within a 5-minute response time from your home to the fire hall.

No facial hair that may interfere with an air mask.

1975 Dodge Mini-pumper Truck

The department is funded through contracts with the townships within the fire protection area, the City of St. Clair and the State of Minnesota. Proceeds from "Charitable Gambling" are used to buy equipment and donations to various charities. The department has a charge for fire calls as well as vehicle accidents, however there is no charge for a medical emergency call.

The 1992 Ford L800 Pumper Truck, that has a 1,000-gallon tank and can pump 1,250 gallons per minute, was purchased at a cost of $130,000. It is also equipped with a "Jaws of Life" unit and a 5,000-watt generator. Donations from the St. Clair American Legion and the St. Clair Actioneers helped purchase equipment for the truck. The 2000 Rescue Truck at a cost of $150,000, as well as 1992 truck, was purchased with the charitable gambling funds. Other equipment the department

1992 Ford Pumper Truck
Standing by the truck is future firefighter Bailey Arndt.

Firefighter Richard Arndt with the 2000 Freightliner Rescue Squad Truck

owns is a 1969 International Pumper Truck, a 1975 Dodge Pumper Truck and a 1978 International Tanker Truck. The department is also well equipped for medical emergencies.

Over the years the members of the fire department have helped with many community functions. They have an annual "steak-fry" in conjunction with St. Clair Days. They also work with the local school and other organizations in fire prevention education. The department offers a pension plan, depending on the number of years of service, as a benefit of being a firefighter. The greatest benefit to each of them is the pride in the service given to their community.

The current officers are: Bill Fitzloff, fire chief, Nathan Mace, assistant fire chief, Rick Huber, president, Troy Goettl, secretary, Charles Grams, treasurer and Bradley Schulz training officer. Dr. Michael Wilcox is the medical director.

Article supplemented with information from Troy Goettl, secretary of the St. Clair Fire Department.

St. Clair Athletic Backers

The St. Clair Athletic Backers was formed in the early 1970's by a group of parents to help with some of the athletic events, such as the elementary wrestling tournament and junior high athletic events. Volunteers helped with staffing the concession stands and selling tickets at athletic events. Fundraisers such as hosting the Minnesota Viking Basketball games and the Baldknobbers were held to help defray some of the expenses relating to sports. This was one of the groups that regularly gets together to promote the school athletic programs and to help out in the community. They help in any way possible, over the years the funds that were raised were used to buy the athletic field lights from MSU, build the concession stand and crow's nest on both the old and new athletic field's. Contributions have been made to the school sign posting upcoming events, new padded chairs for the players, ice machine, assortment of sports equipment, equipment for the new weight room, junior high uniforms and assisted in the purchase of new wrestling mats and lifts. Also included are many, many hours of volunteer labor. The group also helps with the athletic achievement awards as well as helping with the "St. Clair Days" celebration.

One of the biggest fundraisers is the raffle held with the St. Clair Day's celebration and a cleanup day project at the Minnesota State Fair. Over one hundred and fifty people have signed up for this in the past. The group has 60 paid members and is always looking for new members.

St. Clair Athletic Backers

These programs are being provided by the St. Clair Athletic Backers in conjunction with listed sponsors.

The St. Clair Athletic Backers mission statement is to enrich the growth of St. Clair Elementary and High School Sports Programs.

The dedicated coaching staff, fans, volunteers, and parents are proud of our students' athletic achievements.

Officers:

President:
Cindy Glamm
Vice President:
Linda Kruse
Secretary:
Noreen More
Treasurer:
Val Levos
Directors:
Mike Denn
Steve More
Myron Schweim

The St. Clair Athletic Backers

would like ***"YOU"*** to join our team! Meetings are held the second Wednesday of every month at 7:00 pm in the St. Clair School Commons.

See You There!

Clever Clover 4-H Club

The Clever Clover 4-H Club was started in 1982, taking the place of the "Husky Helper" Club. The Clever Clovers Club consists of 33 members from the St. Clair-McPherson Township as well as other surrounding townships. Members can live in town and also in rural areas. The 4-H program actually has been around for over 100 years and there have been many clubs in the area. 4-H involves youth along with adults to get involved in the community, learn about new projects and offers many volunteer and leadership opportunities.

Members learn about many things from farm safety, how to raise livestock, learning how to sew, cook, build rockets, about horticulture, building-wood working projects, photography and much more. Participants receive the opportunity to show at the Blue Earth County Fair in Garden City, Tri-County Fair in Mankato and even the "Great Minnesota get-togethers," the Minnesota State Fair. Every month meetings are held to discuss community events and issues and even to have a little old fashioned fun! The Clever Clovers meet the second Sunday of each month at the St. Clair Fire Hall at 5 p.m. There are also many countywide meetings where the Clever Clovers have youth participate in making county decisions.

Club members also work on many volunteer projects. The 4-H year's starts off in October with a "county awards" banquet where the youth are honored for all their accomplishments. The club rakes leaves, hosts Halloween and Christmas parties and even performs skits. Every February the members also make 300 valentines and deliver them to area nursing homes. Members also help at benefits for community members and eagerly help with projects through out the community including St. Clair Days.

With smiles on their faces the 4-Hers are always up for a new challenge.

by current secretary Heather Lynch

Women of Today

The St. Clair area Women of Today Chapter was organized in October 1981 as the St. Clair Area Jaycee Women. The chapter was started with 8 charter members. In July 1985 the Jaycee Women name was changed to Women of Today and this is what the chapter is known as today.

One of the first big projects the chapter did was to organize and hold a Community Wide Garage sale that was held at the school cafeteria to raise money for new playground equipment at the school. With the community donations the cafeteria at the school was packed full of items and there was roughly $6,000 raised to buy the new equipment. This gave the chapter the feel of community support to get off the ground and running. From this time on the Women of Today chapter has supported the school by giving donations to various groups each year to help with projects. Some of them are Close Up Program, After Graduation Party, After Prom Party, Accelerated Reader Program, Project Charlie, I'm A Thumbody Program, Spanish Trip, Choir and Band Trips to name a few. We have also donated school supplies for children in need at the St. Clair School in the elementary grades. At Christmas time we purchased gifts for children that may not have had a Christmas and wrap them for the school to deliver.

In 1984 the Jaycee women worked together with the Jaycee men chapter to again start the St. Clair Days Celebration. It was started with a softball tournament, concession stand, quilt raffle and a parade. There have been many different activities added to the celebration over the years, but we have been able to keep the town celebration happening since it was reorganized.

Other community events that the Women of Today have sponsored are Easter with the Easter Bunny, shopping with Mrs. Claus with the appearance of Santa and Mrs. Claus, donating to the Sharing Tree, City Wide Garage Sales in the spring and fall. We also give a scholarship each year and have given donations to people in the community in need. We also get our exercise by doing "Adopt A Highway" for a two-mile stretch just outside of St. Clair.

The St. Clair Area Women of Today have been very active in the community over the 23 years they have been in existence and the community has helped support the chapter in its projects in return. (Additional Note: A big THANK YOU to all who provide these services to our community.)

by Cindy Glamm

St. Clair Post Office

In 1856 Henry Foster, the Indian Agent, was appointed the first postmaster in the McPherson-Winnebago Agency area. In 1862, James B. Hubbell was appointed to replace him and he served until May 1863 at which time Lucius Dyer purchased the land as well as the agency house and thus succeeded him. The post office was known as the "Winnebago Agency." In 1865, J. L. Cook was serving as postmaster. In March 1865 Lucius Dyer sold the land and agency buildings to Josiah C. Truman who also then served as the postmaster.

On August 1865 Aaron Hilton laid out a townsite in section 8 of McPherson Township. He named it "Hilton." The "Winnebago Agency" post office was then moved to

St. Clair Post Office

the Brown Brothers General Store at this location. Six weeks later Charles O'Connor suggested changing the name to St. Clair. A vote was taken and the name of the city as well as the post office was changed. Mr. O'Connor was serving as postmaster and he felt there was too much confusion between "Winnebago Agency" and Winnebago, Minnesota. In May 1869, James E. Brown was appointed postmaster and he was succeeded in August 1861 by Henry Mohr. In 1873 the "Belleview" Post Office was established. It was located in Section 32 of McPherson Township. James H. Eastman was the first postmaster and served until January 1876. Amos H. Easton was then put in charge. In 1879 Asahel B. Preston took over as postmaster. It was closed shortly after this time. In February 1890, Joseph H. Gebbard was appointed postmaster who later was succeeded by Fred Gerlich. In December 1898, Mel. G. Rasdall was noted to be serving as postmaster in St. Clair. The post office remained at the Brown Brothers store for some time. Charles Schweitzer later succeeded Mr. Rasdall. In 1909 Dr. Richard Juliar, MD came back to practice medicine in St. Clair and had purchased the drugstore. In 1914, President Wilson appointed him the postmaster, and he then moved the post office over to the drug store. He remained at this post until 1935. In 1931 Dr. Juliar sold the drugstore to Marvin E. Rohrer and Mr. Rohrer then in 1935 served as postmaster. Later the post office was moved to the E. Duemeland General Store and it remained there after Wm. Godeman purchased the store.

In 1949 Robert Fritzke came to St. Clair and began his service as postmaster. After Dr. Juliar's medical office closed at the drug store, then operated by Olga Fitzloff, Mr. Fritzke again moved the post office to this location. In 1968 the present post office building was built. Mr. Fritzke retired in 1977. Sharon O'Connor, who had worked as postal clerk with Robert Fritzke for several years, was then appointed postmistress. Denise Gjerde

McPherson Farmer's Mutual Insurance Company

was appointed "officer in charge" in 1997 and postmistress in 1998. She is still serving the St. Clair community today.

by Robert Fritzke

McPherson Farmers Mutual Fire Insurance Company

McPherson Farmers Mutual Fire Insurance Company was incorporated on June 6, 1881, and has faithfully served the community ever since. James Riese served as its president in 2004. Other officers were Dale Westphal, vice president and Clarice L. Germo secretary/treasurer. The directors were Jeff Boesch, Russell Christensen, Ronald Marzinske and Todd Stencel. Karon Storjohann was the manager with Margaret Zabel and Adrienne Verschelde the office secretaries. Doug Eustice serves as the fire safety representative.

On January 1, 2004, there were 1,319 policies in force with $447,250,635 in coverage on these policies.

At the annual meeting, which was held in March 2005, the name of the company was changed to McPherson Farmers Mutual Insurance Company. Clarice Germo retired and was recognized for 42 years of service as a

St. Clair State Bank

director. Newly elected directors are Robert Kruse and Jason Witt.

The office building is on Main Street and was the former medical clinic.

St. Clair State Bank

St. Clair State Bank has served this community since it was organized in 1906. The building has seen several structural changes over the years but the objectives of the business have remained the same. The current officers are CEO-Dale Stolt, president-Michael Hagen, senior vice-president-Robert Kruse, executive vice president-William Miller, and director-Lloyd "Butch" Thrun.

UpTown Tavern

The building, which currently houses the UpTown Tavern Bar and Grill, has been in the "beverage" business many years. Wm. Franz & Walter O'Brien owned it at one time as well as several others including Harvey and Dorothea (Froehlich) Amlund as well as Gerald and Muriel (Froehlich) Mace. For some years it was owned by the City of St. Clair and operated as the St. Clair Municipal Liquor Store. Glenn Thompson, Eugene Phillips and Henry Holtz were managers over the years. In 1997 Troy and Kelly Zabel purchased it from the city and operated it as a tavern. After the local café disbanded they added more food services and in 2001 put in a grill. It is known for its hometown atmosphere - a place to enjoy a cup of coffee, bar drinks, food and conversation. They host special occasion parties and also occasional features live entertainment.

L to R: Cathy Walser, Dan Bezdichek, Kelly Miller, Bill Miller, Julie Meyer, Lloyd "Butch" Thrun, Shelly Loeffler, Lana Kruse, Sarah Priem, Dale Stolt, Mike Hagen and Bob Kruse.

Troy Zabel, owner of the UpTown Tavern, with Dale Westphal (left)

UpTown Tavern and apartments

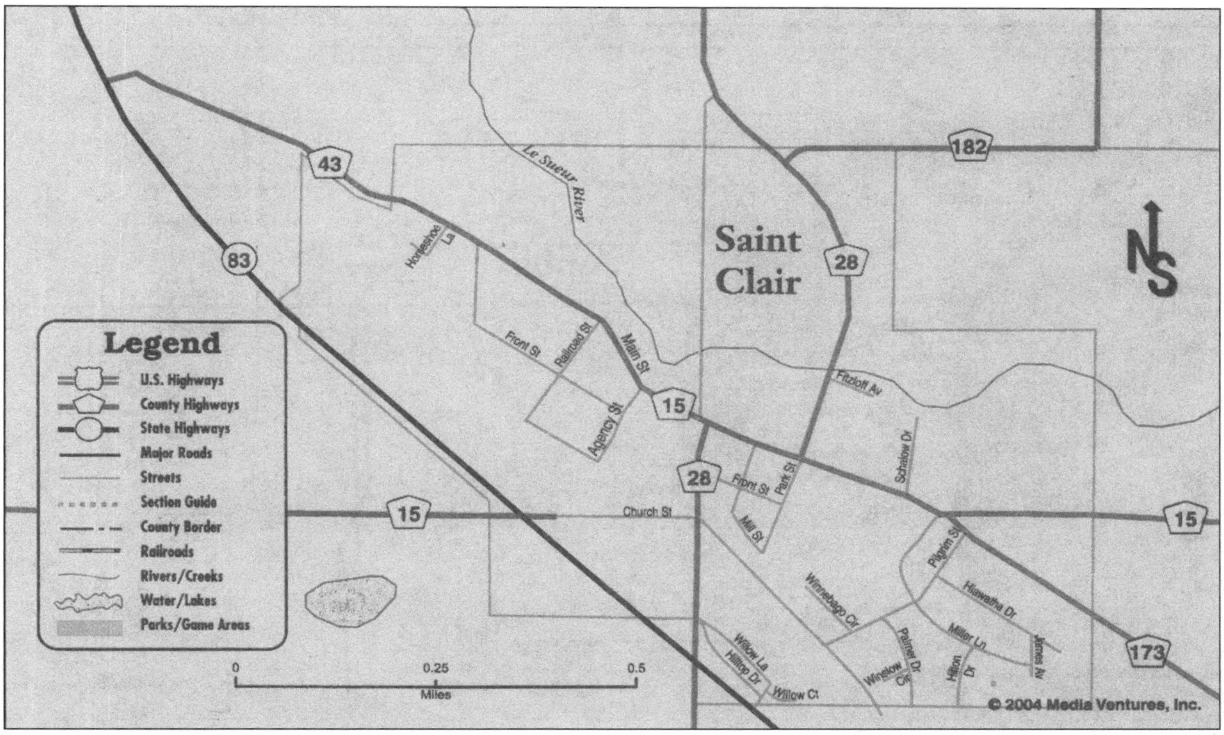

St. Clair City Map

St. Clair Water Tower

St. Clair Sewage Treatment Plant

St. Clair Sewage Treatment Plant

South side of Main Street looking west

Fitzloff's Main Street Auto Repair & Car Wash
Dick & Cheryl Fitzloff, owners

Marquardt's Cowlectables

St. Clair Business Center:
Mankato Realty (Kelly Schreader)
Michelle's Wild Hair (Michelle Thom)
On Gerry's Table (Gerry Baynard)
Seven Ways (Beverly Elmer)

North side of Main Street looking west

Apartments

Jeff's Auto Repair
Jeff & Connie McCollum, owners

North side of Main Street looking east

4 Flags over Aspen

Blue Earth County Highway Department Shop

South side of Main Street looking east

Memorial Park

Palmer Bus Shed
Floyd and Lois Palmer, owners

Schalow Apartments

Schalow Apartments

The Bell Tower
Jonas & Angie Nissen, owners

Margie's Beauty Shop
Margie Hoppe, owner

Main Street Auto Sales
Dick & Cheryl Fitzloff, owners

Winkelman Feed Mill
James & Myrna Winkelman, owners

The Country Register
Linda Lynch, Editor

Other St. Clair Businesses

Cabletime
Filter Rite (Kevin and Shelli Allen, owners)
Jamie's Masonry (Jamie Will, owner)
John M. Gustafson, Attorney

McPherson Township Hall

2004

T-107-N MCPHERSON PLAT R-25-W
(Landowners)

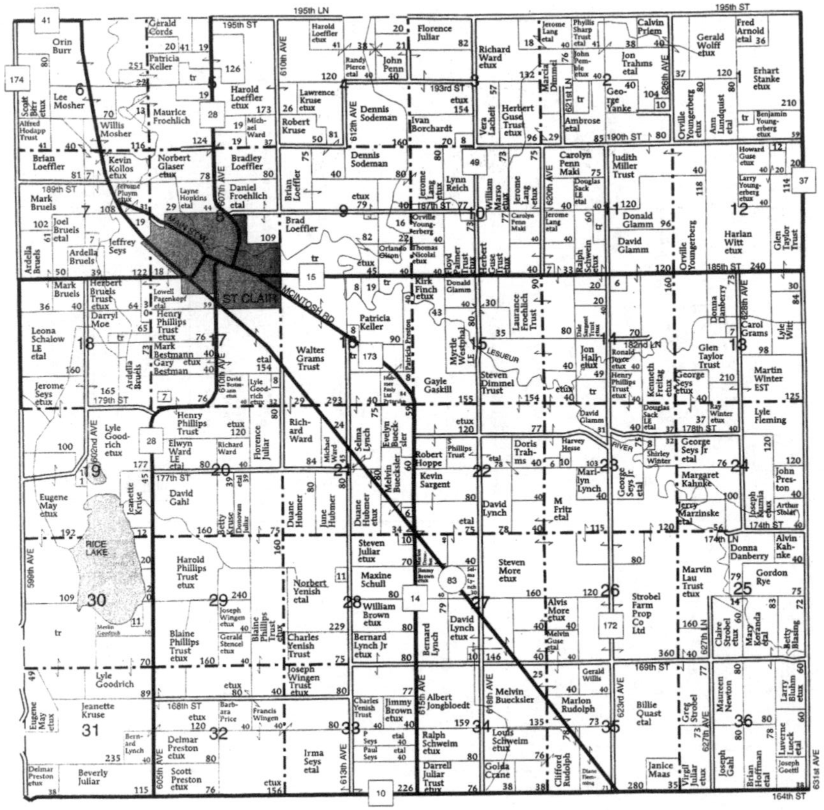

T-107-N MCPHERSON DIRECTORY R-25-W
(Residents - Owners or Renters)

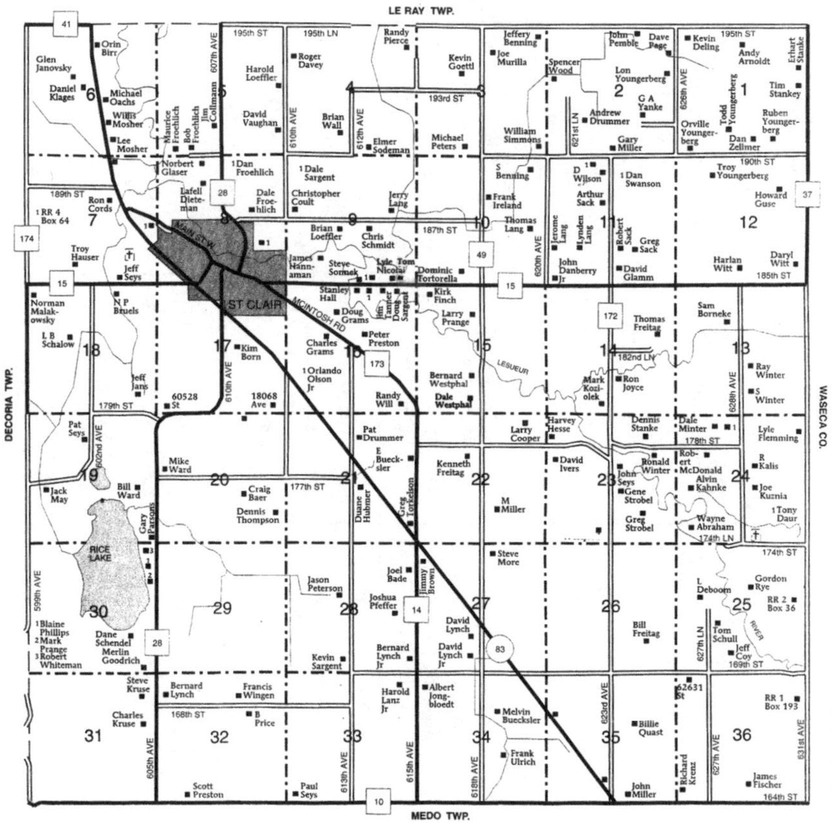

2004-2005

McPherson Township Board in 2005
L to R: Bernard Westphal, Clerk; Steve Kruse, Supervisor; David Lynch, Jr. Supervisor; Steve More, Treasurer
Missing from picture - Retiring supervisor Alvin Kahnke and newly elected supervisor Kevin Deling.

McPherson Township

McPherson Township completely surrounds the City of St. Clair. The McPherson Township Hall is located on the eastern edge of St. Clair, Minnesota. The purpose of this government body is to provide services to the township residents. These services include road maintenance, refuse and recycling pickup, contributions to local fire departments and providing voting facilities. There are 37.5 miles of township roads, 151 households with a population of 474. The 2004-2005 board consists of Alvin Kahnke, chairman, David J. Lynch, supervisor, Steven Kruse, supervisor, Steven More, treasurer and Bernard Westphal, clerk. Dale Westphal is the road grader and snowplow operator. The annual budget is $82,500.

At the 2005 Annual Meeting, supervisor Alvin Kahnke retired after 33 years of service. Kevin Dehling was elected to this position.

McPherson Township Motor Patrol
Businesses in McPherson Township

Minnesota Elevator, Inc./Vertitron Midwest, Inc.

Minnesota Elevator Inc. (MEI) began in 1971 in a rented farm building which was owned by Lee Mosher along Minnesota State Highway 83, about 2 miles north of St. Clair, MN. A year later, property (a farm place) was purchased from Roger Fisher. MEI then moved "across the river" to their present location about 1½ miles north of St. Clair on BE County Rd. 28. In the beginning, MEI serviced and repaired passenger and freight elevators in approximately a 50-mile radius. Since 1971, MEI has experienced considerable growth and now specializes in

Minnesota Elevator, Inc/Vertitron Midwest, Inc.

Minnesota Elevator, Inc.

the manufacture, installation, modernization, and servicing of various types of elevators within the five-state region. MEI's National Sales markets their elevator equipment to many independent elevator contractors and also the major elevator companies. Through their National Sales, their elevator equipment is found in nearly every state as well as several foreign countries, including Korea, China, Iceland, Mexico, Canada, Afghanistan and Puerto Rico. MEI equipment is installed in major airports, sports stadiums, convention centers, churches, schools, hospitals, hotel complexes, government building, shopping malls and industrial plants.

In 1989, Vertitron Midwest, Inc. (VMI), a California based manufacturer of microprocessor based elevator control systems was purchased and moved to Minnesota and now shares the same facility with MEI. They provide

John Danberry Construction

Lone Pine Treasures & Custom Woodworking
Brian & Mary Sader, owners

Ron's Welding
Ron & Beth Winter, owners

West Side Storage
Brian & Mary Sader, owners

Nicolai Masonry
Thomas & Katie Nicolai, owners

Winterhaven Vineyard & Nursery
Ray & Lisa Winter, owners

David Glamm Dairy Farm

Steve & Lynda Kruse Hog Farm

Mike & Tara Ward Dryer Setup

Hog Confinement Lot
Greg & Robin Strobel, owners

John Deere 9650
John Preston, owner

John Preston Grain Storage

elevator control systems for MEI and many independent elevator contractors and also the major elevator companies.

In 2002, MEI became an employee owned company through an Employee Stock Ownership Program (ESOP) with John Romnes, MEI/VMI owner, selling 30% of his MEI stock to the ESOP.

Both MEI and VMI continue to grow. They have made several expansions to their facility and presently have approximately 90,000 square feet of office and plant space, at their rural St. Clair, MN location. They also have offices/representation in the Twin Cities, St. Cloud, Rochester, Duluth, Sioux Falls, SD, and Dallas, TX. They presently have over 200 employees with combined annual sales in excess of 40 million dollars.

by John Romnes

John Deere 8220 Track Tractor-Brent Grain Cart
John Preston, owner

John Deere 4455 Tractor with loader & chopper
John Preston, owner

John Deere 9300 Tractor with DMI Chisel Plow
John Preston, owner

Return, Reunion and Renewal

On May 7, 2005, a group of the "Hochunk" better know to us as the Winnebago Indians, from the Winnebago Indian Reservation in Winnebago, Nebraska, visited the St. Clair area. They visisted Land of Memories Park and toured the Blue Earth County Historical Socitey in Mankato. In St. Clair they visited the Winnebago Agency site, a cemetery and then traveled to the Joseph May farm where they enjoyed a picnic lunch and visited village sites on the old rerservation. They then traveled to the Rapidan area. Accompanying them was Jim Snow whose mother used to tell him stories about the appealing scenery and prime cropland that is now Blue Earth County. These stories have followed from one generation to another. The stories were very pleasant compared to those told about the tribe's trip to the Mankato area in 1855 and its banishment to the harsh lands of central South Dakota about seven years later. Chief Elder Barry Blackhawk who toured with the group, was remembered by Nicholas Cords and Dean Rasmussen. They connected with him during their teaching careers. Chief Elder Blackhawk graduated from Mankato State College back in the sixties.

History cannot be changed, but ancestors of all area people can take part in the healing and the understanding that can last for centuries.

Additinal Businesses

Cheryl's Custom Sewing & Alterations
(Cheryl Klages, owner)
Frank Ireland Construction
Nicolai Cabinetry (James & Sherry Nicolai, owners)
Norm's Soft Water
(Norm & Greg Malakowsky, owners)

Standing - (L to R): St. Clair Mayor Brian Lynch, Jack and Lisa May, and Bruce Dowlin
Seated: Chief Elder Barry Blackhawk and Lyle Goodrich

Barry Blackhawk, Hochunk Chief Elder, offers a prayer and sprinkles ritual tobacco leaves at the site of the Winnebago Indian Agency, one mile east of St. Clair. Photo taken May 7, 2005 by Jack Madsen.

CHAPTER TWELVE

Closing Thoughts...

SOME THINGS YOU KEEP

Like good friends. Warm coats. Old jeans. They're good for you, reliable and practical and so necessary that to throw them away would make the garbage man nothing more than a thief. So you hang on, because something old is sometimes better than something new.

These are my thoughts, they make me sound old & tame, or dull at a time when everybody else wants to be risky, loud and flashy. They're looking for new and improved things in their lives.

New careers, new thoughts, new hair, and new cars. The world is dizzy with trade-ins. I could keep track, but I don't think I want to.

I grew up with practical parents, — a mother, God bless her — who washed aluminum foil after she cooked in it, then reused it. She recycled everything. Which meant hand me down clothes. A father who was happier getting his old shoes fixed than buying new ones.

They weren't poor, my parents, they were just satisfied. Their marriage was good, their dreams were focused. Their best friends lived barely a wave away. I can see them now, Dad in his jeans and tee shirt, Mom in an old blouse, garden hoe in one hand, fishing rod in the other. It was a time for fixing things – a curtain rod, Grandpa's radio, the screen door, the oven door, the hem in a dress.

Good things you keep. It was a way of life, and sometimes it made me crazy. All that re-fixing, reheating, renewing. I wanted just once to be wasteful. Waste meant affluence. Throwing things away meant there'd always be more. But then my father died, and on that day, I remember the chill of the hospital room. I remember my mother's last days at the nursing home. The struggles she endured at the end of her life. Watching her take a deep breath, only later to realize that it had been her last. I was struck with the pain of learning that sometimes there isn't any "more".

I didn't see the angels come, but I know they did, because they're both gone. Because of their faith, I have no doubts that they're in heaven, catching big fish and raising cucumbers in their garden.

Sometimes what you care about most gets all used up and goes away, never to return. So, while you have it, it's best to love it and care for it – fix it when it's broken… heal it when it's sick. You keep them because they're worth it, because you're worth it.

Some things you keep. Like a best friend that moved away or a classmate you grew up with, there's just some things that make life important.

So this is more than a brick, because St. Clair is more than just a school. It's a memory! Cherish it!

by Gene Braam (Class of 1971)
(accompanied with a brick from the old school house)

Almighty Smoke Stacks
May 2002

After demolition
June 2002

Bibliography

BOOKS:

Blegan, Theodore C. Minnesota, A History of a State, St. Paul, MN: University of Minnesota Press, 1963.

Carpenter, Bonnie. District 75, St. Clair, Minnesota, 1986.

Child, James E. Child's History of Waseca County, Owatonna, MN: Press of the Owatonna Chronicle, 1905.

Theodore Christianson. Minnesota The Land of Sky-Tinted Waters: A History of The State and Its People, 1935.

Glamm, Donald. South Central Holstein Scrapbook, 1996-1998.

Hughes, Thomas. History of Blue Earth County, Chicago, IL: Middle West Publishing Company, 1909.

Hughes, Thomas. Indian Chiefs of Southern Minnesota, Minneapolis, MN: Ross & Haines, Inc., 1969.

Newell, Ronald J. Where the Winding Maple Flows, Mankato, MN, 2003.

Schrader, Julie Hiller. The Heritage of Blue Earth County, Dallas, TX, Curtis Media, 1990.

Upham, Warren. Minnesota Geographic Names: Their Origins and Historic Significance, St. Paul, MN: Minnesota Historical Society, 1969.

NEWSPAPERS:

Blue Earth County Enterprise, Mapleton, MN
Free Press, Mankato, MN
Mankato Review, Mankato, MN
Mapleton Enterprise, Mapleton, MN
Minneapolis Tribune, Minneapolis, MN
The Janesville Argus, Janesville, MN
The Lake Region Times, Madison Lake, MN
The Land, Mankato, MN

ATLAS & MAPS:

Blue Earth County Atlas – various years
Blue Earth County Plat Books – various years

OTHER:

Anderson, Marian, Artist
Files of the Blue Earth County Historical Society, Mankato, MN
Lifetouch Church Directories and Portraits
Miller, Emm, Artist
St. Clair Church Directories, Various dates

Quinn Oil Company, 1931

Index

4 Flags over Aspen, 346
A.G. Phillips & Co., 80
Abeerbaum, August, 51
Actelle, A.D., 80
Acters, Christ, 93
Adams, Donald, 161
Adams, Karma (Lang), 161
Adams, Lorna (Oldenberg), 161
Adams, Molly, 161
Adams, Robert, 161
Adams, Sam, 161
Ady, Joshua, 17
Ady, Mrs. J., 46
Agency Road, 10
Ahl, Herbert, 288
Ahlstrom, Lincoln, 69
Ahner, Pastor G.E., 51
Albert Lea Tribune, 90
Albert Lea, MN, 33, 93, 96, 129
Alden, John, 215-216
Alden, Priscilla (Mullens), 215-216
Alden, Ruth, 215
Alexander, Bertha (Timmerman), 110, 161, 280
Alexander, Fred, 161, 280, 296
Alexander, James L., 17, 46
Alexander, Joseph, 161, 260, 296
Alexander, Mary (Myott), 161, 260
Alexander, Newell, 161
Allen, Kevin, 332, 348
Allen, Shelli, 348
Alma City, MN, 76, 81
Alphabet Railroad, 33, 90-91, 93, 96
Alton Township, 1
Amberfield Place, 156
Amberg, Frances, 303, 307-308
Amberg, Frank, 294-295, 303, 307
Amboy, MN, 53
American House, 80, 113, 330
Amlund, Dale, 202
Amlund, David, 202
Amlund, Dorothy (Froehlich), 202, 342
Amlund, Harvey, 202, 342
Anderson, A., 137
Anderson, Anna, 170
Anderson, Butch, 332
Anderson, Christ, 161
Anderson, Harold, 161
Anderson, Holger, 276
Anderson, Lena, 161
Anderson, Marian, 62, 153-154
Anderson, Martha (Schwanke), 276
Anderson, Mary (Kollos), 110, 161, 228, 295
Anderson, Mary, 110
Anderson, Nels, 170
Anderson, Oscar, 161, 228
Anderson, Verna (Herzberg), 161
Andrews, A.T., 33, 93
Andrews, Anna (Schalow), 295
Andrews, Asa, 92, 95, 244, 295
Andrews, Dwight (Dewey), 295
Andrews, Eliza, 80
Andrews, Fannie (Wheeler), 244, 295
Andrews, Genevieve, 295
Andrews, Ida, 295
Andrews, Jim, 295
Andrews, Mame, 295
Andrews, Thelma, 295
Andrews, Una, 295
Andrews, Verna, 120
Appel, Anna (Schwartz), 261
Appel, Conrad, 261
Arend, Emily (Wenner), 168, 283
Arend, John, 168, 283
Arens, Father Patrick, 47
Ario, Edward, 208, 295
Ario, Frank, 87, 113, 295
Ario, John, 104, 295
Ario, Lena, 295
Ario, Rudolph, 113, 295
Armistice Day storm, 123
Arndt, Bailey, 228
Arndt, Jodi (Kollos), 228
Arndt, Richard, 228
Arnold, A., 83
Aufenkalk, Father, 46
Aura, John, 290
Aura, Olive Ione (Wolcott), 290
Autrey, Charles, 254
Autrey, Charlotte (O'Connor), 254
Autrey, Doc, 296
Autrey, Felix, 254
Autrey, Ike, 296
Autrey, Issac, 254
Autrey, James, 254
Autrey, John, 254
Autrey, Paul, 254
Autrey, Scott, 296
Autrey, Thomas, 254
Axrel, Arthur, 86
Axtelle, Mrs. E.W., 80
Babbit, Corba, 276
Babcock, Maude (Preston), 262
Babcock, Merritt, 262
Babcock, S.S., 88
Baer, Augusta (Buesing), 123, 161-162, 336
Baer, Bonnie, 331
Baer, Elwin, 162
Baer, Eugene, 162, 331
Baer, Fredrick W., 161-162, 295
Baer, Lester, 162
Baer, Marlene, 162
Baker, Brandt, 243
Baker, Denise (McCollum), 243
Baker, Thomas, 243
Baker, Timothy, 243
Balcome, A.D., 9, 17
Baldwin School, 78
Bangerter, B. Jr., 194
Banta, Johnny, 232
Banta, Violet (Lang), 232
Bard, Dan, 77
Barlow, J.H., 32, 78
Barneke, August, 186, 188
Barnes, Joel, 169
Barnes, Marcella (Bruels), 169
Barneske, August, 51
Bartelt, Elsie (Schnoor), 215
Bartelt, Herb, 215
Bartlett, R.O., 17
Bartsch, Donnave (Preston), 262
Bartz, Connie (Winter), 288
Bartz, Matt, 288
Batdorf, Dr. Niles, 252
Bauman, Father, 46
Baumgartner, Debra (Seys), 285
Baumgartner, Wayne, 285
Baynard, 344
Bear Lake, 295
Beauford Township, 1, 73, 79
Beauford United Brethren in Christ Church, 54
Beccue, August Carl, 107, 272
Beccue, Beverly (Penhiter), 272
Beccue, David, 272
Beccue, Edie, 123
Beccue, Farleigh, 272
Beccue, Florine, 120
Beccue, Marcella (Weber), 272
Beccue, Mary L. (Schmidt), 272
Beccue, Sharon, 69

Beccue, William, 104, 126, 231, 325
Becker, Amy (Stolt), 279
Becker, Cadence, 279
Becker, Seth, 279
Beckman, Jacob, 163, 276
Beckman, Johanna (Shoeder), 163, 276
Beelow, Harold, 69
Beelow, Orville, 69
Behnke, Rick, 63
Bell Tower Place, 54, 157
Belleview School, 75, 111
Belleview, 17, 76, 341
Bemis, Jeanette (Chase), 175
Bennett, Donald, 197
Bennett, Ordella (Freitag), 197
Bennett, Tammy, 197
Benning, Rodney, 232
Benning, Sharon (Lang), 232
Berentson, Kate, 214
Berentson, Simon, 214
Berg, Ken, 16
Berg, Lyall, 272
Berg, Marie (Marzinske), 272
Berndt, Helena (Youngerberg-Schostag), 274
Berndt, Robert, 274
Besser, Martha (Schmidt), 272
Besser, Sylvester, 272
Bestman, Ada (Fields-Dalton), 144, 162, 184, 252, 295, 336
Bestman, Anna, 162
Bestman, August, 55
Bestman, Charles H., 162, 296
Bestman, David, 162
Bestman, Eileen (Juliar), 162, 223
Bestman, Frederick J. (Fritz), 53, 59, 68, 162, 298, 300
Bestman, Gary, 162
Bestman, Helen (Krause), 162
Bestman, Helena A., 162
Bestman, Henrietta (Beyersdorf), 162, 296
Bestman, Henry, 162
Bestman, Herbert F., 162, 296
Bestman, John, 33, 79, 83, 86, 90, 95-96, 99, 101, 162, 223, 296
Bestman, Lena (Krause), 107, 296
Bestman, Steve, 162
Beveridge, Francis, 57
Bezdichek, Dan, 342
Big Woods, 8-9, 13
Biggins, Cecelia (Hager), 300
Biggins, Mrs Forrest (Schultz), 276
Biggins, Roy, 101
Bingham, Michelle (Winter), 288
Bingham, Shawn, 288
Birr, Carl, 212
Birr, Conley, 248
Birr, Ida (Schull), 248
Birr, Johanna (Weizig), 212
Birr, Orin, 296
Bjornson, Evelyn (Anderson), 161
Blackhawk, Chief Elder Barry, 355
Blank, Adolph, 151, 162-163
Blank, Barbara, 66
Blank, Charlotte (Oftedahl), 162-163
Blank, Elfrieda (Bollman), 162
Bleess, Chad, 288
Bleess, Cheryl, 288
Blegen, Theodore C., 4
Block, Wayne, 168, 283
Bloenke, Lois, 150
Bloomfield, Arnold, 196
Bloomfield, Louise (Franz), 196
Blue Earth County Fair, 181
Blue Earth County Highway Department Shop, 324, 346
Blue Earth County Historical Society, 54, 222, 304, 355
Blue Earth County Public Works Department, 18
Blue Earth County Sheriff's Department, 34
Blue Earth County, 1, 3, 5-6, 8-9, 13, 17, 34, 73-74, 81, 83, 86, 105, 355
Blue Earth River, 1, 8, 45
Blume, Barbara (Kruse), 231
Blume, Merlyn, 231
Blume, Paul, 231
Boesch, Jeff, 157, 341
Boettcher, Herman, 259
Boettcher, Louise (Mueller), 259
Bohan, Rella, 254
Bohnhof, Hans, 203
Bohnhof, Lilly (Glamm), 203
Bollman, Eliza, 163
Bollman, Juergen, 163
Bollmann, Agatha (Oftedahl), 14, 163-164, 220
Bollmann, Albert, 14, 163
Bollmann, Alma, 163
Bollmann, Bonnie (Horazdovsky), 164
Bollmann, Carol (Patton), 14, 164
Bollmann, Charles, 164
Bollmann, Douglas, 164
Bollmann, Elsie, 163
Bollmann, Helen, 163
Bollmann, In Suk Yi, 164
Bollmann, James, 164
Bollmann, Janet (Maureen), 164
Bollmann, John, 163
Bollmann, Judith, 164
Bollmann, Larry, 164
Bollmann, Lawrence, 163
Bollmann, Mable, 163
Bollmann, Marcella, 163
Bollmann, Marie, 163
Bollmann, Martha (Beckmann), 109-110, 163, 200
Bollmann, Mary (Morrison), 164
Bollmann, Mildred (Radford), 164
Bollmann, Nancy (Etta), 164
Bollmann, Patricia (Roberts), 164
Bollmann, Paul, 163
Bollmann, Pearl, 163
Bollmann, Peter C., 109-110, 163, 200, 321
Bollmann, Peter III, 164
Bollmann, Peter Jr., 163-164
Bollmann, Tammy (Enger), 164
Bollmann, Thomas, 164
Bollmann, Timothy, 164
Bollmann, Vera (Schostag), 123, 164
Bollmann, Violetta, 163
Bollmann, William John, 163-164
Bolte, Edward, 246
Bolte, Gertrude (Miller), 246
Boone, Daniel, 264
Borchard, John, 53
Borchardt, Donna Jean (Nicolai), 251
Borchardt, Ivan, 251
Borchert, Marie (Koentop), 227
Borchert, William, 227
Borgwardt, Anna (Friday), 164
Borgwardt, Carl, 164
Borgwardt, Henry, 126, 164, 331
Born, Beverly (Myers), 129-130, 157, 220, 249-250
Born, Dean, 164, 302
Born, George, 164, 249
Born, Herman, 141
Born, Ila Mae (Kopke), 164, 229, 303
Born, Judy, 144
Born, Karen, 164
Born, Martha, 164, 249
Born, Randy, 164, 332
Born, Roland, 164, 229
Born, Wayne, 249-250
Borneke, Anna (Johnson), 198
Borneke, Clarence, 198
Boswell, Clay, 11-12, 68, 106, 165, 279, 294-296, 325
Boswell, Edgar, 165
Boswell, Elizabeth (Truman), 165, 280
Boswell, George, 165
Boswell, Hannah, 165
Boswell, Harold, 14, 103,165-166, 208, 298
Boswell, Hazel (Kenward), 165-166, 209
Boswell, John H., 10, 14, 76, 164-165, 280, 294
Boswell, Josephine, 165
Boswell, Julius, 165

Boswell, Marian, 120
Boswell, Mary, 165
Boswell, Nettie M. (Scott), 165
Boswell, Oscar, 165
Boswell, Tutie (Grignon-Rasdall), 290
Boswell, Viva Estelle (Thielman), 165, 279, 294
Boswell, William, 84, 97, 99, 165, 295, 337
Botsford Lumber Company, 33, 93, 104, 111, 332
Bowe, Ada, 47
Bowe, Ellen (Morris), 166
Bowe, Francis Henry, 166
Bowe, John D., 166
Bowe, Margaret (Dumey), 166
Bowe, Martin, 46
Bowe, Patrick H., 33, 93, 166
Bowe, Theresia (Huettl), 166, 235-236, 238
Bowe, Thomas Sr., 166, 235-236, 238
Bowe, Thomas, 33, 90
Braam, Gene, 357
Bradley, Rev., 80
Brand, Rev. Edward F., 132
Brandenberg, Frank, 88
Brandenburg, Albert, 186
Brandenburg, Sophia (Fitzloff), 186
Brandt, Etta (Borcutt), 166
Brandt, Grace (Glasgow), 295
Brandt, Henry W., 166
Brandt, William A., 80, 166, 295
Brenner, Adella (Lubke), 235
Brenner, Harold G., 235
Brewer, Charles H., 166-167
Brewer, Cyril, 167
Brewer, Daniel D., 166-167
Brewer, E. Gertrude (Miller), 167
Brewer, Gerald, 167
Brewer, James, 167
Brewer, Jennie, 166
Brewer, Julia, 166
Brewer, Laura (Ward), 128, 166-167, 297-298
Brewer, Marcella (Pestka), 167, 301
Brewer, Mary (Getty), 166-167
Brewer, May (Rodgers), 167
Brewer, Violet (Rocker), 167
Breymann, Father, 46
Britton, Rick, 332
Broas, Arvellis (Brummound), 169
Broas, Willmer, 169
Brooks, Irma, 327
Brown Brothers General Store, 31, 74, 341
Brown, Effie (Rasdall), 265-266
Brown, Father Syl, 47
Brown, George, 31, 74
Brown, James E., 31, 74, 341
Brown, Jeremy, 232
Brown, Linda (Ulwelling), 232
Brown, Nathan, 232
Brown, Robert, 265
Brown, Sarah, 232
Brown, William, 232
Bruce, Rev. Wallace, 45
Bruels, Andrew, 168
Bruels, Anna Katharine, 167
Bruels, Ardella (Oftedahl), 169
Bruels, Arline (Cuddy), 169
Bruels, Clement, 168
Bruels, Elizabeth (May), 167-169, 242
Bruels, Florence (Collins), 103, 168, 269
Bruels, Herbert, 46, 169, 247-248, 282
Bruels, Hubert, 83, 86, 99, 103, 167-168, 242
Bruels, Joan (Oftedahl), 131
Bruels, Johann, 167
Bruels, John, 168-169
Bruels, Joseph, 168, 247, 269
Bruels, Judith (Fasnacht), 168
Bruels, Kristine (Kline), 168
Bruels, Leland
Bruels, Leon, 131, 169, 295
Bruels, Lucia (Ross), 168
Bruels, Mark, 168
Bruels, Mrs. Hubert, 101
Bruels, Nicholas, 167
Bruels, Nicholas, 168
Bruels, Norma (Kott-Moe), 146, 169, 247-248, 269, 283
Bruels, Patricia (Sahli), 169
Bruels, Raymond, 168-169
Bruels, Rose (Fallenstein), 168, 247, 269
Bruels, Warren, 169, 298
Bruender, Kim, 47
Brummound, Anna (Urban), 169
Brummound, Arlynd C.H., 169
Brummound, Arnold, 169
Brummound, Arthur, 169
Brummound, LaDonna (Schwantes), 169
Brunz, Richard, 282
Buck, Daniel, 4
Buckholtz, John, 53
Buckholtz, Lou, 304
Buecksler, Albert Carl, 169, 170-172
Buecksler, Amelia, 170
Buecksler, Arthur, 170
Buecksler, Dennis, 171
Buecksler, Edith (Ehmke), 169-170
Buecksler, Ella (Schroeder), 170-172
Buecksler, Evelyn (Radke), 171
Buecksler, Ferdinand, 169-170
Buecksler, Lawrence, 170-171
Buecksler, Leonard, 170-171
Buecksler, Melvin, 170-171
Buecksler, Oscar, 170
Buecksler, Otto, 170
Buecksler, Paul, 170
Buecksler, Phyllis (Roland), 171
Buecksler, Ralph, 170
Buecksler, Robert, 170
Buecksler, Walter, 170
Buecksler, William, 170
Buesing, Anna (Beckmann), 163, 172
Buesing, August, 163, 172
Buesing, Bea, 336
Buesing, Caroline, 172
Buesing, Charles, 169
Buesing, Clotilda (Bruels), 169
Buesing, Diedrich, 114
Buesing, Emma (Abraham), 172
Buesing, Henry, 172
Buesing, Herbert, 117, 162, 172-173, 177, 324, 331
Buesing, Marianna, 114
Buesing, Michael, 173
Buesing, Orville, 173
Buesing, Ralph, 172, 331
Buesing, Ruth, 336
Buesing, Violet (Gekeler), 172-173
Buesing, Warner, 120
Buesing, William, 172
Buesing, Winnie (Renneke), 148, 173
Buffalo Bill, 254
Bunde, Debbie, 168
Bunde, Joan (Wenner), 168, 283
Bunde, Michael, 168, 283
Bunde, Ralph, 164
Bunde, Richard, 168, 283
Bunde, Velma (Borgwardt-Friedrichs), 164
Bunde, Walter, 168, 283
Bunker Hill Cemetery, 54
Bureau of Indian Affairs, 12
Burgess, Evelyn, 247
Burgess, J.L., 18
Burgess, Lowell, 247
Burgess, Maurice, 247
Burgess, Mildred, 247
Burgess, Milton, 247
Burgess, Vaughn, 247
Burnett, Donald, 141, 144
Burt, Charles, 235
Burt, Doris (Kittleson), 235
Burtness, Mabel (Schwanke), 276
Burtness, Oscar, 276
Buse, Cathy (Grams), 209
Buse, Patrick, 209
Bushine, Arnold, 296
Bushine, Bertha (Scheiding), 295

Bushine, Frank, 295-296
Butzer, Mary Lou, 144
Buysse, Andy, 173
Buysse, Brent, 173
Buysse, Dorothy (Priester), 173
Buysse, James P., 62, 173-174, 332
Buysse, Margie (Cordes), 173
Buysse, Paul, 173
Bycees, George, 169
Byersdorf, Albert, 296
Byersdorf, Eddie, 296
Byersdorf, Flora (Schroeder), 296
Byron, Father, 332
Cable TV, 34
Cabletime, 348
Caldwell, Bertha (Fitzloff), 81,174, 192
Caldwell, Curtis, 174
Caldwell, Donald, 174
Caldwell, George Becker, 32, 74, 81, 83, 85, 174, 192, 330
Caldwell, George Jr., 174
Caldwell, Gladys, 88, 174
Caldwell, Howard, 174
Caldwell, James, 174
Caldwell, Ruth, 174
Callaghan, Anthony, 46
Callen, Ansen W., 17, 67, 73
Callis, Alvina (Schostag0DeRemer-Jones), 275
Callis, Robert, 275
Camp Porter, 5
Campbell & Wolcott, 98
Campbell, Arleigh, 175
Campbell, Glenn, 107, 174-175
Campbell, Henry, 85, 113-114, 174, 196, 290
Campbell, Lydia (Foster), 100, 174, 195-196
Campbell, Neal, 175
Candee, Asa, 259
Candee, Mary (McAlpine), 259
Carlson, Arlene (Westphal), 284
Carlson, Larry, 332
Carlson, Stanley, 284
Carlstrom, R.W., 62
Carpenter, Earl, 111, 226
Carpenter, Lucile, 120
Catholic Sisterhood, 45
Cattnach, Penny (Marzinske), 241
Cattnach, Steven, 241
Cenex C-Store, 155
Chamberlain, Paul, 282
Champlin, L.L., 103
Chaplin, Charlie, 224
Chase, Alice (Juliar), 176
Chase, Duane, 100, 175-176
Chase, Edith (Foster), 175, 195-196, 322-323
Chase, Frank Madison, 10, 14, 77, 175, 265, 293-294
Chase, George, 175
Chase, Grace Estelle (Rasdall), 10, 14, 175, 265, 293-294
Chase, Grace Foster, 58, 137
Chase, Jacob W., 33-34, 84-86, 93, 95, 175-176, 196, 290, 295, 322, 337
Chase, Kenneth, 109, 175-176
Chase, Mary, 175
Chase, Mrs. F.M., 100
Chase, Rev. J.E., 83
Chase, Stanley, 175-176
Chen, Jamie, 47
Cheryl's Custom Sewing & Alterations, 355
Chevrolet Garage, 115
Chicago & Milwaukee Line, 33
Chicago, Milwaukee, St. Paul & Pacific System, 33, 78, 96
Chief Big Bear, 10
Chief Coming Thunder, 10
Chief Decora, 4, 8, 12
Chief Four Cloud, 4, 7
Chief Good Thunder, 4, 7
Chief Little Crow, 4, 74
Chief Little Priest, 4-5, 7-8, 10
Chief Rogue, 113
Chief Waukon, 8
Chief Winneshiek, 4-5, 7-8, 10
Chief Yellow Bank, 4, 7
Child, James E., 1
Childs, Harold, 136, 167
Childs, Lydia (Brewer), 167
Chippewa Tribe, 4
Christensen, Russell, 157, 341
Christnagel, Esther (Schuldt), 220, 276
Christnagel, Orville, 68, 144, 146, 204, 276
Christnagel, Patty, 66
Christnagel, Rosalie, 66
City Economic Development Committee, 34
Civil War, 3, 74
Clement, Toby, 281
Clement, Wendie (Walton), 281
Clever Clover 4-H Club, 340
Clifton House, 89
Cloud, Rev. Henry Roe, 6
Coffin, Rev. B.Y., 17-18, 57
Coggershall, Ed, 329
Coker, J.B., 169
Coker, Marion (Bruels), 169
Coleman, Dr., 10
Coleman, Father, 311
Collins, Abby, 193
Collins, Betsie, 193
Collins, Danni, 193
Collins, Tamie (Fossum), 193
Collins, Tim, 193
Collman, James, 201
Collman, Marcella (Froehlich Taber), 201
Compton, Guy, 126
Comstock, Hattie, 78
Congregational Church, 45, 76, 105, 108
Connolly, Father Kevin, 47
Consumers Power & Light Company, 100
Conway, John, 252
Conway, Laura (Kelly), 254
Conway, Ralph, 244
Conway, Shirley (McComb), 179, 244
Cook, D., 79
Cook, Frank, 176
Cook, J.C., 32
Cook, J.L., 79, 176, 340
Cook, Jennie A. (Stearns), 176
Cooperative Oil Company, 118
Copham, Pauline (Grams), 207
Cordes, Elvin, 173
Cordes, Lois, 173
Cords & Chase Sawmill, 87
Cord's Barber Shop, 327
Cords, Alma, 336
Cords, Arthur Oscar, 158, 176-179, 303, 326
Cords, Betty Marie, 178-179, 303, 305
Cords, Charles, 299
Cords, Charley, 113
Cords, Clara (Casper), 177-178, 180
Cords, Clarissa (Nelson), 180-181
Cords, Daisy, 177
Cords, Dan, 180
Cords, Darlene, 66, 68
Cords, Eddy, 137
Cords, Erna, 112
Cords, Ernest, 137
Cords, Ervin, 177
Cords, Frank W., 69, 94, 114-115, 176, 180-181
Cords, Frederick Jr., 176-177
Cords, Frederick, 51
Cords, Henry, 176
Cords, Jim, 179
Cords, Joan, 178, 303
Cords, John, 176-177, 179-180
Cords, Ken, 295
Cords, Lauretta (Lynch), 178-179, 303, 307-312
Cords, Laurie (Hawker), 213
Cords, Maggie (Hurley), 177, 179
Cords, Matilda (Frank), 299
Cords, Mrs. Harold, 129
Cords, Nicholas John, 157, 176-181

Cords, Nick, *iii*, 55, 179, 303-305, 312, 355
Cords, Randall, 213
Cords, Sophia (Ehlers), 176-177
Cords, Steve, 209
Cords, Verna L., 180-181
Cords, Vernie, 177-178
Cords, Viva, 177-178
Cords, Willard E., 180-181
Cotter, Bishop Joseph B., 46
Coult, Hilda (Schostag), 275
Coult, Lou, 118
Coult, Lyle N., 275
Coult, Robin, 155
Coult, Wanda, 155
County Line Bridge, 93
Covel, Albert, 182
Covel, Alpheus, 18, 182
Covel, Benjamin, 182
Covel, Charles, 182
Covel, Cordelia, 182
Covel, David, 182
Covel, Eliza Jane (Nash), 18, 182
Covel, Ella (Reynolds), 18, 182
Covel, George, 18, 182
Covel, Harriet, 182
Covel, Harvey, 182
Covel, Martha, 182
Covel, Mary, 182
Covel, Orin, 182
Covel, William, 182
Cowell, J.Y., 17
Cox-Townsend, Dennis, 332
Coyne, Rev. James, 46
Cramton, Catherine, 54
Cray, Archie, 164, 331
Cray, Myrtle (Borgwardt McKibben), 164
Cream, 90
Crods, Ed, 68
Crown, Lillian (Schalow), 271
Crystal Ballroom, 326
Culle, Major, 10
Cullen, W.J., 17, 73
Culver, George, 17
Currah, Dr., G.R., 95
Cut Nose, 7
Cyphers, Margaret, 144
D & D Service Station, 77
D & L Diner, 149, 211
Daby, Ben Otto, 288
Daby, Marvel (Jessup), 288
Dagen, Donald, 220
Dagen, Gladys, 220
Daigneau, Mr., 80
Dalton, M.C., 93, 329
Danberry Bridge, 26
Danberry, Amy (Bollmann), 164
Danberry, Bradley, 243
Danberry, Connie (McCollum), 243
Danberry, Donna (DeMars), 157, 182-183
Danberry, Elmer, 58
Danberry, Henry, 182
Danberry, Jared, 243
Danberry, John (Jack), 121, 152, 182-183
Danberry, John Jr., 182
Danberry, Lillian, 144, 182, 336
Danberry, Marie, 182
Danberry, Megan, 243
Danberry, Michael, 182
Danberry, Nicholas, 243
Danberry, Tim, 164
Danberry, Wendy, 182
Danner, John, 284
Danner, Rita, 284
Dauk, Sharon (Rose), 269
Dauk, Thomas, 269
Davis, Dr., 297
Davis, Lennie, 250
Davis, Lucinda (Born), 220, 250
Davis, Wilmar, 132
Dawley, Julius, 18
Day, Harriet, 336
Debough, Dennis, 168, 282
Debough, Rita (Wenner), 168, 282
Decoria Township, 1, 6, 32, 73, 79, 81, 84, 113-114
Deling, Derek Allan, 182
Deling, Diane (Parker), 182
Deling, John, 182
Deling, Judy, 182
Deling, Kelly Jean, 182
Deling, Kevin Jon, 182, 351
Delya, John, 331
DeMars - St. Clair Bar, 129
DeMars, Antonia (Tonie), 182-183, 189, 331
DeMars, Hazel (Frank), 130, 183, 196, 299
DeMars, Hotel, 302
DeMars, LaVerne, 196
DeMars, Leo, 182-183, 189, 330-331
DeMars, Martin, 240
DeMars, Virginia (Macomber), 120, 240, 325
Demert, Len, 63
Denn Addition, 34
Denn, Aloysius, 272
Denn, Bert, 68, 141
Denn, Cy, 332
Denn, Ed, 148
Denn, Esther (Koch), 272
Denn, Henry, 287
Denn, Hildegard, 141
Denn, Leona (Wingen), 287
Denn, Mike, 148, 339
Denn, Tricia, 281
Depuydt, Connie Holtz, 217
Depuydt, Daniel, 217
Depuydt, Kimberely, 217
Depuydt, Leonard, 173
Depuydt, Mr., 37
Depuydt, Roger, 217
DeRemer, Hallie, 275
Desmond, Anne (Bruels), 168
Desmond, Walter, 168
Deveraux & Davis, 83
Dickinson, Clark, 183, 216
Dickinson, Sally, 183
Dieteman, Jodi (Miller), 246
Dieteman, Steve, 246
Dietman, Art, 205
Dieudonne, Emil, 273
Dillinger, John, 180
Dimmel, Andy, 318
Dimmel, Caroline, 318
Dimmel, Corrine (Haugen), 179, 312
Dimmel, David, 318
Dimmel, Frederick, 206
Dimmel, Lena (Kruse), 231
Dimmel, Marcia (Schatzke), 318
Dimmel, Marvin, 318
Dimmel, Melvin, 231
Dimmel, Sophie, 206
Dimmel, Steven, 156, 318
Dimmel, Walter, 231
Dittman, Arthur, 126, 183
Dittman, Carl, 51, 53, 88
Dittman, Frederick, 183, 295
Dittman, Hannah, 183-184, 295, 301
Doede, Rev. J.D., 53
Doescher, Fred, 218
Doescher, Keturah (Hubmer), 218
Doland, Ann (Farmer), 184
Doland, Annie, 184
Doland, Carrie, 184
Doland, Eliza, 184
Doland, Ellen, 184
Doland, George, 184
Doland, John, 184
Doland, Lizzie, 184
Doland, Mary, 184
Doland, Nettie, 184
Domeier, Wanda, 156
Donahue, Sheriff, 91
Donald, George, 75
Donaldson, Judge, 4
Dooley, Lucille (Pagenkopf), 257
Dooley, Patrick, 109, 257
Doss, Alma (Schmidt), 272
Doss, Carl, 272
Doss, Charles, 272

Doss, Dallas, 272
Doss, Elnora (Marzinske), 272
Doss, Elsie (Wille), 272
Doss, Ervin, 272
Doss, Evert, 208, 272
Doss, Hazel (Marzinske), 272
Doss, Helen, 272
Doss, Herman, 272
Doss, Isabella, 114
Doss, Leona (Grams), 208, 272
Doss, Rose (Manthe), 272
Dotson, Angeline (Managie), 241, 296
Dotson, Henry, 241, 296
Dotson, John, 296
Dougherty, Geraldine (Schmidt), 273
Dougherty, Richard, 273
Dowlin, Bruce, 355
Downing, Lewis, 121
Draeger, Delbert, 233
Draeger, Linda (Lindloff), 233
Drager, Melvin, 247
Drager, Mildred (Moe), 247
Drake, Jeanette (Nyquist), 144, 179, 184, 252
Drake, Mary (Delaney), 184
Drake, Merton, 184
Drake, Michael, 184
Drake, Scott, 184
Drake, Stanley, 150-151, 177, 184, 249, 252, 295, 300
Drake, Sue, 184
Drake, Vonna, 184
Drake's Station, 147
Drescher, Donald, 186
Drescher, Marion (Fitzloff), 186-187
Dresendorfer, Mr., 96
Duehn, Percy, 114
Duemeland, Dorothea (Gibbons), 185
Duemeland, E.F., 33
Duemeland, Ernest A., 32, 86, 93, 123, 184-185, 195
Duemeland, George A., 185
Duemeland, Gus, 214, 295
Duemeland, Henry J., 185
Duemeland, Henry, 185
Duemeland, Mary (Lane), 185
Duemeland's General Store, 32, 79, 123, 184, 206, 301, 341
Duenes, Marcelle, 190
Duluth, St. Cloud, Glencoe & Mankato Line, 33
Dumbeck, Charles, 82
Dumbeck, Elizabeth (Schalow), 271
Dumbeck, H.H., 95
Dumbeck, Harry, 111, 271
Dumbeck, Will, 104
Dumdei, Gene, 58
Dungan, Martin B., 18
Dyer, Lucius, 9-10, 14, 17, 185, 280, 293 , 340
Dysterheft, Julius, 86
E.B.G. Norton
Eager, Phil, 133
Eagle Lake, MN, 83
Easley, Grace E., 64
East Lake, 12
Eastman, A.J., 75
Eastman, Alfred, 75
Eastman, Amos H., 17
Eastman, David, 18, 76
Eastman, Elizabeth (Haynes), 213
Eastman, H., 75, 213
Eastman, James H., 17, 75, 341
Easton, Amos,H., 341
Eaton, Dr. J.S., 238
Eaton, Dr. Joseph, 32, 165, 297
Eaton, Hanna (Boswell), 238
Eaton, James, 144
Eaton, Sadie, 94
Ebenezer, C. Wood, 54
Ehmke, Emil, 169
Eilrich, Debbie, 155
Ellis, Janice, 183
Ellis, Lowell, 183
Elmer, Beverly, 344
Elysian Hardware Store, 113
Elzea, S., 75
Engel, Arline (Doss), 272
Engel, Hugo, 272
Engeleby, 151
Engelerth, Dick, 126
Eolian, 5
Erickson, Arnold, 69
Erickson, E.J., 129, 133
Erickson, Fred, 330
Escott, Leona (Preston), 262
Esser, Alan, 250
Esser, Melanie (Born), 220, 250
Eustice, Douglas, 157, 341
Evan, Edward, 291
Evan, Thelma (More), 291
Evangelical United Brethren Church, 54, 135
Evert, Edward, 223
Evert, Esther, 223
Ewert, Eldo Bruno, 124, 164, 296
Ewert, Erich C., 250
Ewert, Ervin, 144, 146, 247
Ewert, Evelyn (Moe), 247
Ewert, Hulda (Nicolai), 250
Ewert, Verlyn (Borgwardt), 164
Faley, Jim, 222
Fancher, M.D., 194
Farm, Donald, 141
Farm, Esther, 141
Farm, Robert, 141
Farmamerica, 15
Farmer's Co-operative Creamery
Insurance Company, 88
Farmer's Elevator Company of St. Clair, 98, 108
Farmer's Mutual Insurance Company, 79, 81
Farmers United Township Mutual Hail
Insurance Co., 84
Fasnacht, Adolf, 246
Fasnacht, Iverna (Miller), 246
Faye, Russell, 332
Felber, John A., 129, 138
Ferch, Karen (Olson), 255256
Ferch, Vern, 256
Fields, Ada, 309
Fields, Charlotte, 80
Fields, Harry C., 104, 185, 309
Fields, Isabelle (Larabee), 155, 162, 185, 252
Fields, James, 88, 295
Fields, Jenny, 309-310
Fields, John, 96, 155, 162, 185, 252, 295
Fields, May, 309
Fields, Millie, 309
Fields, Nona, 309
Fields, Sadie, 309
Fields, Sidney, 237
Fields, Susan (Kelly), 254
Fields, William, 235, 295
Filter Rite, 348
Fisher, Alfred, 186
Fisher, Amanda (Johnson), 186
Fisher, Anna (Pietsch), 185
Fisher, August, 53, 185
Fisher, Bertha, 186
Fisher, Carl, 186
Fisher, Charles, 186, 202
Fisher, Emma, 186
Fisher, Frank, 108, 138, 185, 235
Fisher, George, 186
Fisher, Gertrude, 186
Fisher, Harry, 53, 185, 298
Fisher, Ida, 186
Fisher, Joyce (Priem), 123, 185
Fisher, Lena (Gerber), 186, 202
Fisher, Leon, 103, 185
Fisher, Lillian (Haack), 186
Fisher, Louann, 293
Fisher, Matilda, 186
Fisher, Mildred (Juliar), 185
Fisher, Roger, 351
Fisher, Sylvia, 109
Fisher, William, 186
Fisk, Angeline, 290
Fisk, Rev., 80
Fitter, Diane (Grams-Goettl-Cords), 209

Fitter, Michael, 209
Fitterer, Alan, 63
Fitzloff, Albert H., 87, 137-138, 142, 186-187
Fitzloff, Alexander, 190, 198
Fitzloff, Anne Francis (McNamara), 188, 191
Fitzloff, Antonius (Tony), 92, 120, 188, 196, 296
Fitzloff, Arlene (Witt), 186-187
Fitzloff, Bertha, 186
Fitzloff, Beverly (Best), 186
Fitzloff, Bill, 188, 339
Fitzloff, Brandon, 190, 198
Fitzloff, Carl W., 34, 68, 100, 146, 186-187, 191, 217
Fitzloff, Carol Ann, 191
Fitzloff, Charles, 134, 141, 186, 192
Fitzloff, Cheryl (Fredenburg), 190-191, 344, 348
Fitzloff, Daniel, 188
Fitzloff, Dawn, 191
Fitzloff, Debbie, 187
Fitzloff, Dick, 158, 190, 344, 348
Fitzloff, Eileen (Krause), 188
Fitzloff, Ella (Jans), 186-187
Fitzloff, Ellen, 188
Fitzloff, Emma (Gerlich), 186, 192
Fitzloff, Eugene Jr. (Tony), 188
Fitzloff, Eugene, 133, 188
Fitzloff, George, 100, 151, 186-187, 295, 332
Fitzloff, Greg, 189
Fitzloff, Harold, 188
Fitzloff, Henriette (Borchardt), 174, 186
Fitzloff, Herman Henry, 19, 81, 93, 96, 106, 186, 188, 190
Fitzloff, Howard, 187-188
Fitzloff, Hulda (Frank), 32, 123, 133, 188, 196, 296, 326, 336
Fitzloff, Jackie, 190
Fitzloff, James Arthur, 130. 183, 189, 315-317, 332
Fitzloff, James Lee, 189-190
Fitzloff, Jason, 189
Fitzloff, Jeffery, 188
Fitzloff, Johan Ludwig, 174, 186, 188
Fitzloff, Johann Carl, 186, 192
Fitzloff, John Wilhelm (Jack), 51, 98, 100-101, 104, 112, 118-119, 124-125, 130-131, 133, 136-137, 177, 186, 188-189, 198-199, 316, 323-324, 330, 335
Fitzloff, Ken, 187
Fitzloff, LaVerne, 132
Fitzloff, Lee James, 189
Fitzloff, Leilah Clara, 188
Fitzloff, Lilly E. (Prange), 68, 123, 186-187
Fitzloff, Lois, 188
Fitzloff, Louis, 186
Fitzloff, Lydia (Proechel), 96, 192
Fitzloff, Mae (Thisted), 191
Fitzloff, Mandy, 174, 190
Fitzloff, Marilyn, 66, 68, 71, 137
Fitzloff, Mark, 191
Fitzloff, Martha (Schiek), 192
Fitzloff, Mary (Kruse), 186-187
Fitzloff, Melody (Weir), 190
Fitzloff, Minnie (Niebauer), 123, 135
Fitzloff, Olga L.(Fritzke), 126, 135, 144, 188, 198-199, 302, 330, 336, 341
Fitzloff, Ottelia (Barueske), 19, 188, 190
Fitzloff, Otto, 186, 191
Fitzloff, Pamela (Johnson), 189
Fitzloff, Ramona (Hager), 34, 188
Fitzloff, Raymond Herman, 191
Fitzloff, Raymond William (Ray), 112, 132, 138, 188, 190-192, 234, 298, 324, 332
Fitzloff, Riley, 190
Fitzloff, Ryan, 190
Fitzloff, Shirley, 183
Fitzloff, Stacey, 189
Fitzloff, Sydney, 103
Fitzloff, Virginia (Reynolds), 188
Fitzloff, William H., 124, 186
Fitzloff's Main Street Auto Repair & Car Wash, 344
Fitzloff's Store, 71
Fitzsimmons, L. (Richards), 192
Fitzsimmons, Patrick, 192
Fitzsimmons, Sarah, 192
Fitzsimmons, Thomas, 192
Fleming, Alvin, 58
Fleming, Lyle, 58
Flemming, Lester, 204
Flemming, Lorene (Glamm), 203
Fletcher, Jonathan E., 1-3, 8, 10, 13, 17, 68
Flitter Bridge, 23-24
Flitter, Albert, 277
Flitter, Anna (Sodeman), 277
Flitter, Arthur, 103, 124
Flitter, Henry, 106
Flitter, John, 51, 113
Flitter, Martin, 113
Flitter, Robert, 212, 228
Flitterer, Carol (Bollmann), 163
Flo, Ronald, 213
Flosi, Beverly Jane (Chase), 176
Flowers, Blake 173
Flowers, Bradley, 173, 332
Flowers, Brandon, 173
Flowers, Brock, 173
Flowers, Bryce, 173
Flowers, Roxanne (Buesing), 173
Folkerts, Doris (Freitag), 157, 198
Folkerts, Wendell, 198
Folven, Donald, 234
Folven, Hermina (Loge), 234
Forrey, Phil, 161
Fort Randall, 6
Fort Ridgley, 7
Fort Snelling, 1, 7, 124
Fossum, John, 68, 131, 141, 177, 192, 246, 288
Fossum, Lowell, 192
Fossum, Mary Lou (Hoppe), 193
Fossum, Robert, 136, 192-193
Fossum, Sadie (Miller), 192, 246
Foster, Abbie, 196
Foster, Amine, 195
Foster, Earl, 196
Foster, Elizabeth (Adkins), 196, 290
Foster, Ethel, 308
Foster, George, 196
Foster, Hazel O. (Foster), 196
Foster, Henry B., 193-194, 265
Foster, Henry P., 195, 275
Foster, Henry, 10, 17, 46, 340
Foster, Lydia A. (Pitcher-Rasdall), 193-194, 261, 264
Foster, Raymond, 196
Foster, S. Jackson, 193, 195
Foster, Sarah (Campbell), 275
Foster, Stephen Sr., 100, 193, 195-196, 290
Foster, Steven Jr., 194-196
Fosters Hall, 77
Fox, Mollie, 254
Foyles, Aaron L., 17
Frahm, Mark, 63
Franciscus, Frank, 8
Frank Addition, 34
Frank Ireland Construction, 355
Frank, Betty M. (Palmer), 196
Frank, Bruce, 278
Frank, Christoph, 259
Frank, Diane E., 196
Frank, Dorthothy (Fitzloff), 188, 196, 336
Frank, Edward, 112, 196, 295
Frank, Gustav, 196
Frank, Harland H., 121, 127, 146, 196
Frank, Henry, 197
Frank, Herman, 112, 127, 188, 196
Frank, Irene (Frase), 299
Frank, Kathy (Strawn), 196
Frank, LaVerne, 183
Frank, Lena (Freitag), 197
Frank, Leo, 126, 196

Frank, Letha (Tenny), 196
Frank, Martha, 196
Frank, Raymond, 299
Frank, Rhonda (Spear), 278
Frank, Robert J., 196
Frank, Wilhelmina (Monthey), 196
Frank, Wilhelmine, 259
Franke, Albert, 126
Franske, Eddie, 101
Franske, Ernst, 277
Franske, Frederice (Sodeman), 277
Franske, Freidrich, 101
Frantum, Dave, 331
Frantum, Harry, 272
Frantum, Leona (Schmidt), 272
Frantz, Louise, 109, 111
Frantz, William, 92, 114, 342
Franz, Billy, 103
Franz, Lydia, 196-197
Franz, Mr., 92
Franz, Rosie (Proehl), 196
Franz, Virginia, 196-197
Franz, William J., 196-197
Franz, William Jr., 196
Fredericks, Clete, 179
Freeborn, MN, 129
Freedom Township, 1
Freitag Bridge, 26
Freitag, Charles, 198
Freitag, Christopher, 198
Freitag, Clara (Grams), 197, 208, 336
Freitag, Doris, 58
Freitag, Dustin, 198
Freitag, Emma (Risto), 198, 212
Freitag, Ervin, 198
Freitag, Esther (Doering), 198
Freitag, Fredericka (Kruse), 197
Freitag, Herman, 197-198
Freitag, Joan (Nelson), 198
Freitag, John A., 101, 197, 212, 335
Freitag, Jon, 198
Freitag, Kenneth, 58, 197-198
Freitag, LaVerne (Borneke), 150, 198
Freitag, Lisa (Long), 198
Freitag, Luann (Thorsen), 198
Freitag, Lydia, 197-198
Freitag, Sarah, 198
Freitag, Steven, 198
Freitag, Thomas, 61, 198, 331-332
Freitag, William, 110, 197-198, 208
French, Andrew, 84
Frey, Barbara (Nagel), 229
Frey, Fred, 229
Friday, Albertina (Papke), 164
Friday, Charles, 164
Friedrichs, Richard, 164
Fritz, Margie (Westphal), 18, 58, 126, 132, 271, 286
Fritz, Scott, 286
Fritzke, Alice (Harms), 199
Fritzke, Arthur, 199
Fritzke, Bertha (Otto), 188, 198-199
Fritzke, Gertrude (Winkelman), 68, 120, 199
Fritzke, Henry, 109
Fritzke, Lenora (Paulsen), 199
Fritzke, Naomi (Kimm), 199
Fritzke, Otto, 199
Fritzke, Pastor Gustav E., 53, 114, 188, 198-199, 332
Fritzke, Robert, 59, 68, 124, 126, 199, 288, 332, 341
Froehlich Brothers Hatchery, 118, 300, 319, 324
Froehlich Hardware, 113
Froehlich, Amelia (Radke), 199
Froehlich, Ann (Peterson), 201
Froehlich, Anthony, 200
Froehlich, Beverly (Linde), 201
Froehlich, Connie (Buecksler), 200
Froehlich, Dale, 200-201
Froehlich, Daniel, 200
Froehlich, Donald, 201
Froehlich, Eda, 199
Froehlich, Edna (Bollmann), 130, 163, 199-201, 258, 336
Froehlich, Edward, 196, 200
Froehlich, Elmer, 118, 200
Froehlich, Emma, 199
Froehlich, Frances (Mosher), 201
Froehlich, Gail, 202
Froehlich, Gertie (Sorenson), 130, 201-202, 294
Froehlich, Herman, 199-200
Froehlich, Jerry, 201
Froehlich, John, 200
Froehlich, Kelsey, 200
Froehlich, Kyle, 200
Froehlich, Laurance, 68, 202, 298
Froehlich, Lempi (Niemela), 201
Froehlich, Linda, 200
Froehlich, Lydia (Jenrich), 201
Froehlich, Maria (Garduno), 200-201
Froehlich, Mark, 200
Froehlich, Martin, 199
Froehlich, Mathilde (Frank), 196, 200
Froehlich, Maurice, 201
Froehlich, Muriel, 130-131
Froehlich, Oscar, 118, 200-201, 258, 297, 300, 319
Froehlich, Otto, 126, 200-201, 239
Froehlich, Paul, 200
Froehlich, Phyllis (Hodapp), 130, 200, 336
Froehlich, Raymond, 200
Froehlich, Rudolph A., 34, 111, 200-202, 295
Froehlich, Sara (Ayes), 200
Froehlich, Thomas, 200
Froehlich, Wanda (Andrews), 68, 202
Froehlich, William, 199-200
Froehlich, Winifred (Grout), 199
Fromm, Corey, 258
Fromm, Jenna (Palmer), 258
Fry, Terry, 241
Fry, Vickie (Marzinske), 241
Fugleberg, Stephanie, 248
Fugleberg, Amanda, 248
Fugleberg, Carl, 248
Fugleberg, Colleen, 248
Fugleberg, Debra (More), 248
Fugleberg, Natalie, 248
Fugleberg, Tim, 248
Funk, William, 91
Furbish, William, 216
Gahl, Ernest, 287
Gahl, Florence (Wingen), 287
Gahl, George, 287
Gahl, Marjorie (Wingen), 287
Gallagher, Catherine (Murphy), 254
Gallagher, Frank, 117
Galler, Frank, 129
Galston, Agnes (Klein), 282
Galston, Ivennie (Wenner), 150-151, 168, 282
Galston, James, 168, 282
Galston, Linda (Oftedahl), 168, 282
Galston, Nancy, 168, 282
Galston, Robert, 282
Galston, William, 168, 282
Gamble, Anne (Massop), 211
Gamble, Calvin, 211, 267
Ganzel, George, 275
Ganzel, Louise (Marzinske), 241
Ganzel, Louise (Schostag), 275
Ganzel, Wayne, 228, 235, 241
Ganzel, Wilhelm, 241
Garden City, MN, 4
Garven, Hal, 68
Gebbard, Joseph H., 32, 81, 341
Gekeler, Caroline, 172
Gekeler, Emma, 123
Gekeler, John, 53, 172
Gekeler, Will, 108
Gekler, Annie, 308-309
Gekler, Charlie, 309
Gekler, Nona, 308
Gekler, Rosie, 308
Gekler, William, 99
Gens, Mark, 47
George, Otillie (Grams), 207
George, William, 207
Gerber, John, 186, 202, 274, 277

Gerber, Larry, 207
Gerber, Linda (Goodrich), 207
Gerber, Louisa, 186, 202, 274, 277
Gerdes, W.R., 77
Gerlach, Herman, 280
Gerlich, Fred, 32, 85-86, 341
Gerlich, Mamie, 103
Germo, Clarice (Phillips), 157, 260, 341
Germo, John, 260
Gherke, Ferdinand, 207
Gherke, Minnie (Grams), 207
Gibson, Chad, 193
Gibson, Cole, 193
Gibson, Karen (Fossum), 193
Gibson, Randy, 193
Gibson, Taylor, 193
Giesche, John, 288
Giesche, Tricia (Winter), 288
Gillmer, Sarah E., 97
Gjerde, Bridget, 202-203
Gjerde, Denise (Lloyd), 202-203, 341
Gjerde, Douglas, 202
Gjerde, Lacey, 202-203
Gjerde, Waldemar, 121, 129
Glamm, Albena, 203
Glamm, Bertha C. (Krause), 203, 229, 246
Glamm, Chris (Wendt), 203
Glamm, Cindy (Little), 155, 204, 339-340
Glamm, David, 204, 332, 353
Glamm, Donald, 58, 203-204
Glamm, Emil, 203
Glamm, Esther (Schroeder), 203-204, 275
Glamm, Fred, 98, 203-204, 246
Glamm, Hannah W. (Borchardt), 202-203
Glamm, Henry, 203
Glamm, Herman, 203, 246
Glamm, Joanne, 204
Glamm, Johann F.L., 202-203
Glamm, John (Fred) F.L., 203
Glamm, John, 204
Glamm, Julia Rose (Flitter), 203
Glamm, Lorene, 58
Glamm, Marcella (Bartlett), 66, 203-204, 258
Glamm, Orga (Strauss), 203
Glamm, Otto Henry Robert, 101, 203-204, 275, 335
Glamm, Richard, 203
Glamm, Tammy, 204
Glamm, Terry, 204
Glaser, Adolph, 204
Glaser, Allan Theodore, 205
Glaser, Ardella (Stanke), 204-206
Glaser, August, 204, 276
Glaser, Colton, 205
Glaser, Coral (Jarbi), 205
Glaser, Elsie (Kohlhoff), 204
Glaser, Emil, 204
Glaser, Jesse Theodore, 205
Glaser, Jessica (Boyer), 205
Glaser, Maria (Schwanke), 204, 276
Glaser, Mary (Bradley), 204
Glaser, Norbert, 127, 204-205
Glaser, Ruth (Anderson), 204
Glaser, Sue (Freyberg), 205
Glaser, Theodore (Ted), 205
Glaser, Theodore, 103, 126-127, 204
Glaser, Travis, 205
Glaser, Trent, 205
Glaser, Wesley, 204
Glasgow, Andy, 295
Glasgow, Phil, 295
Glendon, Father James, 46
Glynn, Eugene, 232, 282
Glynn, Mary Alice (Conway), 232, 282
Godeman, Herman F., 111, 206
Godemann, Alvina, 206
Godemann, Carl, 206-207
Godemann, Christian, 206
Godemann, Clara, 206
Godemann, Ella (Jeddloh), 206
Godemann, Elma (Oftedahl-McComb), 206
Godemann, Emma, 58, 109, 128, 206-207, 323
Godemann, Fred, 206-207, 259
Godemann, Friedrich, 206
Godemann, Hattie (Schumacker), 206-207
Godemann, Herman, 245
Godemann, Louise (Dimmel), 206
Godemann, Louise (Oftedahl-McComb), 244-245
Godemann, Ludwig, 206
Godemann, Marie, 206, 259
Godemann, Sophia (Hagge), 206
Godemann, William J., 32, 206, 341
Godemann, William R., 206
Godemann's Grocery Store, 300
Goebel, Eillen (Hodapp), 157
Goettl, Barbara (Lotton), 155
Goettl, Eugene Jr., 209, 336
Goettl, Troy, 339
Gollmar Brothers Show, 221
Gollmar, Edward G., 221-222
Gollmar, Mary (Juliar), 87, 91, 221
Gollmar, Sarah (Juliar), 221-222
Good Heart, 4
Good Templars, 80
Good Thunder, MN, 33, 81
Goodrich Housing Additions, 34, 155
Goodrich, Allan, 182, 209
Goodrich, Bruce, 332
Goodrich, Dean, 182
Goodrich, Elmay (Geyer), 18, 207
Goodrich, Evans, 10
Goodrich, Everilda (Anton), 182
Goodrich, George, 18, 182, 207
Goodrich, Gertrude (Grams), 182, 209
Goodrich, James, 207
Goodrich, Jon, 207
Goodrich, Joyce, 207
Goodrich, Keith, 182
Goodrich, LaVera (Dallman), 182
Goodrich, Lottie (Covel), 12, 18, 182, 207
Goodrich, Lyle, 18, 34, 146, 182, 207, 217, 324
Goodrich, Merlin, 12, 18, 207
Goodrich, Stella (Grams), 18, 182, 207-208, 324
Gordon, Alma (Kopke), 228-229
Gordon, Don, 149-150
Gordon, Harv, 229
Gorman, Cecelia, 119
Gorman, Gov., 3
Gottschalk, Carolyn (Grams), 208
Gottschalk, Wayne, 208
Goyne, Jeffery, 164
Goyne, Terri (Bollmann), 164
Grafweg, Father, 46
Grams, Alvin, 208
Grams, Amelia (Doege), 207
Grams, Anita, 58
Grams, Anna, 207
Grams, August, 197, 207-208
Grams, Barbara (Hunt), 208
Grams, Bernard, 207
Grams, Bill, 209
Grams, Carl, 209
Grams, Carol (Schubbe), 209
Grams, Charles, 47, 296, 339
Grams, Chris, 207
Grams, Christopher, 101, 207
Grams, Chuck, 209
Grams, Darlene (Seys), 209
Grams, Donald, 209
Grams, Dora (Santo), 208, 228
Grams, Douglas, 209, 265
Grams, Edna (Schoenfeld), 208
Grams, Emil, 208, 228
Grams, Emma (Jeseritz), 197, 207-208
Grams, Eric, 208
Grams, Evelyn (Leifermann), 209
Grams, Gertrude (Mittelsteadt), 208
Grams, Hannah (Koopman), 208
Grams, Helen (Hirte), 209
Grams, Irene (Vierguts), 208-209
Grams, Jane (Salstrom), 209
Grams, Jerry, 209

Grams, Jodell, 209
Grams, Julia (Hoehn), 209
Grams, Julie (Hagen), 209
Grams, Karen, 208, 331
Grams, Karl, 58, 208
Grams, Louie, 309
Grams, Ludwig, 34, 158, 175, 207-208, 235, 283, 295, 335
Grams, Mabel (Prechel), 128, 207, 214, 298
Grams, Marcella, 208
Grams, Margaret, 46
Grams, Marie (Cuddy), 209
Grams, Marie (Westphal), 207-208, 283, 335
Grams, Mark, 209
Grams, Marlene, 208
Grams, Mary Margaret (Maloney), 166, 209
Grams, Michael, 209
Grams, Nadine, 208
Grams, Norma, 209
Grams, Otto Karl, 208
Grams, Otto, 208
Grams, Pam (Torberg), 209
Grams, Paul, 207, 214, 298-299
Grams, Raymond, 209
Grams, Renee (Fick), 209
Grams, Robert, 157, 209
Grams, Walter E., 208-209, 265
Grams, Walter H., 46, 59, 166, 209
Grams, Wayne, 209
Grams, William Heinrich, 101, 103, 207-208, 296, 335
Grams, William Jr., 209
Grams, William, 209
Grams, Wilma (Shutt), 209
Grawunder, Ida (Mueller), 210
Grawunder, William, 94, 108, 210
Grey, Lita, 224
Grignon & Coughour, 32, 82, 113
Grignon & Greener, 79
Grignon, Belle, 210
Grignon, Henry, 88, 210
Grignon, Jennie (Phillips), 210
Grignon, N.R., 82
Grignon, Virginia, 210
Grim, George, 135
Groebner, Ann Marie, 288
Groebner, David, 288
Groebner, Frank, 288
Groebner, Gretchen (Winkelman), 288
Groebner, Jerry, 34, 267
Groebner, Marie, 34
Groll, William, 335
Groskreutz, Cindi (Phillips), 260
Groskreutz, Darrin, 260
Guddal, Donald, 244
Guddal, Margaret (McComb), 244
Gulden, Mary Lou (Grams), 209
Gulden, Patrick, 209
Gullerud, Dagny, 327
Gunsolus, Sylvia, 66
Guse, Emil, 206
Guse, Herman, 288
Guse, Martha (Godemann), 206
Gusso, Henry, 85
Gustafson, John M., 348
Guyer, Ed, 257
Guyer, Rosa (Pagenkopf), 257
Gwilt, Marni, 241
Haack, John, 6
Haedt, Emma (Juliar), 97, 221-222
Haedt, H.S., 33
Haedt, R.S., 90
Haedt, Robert A., 221
Hagen, Michael, 342
Hager, Aaron, 146, 211
Hager, Amelia, 211
Hager, Anna (Schultz), 300
Hager, Bill, 11, 72, 125, 133
Hager, Cecelia, 157
Hager, Clay, 146, 211
Hager, Clifford, 300
Hager, Collin, 211
Hager, Ernest F., 68, 111, 117, 118, 125-126, 210-211, 275-276, 300, 330, 324
Hager, Esther (Schroeder), 117, 123, 189, 210, 275-276, 300
Hager, Joseph, 210
Hager, Katherine (Yaeger), 210
Hager, Linda (Stevens), 211
Hager, Marie (Baynes), 188
Hager, Mary Jane (Verschelde), 129, 149-150, 210-211
Hager, Mikayla, 211
Hager, Rachel (Rudisill), 211
Hager, Raymond, 188
Hager, William (Bill), 68, 130, 149, 155, 210-211, 217, 276, 325
Hager's Diner, 150-152, 154
Hager's Our Own Hardware Store, 118, 136, 139, 145, 147, 300, 302, 327
Halberg, Lyle, 190
Halberg, Shirley (DeMars Fitzloff), 183, 188-190
Hall, Bessie (Russell), 214
Hall, Carolyn (Glamm), 204
Hall, Curtis, 204
Hall, Daphne (Schmidt), 212
Hall, Dr. Richard, 136
Hall, Edwin, 214
Hall, Elvera (Freitag), 155, 198, 211-212, 232, 298
Hall, Harold, 211
Hall, Harry, 78
Hall, Inga (Finstad), 211
Hall, Jeanette (Lang), 212, 232
Hall, Jerome, 212
Hall, Jody (Bollmann), 164
Hall, John, 103
Hall, Jon, 212, 232
Hall, Katrina, 232
Hall, Keri Anne, 232
Hall, Kristine, 212
Hall, Larry, 164
Hall, Marcus, 212
Hall, May (Foster), 195-196
Hall, Mrs. Edwin, 336
Hall, Samuel, 232
Hall, Stanley, 198, 211-212, 232, 258
Hall, Stella (Rasdall), 265
Hall, Thomas Willie, 85, 196
Hall, Timothy, 212
Hall, William, 85, 265
Hamilton, Charles, 265
Hamilton, Lulu Pearl (Rasdall), 265-266
Hanson, Andrew, 90
Hanson, Brad, 136
Hardie, Shirley (Rose), 269
Hardie, William, 269
Harrison, W.H., 286
Harvest States Elevator, 144
Harvey, Bennett, 182
Harvey, Eunice (Covel), 182
Haskell, Spike, 179
Haugen Meat Market, 111, 154, 269, 327
Haugen, Elmer, 53, 123, 126, 144, 177, 302, 312-318, 335
Haugen, Ingeborg, 312
Haugen, Iver, 312
Haugen, Julia (Braaten), 144, 312-318, 336
Haugen, Kari (Wiste), 312
Haugen, Marlon O., 213-318
Haugen, Ole, 312
Haugen, Oscar, 312
Hawker, Alvin, 132, 211-213, 285
Hawker, Dale, 132, 213
Hawker, Deaney, 132
Hawker, Elenora (Maass), 128-129, 212-213
Hawker, Eliza (Birr), 212, 285
Hawker, Harold William, 124, 132, 212
Hawker, John, 212
Hawker, Judy, 212-213
Hawker, Lillia (Rudolph), 212
Hawker, Lyle, 132, 212
Hawker, Marvin, 213
Hawker, Mildred (Flitter), 212
Hawker, Phyllis, 213
Hawker, Rosella (Drummer), 212
Hawker, Susan (Bruels), 213

Hawker, Wayne, 213, 285
Hawker, Wilbur L., 212
Hawker, William, 212, 285
Hawkins, J.D., 75-76, 79, 213
Hawkins, Paulina (Hill), 213
Hayes, John, 46
Hayes, Joseph, 46, 79
Haynes Hall, 83
Haynes, Celia (Rogers), 213
Haynes, Dr. E.B., 32, 213, 295, 297
Haynes, Elizabeth (Camp), 213
Haynes, Mrs., 83
Healy, Jackie (Danberry), 183
Healy, Mark, 183
Hegle & Reader, 31
Heiman, Mildred, 109
Heinbaugh, Cole, 213
Heinbaugh, Hunter, 213
Heinbaugh, Phillip, 213
Heinbaugh, Tracy, 213
Heinze, Mrs. Theodore (Schultz), 276
Heinze, Theodore F., 90
Hemingover, Kate, 58
Hemingover, Laverna, 58
Hemingover, Ronnie, 58
Hemshrot Grocery, 61, 79, 152, 154, 214
Hemshrot, Anna (Gekler), 213
Hemshrot, Deborah, 214
Hemshrot, George, 213
Hemshrot, Kent, 214
Hemshrot, Lucille (Hall), 32, 213-214, 246
Hemshrot, Marvin (Murph), 32, 144, 146, 213-214, 246
Henzie, Louis, 103
Heritage of Blue Earth County, 10, 118, 294
Herman, Elizabeth, 218
Herman, Melissa (Hubmer), 218
Herman, Nathan, 218
Herman, Thomas, 218
Herniman, John, 238
Herrig, Bradley, 168, 283
Herrig, Lois (Wenner), 168, 283
Hesse, Ada, 214
Hesse, Beverely (Bartelt), 214-215, 269
Hesse, Dorothy (Berentson), 1128, 44, 214-215, 298-300
Hesse, Franzska, 214
Hesse, Harvey, 63, 214-215, 269, 299
Hesse, Jeffrey, 214, 299
Hesse, Keri, 215
Hesse, Kile, 215
Hesse, Kristina, 215
Hesse, Lea (Giles), 214
Hesse, Michael, 215
Hesse, Norla, iii, 214-215, 298-299
Hesse, Paul, 214
Hesse, Susan (Prange), 215
Hesse, Sylvia, 214, 299
Hesse, William, 207, 214-215, 298
Hicks, Gerald, 148
Highes, Father Robert, 46
Hilks, Alvin, 262
Hill, Ernest, 183
Hill, Joyce, 183
Hill, N.S., 75
Hiller, August, 272
Hiller, Elnora (Hadel), 272
Hiller, Johann, 272
Hiller, William Jr., 272
Hiller, William, 272
Hilton Bridge, 19-20, 77
Hilton, 31-32, 51, 74, 79-80, 83, 215, 295, 340
Hilton, Aaron I, 215, 340
Hilton, Aaron II, 31, 74, 76, 215-216
Hilton, Charley, 217, 295
Hilton, Ebenezer, 295
Hilton, Edward, 215
Hilton, Even, 217
Hilton, Grace (Buckholz), 295
Hilton, Gustav, 295-296
Hilton, Harriet A'Della, 216
Hilton, Henry S., 80, 216-217, 295
Hilton, Huldah (Dickinson), 183, 216, 265
Hilton, Jane Bailey (Gould), 215-216
Hilton, Joseph, 216
Hilton, Katherine (Donahue), 217
Hilton, Libby, 217, 295
Hilton, Lydia (Webb), 215
Hilton, Margaret, 217, 295
Hilton, Ralph, 132, 136, 217, 295
Hilton, Sarah (Smith), 216
Hilton, Sumner Charles, 87-88, 216, 265, 295-296, 337
Hilton, William, 215, 217, 295
Hinton, Alice (Grams), 209
Hinton, Guy, 209
Hinton, William, 86
Hintze Liquor Store, 81
Hintze, Charles, 217
Hintze, Clara, 59, 125, 217, 304
Hintze, Hazel, 308
Hintze, John, 86, 217
Hintze, Louis, 217, 310
Hintze, Marie, 217
Hintze, Robert, 217
History of Blue Earth County, 3, 10-11, 162, 165, 167, 185, 217, 222, 242, 255
History of Waseca County, 1
Hockstra, Heidi (Storjohann), 279
Hockstra, Perry, 279
Hodapp, Alfred, 209
Hodapp, Alice (Grams), 209
Hodapp, Anna (May), 242
Hodapp, Anna Katherina (Bruels), 167
Hodapp, Bernard, 69
Hodapp, Edmund, 209
Hodapp, Eva (Grams), 209
Hodapp, Henry, 99
Hodapp, Herbert R., 217
Hodapp, Hubert, 111, 217, 335
Hodapp, Joe, 297
Hodapp, Louise (Frederick), 235
Hodapp, Ludgart (Baumgartner), 217
Hodapp, Lyle, 235
Hodapp, Phillip, 167
Hodapp, Roy, 335
Hodapp, Wendal, 242
Hoechst, Margaret, 284
Hoechst, Woodrow, 284
Hoehn, Candy (Vaske), 213
Hoffman, Albert, 170-171
Hoffman, Annette (Manthey-Ward-Chamberlain), 282
Hoffman, Duane, 170-171
Hoffman, Ellen (Schwanke), 276
Hoffman, Gary Scott, 165
Hoffman, Gerald, 170-171
Hoffman, Gerda, 171
Hoffman, Gloria (Kraske), 171
Hoffman, Henry, 228, 276
Hoffman, Ida (Buecksler), 170-171
Hoffman, John, 282
Hoffman, Karen L., 165
Hoffman, Marion L. (Boswell), 14,165-166, 240, 265, 268, 280, 294
Hoffman, Noel, 165
Hoffman, Norman, 170-171
Hoffman, Vonnie, 171
Hohenstein, Carrie, 278
Hohenstein, Otto, 278
Holasek, Alan, 196
Holasek, Fred W., 196
Holasek, Jane M. (Frank), 196
Holasek, Jay, 196
Hollister, Mr, 121
Holm, Bill, 179
Holman, Dr. Carl J., 87, 95, 297
Holmgren, Harold, 336
Holtan, Pastor Jeffrey, 53
Holthus, Leona (Schroeder), 275
Holthus, Ray, 275
Holtz, Andria, 217
Holtz, Augusta, 217
Holtz, Frederick, 217
Holtz, Henry E., 217, 220, 342
Holtz, Julie (Hoffmann), 217
Holtz, Kristin, 217
Holtz, Larry, 217

Holtz, Matthew, 217
Holtz, Viona (Sohre), 217
Honisch, Elroy, 231
Honisch, LaJune (Kruse), 231
Honish, Elroy Wayne, 128
Honk Honka, 11
Hookemeyer Hotel, 295
Hoppe, Margie, 348
Hoppe, Merrill, 193
Hoppe, Monica, (Hodapp), 193
Hormel, George, 316
Horowitz, Adelyne (Juliar), 223
Horowitz, Harry, 223
Horsager, Barbara (Lewis-Juliar), 233
Horsager, Jerry, 233
Houghton, Newell, 10-11, 17
Hounka, 4
Howley, Elzada (Juliar), 223-224, 330
Howley, John, 223-224, 330
Howley, Mark, 224
Hubbard Mill, 5
Hubbell, James B., 17, 340
Huber, Rick, 339
Hubmer, Alma, 218, 255
Hubmer, Beryl (Cornell), 218
Hubmer, Bruce, 218
Hubmer, Clarence, 218
Hubmer, Courrier G., 10,15, 53, 59, 68, 138, 168, 218, 296, 327
Hubmer, David, 218
Hubmer, Dora (Hoffman), 218
Hubmer, Duane Arnold, 218
Hubmer, Edward, 218
Hubmer, Gayle, 68
Hubmer, George H. , 34, 53, 58, 68-69, 96-97, 100, 106, 110, 123, 133, 136, 218, 248, 295, 300, 337
Hubmer, Gloria (Thorn), 218
Hubmer, H.A., 33, 90, 97, 329
Hubmer, Hattie, 218
Hubmer, Herman A., 218, 221-222
Hubmer, Irma (Ott), 218
Hubmer, June (Mohlke), 218
Hubmer, Katurah, 120
Hubmer, Lois, 120
Hubmer, Lydia (Courrier), 218
Hubmer, Marcus, 218
Hubmer, Marlin B., 218-219
Hubmer, Martin, 218
Hubmer, Mary (Juliar), 218, 221-222
Hubmer, Norma (Oelke), 218
Hubmer, Otto, 218
Hubmer, Pershing, 121, 218, 240
Hubmer, Roger, 218
Hubmer, Roy, 112, 218, 226, 244
Hubmer, Ruth (Oliver), 219
Huck, Pam, 155
Huettl, Claud, 208
Huettl, Joseph, 166
Huettl, Josephine (Wingen), 287
Huettl, Louis, 287
Huettl, Maximilian (Magel), 166
Huggenin, Mrs. L., 101
Hughes, Father Daniel, 46
Hughes, Thomas, 3, 8, 10-11, 113, 162, 165, 167, 185, 217, 222, 242, 265
Hughes, William F., 85
Hulseman, Lydia Marie (Fitzloff), 188
Hulseman, Oscar T., 96, 188
Hunter, Alyce (Coverstone), 219
Hunter, Ivadell (Myers), 129-130, 146, 155, 219-220, 249-250
Hunter, James E., 219-220, 249
Hunter, Joleen (Rathai), 220
Hunter, Keith, 220
Hunter, Lisa, 220
Hunter, Tanner, 220
Huntting Elevator Company, 33, 93-94, 98, 111
Hunziker, Eugene, 66
Hurt, Ivan F., 128
Husky Helper 4-H Club, 340
Hussey, George, 97, 105, 107, 337
Imm, Janelle (Schull), 248
Imm, John, 248
Immaculate Conception Catholic Cemetery, 54
Immaculate Conception Catholic Church, 45-50, 54, 74, 76, 83, 88, 98-99, 102-103
Indian Chiefs of Southern Minnesota, 8
Indian School, 45
Inkpadutah, 11
Insley, Dr., 297
Ireland, Abby, 47
Ireland, Daniel, 47, 332
Ireland, Frank T., 172, 332
Ireland, H.J., 335
Ireland, John, 236
Ireland, Lawrence, 119, 121, 258
Ireland, Mary (Foley), 236
Ireland, Ralph, 121, 295
Irwine, Durward, 124
Itzke, Rev., 86
Jager, Dorothy (McComb-Walera), 244
Jager, Ruben, 244
James, Elaine (Wenner), 168, 282-283
James, Frank, 101
James, Merle, 168, 282-283
Jamie's Masonry, 348
Janesville Argus, 13, 76, 78-83, 86, 148, 200, 228, 280
Janesville, MN, 66, 69, 77, 82, 92
Jannike, Cole, 270
Jannike, James, 270
Jannike, Jennie, 270
Jannike, Kimberly (Savik), 270
Jeff's Auto Repair, 345
Jenkins, Mrs. John, 263
Jennings, Tom, 331
Jenrich, Mrs. Albert (Hintze), 217
Jeseritz, Auguste (Grams), 207
Jeseritz, Rudolph, 207
Jesuit Sisters, 57
Jindra, Duane, 198
Jindra, Zandra (Freitag), 198
Jobe, Elizabeth, 225
Johannsen, George, 172
Johannsen, Peggy, 172
John Danberry Construction, 352
Johns, Connie, 63
Johnson, Alma (Fisher), 186
Johnson, Andrew, 220
Johnson, Carol (Frank), 300
Johnson, Darcy, 331
Johnson, Dustin, 282
Johnson, Dylan, 282
Johnson, Faye (Froehlich), 200-202
Johnson, Gregory, 220
Johnson, H. Luei, 208
Johnson, Harry, 107, 129
Johnson, Hollie (Palmer), 258
Johnson, Hubert, 68, 158, 176, 220, 223, 295, 336
Johnson, Jeffrey, 282
Johnson, Jerome, 300
Johnson, Joel, 220
Johnson, John, 17
Johnson, Kathy, 63
Johnson, Kelly (Ward), 282
Johnson, Ken, 202
Johnson, Kourtney, 282
Johnson, Lisa (Dorland), 300
Johnson, Marlys (Juliar), 220, 223
Johnson, Mary (McLaughlin), 245
Johnson, Michael, 300
Johnson, Rick, 258
Johnson, Roland F., 133
Johnson, Wallace, 245
Jones, Clark, 237
Jones, Elmer, 114
Jones, Hazel, 285
Jones, Ivor, 275
Jones, Lillian (Lynch), 237
Jones, Loren, 285
Jongbleodt, Pharilda, 236
Jongbloedt, Albert J., 223
Jongbloedt, Aloysius, 255
Jongbloedt, Charles, 223
Jongbloedt, Charlotte (Page), 155
Jongbloedt, Denise, 223
Jongbloedt, Julie, 223
Jongbloedt, Lila (Juliar), 223
Jongbloedt, Ronald, 223

Jongbloedt, Susan, 223
Jongbloedt, Thomas, 223
Jongbloedt, Willaert, 236
Joos, Loyal, 65, 68-69
Jost, Margaret (Lang), 220
Jost, Mathias, 32, 77, 220
Joyce, Bernard, 254
Joyce, Eleanor (Murphy), 254
Joyce, Joe, 254
Joyce, Roderick, 254
Joyce, Sabinus, 254
Juliar, Aaron, 222-223
Juliar, Albert A., 33, 90, 97, 221-222
Juliar, Albert Jr., 223
Juliar, Albert Sr., 223
Juliar, Alma (Knutson), 224
Juliar, Barbara (Lewis), 223
Juliar, Bertha (Schostag), 223
Juliar, Beverly (LeBrun), 223
Juliar, Catharine (Stevens), 218, 221
Juliar, Charlotte (Muelhausen), 222-223
Juliar, Clara (Oelke), 223
Juliar, Constance (Hussey), 224
Juliar, Dale, 224
Juliar, Darlene, 224
Juliar, Darrell, 221-223
Juliar, Dean, 223
Juliar, Delmar, 223
Juliar, Dennis, 223
Juliar, Donald, 224
Juliar, Donovan, 223
Juliar, Earl, 223
Juliar, Elaine, 223
Juliar, Elroy, 151, 220, 223, 275
Juliar, Emma (Ewart), 223
Juliar, F.E., 58
Juliar, F.F., 90
Juliar, Florence (Coleman), 223-225, 244, 293, 336
Juliar, G.J., 33
Juliar, Genevieve (Hernlundt), 222
Juliar, George A., 223
Juliar, George F., 97, 126, 222-224
Juliar, Gordon, 134, 136, 155, 223, 233
Juliar, Grace (Larsen), 223
Juliar, Harold, 224
Juliar, Harry H., 97, 109, 221-222, 224
Juliar, Helen (Raves), 224
Juliar, Henry, 222
Juliar, Inez (Walters), 162, 223, 281
Juliar, Iona, 223
Juliar, Irving, 223
Juliar, James, 223, 332
Juliar, Janet, 223
Juliar, Jeanne, 223
Juliar, Jeff, 223, 332
Juliar, Jerome, 223
Juliar, Joan (Toogood), 223
Juliar, Joe, 223
Juliar, John, 162, 222-223, 281
Juliar, Joyce, 223
Juliar, Judy, 223
Juliar, June (Crane), 223
Juliar, LaMarr, 223
Juliar, Lawrence, 222-223
Juliar, Lila (Schull), 224
Juliar, Lorin, 223
Juliar, Lottie, 123, 325
Juliar, Louise (Muehlhausen), 176, 185, 222
Juliar, Lydia (Hagemeister), 223
Juliar, Mabel (Nisbet), 58, 108
Juliar, Magdalen (Eiding), 221
Juliar, Marvin, 224, 298
Juliar, Melbourne, 223
Juliar, Merle, 223
Juliar, Merton, 223
Juliar, Mildred, 53
Juliar, Milton, 109, 183, 224
Juliar, Myrtle (McWhorter), 223
Juliar, Nettie (Mehlhouse), 224
Juliar, Nicholas (Nick), 126, 136, 223-225, 244, 293, 297, 329
Juliar, Nicholas L., 222
Juliar, Nicholas, 33, 58, 68, 83-84, 86, 90-91, 97, 99, 105, 108, 177, 218, 221-222
Juliar, Orvis, 223
Juliar, Otto O., 34, 90, 97, 123, 176, 185, 221-222
Juliar, Ralph, 223, 275
Juliar, Richard O., M.D., 33, 97-98, 100, 103, 108, 118, 221-224, 297, 300, 302, 318, 325-326, 329, 341
Juliar, Rosalie (Schroeder), 223, 275
Juliar, Rose (Hagemeister), 222-223
Juliar, Russell, 223
Juliar, Sharon, 155
Juliar, Silas, 97, 221-222
Juliar, Terry, 223
Juliar, Verna (Ramsden), 100, 124, 137, 223
Juliar, Vernon, 223
Juliar, Viola (Schroeder), 220, 223, 275
Juliar, Virgil, 121, 223
Juliar, Wilmar, 222
Junior Red Cross, 101
Kafka, Robert V., 68, 327
Kahn, Hazel (Schostag), 275
Kahn, Herbert, 275
Kahnke, Alvin, 351
Kahnke, Regina (Schmidt), 273
Kahnke, Sib, 273
Kalbus, Walter, 121
Kamrath, Bertha (Froehlich), 199
Kamrath, John, 199
Kapinske, Alma (Schostag), 274
Kapinski, John, 274
Karels, Allie, 226
Karels, Andrew, 225
Karels, Brandon, 224
Karels, Carrie (Mangen), 225-226
Karels, Christopher, 225-226, 332
Karels, Jordan, 224
Karels, Maci, 225
Karels, Mary (Hawker), 225
Karels, Morgan, 225
Karels, Regina (Jobe), 225-226
Karels, Sarah (Melby), 225
Karels, Sheila (Bohm), 225
Karels, Stacey, 225, 332
Karels, Thomas Jr., 225-226
Karels, Thomas Sr., 225, 331-332
Karels, William, 225, 332
Karst, Aimee McGinn, 254
Kasch, Meta (Klingbeil), 226
Kasch, Willia, 226
Kasota, MN, 117
Kathy's Café, 156
Kell, Pastor Arthur, 53, 302
Keller, James, 262
Keller, Patricia (Rahbeck-Preston), 10, 16, 262
Kelly, Alice (O'Connor), 254
Kelly, Alice, 254
Kelly, Clara, 254
Kelly, Ira, 296
Kelly, James, 254
Kelly, John, 254
Kelly, Lawrence, 296
Kelly, Margaret (Manaige), 241, 296
Kennedy, Frank, 46
Kenward, Elsie (Gekler), 166
Kenward, Helen (Schostag), 240, 275, 305, 325-326
Kenward, Howard, 275
Kenward, Robert, 165-166
Kern, Ben, 12
Keysor, Captain Clark, 7
Kiecker, Elmer John, 251
Kiecker, Gertrude (Seehusen), 251
Kiley, Father, 310-311
King, Albert, 115
King, Alexander, 233
King, Bertha (Schoettler), 226, 231
King, H.R., 32, 77, 226
King, Helen (Menk), 226
King, James, 233
King, Julia, 233
King, Maggie J. (Geddes), 226
King, Mary Kay (Lang), 233
King, Nichlaus, 226, 231
King, Richard, 233
King, Terry, 233

King, Walter E., 226
Kirkey, James, 125
Kittleson, Marley, 258
Klaesus, Janet (Kruger), 168
Klaesus, Joseph, 168, 283
Klaesus, Linda (Wenner), 168, 283
Klaesus, Steven, 168
Klages, Cheryl, 355
Klages, Jenna, 235
Klages, Julie (Lynch), 235
Klages, Kylie, 235
Klages, Matt, 235
Kleeman, Charles, 249
Kleeman, Minnie (Koplen), 249
Klingbeil, Alan, 227
Klingbeil, Donald, 226
Klingbeil, Emilie (Burmeister), 227, 275
Klingbeil, Eva, 226
Klingbeil, Herman, 56, 226-227, 275
Klingbeil, Joan (Hudson), 227
Klingbeil, Leona, 226
Klingbeil, Louis H., 210, 226
Klingbeil, Lydia (Grawunder-Silkey), 210, 227
Klingbeil, Reinhart, 226
Klinkner, Renee, 63
Klint, Jane (Danberry), 182
Klint, Jody, 182
Klugherz, Deputy, 91
Knebel, Rev. G.H., 54
Knights of the Forest, 4, 67-68
Knutson, Bob, 132
Koch, Albert, 272
Koch, Fred, 51, 228
Koch, Ida A. (Schmidt), 272
Koch, Martha (Kopke-Flitter), 212, 228
Kock, Pastor David, 53
Koehler, Mr., 31
Koehler, Theodore, 85
Koentop, Agnes, 228
Koentop, August, 227
Koentop, Edward, 227
Koentop, Ella, 227
Koentop, Emil, 227
Koentop, John, 227
Koentop, Karl, 228
Koentop, Minnie (Sodeman), 227, 277
Koentop, Wilhelm F., 227, 277
Koholoff, Willie, 205
Kollos, Anita (Grams), 128, 228
Kollos, Anna (Lubke), 228
Kollos, Augusta (Schroeder), 161, 228, 275
Kollos, Bertha (Glamm), 203
Kollos, Clements, 112, 161, 228, 275
Kollos, Dee (Bjornson), 228
Kollos, E.G., 92
Kollos, Fred, 128, 203, 280
Kollos, George F., 128
Kollos, Gerald, 144, 146, 228, 295
Kollos, Harvey, 231
Kollos, Herman, 144, 146, 228
Kollos, Ida (Timmerman), 280
Kollos, Jamie, 228
Kollos, Jeffrey, 228
Kollos, Kevin, 228
Kollos, Michael, 228
Kollos, Sidney, 121,128
Kopke Flour Mill, 302
Kopke, Anna (Lubke), 235
Kopke, August C., 51, 186, 235, 295, 302
Kopke, Ida (Frey), 164, 229
Kopke, Johnas (John), 164, 229
Kopke, Karl, 228
Koplen, Amelia, 283
Koplen, William, 283
Koppen, Joe, 81, 296
Korth, Louis, 51
Kortuem, John, 278
Kortuem, Rose (Mach), 278
Kott, Ernest, 247
Kott, Wanda, 247
Kotz, Bernice (Covel), 182
Kramer, Elaine (Gehring), 288
Kramer, Francis F., 288
Kramer, Marlee Jo (Winkelman-Seys), 285, 288
Kramer, Ronald, 288
Krause, Alvin, 284
Krause, Esther (Vandrey), 284
Krause, Gertrude (Popham), 188
Krause, Henry, 204, 229
Krause, William, 188
Kreig, Holly (Gjerde), 202-203
Kreig, Kelsey, 203
Kreig, Michael, 203
Krenke, Louis, 172
Kroc, Jill (Zabel), 291
Kroc, Michael, 291
Kroc, Riley, 291
Kroenke, Amelia (Zellmer), 229
Kroenke, Angela, 230-231
Kroenke, Clay, 230
Kroenke, Dale, 231
Kroenke, Daniel, 230231
Kroenke, David Thomas, 229-230
Kroenke, Edward Dale, 155, 229-231, 335
Kroenke, Emilia (Zellmer), 244
Kroenke, George Robert, 121, 165, 229-230
Kroenke, Herman, 119, 229-230, 244, 300, 302, 324
Kroenke, James, 231
Kroenke, Jane Ann (Boswell), 14,165, 230
Kroenke, Kathleen (Kremer), 229-231
Kroenke, Kenneth Herman, 157, 229-231, 296, 325
Kroenke, Lori, 231
Kroenke, Mary, 230
Kroenke, Michael, 229-230
Kroenke, Patrick, 230
Kroenke, Ralene (Schaub), 231
Kroenke, Ramona, 230-231
Kroenke, Selma (Rosenthal), 231
Kroenke, Thomas, 61, 230
Kruckelberg, Marge, 248
Kruckelberg. Merville, 248
Kruse, Adelle (Zahn), 108
Kruse, Ardela, 58
Kruse, Bertha (Frank), 231, 300
Kruse, Bertha (King), 231
Kruse, Betty Lou (Mabee), 70, 155, 223, 231
Kruse, Bradley, 248
Kruse, Carl F., 51, 231, 296
Kruse, Charles, 248
Kruse, Dennis, 271
Kruse, Derek, 249
Kruse, Edith, 141
Kruse, Ervin, 231
Kruse, Fred, 52, 123, 188
Kruse, Fredrick Albert, 231
Kruse, Fredrick John, 231
Kruse, Hedwig (Hattie Fitzloff), 188
Kruse, Jeannette, 248, 296
Kruse, John, 112
Kruse, Kendra, 249
Kruse, Lana, 342
Kruse, Laurence, 103
Kruse, Lawrence, 223, 231
Kruse, Leo, 141, 295
Kruse, Lester F., 128
Kruse, Lynda (More), 248-249, 339, 353
Kruse, Maria, 249
Kruse, Mark, 271, 296
Kruse, Mary (Armstrong), 231
Kruse, Raymond, 100, 295
Kruse, Robert, 231, 342
Kruse, Steven, 248-249, 351, 353
Kruse, Verna, 231
Kubista, Collin, 208
Kubista, Jordan, 208
Kubista, Kevin, 208
Kuhn, Rev. Albert, 51
Kuhns, Louie, 190
Kukuk, Awald, 227-228
Kukuk, Ida (Koentop), 227
Kulseth, Darlene (DeMars), 183
Kulseth, Robert, 183
Kunkel, Donna (Pagenkopf), 179, 258

Kunkel, Jess, 258
Kunkel, Kathleen, 258
Kunkel, Scott, 258
Kurth, Karl, 51
Kurth, Laura, 308
Kurth, Wilhelmine, 55
Kurtzbein, Dorothy (Kollos), 228
Kurtzbein, Robert, 228
Kuske Harness, Leather & Hardware, 33, 77, 98, 118, 295
KYSM, 130
Lachelt, Emma (Grams), 207, 231
Lachelt, Herbert, 207, 231-232
Lachelt, Luella (Priebe), 207, 231-232
Lachelt, Reinhold, 207, 231
Lachelt, Sam, 170
LaCrosse, WI, 92
Ladies Sewing Club, 110
Laird, Danielle (Rollings), 206
Laird, Ean Joseph, 206
Laird, Sean, 206
Lake Elysian, 4
Lake Region Times, 34, 267, 321
Land of Memories Park, 355
Lang, Agnus (Soukup), 232
Lang, Anna (Wingen), 286
Lang, Anton, 18, 94, 232-233
Lang, Clair Marie, 233
Lang, Clyde, 161
Lang, Dorothy (Rudenick), 232
Lang, Jerome Anton, 232-233
Lang, Jerome Lynden, 212, 232-233
Lang, Kathy (Gens), 232
Lang, Kristine (Majeres), 18, 232-233
Lang, Laura (O'Connor), 254-255
Lang, Leon, 232
Lang, Lynden, 18, 232-233
Lang, Marcella (Willard), 232
Lang, Marian, 232
Lang, Mary Alice (Glynn), 18, 212, 232
Lang, Mildred (Rudnick), 18, 232-233
Lang, Neal Todd Lynden, 233
Lang, Nick, 32
Lang, Otto, 232
Lang, P.A., 54
Lang, Paul Anton, 233
Lang, Ruth (Thompson), 161
Lang, Sophia, 232
Lang, Thomas, 232
Lang, Wilbur, 232
Lange, Helen, 313
Lange, Marcella, 80
Lans, Vernon, 118
Lanz, Harold Jr., 239
Lanz, Suzanne (Mace), 239
LaPointe, Cora (Wingen), 287
Larsen, Allison Marie, 218
Larsen, Kevin, 218
Larsen, Michelle (Hubmer), 218
Larson, Arnold, 277
Larson, Don, 62
Larson, Gertrude (Sodeman), 277
Larson, John, 92
LaSallieur, Baptiste, 3-4
Lassow, Albert, 296
Lassow, F.W., 33, 79, 90, 195
Lassow, Frank, 83, 296
Lassow, Fred, 51, 83
Lassow, George, 296
Lassow, Irna, 296,
Latusek, Jared, 211
Latusek, Lani (Hager), 146, 150, 211
Latusek, Paul, 211
Latusek, Timothy, 211
Lavitzke, Dean, 248
Lavitzke, Joan (Schull-Preis), 248
Le Sueur Creamery, 141
Le Sueur River Bridge, 22
Le Sueur River Streambank Erosion Project, 34
Le Sueur River, 8, 11, 12, 18-20, 31, 57, 67, 83
Leary Hotel, 119-120
Leary, J., 329
Leary, Patrick, 46
Lebens, Rich, 332
Lentz, Elmer, 186
Lentz, Marie (Fitzloff), 186
Lenz, Kenneth, 258
Leo Hardware Company, 100
LeRay Township, 3
Levos, Val, 339
Lewis, Donald, 68, 233, 304
Lewis, Jarrett (Jerry), 233
Lewis, Laura (Jones), 233
Lewis, Molly (Stockstad), 233
Lewis, Nadine (Robertson), 68, 233, 252
Lewis, Patricia (Thrun), 233
Lewis, Roy, 37, 69, 233, 252, 300
Lewis, William, 233
Lillo, Jason, 215
Lillo, Jennifer, 215
Lillo, Jessica, 215
Lillo, Joni, 215
Lillo, Larry, 215
Lillo, Londa (Hesse), 215
Lincoln, Patricia (Bunde), 168, 283
Lincoln, President Abraham, 17, 242, 261, 315
Lincoln, William, 168, 283
Lind, Mr., 81
Lindberg, Carrie Lea, 270
Lindberg, Cheryl Ann (Sargent), 270
Lindberg, Nathan Dale, 270
Lindberg, Terrance F., 270
Linde, Gloria (King), 155, 226
Linde, Harold, 226, 259
Linde, Laura, 63
Linde, Robert, 155
Lindloff, Elsie (Grimm), 233
Lindloff, Mrs. Donald, 233
Lindloff, Rev. Donald W. 53, 233
Lindloff, Rev. William, 233
Lindrud, Cathleen, 164
Lindrud, Charles, 164
Lindrud, Cory, 164
Lindrud, Robin, 164
Lindrud, Valera (Bollmann), 163-164
Lindrup, John, 84, 295
Linnell, Anne (Remington), 234
Linnell, Donna, 233
Linnell, Eric James, 234
Linnell, Kelsey Anne, 234
Linnell, Oswald, 233
Linnell, Rick, 63, 233-234
Little Decora, 6
Loeffler, Bradley, 234
Loeffler, Brian Harold, 234, 332
Loeffler, Bruce, 234
Loeffler, Corine (Frank), 234, 300
Loeffler, Courtney, 234
Loeffler, David, 234
Loeffler, Dominic, 189
Loeffler, Elenora, 234
Loeffler, Harold, 234, 300
Loeffler, Heather, 189
Loeffler, James, 183
Loeffler, Jessica, 234
Loeffler, Logan, 189
Loeffler, Robert, 189
Loeffler, Rose (DeMars), 183
Loeffler, Shelly (Boehler), 234, 342
Loeffler, Stephanie, 189, 234
Loge, Eric, 234
Loge, Florence (Klatt), 234
Loge, Herman, 141, 234
Loge, Katharine (Beyer), 234
Loge, Linda (Zawacki), 234
Loge, Lorelee, 234
Loge, Loren (Chet), 234
Loge, Marlyn, 234
Loge, Matthew, 234
Loge, Michael, 234
Lone Pine Treasures & Custom Woodworking, 352
Long Prairie Reservation, 1, 8
Long Prairie, MN, 1-2, 14-15, 45
Lorentz, Isabelle, 155
Loretta Zelasney, 47
Lorse, Leslie, 130
Lower Agency School, 80
Lower Sioux Agency, 4, 10

Lubke Wagon & Blacksmith Shop, 77, 314
Lubke, Anetta, 235
Lubke, Arlin, 235
Lubke, Delois, 235
Lubke, Dorothy, 235
Lubke, Edward, 235
Lubke, Ernest, 234-235, 275
Lubke, Genevieve (Feipel), 235
Lubke, Helena, 235
Lubke, Henry F., 33-34, 58, 93, 97, 111, 228, 235, 303, 329, 337
Lubke, Hulda (Dahlem), 235
Lubke, John, 235
Lubke, Mary/Marie (Tress), 234-235, 275
Lubke, Odella, 103
Lubke, Oscar, 58, 108, 235
Lubke, Selma (Kopke), 128, 228, 235
Lubke, William, 235
Ludvig, Jeff, 332
Lueck, Leslie, 272
Lueck, Lila (Marzinske), 272
Lueck, Louis, 272
Lueck, Marie (Doss), 272
Luenebury, Fred, 51
Lumberg, Frederick, 53
Lumberg, Jessie (Ira), 297
Luther, Dr. Martin, 53
Lutheran Cemetery Association, 53
Luthultz, Anna (Kopke), 228
Luthultz, Charles, 228
Lynch Garage, 114
Lynch, Agnes, 237
Lynch, Alice, 87
Lynch, Allan, 237
Lynch, Ann (Dooley), 237
Lynch, Audrey (Goettl), 237
Lynch, Bernard Jr., 235
Lynch, Bernard Sr., 235
Lynch, Bill, 120
Lynch, Brian, iv, 34, 235
Lynch, Cecelia (Thissen), 123, 237, 239
Lynch, Clara (Bruels), 168
Lynch, Clements, 235
Lynch, Collette, 237
Lynch, Danielle, 235
Lynch, David Jr., 236-237, 351
Lynch, David Louise, 127, 131, 236-237
Lynch, Edward, 46
Lynch, Eileen, 236
Lynch, Ella (Lindeberg), 237
Lynch, Everett G., 128, 237
Lynch, Genevieve (Phillips), 235
Lynch, George, 132, 237, 239
Lynch, Grace (Biggins), 237
Lynch, Guy, 100, 235
Lynch, Harry, 295
Lynch, Heather, 237, 340
Lynch, Henry, 69, 235-236
Lynch, Ignatius, 235
Lynch, Irenus, 235-236
Lynch, James, 155, 185, 237, 252
Lynch, Jane (Bowe), 166, 235
Lynch, Jennie, 123
Lynch, Jerome (Jerry), 108, 115, 210, 237, 298, 326
Lynch, Joanne, 236
Lynch, Joseph, 235
Lynch, Karen (Tacheny), 235
Lynch, Katherine (Thissen), 235
Lynch, Kim, 235
Lynch, Lauretta (Schalow), 237
Lynch, Lawrence, 236
Lynch, Leo, 168
Lynch, Linda (Kruse), 235-237, 348
Lynch, Linus, 166, 235-236
Lynch, Lorraine, 236
Lynch, Louise Ignatius, 100, 236
Lynch, Marcus, 235
Lynch, Marilyn (Manthey), 237
Lynch, Mark, 237
Lynch, Mary (Fields), 235
Lynch, Matthew, 237
Lynch, Michael, 237
Lynch, Nicholas, 179, 236
Lynch, Nicole, 235
Lynch, P., 86
Lynch, Raymond, 235
Lynch, Robert, 235
Lynch, Rose (Ireland), 100, 236
Lynch, Rose E. (Bowe), 236
Lynch, Rosella, 235
Lynch, Sadie (Fields), 155, 185, 237, 252
Lynch, Sally, 237
Lynch, Sandra (Burt), 235
Lynch, Scott, 237
Lynch, Selma (Jongbloedt), 131, 236-237
Lynch, Shari (Hodapp), 235
Lynch, Shelly, 237
Lynch, Thomas, 237
Lynch, Todd, 237
Lynch, Viola, 236
Lynch, William, 235, 237, 241
Lyons, Ben, 220
Lyons, Vivian (Hunter-Stelter), 220
Lyra Township, 1, 73, 76
Lysdale, Vera, 144
Maass, Frank, 213
Maass, Marie (Holtz), 213
Macbeth, Albert, 238
Macbeth, Ann (Herniman), 238
Macbeth, Carrie, 238
Macbeth, Charles C., 237-238
Macbeth, Colin, 238
Macbeth, Dr. Jesse Lynn, 95, 97, 107, 237-238, 297, 303, 325
Macbeth, George, 237-238
Macbeth, James, 238
Macbeth, Kenneth, 237
Macbeth, Lol May (Pressnall), 237
Macbeth, Lyle, 237
Macbeth, Mary, 238
Macbeth, Matilda, 238
Macbeth, Nellie, 238
Macbeth, Sadie (Eaton), 238
Macbeth, Walter, 238
Macbeth, William, 238
Mace, Betty (Smith), 239
Mace, Brandon, 201, 239
Mace, Carl, 239, 271
Mace, Claud H., 238
Mace, Clements (Bud), 69, 121, 127-128, 132, 235, 238-239, 272
Mace, F.S., 75
Mace, Gary, 239-240, 271, 332, 336
Mace, Gerald, 131, 201, 238-239, 342
Mace, Isabelle (Todd), 138
Mace, Jacob, 238
Mace, Jay N., 238
Mace, Leona (Schalow), 112, 120, 166, 235, 238-240, 271-272, 336-337
Mace, Marvin, 238
Mace, Mary (Faltersack), 238
Mace, Mary (Gilronan), 238
Mace, Muriel Ruth (Froehlich), 68, 153, 200-202, 220, 239, 301-302, 342
Mace, Myron, 238
Mace, Nathan Jacob, 166, 201, 238-239, 339
Mace, S.J., 90
Mace, Shawn (Kawell), 201, 239
Mace, Tanner, 201, 239
Mace, Theresia (Bowe), 166, 201, 238
Mace, Willis, 238
Mace's Café, 131, 300, 302
MacKay, Jack, 179
Mackdanz, Mrs. A.H., 129
Mackdanz, Rev. A.H., 53, 302
Macomber, Andrew Hamlin, 240
Macomber, Clara Evelyn (Reedstrom), 123, 240
Macomber, Geneva Grace, 240
Macomber, George Reed, 34, 109, 124, 135, 177, 240, 316
Macomber, Norma Winfred (Macomber), 120, 240
Macomber, Reed, 179, 316
Madelia, MN, 11, 113
Madigan, Francis, 246
Madigan, Marion (Miller), 246
Madison Lake, MN, 88

Mahowald, Steve, 141
Main Street Auto Sales, 348
Majeres, Maynard, 232
Majeres, Patricia (Larson), 232
Maki, Carolyn (Penn), 259
Maki, David, 259
Maki, Jason, 259
Maki, John, 259
Malakowsky, Greg, 355
Malakowsky, Norm, 355
Mallon, Frank, 85
Maloney, Catherine, 166
Maloney, Cornelius, 68, 166
Maloney, Francis, 166, 209
Maloney, Gertrude, 166
Maloney, James, 46, 166, 209
Maloney, Julian (Cotter), 166, 209
Maloney, Lauretta, 254
Maloney, Marcella, 166
Maloney, Margaret (Bowe), 166, 209
Maloney, Mary, 46
Maloney, Neil, 69
Manaige, A. (Decorah), 241
Manaige, Andrew, 241, 296
Manaige, Archie, 241
Manaige, Charles, 241
Manaige, Charles, 46
Manaige, Ed, 296
Manaige, Edward, 85, 241
Manaige, Frank, 240
Manaige, Hattie (Stocker), 241
Manaige, Henry, 241, 296
Manaige, Josephine, 241, 296
Manaige, Louis, 240, 296
Manaige, Paul, 241, 296
Manaige, Peter, 17, 46, 241, 296
Manaige, Richard, 241, 293, 296
Manaige, Rose, 296
Manaige, William Lweis, 241
Manaige,Teressa, 241
Mankato & Wells Railroad, 76, 78
Mankato Canvas Company, 119
Mankato Citizens Telephone Company, 132
Mankato Free Press, 6, 8, 16, 65, 68, 81, 120, 123-125, 132, 245, 253, 259, 299, 303
Mankato House, 11
Mankato Journal, 113
Mankato Mineral Springs, 299
Mankato Mission, 53
Mankato Reality, 344
Mankato Record, 265
Mankato Review, 194
Mankato Saddle Club, 148
Mankato Semi-Weekly Record, 4
Mankato State University, 61
Mankato Weekly Record, 3
Mankato, MN 1-8, 10, 14, 17, 32-33, 45, 66, 74-78, 80, 83, 86, 92, 136
Manley, Hugh, 127
Mansfield, Charles, 17, 67, 73
Manthe, Arlene (Buecksler), 170-171
Manthei, Jane (Grams), 209
Manthei, Tim, 209
Manthey, C. Raymond, 237
Manthey, Doris (Braun), 237
Manthey, Herman, 282
Manthey, Maggie (Carpenter), 282
Mapleton Enterprise, 87
Mapleton, MN, 31, 76, 132
Margie's Beauty Shop, 348
Marquardt, Carl, 170
Marquardt, Clara (Buecksler), 170
Marquardt's Cowlectables, 330, 344
Marsh, Captain, 7
Martinez, Donna (Bollmann), 164
Martinez, Johnny, 164
Marzinske, Amanda (Schmidt), 241, 272
Marzinske, Carl, 53, 241
Marzinske, Charles, 241
Marzinske, Chester, 241
Marzinske, Della (Lade), 241
Marzinske, Edwin, 272
Marzinske, Elaine, 61
Marzinske, Evelyn (Dumdei), 272
Marzinske, Gert, 130
Marzinske, Goldie (Putsch), 241
Marzinske, Jerry, 241, 331-332
Marzinske, Jill, 241
Marzinske, Lawrence, 121
Marzinske, Marie (Klampe), 272
Marzinske, Marjorie (Knowles), 241
Marzinske, Mrs. Clifford, 129
Marzinske, Richard, 241
Marzinske, Robert, 241, 272
Marzinske, Ronald, 157, 341
Marzinske, Walter, 272
Marzinske, Wendy (Reed), 241
Marzinske, Wilhelmine (Krueger), 241
Marzinske, William, 241, 272
Masel, Barbara (Blank), 163
Masel, Walt, 163
Mason, Delhin, 243
Matawan, MN, 129
Matheson, Carlyle, 234
Matheson, Donna (Loge), 234
Matteson, Mrs. A.H., 101
Mauer, Dorothy (Schweim), 258
Maurer, Alvin, 258
Maxon, Barbara, 123, 179
Maxson, Linda (Witt), 289
Maxson, Richard, 289
May Bridge, 26
May, Aloysius, 242
May, Andrew, 242
May, Anna, 242
May, Catherine, 18, 168-169
May, Chester, 242
May, Colleen, 243
May, Edward, 18, 242, 287
May, Eugene, 18, 241-243
May, Frances (Wingen), 18, 242-243, 287
May, Francis, 242
May, Gene, 242-243
May, George, 18, 33, 90, 242-243
May, Jack, 18, 241, 242-243
May, Joseph, 18,168-169, 241-242, 355
May, Karl, 242
May, Katherine (Robel), 242
May, Katherine (Trout), 242
May, Kathleen, 243
May, Lisa (Keepers), 18, 241, 243
May, Marie, 242
May, Mary (Hodapp), 18, 242
May, Michelle, 243
May, Ottilia, 242
May, Patricia (Sexton), 18, 242-243
May, Phillip, 242
May, Stephen, 242
May, Thomas, 243
May, Viola (Ireland), 242
Maynard, Frank, 80
McCall, Betty, 68
McCarthy, Carrie (Brewer), 167
McCarthy, Charles, 83
McCarthy, Oscar, 167
McCarty, Georgina (Hilton), 217, 295
McCarty, Thomas, 217
McClellan, General George B., 74
McCollum Lake, 295
McCollum, Amanda, 243
McCollum, Arch, 295
McCollum, Bernard, 243
McCollum, Brendan, 243
McCollum, Caleb, 243
McCollum, Carol Jane (Hiller), 243
McCollum, Connie (Goettl), 243, 345
McCollum, Deborah (Riemann), 243
McCollum, Desiree, 243
McCollum, Dylane (Miller), 149, 211, 243
McCollum, Eric, 243
McCollum, Ginger, 243
McCollum, Jeff, 243, 267, 345
McCollum, Jesse, 243
McCollum, Joshua, 243
McCollum, Justin, 243
McCollum, Katelyn, 243
McCollum, Kristen, 243
McCollum, Lena (Widmen), 243
McCollum, LeRoy, 243
McCollum, Lester, 136, 243, 324

McCollum, Lidanne, 295
McCollum, Lloyd, 149, 243, 247
McCollum, Marlyn, 243
McCollum, Mike, 243
McCollum, Steve, 243
McCollum, Tammy, 243
McCollum, Tim, 243
McCollum, Tonia, 243
McCollum, Trenton, 243
McCollum, Victoria, 243
McComb Sisters, 244
McComb, Agnes (Frasier), 243, 263
McComb, Alvin, 244
McComb, Anna (Kroenke),103, 243-244
McComb, Claude, 104
McComb, Cora (Neller), 243
McComb, Elizabeth, 243
McComb, Frank, 243-244
McComb, George, 100, 243
McComb, Ida (Andrews), 243-244
McComb, Jeanne (Ellis), 245
McComb, John, 243, 263
McComb, Lincoln, 243
McComb, Mary, iii, 245, 263, 304
McComb, Mrs. Wm., 128
McComb, Roy, 103, 243-244
McComb, Samuel, 102, 243
McComb, William (Bill), 125, 244-245
McDuff, Curtis, 125
McGannon, James, 285
McGinn, Margaret (O'Connor), 254
McGinnis, Emma Dagen, 95
McGovern, Augusta (Wingen), 95, 286
McGovern, Chris, 295
McGovern, Frank, 295
McGovern, Jack, 295
McGovern, Jane, 295
McGovern, Jennie (Quinn), 263
McGovern, Jim, 295
McGovern, Kate, 295
McGovern, L.F., 86
McGovern, Lawrence (Larry), 295
McGovern, Mike, 295
McGovern, Peter, 295
McGovern, Sadie, 295
McGovern, Thomas, 18, 263
McGovern, Winford, 18
McIntosh, Isabel, 58
McKibben, Ralph, 164
McLaughlin, Alice (Carrigan), 245
McLaughlin, Dr. Raymond, 245
McLaughlin, Mark, 245
McLaughlin, Nova (Donovan), 245
McLaughlin, Thomas, 245
McMaster, Col, John, 124
McMillian, L.E., 106
McMullen, Francis, 275
McMullen, Viola (Schostag), 275
McNamara, Agnes (Collins), 191
McNamara, Robert, 191
McPherson Cemetery Association, 55
McPherson Farmers Insurance, 119
McPherson Farmers Mutual Fire Insurance Company, I, 69-70, 88, 97, 99, 106, 157, 341
McPherson Glee Club, 77
McPherson Mutual Fire Association, 83
McPherson Mutual Insurance Company, 87
McPherson Township Bridges, 18
McPherson Township Hall, 32, 86-87, 144, 337, 348
McPherson Township, 1, 3, 17, 27-29, 30, 54, 57, 73-76, 78-87, 90-93, 115-116, 140, 143, 351
McPherson, Gen. James B., 74, 245
McPherson/Union Cemetery, 55
McRobert & His Troupers, 119
McWhorter, Eliza (Quinn), 263
Meany, Donald, 121, 245, 316
Meany, Roy A., 129, 245-246, 316
Meany, Sarah (Bluhm), 128, 144, 245, 255, 336
Meany, Thomas, 177, 245, 317
Meany, William, 245
Medaris, Amalia (Kopke), 228
Medaris, Henry, 228
Medo Township, 1, 17, 79
Medo, 75, 93
Medo-McPherson Cemetery Association, 75
Memorial Park, 34, 331, 346
Meridan, MN, 4
Merrill, Mrs. Lewis (Wingen), 287
Merseth, Juel, 234
Merseth, Lynette (Loge), 234
Messenger, 32, 78
Mettler, Bill, 191
Mettler, Edith Ann (Fitzloff), 191
Mettler, Frank, 92
Metz, Christian, iii
Metzler, Judith (King), 226
Metzler, Marvin, 226, 273
Meurer, Emil, 330
Meyer, Adam, 273
Meyer, Anieta (Grams), 208, 273, 300
Meyer, Brad, 273
Meyer, F.A., 90
Meyer, Jessica, 273
Meyer, Joan (Schneider), 273
Meyer, Julie, 342
Meyer, Marsha, 144
Meyer, Marvin, 208
Meyer, Ruth (Grams), 208
Meyers, Adolph, 170
Meyers, Anieta (Grams), 300
Michelle's Wild Hair, 344
Michels, Helen (Sodeman), 277
Michels, Jerome, 277
Miely, A.B., 79, 246
Miely, Amanda, 246
Miely, Anne E. (Crabbe), 246
Miely, Fred L., 246
Miely, Louis, 246
Miely, Mabel L., 246
Miely, Ray B., 246
Miller, Alan, 331
Miller, Ann, 236
Miller, Anna (Woefel), 192, 236, 246, 289
Miller, Anne, 246
Miller, Arthur, 203, 246
Miller, Ben, 246-247
Miller, Bruce G., 151, 247
Miller, Corrine (Pickel), 247
Miller, D.P., 95
Miller, Daniel, 247
Miller, Douglas, 247, 332
Miller, Edward, 82, 192, 236, 246, 289
Miller, Ella (Glamm), 203, 246
Miller, Emm, ii
Miller, Ernest, 83, 99
Miller, Frank, 246
Miller, Fred, 203, 246
Miller, Gary, 214, 246-247
Miller, George, 34, 103, 137, 217, 246-247
Miller, Gertrude (Lynch), 236, 246
Miller, Greg, 246
Miller, Harry L., 32, 34, 53, 77, 80, 295
Miller, Helen, 236
Miller, James, 125
Miller, Janice, 246
Miller, Jason, 237
Miller, Jeff, 237
Miller, John, 246-247
Miller, Judy (Hemshrot), 203, 214, 246-247
Miller, Kate (Klebel), 246
Miller, Kelly (Stolt), 279, 342
Miller, Leo, 236
Miller, Margaret, 246
Miller, Mary (Lynch), 236-237
Miller, Mathilda (Block), 246
Miller, Nancy (Wilder), 247
Miller, O.P., 329
Miller, Patrick, 237
Miller, Rose, 236
Miller, Sam, 247
Miller, Sandra, 66
Miller, Scott, 279
Miller, Sharon (Huseman), 247
Miller, Sue (Manthe), 247
Miller, Todd, 279

Miller, Tony, 247
Miller, Val, 247
Miller, Viola (Schuldt), 276
Miller, Willard, 276
Miller, William, 246-247, 342
Miller's Livery, 115
Miller's Produce, 71, 300, 302
Milwaukee Railroad, 61
Milwaukee Road, 148
Minneapolis Tribune, 12, 151
Minnesota Central Railway, 78
Minnesota Elevator, Inc., 148, 351-352, 354
Minnesota Geographic Names, 1
Minnesota Historical Society, 1
Minnesota Lake, MN, 10, 14, 74-75, 120
Minnesota River, 7
Minnesota State Fair, 131
Minnesota State Register of Historic Places, 15
Minnesota Territory, 73
Minnesota Vikings, 153
Minnesota, A History of the State, 4
Minnesota, the Land of Sky-Tinted Waters, 181
Mission, 46
Mississippi River, 7
Missouri River, 7, 45
Mix, Major Charles H., 3, 9, 17, 73, 193
Moe, Agnes (Larsen), 247
Moe, Bridgette, 248
Moe, Cassie, 248
Moe, Darryl, 247-248
Moe, Dennis, 193, 247-248
Moe, Donald, 247
Moe, Emil, 247
Moe, Mayme (Burgess), 247
Moe, Susan (Kruckelberg), 248
Moe, Vernell (Oftedahl), 247
Moe, Vernon, 247
Moede, Carl, 55
Moede, Rev. John, 97
Mohn, Lowell, 281
Mohn, Pat (Walton-Denn), 148, 281
Mohr, Charles, 186
Mohr, Henry, 31, 341
Mohr, Lena (Gerber Fisher), 186
Mondale, Walter, 313
Monson, O.S., 54
Moore, Marcus, 4
More, Alicia (Dauk), 47, 249
More, Allison, 249
More, Alvis, 149, 156, 248
More, Andrew, 249
More, Brian, 248
More, Carol (Schull), 248, 302
More, Fay, 248
More, Helen (Burnell), 248
More, Jeffrey, 248
More, Jennifer, 248
More, Jessica, 248
More, Jodi, 248
More, Joshua, 248
More, Julie (Kietzer), 248
More, Justin, 248
More, Larry, 249
More, Lori (Rieser), 249
More, Marcus, 54
More, Marvin, 248
More, Matthew, 249
More, Melissa, 248
More, Noreen (Pfeffer), 248, 339
More, Steven, 248, 339, 351
Morrell, Frank, 92
Morrison, A.M., 113
Morrison, Mrs. A,M., 113
Morrisson, Mrs. Sterling (Hubmer), 218
Morrow, Arvellis (Brummound), 169
Morrow, William, 169
Morse Minneral Springs, 3
Morse, Daniel, 3
Morse, F.E., 114-115
Morse, Harriet, 144, 327
Mosher, Dawn, 243
Mosher, Dean, 243
Mosher, Debbie, 243
Mosher, Deloris, 243
Mosher, Joe, 324
Mosher, Lee, 351
Mountain, Bobby, 296
Mountain, Charlotte, 296
Mountain, Father Edward, 47
Mountain, Father Harold, 47
Mountain, Jean, 296
Mountain, Jim, 296
Mountain, Mrs. Edward, 241
Mountain, Sybil (Manaige), 296
Mueller, August, 94, 210, 283
Mueller, Ernest, 106
Mueller, Ernestine (Manthe), 210, 283
Mueller, Geneva (Mace), 201, 239
Mueller, Gretchen, 201, 239
Mueller, Heidi, 201, 239
Mueller, Henry, 51
Mueller, Joseph, 201, 239
Mueller, Pastor Reinhold J., 52
Mueller, Paul, 201, 239
Mueller, Rev. Paul, 54
Mullerleile, Shelby, 69
Municipal Liquor Store, 34
Murphy & Thielman, 84
Murphy, Agnes (O'Connor), 254
Murphy, Audrey (O'Brien), 252
Murphy, Cash, 115
Murphy, Ethel, 102
Murphy, Eulalia, 254
Murphy, Francis, 254
Murphy, John, 279, 296
Murphy, Margaret Jane (O'Connor), 254
Murphy, Richard, 252
Murphy, Stephen, 254
Myers, Bill, 104, 144, 288
Myers, Emma (Rick), 249
Myers, Irene (Snyder), 249
Myers, Ivadell, 129-130
Myers, Jay, 209
Myers, Laura (Grams), 209
Myers, Margaret (Kleeman), 104, 128, 130, 184, 219, 249-250
Myers, Wallace, 249
Myers, William, 219, 249-250, 300
Nahlovsky, Joanne (McComb), 245
Nahlovsky, Robert, 245
National Register of Historic Places, 8, 15
National Youth Organization (NYO), 59
Near, A.E., 97, 337
Neary, M. 86
Neary, Mary, 308
Neher, Mary (James), 168, 282
Neher, Rodney, 168, 282
Nelson, Dwight, 184
Nelson, Elias, 181
Nelson, Nancy (Drake), 184
Nelson, W.E., 58
Nenno, Leo, 69
Nesbit, Jim, 295-296
Nett, Kristin, 47
Netzke, Rev. Otto K., 112
New Ulm, MN, 6-7, 11
Newell, Don, 227
Newell, Lois (Klingbeil), 66,71,227
Nicolai Cabinetry, 355
Nicolai Masonry, 352
Nicolai, Abigail, 251
Nicolai, Albert Jr., 199
Nicolai, Arthur, 250
Nicolai, August Sr., 250
Nicolai, Clarence, 124, 250, 276
Nicolai, Delgene Louis, 246, 250
Nicolai, Edna Anna (Schuldt), 250, 276
Nicolai, Elmer, 250-251, 295
Nicolai, Emma (Heinze), 250
Nicolai, Everett, 251
Nicolai, Florentina, 250
Nicolai, Helen (Ward), 251
Nicolai, James, 251, 355
Nicolai, Joseph, 251
Nicolai, Katherine (Arnoldt), 251, 352
Nicolai, Kendall, 251
Nicolai, Louis, 103
Nicolai, Louise (Froehlich), 199
Nicolai, Ludwig, 250

Nicolai, Lyle C., 68, 250-251
Nicolai, Marshall, 251
Nicolai, Marvin, 251
Nicolai, Particia (Daubler), 251
Nicolai, Pauline (Krueger), 250
Nicolai, Ruth (Kiecker), 153, 251
Nicolai, Sherry (Kreft), 251, 355
Nicolai, Steven, 251
Nicolai, Thomas, 251, 352
Nicolai, Yun Yim, 251
Nicollet, MN, 51, 66
Nisbet, Mabel Juliar, 151
Nissan, Percy, 331
Nissen, Angie, 54, 157
Nissen, Jonas, 54, 157
Nixon, Lra, 296
Norm's Soft Water, 355
North Mankato, MN, 96
Northfield Bank, 101
Norton, Amy, 94
Norton, W.H., 75
Novotny, Dennis, 209
Novotny, Dorothy (Grams), 209
Nutting, Dr., 81-82, 297
Nutting, J.C., 32
Nutting, Mrs. J., 113
Nyhusmoen, Sandra (Brewer), 167
Nyhusmoen, Sydney, 167
Nyquist Addition, 34
Nyquist, Alma (Fields), 185
Nyquist, Dean, 139, 141-142, 144, 252, 280, 288, 321
Nyquist, Elmo, 107, 184-185, 249, 252-253, 259, 335
Nyquist, Emil, 226
Nyquist, Harry, 252
Nyquist, Marjorie (Timmerman), 179, 252, 280, 288, 321
Nyquist, Nona (Fields), 123, 184, 252, 298
Nyquist, Ruth (Lamont-Schwichtenberg), 68, 70, 220, 252, 276-277
Oachs, Gloria (Rosin), 288
Oachs, Roger, 288
O'Brien, Audrey, 293
O'Brien, Delmar, 272
O'Brien, Edna (Koch), 272
O'Brien, Elizabeth, 252
O'Brien, Elsa (Grams), 207
O'Brien, Elzada, 109
O'Brien, Everad, 114, 136, 138, 209, 252
O'Brien, Everett, 114, 209
O'Brien, John, 207
O'Brien, Kevin, 58, 108
O'Brien, Lucile (Conway), 252
O'Brien, Mrs. Walter, 123
O'Brien, Ragina (Fitzgerald-Sandick), 252-253
O'Brien, Walter, 58, 126, 197, 252, 265, 342
O'Connor Bridge, 20-22, 80
O'Connor, Arthur, 253-255, 296
O'Connor, Charles, 32, 77, 79-80, 86, 93, 95, 9, 107, 111, 253-255, 329, 337, 341
O'Connor, Cyril, 296
O'Connor, Edward, 254
O'Connor, Emma (Laflin), 254
O'Connor, Father T.A., 175, 325
O'Connor, Francis, 254-255
O'Connor, George, 254
O'Connor, James, 46
O'Connor, John, 46, 253, 309
O'Connor, Josie (Bushine), 296
O'Connor, Judge Chase, 58, 296
O'Connor, Margaret (McDermott), 254-255, 296
O'Connor, Martha (Tracey), 254
O'Connor, Mary Ann (Sheeran), 254
O'Connor, Maurice, 114, 296
O'Connor, Paschal J. (Pat), 252, 296
O'Connor, Patrick R., 46, 253-255
O'Connor, Rev., 100
O'Connor, Sharon, 341
O'Connor, Susan (Goodwin), 253-254
O'Connor, Thomas, 254
O'Connor, William E., 254-255
Oddy, Bonnie (Lynch), 236-237
Oftedahl, Alick, 90
Oftedahl, Bertina (Quam), 162-163
Oftedahl, Casper, 96
Oftedahl, Duane, 171
Oftedahl, Gerhard, 162-163
Oftedahl, Ovidia (Holm), 244
Oftedahl, Peter J., 244
Oftedahl, Ted, 119-120
Ogle, Isabel, 109
O'Herin, Dan, 141
O'Herin, Mrs. Dan, 298
Ojibwa Tribe, 1
O'Leary, Nora, 295
Olmsted, David, 1
Olsen, Alice (Brummound), 169
Olsen, Harold, 169
Olson, Allen, 332
Olson, Beverly (Blank), 163, 256
Olson, Cindy (Parkins), 245, 256
Olson, Donna (Sieberg), 256-257
Olson, Frederick J. (Fritz), 255-256
Olson, Howard, 163, 255
Olson, Jean, 255-256
Olson, Jerry, 62
Olson, Kelsey, 257
Olson, Mildred, 144, 255-256
Olson, Nick, 257
Olson, Orlando Jr. (Lenny), 256-257
Olson, Orlando, 256-257
Olson, Ruth (Bartsch), 256-257
Olson, Sievert, 144
Olson, Steve, 245, 255
Olson, Terese (Sontag), 257
Olson, Terry, 257
Omaha Reservation, 9
On Gerry's Table, 344
O'Neil, Rita (Lynch), 236-237
Order of the Iron Cross Lodge, 83
O'Rielly, John, 168
O'Rielly, Margaret (Bruels), 168
Ott, Jake, 100
Otto, Mrs. Fred, 112
Owens, Amos, 153-154
Page, Francis, 223
Page, Mary (Juliar), 223
Pagenkkopf, C.J., 85, 90, 195
Pagenkopf, Abbie (Thielman), 144, 257-258, 279, 319, 336
Pagenkopf, Albert, 84
Pagenkopf, Belle (Wingen), 257, 287
Pagenkopf, Carl, 51, 257, 311
Pagenkopf, Charles J., 84, 86, 97, 100, 257, 296, 311-312, 319, 337
Pagenkopf, Earl W., 34, 101, 107, 126, 177, 257-258, 279, 311, 319, 335
Pagenkopf, Lillian (Rusch), 257
Pagenkopf, Lowell, 68, 179, 200, 231, 258, 293, 304, 317-321
Pagenkopf, Lucile (Dooley), 58, 108
Pagenkopf, Margaret Joan (Froehlich), 130, 164, 200, 258, 318-321
Pagenkopf, Mary (Krueger), 257, 319
Pagenkopf, Sophia, 120, 257, 311
Pagenkopf, Walter C., 94, 257, 287, 311
Pagenkopf's General Store/Peg's Grocery, 33, 84, 100, 117-118, 136, 257-258, 300, 302, 311, 318-321, 327, 331
Painter, Dobie, 336
Palmer Bus Service, 258, 347
Palmer, Amber, 258
Palmer, Floyd, 258-259, 332, 347
Palmer, Ida (Ringling), 103
Palmer, Leah, 258
Palmer, Lois (Schweim), 258, 347
Panzram, George, 327
Panzram, Patricia (Antonson), 297, 327-328
Parker, Audrey, 182
Parker, Don, 182
Passer, James, 257
Passer, Judy (Olson), 257
Payer, Alexander, 17
Payr, Symion, 296

Pederson, Curtis, 68
Peik, Gladys, 120
Pemberton Lumber Company, 332
Pemberton, MN, 66, 96, 129
Pemble, Ardella Lynn (Glaser), 205-206
Pemble, Phil, 205
Penn, Alvina (Boettcher), 128
Penn, Bess (Ellison), 259
Penn, Dr. George, 106, 205, 259
Penn, Emily, 259
Penn, Gottleib, 259
Penn, Herman, 259
Penn, Ida (Godeman), 144, 255, 259, 336
Penn, John (Jack), 259
Penn, Karl Fredirk Wilhelm (William), 259
Penn, Lindsey, 259
Penn, LuVern (Steinke), 259
Penn, Marie (Frank), 259
Penn, Mary, 259
Penn, Nancy, 259
Penn, Theodore G., 101, 110, 144, 255, 259, 335
Penn, Wihlemina (Ruda), 259
Penn, William, 259
Pepper, Tom, 332
Perch Lake, 302
Pestka, Agnes, 287
Pestka, Catherine, 109
Pestka, Joseph, 100
Pestka, Marcella, 100, 109
Pestka, Marie, 308
Pestka, Matt, 100
Pestka, Matthias, 287
Peters, Michael, 295
Peterson & Perry Meat Market, 80
Peterson, Art, 185
Peterson, Carl, 136
Peterson, Edward, 196
Peterson, Ethel (Foster), 196
Peterson, Gwen, 150
Peterson, Sylvia (Fisher), 109, 185
Petit, Alice, 254
Pettit, Jennie (O'Connor), 254
Pettit, Joe, 254
Pettit, Lurene, 254
Pfaff & Hilton Mill, 77
Pfaff, Peter, 31
Pfarr, Robert, 136
Phelps, Amy, 260
Phelps, Asa, 260
Phelps, Bill, 209
Phelps, Byron, 260
Phelps, Charlotte, 260
Phelps, Claud, 260
Phelps, Daniel, 260
Phelps, Emily, 259
Phelps, Ephraim, 259-260
Phelps, Erica, 259
Phelps, Francis, 260
Phelps, Glenn, 260
Phelps, Hannah (Alexander), 161
Phelps, Hollie, 260
Phelps, Holly Marie, 161
Phelps, Jane (Candee), 259
Phelps, John, 260
Phelps, Lige, 296
Phelps, Louisa, 260
Phelps, Luella, 260
Phelps, Maria (Alexander), 260
Phelps, Mary, 259
Phelps, Myron, 260
Phelps, Oddo, 161, 259
Phelps, Ruth, 260
Phelps, Sallie (Spike), 259
Phelps, Sara (Grams), 209
Phelps, Silas, 259-260
Phillips, Anna, 18, 260
Phillips, Anthony, 260
Phillips, Anton, 18
Phillips, Arlene, 141
Phillips, Brenda Lee (Phillips), 155, 260
Phillips, Carol, 66
Phillips, Clete, 141
Phillips, Elise (Gerlach), 260
Phillips, Elsie (Hager), 127, 220, 260
Phillips, Eugene, 68, 151, 260, 342
Phillips, Geo, 85
Phillips, Harold, 141
Phillips, Harry, 18, 103, 235, 260
Phillips, Henry, 141, 178
Phillips, Jerry, 61-62, 156, 331
Phillips, Joanne (O'Herin), 107, 260
Phillips, Lucille (Hodapp), 18, 235, 260
Phillips, Mable, 281
Phillips, Mary (Wingen), 260, 286
Phillips, Nicholas, 260
Phillips, Nick, 141, 281
Phillips, Norman H., 260-261, 295
Phillips, Paul (Pete), 111, 260
Phillips, Ruth, 141
Phillips, Sandra Lee (Nolan), 260
Phillips, Tim, 260
Phillips, Todd, 260
Phillips, Vera, 18, 141
Pickel, Bergene (Oftedahl), 247
Pickel, Henry C., 247
Pickie, Carl, 107
Pierce, Donna, 58
Pierce, Glenn, 58
Pierce, LuJune, 58
Pietsch, Leslie, 141
Pietsch, Rose, 141
Pint Garage, 136, 261, 300, 324, 327
Pint, Edna (Appel), 261
Pint, Jack, 115, 132, 177, 260, 288
Pischner, Anna Marie, 69
Pitcher, L.O., 194
Pitcher, Miranda (Woodruff), 261
Pitcher, Orrin, 193-194, 261, 264
Pohl, Clarence, 69
Point, Delbert, 332
Polchow, Anna (Schroeder), 275
Polinska Clara (Schwanke), 276
Polinska, Paul, 276
Pomeroy, 5
Pope, Gen., 4
Porter, John J., 5
Porter, Mrs. E.D.B., 8
Possin, Bertha (Schendel), 289
Possin, Toot, 289
Powaser, Christine (Bruels), 169
Prahl, Nancy (Danberry), 182
Prahl, Rick, 182
Prail, Lester, 106
Pray, Quinton, 216
Precht, Fred, 95, 106, 111
Precht, Viola, 111
Preis, Eldon, 248
Prescher, Ernestine (Pockrandt), 261
Prescher, Julie, 261
Prescher, Julius, 261
Prescher, Lisa, 261
Prescher, Lorrie (Neubert), 261
Prescher, Robert, 261, 332
Prescht, Anna, 103
Pressnall, Alexander, 237
Preston, Alicia, 262
Preston, Arthur, 262
Preston, Asahel Brewster, 17-18, 75, 261-262, 341
Preston, Carrie (Stroebel), 262
Preston, Chester Asahel, 262, 298
Preston, Clark Howard, 18, 262, 335
Preston, Dale, 262
Preston, Daniel, 262
Preston, Delmar, 18, 262, 336
Preston, Deloris, 157, 261
Preston, Derward, 262
Preston, Dorothy (DeRemer), 262
Preston, Earl, 262
Preston, Eleanore (Albrecht), 262
Preston, Elizabeth, 261
Preston, Gary, 262
Preston, George, 261
Preston, Gerald, 127, 262
Preston, Glenn, 262
Preston, Grace Elizabeth, 262
Preston, Guy, 262
Preston, Hannah (Jarman), 261-262
Preston, Harold Mark, 171, 262
Preston, Hazel (Danner), 262
Preston, Howard, 261-262

Preston, Jacob, 262
Preston, James. 262
Preston, Janet, 262
Preston, Joan (Danberry), 15, 182, 262
Preston, Joel, 262
Preston, John Jr., 262
Preston, John Sidney Sr., 127, 261, 353-354
Preston, LaVerne, 262
Preston, Leslie, 262
Preston, Lila Mae, 262
Preston, Lillie (Frey), 18, 262
Preston, Marvin, 10-11, 13, 16, 258, 262
Preston, Mary (Fox), 262
Preston, Mary (McCarthy), 262
Preston, Mary, 261
Preston, Nora (Albrecht), 262
Preston, Norma, 18
Preston, Peter, 182, 262
Preston, Phyllis, (Jongbloedt), 262
Preston, Ralph George, 10, 15, 262
Preston, Robert, 262
Preston, Rosella (McMahan), 262
Preston, Samuel Merritt, 261-262
Preston, Scott, 262
Preston, Sharon, 262
Preston, Susie (St. John), 262
Preston, Tillie (Buck), 262
Preston, Verna (Buecksler), 170, 262
Preston, William, 262
Price, Dean, 224
Price, Louisa, 80
Price, Mabel (Juliar), 224
Priem, Albert, 208
Priem, Anna (Grams), 208
Priem, Ella (Timmerman), 280
Priem, George, 185
Priem, Louis, 280
Priem, Nellie, 185
Priem, Sarah, 242
Pritchard, Neuton, 226
Proechel, Bonnie (Witt), 289
Proechel, Merlyn, 289
Proechel, Waldemar, 52
Proechl, Ernest, 108
Ptitchard, Edith (Klingbeil), 226
Puckett, Kirby
Purde, Felix, 296
Purdy, Addie L., 263
Purdy, Dana L., 263
Purdy, Daniel, 262-263
Purdy, E. (Owen), 263
Purdy, Walter L., 263
Purdy, Winfred L., 263
Quade, Henry, 129
Quinlan, John, 11
Quinn Oil Company, 118, 263
Quinn, Andy M., 32, 82, 98, 118, 243, 270, 295, 303-304, 337
Quinn, Hannah, 263
Quinn, James, 263
Quinn, Kathryn Kate (McComb), 82, 123, 243, 263, 303-307
Quinn, Krystal, 16
Quinn, Sarah (Annis), 263
Ragsdale, Godfrey, 264
Ragsdale, William, 263-264
Railroad Street, 37
Ramsden, J.L., 124
Ramsden, Marvin Lee, 124
Ramsden, Naomi, 224
Ramsden, William, 224
Ramsey, Justus C., 5
Rapidan Township, 1, 73
Rapidan, MN, 108, 355
Rasdall, Abel, 194, 261, 264-265
Rasdall, Alice J. (Hilton), 216, 266
Rasdall, Alice Jane (Faley), 264-266
Rasdall, Charles, 264-265
Rasdall, Duane Franklin, 10, 14, 78, 82, 89-90, 193-195, 261, 264-265, 293-294
Rasdall, Elizabeth (Wright), 264
Rasdall, Frank, 265
Rasdall, Grant Arthur, 264-266
Rasdall, Hubert or Hobart, 193, 261, 264
Rasdall, Jane, 10, 14
Rasdall, Jean (Fisher Hutchinson), 266
Rasdall, Jessie, 82
Rasdall, Lee Sumner, 264-266
Rasdall, Lydia Ann (Pitcher), 261, 264-265
Rasdall, Mark, 265
Rasdall, Mel G., 32, 341
Rasdall, Melvin B, 32, 76, 83, 113, 193-194, 216, 261, 264-265, 295-296
Rasdall, Robert, 263-264
Rasmussen, Dean V., 266-267, 355
Rathman, Alma (Koentop-Schmitt), 227-228
Rathman, Ben, 228
Ravoux, Msgr. Augustine, 45
Ray, C. Wilbur, 32
Ray, Dr., 83, 297
Red Ribbon Club, 78
Redner, A.L., 75
Redwood Agency, 7
Redwood County, 10
Redwood Ferry, 7
Redwood, MN, 7
Reed, Augusta (Marzinske), 241
Reed, Joseph, 241
Reedstrom, Charles, 240
Reedstrom, Eva (Nelson), 240
Reedstrom, Frank, 288
Reedstrom, Lydia (Kriel), 288
Reich, Bradley, 282
Reich, Caleb, 282
Reich, Colleen (Ward), 282
Reich, Joshua, 282
Reich, Kaden, 282
Reichard, Andy, 278
Reichard, Robin, 278
Reichel, Cecelia (Miller), 246
Reichel, Cel, 103
Reichel, Josie (Kelly), 296
Reichel, Raymond, 246
Remington, Eldon, 182
Remington, Lila (Goodrich), 182
Rice Lake, 12, 17, 65, 67, 73, 103, 129
Rice, Frank, 82
Rice, H., 1
Richards, Father Herman, 46, 86
Riese, Andy, 58
Riese, August, 272
Riese, Bob, 134
Riese, Carl, 228
Riese, Donna, 179
Riese, James, 68, 72, 134, 136, 152, 155, 157, 341
Ringling Brothers & Barnum & Bailey Circus, 78, 85-87, 99, 221-222
Ringling, Al, 221
Ringling, Henry, 103
Ringling, Salome (Juliar), 221
Ripplinger Hardware, 156
Ripplinger, JoAnn, 267
Ripplinger, Leo, 243, 267, 332
Ristow, Pastor LeRoy, 53
Ritter, John P., 270
Ritter, Mary C. (Horvat), 270
Roalson, Andrew, 201, 239
Roalson, Bonnie (Mace), 201, 239
Roalson, James, 201, 238
Roalson, Ronald, 201, 239
Roberts, Bruce Dean, 191
Roberts, Colleen Rae (Fitzloff), 188, 191-192
Roberts, Dean, 191
Roberts, Julie Ann, 191
Robertson, Robert, 233
Robertson, Viola (Hurst), 233
Rodgers, Charles, 82, 84
Roemer, Adeline, 100
Roemhildt, Hugo, 274
Roemhildt, Mabel (Schostag), 274
Roerig, Emma (Sodeman), 277, 295
Roerig, John, 104
Roerig, Peter, 277
Roessler, Andrea (Froehlich), 202
Roessler, Curtis, 202
Rogers, Blanche, 294

Rogers, Charlie, 295-4
Rogers, Hazel, 294
Rohrer Drug Store, 268, 300, 341
Rohrer, Chris, 268
Rohrer, Marvin E., 118-119, 268-269, 300, 330, 341
Rollings, James (Fred), 205-206
Rollings, Lucas, 206
Rollings, Melinda Sue (Glaser), 205-206
Romnes, John, 354
Ron's Welding, 352
Rose, Ardys (Stoltzman), 215, 269
Rose, Carl, 34, 124, 146, 169, 177, 225, 269, 300
Rose, Dale, 269
Rose, Dean, 215, 269
Rose, Dorothy (Hanson), 269
Rose, Elizabeth (Jaeger), 269
Rose, Florence (Bruels), 169, 269
Rose, Frederick, 269
Rose, Gary, 269
Rose, Gerald, 215, 269
Rose, Janice (Pufahl), 269
Rose, Judy (Spiess), 269
Rose, Megan, 215
Rose, Patrick, 269
Rose, Ron, 168, 282
Rose, Rosemary (Galston-Fredrick-Bohnert), 168, 282
Rose, Tayton, 215
Rose, Terrance, 269
Rose, Vicki (Hesse), 215, 269
Rose's Meat Market, 139, 300, 302, 326
Rosin, Elmer, 284
Rosin, Mavis (Westphal), 284
Ross, Majorie J., 171
Routh, Bart, 278
Routh, Rochell, 278
Rowell, Charlie, 296
Rowell, George, 296
Rowell, Lillian, 296
Rowell, Mae, 295-296
Rowell, Mary Olive, 269
Rowell, Nell, 296
Ruethenbeck, Walter, 123
Russell, Annie (Nesbit), 269
Russell, Charles, 68, 269, 295
Russell, Darla, 269
Russell, Father James, 47
Russell, Hugh, 59, 109, 123, 126, 240, 269, 295, 330, 332
Russell, Lloyd, 335
Russell, Mae (Westmack), 269
Russell, Sandra, 269
Russell, Steve, 269
Rutt, Dorothy (Grams), 208
Rutt, Eddie, 208
Ryan, Dora, 295
Ryan, Father E.M., 46
Ryan, Jim, 295-296
Ryan, Sarah (Quinn), 295
Ryan, Thomas, 82
S.P. Morrison & Co., 79
Sack, Adolph, 204
Sader, Brian, 269-270, 332, 352
Sader, Jerry, 61-62
Sader, Mary, 269-270, 352
Sahli, Mary Lou (O'Brien), 252
Sahli, Robert, 252
Sanborn, Bernice, 304
Sanborn, Duane, 68
Sanborn, John P. (Jack), 69, 126, 144, 177, 317-318, 332, 335
Sanborn, Mrs. John, 144, 336
Sanborn, Phyllis, 120
Sanborn, Warren, 121
Sandberg, Lloyd, 66
Sandick, Robert, 253
Sandick, Ronald, 253
Sandick, Terrance, 253
Sandon, William, 69
Sargent, Amanda Rae, 270
Sargent, Angela Lynn, 270
Sargent, Calvin James, 270
Sargent, Cassidy Marie, 270
Sargent, Catherine (Anderson), 47, 270
Sargent, Dale, 118, 258, 270, 332
Sargent, Douglas Scott, 270
Sargent, Eleanore (Schumacker), 270
Sargent, Frances L. (Ritter), 118, 270, 332
Sargent, JoAnn (Frissel), 270
Sargent, Jonathan, 270
Sargent, Julie (Amundson), 270
Sargent, Kevin John, 270
Sargent, Mary (Reichwald), 270
Sargent, Patrick Jacob, 270
Sargent, Robert John, 270
Sargent, Terry, 270
Sauer, Arnold, 229
Saulpaugh Hotel, 117
Saunders, Ray, 179
Savick, Ardyth (Pogatchnik), 150, 270
Savik, Richard, 270, 327
Scampoli, James Jr., 251
Scampoli, James, 251
Scampoli, Jonathan, 251
Scampoli, Laura (Nicolai), 251
Schaaf, Father, 46
Schalow Apartments, 34, 347
Schalow Bridge, 26
Schalow, Ben, 271
Schalow, Carl B. (Charlie), 98, 104, 112, 124, 141, 270-272, 286
Schalow, Charles, 272
Schalow, Duane, 131, 271-272
Schalow, Emilie (Hoppe), 270
Schalow, Emma, 270
Schalow, Evelyn, 103
Schalow, Georgia, 272
Schalow, Heinrich (Henry), 88, 98, 102, 104, 158, 239, 288
Schalow, Henry Jr. (Hank), 271
Schalow, Ida (Voight), 110, 270-272, 286
Schalow, Julie, 272
Schalow, Leona (Buhr), 272
Schalow, Leonard, 272
Schalow, Malizabeth (Harris), 270
Schalow, Paul, 270-271
Schalow, Sadie, 271
Schalow, Sharon, 272
Schelbach, Prof., 83
Schenk, Alvin, 52
Schenk, David, 252, 280
Schenk, Mary Lee (Nyquist), 252, 280, 321-332
Scherer, Arthur, 182
Scherger, Rowena (Goodrich), 182
Schimmel, Naomi, 273
Schimmel, William, 273
Schmahl, Delma (O'Brien), 157
Schmahl, Julius, 96
Schmidt, August, 272
Schmidt, Augusta (Veigel), 272
Schmidt, Benjamin, 273
Schmidt, Carl, 272
Schmidt, Caroline (Ratloff), 273
Schmidt, Clifford, 273
Schmidt, Daniel Jr., 273
Schmidt, Elizabeth (Schimmel), 273
Schmidt, Ellen, 58
Schmidt, Emily, 273
Schmidt, Emma, 272
Schmidt, Ernest, 273
Schmidt, Esther, 272
Schmidt, Frank, 273
Schmidt, Fred, 74
Schmidt, Genevieve, 272
Schmidt, Grace, 273
Schmidt, Harry, 273
Schmidt, Henry William, 273
Schmidt, Ida Frieda, 272
Schmidt, Irene, 272
Schmidt, Jacob, 273
Schmidt, John, 272
Schmidt, Leo, 273
Schmidt, Lester, 272
Schmidt, Lydia, 272
Schmidt, Margaret, 123
Schmidt, Martha, 58
Schmidt, Mary (Lambrecht), 273
Schmidt, Mary Lou, 273
Schmidt, Mildred (Zechek), 272-273

Schmidt, Milton, 273
Schmidt, Monica (Grams), 209
Schmidt, Oscar, 272
Schmidt, Otto, 101, 273
Schmidt, Pastor Daniel, 53, 273
Schmidt, Robert, 331
Schmidt, Rose, 273
Schmidt, Roy, 273, 335
Schmidt, Syvella, 272
Schmidt, Terry, 209
Schmidt, Viola, 114
Schmidt, Virginia, 273
Schmidt, Wilhelmina (Hiller), 272
Schmidt, William, 273, 335
Schmitt, Peter, 228
Schnackenberg, Dorothy (Rohrer), 269, 327
Schneider, Clifford, 47, 273
Schneider, Dan, 273
Schneider, Ed, 273
Schneider, Justine, 273
Schneider, Monica, 273
Schneider, Pam (Howe), 273
Schneider, Tami (Heller), 273
Schneiderhan, John, 287
Schneiderhan, Laura (Wingen), 287
Schnitzler, Father, 46
Schoffman, Sophia (Wingen), 287
Schoffman, Toot, 123
Scholljergerdes, Robert, 197
Schonrock, Erna (Wingen), 287
Schonrock, Herman, 229
Schonrock, Ida (Nitschke), 229
Schonrock, Janice, 229
Schonrock, Lita (Kopke), 229
Schonrock, Marlys, 229
Schonrock, Merlin, 229
School District #70, 51, 53
School District #75, 59-64, 69, 154
School, 33, 56-64, 73, 103, 107
Schostag Hotel & Bar, 120, 295, 327
Schostag Mill, 74-75
Schostag, Albert, 274-275
Schostag, Alfred, 275
Schostag, Alvina, 274
Schostag, Anna (Klingbeil), 120, 123, 226, 274-275, 300, 324, 330
Schostag, Carl (Charlie), 202, 273-275
Schostag, Charles, 92, 95, 274
Schostag, Christian, 273
Schostag, Clara (Struz), 274
Schostag, Dorothy (Lubke), 274-275
Schostag, Eda (Frank), 196
Schostag, Ellen (Anderson), 275
Schostag, Everett, 274
Schostag, Fred, 92, 164, 196, 296
Schostag, Fredericka, (Gerber), 202, 274-275
Schostag, George, 92, 274
Schostag, Glen, 258
Schostag, Goldie (Foster), 196
Schostag, Gotfried, 74
Schostag, Gottlieb, 92
Schostag, Gus, 126, 295
Schostag, Helen, 120, 274
Schostag, Ida (Frank), 164
Schostag, Ida (Gensmer), 274
Schostag, John, 196
Schostag, Juliane (Kindler), 273
Schostag, Julie, 75
Schostag, Lucy (Kastner), 275
Schostag, Merle, 274
Schostag, Mrs. Gus, 123
Schostag, Myrtle, 274
Schostag, Robert, 120, 177, 196, 226, 274-275, 300-301, 324-325, 330
Schostag, Theodore, 274
Schostag, Vera, 103, 114
Schostag, Walter, 325
Schostag, Winnefried Fay (Foster), 196, 274-275
Schrader, Julie, 18, 34, 273
Schroeder Mercantile Store, 106
Schroeder, Albert, 275
Schroeder, Alfred, 275
Schroeder, August F., 203, 228, 275-276
Schroeder, Beulah, 109
Schroeder, Bill, 121, 240
Schroeder, Buddy, 179
Schroeder, Caroline (Franz), 197, 203, 275
Schroeder, Charles, 275, 296
Schroeder, Daisy, 114
Schroeder, Dean, 317
Schroeder, Ernestine (Bocholtz), 275
Schroeder, Esther, 107, 204
Schroeder, Florentine, 275
Schroeder, Frank, 210, 275
Schroeder, Johanna, 228
Schroeder, Kelly, 344
Schroeder, Kevin, 332
Schroeder, Lizzie, 296
Schroeder, Louisa, 275
Schroeder, Mary (Matthies), 210, 275
Schroeder, Minnie, 275
Schroeder, Ole, 302
Schroeder, Otto, 204
Schroeder, Robert, 275
Schroeder, William, 275, 296
Schroeder's Grocery Store, 117
Schuab, James, 32
Schuab, Randy, 332
Schubbe, Elwin, 209
Schubbe, Marvin, 144
Schubbe, Melinda (Benz), 209
Schuenemann, Paul, 100
Schuldt, Helene (Beckmann), 123,163, 250, 276, 336
Schuldt, Jacob, 163, 250, 276
Schuldt, Walter, 121, 276
Schull, Edna (Fesselt), 248, 302
Schull, Richard, 248, 302
Schultz, Amelia (Splinter), 276
Schultz, Ervin, 104
Schultz, Fred A., 276, 310
Schultz, Frederick C., 33, 90, 276
Schultz, Fredrich, 55, 108
Schultz, Otto, 53
Schultz, R., 101
Schultz, Roy, 69, 121, 223
Schultz, Velma (Juliar), 223
Schultz, Walter, 223
Schulz, Bradley, 339
Schulz, Frederick, 287
Schulz, Minnie (Kurth), 287
Schwandt, Maynard, 62
Schwanke, Aaron, 177, 276
Schwanke, Gustof, 276
Schwanke, Hank, 177
Schwanke, Ruth (Gomsrud), 276
Schwartz, Brian, 257
Schwartz, Diane (Olson), 257
Schwartz, Greg, 257
Schwartz, Jen, 257
Schwartz, Jerry, 257
Schwartz, McKayla, 257
Schwartz, Mrs. Harold, 107
Schwartz, Trevor, 257
Schweim, Andrew, 251
Schweim, Chelsea, 251
Schweim, Debbie (Phillips), 260
Schweim, Elizabeth (Nicolai), 251
Schweim, Jeff, 260
Schweim, Mallory, 251
Schweim, Myron, 251, 339
Schweim, Ryan, 251
Schweitzer, Charles, 341
Schwichtenberg, Dennis, 277
Schwichtenberg, Donovan, 68, 138, 277
Schwichtenberg, Jeanne (Wrightson), 277
Schwichtenberg, Leon, 277
Schwichtenberg, Marlene (Pawlicki), 277
Schwichtenberg, Myrna (Rixman), 276
Schwichtenberg, Paul, 68, 252, 255, 276-277
Schwitchenberg, Carl, 114
Scott, Collin, iv
Scott, Edward James, 165
Scott, Margaret, 99
Seaman, F.W., 329
Seepaniak, Father Russell, 47
Seewald, H.E., 185, 252

Seewald, Maxine, 120
Seewald, May (Fields), 185, 252
Seven Ways, 344
Severson, Harold, 120, 222
Seys, Chris, 285
Seys, Colleen (Preston), 285
Seys, Donna, 285
Seys, George Jr., 285
Seys, George, 285
Seys, Henry, 230, 335
Seys, James, 269
Seys, Janice (Thurn), 152, 155, 291
Seys, Jeffrey, 189
Seys, Jerome, 291
Seys, John, 285
Seys, Kathy, iv, 34
Seys, Kay, 285
Seys, Kim (Baumgartner), 285
Seys, Kimberly (Rose), 269
Seys, Oscar, 128
Seys, Roxanne (Fitzloff-Loeffler), 189
Seys, Steve, 278
Shaver, Allene, 135
Shaver, Craig, 135
Shaver, Emma, 135
Shaver, Gary, 135
Shaver, Kevin, 135
Shaver, Victor, 59, 135
Shaw, Kathleen (Grams), 209
Shaw, Randy, 209
Shea, Helen, 46
Sherman, 75
Shirley, John, 68
Sibley County, 11
Sibley Park Zoo, 120
Sibley Park, 7, 296
Sibley, General Henry H., 4, 7, 176
Sieberg, Matt, 47
Siebert, Mrs. William, 228
Sigg, Father, 46
Silkey, Fred, 210
Silkey, Ludwig, 283
Silkey, Ottilie (Santo), 283
Simpson, Darlene (Preston), 262
Sioux Tribe, 1, 5-8, 10-12, 67
Sioux Uprising, 3-5, 9, 11, 74
Sjostrom, Cora (Juliar-Schultz), 222-223
Sjostrom, Herbert, 223
Small, W.F., 58
Smelling, Erv, 232
Smelling, Stella (Lang), 232
Smestad, Deloris (Stine), 277
Smestad, Esther, 277
Smestad, Jacob D., 277
Smestad, Leonard, 277
Smestad, Stephen, 277
Smestad, Zachary S., 277
Smith, Austen, 167
Smith, Charlie, 107
Smith, Dr. W.S., 32, 83, 86-87, 297
Smith, Elizabeth, 46
Smith, Esther, 167
Smith, Gordon, 68
Smith, Mrs. William, 263
Smith, Rev. Robert, 78
Smith, Roy, 103
Smith's Mill, 53, 92, 113
Smyth, Bert, 185
Smyth, Delores (Fisher), 185
Snow, Jim, 355
Sodeman, Abbie (Gleason), 277
Sodeman, Anna (Andrews), 277, 304
Sodeman, Christian, 80-81, 202, 227, 277
Sodeman, Dennis, 278
Sodeman, Elizabeth (Strobel), 277
Sodeman, Elmer, 103, 277-278
Sodeman, Frank, 204. 277-278, 295
Sodeman, Henry, 103, 277
Sodeman, Ida (Glaser), 204, 277-278
Sodeman, Karl, 204, 277
Sodeman, Margaret (Bradley), 277
Sodeman, Marie (Gerber), 227, 277
Sodeman, Mary, 202
Sodeman, Robert, 104, 277, 295, 335
Sodeman, Verna (Hohenstein), 202, 228, 276-277
Sohre, Arthur, 217
Sohre, Martha, 217
Sommereisen, Father, 46, 74
Sonday, Daniel, 201, 239
Sonday, David, 201, 239
Sonday, Geraldine (Mace), 201, 239
Sonday, Jennifer, 201, 239
Sonday, Jeremy, 201, 239
Songe, Chris, 291
Songe, Tracy (Zabel), 291
Sonnek, Scott, 63
Sorenson, Peder, 201
Sour, Dr., 87
Southern Valley/Crystal Valley Fertilizer Plant, 157
Spear, Betty (Drager), 278
Spear, Cathy (Depuydt), 61-62, 278
Spear, Clara (Guenther), 278
Spear, Clifford, 278
Spear, Jordan, 251
Spear, Julie (Nicolai), 251, 278
Spear, Nicole, 251
Spear, Randy, 251, 278
Spear, Rick, 278
Spear, William J., 278
Speck, Herman, 282
Speck, Juanita Jane (Ward-Brunz), 282
Splinter, Agnes, (Kortuem), 278
Splinter, Barbara, 278
Splinter, Dennis, 278
Splinter, Frank, 278
Splinter, John, 278
Splinter, Katherine (Pollei), 278
Splinter, Lorraine, 278
Splinter, Lyle, 45, 68, 69, 115, 146, 278, 288, 337
Splinter, Raymond, 278
Splinter's Garage, 147-148, 152
Sprague, Lisa Ann (Mettler), 191
SS Peter & Paul's Catholic Church, 46
St. Clair American Legion Hall, 144, 155
St. Clair American Legion Post #475 Auxiliary, 130, 144, 336
St. Clair Area Actioneers, 34, 331
St. Clair Area Jaycees, 331
St. Clair Area Women of Today, 340
St. Clair Athletic Backers, 61, 149, 339
St. Clair Bellview Telephone Company, 32, 88
St. Clair Catholic Church, 46
St. Clair Centennial, 65-72
St. Clair City Hall & Fire Department, *iv*, 34, 88
St. Clair City Park, 61
St. Clair Commercial Club, 68, 99, 123, 136, 325, 329-330
St. Clair Creamery, 33, 82, 88, 90, 111, 117, 141, 151
St. Clair Dance Pavillion, 117
St. Clair Days, 34, 339-340
St. Clair Elevator, 156
St. Clair Feed Mill, 71
St. Clair Garage, 111
St. Clair Grams-Schmidt American Legion Post 475, 68, 126, 130-131, 144, 153, 335
St. Clair High School, 58, 109, 120-121, 129-130, 133, 141, 149, 153, 155, 358
St. Clair Hotel & Cafe, 119, 126, 326, 330
St. Clair Ice Company, 103
St. Clair Lumber Yard, 332
St. Clair Main Street, 30, 32-33, 35-40, 42-43, 102, 108, 113, 138, 147-148, 344-346
St. Clair Mercantile, 111
St. Clair Municipal Liquor Store, 147, 342
St. Clair Post Office, 340-341
St. Clair PTA, 128, 135
St. Clair Red Cross, 100
St. Clair Roller Mill, 113
St. Clair Sewage Treatment Plant, 343
St. Clair Star, 32, 84-85, 87

St. Clair State Bank, I, 33, 90, 93, 95-97, 106-111, 120-121, 123, 145, 326, 342
St. Clair Telephone Company, 132-133
St. Clair Town Hall, 99, 107-108, 130
St. Clair Volunteer Fire Department, iv, 33, 82, 97, 151, 337-339
St. Clair, General, 6, 80
St. Clair's Cottonwood Tree, 149-151, 331
St. Cyr, M., 113
St. Cyr, Michael, 46
St. Cyr, Valentine, 296
St. Cyr, Vinsante, 296
St. John (Bestman) Cemetery, 55
St. John's Evangelical Lutheran Cemetery, 55
St. John's Evangelical Lutheran Church, 40, 44-45, 51-53, 55, 74, 76, 80, 93, 101, 106, 108, 111
St. John's Lutheran Ladies' Aid, 128, 130
St. John's Lutheran Pre-school, 53
St. Paul, MN, 57, 76, 80-81
St. Peter Land Office, 74
St. Peter, MN, 5
Stalberger, Jerry, 247
Stalberger, Joan (Miller), 247
Staloch, Patricia, 183
Staloch, Tony, 183
Stanke, Fred, 204
Stanke, Lena, 204
Stassen, Harold (Red), 224
Stavenau, Edgar, 171
Stavenau, Gertrude (Buecksler), 170-171
Steck, Conrad, 247
Steck, Delores (Moe), 247
Steckelberg, Cora (Juliar), 223
Steckelberg, Harry, 223
Steckelberg, Henry, 223
Steckelberg, Marion, 223
Steel, Ardis (Seifert), 278
Steel, David, 260, 278
Steel, Doris, 155
Steel, Marvin, 119, 138, 278
Steel, Mary, 327
Steel, Savallah (Phillips), 260, 278
Steel, Stanley, 119, 121, 298
Stegemeier, Joe, 181
Stelter, Dan, 220, 331
Stelter, Lindsey, 220
Stencel, Todd, 157, 341
Sterle, Cynthia (Rose), 269
Sterle, Lawrence, 269
Stevens, Mrs. C., 82
Stevenson, Andrew, 244
Stevenson, Blanche Estelle (Foster), 193-194-5
Stevenson, Capitola (McComb), 120, 179, 244
Stewart, Duane, 91
Stine, Lee, 277
Stine, Leonard, 277
Stoffel, Irene (Kruse), 231
Stoffel, Jerry, 231
Stoffel, Patty, 66
Stolt, Dale, iii, 149, 278-279, 342
Stolt, Mary Ann, 149, 279
Stolt, Scott, 149
Storjohann, Bethany (Smith), 279
Storjohann, Fredrick J.. 279
Storjohann, Henry (Hank), 279
Storjohann, Ida (Berndt), 279
Storjohann, Jerry, 279
Storjohann, Karon (O'Donnell), 157, 279, 341
Stradtmann, William, 110
Strobel, Gregory J., 170-171, 353
Strobel, Robin, 353
Stroebel, John Jr., 89
Student Prints, 120, 129
Studer-Johnson, Marian, 16
Suddendorf, Carol (Sodeman), 278
Suddendorf, Thomas, 278
Sullivan, Ellen Marie Hayes, 101
Sullivan, John, 81
Sullivan, Tim, 101
Sullivan, Vera (Kruse), 157
Sumcoe, Anna (Schalow), 270
Sunshine Golf Course, 118, 332
Sunshine Turkey Farms & Hatchery, 118
Surplus Marketing Administration (SMA), 58, 125
Svein, Carol (Schmidt), 273
Svien, John, 273
Swan, Ardyce (Juliar), 223
Swan, Duane, 223
Tabeau, Louis, 88
Taber, Allan, 2015
Tacheny, Dale, 157, 304
Tacheny, John, 335
Tacheny, Nick, 296
Taylor, Henry, 169
Taylor, Marion (Bruels), 169
Teff, Jean (Hemshrot), 214
Teff, Larry, 214
Temple, Floyd, 121
Tenish, Mr., 88
Terhurne, Darlene (Hawker), 132, 213
Terhurne, David, 213
Tharp, Kathleen
The Aborigines of Minnesota, 1, 3
The Bell Tower, 347
The Country Register, 235, 348
The Land, 222
Thebow, Louie, 296
Thebow, Margaret (Managie), 296
Thielman, Henry, 32-33, 88, 90, 93-95, 97, 99, 118, 123, 126, 165, 258, 264, 279, 319, 337
Thielman, Jessie (Rasdall), 165, 258, 264, 279, 319
Thielman, Peter, 279
Thielman, Sophia (Dorweiler-Wingen), 279
Thielman's St. Clair Mercantile, 32, 106, 319
Thielscher, Judy (Roher), 268
Thissen, Catherine, 18, 123
Thissen, Frances (Fredrickson), 235
Thissen, Fred, 18
Thissen, Gerhart, 235
Thissen, Katie, 18
Thissen, Mary, 18
Thissen, Monica, 109
Thissen, Patrick, 18
Thissen, Severin, 18
Thom, Michelle, 344
Thompson, Blake, 258, 320
Thompson, Christine (Fossum), 193
Thompson, Claire, 193
Thompson, Clark W., 6
Thompson, Glen, 331, 342
Thompson, Mike, 193
Thompson, Rachael, 193
Thompson, Rebecca (Pagenkopf), 258, 320-321
Thompson, Slade, 258, 320
Thompson, Tom, 258, 320-321
Thordahl, Amy, 198,
Thordahl, Anton, 198
Thordahl, David, 198
Thordahl, Eric, 198
Thordahl, James, 198
Thordahl, Judy, 198
Thordahl, Karen, 198
Thordahl, Lorraine (Freitag), 198
Thordahl, Susan, 198
Thoreson, Angela (Seys), 285
Thoreson, Brent, 285
Thorson, Lowell, 150-151
Thurn, Lloyd (Butch), 342
Tillman, Theodore, 335
Tillotson, Doc, 296
Tillotson, Francis, 80
Tillotson, Mabel, 296
Tillotson, Oliver, 296
Tillotson, Scott, 296
Tillotson, Summer, 12
Tillotson, William, 296
Timm, Julie (Miller), 246

Timm, Kevin, 246
Timmerman, Anna (Gerlach), 161, 280
Timmerman, Evelyn (Kollos), 110, 121, 228, 252, 280, 321
Timmerman, Fred, 228, 280
Timmerman, Herman, 280
Timmerman, Ida (Kollos), 228, 280
Timmerman, John, 103, 161, 280
Timmerman, Louis, 121, 139, 228, 252, 280, 302, 321
Timmerman, Raymond, 280
Timmerman, Unetta, 280, 321
Timmerman, Walter, 280
Tivoli Bridge, 327
Tivoli Cemetery, 12
Tivoli, 11, 75
TJ's Café, 157
Tobie, E.L., 91
Tolzman, Walter, 94
Tolzmann, Alma, 102
Tortorella, Dominic Jr., 270
Tortorella, Dominic Sr., 270
Tortorella, Mario, 270
Tortorella, Vicki (Savik), 270
Tosch, Clarence, 69
Trahms, Ellen Emma Anne (Fitzloff), 188
Trahms, George, 188, 190
Trainor, Father, 311
Treaty of Traverse des Sioux, 73
Trembley, Don, 175
Treutner, Mr., 88-89
Trinity Evangelical Lutheran Church, 112
Trio, Allie, 141
Truman, Edward, 280
Truman, Hannah, 280
Truman, Henry, 9, 14, 164, 264, 280, 294
Truman, Josiah C., 9, 14, 17, 31, 46, 185, 280, 293, 340
Truman, Mary (Smith), 280
Truman, Susan, 280
Tuttle, Depot Agent, 96
Twedten, Mildred, 336
Tweeten Corner Stop, 157-158
Tweeten, Arlo, 158
Tweeten, Judy, 158
Twirling Thunder, 113
Udelhofen, Heinie, 130, 179
Ulman, Harlen, 188
Ulman, Leona (Fitzloff), 188
Ulrich, Lena (Wingen), 286
Ulrich, Sophia (Wingen), 286
Uncle Albert's Café, 155-156
Union House, 80, 330
United Brethren in Christ Church, 54
Upham, Warren, 1
Upper Agency School, 80
Upper Sioux Agency, 15
UpTown Tavern, 34, 197, 325-326, 342
Urban, Gerald, 234
Urban, Sandra (Loge), 234
Van Brunt Addition, 10
Van De Mark, Betty (Cords), 303, 305
VanErdwyk, Katie (Rollings), 206
VanErdwyk, Korey, 206
Varpness, Audrey (Phillips), 260
Varpness, Don, 260
Vaske, Amber, 213
Vaske, Clifford, 213
Vaske, Clint, 213
Vaske, Gabrielle, 213
Vaske, Linda, 213
Vaske, Maribeth, 213
Velin, Esther (Kruse), 231
Velin, John, 231
Veroven, Sam, 331
Veroven, Stacey, 332
Verschelde, Adrienne, 150, 157, 341
Verschelde, Herman, 211
Verschelde, Mary (Hollobusch), 211
Vertitron Midwest, Inc., 351-352, 354
Vierguts, Ida (Kruger), 208
Vierguts, William, 208
Village Bakery, 156
Vivaldi, Father Francis, 45
Vogel, Eugene, 253
Vogel, Valeria (Sandick), 253
Voight, Franz, 271
Voight, Howard, 112
Voight, Wilhelmina (Ehrenberg), 271
Volkmann, Alvin, 204
Volkmann, Virgene (Glamm), 157, 204
Von Arb, Ronald, 247
Von Arb, Sondra (Miller), 246-247, 290
W.O. Lovell & Co., 96
Wabasha III, 1
Wagner, Daisy (Schroeder), 275
Wagner, Robert, 275
Waldera, Francis, 244
Waldorf, MN, 129
Waldorf-Pemberton School District, 61
Walechka, Aaron, 208
Walechka, Austin, 208
Walechka, Benjamin, 208
Walechka, Holly (Grams-Kubista), 207-208
Walechka, L. Rick, 208
Wall, Brian, 332
Walser, Cathy, 342
Walton, Alvin, 187
Walton, Birdie, 281
Walton, Dr. Michael, 281
Walton, Elaine (Phillips), 281
Walton, Harold, 59, 258, 281, 328
Walton, Lewis, 281
Walton, Luci, 281
Walton, Marilyn (Fitzloff), 187
Walton, Nancy, 281
Walton, Tom, 281
Ward, Annette (Manthey), 282
Ward, Bernice (Juliar), 223, 281-282
Ward, Charles H., 251, 281
Ward, Clara (Mann), 282
Ward, Curly, 296
Ward, Daniel, 282
Ward, Doris (Armes), 282
Ward, Elwyn, 223, 281-282
Ward, George, 69. 167, 175
Ward, Helen (Glynn), 149, 282
Ward, J.W., 32, 85
Ward, Jalen, 282
Ward, Kristi (Tolman), 282
Ward, Lial Lee, 282
Ward, Merle N., 282
Ward, Michael, 282, 353
Ward, Millie (Brazier), 251, 281
Ward, Norman Lee, 282
Ward, Patricia (O'Herin), 282
Ward, Pearl E. (Foster), 196
Ward, Raymond L., 282
Ward, Richard, 149, 282
Ward, Rose (Beise), 167
Ward, Sue (Wilder), 282
Ward, Tara (Krautbauer), 282, 353
Ward, W.J., 84
Ward, William, 282
Warner, Alice (Frank), 196
Warner, Charles, 196
Warren Addition, 10
Warwick, Dolly Mae (Wolcott), 290
Warwick, William, 290
Waseca County, 1, 8, 13
Waseca, MN, 15, 66, 82-83, 85, 110
Water Tower, 33, 96, 100, 317, 343
Watson, Donald, 186
Watson, Donna (Fitzloff), 186
Waugh, Lawrence, 272
Waugh, Sadie (Schmidt), 272
Webb Oil Station, 118
Webb, Carol (Phillips), 260
Webb, William, 260
Webster, Jerome, 136
Wellcome, G.T., 80
Wells, J.C., 79
Wells, MN, 76
Wenner, Agnes (Klein), 168, 282
Wenner, Bernard, 168, 282
Wenner, Berneil (Flores), 168, 283
Wenner, Debra (Eckstein), 168, 282
Wenner, Edwin, 168, 282
Wenner, Elizabeth (Brunner), 168, 282
Wenner, Gerald, 168, 282

Wenner, Harbert (Harry), 141,168, 282
Wenner, Harold, 168, 282
Wenner, Irene (Brown), 168, 283
Wenner, Janet (Kruger), 168, 283
Wenner, Joyce, 168, 283
Wenner, Kathy (Janssen), 168, 282
Wenner, Kristine (Kline), 282
Wenner, Leland, 168, 283
Wenner, Leon, 168, 283
Wenner, Lester, 168, 282
Wenner, Mark, 168, 282
Wenner, Neil, 168, 283
Wenner, Robert, 168, 282
Wenner, Rose Marie (Bruels), 100, 141, 168, 282
Wenner, Stanley, 168, 282
Wenner, Steven, 168, 283
Wenner, Victoria (McCormick), 168, 282
Wenner, Wendy (Sawatzky), 168, 283
Weppler, Carl, 199
Weppler, Marie (Fritzke), 199
Werdin, Clara (Koplen), 283
Werdin, Edward, 283
Werdin, Faith, 283
Werdin, Hazel (Abraham), 283
Werdin, Wilfred, 283
Werth, Fred, 94
West Side Storage, 352
West, Connie (Walton), 281
West, Dodie, 288
West, Gary, 281
West, Ronald, 288
Westphal, Aaron, 284
Westphal, Adeline (Schalow), 18, 112, 114, 141, 271-272, 286
Westphal, Alma (Kriesh), 283
Westphal, Anna (Mueller), 18, 102, 283
Westphal, Arthur, 113, 283
Westphal, August, 120, 131-132, 252, 283-284
Westphal, Bernard, 18, 22, 132, 149, 155-156, 253, 284, 351
Westphal, Beth (Jones), 285
Westphal, Betty Lou, 285
Westphal, Dale, 63, 157, 285, 341-342, 351
Westphal, Donald, 285
Westphal, Douglas, iv, 284-285
Westphal, Edna (Dimmel), 283
Westphal, Emil, 283
Westphal, Eric, 22, 285
Westphal, Florence (Bluhm), 283
Westphal, Frieda (Hawker), 18, 114, 128, 130, 212, 285
Westphal, Janice (Schull), 248
Westphal, Jerry, 213
Westphal, John (Jack), 18, 132, 212, 283, 285
Westphal, Joshua, 284
Westphal, Kathryn Sadie (McGannon), 285
Westphal, Laura, 285
Westphal, Lena (Silkey), 145, 252, 283-284
Westphal, Leona (Drager), 283
Westphal, Leona (Santo), 283
Westphal, Linda (Danner), 284-285
Westphal, Marilyn (Hoechst), 284
Westphal, Marion (Hawker-Flo), 132, 213
Westphal, Mavis (Rosin), 285
Westphal, Megan, 285
Westphal, Michael, 145, 284
Westphal, Myrtle (Krause), iii, 18, 156, 233, 253, 284, 286
Westphal, Otto, 283, 285
Westphal, Paul (Pete), 131-132, 141, 283, 286
Westphal, Paul Marion Sr., 18, 94, 107-108, 272
Westphal, Reinhart, 94, 283
Westphal, Thomas, 285
Westphal, Walter, 94, 101-102, 113, 283
Westphal, William, 283
Westphal, Willis, 248
Weyrauch, Leo, 218
Weyrauch, Valera (Hubmer), 218
Wheaton, Michael, iv
Wheeler & Levi Blacksmith, 82
Wheeler, Jim, 295-296
Wheeler, Savallah (Rowell), 295
White, Asa, 10, 17, 295
Whiting, Darlene, 141
Whiting, Robert, 141
Wickersham, Dr. M.R., 8
Wilcox, Dr. Michael, 339
Wilder, Judy (Nicolai), 153, 251
Wilder, Richard, 251
Wilder, Robert, 289
Wilder, Sharon (Witt), 289
Wiley, Cheryl (Bunde), 168, 283
Wiley, Kenneth, 168, 283
Wilking, Jerilyn, 247
Wilking, Jerry, 247
Wilkins, Clara L., 286
Wilkins, Frank, 18, 286
Wilkins, Grace E., 286
Wilkins, Matilda (Abbott), 286
Wilkins, Morris, 18
Wilkins, William E., 286
Will, Brian, 168
Will, Jamie, 168, 248, 348
Will, Kristin, 168
Will, Ramona (James), 168, 283
Will, Randy, 168, 283
Will, Sara (More), 168, 248
Wille, Albert G., 272
Wille, Carl, 169, 171
Wille, Emil, 272
Wille, Emma (Schmidt), 272
Wille, Otto, 272
William Field & Son, 32, 79
Williams, Burton, 186
Williams, Dr., 138
Williams, James, 332
Williams, John H., 272
Williams, LaVerne (Fitzloff), 186
Williams, Minnie (Schmidt), 272
Williams, Ralph, 272
Willie, Johanna (Buecksler), 169, 171
Willow Creek, 53
Wills, Charles, W., 286
Wills, Eva (Crick), 286
Wills, J. C., 286
Wills, Sylvester, 296
Wilmes, Delores, 299
Wilmes, Stanley, 299
Wilmes, Steve, 331
Wilson, Art, 226
Wilson, Danny, 150
Wilson, Eliza, 18
Wilson, S.B., 33
Wingen, Agnes, 123
Wingen, Alonzo J., 287
Wingen, Anthony J., 286-288
Wingen, Edward, 287
Wingen, Fred W., 34, 90, 99, 117, 286-287
Wingen, Frederick, 287
Wingen, Jacob, 260, 286-287
Wingen, Joseph, 87, 242, 286-287
Wingen, Josie, 310
Wingen, Katherine (Phillips), 287
Wingen, Kathy, 144
Wingen, Louise (Burscke), 287
Wingen, Mary (Phillips), 287
Wingen, Minnie (Schulz), 287-288
Wingen, Sophia (Dorweiler), 260, 286
Winkelman Feed Mill, 348
Winkelman, Arthur, 37, 177, 199, 270, 288, 332
Winkelman, James, 69, 179, 288, 332
Winkelman, Jeffrey James, 288
Winkelman, JoHanna (Apple), 123, 199, 288
Winkelman, Mary (Oachs), 288
Winkelman, Melody (West), 288
Winkelman, Myrna (Daby), 146, 288
Winkelman, Thomas Mark, 288
Winnebago Agency House, ii, 8-9, 13-14, 16, 31, 73, 153

Winnebago Agency, 3, 5-6, 9-11, 15-17, 45, 51, 53, 57, 65, 67, 74-79, 83, 113, 293, 340-341, 355
Winnebago Reservation, 2-9, 17, 73, 86, 88
Winnebago Tribe, iii, 1-12, 17, 45, 67-68, 73, 113, 355
Winona, MN, 8, 123
Winslow, Ben, 34, 229
Winslow, Emma (Kopke-Wood-Sauer), 228-229
Winter, Angela, 289
Winter, Beth (Frazen), 289, 352
Winter, Brent, 288
Winter, Cathryn (Anderson), 289
Winter, Christine, 289
Winter, Darwin, 164
Winter, Eric, 289
Winter, Frieda (Schulz), 288
Winter, Gloria (James-Block), 168, 283
Winter, Joseph, 168, 283
Winter, Judy Ann (Nyquist), 252, 280, 288
Winter, Linda (Faltersack), 288
Winter, Lisa (Barnes), 289, 352
Winter, Lyless (Lindloff), 233
Winter, Martin E., 288
Winter, Martin P. (Marty), 137, 288
Winter, Penny (Bollmann), 164
Winter, Ray A., 289, 352
Winter, Rev. Ronald, 233
Winter, Richard D., 129, 252, 280, 288
Winter, Robert M., 288
Winter, Ronald L., 288-289, 352
Winter, Russell J., 289
Winter, Shirley (Reedstrom), 288-289
Winter, Susan, 289
Winter, Thomas, 289
Winter, Tom, 137
Winter, Tyler, 289
Winterhaven Vineyard & Nursery, 352
Wise, John C. Jr., 265
Wiste, Anne, 312
Wiste, Ole, 312
Wiste, Oliver, 312-313
Witt, Bertha (Rost), 289
Witt, Carol (Lee-Grams), 208
Witt, Clarence, 289
Witt, Daryl, 289, 331
Witt, Elsie (Grams), 208
Witt, Erick, 187
Witt, Gertrude (Lachelt), 120, 123, 129-130, 207
Witt, Harlan, 260, 289
Witt, Jason, 342
Witt, Judy (Phillips), 260, 289
Witt, Lenora (Possin), 289
Witt, Lisa (Linn), 289
Witt, Lotie, 187
Witt, Lyle, 208
Witt, Maxine, 66
Witt, Otto, 134, 207, 231, 295
Witt, Robert, 289
Witt, Water, 208
Wm Frantz Soft Drink Parlor, 114
Wobschall, Carl, 196
Wobschall, Norma (Frank), 196
Woelfel, Anna, 289
Woelfel, Anton, 289
Woelfel, Charles, 246, 289, 290
Woelfel, Christina (Troske), 289
Woelfel, Fracis Charles (Carl), 290
Woelfel, Helen (Gales), 290
Woelfel, Joseph, 289
Woelfel, Maria, 289-290
Woelfel, Philomena (Bolnig), 246, 289
Woelfel, Teresa Marie, 290
Wohlrabe, Dr. A., 97
Wohlrabe, Dr. John, 136-137, 297
Wohlrabe, J.C., 59
Woites, Cy, 220
Wolcott Brothers, 32
Wolcott, Claire (Pete), 32, 79, 106, 214, 290-291
Wolcott, Cora (Head), 290
Wolcott, Foster Fernley (Jack), 106, 290
Wolcott, Grocery Store, 139, 302
Wolcott, Harold, 32, 68-69, 106, 109, 138, 214, 290-291
Wolcott, John Fremont, 113-114, 195, 290
Wolcott, John Henry, 290
Wolcott, Lester Allen, 124
Wolcott, Lloyd Earl, 290
Wolcott, Minnie Olive (Foster), 195, 290
Wolcott, Ruth (Swart), 290
Wolcott, Theodore, 106, 290
Wolf, Ernestine (Frank), 196
Wolf, Joseph, 196
Wolff, Gustave, 262
Wolff, Mary, 260
Wolff, Maude Charlotte (Preston), 261-262
Wolff, Pete, 260
Wolner, Julie (Klingbeil), 227
Wolner, Steve, 227
Womack, Gene, 168
Womack, Katherine (Bruels), 168
Women Jaycees, 34
Women of today, 155
Wood, Dale, 229
Wood, Delores, 229
Wood, John, 229
Wood, Kathleen, 228-229
Wood, Ralph, 229
Wood, Spencer, 163
Woodruff, Matthew, 261
Works Progress Administration (WPA), 58, 125
Wright, Kathy (DeMars), 183
Wright, Thomas, 183
Yackel, Stella (McComb), 244
Yackel, Wilbur, 244
Yackley, Evelyn (Preston), 262
Yellow Blanket, 12
Yellow Medicine County, 15
Yellowbank, James, 88
Yenish, Charles J., 121,128
Yenish, Norbert, 121
Young Peoples League, 53
Young, Charles, 32, 77
Young, Louise (Westphal), 283
Young, Paul, 283
Younger Brothers, 254
Younger, Bob, 101
Youngerberg, Gottlieb, 274
Youngerberg, Herman, 203
Youngerberg, Hulda (Meyer), 274
Youngerberg, Isabella (Doss), 272
Youngerberg, Martha (Glamm), 203
Youngerberg, Sylvester, 131, 272
Zabel, Dennis, 34, 291
Zabel, Donald, 291
Zabel, Edie (Guise), 291
Zabel, Haley, 291
Zabel, Katie, 291
Zabel, Kelly (Seys), 34, 291, 342
Zabel, Margaret, 157, 191, 341
Zabel, Peyton, 291
Zabel, Shaya, 291
Zabel, Troy, 34, 158, 291, 342
Zavoral, Florence (Hubmer), 218
Zavoral, Robert, 53, 138, 183, 218, 300, 331
Zell, Darla, 156
Zell, Heather, 156
Zenzen, Ben, 271
Zenzen, Edith (Schalow), 271
Zieske, Rev. 175
Zion Evangelical Church in St. Clair, 54, 76, 98
Zion United Methodist Church, 53, 74, 111, 157

Sesquicentennial Memories